PEARSON CUSTOM
Education

Becoming a Teacher, 8th Edition

Forrest W. Parkay

Beverly Hardcastle Stanford

Florida Version

PEARSON

Custom
Publishing

Sponsoring Editor: Natalie Danner
Development Editor: Abbey Briggs
Editorial Assistant: Jill Johnson
Marketing Manager: Amy Dyer
Operations Manager: Eric M. Kenney
Production Manager: Jennifer M. Berry
Rights Editor: Francesca Marcantonio
Art Director: Renée Sartell
Cover Designers: Kristen Kiley

Cover Art: "Textbooks and apple" used by permission of istock; "Teacher and students" used by permission of istock; "Classroom, globe on desk, US flag hanging from blackboard" Copyright © 1999-2008 Getty Images, Inc. All rights reserved.

Please visit our websites at *www.pearsoncustom.com* and *www.customliterature.com*.
Attention bookstores: For permission to return any unsold stock, contact us at *pe-uscustomreturns@pearsoncustom.com*.

ISBN-13: 9780558154813
ISBN-10: 0558154816

Package ISBN-13: N/A
Package ISBN-10: N/A

PEARSON CUSTOM PUBLISHING
501 Boylston Street, Suite 900, Boston, MA 02116
A Pearson Education Company

Contents

If you want your students to **get better grades** and to **become better teachers**

adopt and assign **MyEducationLab** today
www.myeducationlab.com

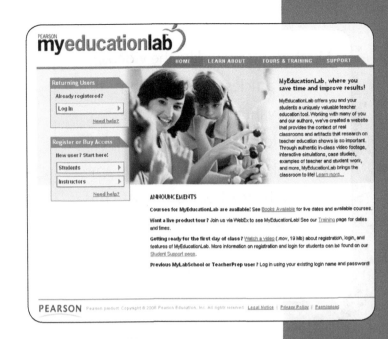

What is MyEducationLab?

MyEducationLab grounds teacher education in real classrooms—among real teachers and students and among actual examples of students' and teachers' work—to prepare your students for the complexities of teaching today's students in today's classrooms:

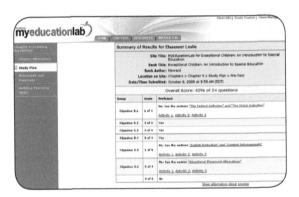

PRACTICE TESTS: These self-paced assessments give students an opportunity to test their knowledge of chapter content. Based on a student's performance on the test, MyEducationLab generates an individual study plan to help each student identify topics for which he or she needs additional study. MyEducationLab then provides the appropriate chapter excerpts and, in some instances, interactive, multimedia activities to help the student master that content.

ASSIGNMENTS AND IN-CLASS ACTIVITIES: Each chapter in MyEducationLab includes assignable Activities and Applications exercises that use authentic classroom video, teacher and student artifacts, or case studies to help students understand course content more deeply and to practice applying that content.

PRACTICE TEACHING: Building Teaching Skills and Dispositions exercises use video, artifacts, and/or case studies to help your students truly see and understand how specific teaching techniques and behaviors impact learners and learning environments. These exercises give your students practice in developing the skills and dispositions that are essential to quality teaching.

> "My students really like the videos, and the articles are interesting and relevant too. I like how the site reinforces the concepts in the textbook in a meaningful way. I am so glad the textbook came with this online resource—it's great!"
>
> — Shari Schroepfer,
> Adams State College

Does it work?

A survey of student users from across the country tells us that it does!

93% MyEducationLab was easy to use.

70% MyEducationLab's video clips helped me to get a better sense of real classrooms.

79% I would recommend my instructor continue using MyEducationLab.

*Percentage of respondents who agree or strongly agree.

Where is it?

- Online at www.myeducationlab.com
- Integrated right into this text! Look for margin annotations and end-of-chapter activities throughout the book.

> "This program will change teaching! Brilliant!"
>
> — Bob Blake,
> SUNY College at Brockport

What do I have to do to use MyEducationLab in my course?

Just contact your Pearson sales representative and tell him/her that you'd like to use MyEducationLab with this text next semester. Your representative will work with your bookstore to ensure that your students receive access with their books.

What if I need help?

We've got you covered 24/7. Your Pearson sales representative offers training in using MyEducationLab for you and your students. There is also a wealth of helpful information on the site, under "Tours and Training" and "Support." And technical support is available 24 hours a day, seven days a week, at http://247pearsoned.custhelp.com.

> "The ability to track students' performance on the MyEducationLab activities has allowed me to easily keep the students' performance records and devote more time to the development of appropriate in-class activities. The technology has made it possible to design a mastery-based learning system and more easily demonstrate evidence-based practices."
>
> — Daniel E. Hursh,
> West Virginia University

Teaching: Your Chosen Profession

2

Teaching: Your Chosen Profession

I feel so passionate and personally called to this wonderful profession called teaching.

—Sara Ferris, third-grade teacher, and author of "A Teacher's Voice: Lost and Found in Paradox" (2008, p. 16).

CLASSROOM CASE
The Realities of Teaching

THE CHALLENGE: Dealing with the everyday challenges of teaching and deciding if you are really meant to be a teacher.

It is your first day of teaching. You enter the classroom full of anticipation. As the students come into the room, chatting easily with one another, you think about how they feel comfortable, accustomed to the routine. You, on the other hand, are anxious, not sure of what to expect.

For a week, you've spent an hour or two a day going over your plans for the first day with your students. You are amazed at the amount of time you've spent preparing for the first day, and you wonder how much time experienced teachers spend preparing for class. Last night, you woke up twice, and each time you mentally rehearsed what you would do during that first day.

Now you are finding out what it is like to be a real teacher. "Can I adjust to the challenges of teaching?" you wonder. You received good grades in your teacher education courses, but you know that putting research and theory into practice is not easy. Right now, it's hard to imagine that you will ever feel as comfortable as your students do in the classroom.

In spite of feeling anxious, you know you have prepared well. You definitely know the material you are going to teach. Thinking about how well prepared you are gives you confidence. "I am a 'real' teacher," you think, just as the bell rings, signaling the start of class. Now you begin to teach.

"Good morning, class. My name is . . . . "

The next several hours seem to fly by. Already, it is afternoon and the dismissal bell has just rung. As the students file out of your room, you take stock of the first day. It's hard to remember everything that happened. Some things went well, you think; others did not go as well.

For the most part, students seemed to be interested and on-task during the day. At other times, however, you could feel their resistance. Some students talked with their neighbors. Others stared out the window. Others yawned openly, as if to say, "I am bored. Why don't we do something interesting?"

Though you had a definite plan for the day, you realize that teaching involves a lot more than just following a plan. Being a good teacher involves a lot. It's more than showing students who's the boss. It's more than being a subject-matter expert. It's knowing what to teach and how to teach it.

5

FOCUS QUESTIONS

1. Why do I want to teach?
2. What are the benefits of teaching?
3. What are the challenges of teaching?
4. What will society expect of me as a teacher?
5. What is the job outlook for teachers?
6. How will I become a highly qualified teacher?

Congratulations on deciding to become a teacher! Teaching is exciting, rewarding, and uplifting. Teachers receive great satisfaction from knowing that they really do make a difference in their students' lives. I hope you share my belief that teaching is the world's most important profession. I also hope your commitment to teaching will become deeper and stronger as you move through your teacher education program. And I hope your experiences will be similar to those a student teacher recently shared with me: "When I came to the university I had various majors—electrical engineering, architecture, journalism—but I wasn't really happy until I went into teaching. Now it's really becoming a passion."

As the opening classroom case suggests, teaching is a challenging but rewarding profession—one that is not for everyone. This book will orient you to the world of teaching and help you answer your own questions about the career you have chosen. What is teaching really like? What rewards do teachers experience? What are the trends and issues in the profession? What problems can you expect to encounter in the classroom? What will you need to know and be able to do to become a highly qualified teacher?

I believe that successful teachers know why they want to teach. They examine their motives carefully, and they understand why, at first, they might have been uncertain about choosing teaching as a profession. This chapter, then, addresses the six focus questions listed above, which will help you decide if teaching is the right profession for you.

The focus questions will address *your future* as a teacher. Answers to these questions will provide you with a reality-based look at the world of teachers, students, classrooms, and schools and their surrounding communities. After reading this text, you will have a broad understanding of one of the most exciting, satisfying, and honorable professions the world has ever known. And you will know if teaching is the right profession for you.

WHY DO I WANT TO TEACH?

You may want to teach for many reasons. Your desire to teach may be the result of positive experiences with teachers when you were a child. You may see teaching as a way of making a significant contribution to the world and experiencing the joy of helping others grow and develop. Or you may be attracted to teaching because the life of a teacher is exciting, varied, and stimulating. Figure 1.1 shows the primary reasons teachers give for entering the profession.

Desire to Work With Children and Young People

As Figure 1.1 shows, the desire to work with young people is the most frequently cited reason teachers give for choosing their profession. Though teaching may be challenging and teachers' salaries modest, most teach simply because they care about students. Teachers derive great satisfaction when their students learn—when they make a difference in students' lives. In fact, 47 percent of teachers in a national survey reported that the personal satisfaction they experienced as a teacher was "better than expected," while 47 percent found it to be "about the same" as they expected (Harris Interactive, 2006, p. 21).

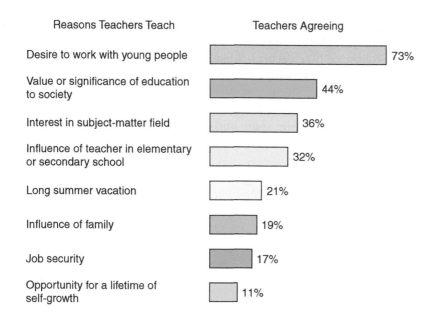

Reasons Teachers Teach   Teachers Agreeing

- Desire to work with young people — 73%
- Value or significance of education to society — 44%
- Interest in subject-matter field — 36%
- Influence of teacher in elementary or secondary school — 32%
- Long summer vacation — 21%
- Influence of family — 19%
- Job security — 17%
- Opportunity for a lifetime of self-growth — 11%

FIGURE 1.1 Why teachers originally decided to enter the profession

Source: National Education Association, Status of the American Public School Teacher, *2003. Data used with permission of the National Education Association © 2003. All rights reserved.*

As a teacher, your day-to-day interactions with students will build strong bonds between you and them. Daily contact will enable you to become familiar with your students' personal and academic needs. Concern for their welfare will help you cope with the difficulties and frustrations of teaching. As the following statements by highly accomplished individuals illustrate, the teacher's potential to make a difference in students' lives can be profound:

The dream begins, most of the time, with a teacher who believes in you, who tugs and pushes and leads you on to the next plateau, sometimes poking you with a sharp stick called truth.

—Dan Rather, national news commentator

Compassionate teachers fill a void left by working parents who aren't able to devote enough attention to their children. Teachers don't just teach; they can be vital personalities who help young people to mature, to understand the world and to understand themselves.

—Charles Platt, science fiction novelist

One looks back with appreciation to the brilliant teachers who touched our human feelings. The curriculum is so much necessary raw material, but warmth is the vital element for the growing plant and for the soul of the child.

—Carl Jung, world-renowned psychoanalyst

Like most teachers, you appreciate the unique qualities of youth. You enjoy the liveliness, curiosity, freshness, openness, and trust of young children or the abilities, wit, spirit, independence, and idealism of adolescents. As one teacher put it, you want to "truly make a difference in the lives of children who [do] not always come 'ready to learn' [and] be a part of helping students see themselves as literate and able to solve problems" (Ferris, 2008, p. 16).

As a teacher, you will also derive significant rewards from meeting the needs of diverse learners. Students from our nation's more than one hundred racial and ethnic groups and students with special needs are increasing in number, so your classroom will be enriched by the varied backgrounds of your students. To ensure that you can experience the satisfaction of helping all students learn, significant portions of this book are devoted to **student variability** (differences among students in regard to their developmental needs, interests, abilities, and disabilities) and **student diversity** (differences among students in regard to gender, race, ethnicity, culture, religion, sexual orientation, and socioeconomic status). Your appreciation for diversity will help you to experience the rewards that come from enabling each student to make his or her unique contribution to classroom life.

Like the following two teachers, a likely reason you have been drawn to teaching is the privilege of working with children and youth, regardless of their stages of development or their life circumstances:

> *Where else can you regularly get hugged, get smeared with fingerpaints, receive handmade cards, wipe tears, share smiles, wiggle loose teeth, share awful cafeteria food, read silly stories, and know that you are changing the world?*

> *The rewards are great, when you see a child suddenly grasp a concept or write that poem that he/she thought [he/she] couldn't, these are the moments that let me know that I am in the right profession!* (Harris Interactive, 2001, p. 118)

A Passion for Teaching

Like 79 percent of the teachers who responded to a MetLife Survey of the American Teacher (Harris Interactive, 2001), you may "strongly agree" that you are passionate about teaching. Why do teachers find teaching so satisfying? What does it mean to be *passionate* about teaching?

A Passion for the Subject

You may be passionate about teaching because you are passionate about teaching in your discipline. In "The Satisfactions of Teaching," Eliot Eisner points out that "teaching provides the occasion to share with others your deep affection for what you teach. When your eyes twinkle with delight at the prospect of introducing students to what you love, you create a sense of contagion and convey your love of what you teach. Your passion for your subject is the sincerest and most powerful invitation you can extend" (March 2006, p. 45).

A Passion for the Teaching Life

Like many teachers, perhaps you always enjoyed school. The life of a teacher appeals to you—to be in an environment that encourages a high regard for education and the life of the mind, and to have daily opportunities to see students become excited about learning. Albert Einstein, for example, regretted that he did not devote his career to the teaching life:

> *Believe it or not, one of my deepest regrets [is that I didn't teach]. I regret this because I would have liked to have had more contact with children. There has always been something about the innocence and freshness of young children that appeals to me and brings me great enjoyment to be with them. And they are so open to knowledge. I have never really found it difficult to explain basic laws of nature to children. When you reach them at their level, you can read in their eyes their genuine interest and appreciation.* (quoted in Bucky, 1992, p. 99)

A Passion for the Teaching-Learning Process

You may be passionate about teaching because you are excited about helping students learn. The prospect of thinking on your feet and capitalizing on teachable moments is appealing. Perhaps you have had expert teachers who made you realize that "teaching well requires improvisation without constraints" and that "teaching is a custom job" (Eisner, 2006, p. 45).

Philip Jackson describes the unpredictability of teaching in his well-known book *Life in Classrooms*: "[As] typically conducted, teaching is an opportunistic process. . . . Neither teacher nor students can predict with any certainty exactly what will happen next. Plans are forever going awry and unexpected opportunities for the attainment of educational goals are constantly emerging" (Jackson, 1990, p. 166).

Research tells us that teachers may make up to 3,000 low-level decisions in a single school day (Jackson, 1990). Most decisions are easy and natural, but some require critical thinking. Stepping into the minds of teachers to see how they turned a negative situation into a positive learning experience for students is the purpose of the Teaching on Your Feet feature. For example, the Teaching on Your Feet feature in this chapter illustrates how a teacher responded to sixth-grade students' initial negative attitudes about learning math and eventually made the subject inviting to students.

Influence of Teachers

The journey toward becoming a teacher often begins early in life. While few people are born teachers, their early life experiences often encourage them to become teachers. With the exception of parents or guardians, the adults who have the greatest influence on children are often their teachers. Perhaps a positive relationship with a teacher was the catalyst for your decision to become a teacher. Like 22 percent of the respondents to the NEA 2002 Teacher Day online ballot (National Education Association, 2002) who indicated they would consider becoming a teacher, the influence of a teacher in elementary or secondary school may be the principal reason you decided to become a teacher.

Similar to most people who become teachers, you may have been more influenced by your teachers as people than as subject-matter experts. Perhaps you had a teacher similar to Salina Gray, who made the following self-reflective observation during her first year of teaching: "I have evaluated my beliefs as a teacher, asking what education should be, what it means, and what I actually show my students. Do my actions show my values to my students? So, I have become a kinder, more honest Ms. Gray. My students have noticed" (Oakes & Lipton, 2007, p. 490). The inspirational memory of earlier teachers may have led you to the teaching profession.

Desire to Serve

You may have chosen teaching because you want to serve others. You want your life's work to have meaning, to be more than just a job. As one prospective teacher said:

> I mostly come to teaching because I love—well, this is going to sound like a cliché, but I love to expand minds. It's great to see someone think about something in a way they never thought about before because of you. See the light bulb go off, it's a pretty cool thing! And you had a hand in that. Rewarding, not like pushing paper, ya' know? (Harris Interactive, 2006, p. 19)

Your decision to serve through teaching may have been influenced by your experiences as a volunteer. One such teacher is Noah Zeichner, profiled in the Teachers' Voices feature for this chapter. His experience as a volunteer teacher in another country led him to the profession of teaching.

After the terrorist attacks of 9/11, many people reported that the uncertainty caused by the attacks led them to consider teaching as a career. According to school officials, the national wave of soul-searching after the attacks swelled the number of people seeking jobs as teachers. Clearly, they saw teaching as a way to serve.

The desire to serve others and give something back to society is a key attraction of the **Teach for America** program, which was developed in 1989 by Wendy Kopp as an outgrowth of her senior thesis at Princeton University. Teach for America volunteers, recent graduates from some of the best colleges and universities in the United States, are assigned to teach for a minimum of two years in urban and rural school districts with severe shortages of science, math, and language arts teachers. Volunteers complete five weeks of intensive training during a summer institute in Atlanta, Houston, Los Angeles, New York City, Philadelphia, or Phoenix. After two years of teaching, being monitored by state and school authorities, and taking professional development courses, Teach for America teachers can earn regular certification. Upon completion of their two-year assignment, volunteers then return to their chosen careers in other fields, though more than half remain in education as teachers, principals, and educational administrators. During 2008, 5,000 Teach for America corps members taught in 26 urban and rural areas across the country (Teach for America, 2008).

TEACHING ON YOUR FEET

MAKING A SUBJECT INVITING TO STUDENTS

I heard rumbling in the back of my sixth-grade classroom and saw that Tony was at the center of it. His temper flaring, he reacted to his math test grade by slapping the test facedown on his desk. "I hate math. It's boring!" he said, loud enough for most of us to hear.

I shot him a stern look and started walking in his direction. He became quiet and busied himself as I approached. Temporarily, the problem was resolved.

Before recess, I put a note on his desk. "Please see me for a few minutes at recess. It won't take long." I didn't want him to view our talk as a punishment.

When the others went to recess, he remained in the room, shifting from one foot to the other. I assured him I only wanted a few minutes and asked him to sit down. We sat in two adjacent student desks, and I began by asking him why he was so upset about his test grade. With some probing, he explained that he wasn't good at math, math was boring, he didn't see the point in it, and the assignments took too long to complete. I listened and nodded, letting him know I understood what he was saying. I made a few comments about the need to know math for future classes and mentioned that math was valuable in life as well. He seemed unconvinced. I thanked him for his time and said that he could go out to recess. He dashed out.

I was determined to motivate Tony to like math. I loved it, found comfort in its consistency and beauty in its amazing patterns. How could I make math more inviting, especially to sixth-grade students who loved recess and sports? "Stating the problem is the first step toward gaining the answer," I always believed. And an answer came. I would combine sports with math and offer students Math Muscle Labs.

The first Math Muscle Lab focused on means, medians, and modes. The school nurse, who had welcomed my invitation to the class, taught the students how to take their pulse. I then had them work with partners to take and record their pulse levels before and after doing 10 sit-ups. I divided the class into two teams, boys versus girls, and told each team to find the mean, median, and mode for their group's before- and after-exercise pulse levels. The competition added excitement to the activity. Soon all were concentrating on their measurements and math operations.

As I watched their positive engagement with math, I relished the moment. "I love teaching," I thought. "I can interact with lively minds and emotions, solve problems, be creative, promote learning, and even change some students' perspectives on themselves!" I was grateful. The Math Muscle Labs became a weekly event for several months and then morphed into a Consumer Math Lab that used local newspaper and catalog advertisements as the text. My students—even Tony—were well on their way to appreciating math. Tony seemed to value the extra effort I took to make math interesting, and I took pleasure in seeing him engage in math fully. Our brief visit yielded results for both of us.

ANALYSIS

Students' misbehavior is a symptom of an underlying problem. Taking time to understand the problem is essential. A brief visit with Tony indicated that his misbehavior (the angry outburst) was related to his lack of success in math, which in turn was related to his lack of interest in math.

Motivating students is an ongoing challenge and part of the art of teaching. Understanding students' interests and figuring out ways to draw on those interests can result in creative lessons that help students learn.

REFLECTION

- How did the teacher initially handle Tony's outburst?
- How did the teacher show that she valued Tony?
- How else might the teacher have responded to Tony's complaints about math?
- What creative math lessons would you use to keep Tony from being bored?
- Think of a time when you were especially motivated to learn in school. What motivated you?

Beverly Hardcastle Stanford
Former Sixth-Grade Teacher
Avon Middle School

PEARSON **myeducationlab** To answer these questions online, go to MyEducationLab at www.myeducationlab.com, select the Activities and Application section, and click on this chapter's Teaching on Your Feet.

TEACHERS' VOICES
Walk in My Shoes

Noah Zeichner's desire to become a teacher was solidified when he studied for a year in Quito, Ecuador. As a volunteer who taught world and Ecuadorian history, he recalls, "I figured if I could be successful there—with 12 students ages 12 to 18—I could do it in the United States." His years of working as a counselor and director in high school summer camps led him toward teaching, but the experience of teaching in another country, something he recommends to other teachers, made the difference: "It opened my eyes and made me think about motivating students who had nothing." He observed that his Ecuadorian students "had the desire to learn, in spite of overwhelming economic hardships."

Noah earned his bachelor's degree at the University of Wisconsin and did his graduate work at the University of Washington, drawn there by the reputation of Walter Parker, a leader in social studies education. Noah appreciates the discussion-oriented, critical-thinking approach to social studies education that he learned from Parker. His first teaching position included tenth-grade world history, Spanish I for ninth- to eleventh-graders, and twelfth-grade American government.

During his first year of teaching, Noah was asked to address the graduating cohort of teachers at his university. His advice included:

- Don't worry or panic about things you can't control—don't let [anyone] distract you from the things you need to do. Be patient. Let things go. You can't solve every problem; [and you] can't get everything right the first year.
- Keep good files on what you learn in your student teaching courses and in your ongoing professional reading and experiences.
- Be reflective and self-evaluative. Reflection was a big focus of my graduate program. It's hard to find the time to [write in a] journal the first year, but devise some system—journal or [Post-it] notes—to monitor how things are going. I wish I had done a better job of keeping a record for how to improve things.

"Be reflective and self-evaluative."

- Build good relationships; they will make teaching so much easier. Make yourself available outside class. Do more listening than talking. Attend basketball, football, and baseball games and concerts. Students really appreciate that. Having a sense of humor is very important—it holds our relationship together. I also show them that I am human; I make mistakes. It's hard to explain how I build relationships. It's an individual process.
- Try not to lose your idealism. A certain amount of idealism is lost when you get into the real job with all the pressures of budgets and layoffs—but try to maintain some idealism.
- Welcome a tough student-teaching assignment; it will better prepare you for the pressures of the first year of teaching.
- Schedule time away from work—with family and friends and for yourself. With 130 students, you will need time to replenish yourself.

Noah's creative teaching of social studies helps his students find lessons meaningful and empowers them to be active citizens. "Gun control" and "music as encouraging violence" are typical issues Noah uses to involve students. In his senior-level government class, he had his students go into the neighborhood to interview people on issues that mattered to them. The students collectively identified one of the issues to focus on, studied it, and came up with action plans that included a solution to the problem. They then combined their ideas into one proposal (in this case, it was affordable housing) that they presented to the city council for consideration. "Students came out with a connection to public life that they didn't have before," Noah notes. First-year teachers can incorporate fresh, motivating, and even life-enhancing lessons, as Noah demonstrates.

Noah Zeichner

Explore your reasons for becoming a teacher. Rate each of the following characteristics and experiences in relation to how each describes your motivation for choosing teaching as a career. Rate each item on a scale from 1–5 (1 = "very applicable"; 5 = "not at all applicable"). Which factors are most applicable to you? What is your strongest reason for becoming a teacher?

	Very applicable		Not at all applicable				Very applicable		Not at all applicable	
1. A passion for learning	1	2	3	4	5	7. Good verbal and writing skills	1 2 3 4 5			
2. Success as a student	1	2	3	4	5	8. Appreciation for the arts	1 2 3 4 5			
3. Good sense of humor	1	2	3	4	5	9. Experiences working with children (camp, church, tutoring, etc.)	1 2 3 4 5			
4. Positive attitude toward students	1	2	3	4	5	10. Other teachers in family	1 2 3 4 5			
5. Tolerance toward others	1	2	3	4	5	11. Encouragement from family to enter teaching	1 2 3 4 5			
6. Patience	1	2	3	4	5	12. Desire to serve	1 2 3 4 5			

FIGURE 1.2 Why do I want to teach?

Explore more deeply your reasons for becoming a teacher by completing the activity presented in Figure 1.2. The figure presents several characteristics that may indicate your probable satisfaction with teaching as a career.

WHAT ARE THE BENEFITS OF TEACHING?

Perhaps you are drawn to teaching by its practical advantages. Teachers' hours and vacations are well-known advantages. While the hours most teachers devote to their jobs go far beyond the number of hours they actually spend at school, their schedules are more flexible than those of other professionals. Teachers who have young children can often be at home when their children are not in school, and nearly all teachers, regardless of years of experience, have numerous holidays and a long summer vacation. On the other hand, teachers at the nation's nearly 3,000 public year-round schools in 46 states have three or four mini-vacations throughout the year (National Association for Year-Round Education, 2008). Teachers at year-round schools welcome the flexibility of being able to take vacations during off-peak seasons.

Salaries and Benefits

Although intangible rewards are a significant attraction to teaching, teachers want the public to acknowledge the value and status of teaching by supporting higher salaries. According to a poll, *A National Priority: Americans Speak on Teacher Quality* (Hart & Teeter, 2002), 83 percent of the public favors increased salaries for teachers, even if it means paying higher taxes. As a result of the public's support for higher teacher salaries, teachers' salaries have increased steadily since the 1990s. The average salaries of all teachers in 1990 was $31,367; for 2006–07, the average salary was $50,816 (National Education Association, December 2007). By 2015–16, it is estimated that teachers' average salaries will increase by 5 percent (National Education Association, December 2007). Table 1.1 shows a state-by-state ranking of salaries for public school teachers for 2006–07.

TABLE 1.1 Estimated average instructional staff and teacher salaries, 2006–07

Region and State	Average Salaries	
	Instructional Staff	Classroom Teachers
U.S. and D.C.	**52,843***	**50,816***
Alabama	45,528	43,389
Alaska	62,448*	54,658*
Arizona	58,283*	45,941*
Arkansas	45,509*	44,245*
California	63,640*	63,640
Colorado	47,987	45,833
Connecticut	63,769*	60,822*
Delaware	57,375	54,680
D.C.	59,000*	59,000*
Florida	46,669	45,308
Georgia	52,403	49,905
Hawaii	53,990	51,922
Idaho	42,798	42,798*
Illinois	58,903	58,246
Indiana	50,569	47,831
Iowa	44,738	43,130
Kansas	44,348	43,334
Kentucky	47,192	43,646
Louisiana	44,768	42,816
Maine	46,216*	41,596*
Maryland	57,882	56,927
Massachusetts	59,556*	58,624
Michigan	60,198*	54,895*
Minnesota	51,981*	49,634*
Mississippi	41,754	40,182
Missouri	43,796	41,839
Montana	40,943*	41,225*
Nebraska	45,013*	42,044
Nevada	47,533*	45,342*
New Hampshire	48,315*	46,527*
New Jersey	63,125*	59,920*
New Mexico	44,472	42,780
New York	59,839*	58,537*
North Carolina	46,410*	46,410
North Dakota	40,171	38,822
Ohio	53,181*	51,937*
Oklahoma	44,025	42,379
Oregon	51,122	50,911
Pennsylvania	56,638*	54,970*
Rhode Island	59,435*	55,956*
South Carolina	47,350*	44,133*
South Dakota	36,743	35,378
Tennessee	45,503	43,816
Texas	47,584	44,897
Utah	44,308*	40,566*
Vermont	49,705*	48,370*
Virginia	46,823*	44,727*
Washington	50,517	47,882
West Virginia	42,249	40,531
Wisconsin	52,116*	47,901*
Wyoming	52,471	50,692

Note: "Instructional staff" includes teachers, principals, consultants or supervisors of instruction, guidance personnel, librarians, psychological personnel, and other instructional staff.

*Data reflect NEA estimates rather than estimates by state departments of education.

Adapted from: Rankings & Estimates: Rankings of the States 2006 and Estimates of School Statistics 2007. Washington, DC: National Education Association, December 2007, p. 67. Data used with permission of the National Education Association © 2007. All rights reserved.

When comparing teachers' salaries state by state, remember that higher salaries are frequently linked to a higher cost of living, a more experienced teaching force, and a more desirable location. In addition, many districts have salary policies that attract the best graduates of teacher education programs, encourage quality teachers to remain in the classroom, or draw teachers into subjects and geographic areas in which there are shortages. These policies can increase a teacher's salary by thousands of dollars. For example, the Southern Regional Education Board reported that states in the region offered annual quality-based incentives from $1,000 to $15,000 during 2006 (Gaines, 2007).

Teachers' salaries are typically determined by years of experience and advanced training, as evidenced by graduate credit hours or advanced degrees. When you become a teacher, you may be able to increase your salary by taking on additional duties, such as coaching an athletic team, producing the yearbook and school newspaper, or sponsoring clubs. In addition, your district may offer limited summer employment for teachers who wish to teach summer school or develop curriculum materials. Additionally, about one-fourth of the nation's nearly 4 million public school teachers moonlight (i.e., hold a second job) to increase their earnings.

Teachers also receive various fringe benefits, such as medical insurance and retirement plans, which are usually given in addition to base salary. These benefits vary from district to district and are determined during collective bargaining sessions. When considering a school district for your first position, carefully examine the fringe benefits package as well as the salary schedule and opportunities for extra pay.

Job Security and Job Outlook

Periods of economic recession often result in layoffs for workers in other sectors of U.S. society; however, teachers tend to enjoy a higher level of job security during such times. In addition, the widespread practice of **tenure** contributes to job security for teachers. Tenure is job security granted to teachers after satisfactory performance for a specified period, usually two to five years.

Clearly, there will be many job opportunities for teachers in the near future. As a result of what researchers call a demographic echo of the baby boom, the school-age population in the United States is expected to reach 48.2 million by 2012. In addition, the total number of pre-K to 12 school teachers is expected to increase from 3,954,000 in 2006 to 4,433,000 in 2016, an increase of 12 percent (U.S. Department of Labor, 2008).

Job opportunities for teachers over the next 10 years should be excellent. Currently, many school districts are luring teachers from other states and districts with bonuses and higher pay. In addition, increasing enrollments of students from minority groups and a shortage of teachers from minority groups are leading to increased efforts to recruit minority teachers. Also, the number of non-English-speaking students has grown dramatically, especially in California and Florida, creating a demand for bilingual teachers and teachers of English as a second language.

In response to a current shortage of teachers in some locations and anticipated teacher retirements, many states are implementing policies that will encourage more college students to become teachers. Some states give large signing bonuses that are distributed over the teacher's first few years of teaching. Some are increasing state scholarships, issuing loans for moving expenses, and implementing loan-forgiveness programs (U.S. Department of Labor, 2008).

The supply of teachers also is expected to increase in response to reports of improved job prospects, more teacher involvement in school governance, and greater public interest in education. The improved job outlook for teachers is reflected in the steadily increased number of bachelor's and master's degrees granted in education. Also, more people are entering the profession from other careers.

WHAT ARE THE CHALLENGES OF TEACHING?

Like all professions, teaching has undesirable or difficult aspects. Frank McCourt, a teacher at four New York City high schools over a 30-year period and a noted author after his retirement from teaching, said a teacher needs to be "a drill sergeant, a rabbi, a disciplinarian, a low-level scholar, a clerk, a referee, a clown, a counselor, and therapist" (McCourt, 2005).

As a prospective teacher, you should consider the challenges as well as the satisfactions you are likely to encounter. You can make the most of your teacher education program if you are informed. Awareness of the realities of teaching will enable you to develop your personal philosophy of education, build a repertoire of teaching strategies, strengthen your leadership skills, and acquire a knowledge base of research and theory to guide your actions. In this manner, you can become a true professional—free to enjoy the many satisfactions of teaching and confident of your ability to deal with its challenges. Table 1.2 shows that teachers must deal with a variety of problems in the schools. The sections that follow discuss three challenges that are part of teachers' daily lives: long working hours, accountability for student learning in a high-stakes testing environment, and motivating today's tech-savvy students.

Long Working Hours

The length of a teacher's workday may appear attractive, but teachers' actual working hours are another matter. Teachers' contracts do not include additional hours for lesson planning and evaluating students' work, nor do they include noninstructional assignments found at all levels of teaching—from recess duty to club sponsorship and coaching. Teachers devote an average of 50 hours a week to their jobs, with approximately 37 hours devoted to required duties, and 12 hours devoted to uncompensated teaching tasks (National Education Association, 2003).

TABLE 1.2 What do you think are the biggest problems with which the public schools of this community must deal?

	1999 Teachers (%)	1996 Teachers (%)	1989 Teachers (%)	1984 Teachers (%)
Parents' lack of support/interest	18	22(1T)	34(1)	31(1)
Pupils' lack of interest/attitudes/truancy	13	16(3)	26(3)	20(3)
Lack of financial support/funding/money	9	22(1T)	27(2)	21(2)
Lack of discipline/more control	7	20(2)	25(4T)	19(4)
Lack of family structure/problems of home life	6	15(4)	8(8)	4(13)
Overcrowded school	4	7(5T)	7(9T)	4(10)
Use of drugs/dope	2	7(5T)	13(7)	5(7)
Fighting/violence/gangs	1	7(5T)	—	—
Moral standards/dress code/sex/pregnancy	*	7	4(15T)	2(22)

Note: Figures add to more than 100 percent because of multiple answers, except 1999 figures, which add to less than 100 percent because all answers are not reported. Parenthetical figures indicate rankings. T indicates a response tied for a given rank.

* Less than 1 percent.

Source: From Carol A. Langdon, "Sixth Poll of Teachers' Attitudes Toward the Public Schools: Selected Questions and Responses," Bloomington, IN: Phi Delta Kappa Center for Education, Development, and Research, Research Bulletin, April 2000, No. 26 (www.pdkintl.org/edres/resbul26.htm).

What might be some of the pressures felt by students and teachers as a result of the emphasis on high-stakes testing?

The need to keep accurate, detailed records of students' academic progress, absences, and lateness, as well as other forms of paperwork, is one of the teacher's most time-consuming tasks. Other nonteaching tasks include supervising students on the playground, at extracurricular events, and in the hallways, study halls, and lunchrooms; attending faculty meetings, parent conferences, and open houses; and taking tickets or selling at concessions for athletic events. Nonteaching responsibilities often are enjoyable and provide opportunities to interact informally with students; however, they can lessen the amount of time and energy teachers have available for teaching-related tasks.

High-Stakes Testing and Increased Accountability

A significant challenge for today's teachers is the emphasis placed on **high-stakes tests.** Each state has mandated a standardized test to assess students' mastery of academic standards. For example, fourth-, seventh-, and tenth-grade students in Washington State must take the Washington Assessment of Student Learning (WASL) based on the state's Essential Academic Learning Requirements (EALRs) in reading, writing, listening, and mathematics. In Texas, students must take the Texas Assessment of Knowledge and Skills (TAKS), which assesses how well they have mastered the Texas Essential Knowledge and Skills (TEKS) in English language arts, mathematics, science, and social studies.

Nationwide, high-stakes tests are used increasingly to determine whether a student can participate in extracurricular activities or graduate, or whether teachers and administrators are given merit pay increases. Similarly, at the national level, efforts are being made to hold schools and teachers more accountable. One teacher describes the pressure she feels to keep track of student progress in mathematics on a daily basis as one of the biggest changes she experienced in ten years of teaching:

> Before, you didn't have four or five groups going in math. . . You didn't give an exit card [formative assessment] at the end of every lesson to see who got it, who didn't, who needs reteaching. And that's a daily thing now, to figure out where you're gonna go tomorrow, who's going on, who's staying here, who's going backwards. . . . Before, you taught a lesson to everybody, and hopefully, everybody got it. (Valli & Buese, 2007, p. 541)

In 2002, President George W. Bush, to fulfill his pledge to "leave no child behind," signed into legislation the **No Child Left Behind (NCLB) Act,** a $26.5 billion comprehensive educational reform bill mandating statewide testing in reading and mathematics each year in grades 3–8. Six years later, in his eighth and final State of the Union address, President Bush stressed the importance of continuing NCLB's emphasis on accountability: "Six years ago, we came together to pass the No Child Left Behind Act, and today no one can deny its results. . . . Now we must work together to increase accountability, add flexibility for states and districts, reduce the number of high school dropouts, provide extra help for struggling students" (U.S. Department of Education, March/April 2008, p. 1).

According to NCLB, schools whose scores fail to improve over a six-year period could lose staff, and low-income students at those schools could receive federal funds for tutoring or transportation to another public school. Also, NCLB requires that, by the end of the academic year 2013–14, public schools guarantee that all students are pre-

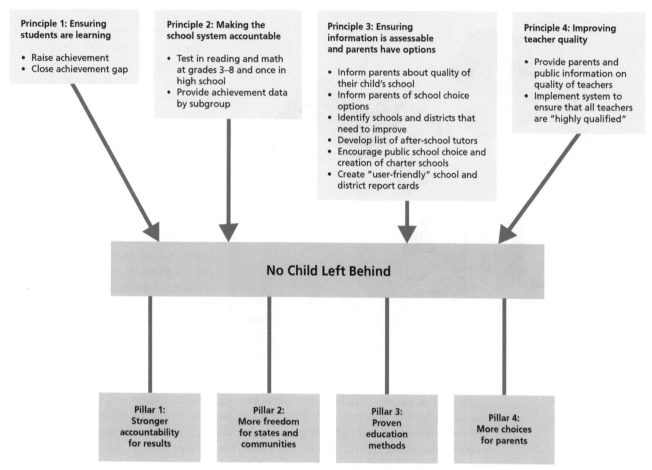

FIGURE 1.3 Four key principles and four pillars of NCLB

pared to pass state proficiency tests. Figure 1.3 illustrates the four key principles and four "pillars" of NCLB.

An additional key provision of NCLB is for schools to provide evidence each year that students are making **adequate yearly progress (AYP).** Schools that fail to make AYP will be identified as "in need of improvement." The first year a school does not make AYP, it must provide transportation for pupils who want to enroll in another public school. If the school fails to make AYP again, it must pay for supplemental services, including tutoring.

AYP is determined by students' performance on machine-scored, multiple-choice tests in math and reading. At least 95 percent of students in grades 3–8 at a school must take the tests. However, schools must do more than improve overall average scores. The federal government requires that AYP be made by students in all subgroups according to age, race, ethnicity, and socioeconomic status. Pressure to meet the requirements of NCLB is a reality for today's teachers, as a middle school principal points out: "We have wonderful teachers. They work hard and do a great job of meeting needs. My concern is the extra, unnecessary pressure added to them due to NCLB. . . . [T]est scores drive teaching now, more than ever, and [NCLB is] increasing the amount of pressure for teachers and principals" (Abernathy, 2007, p. 99).

Today's Tech-Savvy Students

Understanding how technology affects students and schools and integrating technology into teaching come easy for some teachers; for other teachers, however, it can be a challenge. Students in your classroom will have grown up in "a techno-drenched atmosphere that has trained them to absorb and process information in fundamentally different

For these students, using computers and advanced technology is an everyday part of their lives. How can teachers remain up-to-date regarding the role that technology plays in their students' lives?

ways" (McHugh, 2005). For example, students in grades 3–12 spend an average of 6 hours and 21 minutes each day using some type of media. Because today's students are skilled at multitasking, the figure jumps to about 8½ hours and includes almost 4 hours watching TV and 50 minutes of videogame play. Homework, however, receives only 50 minutes of their time (Rideout, Roberts, & Foehr, 2005).

Schools have not kept up with the rapid changes in technology. "For this digital generation, electronic media is increasingly seductive, influential, and pervasive, yet most schools treat the written word as the only means of communication worthy of study" (George Lucas Educational Foundation, February 9, 2008). Today's students have iPods, cell phones, video cameras, laptops, and digital cameras. Websites like Facebook and MySpace are changing the way students communicate, socialize, and network. Sites like YouTube and iTunes bring media to students seamlessly, whether at home, school, or on the move. Media content comes into schools through cell phones, the Internet, e-mail, text messages, and general entertainment (music, video, and blogs, for example).

To keep up with the media and technology environment today's students inhabit outside school, teachers must integrate technology into their teaching. For example, students of Diane Hamstra, a teacher at Park Tudor School in Indianapolis, use software called *DyKnow Vision* to analyze passages from American literature on computer screens at their desks. She then posts their work on a large-screen monitor at the front of the classroom, and students discuss the displayed examples.

Hamstra has also had students analyze similar passages using pen and paper; however, she found that, using the software, the students' responses "were deeper than with pen and ink. The focus is really sharp. There's something about changing over to an electronic medium, something about that screen. It's psychological. It's a generational thing" (George Lucas Educational Foundation, 2005).

Another teacher who has integrated technology into teaching is John Blake, a teacher at North Whiteville Academy, an alternative school in North Whiteville, North Carolina. Blake realized that "kids are bombarded by media. They're completely high tech, and they don't know a different way. When you hand them a book, they're going to say, 'Is this all there is?'" (George Lucas Educational Foundation, 2005).

Blake uses Moodle software to manage class-related conversations, homework assignments, and quizzes. He also encourages students to keep blogs (short for "web log") using *BlogMeister*, an online publishing tool developed specifically for classroom use. So all school-related activity can be viewed in one place, Blake links material from Moodle and BlogMeister using Bloglines.

"This is a mix-and-match generation," Blake says. "I'm looking at these things as a way to hook into what they're doing outside the classroom. When they see that I know how to use the technology, they think, 'This is going to be cool.'" On Blake's class wiki (online software that allows users to create, edit, and link web pages easily), a student notes that we "are learning how to micromanage an array of elements while simultaneously balancing short- and long-term goals" (George Lucas Educational Foundation, 2005).

Effective teachers recognize that technology can be a powerful tool for enhancing students' inquiry, reflection, and problem solving. They also realize that technology cannot be grafted onto existing teaching strategies; it must be integrated into those strategies. The Technology in Action feature demonstrates practical applications of technology in real classrooms, by real teachers. It includes technology-based learning activities designed to give you hands-on experience at integrating technology into teaching. The Technology in Action feature on the next page explains how your classmates can create a wiki to use during the term to discuss issues and content presented in this text.

WHAT WILL SOCIETY EXPECT OF ME AS A TEACHER?

The prevailing view within our society is that teachers are public servants accountable to the people. As a result, society has high expectations of teachers—some would say too high. Entrusted with our nation's most precious resource, its children and youth, today's teachers are expected to have advanced knowledge and skills and high academic and ethical standards. Although promoting students' academic progress has always been their primary responsibility, teachers are also expected to further students' social, emotional, and moral development and to safeguard students' health and well-being. Increasingly, the public calls on teachers and schools to address the social problems and risk factors that affect student success.

The Public Trust

Teaching is subject to a high degree of public scrutiny and control. The level of trust that the public extends to teachers as professionals varies greatly. The public appears to have great confidence in the work that teachers do. Because of its faith in the teaching profession, the public invests teachers with considerable power over its children. For the most part, parents willingly allow their children to be influenced by teachers and expect their children to obey and respect teachers. However, the public trust increases and decreases in response to social and political changes that lead to waves of educational reform. Table 1.3 shows how people rated their public schools in selected years between 1983, just after the release of *A Nation at Risk,* and 2007.

TABLE 1.3 Ratings given the local public schools (in percent)

	2007	2005	2002	2001	1999	1998	1995	1993	1991	1989	1987	1985	1983
A and B	45	48	47	51	49	46	41	47	42	43	43	43	31
A	9	12	10	11	11	10	8	10	10	8	12	9	6
B	36	36	37	40	38	36	33	37	32	35	31	34	25
C	34	29	34	30	31	31	37	31	33	33	30	30	32
D	14	9	10	8	9	9	12	11	10	11	9	10	13
Fail	5	5	3	5	5	5	5	4	5	4	4	4	7
Don't know	2	9	6	6	6	9	5	7	10	9	14	13	17

Sources: Alec M. Gallup, Lowell C. Rose, and Stanley M. Elan, "The 24th Annual Gallup Poll of the Public's Attitudes Toward the Public Schools," Phi Delta Kappan, September 1992, p. 32; Stanley M. Elam and Lowell C. Rose, "The 27th Annual Phi Delta Kappa/Gallup Poll of the Public's Attitudes Toward the Public Schools," Phi Delta Kappan, September 1995, p. 42; Lowell C. Rose and Alec M. Gallup, "The 30th Annual Phi Delta Kappa/Gallup Poll of the Public's Attitudes Toward the Public Schools," Phi Delta Kappan, September 1999, p. 45; Lowell C. Rose and Alec M. Gallup, "The 34th Annual Phi Delta Kappa/Gallup Poll of the Public's Attitudes Toward the Public Schools," Phi Delta Kappan, September 2002, p. 43 (http://www.pdkintl.org/kappan/k0209pol.htm#1a); and Lowell C. Rose and Alec M. Gallup, "The 37th Annual Phi Delta Kappa/Gallup Poll of the Public's Attitudes Toward the Public Schools," Phi Delta Kappan, September 2005, pp. 41–57, "The 37th Annual Phi Delta Kappa/Gallup Poll of the Public's Attitudes Toward the Public Schools," Phi Delta Kappan, September 2007, pp. 33–48.

TECHNOLOGY in *ACTION*

Wikis in 10th-Grade Social Studies

Maria Valquez has asked her 10th-grade social studies students to track and report on national election activities. She has organized her four social studies classes into 28 groups of 3 students each. Each group is assigned an aspect of the election to cover, such as specific political parties, an individual candidate, hot topic issues, media campaign messages, and so on. Maria wants students to be able to share the information they find among the four classes, with the rest of the school, and even with the community. In addition to researching election activities, she hopes that students will strive to find common ground and form a consensus on controversial issues. To facilitate this communication and sharing of information, Maria needs a technology tool that is not controlled by a single group or individual. She needs a tool that allows all students in her social studies classes to have an equal say. She decides to use a wiki.

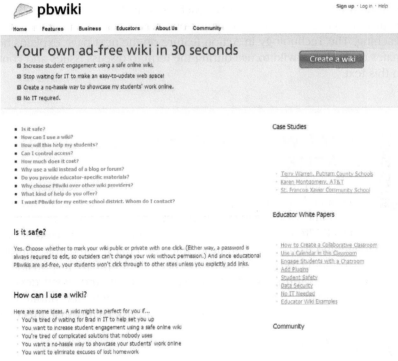

Source: PBWiki, Inc., http://www.pbwiki.com (accessed May 3, 2008). Used by permission.

WIKIS: Coming out of the social web movement, wikis follow the logic that many voices are better than one. A wiki is a website that allows collaborative work by various authors. A wiki website allows anyone or designated members of a group to create, delete, or edit the content on the website.

VISIT: http://pbwiki.com/education.wiki. Several free wiki services are available to educators. A simple Google search yields promising results. Although you can choose any tool that feels right to you, for the purpose of this discussion we will use PBwiki. It is one of the most popular and it is free to educators (at the time of publication anyway). According to the authors of the site, "PBwiki lets you quickly set up your own free, hosted, password-protected wiki to edit and share information. It's as easy as a peanut butter sandwich." In addition to creating your own wiki, you can see how others have used wiki tools to increase student engagement.

POSSIBLE USES: By using a wiki, students can explore a book, an events calendar, a field trip, and so on. A wiki can be a long-term exploration—such as the results of a newly formed conservation club—or a short-term event—like your high school basketball team going to the state tournament. View the example of Terry Warren, at Putnam County School, who was looking for a way to showcase his student's work: http://pbwiki.com/content/casestudy-terrywarren.

TRY IT OUT: First, visit http://pbwiki.com/education.wiki and click on Create a WIKI. Then complete the wiki form—which consists of your e-mail address, a password, the name of the wiki site that you want to create, and the purpose of your wiki site. Hit Submit, and then instructions are e-mailed to you. It's that easy.

Teacher Competency and Effectiveness

Society believes that competent, effective teachers are important keys to a strong system of education. As a teacher, you will be expected to be proficient in the use of instructional strategies, curriculum materials, advanced educational technologies, and classroom management techniques. You will also be expected to have a thorough understanding of the developmental levels of students and a solid grasp of the content you teach. To maintain and extend this high level of skill, you will be expected to keep informed of exemplary practices and to demonstrate a desire for professional development.

Teacher competency and effectiveness include the responsibility to help all learners succeed. Although today's students come from diverse backgrounds, society will expect you to believe in the potential of *all* children. Regardless of your students' ethnicity, language, gender, socioeconomic status, sexual orientation, religion, family backgrounds and living conditions, abilities, and disabilities, you will have a responsibility to ensure that all students develop to their fullest potential. To accomplish this, you will be expected to have a repertoire of instructional strategies and resources to create meaningful learning experiences that promote students' growth and development.

Teacher Accountability

Teachers must also "be mindful of the social ethic—their public duties and obligations embodied in the practice of teaching" (Hansen, 1995, p. 143). Society agrees that teachers are primarily responsible for promoting students' learning, although different members of society are not always in agreement about what students should learn. As a teacher, you will be expected to understand how factors such as student backgrounds, attitudes, and learning styles can affect achievement. You will be expected to create a safe and effective learning environment for your students, and you will be accountable for equalizing educational opportunity and maintaining high professional standards.

WHAT IS THE JOB OUTLOOK FOR TEACHERS?

When you think ahead to a career in teaching, a question you are likely to ask yourself is, What is the job outlook for teachers? From time to time, **teacher supply and demand** figures have painted a rather bleak picture for those entering the teaching profession. At other times, such as now, finding a position has not been difficult. For example, the U.S. Department of Education projects that the number of elementary through secondary teachers will increase from 3.5 million in 2004 to almost 4.2 million in 2016, an increase of 18 percent (National Center for Education Statistics, December 2007).

Even during times of teacher surplus, talented, qualified teachers are able to find jobs. Teaching is one of the largest professions in the United States; out of a national population of nearly 304 million, about 49.6 million attended public and private elementary and secondary schools during 2007–08, where they were taught by nearly 4 million teachers (National Center for Education Statistics, February 28, 2008). Within such a large profession, annual openings resulting from retirements and career changes alone are numerous.

For the foreseeable future, there will be exceptional job opportunities for teachers from diverse racial and ethnic backgrounds and for teachers with disabilities. Students from diverse racial, ethnic, and cultural backgrounds and students with disabilities benefit from having role models with whom they can easily identify. In addition, teachers from diverse groups and teachers with disabilities may have, in some instances, an enhanced understanding of student diversity and student variability that they can share with other teachers.

Demand for Teachers of Color

Approximately 42 percent of public school students were considered part of a minority group during 2004, an increase of 20 percent from 1972 (National Center for Education Statistics, September 2007). Before the middle of this century, more than half of the nation's students will be minority-group members (U.S. Bureau of Census, 2008). In the nation's 25 largest cities, students of color represent half or more of the student population (Ladson-Billings, 2005).

When contrasted with the diverse mosaic of student enrollments, the backgrounds of today's teachers reveal less diversity. Teachers of color represent about 12 percent of public school teachers in the United States (Ladson-Billings, 2005), and that percentage is expected to drop to less than 5 percent (Jorgenson, 2001). This shortage is due in part to the fact that minority students frequently attend our nation's most impoverished schools. At such schools, students receive little motivation to become teachers. If their school experiences are negative, they have little incentive to pursue a career in teaching. To attract more minority candidates to teaching, Jorgenson (2001) suggests that districts

- prioritize the recruitment of ethnic educators
- consider nontraditional sources of teacher recruitment
- expedite the application materials of ethnic applicants
- discuss the possibility of offering hiring bonuses for ethnic candidates
- develop a paraprofessional-to-teacher program
- understand how ethnically diverse employees perceive the district
- create a support network for educators of color

The typical undergraduate candidate preparing to teach is a young, white female who recently graduated from high school and is attending college full-time. Postbaccalaureate-level individuals preparing to teach tend to be older, to include slightly more people of color and more males, to be transitioning into teaching from an occupation outside the field of education, to have prior teaching-related experience, and to be attending college part-time (Feistritzer, 1999). Figure 1.4 illustrates the differences between the racial and ethnic composition of students enrolled in U.S. public schools and that of teacher-preparation students in undergraduate and graduate programs.

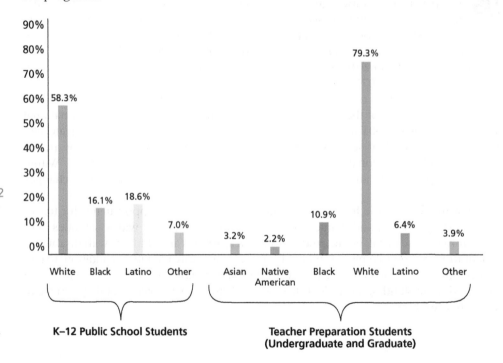

FIGURE 1.4 Racial and ethnic distribution of K–12 public school and teacher preparation students
Sources: Based on data from (1) U.S. Department of Education, National Center for Education Statistics, The Condition of Education 2002–05. Washington, DC: Author, 2005. (2) C. Emily Feistritzer, A Report on Teacher Preparation in the U.S. Washington, DC: National Center for Education Information.

Demand for Teachers with Disabilities

Contrary to what some people may think, research indicates that people with disabilities can be effective teachers (Educators with Disabilities Caucus, Council for Exceptional Children, 2008). In addition, as Amanda Trei, an elementary school teacher with disabilities, points out, teachers with disabilities have an "advantage" in working with special education students: "I have a one-up on anybody who can walk, because I can see what my students need, and I can see the struggles they're going to face. Somebody who isn't disabled—they can read about it, they can watch it, but if they never live through it, they never really know" (Wills, September 2007).

Teachers with disabilities can also be inspirational to students without disabilities, as Tricia Downing, a competitive athlete paralyzed from the waist down and a teacher at a magnet high school, points out: "Sometimes, students get stuck in their teenage world, where everything's a crisis. I've been able to get across to students that the world is bigger than their problems. My message is that life is full of challenges, but if you're willing to try to overcome them, you can find the resources within yourself" (Wills, September 2007).

The percentage of children with disabilities receiving special education in public pre-K to 12 schools is approximately 10 percent (Hardman, Drew, & Egan, 2007), and the current critical need for special education teachers is expected to continue for the next few decades.

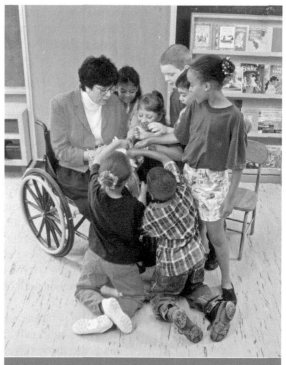

Teachers with disabilities can be highly effective at teaching students in "regular" classrooms. In what ways can teachers with disabilities be role models for students without disabilities?

Demand for Teachers by Geographic Region and Specialty Area

Public elementary and secondary school enrollments are projected to rise by more than 4 percent between 2001 and 2013, and growth will vary widely across the nation. Enrollment will increase in the western and southern regions by 13.2 percent and 3.9 percent, respectively. On the other hand, a decrease of 1.8 percent is projected for the northeastern region, while the midwestern region will show no change in enrollment (National Center for Education Statistics, 2008). The ease with which you will find your first teaching position is also related to your area of specialization. In 2008, for example, job seekers able to teach bilingual education, special education, English as a second language (ESL), mathematics, chemistry, or physics were in an especially favorable position.

HOW WILL I BECOME A HIGHLY QUALIFIED TEACHER?

"Quality teachers have a greater influence on pupil achievement than any other school-based factor," according to *Teachers for a New Era*, a teacher education reform effort led by the Carnegie Corporation of New York (2008). **Highly qualified teachers (HQTs)** for all students is also a key provision of NCLB. As shown in Figure 1.3 on page 17, Principle 4 of NCLB calls for "highly qualified" teachers—that is, teachers who have (1) a bachelor's degree, (2) full state certification, and (3) knowledge of each subject they teach. NCLB also requires states to report progress toward the goal of highly qualified teachers for all students.

How will you make the transition from being a student to being a highly qualified teacher? At this point in your journey to become a teacher, you can do a great deal to make your entry into teaching professionally rewarding and to ensure that you will become a highly qualified teacher. During your journey toward becoming a highly qualified teacher, you will become immersed in the world of professional standards.

Professional Standards

To ensure that all students are taught by highly qualified teachers, several professional associations and state departments of education have developed standards that reflect what teachers should know and be able to do. Most likely, the teacher education program in which you are enrolled will use one or more of these sets of standards to evaluate your progress toward becoming an effective teacher. During your training, you are sure to hear repeatedly about plans instituted by state departments of education to assess teachers and students alike on an ongoing basis. After you become a teacher, you may learn even more about state standards if you have a mentor like Jane Ching Fung, author of this chapter's Teachers' Voices: Research to Reality and a National Board Certified Teacher at a public school in Los Angeles. Fung started the Early Literacy Club, a support network for new teachers at her school. She conducted a research project on how a teacher network supports new teachers as they implement state standards in the classroom.

The professional standards that have had the greatest impact on teacher education programs nationally (as well as on teachers' ongoing professional growth and development) are those developed by the **Interstate New Teacher Assessment and Support Consortium (INTASC)**, the **National Council for Accreditation of Teacher Education (NCATE)**, the **Praxis Series** and the **Professional Assessments for Beginning Teachers,** and the **National Board for Professional Teaching Standards (NBPTS).** Figure 1.5 provides an overview of their standards. How have these standards influenced the teacher education program in which you are enrolled? Does your state have a set of professional standards that also applies to your teacher education program?

INTASC Standards

INTASC is a consortium of more than 30 states that has developed standards and an assessment process for initial teacher certification. INTASC model core standards are based on 10 principles evident in effective teaching regardless of subject or grade level. The principles are based on the realization that effective teachers integrate content knowledge with pedagogical understanding to ensure that all students learn (INTASC, 1993).

1. Knowledge of subject matter
2. Knowledge of human development and learning
3. Adapting instruction for individual needs
4. Multiple instructional strategies
5. Classroom motivation and management
6. Communication skills
7. Instructional planning skills
8. Assessment of student learning
9. Professional commitment and responsibility
10. Partnerships

NCATE Standards

NCATE standards are for the accreditation of colleges and universities with teacher preparation programs. Currently, fewer than half of the 1,300 institutions that prepare teachers are accredited by NCATE. While NCATE standards apply to teacher education programs, not to teacher education students per se, NCATE believes that the new profe ssional teacher who graduates from a professional accredited school, college, or department of education should be able to" do the following (NCATE, 2002a):

- Help all prekindergarten through twelfth grade (P–12) students learn
- Teach to P–12 student standards set by specialized professional associations and the states
- Explain instructional choices based on research-derived knowledge and best practice
- Apply effective methods of teaching students who are at different developmental stages, have different learning styles, and come from diverse backgrounds
- Reflect on practice, act on feedback, and integrate technology into instruction effectively

(continues)

FIGURE 1.5 Professional standards for teachers: What should teachers know and be able to do?

NBPTS Standards

This board issues professional certificates to teachers who possess extensive professional knowledge and the ability to perform at a high level. Certification candidates submit a portfolio including videotapes of classroom interactions and samples of student work plus the teacher's reflective comments. Trained NBPTS evaluators who teach in the same field as the candidate judge all elements of the assessments. NBPTS has developed five "core propositions" on which voluntary national teacher certification is based (NBPTS, 1994):

1. Teachers are committed to students and their learning.
2. Teachers know the subjects they teach and how to teach those subjects to students.
3. Teachers are responsible for managing and monitoring student learning.
4. Teachers think systematically about their practice and learn from experience.
5. Teachers are members of learning communities.

Praxis Series

Based on knowledge and skills states commonly require of beginning teachers, the Praxis Series assesses individual development as it corresponds to three steps in becoming a teacher. These three areas of assessment are Academic Skills Assessments: entering a teacher education program (Praxis I); Subject Assessments: licensure for entering the profession (Praxis II); and Classroom Performance Assessments: the first year of teaching (Praxis III). Praxis III involves the assessment of actual teaching skills in four areas (Danielson, 1996):

1. Planning and preparation
   - Demonstrating knowledge of content and pedagogy
   - Demonstrating knowledge of students
   - Selecting instructional goals
   - Demonstrating knowledge of resources
   - Designing coherent instruction
2. The classroom environment
   - Creating an environment of respect and rapport
   - Establishing a culture for learning
   - Managing classroom procedures
   - Managing student behavior
   - Organizing physical space
3. Instruction
   - Communicating clearly and accurately
   - Using questioning and discussion techniques
   - Engaging students in learning
   - Providing feedback to students
   - Demonstrating flexibility and responsiveness
4. Professional responsibilities
   - Reflecting on teaching
   - Maintaining accurate records
   - Communicating with families
   - Contributing to the school and district
   - Growing and developing professionally

FIGURE 1.5 Continued

Certification

Successful completion of a college or university teacher preparation program will not automatically enable you to teach. State certification is required for teaching in the public schools and in many private schools as well. In some cases, large cities (e.g., Chicago, New York, Buffalo) have their own certification requirements that must be met. And certain local school districts have additional requirements, such as a written examination, before one can teach in those districts.

TEACHERS' VOICES RESEARCH TO REALITY

Jane Ching Fung

THE EARLY LITERACY CLUB: BUILDING EXCELLENCE THROUGH COLLABORATION

Every year, California hires thousands of brand-new teachers for its teaching positions. Many of those newly hired teachers enter the classroom with little or no training in the field of education. My concern, as a mentor teacher and former emergency credential teacher, is that these new educators receive adequate support and are provided with professional development opportunities to help them become effective members of our profession.

I teach in an urban primary school located near downtown Los Angeles. Approximately 85 percent of our school population consists of limited-English-speaking students. Almost all of our students receive free or reduced-price meal tickets. Over 60 percent of the teachers at my school are on emergency credentials and have taught less than three years. Although these new teachers are eager to learn and develop their craft, there are few opportunities in our district and at the school site to meet and collaborate on an ongoing basis.

[A] group of new teachers and I created the Early Literacy Club (ELC), a teacher network at our school. Initially, the goal of the ELC was to provide much-needed instructional and emotional support for the overwhelmed new teacher.

Teachers need to discuss their teaching and have ongoing professional discussions with peers, not just read or hear about best practices. New teachers must be given opportunities to see what quality teaching looks like in action and be given feedback on their own teaching. [Teachers] and schools involved in these forms of professional development have frequently shown increased student achievement.

The more knowledgeable and successful we are as educators, the more our students will achieve. My study shows the importance of ongoing support and collaboration in the training and retention of new teachers. Networks are one way to improve our teaching practices and train new teachers in a comfortable, risk-free environment.

The network is now a cross-school network and has increased its membership to fourteen. Membership includes National Board Certified teachers, mentor teachers, literacy and math facilitators, and teacher leaders. The network continues to meet regularly, and members' teaching experience ranges from 3 weeks to 14 years. The current focus of the network is individual teacher action research. The network's motto remains: *The Early Literacy Club: Building Excellence Through Collaboration.*

QUESTIONS

1. In what ways might a teacher network support a new teacher during his or her induction into the profession?
2. Why is it important for teachers to "discuss their teaching and have ongoing professional discussions with peers"?
3. Fung started an in-school teacher network focusing on action research and providing support for new teachers. On what other areas might an in-school teacher network focus?

Jane Ching Fung is in her 15th year of teaching. She is a MetLife Fellow in the Teachers Network Policy Institute. Her article appeared in Ellen Meyers and Frances Rust (Eds.), *Taking Action with Teacher Research*, Portsmouth, NH: Heinemann, 2003, pp. 41–62.

A **teaching certificate** is actually a license to teach. The department of education for each of the fifty states and the District of Columbia sets the requirements for certification. A certificate usually indicates at what level and in what content areas one may teach. One might be certified, for example, for all-level (K–12) physical education or art, secondary English, elementary education, or middle-level education. Currently, about two-thirds of the states offer certification for teaching at the middle school or junior high level—an increase from 1987 when about half of the states offered such certification. In addition, a certificate may list other areas of specialization, such as driver's training, coaching, or journalism. If you plan to go into nonteaching areas such as counseling, librarianship, or administration, special certificates are usually required.

The Praxis Series

Thirty-five of the forty-three states that include tests as part of their licensure process require completion of the **Praxis Series: Professional Assessments for Beginning Teachers** developed by Educational Testing Service (ETS) in consultation with teachers, educational researchers, the National Education Association, and the American Federation of Teachers. The Praxis Series (*praxis* means "putting theory into practice") enables states to create a system of tests that meet their specific licensing requirements.

The Praxis Series, which replaced the National Teacher Examination in the mid-1990s, consists of three components:

Praxis I: Academic skills assessments—Praxis I covers the enabling skills in reading, writing, and mathematics that all teachers need, regardless of grade or subject taught. Two formats, computer-based and pencil-and-paper, are available for the Praxis I assessment, which is given early in a student's teacher education program. To help students pass Praxis I, ETS offers online practice test items. Additionally, for students who need help in improving basic academic skills, LearningPlus is an interactive computer software program that provides instruction and diagnostic placement tests in reading, writing, and mathematics.

Praxis II: Subject assessments—Praxis II measures teacher education students' knowledge of the subjects they will teach. In most cases, Praxis II tests are taken after completion of an undergraduate program. The tests, available in more than 70 subject areas, have a core content module required by every state, with the remaining modules selected on an individual basis by the states. Each state can base its assessment on multiple-choice items or on candidate-constructed response modules. In addition, Praxis II includes the Principles of Learning and Teaching (PLT) test and the Professional Knowledge test; each is a two-hour test to assess teachers' professional knowledge. The PLT is available in three versions: K–6, 5–9, and 7–12.

Praxis III: Classroom performance assessments—Praxis III is a performance-based assessment system, not a test. Developed after extensive job analyses, reviews of research, and input from educators, Praxis III involves the assessment of the actual teaching skills of the beginning teacher. The assessments focus on the four domains of the Praxis Series, which are illustrated in Figure 1.5: planning and preparation, the classroom environment, instruction, and professional responsibilities. In addition, Praxis III assesses the teacher's sensitivity to developmental levels and cultural differences among students. In-class assessments and pre- and post-observation interviews conducted by trained state and local personnel are the main components of Praxis III. The observations are supplemented by work samples—for example, lesson plans. Following Praxis III assessments, which normally are completed by the end of the first year of teaching, the state makes a decision about whether to grant a license to teach.

State Licensure Certification Requirements

For a person to receive a license to teach, all states require successful completion of an approved teacher education program that culminates with at least a bachelor's degree. To be approved, programs must pass a review by the state department of education approximately every five years. In addition to approval at the state level, most of the nearly 1,300 programs in the nation have regional accreditation, and more than 600 voluntarily seek accreditation by the **National Council for Accreditation of Teacher Education (NCATE)** (February 28, 2008). Currently, all states require an average of six to eight semester credits of supervised student teaching. Alabama, Colorado, Idaho, Indiana, Nevada, New York, and Virginia require a master's degree for advanced certification; and Arizona, Maryland, Montana, Oregon, and Washington require either a master's degree or a specified number of semester credits after certification (Kaye, 2001). Additional requirements may also include U.S. citizenship, an oath of loyalty, fingerprinting, or a health examination.

A few states, including Iowa, New Mexico, North Carolina, and Oklahoma, waive state licensing requirements for teachers certified by the National Board for Professional Teaching Standards (NBPTS). About half of the states issue a license to a person from another state who holds a valid NBPTS certificate. For a current listing of state and local action supporting NBPTS certification, visit NBPTS at http://nbpts.org/.

Nearly all states now require testing of teachers for initial licensure. States use either a standardized test (usually Praxis) or a test developed by outside consultants. Areas covered by the states' tests usually include basic skills, professional knowledge, and general knowledge. Many states also require an on-the-job performance evaluation for licensure.

Today, most states do not grant a teaching license for life. Some states issue three- to five-year licenses, which may be renewed only with proof of coursework completed beyond the bachelor's degree. And, amid considerable controversy, several states, including Connecticut, Maryland, Massachusetts, New Hampshire, Rhode Island, South Carolina, and Wisconsin, have enacted testing for recertification of experienced teachers. New Hampshire and South Carolina, for instance, require that teachers pursue professional development in their subject areas, as well as in technology, to become recertified (Boser, 2000).

PEARSON
myeducationlab

Go to MyEducationLab and select Resources, *then* Licensure and Standards *to view the certification offices in the United States.*

Licensure requirements differ from state to state, and they are frequently modified. To remain up-to-date on the requirements for the state in which you plan to teach, it is important that you keep in touch with your teacher placement office or certification officer at your college or university. You may also wish to refer to *Requirements for Certification for Elementary and Secondary Schools* (The University of Chicago Press), an annual publication that lists state-by-state certification requirements for teachers, counselors, librarians, and administrators. Or you may contact the teacher certification office in the state where you plan to teach. (See the "Directory of State Teacher Certification Offices in the United States," at myeducationlab.com).

Currently, 47 states and the District of Columbia are members of the **National Association of State Directors of Teacher Education and Certification's (NASDTEC) Interstate Agreement,** a reciprocity agreement whereby a certificate obtained in one state will be honored in another. If you plan to teach in a state other than the one in which you are currently studying, you should find out whether both states are members of the NASDTEC Interstate Agreement.

More than 464,000 teachers, many of whom are noncertified, teach in the growing system of private, parochial, for-profit, and charter schools in the United States (National Center for Education Statistics, February 28, 2008). Private and parochial schools supported largely by tuition and gifts, and for-profit schools operated by private educational corporations, usually have no certification requirements for teachers. Also, teacher-created and teacher-operated charter schools, although they are public, are often free of state certification requirements. A school's charter (an agreement between the school's founders and its sponsor—usually a local school board) may waive certification requirements if the school guarantees that students will attain a specified level of achievement.

Alternative Certification

Despite the national movement to make certification requirements more stringent, concern about meeting the demand for 2 million new public school teachers during the next decade (National Education Association, 2008) and attracting minority-group members into the teaching profession has resulted in increasing use of **alternative teacher certification** programs. In 1983, only eight states offered alternatives; by 2008, each state had an alternative route to certification (Feistritzer, 2008).

Alternative certification programs are designed for people who already have at least a bachelor's degree in a field other than education and want to become licensed to teach. In 2006, more than 50,000 people were licensed through alternative certification programs (Feistritzer, 2008). Most alternative certification programs are collaborative efforts among state departments of education, teacher education programs in colleges and universities, and school districts. For example, Washington State University, in collaboration with area school districts, has a federally funded program to prepare paraprofessional educators (teachers' aides, for example) in southwest Washington to become bilingual/ESL teachers. Compared with recent college graduates who enter teaching directly from a traditional college-based teacher preparation program, those who enter teaching through alternate routes tend to be "older, more diverse, and more willing to teach wherever the jobs are and in high-demand subjects than are traditionally trained teachers" (Feistritzer, 2008, p. 126).

SUMMARY

Why Do I Want to Teach?

- Individual reasons for becoming a teacher may be intrinsic (desire to work with young people, passion for the subject, a desire to serve others and society) as well as extrinsic (work hours, vacations, job security).

What Are the Benefits of Teaching?

- Practical benefits of teaching include on-the-job hours at school, vacations, increasing salaries and benefits, job security, and a feeling of respect in society.
- In contrast to the diversity of student enrollments, the backgrounds of today's teachers are less diverse; thus, teachers from diverse racial and ethnic backgrounds and teachers with disabilities will experience exceptional opportunities for the foreseeable future.

What Are the Challenges of Teaching?

- The challenges of teaching include long working hours, meeting the accountability demands of high-stakes testing and No Child Left Behind (NCLB), and understanding the pervasive influence of technology on today's children and youth.

What Will Society Expect of Me as a Teacher?

- Society expects teachers to be competent and effective, and it holds teachers accountable for student achievement, for helping all learners succeed, and for maintaining high standards of conduct.

What Is the Job Outlook for Teachers?

- The job outlook for teachers will be very positive for the foreseeable future.
- Teacher supply and demand in content areas and geographic regions influence finding a teaching position.

How Will I Become a Highly Qualified Teacher?

- Four sets of professional standards had a great impact on teacher education programs nationally (as well as on teachers' ongoing professional growth and development): standards developed by the Interstate New Teacher Assessment and Support Consortium (INTASC), the National Council for Accreditation of

Teacher Education (NCATE), the Praxis Series: Professional Assessments for Beginning Teachers, and the National Board for Professional Teaching Standards (NBPTS).

- State certification is required for teaching in public schools and in many private schools. Some large cities and local school districts have additional criteria for certification. Certification requirements for teachers vary from state to state and are frequently modified. Some states waive licensing requirements for teachers certified by the National Board for Professional Teaching Standards (NBPTS).
- Most states require testing of teachers for initial certification, and some require recertification after a three- to five-year period.
- States that are members of the Interstate Certification Agreement Contract honor teaching certificates granted by certain other states.

PROFESSIONAL REFLECTIONS AND ACTIVITIES

Teacher's Journal

1. What significant experiences in your life have contributed to your decision to become a teacher? What have you learned from these experiences?
2. Do you think teachers at the elementary level (grades K–5), middle level (grades 6–8), and secondary level (9–12) have different reasons for becoming a teacher? Do you think teachers in different content areas have different reasons for becoming a teacher? Explain your answers to these questions.

Teacher's Research

1. Compare professional standards for teachers according to state boards of education, national standards organizations, and teacher and subject-area organizations. Begin by locating the following organizations online and information about your school's education program in relation to state and national standards:
    National Association for State Boards of Education (NASBE)
    National Association of State Directors for Teacher Education and Certification (NASDTEC)

National Board for Professional Teaching Standards (NBPTS)
National Council for Accreditation of Teacher Education (NCATE)

2. Formulate a research question concerning demographic aspects of teachers in the United States. Your question might relate to one or more of the following topics:
   - Attitudes of teachers
   - Characteristics of the teaching force
   - Teacher recruitment
   - Teacher shortages
   - Teaching salaries and benefits
   Begin your data search at the U.S. Department of Education's National Center for Education Statistics (nces.ed.gov). Present a brief oral report to the rest of your class that summarizes the results of your data search.

Observations and Interviews

1. Observe the first day of classes at a local school. What strategies did the teachers use to begin the year on a positive, task-oriented note?
2. Interview one or more teachers at a local elementary, middle, junior, or senior high school. Ask the teacher(s) what advice they would give to beginning teachers.

myeducationlab To complete additional observations and interviews, go to MyEducationLab at www.myeducationlab.com, select the Virtual Field Experience section, and click on this chapter's Observations and Interviews.

Professional Portfolio

To help you in your journey toward becoming a teacher, each chapter in this textbook includes suggestions for developing your professional portfolio, a collection of evidence documenting your growth and development while learning to become a teacher. At the end of this course, you will be well on your way toward a portfolio that documents your knowledge, skills, and attitudes for teaching and contains valuable resources for your first teaching position.

For your first portfolio entry, expand on Teacher's Journal entry 1, which asks you to identify significant experiences in your life that have contributed to your decision to become a teacher. In your entry (or videotaped version), discuss your reasons for becoming a teacher and the rewards teaching will hold for you. Also describe the aspects of teaching that you will find challenging.

myeducationlab Now go to MyEducationLab at www.myeducationlab.com to test your understanding of chapter content by completing this chapter's Study Plan.

Today's Teachers

3

From Chapter 2 of *Becoming a Teacher*, 8/e. Forrest W. Parkay. Beverly Hardcastle Stanford.
Copyright © 2009 by Pearson Merrill. All rights reserved.

Today's Teachers

CLASSROOM CASE
The Realities of Teaching

THE CHALLENGE: Learning to deal with the complexities and ambiguities of teaching.

You are a first-year teacher at a school in a city of about 200,000 in the Midwest. It is the first day after the winter break, and students are just entering your classroom. There is a lot of talking and laughing. Students are obviously glad to see their friends again at school.

You are proud to have survived several months as a real teacher. You had some ups and downs, but, overall, the beginning of your teaching career has been positive. You are beginning to feel more comfortable in your role as a teacher. It has been very rewarding to see students make definite progress in their learning.

With the exception of occasional small-group activities, you have used whole-group instruction until now. Your mentor teacher in the classroom next door, however, uses a cooperative learning approach. Several times you have observed her classes and talked with her about the advantages of cooperative learning. Now, you've decided to give it a try.

Early this morning, you set up your classroom for cooperative learning. Five octagonal tables are distributed evenly around the room. Students at each table will make up a team. Although students will work in teams, you plan to deemphasize competition among the teams.

As students select tables at which to sit, you sense their excitement at being involved in a new approach to learning. You also notice that students seem to be clustering according to ability levels—your highest ability students are at one table and the lowest ability students at another table. Now, you wonder if it was a good idea to allow students to select their tables. Perhaps you should have assigned tables so that each one had students with different ability levels.

You realize that cooperative learning, compared to whole-group instruction, is a more complex approach to teaching. You wonder if you can handle the unforeseen challenges that will emerge. Fortunately, your mentor teacher is next door, and you are confident that she can help you think through how to meet those challenges.

FOCUS QUESTIONS

1. Who are today's teachers?
2. What do teachers *do* in the classroom?
3. What knowledge and skills do today's teachers need?
4. To what extent is teaching a full profession?
5. To what professional organizations do teachers belong?
6. How do teachers help to build learning communities?
7. How do teachers participate in teacher collaboration?

WHO ARE TODAY'S TEACHERS?

The answer to this question is not as simple as you might think. Today's teachers teach in schools with different grade configurations, they teach in different subject-matter and specialized areas, and they teach students with different types of learning needs.

Teaching is the largest profession in the United States. Pre-K, elementary school, middle school, and secondary school teachers, not including special education teachers, totaled about 4.0 million in 2006. Of those teachers, about 1.5 million were elementary school teachers, 1.1 million were secondary school teachers, 674,000 were middle school teachers, 437,000 were preschool teachers, and 170,000 were kindergarten teachers (U.S. Department of Labor, 2008).

Table 2.1 shows that, compared to 1971, today's teachers are better educated—more than half (56 percent) have a master's degree, and the average teacher has 15 years of classroom experience. The table also shows that today's teachers are mostly white and female. Classrooms today are much more diverse than they were in 1971; however, diversity among the teaching force has remained about the same.

Today's teachers also have higher grade point averages (GPAs) and standardized achievement test (SAT) scores than teachers did several years ago. According to a study by the developers of the Praxis test, the percentage of teacher candidates who took the Praxis and reported a 3.5 GPA or higher increased from 27 percent during 1994–97 to 40 percent during 2002–05. Additionally, candidates' verbal SAT scores rose 13 points and math scores rose 17 points (Educational Testing Service, December 17, 2007).

Schools and Grade-Level Designations

Teachers in U.S. schools teach students who are approximately 3 through 17 years of age and attend schools from the pre-kindergarten (pre-K) through high school levels. Figure 2.1 shows that pre-K, elementary, middle, and high school programs in the United States have various grade configurations. A common arrangement is elementary schools that include pre-kindergarten or kindergarten through fifth-grade levels, middle schools that include sixth- through eighth-grade levels, and high schools that include ninth- through twelfth-grade levels. A less common arrangement beyond the elementary level is junior high schools that include sixth- through ninth-grade levels, and senior high schools that include tenth- through twelfth-grade levels.

Pre-K Teachers

The ages included in **pre-K education** (also termed **early childhood education** and, less frequently, nursery school education), according to the National Association for the Education of Young Children (NAEYC), range from birth to age 8. Pre-K teachers play a critical role in the development of children. What children learn and experience during their early years shapes their views of themselves and the world and influences their later success in school, work, and their personal lives.

TABLE 2.1 Teachers in the United States`

Highest Degree Held	1971(%)	2001(%)
Less than bachelor's	3	0
Bachelor's	70	43
Master's or six years	27	56
Doctor's	0	1
Median Years of Experience	**Number of Years**	**Number of Years**
All teachers	8	14
Males	8	14
Females	8	14
Teachers Teaching for First Year	**1971(%)**	**2001(%)**
All teachers	9	3
Males	10	4
Females	9	3
School Level of Teachers	**1971(%)**	**2001(%)**
Elementary	49	53
Middle/junior high school	19	22
Senior high school	26	25
Subjects Taught by Secondary Teachers	**1971(%)**	**2001(%)**
Agriculture	1	1
Art	4	3
Business education	6	2
English	20	22
Foreign language	5	5
Health, physical education	8	4
Home economics	5	2
Industrial arts	4	0
Mathematics	14	18
Music	5	3
Science	11	15
Social studies	14	5
Special education	1	4
Other	0	5
Race	**1971(%)**	**2001(%)**
Black	8	6
White	88	90
Hispanic, Asian, other	4	5
Sex	**1971(%)**	**2001(%)**
Male	34	21
Female	66	79
Marital Status	**1971(%)**	**2001(%)**
Single	20	15
Married	72	73
Widowed, divorced, separated	9	12

Source: Based on data from Status of the American Public School Teacher 2000–2001. *National Education Association, 2003, pp. 5–8.*

If you had a pre-K educational experience, you probably remember learning through play and interactive activities. Your pre-K teacher(s) most likely used play to further your language and vocabulary development (storytelling, rhyming games, and play acting, for example), improve your social skills (cooperating with other children to build a small town in a sandbox), and introduce scientific and mathematical concepts (learning to balance and count blocks when building a skyscraper or mixing colors for fingerpainting).

Pre-K teachers use a less structured approach than teachers of older students. Children at the pre-K level are involved in small-group lessons; one-on-one instruction;

Go to MyEducationLab, select Chapter 2 and then Activities and Applications to watch the video Appropriate Learning Environments.

FIGURE 2.1 The structure of education in the United States

Source: U.S. Department of Education, National Center for Education Statistics. Retrieved April 9, 2008, from: http://nces.ed .gov/programs/digest/d01/fig1 .asp.

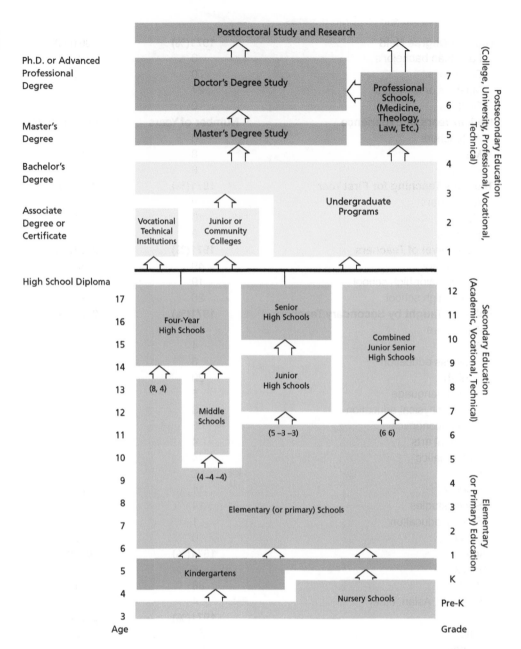

Note: Adult education programs, while not separately delineated above, may provide instruction at the elementary, secondary, or higher education level. Chart reflects typical patterns of progression rather than all possible variations.

and learning through creative activities such as art, dance, and music. To see how an early childhood classroom is organized, go to MyEducationLab, where you will see the indoor and outdoor areas of a developmentally appropriate environment for early childhood education.

Play and hands-on activities are used also by kindergarten teachers; however, academic learning becomes more important in kindergarten classrooms. Letter recognition, phonics, numbers, and basic understanding of nature and science are introduced at the kindergarten level.

Elementary Teachers

Elementary school teachers usually teach one class, from grades 1 through 6, of about 25 children in several subjects. In some elementary schools, two or more teachers work as a team with a group of students in at least one subject. In other elementary schools, a teacher may teach one subject—often music, art, reading, science, arithmetic, or physical education—to a number of classes. An increasing number of teachers teach in **multi-age,** or multigrade, **classrooms,** with students from different grade levels. Elementary school teachers introduce children to mathematics, language, science, and social studies. They use games, music, artwork, films, books, computers, and other tools to teach basic skills.

Elementary school teachers write daily lesson plans based on school or state requirements, and they record student attendance each day. They assign homework, grade papers, and record grades on tests and homework. At regular intervals they evaluate each child's academic progress and write progress reports for parents. On the progress report, they note any behavioral or social problems and disciplinary actions. Elementary teachers also supervise activities on playgrounds, in cafeterias, and other areas of the school.

Elementary teachers also meet with parents or guardians to discuss student progress or problems. If a child is not adjusting well to school, teachers work with the child; administrators; and parents, guardians, or other family members to find solutions.

Some elementary school teachers teach subjects such as art or music. Art teachers develop art projects, maintain art supplies, and help children develop art skills. Music teachers teach music and lead singing groups, and sometimes they direct the school band. Other teachers teach physical education to help children develop physical coordination. Often, these teachers work at several schools during a week. Some elementary teachers coordinate volunteer groups and/or oversee special projects in addition to their regular duties.

Elementary teachers frequently work with parent volunteers in the classroom. They also attend in-service workshops to learn about new instructional methods and materials. Typically, elementary teachers meet regularly with other staff members to discuss school issues. For example, you can watch fifth-grade teachers at an urban elementary school conduct a team meeting by going to MyEducationLab.

myeducationlab
Go to MyEducationLab, select Chapter 2 and then Activities and Applications to watch the video The Organization of Schools.

Middle School Teachers

Middle school teachers help students learn more about the subjects studied in elementary school. Most middle school teachers specialize in a specific subject, such as English, mathematics, or science, and they teach several classes a day in that subject area. However, some middle school teachers work in self-contained classrooms and teach all major subjects to one group of students.

During the middle school years, young adolescents are at a unique stage of life. They are dealing with an array of physical, intellectual, emotional, and social challenges. Some mature rapidly, while others mature more slowly. Some may be physically mature yet socially immature. Middle school students have very different developmental needs. Middle school teachers understand these needs and are skilled at providing students with developmentally appropriate learning activities. One example of such a teacher is Mr. Shipley, a sixth-grade science and social studies teacher at a middle school. To read a student's essay about the influence Mr. Shipley had on her and how he had a "special bond with kids," go to MyEducationLab.

myeducationlab
Go to MyEducationLab, select Chapter 2 and then Activities and Applications to analyze the artifact The Effective Teacher.

High School Teachers

Most high school teachers teach four or five courses within a single content area. For example, a high school math teacher might teach two classes of Algebra I, a trigonometry class, and two geometry classes. An English teacher might teach two classes of sophomore English, one advanced-placement (AP) English literature class for which students receive college credit, one honors English class, and one journalism class.

You probably have clear memories of your own high school teachers. You might want to contrast those memories with videos of high school classrooms available at MyEducationLab. For example, you can watch a high school math teacher explain how he uses Geometer's Sketchpad to enhance his students' learning of geometry. Then the video shows the teacher in the classroom, helping his students use inductive reasoning to solve a problem.

myeducationlab
Go to MyEducationLab, select Chapter 2 and then Activities and Applications to watch the video Geometer's Sketchpad for Inductive Reasoning.

In addition to teaching, some high school teachers monitor study halls and homerooms or supervise extracurricular activities. On occasion, they may supervise events such as school dances or athletic contests or accompany students on field trips. They may also counsel students regarding classes to take at the high school and/or plans for college, training, or employment after high school.

High school teachers also participate in faculty meetings, professional development workshops, and educational conferences. If they have students with behavioral or academic problems, they may meet with those students, their parents or guardians, and administrators to resolve those problems. They may also identify students with physical or mental problems and refer them to the school counselor, special education teacher(s), or other professionals.

Teachers in Nontraditional School Settings

In addition to teachers who work in pre-K, elementary, middle, and high school programs, some teachers teach in nontraditional school settings, such as private schools, charter schools, alternative schools, and magnet schools.

Private School Teachers

Teachers in private schools often have smaller class sizes and more control over determining the curriculum and standards for performance and discipline. Their students also tend to be more motivated because private schools can be selective in their admissions processes. Although private school teachers may earn less than public school teachers, they may have other benefits, such as free or subsidized housing.

Many private schools are affiliated with religious institutions, and almost all religious sects operate schools across the country. There are schools founded on the Christian, Jewish, Muslim, Quaker, and Seventh Day Adventist faiths, to name a few. The Catholic Church has one of the largest networks of religious schools in the country—almost 6,300 elementary/middle schools and more than 1,200 high schools. Total Catholic school student enrollment for the 2006–07 academic year was more than 1,682,000 at the elementary/middle level, and more than 638,000 at the secondary school (National Catholic Education Association, April 11, 2008). Other Christian denominations operate more than 1,000 schools across the country, and the Jewish faith operates more than 8,000 (http://privateschool.about.com, April 9, 2008).

Charter School Teachers

Charter schools are independent public schools, often founded by teachers, that are given a charter to operate by a school district, state, or national government. For a charter school to be approved, the school must agree to document students' mastery of predetermined outcomes. To some extent, teachers at charter schools have freedom from many of the regulations that apply to traditional public school teachers. However, charter school teachers must account—usually to a state or local school board—for producing positive academic results and adhering to the charter contract.

Since the first charter school opened in Minnesota in 1992, the charter school movement has grown to more than 3,940 schools operating nationwide in 2007 and serving over 1,150,000 students. Students served by charter schools are 53 percent minority and 54 percent low income (Center for Educational Reform, April 2007).

Alternative School Teachers

To find better ways to educate all students and to reduce problems with violence, weapons, and drugs in schools, many school districts have established alternative schools. There is no single commonly accepted definition for an **alternative school** or program (Lange & Sletten, 2002); however, an alternative school is usually a small, highly individualized school separate from the regular school. Thirty-nine percent of public school districts have at least one alternative school or program for at-risk students (National Center for Education Statistics, August 2002).

Alternative schools are designed to meet the needs of students at risk of failure and dropping out. In general, students are referred to alternative schools and programs if they are at risk of education failure, as indicated by low grades, truancy, disruptive behavior, suspension, pregnancy, or similar factors associated with early withdrawal from school (Spring, 2008).

Because they often have small class sizes and the freedom to be creative in meeting students' needs, alternative school teachers usually find their work very satisfying. As a teacher at one alternative school said, "Here, you finally have a sense of ownership as a teacher. You have to come in the morning and create something and keep working at it, and it's a tremendous experience" (Firestone, 2008).

Magnet School Teachers

A **magnet school** offers a curriculum that focuses on a specific area such as the performing arts, mathematics, science, international studies, or technology. Magnet schools, which often draw students from a larger attendance area than regular schools, are frequently used to promote voluntary desegregation. In 2004, teachers taught at over 1,800 magnet schools in the United States (National Center for Education Statistics, February 2006, p. 23).

Some evidence suggests that teachers at magnet schools may experience greater levels of autonomy, influence on school policies, and professional development than teachers at traditional schools (Evans, 2002). One example of a professional magnet school teacher is Thomas Brodnitzki, a social studies teacher at the Metropolitan Learning Center in Bloomfield, CT. Influenced by "an eleventh-grade history teacher that taught the subject with enthusiasm," Brodnitzki received a $25,000 National Educator award from the Milkin Family Foundation in 2007. He also received a Fulbright Award, which included a visit to China in 2000, and he lobbied in Washington, DC, on behalf of the National Geographic Society to request legislation for more funds for geographic education (Woodman, October 18, 2007).

Teachers in Specialized Areas

Some teachers, regardless of level, teach in specialized areas such as art, vocational education, music, or physical education. Others teach in areas differentiated according to the learning needs of students in various groups, for example, special education teachers who specialize in teaching students with disabilities and/or special needs. Other teachers specialize in teaching students whose first language is not English (often called English language learners [ELLs]). The following sections present brief job descriptions for teachers in these specialized areas.

Art Teachers

From elementary school through high school, art teachers teach students the visual arts—painting, sketching, designing, and sculpting, for instance. Art teachers may specialize in teaching one or more areas of art, such as illustration, art history, or commercial art, and at times they may organize student art contests or arrange for student artwork to be exhibited. In some cases, art teachers travel from school to school.

More than other areas of the curriculum, art and music (discussed in the following subsection) have had an insecure position. When schools face budget cutbacks or increased pressure to prepare students for high-stakes tests, eliminating art and music is often considered.

Music Teachers

Music teachers instruct students in vocal or instrumental music and foster music appreciation. Elementary and secondary school music teachers often direct the school chorus, choir, orchestra, or marching band, as well as give group and private lessons. They instruct students in the technical aspects of music, conduct rehearsals, and evaluate student performances. School music teachers sometimes take students on field trips to musical presentations, or the students may perform off campus under the direction of the teacher.

Vocational Education Teachers

Vocational education teachers (sometimes called vocational/technical education [vo-tech] teachers) train students to work in fields such as healthcare, business, auto repair, communications, and technology. About 16,000 teachers taught vocational education at the middle school level in 2006, and 96,000 taught at the high school level (U.S. Department of Labor, 2008). They often teach courses that are in high demand by area employers, who may provide input into the curriculum and offer internships to students. Many vocational teachers play an active role in developing and overseeing these internships. To prepare students for the real world of specific vocational or technical careers, vocational education teachers use a hands-on approach to teach academic and vocational skills.

Physical Education Teachers

Physical education teachers teach students from the elementary through high school levels. The ultimate aim of their teaching is to introduce students to physical activities that develop within them a desire to maintain physical fitness throughout life.

At the high school level, physical education teachers often teach one or two classes of health, coach one or more sports, or teach driver education. Physical education teachers teach individual and team sports that promote the development of students' physical abilities. They organize and referee indoor and outdoor sports, such as volleyball, football, baseball, and basketball. They teach students beginning or advanced calisthenics, gymnastics, or corrective exercises. They teach and demonstrate the use of gymnastic and training equipment such as trampolines and weight-lifting equipment.

At one time, physical education teachers placed greater emphasis on highly competitive team sports. Many students, however, did not do well at such sports and may have experienced a lowered sense of self-esteem as a result. Today's physical education teachers offer activities to meet the needs and abilities of all students, not just the athletically talented. In addition to traditional team sports such as football, basketball, and baseball, and individual sports such as swimming and wrestling, students participate in activities such as aerobics, badminton, gymnastics, volleyball, golf, soccer, and yoga.

Special Education Teachers

Special education teachers work with children and youth who have a variety of disabilities. Special education teachers held a total of about 459,000 jobs in 2006. About 219,000 worked at the preschool, kindergarten, and elementary level; 102,000 worked at the middle school level; and 138,000 worked at the high school level. Most special education teachers work in public and private educational institutions. A few work for individual and social assistance agencies or residential facilities, or in homebound or hospital environments (U.S. Department of Labor, 2008).

Special education teachers often specialize in working with students who have specific disabilities—learning disabilities, autism, and brain injuries, for example. Special education teachers must develop Individualized Education Programs (IEPs) for students. Special education teachers work collaboratively with regular classroom teachers, parents, social workers, school psychologists, and other school staff.

Special education teachers are trained to use advanced educational technologies—for example, word prediction software, voice recognition computers, and speech synthesizers—to help students with special needs learn. To see two classrooms where teachers use SmartBoards to teach students with hearing impairments, go to MyEducationLab.

PEARSON myeducationlab

Go to MyEducationLab, select Chapter 2 and then Activities and Applications to watch the video Smartboards for Students with Hearing Impairments.

As schools become more inclusive, special education teachers and general education teachers increasingly work together in general education classrooms. Special education teachers help general educators adapt curriculum materials and teaching techniques to meet the needs of students with disabilities. They coordinate the work of teachers; teacher assistants; and related personnel, such as therapists and social workers, to meet the individualized needs of the student within inclusive special education programs. A large part of a special education teacher's job involves communicating and coordinating with others involved in the child's well-being, including parents, social workers, school psychologists, occupational and physical therapists, school administrators, and other teachers.

Special education teachers work in a variety of settings. Some have their own classrooms and teach only special education students. Others work as special education resource teachers and offer individualized help to students in general education classrooms. And others teach alongside general education teachers in classes that have both general and special education students. Some teachers work with special education students for several hours a day in a resource room, separate from their general education classroom.

Teachers of English Language Learners (ELLs)

Many teachers, whether they have specialized training or not, teach students whose first language is not English (often called English language learners [ELLs]). About 11 percent (3.8 million) of the nation's total school enrollment were **English language learners (ELLs)** during the 2003–04 school year. Most ELL students were in California (1.6 million, or 26 percent of that state's total enrollment) and Texas (0.7 million, or 16 percent of that state's total enrollment) (National Center for Education Statistics, 2006).

Only 30 percent of teachers who instruct ELL students have received training to teach ELL students, and less than 3 percent have earned a degree in English as a Second Language (ESL) or bilingual education (National Center for Education Statistics, 2006). Nevertheless, as comments by the following teacher who has no ELL training illustrate, professional teachers are committed to teaching *all* their students: "They [ELL students] need to be in the classroom . . . My job is to teach the kids. If they don't know English, that's my job" (Valli & Buese, 2007, p. 532).

Seeing ELL students develop as learners can be very rewarding, as first-grade ELL teacher Jacqueline Gallo points out: "I have three different languages [in my classroom]—Spanish, Somali, and Russian. [Now students are] starting to understand and participate. It's getting to be fun. They're starting to really interact with the lessons" (Blair, November/December 2005). Similarly, at the high school level, Karen Christenson emphasizes the rewards she has experienced as a teacher of ELL students: "They're good kids. They want to learn and they're very cooperative" (Blair, November/December 2005).

WHAT DO TEACHERS *DO* IN THE CLASSROOM?

At first, this question may appear easy to answer. From your own experiences as a student, you know that teachers assign learning tasks. They ask questions and evaluate students' responses. They lecture and, on occasion, demonstrate what students are to do. They assign chapters to read in the text and then conduct recitations or give quizzes on that material. They praise some students for right answers or good work, and they prod, chastise, and at times embarrass others in the hope that their work will improve. And near the end of the term or semester, they decide who has passed and who has failed. However, the role of today's teachers includes responsibilities that go beyond actual teaching in the classroom. For examples of some of these responsibilities, go to MyEducationLab, where you can watch a video of elementary

myeducationlab

Go to MyEducationLab, select Chapter 2 and then Activities and Applications to watch the video Grade Level Meeting.

teachers at a grade-level meeting. Their discussion covers a diverse array of topics, including a budget cut that affects the purchase of grade-level supplies, recruitment strategies for the parent-teacher association (PTA), students' academic performance, and a forthcoming field trip.

Teaching is more than the sum of the behaviors that you have observed in your own teachers. As you move ahead in your journey toward becoming a teacher, you will discover that teaching involves more than performing certain behaviors in front of a group of students. A significant portion of the teacher's work is mental and involves problem solving in response to unforeseen events that emerge in the classroom (Martinez, 2006).

Teaching is a creative act in which teachers continually shape and reshape lessons, events, and the experiences of their students. A former teacher and now head of an organization that creates small, personalized, public high schools in collaboration with their communities describes the creative dimensions of teaching this way: "The act of being a teacher is the act of . . . using your skills and love for kids to figure out how to create the best environment to help your students [learn]" (Littky, 2004, p. 12).

Although your teachers reflected different personalities and methods, your experiences as a student are similar to the experiences of other students. Our recollections about teachers who were good or bad, easy or hard, interesting or dull are drawn from a commonly shared set of experiences. The universality of these experiences leads us to conclude that we know "the way teaching is" and what teachers do. However, in a seminal article aptly titled "The Way Teaching Is," noted educational researcher Philip Jackson points out that teaching is "fleeting and ephemeral" because of the "fragile quality of the psychological condition that is created by the teacher" (Jackson, 1965, p. 62).

The following sections examine three dimensions of teaching that illustrate how, on the one hand, teaching involves "enduring puzzlements, persistent dilemmas, complex conundrums, [and] enigmatic paradoxes" (Eisner, 2006, p. 44) while, on the other, it offers opportunities for "saving lives, rescuing a child from despair, restoring a sense of hope, soothing discomfort" (p. 46). Effective teachers understand that they are role models for students, spontaneous problem-solvers, and reflective thinkers.

Teacher as a Role Model for Students

Clearly, teachers are role models for their students. In the elementary grades, teachers are idolized by their young students. At the high school level, teachers have the potential to inspire students' admiration if they model positive attitudes and behaviors. Actually, teachers teach "not only by what [they] say but also by what [they] do" (Ormrod, 2003, p. 342). Teachers are "active agents whose words and deeds change lives and mold futures, for better or worse. Teachers can and do exert a great deal of power and influence in the lives of their students" (Nieto, 2003, p. 19).

In *Listening to Urban Kids: School Reform and the Teachers They Want* (Wilson & Corbett, 2001), students express the following expectations about their teachers' attitudes and behaviors:

> I heard teachers talking about people, saying "Those kids can't do nothing." Kids want teachers who believe in them. (p. 86)

> A good teacher to me is a teacher who is patient, willing to accept the fact that she might be dealing with students who have problems. (p. 87)

> Since this is one of his first year's teaching, I give him credit. He relates, but he also teaches. . . . He advises us. He not only tries to teach but gets involved with us. (p. 88)

A high school teacher explains why developing positive relationships with students is so important: "[The] relationship between teachers and students is becoming one of the most important aspects of teaching. [In] a world of broken homes and violence, the encouragement of their teachers may be the only thing students can hold onto that makes them feel good about themselves" (Henry et al., 1995, p. 127).

Teachers also model attitudes toward the subjects they teach and show students through their example that learning is an ongoing, life-enriching process that does not end with diplomas and graduations. Their example confirms the timeless message of Sir Rabindranath Tagore that is inscribed above the doorway of a public building in India: "A teacher can never truly teach unless he is still learning himself. A lamp can never light another lamp unless it continues to burn its own flame."

Teacher as a Spontaneous Problem-Solver

In the classroom, teachers must respond to unpredictable events that are rapidly changing, multidimensional, and fragmented. Furthermore, "day in and day out, teachers spend much of their lives 'on stage' before audiences that are not always receptive. . . . Teachers must orchestrate a daunting array of interpersonal interactions and build a cohesive, positive climate for learning" (Gmelch & Parkay, 1995, p. 47).

When teachers are preparing to teach or reflecting on previous teaching, they can afford to be consistently deliberate and rational. Planning for lessons, grading papers, reflecting on the misbehavior of a student—such activities are usually done alone and lack the immediacy and sense of urgency that characterize interactive teaching. While working face-to-face with students, however, you must be able to think on your feet and respond appropriately to complex, ever-changing situations. You must be flexible and ready to deal with the unexpected. During a discussion, for example, you must operate on at least two levels. On one level, you respond appropriately to students' comments, monitor other students for signs of confusion or comprehension, formulate the next comment or question, and remain alert for signs of misbehavior. On another level, you ensure that participation is evenly distributed among students, evaluate the content and quality of students' contributions, keep the discussion focused and moving ahead, and emphasize major content areas. In the Teaching on Your Feet feature for this chapter, you can see how one teacher responded to several unpredictable events in the classroom.

During interactive teaching, the awareness that you are responsible for the forward movement of the group never lets up. Teachers are the only professionals who practice their craft almost exclusively under the direct, continuous gaze of up to 30 or 40 clients. Jackson (1990, p. 119) sums up the experience: "The immediacy of classroom events is something that anyone who has ever been in charge of a roomful of students can never forget."

Teacher as a Reflective Thinker

Teaching involves a unique mode of being between teacher and student—a mode of being that can be experienced but not fully defined or described. On your journey to become a teacher, you will gradually develop your capacity to listen to students and to convey an authentic sense of concern for their learning. Unfortunately, there is no precise, easy-to-follow formula for demonstrating this to students. You will have to take into account your personality and special gifts to discover your own best way for showing this concern.

One reason it is difficult to describe teaching is that an important domain of teaching, teachers' thought processes (including professional reflection), cannot be observed directly. Figure 2.2 shows how the unobservable domain of the teacher's "interior reflective thinking" interacts with and is influenced by the observable domain of the teacher's "exterior reflective action." Teachers' thought processes include their theories and beliefs about students and how they learn, their plans for teaching, and the decisions they make while teaching. Thought processes and actions can be constrained by the physical setting of the classroom or external factors such as the curriculum, the principal, or the community. On the other hand, teachers'

TEACHING ON YOUR FEET

RESPONDING TO MULTIPLE PROBLEMS THAT EMERGE SIMULTANEOUSLY

Tony's outburst did not occur in isolation. Twenty-nine other students observed his angry outburst over his math test grade. The problem seemed to be resolved temporarily when I walked toward Tony's desk and looked at him sternly; however, other problems emerged at that moment.

"Tony's upset 'cause you flunked him in fifth grade," Leroy called out, stopping me in my tracks.

"Now just a minute!" I was upset now. "This is between me and Tony."

Leroy and Carlos spoke at once. "That's okay, most of us are behind a grade." Other boys around the room nodded and then started laughing among themselves. "Our parents kept us back so we would be bigger for the football team," one called out. My mouth dropped open at what I just heard.

Hiding my disapproval, I searched for a way to handle the situation. I weighed the problems at hand: Tony's angry outburst, Leroy's inappropriate comment, other students calling out and laughing, my disapproval of their parents' reason for retaining them, and the fact that Tony, and perhaps others, thought math was boring.

After his classmates spoke out, Tony no longer seemed angry—he, Leroy, Carlos, Mike, and Ron sat taller in their seats and exchanged smiles. "They're visualizing themselves on the football team," I thought. I still needed to talk to Tony about his outburst, but that would be in private, later, not in front of his peers.

Leroy's initial comment was not as serious as I first thought, since he, too, had failed the fifth grade. Even so, his comment needed to be addressed. Again, I would do that later, in private.

The other students who called out actually did so in a helpful way, because now I understood why so many boys in my class were behind a grade. To remind them of our previously discussed rules about talking in class seemed inappropriate under the circumstances.

Regarding my students' parents, I knew I needed to respect their actions. I also suspected that the reasons for

thought processes and actions may be influenced by unique opportunities, such as the chance to engage in curriculum reform or school governance. The model also illustrates a further complexity of teaching—namely, that the relationships among teacher behavior, student behavior, and student achievement are reciprocal. What teachers do is influenced not only by their thought processes before, during, and after teaching but also by student behavior and student achievement. This complexity contributes to the uniqueness of the teaching experience.

In this chapter's Teachers' Voices: Research to Reality feature, Jeff Huntley reflects on his year-long student teaching experience at Mark Twain Middle School, an urban professional development school in San Antonio. Now a successful sixth- to eighth-grade reading teacher, Huntley recognized early in his career that applying what he learned in education classes would not be easy, "that action and reflection in teaching can be worlds apart." To his credit, though, he was quick to learn that the hallmark of a professional teacher is the ability to reflect upon one's experiences in the classroom. He learned that teaching is a complex act—one that requires thoughtfulness, insight into the motivations of others, and good judgment.

Among the factors that enabled Huntley to have a constructive, meaningful student teaching experience were his ability to draw from what he learned in a fifth-year master of arts in teaching (MAT) program and the support, guidance, and encourage-

TEACHING ON YOUR FEET

my students being retained were probably more complex than what was shared.

In the final analysis, the problem that remained was that Tony, and probably others, saw math as boring. I loved math and wanted my students to love it as well. So, with a smile I said, "Well, tomorrow's lesson will show you that math is not boring!"

ANALYSIS

Teachers need to make spur-of-the-moment decisions about problems that can emerge simultaneously in the classroom. Research tells us that teachers may make up to 3,000 low-level decisions in a single school day. Most problems are easily solved, but some require careful, critical thinking. Stepping into the minds of teachers to see how they turn negative situations into positive situations is the purpose of this feature.

In this situation, multiple problems emerged simultaneously. The teacher needed to consider two audiences—individual misbehaving students and the class as a whole. She responded to Tony's misbehavior by using proxemics (walking toward him) and nonverbal communication (the stern look). When Leroy made his inappropriate comment, she used nonverbal communication (an upset expression) and orally communicated her disapproval. She also planned to speak privately with the two misbehaving students later.

Regarding the class as a whole, she listened to students' explanations about why they were retained, and she monitored the changing classroom atmosphere as the tension dissolved. Rather than remind the class of rules for classroom conduct at that point, she chose to move the group in a positive direction. And she provided closure on the situation nonverbally (her smile) and with a friendly challenge ("tomorrow's lesson will show you that math is not boring!").

REFLECTION

- Why would the teacher plan to talk with Tony and Leroy separately and in private?
- Why did the teacher orally convey disapproval of Leroy's misbehavior and not treat Tony's misbehavior the same way?
- What would guide you in prioritizing multiple problems that emerge simultaneously in the classroom?

Beverly Hardcastle Stanford
Former Sixth-Grade Teacher
Avon Middle School
Avon, New York

myeducationlab *To answer these questions online, go to MyEducationLab at www.myeducationlab.com, select the Activities and Application section, and click on this chapter's Teaching on Your Feet.*

ment he received from a mentor teacher at the school. By the end of his internship, Huntley was well on his way to developing an understanding of the teacher's complex role.

WHAT KNOWLEDGE AND SKILLS DO TODAY'S TEACHERS NEED?

Just as people hold different expectations for schools and teachers, there are different views of the knowledge and skills teachers need to teach well. In addition to being knowledgeable about the subjects they teach, teachers must have the ability to communicate, inspire trust and confidence, and motivate students, as well as understand their students' educational and emotional needs. Teachers must be able to recognize and respond to individual and cultural differences in students and employ different teaching methods that will result in higher student achievement. They should be organized, dependable, patient, and creative. Teachers must also be able to work cooperatively and communicate effectively with other teachers, support staff, parents, and members of the community.

To respond effectively to the complexities of teaching, you must have four kinds of knowledge: knowledge of yourself and your students, knowledge of subject, knowledge of educational theory and research, and knowledge of how to integrate

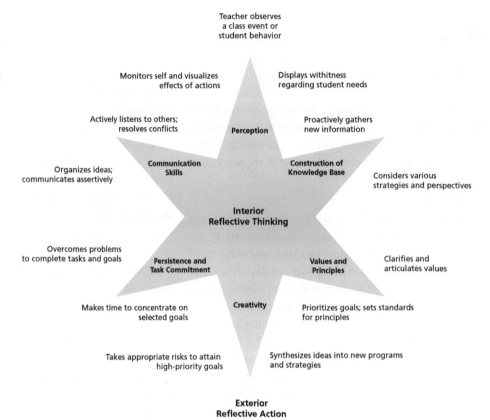

technology into teaching. The following sections examine these four forms of essential knowledge.

Self-Knowledge

Effective teachers understand themselves and are sensitive to students' needs. "They recognize that the child's personality is a fragile work in progress" (Erickson, 2008, p. 225). Naturally, you should understand your students as much as possible. What is the connection, however, between self-knowledge and the ability to promote student learning? If you understand your own needs (and can satisfy those needs), you are in a better position to help students learn. A teacher's self-understanding and self-acceptance help students to know and accept themselves.

Your self-evaluations as a teacher are influenced by the feelings you may experience while teaching—feelings that may range from great joy and satisfaction to anxiety or loneliness, for example. As the classroom case at the beginning of this chapter suggests, anxiety is a common feeling to experience when starting to use a new, more complex teaching strategy.

As a teacher, you will experience feelings of happiness, excitement, and wonder as a result of the time you spend with students. You may also experience occasional feelings of loneliness or isolation because most of your time will be spent with children and youth, not adults. Though teachers are behind the classroom door most of the day, today's teachers have more opportunities to collaborate with their colleagues, whether it be serving on a school improvement committee, developing new curricula, or mentoring new teachers.

Knowledge of Students

Without doubt, knowledge of your students is important. Student characteristics such as aptitudes, talents, learning styles, stages of development, and readiness to learn new

TEACHERS' VOICES RESEARCH TO REALITY

ACTION AND REFLECTION IN TEACHING

To be a teacher you must be able to step outside yourself and look at the situation. . . .

Jeff Huntley

I experience the tension between the rolled-up-sleeves feeling of teaching in action and the higher philosophical aims I formulate about what I do. It's as if there are two opposing worlds for education, one seething with organic activity, the other a pristine latticework of ideas and beliefs. When I started my internship at Twain (Middle School), experienced teachers laughed knowingly as I told them about the theories we were studying in our night classes. "All that philosophical thinking about education is interesting," they would say, "but you'll find it isn't worth squat in the classroom. That's teaching."

Meanwhile, in the seminar rooms at [the university], I was being told to challenge that opinion. I needed to bring my philosophical beliefs into the classroom and act upon them as I taught. "That's professionalism," my professors said.

"Okay," I thought, smart-aleck just out of college and full of ideas. "I'll try it."

Very quickly I found out for myself that action and reflection in teaching can be worlds apart. The smell of a middle school; the whirlwind appearance of the classroom; the things there that have been touched, chewed, stepped on by adolescents—these things drive clean, well-crafted, long-prepared ideas from the building screaming in terror. Oh, you could probably heavily Scotch-Guard the ideals and smuggle them in, but don't expect miracles. "Be pessimistic," I hear teachers say in their hesitant suggestions about my grand ideas. "That way, you won't be disappointed when they don't work."

Do I dare put my emotional and intellectual foundations on the line every day by attempting to reflect on my deepest beliefs in the daily tempest of middle school? Is self-preservation a good enough excuse to answer, "No"?

I don't think I'm ready. . . . But don't count me out yet. I still take great pleasure in returning to the safety of my home, where I can face the things I believe at the bottom of my heart. . . . I tell myself, "I am a teacher." My ideals intact . . . I sit and reflect upon the day that, once the laughter and the tears have been wiped away, becomes a tool with which I may better myself. For now, it's the most professional thing I can do. (Henry et al., 1995, pp. 106–107)

QUESTIONS

1. What does Huntley mean when he says that reflecting on his day in the classroom "becomes a tool with which I may better myself"?
2. After you become a teacher, how will you use the theoretical knowledge you have acquired in your teacher education program?

---

material are among the essential knowledge you must have. The importance of this knowledge is evident in comments made by an intern at a middle school: "To teach a kid well you have to know a kid well. . . . Teaching middle school takes a special breed of teachers who understand the unique abilities and inabilities . . . [of] those undergoing their own metamorphosis into teenagers" (Henry et al., 1995, pp. 124–125). After you become a teacher, you will expand your knowledge of students through additional study, observation, and interactions with students.

Knowledge of Subject

Teachers are assumed to have extensive knowledge. People who are not teachers expect a teacher to have knowledge far beyond their own. Without doubt, teachers who have extensive knowledge of their subjects are better equipped to help students learn.

However, knowledge of subject matter does not translate into an understanding of how to impart that knowledge to students—a point illustrated in a case study conducted by the National Center for Research on Teacher Learning. The case focused on "Mary," an undergraduate literature major enrolled in a teacher education program at a major university. By any standards, Mary was a subject-matter expert—she was valedictorian of a large, urban high school; had straight A's in the literature courses she had taken; and had a sophisticated understanding of literature, especially poetry. The case study revealed that Mary had little understanding of classroom activities that would show her students how to read with sophistication and concluded that "some prospective teachers may come to teacher education unaware of how they have learned the processes they use and that render them expert. Unaided by their disciplines in locating the underpinnings of their expertise, these skilled, talented, and desirable recruits may easily become, ironically, those who can do but who cannot teach" (Holt-Reynolds, 1999, p. 43).

Extensive knowledge of subject matter, as the National Board for Professional Teaching Standards (2002, pp. 10–11) puts it, "entails more than being able to recite lists of dates, multiplication tables, or rules of grammar. [Accomplished] teachers possess what is sometimes called '**pedagogical content knowledge.**' Such understanding is the joint product of wisdom about teaching, learning, students and content. It includes knowledge of the most appropriate ways to present the subject matter to students through analogies, metaphors, experiments, demonstrations and illustrations."

Knowledge of How to Use Educational Theory and Research

Theories about learners and learning will guide your decision making as a teacher. Not only will you know that a certain strategy works, you will also know why it works. Because you realize the importance of theories, you will have a greater range of available options for problem solving than teachers who do not have a repertoire of theories. Your ultimate goal as a professional is to learn how to apply theoretical knowledge to the practical problems of teaching.

Research on students' learning does not set forth, in cookbook fashion, exactly what you should do to increase students' learning. Instead, it may be helpful to think of educational research as providing you with "rules of thumb" to guide your practice, or, to recall a comment by noted educational psychologist Lee Cronbach (quoted in Eisner, 1998, p. 112), "[educational research] is to help practitioners use their heads."

Educational researchers are still learning *what* good teachers know and *how* they use that knowledge. As a result, many people believe that a knowledge base for teaching should consist of not only what educational researchers have learned about teaching but also what teachers themselves know about teaching—often called teachers' craft knowledge or practitioner knowledge (Hiebert, Gallimore, & Stigler, 2002; Kennedy, 1999; Leinhardt, 1990). **Teachers' craft knowledge** is developed by teachers in response to specific problems of practice.

Knowledge of How to Integrate Technology Into Teaching

As a teacher, you will be expected to know how to integrate technology into your teaching. And throughout your teaching career, you will be expected to be familiar with newly emerging technologies and how they can be used in the classroom. To increase your skills in using advanced technologies to enhance student learning, this chapter's Technology in Action feature focuses on e-portfolios. E-portfolios not only show the finished product, which could be a paper, artwork, project, musical score, and so on; they also highlight the process that the student engaged in and the stages the work went through to achieve the finished product.

Using technology to enhance students' learning requires more than knowing how to use the latest hardware and software. Conducting classroom demonstrations augmented with multimedia, using presentation graphics to address students' varied learning styles, and designing lessons that require students to use technology as a tool for inquiry should be second nature for teachers.

The technology component of No Child Left Behind (NCLB), Title II, Part D, calls on teachers to use technology to "close the achievement gap." According to a study of the implementation of NCLB, "highly qualified" teachers are achieving this goal when they have knowledge and skills in the following areas:

- software, web courses, virtual learning, and other technology-based learning solutions that are aligned to standards, strengthening basic skills and increasing student achievement.

- digital tools, which are used to broaden and strengthen learning and teaching through authenticity, real-world problem solving, critical thinking, communication, and production for students; as well as support . . . through online courses, communities of practice, and virtual communication.

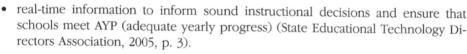

Knowledge of how to integrate technology into teaching is essential for today's teachers. What steps can you take to remain technologically up to date?

- real-time information to inform sound instructional decisions and ensure that schools meet AYP (adequate yearly progress) (State Educational Technology Directors Association, 2005, p. 3).

Reflection and Problem Solving

The preceding discussion of essential knowledge and skills for teaching highlights the fact that teaching is complex and demanding. As you use your knowledge and skills to meet the challenges of teaching, you will be guided by reflection and a problem-solving orientation. As Figure 2.3 shows, reflection and problem solving will enable you to determine how to use knowledge of self and students (including cultural differences),

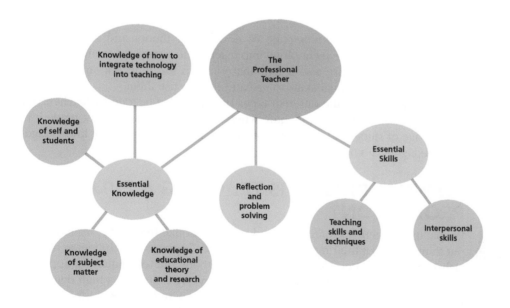

FIGURE 2.3 Essential knowledge and skills for the professional teacher

TECHNOLOGY in *ACTION*

E-Portfolios in 12th-Grade Industrial Arts

Bill Thompson had taught in the industrial arts automotive technology program for over a year. His student population was quite diverse in terms of interest, gender, and ethnicity. The students' one common characteristic was pride in the work that they did in Mr. Thompson's classes. He understood that his students did not just rebuild engines. They were required to problem-solve; work in teams; and think critically about the possible effects of the decisions they made on safety, the environment, and personal finances. However, Mr. Thompson was troubled that the school and even his own students labeled these students as "gear-heads."

Mr. Thompson wanted to demonstrate to the school and his students that the outcomes of his program went beyond just building a pretty car. Over lunch he was talking with Mrs. Watson, the technology coordinator for the school, and she suggested that his students might enjoy creating an e-portfolio to share with others. She explained that an e-portfolio is an electronic portfolio of a student's work. Students could upload text, video, audio, and graphics of indi-

vidual projects that they worked on, and then share that site with other students in their class, the school at large, or even the community. The next day, Mr. Thompson explained to his

---

Go to MyEducationLab, select Chapter 2 and then the Activities and Applications to watch the video Types of Professional Knowledge.

knowledge of subject matter, knowledge of educational theory and research, and knowledge of how to integrate technology into teaching to create optimum conditions for student learning. The figure also shows that you can use reflection and problem solving to decide which essential skills to use and how to use them.

For a video example of the different types of knowledge needed by teachers, go to MyEducationLab. See if you can identify where two teachers at different grade levels use knowledge of students, knowledge of subject, pedagogical content knowledge, and general pedagogical knowledge.

TO WHAT EXTENT IS TEACHING A FULL PROFESSION?

People use the terms *professional* and *profession* quite frequently, usually without thinking about their meanings. Professionals "possess a high degree of specialized theoretical knowledge, along with methods and techniques for applying this knowledge in their day-to-day work. . . . [And they] are united by a high degree of in-group solidarity, stemming from their common training and common adherence to certain doctrines and methods" (Abrahamsson, 1971, pp. 11–12).

students that they would all be required to build an e-portfolio of their classwork over the school year. Students were to use the e-portfolio to document work, explain processes and decisions, show and discuss stages of work for each project, and provide a personal reflection statement about their group work. Outside his office, he provided a computer workstation that used an e-portfolio website called Epsilen as a home page. He also provided a digital camera, a video camera, and a microphone.

Over the course of the school year, students began building their e-portfolios. Mr. Thompson shared some of the e-portfolios with his principal, who shared them with the school board. Some of the students even used their e-portfolio to secure a summer job because they shared them with prospective employers.

E-PORTFOLIO: An e-portfolio is an electronic collection of work. The purpose of an e-portfolio is not merely to show the finished product, which could be a paper, artwork, project, musical score, etc., but also to highlight the processes that the student engaged in and the stages the work went through before becoming the finished product. Students use text, audio, visuals, and web links to describe what they have done. Some e-portfolios allow visitors to ask questions of the e-portfolio owner.

VISIT: http://www.epsilen.com/Epsilen/Public/Home.aspx. Free e-portfolio services are available on the Web. If you need more features and options, you can purchase services as well. To get an idea of how to use an e-portfolio, visit Epsilen—a free service.

POSSIBLE USES: The primary use of an e-portfolio is to document student work. The documentation of this work can be used for college admission, for employment, and as a way to update parents on student work. Students can document their growth in writing performance; highlight various research projects they conducted; document their artistic expression with digital stills of their work; and then provide context with narrative text, audio/video, and supporting images and documents.

TRY IT OUT: Visit http://www.epsilen.com/Epsilen/Public/Home.aspx and click on "Create EPORTFOLIO." You will be directed to a page that asks for your e-mail address and personal information, and to accept the terms of agreement. Once completed, you will be asked for detailed information. Here, you will decide whom you would like to view your work—from private (no one can see it) to open access to everyone and a few points in between. Then you will be asked to list your interests and write a biography. When complete, click "complete registration." You will be sent an e-mail that will ask you to verify your registration. Once you click on that link in the e-mail, you will be prompted to create a password, and from there you will be directed to your new e-portfolio page. Good luck!

■ ■ ■ ■ ■ ■ ■ ■ ■ ■

From several sociologists and educators who have studied teaching come additional characteristics of occupations that are highly professionalized; these characteristics are summarized in Figure 2.4. Before reading further, reflect on each characteristic and decide whether it applies to teaching. Then continue reading about the extent to which teaching satisfies each of these commonly agreed-upon characteristics of full professions. Do our perceptions agree with yours?

Institutional Monopoly of Services

On one hand, teachers do have a monopoly of services. As a rule, only those who are certified members of the profession may teach in public schools. On the other hand, varied requirements for certification and for teaching in private schools weaken this monopoly. (Although state certification and teacher education courses are generally not required to teach in private schools, a college degree is a minimum requirement.)

Any claim teachers might have as exclusive providers of a service is further eroded by the practice of many state systems to approve temporary, or **emergency**

FIGURE 2.4 Does teaching meet the criteria for a profession?

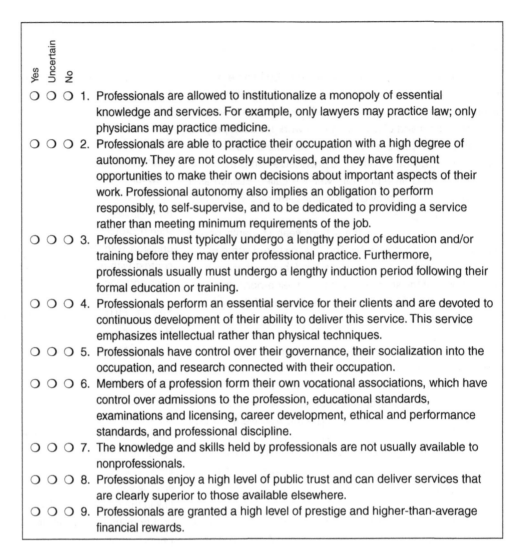

Yes / Uncertain / No

○ ○ ○ 1. Professionals are allowed to institutionalize a monopoly of essential knowledge and services. For example, only lawyers may practice law; only physicians may practice medicine.

○ ○ ○ 2. Professionals are able to practice their occupation with a high degree of autonomy. They are not closely supervised, and they have frequent opportunities to make their own decisions about important aspects of their work. Professional autonomy also implies an obligation to perform responsibly, to self-supervise, and to be dedicated to providing a service rather than meeting minimum requirements of the job.

○ ○ ○ 3. Professionals must typically undergo a lengthy period of education and/or training before they may enter professional practice. Furthermore, professionals usually must undergo a lengthy induction period following their formal education or training.

○ ○ ○ 4. Professionals perform an essential service for their clients and are devoted to continuous development of their ability to deliver this service. This service emphasizes intellectual rather than physical techniques.

○ ○ ○ 5. Professionals have control over their governance, their socialization into the occupation, and research connected with their occupation.

○ ○ ○ 6. Members of a profession form their own vocational associations, which have control over admissions to the profession, educational standards, examinations and licensing, career development, ethical and performance standards, and professional discipline.

○ ○ ○ 7. The knowledge and skills held by professionals are not usually available to nonprofessionals.

○ ○ ○ 8. Professionals enjoy a high level of public trust and can deliver services that are clearly superior to those available elsewhere.

○ ○ ○ 9. Professionals are granted a high level of prestige and higher-than-average financial rewards.

certification measures (or waivers) to deal with teacher shortages. According to the U.S. Department of Education's *Fourth Annual Report on Teacher Quality,* 3.5 percent of teachers were on waivers in 2005, with more teachers on waivers in high-poverty districts (5.2 percent) than in all other school districts (3.1 percent) (U.S. Department of Education, Office of Postsecondary Education, 2005). To address the use of waivers, the goal of No Child Left Behind (NCLB) is to have a "highly qualified teacher" (a teacher with "full state teacher certification") in every classroom. In addition, emergency certification is strongly resisted by professional teacher organizations and several state departments of education.

The widespread practice of out-of-field teaching also weakens teachers' monopoly of services. For example, about one out of four teachers in grades 7–12 lack even a college minor in the subject being taught. In high-poverty schools, the rate of out-of-field teachers is 34 percent, compared to about 19 percent in low-poverty schools (Education Trust, 2002). Thus, teaching is the only profession that allows noncertified individuals to practice the profession.

Perhaps the most significant argument against teachers claiming to be the exclusive providers of a service, however, is the fact that a great deal of teaching occurs in informal, nonschool settings and is done by people who are not teachers. Every day, thousands of people teach various kinds of how-to-do-it skills: how to water-ski, how to make dogs more obedient, how to make pasta from scratch, how to tune a car's engine, and how to meditate.

Teacher Autonomy

In one sense, teachers have considerable autonomy. Teachers usually work behind a closed classroom door, and seldom is their work observed by another adult. In fact, one of the norms among teachers is that the classroom is a castle of sorts, and teacher privacy a closely guarded right. Although the performance of new teachers may be observed and evaluated on a regular basis by supervisors, veteran teachers are observed much less frequently, and they usually enjoy a high degree of autonomy.

Teachers also have extensive freedom regarding how they structure the classroom environment. They may emphasize discussions as opposed to lectures. They may set certain requirements for some students and not for others. They may delegate responsibilities to one class and not another. And within the guidelines set by local and state authorities, teachers may determine much of the content they teach.

However, there are constraints placed on teachers and their work. Teachers, unlike doctors and lawyers, must accept all the "clients" who are sent to them. Only infrequently does a teacher actually reject a student assigned to him or her.

Teachers must also agree to teach what state and local officials say they must. And the work of teachers is subject to a higher level of public scrutiny than that found in other professions. Because the public provides "clients" (students) and pays for schools, it has a significant say regarding the work of teachers. Nevertheless, it has been suggested that some leveling of professions will occur in the future: "More of the work of the traditional high-status professions, particularly medicine, will occur in bureaucratic or large organizational settings under the watchful eye of managers. [While] doctors are accepting more and more regulation, school teachers . . . will slowly break out of long-established bureaucratic hierarchies and share more of the autonomy previously enjoyed by members of the high-status professions" (Grant & Murray, 1999, pp. 231–232).

Years of Education and Training

As sociologist Amitai Etzioni (1969) points out in his classic discussion of the "semiprofessions," the training of teachers is less lengthy than that required for other professionals, for example, lawyers and physicians. The professional component of teacher education programs is the shortest of all the professions—only 15 percent of the average bachelor's degree program for a high school teacher is devoted to professional courses. However, several colleges and universities have begun five-year teacher education programs. Similarly, the National Commission on Teaching and America's Future recommended that teacher education be moved to the graduate level. If the trend toward five-year and graduate-level teacher education programs continues, the professional status of teaching will definitely be enhanced.

In most professions, new members must undergo a prescribed induction period. Physicians, for example, must serve an internship or a residency before beginning practice, and most lawyers begin as clerks in law firms. In contrast, teachers usually do not go through a formal induction period before assuming full responsibility for their work. Practice teaching comes closest to serving as an induction period, but it is often relatively short, informal, and lacking in uniformity.

Provision of Essential Service

Although it is generally acknowledged that teachers provide a service that is vital to the well-being of individuals and groups, the public does need to be reminded of this fact from time to time. This importance was driven home on a large scale during the early 1980s when reports such as *A Nation at Risk* linked the strength of our country to the quality of its schools.

The ability to function as the spark that stimulates young people to learn and grow can give teachers a sense of meaning and fulfillment they might not find in other professions. A foreign language teacher who immigrated to this country describes what many teachers feel about their profession: "I feel that I get satisfaction . . . that I am a useful member of the society. I feel this is the field in which . . . I can contribute more to society than in any other field. . . . I am doing a job which is good [for] the American society" (Parkay, 1983, pp. 114–115).

Degree of Self-Governance

Without doubt, if members of a profession feel empowered, they have higher morale. If they participate in decisions about job-related policies and if their expertise is acknowledged, they are more invested in their work. The limited freedom of teachers to govern themselves, however, has detracted from the overall status of the profession. In many states, licensing guidelines are set by government officials who may or may not be educators, and at the local level, decision-making power usually resides with local boards of education, largely made up of people who have not taught. As a result, teachers have had little say over what they teach, when they teach, whom they teach, and—in extreme instances—how they teach.

However, recent efforts to empower teachers and to professionalize teaching are creating new roles for teachers and expanded opportunities to govern important aspects of their work. At schools throughout the country, teachers are having a greater voice in decisions related to curriculum development, staffing, budget, and the day-to-day operation of schools. "Teachers in the U.S. today are developing leadership skills to a degree not needed in the past" (Parkay et al., 1999, pp. 20–21). Figure 2.5 shows that teachers believe they have the most influence over practices in their own classrooms—for example, establishing curriculum, setting performance standards for students, determining their own professional development, and setting discipline policies. They believe they have less influence over decisions related to hiring, budget, and teacher evaluation.

Although teachers differ significantly in the amount of influence they believe teachers have, teachers should experience greater self-governance as principals respond to increasing pressure to become more effective at facilitating collaborative, emergent approaches to leadership. Increasingly, principals realize that "leadership in instructional matters should emerge freely from both principals and teachers. After all, teachers de-

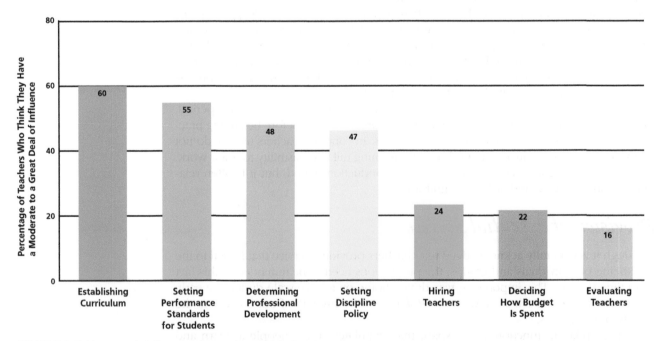

FIGURE 2.5 How much influence do teachers think they have?

Source: Editorial Projects in Education, 2008. Quality Counts (27)18, January 10, 2008, Education Week, p. 34.

liver the instruction in the classroom; they have expertise in curriculum and teaching, and they have mastered a substantive body of knowledge" (Hoy & Hoy, 2009, p. 2).

Professional Associations

Like other professionals, teachers have formed vocational associations that focus on issues such as admission to the profession, educational standards, examinations and licensing, career development, ethical and performance standards, and professional discipline. It is clear, though, that national teacher organizations have not progressed as far as other professions have in gaining control of these areas.

Professional Knowledge and Skills

Professionals are granted a certain status because they possess knowledge and skills not normally held by the general public. Within the profession of teaching, however, the requirements for membership are less precise. In spite of the ongoing efforts of educational researchers, there is less than unanimous agreement on the knowledge and skills considered necessary to teach. This lack of agreement is reflected in the varied programs at the 1,300 or so colleges and universities that train teachers.

Since it was established in 1987, the National Board for Professional Teaching Standards (NBPTS) has made significant progress toward clarifying the knowledge base for teaching and enhancing the status of the profession. The NBPTS (the majority of whose members are teachers) offers board certification to teachers who possess a high level of NBPTS-identified knowledge and skills. Since 1987, the NBPTS has granted national certification to nearly 64,000 teachers (National Board for Professional Teaching Standards, December 3, 2007).

According to the president of NBPTS, "National Board Certification is the most prestigious credential a teacher can earn. Like board-certified doctors and accountants, teachers who achieve National Board Certification have met rigorous standards through intensive study, expert evaluation, self-assessment and peer review" (National Board for Professional Teaching Standards, December 3, 2007). Similarly, a teacher comments on the rigor at board certification: "The National Board Certification process was a powerful and worthwhile professional experience. It drastically refined my practice as an educator." (National Board for Professional Teaching Standards, 2007).

Level of Public Trust

The level of trust the public extends to teachers as professionals varies greatly. On the one hand, the public appears to have great confidence in the work that teachers do. Because of its faith in the teaching profession, the public invests teachers with considerable power over its children. For the most part, parents willingly allow their children to be molded and influenced by teachers, and this willingness must be based on a high degree of trust. In addition, most parents expect their children to obey and respect teachers.

Although all professions have some members who might be described as unprofessional, teaching is especially vulnerable to such charges. The sheer size of the teaching force makes it difficult to maintain consistently high professional standards. Moreover, teaching is subject to a level of public scrutiny and control that other, more established professions traditionally have not tolerated. However, the era of widespread public trust may be running out for these other professions as well. The mushrooming number of malpractice suits against doctors, for example, may be a sign that here, too, public confidence has significantly eroded. Table 2.2 shows that the public considers teachers to be highly trustworthy.

Prestige, Benefits, and Pay

While "many teachers and school administrators . . . are thought to be of a more elite social class than the majority of the population in the United States" (Parker & Shapiro,

TABLE 2.2 Whom would you generally trust?

"Would you generally trust each of the following types of people to tell the truth, or not?"

	Would Trust (%)	Would Not (%)	Not Sure/Refused (%)
Doctors	85	12	3
Teachers	83	15	2
Scientists	77	19	4
Police officers	76	21	3
Professors	75	19	6
Clergy or priests	74	22	4
Military officers	72	26	3
Judges	70	24	5
Accountants	68	28	3
Ordinary man or woman	66	26	8
Civil servants	62	32	6
Bankers	62	34	3
The president	48	47	4
TV newscasters	44	51	5
Athletes	43	47	10
Journalists	39	58	3
Members of Congress	35	63	3
Pollsters	34	54	12
Trade union leaders	30	60	10
Stockbrokers	29	63	8
Lawyers	27	68	5
Actors	26	69	5

Source: The Harris Poll® #61, August 8, 2006. Based on telephone interviews of 1,002 U.S. adults, July 10–16, 2006.

1993, p. 42), this higher status is based on level of education attained rather than wealth. Thus, teachers have not received salaries in keeping with other professions requiring approximately the same amount of schooling. Nevertheless, there is significant support for reducing the salary gap—83 percent of the public favor increased salaries for teachers, even if it means paying higher taxes (Hart & Teeter, 2002).

TO WHAT PROFESSIONAL ORGANIZATIONS DO TEACHERS BELONG?

The expanding leadership role of teachers has been supported through the activities of more than 500 national teacher organizations (*National Trade and Professional Associations of the United States,* 2008). These organizations and the scores of hardworking teachers who run them support a variety of activities to improve teaching and schools. Through lobbying in Washington and at state capitols, for example, teacher associations acquaint legislators, policymakers, and politicians with critical issues and problems in the teaching profession. Many associations have staffs of teachers, researchers, and consultants who produce professional publications, hold conferences, prepare grant proposals, engage in school improvement activities, and promote a positive image of teaching to the public. Two national organizations have led the quest to improve the professional lives of all teachers: the National Education Association (NEA) and the American Federation of Teachers (AFT). These two groups have had a long history of competition for the allegiance of teachers.

The National Education Association

Membership in the National Education Association (NEA), the oldest and largest of the two organizations, includes both teachers and administrators. Originally called the National Teachers Association when it was founded in 1857, the group was started by forty-three educators from a dozen states and the District of Columbia (Laurence, 2000).

The NEA has affiliates in every state plus Puerto Rico and the District of Columbia, and its local affiliates number more than 14,000. About two-thirds of the teachers in this country belong to the NEA. More than 78 percent of NEA's 3.2 million members are teachers; about 12 percent are guidance counselors, librarians, and administrators; almost 3 percent are university professors; about 2 percent are college and university students; about 3 percent are support staff (teacher aides, secretaries, cafeteria workers, bus drivers, and custodians); and about 2 percent are retired members (National Education Association, April 29, 2008).

To improve education in this country, the NEA has standing committees in the following areas: affiliate relationships, higher education, human relations, political action, teacher benefits, and teacher rights. These committees engage in a wide range of activities, among them preparing reports on important educational issues, disseminating the results of educational research, conducting conferences, working with federal agencies on behalf of children, pressing for more rigorous standards for the teaching profession, helping school districts resolve salary disputes, developing ways to improve personnel practices, and enhancing the relationship between the profession and the public.

Currently, more than two-thirds of states have passed some type of collective bargaining laws that apply to teachers. There is little uniformity among these laws, with most of the 31 states permitting strikes only if certain conditions have been met. The NEA has gone on record as supporting a federal statute that would set up uniform procedures for teachers to bargain with their employers.

The NEA continues today to focus on issues of concern to teachers, primarily in the area of professional governance. Efforts are being made to broaden teachers' decision-making powers related to curriculum, extracurricular responsibilities, staff development, and supervision. To promote the status of the profession, the NEA conducts annual research studies and opinion surveys in various areas, and publishes *NEA Today* and *Tomorrow's Teachers* for NEA student members.

The American Federation of Teachers

The American Federation of Teachers (AFT) was founded in 1916. Three teachers' unions in Chicago issued a call for teachers to form a national organization affiliated with organized labor. Teacher unions in Gary, Indiana; New York City; Oklahoma; Scranton, Pennsylvania; and Washington, DC, joined the three Chicago unions to form the AFT.

The AFT differs from the NEA because it is open only to teachers and nonsupervisory school personnel. The AFT is active today in organizing teachers, bargaining collectively, fostering public relations, and developing policies related to various educational issues. In addition, the organization conducts research in areas such as educational reform, bilingual education, teacher certification, and evaluation, and also represents members' concerns through legislative action and technical assistance.

The AFT has more than 1.4 million members who are organized through 43 state affiliates and more than 3,000 local affiliates. The AFT is affiliated with the American Federation of Labor–Congress of Industrial Organizations (AFL-CIO), which has over 13 million members. To promote the idea that teachers should have the right to speak for themselves on important issues, the AFT does not allow superintendents, principals, and other administrators to join. As an informational brochure on the AFT states, "Because the AFT believes in action—in 'getting things done' rather than issuing reports, letting someone else do the 'doing'—a powerful, cohesive structure is necessary."

Unlike the NEA, the AFT has been steadfastly involved throughout its history in securing economic gains and improving working conditions for teachers. Although the AFT has been criticized for being unprofessional and too concerned with bread-and-butter issues, none other than the great educator and philosopher John Dewey took out the first AFT membership card in 1916. After twelve years as a union member, Dewey made his stance on economic issues clear:

> It is said that the Teachers Union, as distinct from the more academic organizations, overemphasizes the economic aspect of teaching. Well, I never had that contempt for the economic aspect of teaching, especially not on the first of the month when I get my salary check. I find that teachers have to pay their grocery and meat bills and house rent just the same as everybody else. (1955, pp. 60–61)

Traditionally, the AFT has been strongest in urban areas. Today, the AFT represents teachers not only in Chicago and New York but in Philadelphia; Washington, DC; Kansas City; Detroit; Boston; Cleveland; and Pittsburgh. NEA membership has tended to be suburban and rural. The NEA has always been the larger of the two organizations, and it is presently more than twice the size of its rival.

The NEAFT Partnership

For decades, many people within both the NEA and the AFT believed that the interests of teachers and students could best be served through a merger of the two organizations. One national teachers' union with enormous political strength, they believed, could do more to advance the teaching profession than two independent, often competing organizations. Until the turn of the century, however, differences between the two organizations thwarted periodic efforts to merge.

By the end of the 1990s, differences between the NEA and the AFT had become less apparent. Collective bargaining and the use of strikes, long opposed by the NEA, were now used by both organizations. Eventually, a "conceptual agreement" to merge the organizations was announced in 1998 by the presidents of the NEA and the AFT. The presidents cited an "assault" on public education in the form of voucher plans, charter schools, and other approaches to school privatization as a primary reason to merge (Bradley, 1998). In 2001, NEA and AFT Unity Discussion Teams and Advisory Committees forged the NEAFT Partnership and endorsed the following goals:

- **Building Relationships** to increase knowledge, promote trust and collaboration and involve leaders and affiliates in both our unions at the national, state and local levels.
- **Making Collaboration Work** to more effectively use our combined resources to focus on promoting the welfare of children, public education and our members.
- **Creating Value** from the power of our collaboration to strengthen our ability to resist the challenges by the enemies of public education and collective bargaining.
- **Demonstrating Visibly** our united strength and ability to improve the institutions in which our members work and further signal our commitment to public education and unionism (NEAFT Partnership, 2002).

The NEA and AFT have found additional common ground in their opposition to No Child Left Behind (NCLB). Both organizations maintain that the law is seriously flawed. In particular, NEAFT believes the NCLB's requirement that schools make AYP is harmful to public schools. NEAFT believes that NCLB does not give enough credit for schools that make academic progress but fail to reach NCLB's AYP standards. NEAFT is also working with other education associations to develop alternatives to what it views as punitive high-stakes testing programs. NEAFT supports high-stakes tests aligned with standards as one, but not the only, tool in student and school assessment.

Other Professional Organizations

In addition to the NEA and AFT, teachers' professional interests are represented by more than 500 other national organizations. Several of these are concerned with improving the quality of education at all levels and in all subject areas. Phi Delta Kappa (PDK), for example, is an international professional and honorary fraternity of educators concerned with enhancing quality education through research and leadership activities. Founded in 1906, Phi Delta Kappa has a membership of about 100,000. Members, who are graduate students, teachers, and administrators, belong to one of 640 chapters. To be initiated into Phi Delta Kappa, one must have demonstrated high academic achievement, have completed at least fifteen semester hours of graduate work in education, and have made a commitment to a career of educational service. Phi Delta Kappa members receive *Phi Delta Kappan*, a journal of education published ten times a year.

Another example is the Association for Supervision and Curriculum Development (ASCD), a professional organization of teachers, supervisors, curriculum coordinators, education professors, administrators, and others. The ASCD is interested in school improvement at all levels of education. Founded in 1943, the association has a membership of about 175,000. ASCD provides professional development experiences in curriculum and supervision; disseminates information on educational issues; and encourages research, evaluation, and theory development. ASCD also conducts several National Curriculum Study Institutes around the country each year and provides a free research information service to members. Members receive *Educational Leadership*, a well-respected journal published eight times a year. ASCD also publishes a yearbook, each edition devoted to a particular educational issue, and occasional books in the area of curriculum and supervision.

Many professional associations exist for teachers of specific subject areas, such as mathematics, English, social studies, music, physical education, and so on, as well as for teachers of specific student populations, such as exceptional learners, young children, and students with limited English proficiency.

myeducationlab

Go to MyEducationLab, select Resources and then Beginning Your Career to see a sampler of professional organizations for teachers.

HOW DO TEACHERS HELP TO BUILD LEARNING COMMUNITIES?

Success in your first year of teaching will be determined by the relationships you develop with students, their families, your colleagues, school administrators, and other members of your school community. Ideally, all of these groups will work together to create a learning community—a school environment "where teachers and principals can continually expand their capacity to create the results that they desire, where emergent patterns of thinking are nurtured, where collective aspiration is liberated and where people are constantly learning how to learn" (Hoy & Hoy, 2009, p. 22). One teacher who participated in her school's learning community is Erin McGee, the fifth-grade teacher profiled in Teachers' Voices: Walk in My Shoes.

Relationships with Students

Without a doubt, your relationships with students will be the most important (and complex) you will have as a teacher. The quality of your relationships with students will depend in large measure on your knowledge of students and commitment to improving your interactions with them. As a first-year teacher put it:

> It is amazing when every student is involved and enjoying the lesson. At moments like these, I realize that I'm educating real people and making a difference in their futures. I really connected with my students because they saw that learning can be fun. They realized that I, too, am a person who cares about them and wants them to succeed. It makes my job feel complete and I know I'm in the right profession. (Hauser & Rauch, 2002, p. 36)

Your relationships with students will have many dimensions. Your primary responsibility as a professional teacher will be to see that each student learns as much as possible. You will need to establish relationships with *all* students based on mutual respect, caring, and concern. Without attention to this personal realm, your effectiveness as a teacher will be limited, as will your ability to have a positive influence on students' attitudes and behaviors.

 TEACHERS' VOICES *Walk in My Shoes*

A SUCCESSFUL NOVICE TEACHER

In her second year of teaching, Erin McGee, a fifth-grade teacher, had won the respect and love of the administration, staff, students, and parents. Her principal described her as "truly exemplary" and having "the whole package—management, curriculum, enthusiasm, and a positive attitude." How did Erin quickly suceed as a novice teacher? And what did she do to earn such a good reputation so early in her career?

Erin credited her teacher education program for preparing her well. In addition to skills and knowledge, the program offered numerous opportunities for hands-on work in elementary school classrooms. The most extensive of these were two 3-month student teaching experiences, in an upper and lower grade. In each setting, she observed and worked alongside the regular classroom teacher, who served as a master teacher in the program.

In her fourth-grade assignment, Erin was impressed by her master teacher and "kept a journal of everything he did." She gradually began teaching lessons and then managing portions of the day. At the end of each day, she and the master teacher would sit down and evaluate how things went, a ritual Erin appreciated. Early on, Erin volunteered to do "something extra" and was permitted to help coordinate a fourth-grade physical education program,  drawing on her undergraduate emphasis in physical education to do so. For the final week of student teaching, Erin taught the whole day without the master teacher present.

Unexpected circumstances caused Erin to teach on her own more in her second student-teaching assignment. After several weeks, her master teacher needed to take a medical leave. Fortunately, Erin had earlier completed the school district's paperwork to become a substitute teacher. And when the principal selected her to be the substitute teacher, she welcomed the opportunity. With initial guidance from the master teacher, she substitute-taught for the next 4 weeks. Reflecting on the time, she says, "I loved it! The kids were wonderful."

Erin's teacher preparation journey was not without bumps. To be credentialed in California, teachers are required to pass a series of tests: the California Basic Education Skills Test (CBEST), the California Subject Examinations for Teachers (CSET), and the Reading Instruction Competence Assessment (RICA). The most difficult of these for Erin was the CSET, which covered a range of subjects: reading, language, literature, history, social studies, science, math, physical education, human development, and visual and performing arts. Erin needed to take one section of it several times. She studied hard every weekend until she passed it, motivated throughout by her passion to teach and the knowledge that she was qualified to teach.

Pressed to mention her greatest challenge when she began teaching, Erin confessed that it was the parents. Being new and young on a staff of well-regarded teachers who had taught 15 to 20 years was stressful. Concerned that the parents were nervous about her and feeling like she was under a spotlight, she decided to woo them with one of her strengths — her knowledge and use of technology. On "Back to School Night," she did a PowerPoint presentation, including the students' pictures to personalize the presentation and take the focus off her. She also used a computer 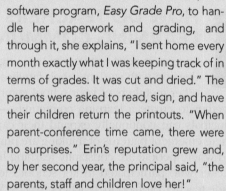 software program, *Easy Grade Pro*, to handle her paperwork and grading, and through it, she explains, "I sent home every month exactly what I was keeping track of in terms of grades. It was cut and dried." The parents were asked to read, sign, and have their children return the printouts. "When parent-conference time came, there were no surprises." Erin's reputation grew and, by her second year, the principal said, "the parents, staff and children love her!"

Erin's early success was aided by collaboration with her two fellow fifth-grade teachers. "My team is incredible! They have been teaching for 20-plus years, and I look up to them and see how they manage their kids. Together we have new and old ideas and mix them." The three regularly plan together, rotate classes for several subjects, and on Fridays gather their students for special events such as a science bee (like a spelling bee) to prepare for state testing or parents' guest lectures that draw on their expertise in curriculum-related topics.

Erin's positive attitude and commitment are keys to her early success. "I just love teaching—love the idea that I have a group of students I can influence for a year; can teach them academic, personal, and social skills and work habits; and can help them to be successful, not just in fifth grade, but also in the future."

Erin McGee

Relationships With Colleagues and Staff

Each working day, you will interact with other teachers and staff members. They can provide much-needed support and guidance, as Georgene Acosta, a first-year teacher, learned: "When I have difficult situations as a teacher, they inspire me to work through those difficulties. They renew my sense of hope and courage by reminding me that I am not alone" (Oakes & Lipton, 2007, p. 489).

From the beginning of your first teaching assignment, let your colleagues know that you are willing to learn all you can about your new job and to be a team player. In most schools, it is common practice to give first-time teachers less desirable assignments (classes that have a greater number of lower-ability students, for example), reserving the more desirable assignments (honors or advanced placement classes, for example) for more experienced teachers. By demonstrating your willingness to take on these assignments with good humor and to give them your best effort, you will do much to establish yourself as a valuable colleague.

It is important that you get along with your colleagues and contribute to a spirit of professional cooperation or collegiality in the school. Some you will enjoy being around; others you may wish to avoid. Some will express obvious enthusiasm for teaching; others may be bitter and pessimistic about their work. Be pleasant and friendly with both types. Accept their advice with a smile, and then act on what you believe is worthwhile.

Relationships With Administrators

Pay particular attention to the relationships you develop with administrators, department heads, and supervisors. Though your contacts with them will not be as frequent as with other teachers, they can do much to ensure your initial success. The following comments illustrate the information new teachers often desire from their school principals:

- "I would like affirmation from my principal that I am doing things OK. If not, I would like to know about it so I can address and correct the situation."
- "I would like to meet monthly with my principal to discuss things like 'hidden agendas,' culture and traditions of the school, expectations, regular events, and what to expect, as well as an opportunity to bitch and gripe a bit."
- "The principal should express the expectations that he has for students in the school. I needed to know about the parameters of the grading system. I needed to know expectations for lesson plans." (Brock & Grady, 2001, pp. 18–19)

Principals are well aware of the difficulties you might encounter as a first-year teacher, and they are there to help you succeed. Because the demands on their time are intense, however, you should not hesitate to be proactive about meeting with them to discuss issues of concern.

The principal of your new school will most likely be the one to introduce you to other teachers, members of the administrative team, and staff. He or she should inform you if there are assistant principals or department heads who can help you enforce school rules, keep accurate records, and obtain supplies, for example. The principal may also assign an experienced teacher to serve as a mentor during your first year.

Relationships With Parents or Guardians

Developing positive connections with your students' parents or guardians can contribute significantly to students' success and to your success as a teacher. In reality, teachers and parents or guardians are partners—both concerned with the learning and growth of the children in their care. As former U.S. Secretary of Education Rod Paige pointed out, "We need to build a bridge between powerful scientific research, homes, and pre-schools and make sure that adults know how vital it is that children have strong cognitive development, even before they enter school. Teachers and

Parents or guardians can be a teacher's greatest partners in determining the success of his or her students. What are some ways you can reach out to know your students' parents or guardians and gain their support?

parents around the country [must work together] to ensure that no child is left behind" (U.S. Department of Education, 2001).

It is important that you become acquainted with parents or guardians at school functions, at meetings of the parent-teacher association (PTA) or parent-teacher organization (PTO), at various community events, and in other social situations. To develop good communication with parents or guardians, you will need to be sensitive to their needs, such as their work schedules and the language spoken at home.

By maintaining contact with parents or guardians and encouraging them to become involved in their children's education, you can significantly enhance the achievement of your students. One research study, based on interviews with the parents and guardians of almost 17,000 K–12 students, showed that parental involvement is associated with higher levels of student achievement, more positive attitudes toward school, greater participation in extracurricular activities, fewer suspensions and expulsions, and fewer grade repetitions (Nord & West, 2001). In light of such significant findings, it is important that you be willing to take the extra time and energy to pursue strategies such as the following for involving parents:

- Parents reading aloud to the child, listening to the child read, and signing homework papers.
- Parents drilling students on math and spelling and helping with homework lessons.
- Parents discussing school activities with their children. Parents can help teach their children at home. For example, a simple home activity might be alphabetizing books; a more complex one would be using kitchen supplies in an elementary science experiment.
- Home suggestions for games or group activities related to the child's schoolwork that the parent and child can play together.
- Parents participating in school activities such as a sports booster club, career day, and music and drama events.
- Parents participating in their children's learning by having them cosign learning contracts and serving as guest speakers.

The Goals 2000: Educate America Act funded parent resource centers in each state plus the District of Columbia (see the Appendix "Parent Information and Resource Centers" at MyEducationLab). To help families get involved in their children's learning, these centers offer training for parents, hotlines, mobile training teams, resource and lending libraries, support groups, and referral networks. The U.S. Department of Education also sponsors the Partnership for Family Involvement in Education, designed to help students act as a link between their teachers/schools and their families/communities. (For information, call 1-800-USA-LEARN.)

Family involvement resources are also available on the Internet through the National Parent Information Network (NPIN, http://npin.org), a project formerly sponsored by the ERIC system. NPIN resources include information for parents on child development, testing, working with teachers, and home learning activities.

Community Relations

Communities provide significant support for the education of their young people and determine the character of their schools. In addition, communities often help their schools by recruiting volunteers, providing financial support for special projects, and operating homework hotline programs. For example, school–community partnerships have been formed through "The Employer's Promise," a national effort to involve communities in supporting the family's central role in children's learning:

- Hancock Financial Services sponsors "Kids-to-Go," a program of day-long supervised activities for employees' school-age children during school holidays in Boston.
- California Edison supports the Parent Institute for Quality Education, which has trained 7,500 parents from East Los Angeles to participate actively in their children's education.
- Packard staggers start times for employees who volunteer at the corporation's on-site elementary school and accommodates the schedules of employees with school-age children.
- College Testing's "Realize the Dream" program provides workshops and resources to involve parents in their children's education.

Martha Guerro, first-year high school social studies teacher in East Los Angeles, says, "I believe that teachers should develop . . . genuine relationships with the community. . . . I interact frequently with my students and their families outside of the classroom. I do countless home visits. I take my students to conferences and work with them on community-related issues . . . we attended a Coalition for Educational Justice conference that focused on overcrowding in inner-city schools and high-stakes standardized testing" (Oakes & Lipton, 2007, p. 414).

HOW DO TEACHERS PARTICIPATE IN TEACHER COLLABORATION?

The relationships that build a learning community involve collaboration—working together, sharing decision making, and solving problems. As a member of a dynamic, changing profession, your efforts to collaborate will result in an increased understanding of the teaching–learning process and improved learning for all students. By working with others on school governance, curriculum development, school partnerships, and educational reform, you will play an important role in enhancing the professional status of teachers.

The heart of collaboration is meaningful, authentic relationships among professionals. Of course, such relationships do not occur naturally; they require commitment and hard work. Friend and Bursuck (2002, pp. 76–77) have identified seven characteristics of collaboration, which are summarized here. Collaboration

- is voluntary; teachers make a personal choice to collaborate.
- is based on parity; all individuals' contributions are valued equally.
- requires a shared goal.
- includes shared responsibility for key decisions.
- includes shared accountability for outcomes.
- is based on shared resources; each teacher contributes something—time, expertise, space, equipment, or other resource.
- is emergent; as teachers work together, the degree of shared decision making, trust, and respect increases.

Schools that support the essential elements of collaboration are collegial schools "characterized by purposeful adult interactions about improving schoolwide teaching and learning" (Glickman, Gordon, & Ross-Gordon, 2004, p. 6). The following sections examine four expressions of teacher collaboration: peer coaching, staff development, team teaching, and co-teaching.

Peer Coaching

Experienced teachers traditionally help novice teachers, but more formal peer-coaching programs extend the benefits of collaboration to more teachers. Peer coaching is an arrangement whereby teachers grow professionally by observing one another's teaching and providing constructive feedback. The practice encourages teachers to learn together in an emotionally safe environment. According to Bruce Joyce and Marsha Weil, peer coaching is an effective way to create communities of professional educators, and all teachers should be members of coaching teams:

> If we had our way, all school faculties would be divided into coaching teams—that is, teams who regularly observe one another's teaching and learn from watching one another and the students. In short, we recommend the development of a "coaching environment" in which all personnel see themselves as coaches. (Joyce, Weil, & Calhoun, 2000, p. 440)

Through teacher-to-teacher support and collaboration, peer-coaching programs improve teacher morale and teaching effectiveness.

Staff Development

Today, teachers often contribute to the design of staff development programs that encourage collaboration, risk-taking, and experimentation. Some programs, for example, give teachers the opportunity to meet with other teachers at similar grade levels or in similar content areas for the purpose of sharing ideas, strategies, and solutions to problems. A day or part of a day may be devoted to this kind of workshop or idea exchange. Teachers are frequently given released time from regular duties to visit other schools and observe exemplary programs in action.

One example of a collaborative staff development program is at Sherman Oaks Community Charter School in San Jose, California. Every school day between 11:30 A.M. and 1 P.M., Sherman Oaks teachers meet for 90 minutes of professional development. The teachers discuss and debate instructional theory and practice, try to solve problems that have come up or are likely to come up in their classrooms, discuss curriculum, seek advice, offer encouragement, or quietly reflect. As one teacher put it, "It's always wonderful stuff—things that get your brain stretched. I feel like a professional" (Curtis, 2000).

Another collaborative program is the Maryland Electronic Learning Community (MELC), a teacher development and support group that provides formal training in technology integration followed by ongoing collaboration and support. Funded in part by the U.S. Department of Education, the MELC project is a coalition of partners who form an electronic learning community using technologies such as digitized video, Internet resources, two-way video and audio for distance learning, and e-mail to support and enhance middle school curriculum and professional development (Fulton & Riel, 1999).

Team Teaching

In team-teaching arrangements, teachers share the responsibility for two or more classes, dividing the subject areas between them, with one preparing lessons in mathematics, science, and health, for instance, while the other plans instruction in reading and language arts. The division of responsibility may also be made in terms of the performance levels of the children, so one teacher may teach the lowest- and highest-ability reading groups and the middle math group, for example, while the other teaches the middle-ability reading groups and the lowest and highest mathematics group.

The practice of team teaching is often limited by student enrollments and budget constraints. As integrated curricula and the need for special knowledge and skills increase, however, the use of collegial support teams (CSTs) will become more common. A collegial support team (CST) provides teachers with a safe zone for professional growth; as one teacher commented:

> [The CST] allows me much discretion as to the areas I'd like to strengthen. Therefore, I am truly growing with no fear of being labeled or singled out as the "teacher who is having problems." I am aware of problem spheres and I work to correct these with the aid of my colleagues. (Johnson & Brown, 1998, p. 89)

The members of a team make wide-ranging decisions about the instruction of students assigned to the team, such as when to use large-group instruction or small-group instruction; how teaching tasks will be divided; and how time, materials, and other resources will be allocated.

Co-teaching

In co-teaching arrangements, two or more teachers, such as a classroom teacher and a special education teacher or other specialist, teach together in the same classroom. Co-teaching builds on the strengths of two teachers and provides increased learning opportunities for all students (Friend & Bursuck, 2002). Typically, co-teaching arrangements occur during a set period of time each day or on certain days of the week. Among the several possible co-teaching variations, Friend and Bursuck (2002) have identified the following:

- One teach, one support—one teacher leads the lesson; the other assists.
- Station teaching—the lesson is divided into two parts; one teacher teaches one part to half of the students while the other teaches the other part to the rest. The groups then switch and the teachers repeat their part of the lesson. If students can work independently, a third group may be formed, or a volunteer may teach at a third station.
- Parallel teaching—a class is divided in half, and each teacher instructs half the class individually.
- Alternative teaching—a class is divided into one large group and one small group. For example, one teacher may provide remediation or enrichment to the small group, while the other teacher instructs the large group.

SUMMARY

Who Are Today's Teachers?

- Teachers teach in schools with different grade configurations, they teach in different subject-matter and specialized areas, and they teach students with different types of learning needs.
- Today's teachers are better educated and more qualified than ever.
- In addition to teachers who work in pre-K, elementary, middle, and high school programs, some teachers teach in nontraditional school settings, such as private schools, charter schools, alternative schools, and magnet schools.
- Some teachers teach in specialized areas such as art, vocational education, music, or physical education. Special education teachers specialize in teaching students with disabilities and/or special needs. Many teachers, whether they have specialized training or not, teach students whose first language is not English (often called English language learners [ELLs]).

What Do Teachers Do in the Classroom?

- What teachers do goes beyond observable behaviors; the effective teacher understands that, simultaneously, he or she must be a role model for students, a spontaneous problem-solver, and a reflective thinker.

What Knowledge and Skills Do Today's Teachers Need?

- Teachers need four kinds of knowledge: knowledge of self and students, knowledge of subject, knowledge of educational theory and research, and knowledge of how to integrate technology into teaching.
- Self-knowledge influences your ability to understand your students; ongoing reflection and a problem-solving orientation continue to guide your instruction.
- Teachers must know their students' aptitudes, talents, learning styles, stages of development, and readiness to learn new material so they can modify instructional strategies based on students' needs.
- Knowledge of educational theory and research enables teachers to know why certain strategies work and offers general guidelines for practice.
- Teachers also use craft knowledge, what they know about teaching as a result of reflecting on their classroom experiences.

To What Extent Is Teaching a Full Profession?

- Of the following nine criteria for a profession, teaching meets some more fully than others: (1) institutional monopoly of services; (2) teacher autonomy; (3) years of education and training; (4) provision of essential service; (5) degree of self-governance; (6) professional associations; (7) professional knowledge and skills; (8) level of public trust; and (9) prestige, benefits, and pay.

To What Professional Organizations Do Teachers Belong?

- As the oldest and largest professional organization for educators, the National Education Association has played a key role in addressing issues of concern to the 78 percent of its members who are teachers.
- Affiliated with organized labor and open only to teachers and nonsupervisory personnel, the American Federation of Teachers has done much to secure greater financial rewards and improved working conditions for teachers.
- The NEA and AFT formed the NEAFT Partnership to work toward shared goals for improving the profession of teaching.
- Teachers are members of professional associations for specific subject areas and student populations.

How Do Teachers Help to Build Learning Communities?

- The learning community includes students, their families, colleagues, and members of the community.
- Training programs, hotlines, referral networks, and partnership programs are among the resources teachers can use to involve parents and members of the community.

How Do Teachers Participate in Teacher Collaboration?

- Teachers collaborate through participation in school governance, curriculum development, school–community partnerships, and educational reform.
- Four approaches to teacher collaboration are peer coaching, staff development, team teaching, and co-teaching.

PROFESSIONAL REFLECTIONS AND ACTIVITIES

Teacher's Journal

1. Recall a teacher who was a role model for you. Describe the influence he or she had on you. Did this teacher have an influence on your decision to become a teacher?
2. Regarding the grade level and subject area for which you are preparing to teach, what do you find most appealing, and why? What do you find least appealing, and why?

Teacher's Research

1. While on the Internet, use your favorite search engine to search for information by keywords or topics such as *teachers' working conditions*, *teacher accountability*, and *teacher professional development*. Report your findings to the rest of your class.
2. Review several recent issues of the NEA publication *NEA Today*, and the AFT publication *American Teacher*. Compare and contrast concerns or issues that each publication addresses. What overall differences do you find between the NEA and AFT publications?

Observations and Interviews

1. Interview a few teachers about their involvement in professional associations and, if applicable, a teachers' union. What benefits do teachers obtain from their professional involvement?
2. Interview a teacher about the knowledge and skills he or she thinks teachers must have. Which of the knowledge and skills discussed in this chapter does the teacher mention? Does he or she mention knowledge and skills not discussed in this chapter? If so, explain.

---

myeducationlab To complete additional observations and interviews, go to MyEducationLab at www.myeducationlab.com, select the Virtual Field Experience section, and click on this chapter's Observations and Interviews.

Professional Portfolio

Go to the Resources section of MyEducationLab to see a sampler of professional organizations for teachers. Begin to gather materials from teacher organizations that are relevant to the grade level and subject area for which you are preparing to teach.

---

myeducationlab Now go to MyEducationLab at www.myeducationlab.com to test your understanding of chapter content by completing this chapter's Study Plan.

Today's Schools

4

Today's Schools

I am a role model for students of color and low socioeconomic status. It is my goal that every one of my students leaves my classroom believing in themselves and their ability to reach college. I treat each student with respect, and I hope to teach them to respect each other and themselves in the same way.

Mark Hill, first-year high school math teacher
Quoted in *Teaching to Change the World*, 2007, p. 27

CLASSROOM CASE
The Realities of Teaching

THE CHALLENGE: Understanding how schools are influenced by their surrounding communities.

You are a teacher at a school located in a poor, high-crime section of a big city. Twenty years ago, the neighborhood around the school was made up of well-kept homes belonging to middle-income families. Today, the neighborhood reveals the scars of urban blight and decay. Most homes in the neighborhood are rundown. Yards overgrown with weeds; wrecked cars in driveways and on the streets; and graffiti on fences, buildings, and street signs reflect the decline that has overtaken the area.

The school, four-stories tall and built at the end of World War II, also shows signs of neglect. Graffiti artists have targeted the school's yellow brick walls. Numerous window panes at the street level are boarded over.

About one-fifth of the students who attend the school are from families where English is not the first language. More than 70 percent of the students are from families on public assistance. The school has a reputation throughout the city for below-average achievement, high absenteeism, and chronic misbehavior.

It is early in the school year, and you are standing at a media cart that holds a computer and projector, ready to begin a PowerPoint overview of a new unit of instruction. Your students, evenly divided between boys and girls, are seated in five parallel rows. Four guiding questions to help students organize the material you will present during the unit are projected on the screen behind you.

Students seated near the front of the room are ready to learn. They are either looking directly at you or writing down the four questions from the PowerPoint slide. Nine students at the back of the room, however, squirm restlessly in their seats. They are involved in various off-task behaviors. One girl matter-of-factly braids the hair of the girl sitting in front of her. A boy seated to the right of her yawns and then places his head on his desk. Two boys look out the window at four youth seated on the stoop of a rundown apartment building across the street. One girl leaves her desk without permission and saunters across the room to deliver a note to a friend.

At this moment, you realize that your students' behavior reflects the surrounding environment. You have two groups of students—those who want to learn and those who don't. You think to yourself, "What is the best way to respond to my students' lack of attention?"

FOCUS QUESTIONS

1. What is the role of schools in today's society?
2. How can schools be described?
3. What are schools like as social institutions?
4. What are the characteristics of successful schools?
5. What social problems affect schools and place students at risk?
6. How are schools addressing societal problems?
7. How can community-based partnerships help students learn?

Schools do not exist in a vacuum. As this chapter's classroom case illustrates, the surrounding community can have a significant influence on daily life within a school. In addition, schools must respond to the changing expectations of students, parents, teachers, communities, and the public at large. As the following section shows, today's schools have a complex, multifaceted role in today's society.

WHAT IS THE ROLE OF SCHOOLS IN TODAY'S SOCIETY?

Among the different perspectives on the role of schooling in U.S. society, the achievement of academic goals is the most universally agreed upon. Most people believe that the primary purpose of schools is to provide students with the academic knowledge and skills needed for schooling beyond high school or for the world of work. Philosophical, political, religious, and cultural beliefs and ideologies aside, people believe that schools should teach academic content. As you will learn, however, disagreement exists regarding the overall *purpose* for learning academic content.

Some people believe that the primary purpose of learning should be to promote the personal growth and development of students. Others, such as the governors and business leaders who attended the 2005 National Education Summit on High Schools in Washington, DC, believe that the primary purpose of schooling is to ensure the success of the United States in a global economy. As noted in a report released at the summit, "High school is now the front line in America's battle to remain competitive on the increasingly competitive international economic stage" (Achieve, Inc., 2005). One year later, in *Answering the Challenge of a Changing World: Strengthening Education for the 21st Century*, U.S. Secretary of Education Margaret Spellings confirmed this viewpoint by stating that "high school reform is not just an 'education issue.' It is also an economic issue, a civic issue, a social issue, and a national security issue" (U.S. Department of Education, 2006).

Schools and Prosocial Values

While debate continues about the primary purpose of schooling in the United States, the public does agree that schools should teach prosocial values such as honesty, patriotism, fairness, and civility. The well-being of any society requires support of such values; they enable people from diverse backgrounds to live together peacefully. For example, in the 670-page No Child Left Behind legislation, a section titled "Partnership in Character Education" calls for teaching the following values:

- Caring
- Civic virtue and citizenship
- Justice and fairness
- Respect

TECHNOLOGY in *ACTION*

Video Editing in Sixth Grade

A unit on study skills has been a mainstay of Rachael Yelmin's sixth-grade language arts class for years. Her students had just entered middle school from elementary school and they seem to struggle to keep up with the pace of middle school. Two years ago, she experimented with a new way to teach language arts. Instead of telling her students about the things they needed to do to be successful in middle school—like time management, social responsibility, reading for comprehension, and so on—she decided to let them tell her.

Ms. Yelmin divided her students into groups of four and asked each group to create a video for fifth-grade students highlighting the skills necessary to survive middle school. Each group was able to check out a video camera, access free video-editing software, access enough hard drive space to store the raw video clips, and save the edited video. They were also given a CD on which to burn their video.

The project began with the student groups writing a storyboard for their video. Here, the students researched, selected topics, and decided their video sequence. This stage allowed students to make important development decisions (with Ms. Yelmin's help) without expending costly development time. After the storyboard was written, students performed in front of the camera, visited important locations, interviewed students and staff, developed graphics, selected music, and wrote text. Then they loaded their raw footage and edited the raw material into a finished video using Windows Movie Maker. When the project was complete, Ms. Yelmin sent the completed videos to fifth-grade classrooms around the community. Ms. Yelmin found that her students who created the study skills video retained the study skills information much better than her students who were merely lectured to. She also found that her incoming students (the fifth-graders who had watched the videos created by "upperclassmen") had a good foundation from which to begin.

VIDEO EDITING: Several technical tools are available when you need to edit video. You need a computer, a video source (such as a camera or already captured video), enough hard drive space to store the raw video, video-editing software such as Windows Movie Maker, and creativity.

VISIT: http://video-editing-software-review.toptenreviews.com/. As mentioned above, a number of video-editing options are available to you. Some are free; others are expensive. The site listed here is a great resource to help you explore video-editing options and features.

POSSIBLE USES: Teachers have used their edited video in many diverse ways. They have used video to present information to students, create virtual field trips to historical sites, create compilations of student work, and allow students to submit research reports in video format—to name a few.

TRY IT OUT: Ms. Yelmin used Windows Movie Maker for her study skills lesson. This tool is usually bundled with current Windows installations. To test-drive this tool in a Windows environment, go to the Start menu, then select "all programs" and locate Windows Movie Maker and select. First, load your video clip(s). You can attach your video camera or you can import an already captured video clip. Once you have your clip(s) in your workspace, drag a clip to the timeline. All of your editing work takes place on the timeline. Here, you can add music, background textures, transition affects, titles, and so on. The rendering process can be lengthy. For a detailed account of all timeline options, click on the Help menu. When you have finished your work on the timeline, save your video. You can now showcase your masterpiece in your classroom, on the Web, or through e-mail.

- Responsibility
- Trustworthiness
- Giving

Support for prosocial values reflects the public's belief that schools should play a key role in promoting the democratic ideal of equality for all. As President George W. Bush stated when he signed the No Child Left Behind Act into law, "[I have a] deep belief in our public schools and their mission to build the mind and character of every child, from every background, in every part of America." The Technology in Action feature for this chapter explains how teachers can use video editing to teach students the importance of study skills and social responsibility.

Schools and Socialization of the Young

Through their experiences in schools, children and youth become socialized—they learn to participate responsibly in our nation's society. The goal of socializing students is evident in countless local schools whose mission statements focus on preparing students for responsible citizenship, further learning, and productive employment in our nation's economy. In effect, schools reflect or mirror society; they reproduce the knowledge, skills, values, and attitudes that society has identified as essential.

Education is the primary means of producing enlightened citizens. Without such a citizenry to hold it together, a society, especially a democratic society, is at risk. The need for each nation to socialize its children and youth was recognized by Emile Durkheim (1858–1917), the great French sociologist and philosopher, when he stated in *Education and Sociology* that "society can survive only if there exists among its members a significant degree of homogeneity; education perpetuates and reinforces this homogeneity by fixing in the child, from the beginning, the essential similarities collective life demands" (Durkheim, 1956, p. 70).

More than any other institution in our society, schools also assimilate persons from different ethnic, racial, religious, linguistic, and cultural backgrounds and pass on the values and customs of the majority. For example, one in every five students today speaks a language other than English at home, and nearly one-third of these students (31 percent) have difficulty speaking English (Oakes & Lipton, 2007). Through the schools, children and youth from such diverse backgrounds learn English and learn about the importance of U.S. holidays such as the Fourth of July and Memorial Day; the contributions of Thomas Jefferson, Abraham Lincoln, and Dr. Martin Luther King Jr.; and the importance of citizenship in a democracy.

Schools and Social Change

Schools also provide students with the knowledge and skills to improve society and to adapt to rapid social change. Thus, "education and social change [are] inextricably tied to one another" (Rury, 2002, p. ix). Not everyone agrees, however, that schools *should* attempt to improve society—as one observer of education in the United States noted: "The school continues to be used in efforts to solve social, political, and economic problems. It is easier for politicians to blame schools for social and economic problems than to try to directly correct these problems. . . . 'Reform the individual rather than society' is the message of those who trust the school to end crime, poverty, broken families, drug and alcohol abuse, and myriad other social problems" (Spring, 2008, p. 32).

Less controversial have been service-learning activities that prepare students to serve others through volunteerism and to participate actively in the political life of the nation. During the late 1990s, some high schools began to require that every student complete a service requirement to help students understand that they are members of a larger community to which they are accountable. The Chicago public schools, the third largest school system in the United States, currently requires that "students must complete a minimum of 40 hours of service between 9th and 12th grade in order to graduate" (Chicago Public Schools, April 30, 2008). Other schools began to introduce service-learning activities into their curricula. Service learning provides students with opportunities to deliver service to their communities while engaging in reflection and study on the meaning of those experiences. Service learning brings young people into contact with the elderly, the sick, the poor, and the homeless, and it acquaints them with neighborhood and governmental issues.

Schools and Equal Educational Opportunity

Ample evidence exists that certain groups in U.S. society are denied equality of opportunity economically, socially, and educationally. For example, if we look at the percentage of children 3 to 4 years old who participate in early childhood programs such as

Head Start, nursery school, and prekindergarten—experiences that help children from less advantaged backgrounds start elementary school on an equal footing with other children—we find that children from lower-income families are less likely to have such opportunities (National Center for Education Statistics, 2008). In addition, there is a positive relationship between parents' educational attainment and their children's enrollment in early childhood programs; also, Latino children are less likely to be enrolled than white or African American children (National Center for Education Statistics, 2008).

The United States has always derived strength from the diversity of its people, and all students should receive a quality education so that they may make their unique contributions to society. To reach this goal, extensive programs at the federal, state, and local levels have been developed to provide equity for all in the United States—regardless of race, ethnicity, language, gender, or religion. For example, the first section of the No Child Left Behind Act, titled "Improving the Academic Achievement of the Disadvantaged," states:

> [A]ll children [should] have a fair, equal, and significant opportunity to obtain a high-quality education and reach, at a minimum, proficiency on challenging State academic achievement standards and state academic assessments. This purpose can be accomplished by . . . meeting the educational needs of low-achieving children in our Nation's highest-poverty schools, limited English proficient children, migratory children, children with disabilities, Indian children, neglected or delinquent children, and young children in need of reading assistance, . . . closing the achievement gap between high- and low-performing children, especially the achievement gaps between minority and nonminority students, and between disadvantaged children and their more advantaged peers.

The goal of providing equal educational opportunity for all has long distinguished education in the United States from that found in most other countries. Since the 1850s, schools in the United States have been particularly concerned with providing children from diverse backgrounds with the education they need to succeed in our society. As James Banks (2008, p. 4) suggests, "Education within a pluralistic society should affirm and help students understand their home and community cultures. [To] create and maintain a civic community that works for the common good, education in a democratic society should help students acquire the knowledge, attitudes, and skills needed to participate in civic action to make society more equitable and just."

HOW CAN SCHOOLS BE DESCRIBED?

Given the wide variation in schools and their cultures, many models have been proposed for describing the distinguishing characteristics of schools. Schools can be categorized according to the focus of their curricula; for example, high schools may be college prep, vocational, or general. Another way to view schools is according to their organizational structure, for example, alternative schools, charter schools, or magnet schools. Other models, such as those addressed in the following section, view schools metaphorically; that is, what is a school like?

Metaphors for Schools

Some schools have been compared to factories; students enter the school as raw material, move through the curriculum in a systematic way, and exit the school as finished products. Terrence Deal and Kent Peterson (1999, p. 21) have suggested that exemplary schools "become like tribes or clans, with deep ties among people and with values and traditions that give meaning to everyday life." Others have suggested that schools are like banks, gardens, prisons, mental hospitals, homes, churches, families, and teams.

In the school-as-family metaphor, for example, the effective school is a caring community of adults who attend to the academic, emotional, and social needs of the children and youth entrusted to their care. One teacher who helped his high school develop a family atmosphere is Matthew Amato Flanders, a first-year history teacher and head coach of the school's water polo team. As Flanders and his assistant coaches explained, "[We] provided a place that students could be comfortable as well as mentally and physically challenged. We connected them to the campus, to the school community . . . however, our involvement did not stop in the pool. We dealt with the issues of alcoholism, drug abuse, pregnancy, sexually transmitted disease, child abuse, and jail time that our student athletes faced" (Oakes & Lipton, 2007, p. 358).

Schools and Social Class

In spite of a general consensus that schools should promote social change and equal opportunity, some individuals believe that schools "reproduce" the existing society by presenting different curricula and educational experiences to students from different socioeconomic classes. Students at a school in an affluent suburb, for example, may study chemistry in a well-equipped lab and take a field trip to a high-tech industry to see the latest application of chemical research, while students at a school in an impoverished inner-city neighborhood learn chemistry from out-of-date texts, have no lab in which to conduct experiments, and take no field trips because the school district has no funds.

In effect, schools preserve the stratification within society and maintain the differences between the haves and the have-nots. As Joel Spring (2008, p. 75) explains: "[T]he economic level of the family determines educational attainment. Children from low-income families do not attain so high a level of education as children from rich families. From this standpoint the school reinforces social stratification and contributes to intergenerational immobility." Moreover, rich families can afford to live in affluent school districts or send their children to private schools. This, in turn, increases the chances that their children will attend the "best" colleges and universities and ultimately maintain or increase the family's social class status.

In addition, children from lower-income families tend to develop "restricted" language patterns with their use of English, while children from more affluent backgrounds tend to develop more "elaborated" language patterns (Bernstein, 1996; Heath, 1983). In many cases, children from lower-income families encounter a mismatch between the language patterns used in the home and those they are expected to use in school. This mismatch can be "a serious stumbling block for working class and non-white pupils" (MacLeod, 1995, p. 18).

To understand the different types of knowledge students bring with them into the classroom and how this knowledge can conflict with the norms and values of schools and teachers, watch four videos available at MyEducationLab. See if you can identify how different cultural behaviors of students are not accepted. In one video, a multicultural expert explains the need for teachers to bridge the gap between the school and the community.

Four Types of Schools

A useful way to talk about the relationship between schooling and social class in the United States is suggested by the four categories of schools that Jean Anyon (1996) described in her study of several elementary schools in urban and suburban New Jersey. Anyon maintains that schools "reproduce" the existing society by presenting different curricula and educational experiences to students from different socioeconomic classes. As a result of their experiences at school, students are prepared for particular roles in the dominant society.

The first kind of school she calls the *working-class school*. In this school, the primary emphasis is on having students follow directions as they work at rote, mechanical activities such as completing mimeographed worksheets. Students are given little opportunity to exercise their initiative or to make choices. Teachers may make negative, disparaging comments about students' abilities and, through subtle and not-so-

PEARSON
myeducationlab

Go to MyEducationLab, select Chapter 3 and then Activities and Applications to watch the video Incorporating the Home Experiences of Culturally Diverse Students into the Classroom, Parts 1–4.

subtle means, convey low expectations to students. Additionally, teachers at working-class schools may spend much of their time focusing on classroom management, dealing with absenteeism, and keeping extensive records.

The *middle-class school* is the second type identified by Anyon. Here, teachers emphasize to students the importance of getting right answers, usually in the form of words, sentences, numbers, or facts and dates. Students have slightly more opportunity to make decisions, but not much. Most lessons are textbook-based. Anyon points out that "while the teachers spend a lot of time explaining and expanding on what the textbooks say, there is little attempt to analyze how or why things happen. . . . On the occasions when creativity or self-expression is requested, it is peripheral to the main activity or it is 'enrichment' or 'for fun' " (Anyon, 1996, p. 191).

Unlike the previous two types of schools, the *affluent professional school* gives students the opportunity to express their individuality and to make a variety of choices. Fewer rules govern the behavior of students in affluent professional schools, and teacher and students are likely to negotiate about the work the students will do.

Anyon provides the following definition of the fourth type of school she identified, the *executive elite school:*

> In the executive elite school, work is developing one's analytical intellectual powers. Children are continually asked to reason through a problem, to produce intellectual products that are both logically sound and of top academic quality. (Anyon, 1996, p. 196)

In the affluent professional and executive elite schools, teacher-student relationships are more positive than those in the working-class and middle-class schools. Teachers are polite to their students, seldom give direct orders, and almost never make sarcastic or nasty remarks.

In applying Anyon's categories to schools in the United States, keep in mind that few schools are one type exclusively and that few schools actually fit the categories in all ways. Instead, most schools probably contain individual classrooms that represent all four types. Also, it is possible for one type of school to exist within a school of another type—for example, an advanced placement program (essentially an affluent professional or executive elite school) within an urban working-class school.

Also keep in mind that Anyon studied a small group of schools in one metropolitan area, and her criteria are linked almost exclusively to socioeconomic status. There are many schools in poor urban areas, for example, whose culture is more like the affluent professional school Anyon describes than the working-class school, and vice versa. Nevertheless, regardless of how schools in the United States are categorized, it seems they do reflect the socioeconomic status of the communities they serve.

WHAT ARE SCHOOLS LIKE AS SOCIAL INSTITUTIONS?

Schools are social institutions. An institution is an organization established by society to maintain and improve its way of life. Schools are the institutions our society has established for the purpose of educating the young. For the last 200 years, schools in the United States have developed complex structures, policies, and curricula to accomplish this mission.

The School as a Reflection of Society

As the first part of this chapter has pointed out, schools mirror the national culture and the surrounding local culture and other special interests. Private, parochial, and religious schools, for example, are often maintained by groups that see the school as a means of perpetuating their preferred way of life. Schools also reflect their location. As Durkheim (1956, p. 68) observed: "do we not see education vary with . . . locality? That of the city is not that of the country." As the following sections illustrate, schools in rural, urban, and suburban settings often have significantly different cultures.

Rural School Settings

Rural schools are often the focal point for community life and reflect values and beliefs that tend to be more conservative than those associated with urban and suburban schools. While the small size of a rural school may contribute to the development of a family-like culture, its small size may also make it difficult to provide students with an array of curricular experiences equal to that found at larger schools in more populated areas. In contrast, large suburban or urban schools may provide students with more varied learning experiences, but these schools may lack the cohesiveness and community focus of rural schools.

Urban and Suburban School Environments

The differences among the environments that surround schools can be enormous. Urban schools found in or near decaying centers of large cities often reflect the social problems of the surrounding area, such as drug abuse, crime, and poverty. One of the most serious problems confronting education in the United States is the quality of such schools. Across the country—in Chicago, New York, Los Angeles, St. Louis, Detroit, and Cleveland—middle-class families who can afford to do so move away from urban centers or place their children in private schools. As a result, students in urban school districts are increasingly from low-income backgrounds.

In *Shame of the Nation*, Jonathon Kozol (2005) documents the startling contrast between the neighborhoods that surround impoverished inner-city schools and those that surround affluent suburban schools. He also examines the significant discrepancy between per-pupil spending for students at the two types of schools. For example, during 2002–03, per-pupil funding for the Highland Park/Deerfield, Illinois, School District, an affluent suburb north of Chicago, was $17,291. Ninety percent of students in the district were white or "other," while 10 percent were black and Hispanic. On the other hand, per-pupil funding for Chicago Public Schools was $8,482. In Chicago, 87 percent of students were black and Hispanic, and 18 percent were white or "other" (Kozol, 2005, p. 321).

In what ways do schools reflect their communities and the wider U.S. society? How might the surrounding neighborhood influence this school? The students who attend it? The teachers who work there?

In Kozol's earlier book, *Savage Inequalities*, he compares New Trier High School in affluent Winnetka, Illinois, and Chicago's DuSable High School, an inner-city school at which the author of this textbook taught for eight years. Kozol points out that New Trier is in a neighborhood of "circular driveways, chirping birds and white-columned homes" (1991, p. 62). In contrast, DuSable's surroundings are "almost indescribably despairing"; across the street from the school is "a line of uniform and ugly 16-story buildings, the Robert Taylor Homes, which constitute . . . the city's second-poorest neighborhood" (1991, pp. 68, 71).

Although the extreme poverty found in some communities may affect their schools in undesirable ways, effective teachers at such schools communicate to students that they are "rich" in ways that go beyond material wealth. Rachel Armour (2006), a former DuSable High School student and resident of the Robert Taylor Homes, describes the grim conditions in her community and the positive impact of some of her caring teachers:

> "Bang! Bang! Bang!" Gunshots rang deep into my eardrums as Mickey Cobras and Gangster Disciples waged deadly war right outside of my rundown building. My brother joined the infamous Gangster Disciples street gang—shootings at DuSable High School, where he attended, became frequent. The war between GDs and MCs was bloodier than ever. My mother couldn't bear the thought of seeing my brother's obituary posted near the graffiti-plastered elevator doors like some of our neighbors.
>
> I remember the good teachers who encouraged me and told me "Black is beautiful," and to "be yourself." On the other hand, I remember the teacher who called nearly every child in class, "dumb and stupid." Educators should make connections with kids [and] take every opportunity to boost every child's self-esteem in the classroom. A simple "you are so smart" or "you have a brilliant mind" goes a long way for a child who may hear "dumb or stupid" in their environments. We need to respect our children in a deeper way by understanding who they are inside, and how they may feel about their situations.

Rachel was fortunate that some of her teachers saw her not merely as a child living in an impoverished neighborhood, but as a child needing validation and support to realize her full potential. Rachel Armour went on to become the founder of Armour Achievement, an integrated marketing communications firm that works with educators and businesses to provide a better education for K–12 students, and she is the winner of numerous awards at the local, regional, and national levels in the areas of public speaking, forensics and debate, community service, public relations, advertising, leadership, academic excellence, and education. Another teacher similar to those who had a positive impact on Rachel is Romaine Washington, who is profiled in the Teachers' Voices: Walk in My Shoes feature for this chapter.

The Culture of the School

Although schools are very much alike, each school is unique. Each has a culture of its own—a network of beliefs, values and traditions, and ways of thinking and behaving that distinguishes it from other schools.

Much like a community, a school has a distinctive culture—a collective way of life. Terms that have been used to describe school culture include *climate, ethos, atmosphere,* and *character.* Some schools may be characterized as community-like places where there is a shared sense of purpose and commitment to providing the best education possible for all students. Other schools lack a unified sense of purpose or direction and drift, rudderless, from year to year. Still others are characterized by internal conflict and divisiveness and may even reflect what Deal and Peterson (1999) term a "toxic" school culture; students, teachers, administrators, and parents may feel that the school is not sufficiently meeting their needs. The following comments by a high school teacher who worked at two different schools during his first year describe the culture at the two types of schools:

> Lincoln High had many well-trained teachers and administrators. Teachers formed small communities among themselves, and one hosted a monthly inquiry meeting. Teachers felt free to speak out at the large monthly staff meetings. We could also give anonymous feedback and ask questions of the principal, and we were given typed-up answers.
>
> Jefferson, in contrast, has had six principals in the last eight years. There is high teacher turnover, and the administration has had a very difficult time finding substitute teachers. Many students sit in the cafeteria waiting for a solution. (Oakes & Lipton, 2007, p. 339)

 TEACHERS' VOICES *Walk in My Shoes*

GIFTED TEACHER IN DIVERSE SETTINGS

Romaine Washington, high school English and French teacher and poet, has taught students in a dramatic contrast of schools and educational settings over her 14 years of teaching. She knows what it is like to teach well-traveled students of privilege, whose goals are to win academic decathlons and attend Stanford, Duke, or universities in the California system and Ivy League and to pursue professional careers. And she knows what it is like to work with students low on hope and trust, from foster homes and broken families, whose parents might be incarcerated or struggling to survive in environments devoid of economic opportunities.

The schools she has taught in range from being designated by the state as an "underperforming school," determined by students' low scores on the SAT-9 (Stanford Achievement Test, Ninth Edition), to being recognized by *U.S. News and World Report* as being among "America's Best High Schools." The latter, Los Osos High School, was named a Silver Medal High School in 2008 because it ranked among the top 2 percent in the country based on "a combination of promise and challenge, overall academic quality, and college readiness."

Washington has taught in unique education programs as well. Through the College Bound Program on the Claremont University campus, she helped prepare eager but unready students to be the first in their families to attend college. In this multidistrict enrichment program, she met weekends with students to teach them junior and senior English and study skills and strategies.

In addition, she taught in the University of California—Riverside Inland Area Writing Project (IAWP), part of a state and national network of professional development projects for educators seeking to improve their teaching of writing across the curriculum by strengthening their own writing skills. The voluntary program was a natural for Washington, a poet since her youth, with an impressive résumé of poetry readings and publications in what she regarded as a parallel second career. Dr. Catherine Humphrey, a leader in the IAWP, recognized her writing gifts, invited her to be an instructor in the program, and became her mentor. Humphrey encouraged Washington to integrate her poetry life and her teaching life, and the results of that have been rich. She became the Poet in Residence at a teacher writing retreat at the famous Mission Inn in Riverside and a facilitator in a six-week summer program, Teachers Teaching Teachers, that assisted teachers with writing and presentation skills.

Washington extended her teaching of adults at a local university. As an adjunct there, she teaches a course entitled "Teaching and Cultural Diversity" in the Teacher Education Program.

In all her teaching experiences, Washington shares with students the same messages she expresses in her poetry—the importance of "seeing the world through a different viewpoint," "having empathy and respect for others," and (drawing on her mentor's example) "believing that there is nothing too difficult to achieve."

Romaine Washington

The following sections discuss three dimensions of schools that have a significant influence on a school's culture: the physical environment, formal practices, and traditions.

The Physical Environment

The physical environment of the school both reflects and helps to create the school's overall culture. "Whether school buildings are squeezed between other buildings or located on sprawling campuses, their fenced-in area or other physical separation distinguishes them from the community-at-large" (Ballantine, 1997, p. 210). Some schools are dreary places or, at best, aesthetically bland. The tile floors; concrete block walls; long, straight corridors; and rows of fluorescent lights often found in these schools contribute little to their inhabitants' sense of beauty, concern for others, or personal comfort.

Other schools are much more attractive. They are clean, pleasant, and inviting, and teachers and students take pride in their building. Overall, the physical environment has a positive impact on those who spend time in the school; it encourages learning and a spirit of cohesiveness.

Formal Practices of Schools

The formal practices of schools are well known to anyone who has been educated in U.S. schools. With few exceptions, students attend school from 5 or 6 years of age through 16 at least, and usually to 18, Monday through Friday, September through May, for 12 years. For the most part, students are assigned to a grade level on the basis of age rather than ability or interest. Assignment to individual classes or teachers at a given grade level, however, may be made on the basis of ability or interest.

These students are participating in the culture of their school. What other behaviors, formal pratices, and school traditions are probably part of their school culture?

The **self-contained classroom** is the most traditional and prevalent arrangement in elementary through secondary schools. In open-space schools, however, students are free to move among various activities and learning centers. Instead of self-contained classrooms, **open-space schools** have large instructional areas with movable walls and furniture that can be rearranged easily. Grouping for instruction is much more fluid and varied. Students do much of their work independently, with a number of teachers providing individual guidance as needed.

In middle schools and junior and senior high schools, students typically study four or five academic subjects taught by teachers who specialize in them. In this organizational arrangement, called **departmentalization,** students move from classroom to classroom for their lessons. High school teachers often share their classrooms with other teachers and use their rooms only during scheduled class periods.

School Traditions

School traditions are those elements of a school's culture that are handed down from year to year. The traditions of a school reflect what students, teachers, administrators, parents, and the surrounding community believe is important and valuable about the school. One school, for example, may have developed a tradition of excellence in academic programs; another school's traditions may emphasize the performing arts; and yet another may focus on athletic programs. Whatever a school's traditions, they are usually a source of pride for members of the school community.

Ideally, traditions are the glue that holds together the diverse elements of a school's culture. They combine to create a sense of community, identity, and trust among people affiliated with a school. Traditions are maintained through stories that are handed down, rituals and ceremonial activities, student productions, and trophies and artifacts that have been collected over the years. For example, Joan Vydra, now principal of Briar Glen Elementary School in Wheaton, Illinois, initiated Care Week as part of the fall tradition at her former school, Hawthorne Elementary. Vydra believed that a tradition of care would nurture student success. On the first day of Care Week, students learned the importance of caring for themselves; on Tuesdays, caring for their families; on Wednesdays, caring for each other; on Thursdays, caring for the school; and on Fridays, caring for those served by local charities (Deal & Peterson, 1999).

The Culture of the Classroom

Just as schools develop their unique cultures, each classroom develops its own culture or way of life. The culture of a classroom is determined in large measure by the manner in which teacher and students participate in common activities. In addition, "the environment of the classroom and the inhabitants of that environment—students and teachers—are constantly interacting. Each aspect of the system affects all others" (Woolfolk, 2007).

The quality of teacher-student interactions is influenced by the physical characteristics of the setting (classroom, use of space, materials, resources, etc.) and the social dimensions of the group (norms, rules, expectations, cohesiveness, distribution of power and influence). These elements interact to shape classroom culture. Teachers who appreciate the importance of these salient elements of classroom culture are more likely to create environments that they and their students find satisfying and growth-promoting. For example, during the second month of student teaching in the second grade, "Miss Martin" reflects on her efforts to create a classroom culture characterized by positive teacher-student interactions:

> I started off with a big mistake. I tried to be their friend. I tried joining with them in all the jokes and laughter that cut into instruction time. When this didn't work, I overcompensated by yelling at them when I needed them to quiet down and get to work. I wasn't comfortable with this situation. I did not think it was like me to raise my voice at a child. I knew I needed to consider how they felt. I realized that if I were them, I'd hate me, I really would. In desperation, I turned to my education textbooks for advice.
>
> This was a huge help to me, but a book can only guide you. It can't establish a personality for you or even manage your classroom for you. You have to do that yourself and as lovingly and effectively as possible. But I had so much trouble finding a middle ground: love them, guide them, talk to them, manage them, but don't control them. (Rand & Shelton-Colangelo, 1999, pp. 8–9)

Similarly, students believe that effective teachers develop positive, task-oriented classroom cultures, while ineffective teachers develop negative cultures. One inner-city school, for example, provides an illustration of these two very different classroom cultures:

> [Sixth-grade] students saw their social studies/language arts teacher as someone they could learn from and relate to well, while they seemed to constantly do battle with their math and science teacher. Students portrayed [the math and science teacher] as overdemanding, impatient, and insensitive; [the social studies/language arts teacher] seemed to be just the opposite. [The math and science teacher], according to one student, "has an attitude problem. She wants us to be so good the first time. She wants us to always be perfect. She has us walk in a line in the hallway. We are the only class in the school to do that. . . . She is the only [teacher] who won't go over things. She never comes in with a smile; she is always evil. By not going over it, we got a bad attitude. I haven't learned nothing in her class." (Wilson & Corbett, 2001, pp. 54–55)

Clearly, the math and science teacher has developed an adversarial, counterproductive relationship with students. The social studies/language arts teacher, on the other hand, recognizes the importance of developing positive relationships with students and understands how such relationships pave the way for student learning.

WHAT ARE THE CHARACTERISTICS OF SUCCESSFUL SCHOOLS?

Like Miss Martin above, you may be uncertain at this point in your professional education of your ability to develop a positive classroom climate at a school. However, a great many schools in all settings and with all kinds of students are highly successful, including inner-city and isolated rural schools and schools that serve pupils of all socioeconomic, racial, and ethnic backgrounds. What are the characteristics of these schools? Do they have commonalities that account for their success?

Measures of Success

First, we must define what we mean by a *successful school*. One measure of success, naturally, is that students at these schools achieve at a high level and complete requirements for graduation. Whether reflected in scores on standardized tests or other documentation of academic learning gains, students at these schools are learning. They are achieving literacy in reading, writing, computation, and computer skills. They are learning to solve problems, think creatively and analytically, and, most important, they are learning to learn.

Another valid measure of success for a school is that it achieves results that surpass those expected from comparable schools in comparable settings. The achievement of students goes beyond what one would expect. In spite of surrounding social, economic, and political forces that impede the educative process at other schools, these schools are achieving results.

Finally, successful schools are those that are improving, rather than getting worse. School improvement is a slow process, and schools that are improving—moving in the right direction rather than declining—are also successful.

Research on School Effectiveness

During the 1980s and early 1990s, much research was conducted to identify the characteristics of successful (or effective) schools. The characteristics of successful schools were described in different ways in several research projects. The following is a synthesis of those findings.

- **Strong leadership:** Successful schools have strong leaders—individuals who value education and see themselves as educational leaders, not just as managers or bureaucrats. They monitor the performance of everyone at the school—teachers, staff, students, and themselves. These leaders have a vision of the school as a more effective learning environment, and they take decisive steps to bring that about.
- **High expectations:** Teachers at successful schools have high expectations of students. These teachers believe that all students, rich or poor, can learn, and they communicate this to students through realistic yet high expectations.
- **Emphasis on basic skills:** Teachers at successful schools emphasize student achievement in the basic skills of reading, writing, and mathematical computation.
- **Orderly school environment:** The environments of successful schools are orderly, safe, and conducive to learning. Discipline problems are at a minimum, and teachers can devote greater amounts of time to teaching.
- **Frequent, systematic evaluation of student learning:** The learning of students in successful schools is monitored closely. When difficulties crop up, appropriate remediation is provided quickly.
- **Sense of purpose:** Those who teach and those who learn at successful schools have a strong sense of purpose. From the principal to the students, everyone at the school is guided by a vision of excellence.
- **Collegiality and a sense of community:** Teachers, administrators, and staff at successful schools work well together. They are dedicated to creating an environment that promotes not only student learning but also their own professional growth and development.

In short, the culture of an effective school encourages teachers to grow and to develop in the practice of their profession. It encourages them to develop knowledge and skills to respond to social problems such as those described in the following sections.

WHAT SOCIAL PROBLEMS AFFECT SCHOOLS AND PLACE STUDENTS AT RISK?

A complex and varied array of social issues affects schools. These problems often detract from the ability of schools to educate students. Furthermore, schools are often charged with the difficult (if not impossible) task of providing a front-line defense against such problems. Nevertheless, effective teachers understand how social issues influence student learning, and they are able to reduce the negative impact of those issues.

One of the most vocal advocates of the role of schools in solving social problems was George S. Counts, who said in his 1932 book *Dare the School Build a New Social Order?* that "if schools are to be really effective, they must become centers for the building, and not merely the contemplation, of our civilization" (p. 12). Many people, however, believe that schools should not try to build a new social order. They should be concerned only with the academic and social development of students—not with solving society's problems. Nevertheless, the debate over the role of schools with regard to social problems will continue to be vigorous. The following sections examine several societal problems that directly influence schools, teachers, and students.

Identifying Students at Risk

An increasing number of young people live under conditions characterized by extreme stress, chronic poverty, crime, and lack of adult guidance. As James Garbarino (1999, p. 19) points out in *Lost Boys: Why Our Sons Turn Violent and How We Can Save Them*: "In almost every community in America, growing numbers of kids live in a socially toxic environment."

Frustrated, lonely, and feeling powerless, many youth escape into music with violence-oriented and/or obscene lyrics, violent video games, cults, movies and television programs that celebrate gratuitous violence and sex, and cruising shopping malls or hanging out on the street. Others turn also to crime, gang violence, promiscuous sex, or substance abuse. Not surprisingly, these activities place many young people at risk of academic failure and eventually dropping out of school. The National Center for Education Statistics (July 2, 2002) has identified the following at-risk factors for today's children and youth:

- Being in the lowest socioeconomic status
- Changing schools two or more times from grades 1 to 8 (except for transitions to middle school or junior high school)
- Having average grades of C or lower from grades 6 to 8
- Living in a single-parent household during grade 8
- Having one or more older siblings who left high school before completion
- Being held back one or more times from grades 1 to 8

Grouped by gender, race, ethnicity, family income, age, and region, students drop out of school at varying rates. Table 3.1, for example, shows that the dropout rate for Hispanic students in 2005 was higher than the rates for other groups. Also, African American students dropped out of school more frequently than their white peers. The data also reveal that students from low-income families are more likely to drop out than their counterparts from middle- and high-income families. Students at risk of dropping out tend to get low grades, perform below grade level academically, are older than the average student at their grade level because of previous retention, and have behavior problems in school. Students at risk need teachers who can recognize opportunities in the classroom to build up their confidence as learners, as Jennifer Michele Diaz illustrates in the Teaching on Your Feet feature for this chapter.

Many youth take more than the typical four years to complete high school, or they eventually earn a high school graduate equivalency diploma (GED). If these alternative

TABLE 3.1 Event dropout rates and number and distribution of 15- through 24-year-olds who dropped out of grades 10–12, by selected background characteristics: October 2005

Characteristic	Event Dropout Rate (Percent)	Number of Event Dropouts (Thousands)	Population Enrolled[1] (Thousands)	Percentage of All Dropouts	Percentage of Population Enrolled
Total	3.8	414	10,870	100.0	100.0
Sex					
Male	4.2	233	5.515	56.3	50.7
Female	3.4	181	5,355	43.7	49.3
Race/ethnicity[2]					
White, non-Hispanic	2.8	196	6,897	47.3	63.5
Black, non-Hispanic	7.3	112	1,538	27.2	14.1
Hispanic	5.0	86	1,717	20.8	15.8
Asian/Pacific Islander, non-Hispanic	1.6!	6!	411	1.5!	3.8
More than one race	4.9!	12!	241	2.9!	2.2
Family income[3]					
Low income	8.9	137	1,544	33.1	14.2
Middle income	3.8	228	5,990	55.2	55.1
High income	1.5	49	3,326	11.7	30.6
Age[4]					
15–16	2.1	72	3,347	17.4	30.8
17	2.4	93	3,797	22.5	34.9
18	3.9	105	2,693	25.3	24.8
19	9.1	64	702	15.4	6.5
20–24	24.4	81	331	19.5	3.0
Recency of immigration					
Born outside the 50 states and District of Columbia					
Hispanic	5.9	25	418	6.0	3.8
Non-Hispanic	5.0	22	440	5.3	4.0
First generation[5]					
Hispanic	5.5	40	738	9.8	6.8
Non-Hispanic	1.2!	9!	759	2.2!	7.0
Second generation or higher[5]					
Hispanic	3.7!	21!	562	5.0	5.2
Non-Hispanic	3.7	297	7,954	71.8	73.2

Source: U.S. Department of Commerce, Census Bureau, Current Population Survey (CPS), October 2005.

!Interpret data with caution. Because of relatively large standard errors, estimates are unstable.

[1]This is an estimate of the population of 15- through 24-year-olds enrolled during the previous year in high school based on the number of students still enrolled in the current year and the number of students who either graduated or dropped out the previous year.

[2]Respondents were able to identify themselves as being "more than one race." The White, non-Hispanic; Black, non-Hispanic; and Asian/Pacific Islander, non-Hispanic categories consist of individuals who considered themselves to be one race and who did not identify as Hispanic. Non-Hispanics who identified as multiracial are included in the "more than one race" category. The Hispanic category consists of Hispanics of all races and racial combinations. Because of small sample size, American Indians/Alaska Natives are included in the total but are not shown separately.

[3]"Low income" is defined as the bottom 20 percent of all family incomes for 2005, middle income is between 20 and 80 percent of all family incomes, and high income is the top 20 percent of all family incomes.

[4]Age when a person dropped out may be 1 year younger because the dropout event could occur at any time over a 12-month period.

Note: The event dropout rate indicates percentage of youth ages 15 through 24 who dropped out of grades 10–12 between one October and the next (e.g., October 2004 to October 2005). Dropping out is defined as leaving school without a high school diploma or equivalent credential such as a General Education Development (GED) certificate. Detail may not add to totals because of rounding.

TEACHING ON YOUR FEET

"THE ABOLISHMENT OF 'I CAN'T'"

Thirty-two little hands burst into the air as I reached into our classroom jar of student numbers to randomly select a student to read aloud. It was the second week of the school year for my fourth-graders, and the second week of my first year teaching. The students were excited and enthusiastic about the possibility of being selected to read aloud from the new brightly colored social studies textbook.

"Congratulations, student number three! Let's follow along as we listen to Anthony read aloud," I directed, when I pulled Anthony's number from the jar. Several students dropped their hands back down to their desks in disappointment. (My students somehow thought that if they raised their hands while slightly lifting their bottoms out of the chair, their student number would magically be selected. Their sense of naïveté melted my heart.)

As a silence fell over the classroom, Anthony gazed at the book. He squirmed in his chair and began to gently rock back and forth. A slight mumble came from his mouth as he began to stumble through the words "The state of California is . . . ." Then he blurted out, "I can't read Miss Diaz," and began to chuckle, perhaps hoping to give the impression that a silly moment of embarrassment was the cause of his inability to read aloud fluently.

Anthony's laughter sparked giggles among his classmates but brought a lump of panic to my throat. I was aware that Anthony had previously been retained. However, the fact that he was a year older than his classmates yet several years behind them in terms of reading ability alarmed me. How can I, as a first-year teacher, tackle the pressing issue of his near-illiteracy?!

Quickly bringing myself back to the immediacy of a classroom of 32 students, I promptly praised Anthony for being courageous enough to read aloud and assisted him in completing the remainder of the short paragraph. Setting the social studies lesson aside, I took the opportunity provided by Anthony's comment to insert a minilesson on the need to eliminate the phrase I can't from my students' vocabulary. I noted that, even though Anthony may have felt that he could not read aloud, he did in fact read (albeit with my guidance).

During my minilesson, one student suggested that we ban the phrase I can't from our classroom. As a class, we then collectively created a list of phrases that could be used instead of I can't when we became frustrated with a

---

routes to high school completion are considered, however, there are still significant differences among racial/ethnic groups. For example, in 2003, 89.4 percent of whites 25 years and over had completed high school, compared to 80.0 percent of African Americans and 57.0 percent of Latinos (U.S. Census Bureau, June 2004).

Many children in the United States live in families that help them grow up healthy, confident, and skilled, but many do not. Instead, their life settings are characterized by problems of alcoholism or other substance abuse, family or gang violence, unemployment, poverty, poor nutrition, teenage parenthood, and a history of school failure. Such children live in communities and families that have many problems and frequently become dysfunctional, unable to provide their children with the support and guidance they need. According to *Kids Count Data Book: 2007*, "Too many children in our country do not succeed because crises leave them without a family to whom they can turn for the kind of help and support that most children take for granted. For a variety of reasons—illness, inadequate housing, substance abuse, poverty, domestic violence, mental health issues, and others—their families have failed to meet their needs" (Annie E. Casey Foundation, 2007).

It is important to remember that at-risk factors are only an indication of *potential* academic problems. The majority of children and youth who live in environments affected by poverty, crime, and other social problems are academically successful. Marian Wright Edelman (April 11, 2008), founder and president of the Children's Defense Fund, describes how such students beat the odds: "On their way to and from school,

TEACHING ON YOUR FEET

challenging task. These phrases included I do not understand . . . ; I think I may be confused about . . . ; *and* I think I need some extra help/extra time with . . . . *Our time quickly ran out, and it was time to go to lunch. As my long line of fourth-graders made its way to the cafeteria, I could hear the voices of several students echoing in the halls as they chanted, "There's no such thing as 'I can't'!" Though our social studies lesson was delayed, it was well worth the boost in confidence and consideration that filled our classroom because Anthony was now encouraged rather than ridiculed.*

ANALYSIS

I was taken aback by the comment Anthony made regarding what he thought was his inability to read. I believe that Anthony was not trying to be humorous or disruptive but that he felt he actually could not read. My goal was to show, not only Anthony but his classmates as well, that he *could* read and that the phrase *I can't* meant nothing in my class. By abolishing *I can't* from my classroom, my students can see that knowledge *is* power and that their inquisitiveness, resilience, and diligence can challenge them to learn and help them be successful in the future.

Anthony's use of *I can't* also served as a green light for me to become an advocate for a student in need of more than what I, as a single teacher, could offer him. At this point, teaching was not about about sinking or swimming as teacher but about stepping outside the classroom and utilizing the resources that are available not only to me, but to Anthony as well.

REFLECTION

- What resources would you locate and draw on to assist a student who exhibited difficulties similar to Anthony's?
- How would you handle a student's embarrassment over not being able to perform in front of the class?
- What programs or strategies can teachers use to help enhance students' self esteem?

Jennifer Michele Diaz
Fourth-Grade Teacher
Westmont Elementary School

myeducationlab *To answer these questions online, go to MyEducationlab at www.myeducationlab.com, select the Activities and Application section, and click on this chapter's Teaching on Your Feet.*

---

they daily walk a gauntlet through mean streets that are thoroughfares for crime and violence. They struggle to learn in underachieving schools. They have reached out for positive goals beyond the low expectations of others. . . . They are . . . beating the odds—every day."

The life experiences of students who are at risk of dropping out can be difficult for teachers to imagine, and as the following comments by a student teacher in an inner-city third-grade classroom illustrate, encountering the realities of poverty for the first time can be upsetting:

> Roughly 85 percent of [students are] living in poverty. The entire school population is eligible for free or reduced lunch. I was horrified. I guess I was a little ignorant of other people's situations.

> [Some] students came in wearing the same clothes for a week. Others would come in without socks on. No pencils, crayons, scissors, or glue. Some without breakfast, lunch, or a snack. My heart bled every day. I found myself becoming upset about their lives. I even found myself thinking about them at night and over the weekend. [I] noticed that they were extremely bright students, but their home life and economic status hindered them from working to their potential. Some of my students couldn't even complete their homework because they had no glue, scissors, or crayons at home. (Molino, 1999, p. 55)

Children and Poverty

Although the United States is one of the wealthiest countries in the world, by no means has it achieved an enviable record with regard to poverty among children (see Figure 3.1). According to *Kids Count Data Book: 2007*, 8 percent of children are members of families that live in "extreme poverty," and 40 percent are members of "low income" families. In addition, more than 726,000 lived in a foster home during 2004. During 2006, 33 percent of children lived in poverty in the District of Columbia, and 46 percent lived in a family where no parent had full-time, year-round employment. Comparable figures for Louisiana were 28 percent and 43 percent; for Texas, 24 percent and 34 percent (Annie E. Casey Foundation, 2007).

Despite the overall high standard of living, homelessness in the United States is a major social problem. Prior to the 1980s, homelessness was largely confined to the poorest areas of the nation's largest cities. Since then, changes in social policies such as welfare, minimum wages, and affordable housing—coupled with economic upheavals and continued unequal distributions of wealth—have swelled the number of homeless people. In addition, homelessness is moving beyond cities to rural areas where single mothers (often migrant farm workers) and their children make up the largest percentage of the homeless population (National Coalition for the Homeless, 2008).

About half of all homeless children do not attend school regularly (Cunningham, 2003). A host of barriers can make it difficult for them to attend school. First is the need to overcome health problems, hunger, and the difficulty of obtaining clothing and school supplies. Second, providing documentation for school enrollment is often almost impossible for homeless guardians. School districts are often reluctant to eliminate requirements for birth certificates, immunization records, and documentation of legal guardianship. Third, homeless shelters and other temporary housing may not be on regular school district bus routes, making it difficult for homeless children to get to and from school. And homeless children can be difficult to identify because they are often highly mobile and may not wish to be identified.

The nation's first law to provide assistance to homeless persons, particularly children, was passed in 1987. The McKinney Act (recently renamed the McKinney-Vento Act) requires states to provide homeless children with free public education. According to the McKinney-Vento Act, schools must remove obstacles to school registration for homeless students—requirements for residency, guardianship, immunization, and previous school records—as well as provide transportation to and from school. In addition, the act requires that each school district have a liaison whose responsibility is to help identify homeless students and to ensure their success in school.

Family Stress

The stress placed on families in a complex society is extensive and not easily handled. For some families, such stress can be overwhelming. The structure of families who are experiencing the effects of financial problems, substance abuse, or violence, for example, can easily begin to crumble. One teacher who reaches out to students' families experiencing stress is Kimberly Min, profiled in the Teachers' Voices: Research to Reality feature for this chapter.

The National Clearinghouse on Child Abuse and Neglect (NCCAN) reported that Child Protective Service (CPS) agencies investigated 3 million reports of alleged child maltreatment involving 5 million children in 2000. Of these children, CPS determined that about 879,000 were victims of child maltreatment. Almost two-thirds of child victims (63 percent) suffered neglect (including medical neglect), 19 percent were physically abused, 10 percent were sexually abused, and 8 percent were psychologically maltreated (National Clearinghouse on Child Abuse and Neglect, 2002). Clearly, the burden of having to cope with such abuse in the home environment does not prepare a child to come to school to learn. Such stress is often associated with health and emotional problems, failure to achieve, behavioral problems at school, and dropping out of school.

Demographic Data

Number of Children: 2006

	NUMBER	PERCENT
Total children under age 18	73,735,562	25%
Total youth ages 10–17	33,608,039	46%

Race and Hispanic Origin of Youth (ages 10–17): 2006

	NUMBER	PERCENT
White*	20,013,455	60%
Black/African American*	5,061,811	15%
American Indian/ Alaskan Native*	314,357	1%
Asian and Pacific Islander*	1,316,652	4%
More than one race*	731,253	2%
Hispanic/Latino	6,170,511	18%

Children in Immigrant Families: 2006

Percent of children in immigrant families	22%

*Non-Hispanic/Latino

Education

Fourth-grade students who scored at or above proficient reading level: 2007	32%
Fourth-grade students who scored at or above proficient math level: 2007	39%
Eighth-grade students who scored at or above proficient reading level: 2007	29%
Eighth-grade students who scored at or above proficient math level: 2007	31%

Economics

Median income of families with children: 2006	$54,500
Children in extreme poverty (income below 50% of poverty level): 2006	8%
Children in low-income families (income below 200% of poverty level): 2006	40%
Children in low-income families that spend more than 30% of their income on housing: 2006	66%

Juvenile Justice[†]

Estimated daily count of detained and committed youth in custody: 2006	92,854

Rate of detained and committed youth in custody (per 100,000 youth ages 10–15): 2006

United States	125

Ratio of rates of youth of color to white* youth in custody: 2006	3:1
Percentage of youth in custody for nonviolent offenses: 2006	66%
Juvenile violent crime arrest rate (arrests per 100,000 youth ages 10–17): 2005	283

[†]Age range varies by state unless otherwise noted.

Child Health

Percentage of children without health insurance: 2005	11%
Number of children without health insurance: 2005	8,144,000
Percentage of children with special health care needs: 2005–2006	14%

FIGURE 3.1 Profile of children in the United States

Source: Kids Count Data Book: 2007. Baltimore: Annie E. Casey Foundation, 2007.

TEACHERS' VOICES RESEARCH TO REALITY

Kimberly Min

BUILDING BRIDGES BETWEEN SCHOOL AND COMMUNITY

I chose to teach at a school in the heart of south Los Angeles. When I told my friends and family where I was teaching, many of them were very concerned about my safety. My only response was that I wanted to be in an area where they needed more credentialed teachers. In fact, this is not the safest place to be.

It is my school, however, and I love to teach here. Once I saw my students for the first time, my full concentration and energies were placed on them. I was able to set aside my anxiety about the school and focus on social justice teaching. I began to explore the community. As a class we took a walking field trip to the library and the fire station, which took us past the park, the banks, and stores. This was a part of the community I had never seen, and I felt more empowered by familiarizing myself with the area.

I visited students' homes early in the day so I would feel safer in the neighborhood. Over the winter break, I visited 16 homes. My brief visits strengthened my communication with parents. I understood better how the harsh conditions in their neighborhoods affected both children and parents. Parents explained their concerns about "gang bangers" down the street, the lack of "safe places" for their children to go, and their reasons for "no open windows or doors." Many parents see the school as "okay," but see their neighborhood as "unsafe, dirty, and full of gang bangin'."

I felt empowered by knowing that I was welcomed and accepted in any of my students' homes. In spite of our cultural and ethnic differences, we are the same in wanting the best for the children that we share. Many parents say that they pray for me, they send their good wishes, their hugs, and kisses of gratitude for the work that I am doing.

Many families have lived in the area for generations. Many of my students' parents are graduates of the school. The roots of the community run deep, and the wisdom and love from the parents and grandparents I encountered give me a surge of energy and a sense of inclusion.

I continue to feel the community's tension, but I am also increasingly grateful for the families' support during the years. I have learned and grown so much. What is so great about this experience is that the people close to me—family and friends—who once thought so poorly about this community have changed their perceptions as they see my work and hear my stories about what my students and school mean to me. I am not the only one growing from this experience.

QUESTIONS

1. In addition to visiting their students' homes, what are other ways for teachers to build bridges between school and community?
2. Reflecting on your own experiences, to what extent did bridges exist between the K–12 schools you attended and the communities within which you lived?

Kimberly Min is a third–grade teacher. This feature is taken from her contribution to Jeanne Oakes and Martin Lipton's *Teaching to Change the World*, 3rd edition, Boston: McGraw-Hill, 2007, pp. 400–401.

With the high rise in divorce and women's entry into the workforce, family constellations have changed dramatically. No longer is a working father, a mother who stays at home, and two or three children the only kind of family in the United States. The number of single-parent families, stepparent families, blended families, and extended families has increased dramatically during the last decade.

The composition of today's families is diverse, and so are the styles with which children are raised in families. Because of the number of working women and single-parent homes, an alarming number of children are unsupervised during much of the day. Between 3 P.M. and 8 P.M. is the most likely time for youth to engage in risk-taking or delinquent behaviors or to be victims of a crime (Cunningham, 2003). It has been estimated that there may be as many as 6 million such latchkey children younger than 13 (Hopson, Hopson, & Hagen, 2002). To meet the needs of latchkey children, many schools offer before- and after-school programs.

In addition, many middle-class couples are waiting longer to have children. Although children of such couples may have more material advantages, they may be impoverished in regard to the reduced time they spend with their parents. To maintain their lifestyle, these parents are often driven to spend more time developing their careers. As a result, the care and guidance their children receive is inadequate, and "[s]ustained bad care eventually leads to a deep-seated inner sense of insecurity and inadequacy, emotional pain, and a troublesome sense of self" (Comer, 1997, p. 83). To fill the parenting void that characterizes the lives of an increasing number of children from all economic classes, schools and teachers are being called on to play an increased role in the socialization of young people.

Substance Abuse

One of the most pressing social problems confronting today's schools is the abuse of illegal drugs, tobacco, and alcohol. Although drug abuse by students moved from the top-ranked problem facing local schools according to the 1996 Gallup Poll of the public's attitudes toward the public schools to the sixth-ranked problem in the 2007 poll, drug use among students remains at alarming levels. The University of Michigan's Institute for Social Research (2006) reported that 65.5 percent of high school seniors had used alcohol, 31.5 percent had used marijuana, and 5.7 percent had used cocaine during 2006 (see Table 3.2). In addition, 84.9 percent said they could obtain marijuana "fairly easily" or "very easily" and 46.5 percent said the same about cocaine.

The use of drugs among young people varies from community to community and from year to year, but overall it is disturbingly high. Mind-altering substances used by young people include the easily acquired glue, white correction fluid, and felt marker, as well as marijuana, amphetamines, and cocaine. The abuse of drugs not only poses the risks of addiction and overdosing, but also is related to problems such as HIV/AIDS, teenage pregnancy, depression, suicide, automobile accidents, criminal activity, and dropping out of school. For an alarming number of young people, drugs are seen as a way of coping with life's problems.

Violence and Crime

The rate of victimization in U.S. schools has decreased since 1992, according to Indicators of School Crime and Safety, 2007, jointly published by the Bureau of Justice Statistics and the National Center for Education Statistics. However, students ages 12 to 18 were victims of about 628,000 violent crimes and 868,000 crimes of theft at school during 2005–06 (Bureau of Justice Statistics and the National Center for Education Statistics, 2007). Eighty-six percent of public schools experienced one or more violent incidents. Figure 3.2 shows the percentage of public schools, by level, with various types of crime and the percentage that reported crimes to the police.

In addition, the U.S. Department of Justice (2002) estimates that there are more than 24,500 gangs and approximately 775,000 gang members. According to *Indicators of School Crime and Safety 2007*, 24 percent of students ages 12 to 18 in public schools reported that there were gangs in their schools. Urban students were more likely to report street gangs at their schools (36 percent) than were suburban and rural students (21 percent and 16 percent, respectively).

Gang membership is perceived by many youth as providing them with several advantages: a sense of belonging and identity, protection from other gangs, opportunities for excitement, or a chance to make money through selling drugs or participating in other illegal activities. Although few students are gang members, a small number of gang-affiliated students can disrupt the learning process, create disorder in a school, and cause others to fear for their physical safety. Strategies for reducing the effect of gang activities on schools include identifying gang members, implementing dress codes that ban styles of dress identified with gangs, and quickly removing gang graffiti from the school.

TABLE 3.2 Drug and alcohol use by high school seniors, and availability of drugs (2006)

(a) Reported drug and alcohol use by high school seniors, 2006[a]

Drugs	Used within the last: 12 Months[b]	Used within the last: 30 Days
Alcohol	66.5%	45.3%
Marijuana	31.5	18.3
Other opiates	9.0	3.8
Stimulants	8.1	3.7
Sedatives	6.6	3.0
Tranquilizers	6.6	2.7
Cocaine	5.7	2.5
Hallucinogens	4.9	1.5
Inhalants	4.5	1.5
Steroids	1.8	1.1
Heroin	0.8	0.4

Source: Bureau of Justice Statistics and University of Michigan News and Information Services, December 21, 2006.

[a]Self-reports of drug use among high school seniors may underrepresent drug use among youth of that age because high school dropouts and truants are not included, and these groups may have more involvement with drugs than those who stay in school.

[b]Including the last month.

(b) Percentage of high school seniors reporting they could obtain drugs fairly easily or very easily, 2006

Marijuana	84.9%
Amphetamines	52.9
Cocaine	46.5
Barbiturates	43.8
Crack	38.8
LSD	29.0
Heroin	27.4
Crystal methamphetamine	26.7
Tranquilizers	24.4
PCP	23.1
Amyl/butyl nitrites	18.4

Source: Bureau of Justice Statistics and University of Michigan News and Information Services, December 21, 2006.

Periodically, the nation's attention is riveted by a shooting that takes place in a school. With each instance of horrific school violence, the recurring question is, Why? and there is a renewed effort to understand the origins of youth violence. The nation has debated gun control measures; the influence of violence in television, movies, and point-and-shoot video games; and steps that parents, schools, and communities can take to curb school crime and violence. To consider the impact a fatal in-school shooting can have on a school, go to MyEducationLab and read a short diary entry written by a student whose best friend was one of two people shot to death that day at school. How might the shooting have affected teachers, other school staff, and students and their families? How can teachers help this student, and others, deal with the tragedy?

As a result of school shootings and the public's concern with school crime and violence, many schools have developed crisis management plans to cope with violent incidents on campus. Many schools have also made students and school personnel familiar with the *immediate* warning signs of violence, such as the following:

- Loss of temper on a daily basis
- Frequent physical fighting
- Significant vandalism or property damage
- Increase in the use of drugs or alcohol

PEARSON
myeducationlab

Go to MyEducationLab, select Chapter 3 and then Activities and Applications to analyze the artifact Tragedy at School (Social Studies 9–12).

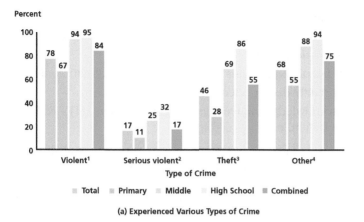

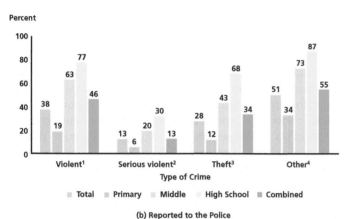

FIGURE 3.2 Percentage of public schools experiencing and reporting incidents of crime that occurred at school, by type of crime and school level; school year 2005–06

Source: U.S. Department of Education, National Center for Education Statistics, 2005–06. School Survey on Crime and Safety (SSOCS), *2006.*

[1]Violent incidents include rape or attempted rape, sexual battery other than rape, physical attack or fight with or without a weapon, threat of physical attack with or without a weapon, and robbery with or without a weapon. Serious violent incidents are also included in violent incidents.
[2]Serious violent incidents include rape or attempted rape, sexual battery other than rape, physical attack or fight with a weapon, threat of physical attack with a weapon, and robbery with or without a weapon.
[3]Theft/larceny (taking things worth over $10 without personal confrontation) was defined for respondents as "the unlawful taking of another person's property without personal confrontation, threat, violence, or bodily harm. Included are pocket picking, stealing a purse or backpack (if left unattended or no force was used to take it from owner), theft from a building, theft from a motor vehicle or of motor vehicle parts or accessories, theft of bicycles, theft from vending machines, and all other types of thefts."
[4]Other incidents include possession of a firearm or explosive device; possession of a knife or sharp object; distribution, possession, or use of illegal drugs or alcohol; and vandalism.

Note: Primary schools are defined as schools in which the lowest grade is not higher than grade 3 and the highest grade is not higher than grade 8. Middle schools are defined as schools in which the lowest grade is not lower than grade 4 and the highest grade is not higher than grade 9. High schools are defined as schools in which the lowest grade is not lower than grade 9. Combined schools include all other combinations of grades, including K–12 schools. Responses were provided by the principal or the person most knowledgeable about crime and safety issues at the school. "At school" was defined for respondents to include activities that happen in school buildings, on school grounds, on school buses, and at places that hold school-sponsored events or activities. Respondents were instructed to respond only for those times that were during normal school hours or when school activities or events were in session, unless the survey specified otherwise. Population size is 83,200 public schools.

- Increase in risk-taking behavior
- Detailed plans to commit acts of violence
- Announcing threats or plans for hurting others
- Enjoying hurting animals
- Carrying a weapon (MTV & American Psychological Association, n.d.)

In addition, students and school personnel are advised to be alert for the following signs of a *potential* for violence over a period of time:

- A history of violent or aggressive behavior
- Serious drug or alcohol use
- Gang membership or a strong desire to be in a gang
- Access to or fascination with weapons, especially guns
- Threatening others regularly
- Trouble controlling feelings like anger
- Withdrawal from friends and usual activities

- Feeling rejected or alone
- Having been a victim of bullying
- Poor school performance
- History of discipline problems or frequent run-ins with authority
- Feeling constantly disrespected
- Failing to acknowledge the feelings or rights of others (MTV & American Psychological Association, n.d.)

As a result of the nation's heightened awareness of school shootings during the last decade, schools have reviewed their ability to provide students, faculty, and staff with a safe environment for learning. Many schools used the "School Safety Checklist" (See Table 3.3), which is excerpted from the National School Safety Center's *School Safety Check Book*.

Bullying

After the 1999 Columbine High School shootings left 14 students and a teacher dead, investigations of school violence brought the problem of bullying in schools to the forefront. According to the *Safe School Initiative*, a collaborative study by the U.S. Department of Education and the Secret Service, "In over 2/3 of the cases, the attackers felt persecuted, bullied, threatened, attacked or injured by others prior to the incident. . . . A number of attackers had experienced bullying and harassment that was longstanding and severe. In those cases, the experience of bullying appeared to play a major role in motivating the attack at school" (October 2000, p. 7).

About 28 percent of 12- to 18-year-old students reported having been bullied at school during the last 6 months. Nineteen percent of students said that the bullying involved being made fun of; 15 percent reported being the subject of rumors; and 9 percent said they were pushed, shoved, tripped, or spit on, with 24 percent of this group

TABLE 3.3 School safety checklist

Give your school a thorough crime prevention inspection now. Use this checklist as a guideline to determine your school's strengths and weaknesses.

	Yes	No
1. Is there a policy for dealing with violence and vandalism in your school? (The reporting policy must be realistic and strictly adhered to.)	___	___
2. Is there an incident-reporting system?	___	___
3. Is the incident-reporting system available to all staff?	___	___
4. Is statistical information about the scope of the problems at your school and in the community available?	___	___
5. Have the school, school board, and administrators taken steps or anticipated any problems through dialogue?	___	___
6. Does security fit into the organization of the school? (Security must be designed to fit the needs of the administration and made part of the site.)	___	___
7. Are the teachers and administrators aware of laws that pertain to them? To their rights? To students' rights? Of their responsibility as to enforcement of and respect for rules, regulations, policies, and the law?	___	___
8. Is there a working relationship with your local law enforcement agency?	___	___
9. Are students and parents aware of expectations and school discipline codes?	___	___
10. Are there any actual or contingency action plans developed to deal with student disruptions and vandalism?	___	___
11. Is there a policy for restitution or prosecution of perpetrators of violence and vandalism?	___	___
12. Is there any in-service training available for teachers and staff in the areas of violence and vandalism and other required reporting procedures?	___	___
13. Is there a policy for consistent monitoring and evaluation of incident reports?	___	___
14. Is the staff trained in standard crime-prevention behavior?	___	___

Source: Excerpted from The School Safety Check Book *by the National School Safety Center, 141 Duesenberg Dr., Suite 11, Westlake Village, CA, 91362, http://www.nssc1.org.*

reporting that they were injured. Seventy-nine percent of students who were bullied said they were bullied inside the school, and 28 percent said they were bullied outside on school grounds (National Center for Education Statistics, 2007, p. 34). To reflect further on the problem of bullying and its consequences, go to MyEducationLab and watch a video of a middle-school teacher talking with her students about their experiences related to bullying and their ideas about what should be done.

Cyberbullying

With the proliferation of personal computers and cell phones, bullying has gone online. **Cyberbullying** involves the use of information and communication technologies to harass or threaten an individual or group. Cyberbullies send harassing e-mails or instant messages; post obscene, insulting, and slanderous messages to online bulletin boards; or develop websites to promote and disseminate defamatory content. As Figure 3.3 shows, an online survey of Internet-using adolescents revealed that 34 percent had experienced cyberbullying, 12 percent had been physically threatened, and 5 percent were afraid for their safety. Cyberbullying is about evenly divided between chat rooms and computer text messages (Patchin & Hinduja, 2006).

Teen Pregnancy

Each year, almost 750,000 U.S. teenagers between the ages of 15 and 19 become pregnant, and more than three-quarters of these pregnancies are unintended (Alan Guttmacher Institute, 2006). Indeed, most teachers of adolescents today may expect to have at least some students who are or have been pregnant.

Since peaking in 1990, the teenage pregnancy, birth, and abortion rates have declined, largely the result of more effective contraceptive practices among sexually active teenagers (Alan Guttmacher Institute, 2006). Nevertheless, teen pregnancies remain a serious problem in society. Because the physical development of girls in adolescence may not be complete, complications can occur during pregnancy and in the birthing process. Also, adolescents are less likely to receive prenatal care in the crucial first trimester; they tend not to eat well-balanced diets; and they are not free of harmful substances such as alcohol, tobacco, and drugs, which are known to be detrimental to a baby's development. "Babies born . . . to teenage mothers are at risk for long-term problems in many major areas of life, including school failure, poverty, and physical or mental illness. The teenage mothers themselves are also at risk for these problems" (The American Academy of Child and Adolescent Psychiatry, July 2004). Because most teen mothers drop out of school, forfeiting their high school diplomas and limiting their access to decent, higher-paying job opportunities, they and their children stay at the bottom of the economic ladder.

Suicide Among Children and Youth

The increase in individual and multiple suicides is alarming. It is the third leading cause of death for young people ages 15 to 24, surpassed only by homicide and accidents, according to the Centers for Disease Control and Prevention (Summer 2007). Almost 17 percent of students, grades 9–12, seriously considered suicide in the previous 12 months, and more than 8 percent reported that they had actually attempted suicide one or more times (Centers for Disease Control and Prevention, Summer 2007).

Although female students are almost two times more likely than male students to have seriously considered attempting suicide during the preceding 12 months, about four times as many male students as females actually commit suicide. Latino students are about two times more likely than white students to attempt suicide, and students in grade 9 are about four times more likely than students in grade 12 to make a suicide attempt that requires medical attention (Centers for Disease Control and Prevention, Summer 2007). Also, lesbian and gay youth are two to three times more likely to attempt suicide than their heterosexual peers, and they account for up to 30 percent of all completed suicides among youth (Besner & Spungin, 1995).

PEARSON myeducationlab

Go to MyEducationLab, select Chapter 3 and then Activities and Applications to watch the video Eliminating Bullies in School.

FIGURE 3.3 Cyberbullying
Source: Patchin, J., & Hinduja, S. (2006). Bullies move beyond the schoolyard: A preliminary look at cyberbullying. Youth Violence and Juvenile Justice, 4(2), 148–169.

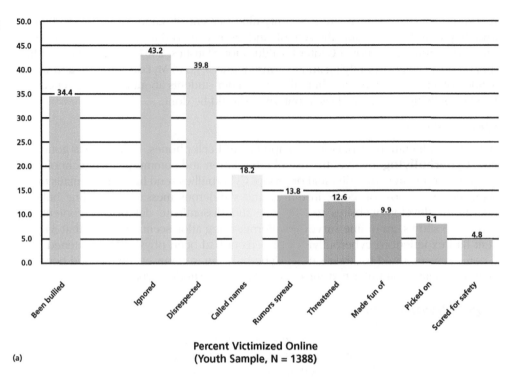

(a)

**Percent Victimized Online
(Youth Sample, N = 1388)**

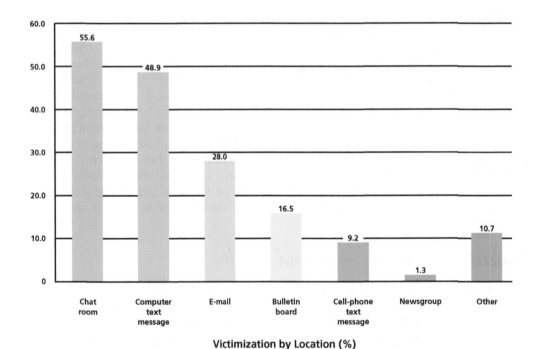

(b)

**Victimization by Location (%)
(Only Those Who Have Been Bullied in Youth Sample, N = 468)**

HOW ARE SCHOOLS ADDRESSING SOCIETAL PROBLEMS?

Responding to the needs of at-risk students will be a crucial challenge for schools, families, and communities during the twenty-first century. Because most children attend school, it is logical that this preexisting system be used for reaching large numbers of at-risk children (and, through them, their families). During the last decade, many school districts have taken innovative steps to address societal problems that affect students' lives.

Although programs that address social problems are costly, most of the public believes that schools should be used for the delivery of health and social services to students and their families. There has been disagreement, however, about the extent to which school facilities should be used for anything but meeting students' educational needs. In isolated instances, community groups and school boards have resisted school-based services such as family planning clinics and mental health services. However, increases in state funding and foundation support to provide school-based health, mental health, and social services have tended to dissipate most of this resistance (Dryfoos, 1998).

Under pressure to find solutions to increasing social problems among children and adolescents, educators have developed an array of intervention programs. In general, the aim of these programs is to address the behavioral, social, and academic adjustment of at-risk children and adolescents so they can receive maximum benefit from their school experiences.

The following sections describe five intervention strategies that have proven effective in addressing academic, social, and behavioral problems among children and adolescents: peer counseling and peer mediation, full-service community schools, school-based interprofessional case management, compensatory education, and alternative schools and curricula.

Peer Counseling and Peer Mediation

To address the social problems that affect students, some schools have initiated student-to-student **peer-counseling** programs—usually monitored by a school counselor or other specially trained adult. In peer-counseling programs, students can address problems and issues such as low academic achievement, interpersonal problems at home and at school, substance abuse, and career planning. Evidence indicates that both peer counselors and students experience increased self-esteem and greater ability to deal with problems.

When peer counseling is combined with cross-age tutoring, younger students can learn about drugs, alcohol, premarital pregnancy, delinquency, dropping out, HIV/AIDS, suicide, and other relevant issues. Here, the groups are often college-age students meeting with those in high school, or high school students meeting with those in junior high school or middle school. In these preventive programs, older students sometimes perform dramatic episodes that portray students confronting problems and model strategies for handling the situations presented.

Peer mediation programs are similar to peer-counseling programs. The focus of **peer mediation** is on cultivating a classroom climate in which students influence one another to be more accepting of differences, not of solving problems per se. In some peer mediation programs, students participate in role-plays and simulations to help them develop empathy, social skills, and awareness of prejudice.

An example of peer mediation can be found at John Marshall Middle School, in Long Beach, California, where students increase their understanding of cultural differences by learning about peer mediation. Students become "diversity ambassadors" by attending workshops on peer mediation, cultural diversity, tolerance, and conflict resolution. The workshops focus on issues of racial and ethnic barriers for fellow students. The diversity ambassadors host a school assembly on school violence in partnership with the Long Beach Police Department's Gang Unit. Marshall school teachers and students report that the diversity ambassadors have improved the school climate (Learning in Deed, 2004).

Full-Service Community Schools

In response to the increasing number of at-risk students, many schools are serving their communities by integrating educational, medical, social, and/or human services. **Full-service community schools,** often called community schools, operate in a public school building before, during, and after school; seven days a week; all year long.

Often located in low-income urban areas, community schools integrate educational, medical, social, and/or human services to meet the needs of children and their families.

Community schools involve collaborative partnerships among school districts, departments of public health, hospitals, and various nonprofit organizations. At full-service community schools, students and their families can receive health screening, psychological counseling, drug prevention counseling, parent education, child-rearing tips, and family-planning information. Parents and community members also participate in adult education and job-training programs at the school, as well as use the school as a site to solve community problems.

An evaluation of 48 community school programs indicates that they contribute to improved student achievement. They are also linked to increased attendance and reduced levels of high-risk behaviors (e.g., drug use and sexual activity). In addition, because community schools support families, family involvement in school programs increases and family functioning improves (Dryfoos & Maguire, 2002).

Another benefit of community schools is that they encourage parents to view the school positively; thus, parents are more likely to support the school in maintaining high expectations for learning and behavior. Community schools also directly support the work of teachers in the classroom. As the Institute for Educational Leadership's Coalition of Community Schools (2002, p. 6) points out: "Teachers in community schools teach. They are not expected to be social workers, mental health counselors, or police officers. Partner organizations do this work, providing teachers with essential support, helping them recognize and respond effectively to student problems, and connecting students and their families with needed community services and opportunities."

School-Based Interprofessional Case Management

To respond to the needs of at-risk students, many schools have developed programs that draw from the resources of community organizations and public services. One such approach to forming new home, school, and community partnerships is known as **school-based interprofessional case management.** The approach uses professionally trained case managers who work directly with teachers, the community, and the family to coordinate and deliver appropriate services to at-risk students and their families. The case management approach is based on a comprehensive service-delivery network of teachers, social agencies, and health-service agencies.

One of the first case management programs in the country is operated by the Center for the Study and Teaching of At-Risk Students (C-STARS) and serves 20 school districts in the Pacific Northwest. Center members include Washington State University, the University of Washington, a community-based organization, and Washington State's Department of Social and Health Services. Working with teachers and other school personnel, an interprofessional case management team fulfills seven functions to meet the needs of at-risk students: assessment, development of a service plan, brokering with other agencies, service implementation and coordination, advocacy, monitoring and evaluation, and mentoring.

C-STARS also provides a combination of the following services customized to the specific needs of each community: after-school educational programs; summer school programs; recreational activities; social and health services; case management services for students and families; and parent resource centers offering educational opportunities such as ESL, computer literacy, and leadership training. Program evaluation data have shown significant measurable improvements in students' attendance, academic performance, and school behavior.

Compensatory Education

To meet the learning needs of at-risk students, several federally funded **compensatory education programs** for elementary and secondary students have been developed, the largest of which is Title I. Launched in 1965 as part of the Elementary and Secondary

Education Act (ESEA) and President Lyndon Johnson's Great Society education program, Title I (called Chapter I between 1981 and 1994) was designed to improve the basic skills (reading, writing, and mathematics) of low-ability students from low-income families. In 2002, ESEA was reauthorized as the No Child Left Behind (NCLB) Act. To assist teachers in meeting the learning needs of students from low-income families, NCLB includes provisions for supplemental educational services. NCLB's Supplemental Educational Services (SES) provision gives parents of eligible children the opportunity and the funding to choose private tutors or other academic support services to help their children succeed in school.

Students who participate in Title I programs are usually taught through pullout programs, in which they leave the regular classroom to receive additional instruction individually or in small groups. Title I teachers, sometimes assisted by an aide, often have curriculum materials and equipment not available to regular classroom teachers.

Research on the effectiveness of Title I programs has been inconclusive, with some studies reporting achievement gains not found in other studies. Recent research has found positive effects on students' achievement in the early grades, but these gains tend to dissipate during the middle grades. Some critics of Title I and other compensatory education programs, such as Head Start for preschool children, Success for All for preschool and elementary children, and Upward Bound for high school students, argue that they are stopgap measures at best. Instead, they maintain, social problems such as poverty, the breakdown of families, drug abuse, and crime that contribute to poor school performance should be reduced.

Alternative Schools and Curricula

To meet the needs of students at risk of education failure because of various social problems, many school districts have developed alternative schools and curricula. These programs are designed to minimize students' high-risk behavior and address concerns about violence, weapons, and drugs in schools. Despite the need for such programs, only about 40 percent of school districts have alternative programs for at-risk students. Sixty-five percent of these districts had only one alternative school during the 2000–01 school year and were unable to meet the demand for alternative schools (Kleiner, Porch, & Farris, 2002).

An **alternative school** is usually a small, highly individualized school separate from the regular school; in other cases, the alternative school is organized as a **school-within-a-school.** Alternative school programs usually provide remedial instruction, some vocational training, and individualized counseling. Because they usually have much smaller class sizes, alternative school teachers can monitor students' progress more closely and, when problems do arise, respond more quickly and with greater understanding of student needs.

One exemplary alternative school is the Buffalo Alternative High School serving at-risk seventh- to twelfth-grade students in the Buffalo, New York, Public School District. To reach students who are not successful at regular schools, the Buffalo program offers individualized instruction, small class sizes, and various enrichment programs delivered in what school staff describe as a "supportive, noncoercive, nontraditional setting." Most students are expected to return to their regular schools after a minimum of four weeks. Students must earn 600 points (based on attendance, punctuality, attitude, behavior, and performance) to return to their regular school.

Another exemplary alternative school is the Beard Alternative School in Syracuse, New York. Students address important community issues such as hunger, domestic violence, the criminal justice system, racism, and gender issues. In partnership with the Center for Community Alternatives and Communities United to Rebuild Neighborhoods, students maintain a flower and vegetable garden on the city's southwest side. The students publish a biannual student newspaper (*Beard News*) that deals with topics relevant to students' lives. Students also participate in classroom learning experiences based on their volunteer activities (Learning in Deed, 2004).

Out-of-School-Time (OST) Activities

One approach to reducing high-risk behaviors among youth is to involve them in **out-of-school-time (OST) activities** (often called *extracurricular activities*). OST activities support and promote youth's development because they (a) place youth in safe environments; (b) prevent youth from engaging in delinquent activities; (c) teach youth general and specific skills, beliefs, and behaviors; and (d) provide opportunities for youth to develop relationships with peers and mentors (Simpkins, 2003). OST programs provide opportunities for growth and development at times when youth are unsupervised and might be tempted to engage in risky behaviors.

Frequently, children living in poverty don't have the same opportunities as other children to participate in music and dance, sports programs, and other OST activities. Students who spend one to four hours in OST activities each week are 49 percent less likely to use drugs and 37 percent less likely to become teen parents than students who do not participate in such activities. However, OST programs met only 25 percent of the demand in urban areas during 2002 (Little & Harris, 2003).

Alternative Curricula

While they don't work in alternative school settings, many highly effective regular teachers have developed alternative curricula to meet the unique learning needs of students at risk. Many teachers, for example, link students' learning to the business, civic, cultural, and political segments of their communities. The rationale is that connecting at-risk students to the world beyond their schools will enable them to see the relevance of education.

HOW CAN COMMUNITY-BASED PARTNERSHIPS HELP STUDENTS LEARN?

The previous section looked at intervention programs that schools have developed to ensure the optimum behavioral, social, and academic adjustment of at-risk children and adolescents to their school experiences. This section describes innovative, community-based partnerships that some schools have developed recently to prevent social problems from hindering students' learning.

The Community as a Resource for Schools

To assist schools in addressing the social problems that affect students, many communities are acting in the spirit of a recommendation made by the late Ernest Boyer: "Perhaps the time has come to organize, in every community, not just a *school* board, but a *children's* board. The goal would be to integrate children's services and build, in every community, a friendly, supportive environment for children" (Boyer, 1995, p. 169). In partnerships between communities and schools, individuals, civic organizations, or businesses select a school or are selected by a school to work together for the good of students. The ultimate goals of such projects are to provide students with better school experiences and to assist students at risk.

Civic Organizations

To develop additional sources of funding, many local school districts have established partnerships with community groups interested in improving educational opportunities in the schools. Some groups raise money for schools. The American Jewish Committee and the Urban League raised funds for schools in Pittsburgh, for example. Other partners adopt or sponsor schools and enrich their educational programs by providing funding, resources, or services.

One example of partnerships with community groups involved the Phenix City (Alabama) schools. Students worked with civic organizations to raise awareness among students and community members about important health issues. The Healthcare Science and Technology (HST) Department and the Western District medical/dental associations taught preventive health skills, including hand washing and oral hygiene, to all kindergarten, first-grade, and special education students in the Phenix City school system. Working with the civic organizations, the students developed and prepared all materials used in the training programs. In addition, students collaborated with the organizations to provide the community with educational programs on diabetes, and they offered blood sugar screenings to the community (Learning in Deed, 2004).

Volunteer Mentor Programs

Mentorship is a trend in community-based partnerships today, especially with students at risk. Parents, business leaders, professionals, and peers volunteer to work with students in neighborhood schools. Goals might include dropout prevention, high achievement, improved self-esteem, and healthy decision making. Troubleshooting on lifestyle issues often plays a role, especially in communities plagued by drug dealing, gang rivalry, casual violence, and crime. Mentors also model success.

Some mentor programs target particular groups. For instance, Concerned Black Men (CBM), a Washington, DC–based organization with 15 chapters around the country, targets inner-city African American male youth. More than 500 African American men in diverse fields and from all walks of life participate as CBM mentors to students in area schools. Their goal is to serve as positive adult male role models for youth, many of whom live only with their mothers or grandmothers and lack male teachers in school. To date, CBM has given cash awards and scholarships to more than 4,000 youth selected on the basis of high academic achievement, motivation, leadership in academic and nonacademic settings, and community involvement.

CBM volunteer mentors receive training and attend class every day, working as teachers' aides, contributing materials, arranging field trips, and running an after-school program for latchkey children. Many volunteers started working with first- and second-graders and saw these same children all the way through their elementary school years. The program's good results have made it a model for mentorship programs in other schools.

Corporate-Education Partnerships

Business involvement in schools has taken many forms, including, for example, contributions of funds or materials needed by a school, release time for employees to visit classrooms, adopt-a-school programs, cash grants for pilot projects and teacher development, educational use of corporate facilities and expertise, employee participation, student scholarship programs, and political lobbying for school reform. Extending beyond advocacy, private-sector efforts include job initiatives for disadvantaged youth, in-service programs for teachers, management training for school administrators, minority education and faculty development, and even construction of school buildings.

Business-sponsored school experiments focus on creating model schools, laboratory schools, or alternative schools that address particular local needs. In Minneapolis, for example, the General Mills Foundation has provided major funding to create the Minneapolis Federation of Alternative Schools (MFAS), a group of several schools designed to serve students who have not been successful in regular school programs. The goals for students who attend MFAS schools include returning to regular school when appropriate, graduating from high school, and/or preparing for postsecondary education or employment.

In addition to contributing more resources to education, chief executive officers and their employees are donating more time; 83 percent of the top managers surveyed by a recent *Fortune* poll said they "participate actively" in educational reform, versus 70 percent in 1990. At Eastman Kodak's Rochester, New York, plant, for example, hundreds of employees serve as tutors or mentors in local schools. In some dropout prevention programs, businessmen and -women adopt individual students, visiting them at school, eating lunch with them once a week, meeting their families, and taking them on personal field trips.

Schools as Resources for Communities

A shift from the more traditional perspective of schools is the view that schools should serve as multipurpose resources for the community. By focusing not only on the development of children and youth, but on their families as well, schools ultimately enhance the ability of students to learn. As Ernest Boyer (1995, p. 168) put it, "No arbitrary line can be drawn between the school and life outside. Every [school] should take the lead in organizing a referral service—a community safety net for children that links students and their families to support agencies in the region—to clinics, family support and counseling centers, and religious institutions."

Beyond the School Day

Many schools and school districts are serving their communities by providing educational and recreational programs before and after the traditional school day and during the summers. Increasingly, educational policymakers recognize that the traditional school year of approximately 180 days is not the best arrangement to meet students' learning needs. As the RCM Research Corporation, a nonprofit group that studies issues in educational change, points out: "Historically, time has been the glue that has bonded the traditions of our public school system—i.e., the Carnegie units, equal class periods, no school during summer months, 12 years of schooling, etc.—and, as a result, the use of time has become sacrosanct, 'We have always done it this way!' How time is used by schools often has more to do with administrative convenience than it does with what is best educationally for the student" (RCM Research Corporation, 1998).

Proposals for year-round schools and educationally oriented weekend and after-school programs address the educational and developmental needs of students affected by social problems. According to the National Association for Year-Round Education, 1,646 year-round schools served 1.3 million students in 1992; by 2007, 2,764 year-round schools served more than 2 million students. In Austin, Texas, for example, schools can participate in an optional extended year (OEY) program that allows them to provide additional instruction in reading and mathematics to students at risk of being retained a grade. Schools participating in OEY can choose from among four school-day options: (1) extended day, (2) extended week, (3) intersession of year-round schools, and (4) summer school (Idol, 1998; Washington, 1998).

Programs that extend beyond the traditional school day also address the needs of parents and the requirements of the work world. As an elementary teacher in Missouri said, "Many of my students just hang around at the end of every day. They ask what they can do to help me. Often there's no one at home, and they're afraid to go home or spend time on the streets" (Boyer, 1995, p. 165).

After-school educational and recreational programs are designed to (1) provide children with supervision at times when they might become involved in antisocial activities, (2) provide enrichment experiences to widen children's perspectives and increase their socialization, and (3) improve the academic achievement of children not achieving at their potential during regular school hours (Fashola, 1999). Ernest Boyer argued that schools should adapt their schedules to those of the workplace so that parents could become more involved in their children's education, and that businesses, too, should give parents more flexible work schedules. Drawing on the model of Japan, Boyer suggested that the beginning of the school year could be a holiday so that parents could attend opening day ceremonies and celebrate the launching and continuation of education in the same way that we celebrate its ending.

For several years, the After-School Plus (A+) Program in Hawaii has operated afternoon enrichment programs from 2:00 to 5:00 for children in kindergarten through sixth grade. The children, who are free to do art, sports, drama, or homework, develop a sense of *ohana*, or "feeling of belonging." Currently, 178 program sites serve nearly 22,000 students (National Governors' Association & NGA Center for Best Practices, 2002). Since the mid-1970s, schools in Buena Vista, Virginia, have operated according to a four seasons calendar that includes an optional summer enrichment program. Buena Vista's superintendent estimates that the district saves more than $100,000 a year on retention costs; although some students take more time, they are promoted to the next grade (Boyer, 1995).

Some research indicates that extended school days and school calendars have a positive influence on achievement (Center for Research on Effective Schooling for Disadvantaged Students, 1992; Gandara & Fish, 1994), but the Center for Research on the Education of Students Placed at Risk (CRESPAR) at Johns Hopkins University concluded that "there is no straightforward answer to the question of what works best in after-school programs" (Fashola, 1999). According to CRESPAR, few studies of the effects of after-school programs on measures such as achievement or reduction of antisocial behavior meet minimal standards for research design. Nevertheless, CRESPAR found that after-school programs with stronger evidence of effectiveness had four elements: training for staff, program structure, evaluation of program effectiveness, and planning that includes families and children (Fashola, 1999).

What approach to the education of students at risk does the scene in this photograph represent? What other risk factors affect children and youth? What are some other effective approaches for helping students succeed in school?

Social Services

In response to the increasing number of at-risk and violence-prone children and youth, many schools are also providing an array of social services to students, their families, and their communities. The following comments by three female students highlight the acute need for support services for at-risk youth who can turn to aggression and violence in a futile attempt to bolster their fragile self-esteem and to cope with the pain in their lives. All three girls have been involved in violent altercations in and around their schools, and all three frequently use alcohol and illegal drugs. Fifteen-year-old "Mary" has been physically abused by both her father and mother, and she was raped when she was 14. "Linda," also 15 years old, was sexually molested during a four-year period by a family acquaintance, and she endures constant physical and psychological abuse from her father. Fourteen-year-old "Jenny" is obsessed with death and suicide, and she aspires to join a gang.

> When you're smoking dope, you just break out laughing, you don't feel like punching people because it's just too hard. It takes too much. . . . You're mellow. . . . You just want to sit there and trip out on everybody. . . . It's even good for school work. When I used to get stoned all the time last year, I remember, I used to sit in class and do my work because I didn't want the teacher to catch me, and this year I'm getting failing marks 'cause I'm not doing my work 'cause I'm never stoned [Mary].

> I just know I got a lot of hatred. . . . And there's this one person [Jenny], and it just kinda happened after she mouthed me off, I was just like totally freaked with her and now I just want to slam her head into something. I wanna shoot her with a gun or something. I wanna kill her. . . . If I could get away with it I'd kill her. I wouldn't necessarily kill her, but I'd get her good. I just want to teach her a lesson. I'd beat the crap out of her. She's pissed me off so badly. I just want to give her two black eyes. Then I'd be fine. I'd have gotten the last word in [Linda].

> I like fighting. It's exciting. I like the power of being able to beat up people. Like, if I fight them, and I'm winning, I feel good about myself, and I

think of myself as tough. . . . I'm not scared of anybody, so that feels good. My friends are scared of a lot of people, and I go "Oh yeah," but I'm not scared of them. . . . All these people in grade eight at that junior high are scared of me, they don't even know me, and they're scared of me. It makes me feel powerful [Jenny]. (Artz, 1999, pp. 127, 136, 157)

Although some believe that schools should not provide social services, an increase in the number of at-risk students like Mary, Linda, and Jenny suggests that the trend is likely to continue. In Seattle, a referendum required that a percentage of taxes be set aside to provide services to elementary-age children. In Florida, Palm Beach County officials created the Children's Services Council to address sixteen areas, from reducing the dropout rate to better child care. From parent support groups, to infant nurseries, to programs for students with special needs, the council has initiated scores of projects to benefit the community and its children.

SUMMARY

What Is the Role of Schools in Today's Society?

- Although the debate about the role of schools continues, many people in the United States believe that schools have a responsibility to socialize students to participate intelligently and constructively in society.

How Can Schools Be Described?

- Schools can be categorized according to the focus of their curricula and according to their organizational structures.

What Are Schools Like as Social Institutions?

- As social institutions that contribute to the maintenance and improvement of society, schools mirror the national U.S. culture as well as the surrounding local culture. Schools often reproduce the existing social class structure, maintaining differences between the haves and have-nots.
- Elements of a school's physical environment such as self-contained classrooms, open-space arrangements, and departmentalization contribute to a school's character and culture. Similarly, each classroom develops its own culture, which is influenced by the physical setting and the social dimensions of the group.
- Three views of successful schools have been suggested: (1) their students manifest a high level of

learning, (2) their results surpass those for comparable schools, and (3) they are improving rather than getting worse.

What Are the Characteristics of Successful Schools?

- Research has identified seven characteristics of effective schools: strong leadership, high expectations, emphasis on basic skills, orderly school environment, frequent and systematic evaluation of student learning, sense of purpose, and collegiality and a sense of community.

What Social Problems Affect Schools and Place Students at Risk?

- In response to life experiences characterized by extreme family stress, poverty, crime, and lack of adult guidance, a growing number of youth are at risk of dropping out of school. Minority at-risk students may also have to contend with intangible obstacles such as language barriers, conflicts with fellow students and teachers, and racism and discrimination.

How Are Schools Addressing Societal Problems?

- Five effective intervention and prevention programs that schools have developed to address social problems are peer counseling and peer mediation, full-service community schools, school-based interprofessional case management, compensatory education, and alternative schools and curricula.

- Since 1965, an array of federally funded compensatory education programs has provided educational services to improve the basic skills of low-ability students from low-income families.
- Many school districts have developed alternative schools or schools within a school that provide highly individualized instructional and support services for students who have not been successful in regular schools. Also, highly effective teachers modify their techniques and develop alternative curricula to meet the needs of students at risk.

How Can Community-Based Partnerships Help Students Learn?

- Schools serve as resources for their communities by providing educational and recreational programs before and after the school day, and by providing health and social services. In addition, community and corporate partnerships can help schools address social problems that hinder students' learning by providing various forms of support.

PROFESSIONAL REFLECTIONS AND ACTIVITIES

Teacher's Journal

1. What evidence suggests that schools reproduce the existing class and social structure in the United States? What evidence suggests that students from the lower socioeconomic classes are not really being prepared for upward social mobility?
2. Using Anyon's four categories of schools (working-class, middle-class, affluent professional, and executive elite), describe the types of schools you have attended. In what ways have those schools contributed to (or detracted from) your own upward mobility within U.S. society?

Teacher's Research

1. Gather data on the Internet about children and/or adolescents that reflect issues of health, safety, and welfare in your state. State government databases are good places to start. Narrow your search to one of the following areas:
   - Childhood poverty and homelessness
   - Student nutrition and health
   - Teen pregnancy
   - Bullying in school
   - Child abuse and neglect
   - Student drug, alcohol, and tobacco abuse
   - School violence and crime
   - Truancy
   - Juvenile delinquency
   - Suicide among children and youth
2. Go to the home page for the National Education Association (NEA). From there, click on the link to NEA's Legislative Action Center. At that site, gather information about federal or state legislation that addresses meeting the educational needs of students

at risk. Send an e-mail message to Congress or one of your state's legislators explaining your position regarding that legislation.

Observations and Interviews

1. Visit a school and interview several teachers in regard to the social issues that affect students at their school. How have the teachers responded to these social issues? From their point of view, what resources would enable them to respond more effectively to these issues?
2. Interview a social worker in your community. According to him or her, what kind of relationship should exist between the schools and social service agencies?

---

myeducationlab To complete additional observations and interviews, go to MyEducationLab at www.myeducationlab.com, select the Virtual Field Experience section, and click on this chapter's Observations and Interviews.

Professional Portfolio

Visit the websites for several organizations that address the needs of at-risk children and youth and compile a set of materials (publications, instructional strategies, videos, training materials, etc.) that address one social issue that places students at risk.

---

myeducationlab Now go to MyEducationLab at www.myeducationlab.com to test your understanding of chapter content by completing this chapter's Study Plan.

The Teaching Profession: Florida-Specific Resources

Objectives:

- Describe teachers in Florida and why they choose to teach.
- Describe what it is like to teach in various grade levels in Florida.
- Compare and contrast the venues of Florida schools.
- Evaluate how cultural diversity impacts Florida classrooms.
- Evaluate how socioeconomic status affects Florida students.

FEAP Competencies:

Continuous Improvement (FEAP #3): The preprofessional student realizes that she/he is in the initial stages of a lifelong learning process and that self-reflection is one of the key components of that process. While his/her concentration is, of necessity, inward and personal, the role of colleagues and school-based improvement activities increases as time passes. The preprofessional student's continued professional improvement is characterized by self-reflection, working with immediate colleagues and teammates, and meeting the goals of a personal professional development plan.

Diversity (FEAP #5): The preprofessional teacher establishes a comfortable environment which accepts and fosters diversity. The teacher must demonstrate knowledge and awareness of varied cultures and linguistic backgrounds. The teacher creates a climate of openness, inquiry, and support by practicing strategies such as acceptance, tolerance, resolution, and mediation.

Human Development and Learning Drawing (FEAP #7): The preprofessional teacher draws upon well established human development/learning theories and concepts and a variety of information about students, the preprofessional teacher plans instructional activities.

Role of the Teacher (FEAP #11): The preprofessional teacher communicates and works cooperatively with families and colleagues to improve the educational experiences at the school.

Important Concepts
- Teacher roles
- Effective teachers
- Grade levels
- School culture
- School venues
- School choice
- School organization
- Cultural diversity

- Multicultural education
- Language diversity
- Family diversity
- Religious diversity
- Socioeconomic diversity
- Students with exceptionalities

Activities

Objective 1: Describe teachers in Florida and why they choose to teach.

The population of Florida is increasing rapidly, second only to Arizona. As a result, the state is in dire need of teachers. The state Department of Education anticipates a 20% increase in the number of teachers it needs by 2008, and a 26% increase by 2013. This means that each year, an additional 20,000 to 30,000 classroom teachers will need to be hired across the state.

As you think about where you would like to teach, look at a district map of Florida at http://www.fldoe.org/eias/flmove/liberty.asp . Click on any district to get additional information.

Questions for Reflection
1. Which districts are you interested in? What factors influence your choice of districts?
2. Choose one school district in the state of Florida and tour the webpage of the district you choose. As you read about the nature of education in this location, identify three reasons why you would be motivated to teach in this district.
3. The Department of Education publishes statistical information about teachers in Florida. Read through this publication at http://www.fldoe.org/eias/eiaspubs/pdf/tchsal05.pdf . Focus on the average salaries by district, located on page 3 of the PDF file above. How do you feel about the average teacher salaries in Florida? Were these numbers higher or lower than you expected?

Objective 2: Describe what it is like to teach in various grade levels in Florida.

In the state of Florida, grade levels are divided up into the following categories for assessment purposes:

> Primary: PreK-2nd grades
> Elementary: 3rd-5th grades
> Middle: 6th-8th grades
> High: 9th-12th grades

Visit the Website for the Sunshine State Standards to get an idea of what will be expected at each level. The site can be located at http://www.fldoe.org/BII/Curriculum/SSS/.

Questions for Reflection
1. Which grade levels and subjects are you most interested in teaching and why?
2. Look at the Sunshine State Standards for this grade level and subject. Pick one expectation and describe it here. Brainstorm some ways to implement this expectation in your classroom.
3. Go back to the list of Sunshine State Standards. Using the same subject, choose a different grade level from the one you used in reflection 1. Compare and contrast the expectation you described above with the new grade level.

Objective 3: Compare and contrast the venues of Florida schools.

The state of Florida generally offers two venues for school options. The first is the traditional public school. There are 67 public school districts in the state of Florida with over 820 schools operating in the 2007-2008 school year. Within the umbrella of the public school system are a number of alternative public school options that are specialized in some way. One example is the magnet school. According to the Florida Department of Education Website, magnet schools are public schools with a particular theme or academic focus, such as mathematics, science, technology, business, or performing arts. In 2007, there are over 350 magnet schools in operation.

Charter schools are another public school option in Florida. There are also over 350 charter schools operating in Florida, serving almost 100,000 students. Virtual charter schools are a new and exciting addition to the Florida public school arena. There are currently two virtual charter schools operating in Florida, Florida Connections Academy and Florida Virtual Academy.

The second venue for schooling in Florida is private education. Private schools exist for many reasons, including religious instruction and prestige.

Questions for Reflection

1. Visit one of the two Florida virtual charter schools, <u>Florida Virtual Academy</u> or <u>Florida Connections Academy</u>.
    - How is this school organized?
    - Describe some features of the school. Which impressed you the most? Why?
    - Research how the school participates in standardized testing. Analyze recent test results. Would you identify this school as effective? Why or why not?
    - What types of subjects are offered for students? Did any of the course offerings surprise you? Why or why not?

2. Cypress Elementary School in Pasco County, Florida, is considered an exemplary traditional public school, winning National Honors from the Kennedy Center Alliance. Visit this school's Website at http://cesonline.pasco.k12.fl.us/.
    - How is this school organized?
    - Describe some features of the school. Which impressed you the most? Why?
    - Research the school's report card and standardized test scores. Would you identify this school as effective? Why or why not?
    - Compare and contrast this traditional school with the virtual charter school you chose for reflection 1. Which would you prefer to teach at and why?

Objective 4: Evaluate how cultural diversity impacts Florida classrooms.

According to the Florida Department of Education's Website, the public school population in Florida is both ethnically and culturally diverse. In proportion to other ethnic groups, the Hispanic population has experienced the greatest growth. In 2006, the population percentages in Florida were:

- White-46.7%
- Hispanic-24.2%
- Black- 23.2%
- Asian-2.3%
- American Indian-0.3%
- Multiracial-3.3%

Florida is home to many different cultures. Take a closer look at the diversity in Florida by locating the listing of the school districts in the state (http://www.fldoe.org/schoolmap/flash/schoolmap_text.asp).

If you are unfamiliar with the names and locations, a geographical region of the state map is provided (http://www.fldoe.org/schoolmap/flash/regionalmap.asp?bhcp=1).

Questions for Reflection

1. Choose one school district in the state of Florida and take a tour of the webpage for the district you choose. As you read about the nature of education in this location, identify aspects of culture and diversity in this district.
2. Pretend that you have been hired to teach in this district. How do you think cultural diversity will affect your classroom?

Objective 5: Evaluate how socioeconomic status affects Florida students.

According to the Florida Department of Education Website, Florida's growing numbers of students eligible for free or reduced-price lunch may be one factor in reflecting the economic status of students' home communities.

In 1998, the number of students who were eligible for free-or reduced lunches was 1,019,815. In 2005, that number rose to 1,223,442.

The poverty rate in Florida has risen from 12.8% in 2005 to 13.1% in 2007. Recent figures show that Escambia County has recently surpassed Miami-Dade as the poorest county in the state.

Questions for Reflection

1. Look at the poverty rates for counties in Florida at http://www.ers.usda.gov/Data/povertyrates/PovListpct.asp?st=FL&view=Percent&longname=Florida. Which counties have the lowest poverty rates? The highest? Would you be willing to work in a county with a high poverty rate? Why or why not?
2. Read through the poverty resources at http://www.tolerance.org/teach/magazine/features.jsp?is=40&ar=777 . How do you think poverty will affect your classroom? How will you deal with this issue in your own classroom?

Important Sources

Florida Educator Accomplished Practices (Pre-professional)
http://www.fldoe.org/dpe/publications/preprofessional4-99.pdf
In Florida, professional educators are required to demonstrate proficiency in twelve sets of skills and practices. These skills are considered essential components of effective teaching. Teacher educators in Florida have re-structured these proficiencies in order to better prepare preservice teachers for the task of meeting the FEAP competencies.

Florida Department of Education

http://www.fldoe.org/

This Website is a vital link for teachers, parents, students, and community members interested in the educational policies, procedures, and resources in Florida.

Teach in Florida

http://www.teachinflorida.com/

Developed by the Florida Department of Education and MyFlorida.com, this Website offers information for prospective teachers in Florida. Information at this site includes searching for jobs, state information, and resources for practicing teachers. Additionally, there is a job search engine, a list of job fairs in the state, and an area to post your teaching resume.

Florida Education Association

http://www.feaweb.org/

This is the Website of the state affiliate of the National Education Association (NEA). The organization dates back to 1886 with the formation of the first professional educators' organization in the state, later known as the Teachers' Union.

Florida School Grades

http://schoolgrades.fldoe.org/

The Florida Department of Education provides a searchable database of state-, district-, and school-wide performances on standardized tests.

Florida Department of Education-No Child Left Behind Site

http://www.fldoe.org/nclb

This component of the FLDOE Website includes reports, information, and fact sheets about the use of NCLB in Florida schools.

The Bureau of Exceptional Education and Student Services

http://www.fldoe.org/ese/linkhome.asp

"Administers programs for students with disabilities and for gifted students. Additionally, the bureau coordinates student services throughout the state and participates in multiple inter-agency efforts designed to strengthen the quality and variety of services available to students with special needs."

Florida State Certification Exam Practice Questions

Directions: The following are 10 multiple-choice questions. Each question prompt is followed by 4 answer choices. Select the response that BEST answers the question.

Question #1

There are many advantages to having classrooms that include students from diverse cultural backgrounds. Which strategies are used by culturally responsive teachers?

- (A)   organizing the class into groups with similar backgrounds
- (B)   expecting students to demonstrate particular traits and characteristics
- (C)   ignoring students' cultural backgrounds in classroom interactions
- (D)   affirming students from the various cultural backgrounds

Question #2

Mrs. Forest decided to focus on enriching her students' communication skills, particularly in written expression. She is aware that some students in her class have been limited in their exposure to writing. Which of these best identifies how she can respond to the needs of her students?

- (A)   Share several samples of good writing with the students and ask them to analyze each. Then, tell the students what they should do when they write.
- (B)   Give the students several samples of writing on a scale of excellent to poor writing. Then, ask the students for examples of good and bad writing practices.
- (C)   Provide several stories for the students to read. Then, requiring students to connect the stories to their own experiences.
- (D)   Ask groups of students to edit pieces of writing for grammar, usage and punctuation. Then, remind the students to include an introduction, body, and conclusion.

Question #3

Teachers, working as a team, are requiring that students create a multidisciplinary report (integrating science, social studies, math, and literature). In order to ensure that students focus on the content, rather than details in the presentation, which step would be most effective?

- (A)   Create a list of topics students must use for the report.
- (B)   Prepare a grading rubric that focuses on content and presentation.
- (C)   Require students to present an outline of the proposed topics.
- (D)   Encourage students to work in small groups and rotate roles on the tasks.

Question #4

Mr. Cho teaches two math classes back-to-back, consisting of students with about the same mathematic abilities as reported on previous records. Additionally, both classes have the same number of students; however, in one class, there are a lot of absences. The class with the fewer absences seems to score better overall, and the class with the most absences has lower grades overall.

Which assessment system offers Mr. Cho a positive and supportive learning environment for all his students when determining grades?

(A)   Mr. Cho should use different standards to determine grades of different abilities for students.
(B)   Mr Cho should provide students feedback based on peer assessments and teacher assessments.
(C)   Mr. Cho should give a variety of measures to assess process, progress, and final products.
(D)   Mr. Cho should administer tests and quizzes with a variety of difficulty levels.

The following scenario should be used in answering questions #5, #6, and #7.

Sammy, age 9, is a new student in Mr. Halfax's class. When Sammy first participated in class two days ago, the students laughed at his response. Now, Sammy sits quietly by himself and does not participate.

Question #5

Mr. Halfax notes that relations between Sammy and other students in the class are beginning to be tense. Which of these is the best response to the observed tensions?

(A)   Provide positive reinforcement for all students who respond to answers.
(B)   Give some type of punishment for students who laugh at others' responses.
(C)   Develop a new seating chart for the classroom with students in small groups.
(D)   Reinforce positive attitudes toward peers and academic success.

Question #6

After a parent conference, Mr. Halfax believes he understands more about Sammy's likes, dislikes, learning styles, moods, family background and personality. If Mr. Halfax talks to Sammy, which of these most likely be a successful tactic?

(A)   Mr. Halfax should focus on the importance of Sammy's family rather than his immediate friends.
(B)   Mr. Halfax should focus on activities Sammy can take place in outside of school and during weekends.
(C)   Mr. Halfax should focus on Sammy's strengths in comparison to other students.
(D)   Mr. Halfax should focus on current ways Sammy can get attention, rather than delayed gratification.

Question #7

Using puppets to role play a similar scenario in his classroom, Mr. Halfax introduced the concern about making friends with new students. The puppets asked his students for suggestions about how to create a caring classroom. What did Mr. Halfax most likely promote in his classroom?

(A)   Mr. Halfax taught students to talk openly about their feelings.
(B)   The puppets allow students to recognize and appreciate new ideas.
(C)   Simulations encourage students to think about how to change their behavior.
(D)   The activity fosters a sense of community and support among students.

Question # 8

Which statistic on an individualized score report is best for comparing students in one district to other students across the U.S.?

(A)   grade equivalent
(B)   normal curve equivalent
(C)   local percentile rank
(D)   raw score

Question #9

What is the meaning of a least restrictive environment?

(A)   a program of education specifically designed for learners of one cultural group so that they develop language skills
(B)   educating students with diversity issues using positive reinforcements, social activity, tangible rewards, and feedback
(C)   educating students with and students without disabilities to the maximum extent possible
(D)   a program of education specifically designed for students with an individualized education plan

Question #10

Which of these characteristics is representative of a good decision maker?

(A)   Relies on intuitive practical considerations.
(B)   Uses a theory to understand a problem.
(C)   Makes deliberate and rapid assumptions.
(D)   Guards choices before selecting a response.

ANSWER KEY

Question Number	Key
1	D
2	B
3	A
4	C
5	A
6	D
7	D
8	C
9	C
10	B

Philosophical Foundations of U.S. Education

6

Philosophical Foundations of U.S. Education

I try to provide opportunities for my students to be active agents in change, which affirms who they are and what they consider important. I also collaborate with students' families, the community, and other social justice educators. Such teaching can shape, transform, and influence individuals whose everyday decisions, in turn, have an impact on the rest of society.

Kimberly Min, third-grade teacher, Quoted in
Teaching to Change the World, 2007, p. 491

CLASSROOM CASE
The Realities of Teaching

THE CHALLENGE: Articulating your educational philosophy and deciding what knowledge is of greatest worth.

Mrs. Pushkov, your mentor teacher, teaches social studies in the classroom next to yours. She takes what she calls a "critical, social justice" approach to teaching—that is, she wants her students to question the status quo. She wants them to learn the important role they can play in improving the world.

To raise her students' level of awareness, Mrs. Pushkov has them think about how race, socioeconomic status, and gender are reflected in political events and human rights violations around the world. Prior to the 2008 Olympics in Beijing, for example, she spent several class sessions explaining to students how Chinese policies in Tibet had led to recent demonstrations in support of Tibet around the world.

Her students often participate in small-group projects, simulations, role-plays, and classroom debates on societal issues. And from time to time, Mrs. Pushkov organizes her students to take action to address local social problems. Last week, as part of a unit on the homeless in the city, her students spent the weekend helping at a neighborhood soup kitchen.

Some of Mrs. Pushkov's fellow teachers are skeptical about her methods. They believe her teaching is "too political" and that she does her students a disservice by making them believe that they can change the world. These teachers also point out that parents want their children to learn the traditional basics rather than learn how to become social activists.

Today, you have just joined Mrs. Pushkov and two other teachers in the teachers' lunchroom. They are discussing strategies for teaching writing. "My kids really got involved in the unit on the homeless," Mrs. Pushkov says. "Now they're working hard to express in writing what they experienced last week at the soup kitchen. They believe they have something to say. Two of my kids even plan to send their papers to the editorial page of the newspaper."

"What do students *really* learn from assignments like that?" asks the teacher seated across the table from Mrs. Pushkov. "I don't think our kids need to be firing off letters to the editor, getting involved in all of these causes. We should just teach them how to write—period. Then if they want to focus on eliminating poverty, crime, or whatever, that should be their decision."

The teacher then looks at you and asks, "What do you think?"

121

FOCUS QUESTIONS

1. Why is philosophy important to teachers?
2. What is the nature of philosophy?
3. What determines your educational philosophy?
4. What are the branches of philosophy?
5. What are five modern philosophical orientations to teaching?
6. What psychological orientations have influenced teaching philosophies?
7. How can you develop your educational philosophy?

As the classroom case for this chapter suggests, teachers can have conflicting views regarding how to answer vital questions about their work. What should the purpose(s) of education be? What knowledge is of most worth? What values should teachers encourage their students to develop? How should learning be evaluated? As difficult as these questions might be, teachers must answer them. To answer these and similar questions, teachers use philosophy.

WHY IS PHILOSOPHY IMPORTANT TO TEACHERS?

Today's schools reflect the philosophical foundations and the aspirations and values brought to this country by its founders and generations of settlers. Understanding the philosophical ideas that have shaped education in the United States is an important part of your education as a professional. This understanding will enable you "to think clearly about what [you] are doing, and to see what [you] are doing in the larger context of individual and social development" (Ozmon & Craver, 2007).

Still, you may wonder, what is the value of knowing about the philosophy of education? Will that knowledge help you become a better teacher? An understanding of the philosophy of education will enhance your professionalism in three important ways. First, knowledge of philosophy of education will help you understand the complex political forces that influence schools. When people act politically to influence schools, their actions reflect their educational philosophies. Second, knowledge of how philosophy has influenced our schools will help you evaluate more effectively current proposals for change. You will be in a better position to evaluate changes if you understand how schools have developed and how current proposals might relate to previous change efforts. Last, awareness of how philosophy has influenced teaching is a hallmark of professionalism in education.

In addition, philosophy can reveal principles that may be used as a guide for professional action. Some teachers disagree and think that philosophical reflections have nothing to contribute to the actual act of teaching (this stance, of course, is itself a philosophy of education). However, as the great educational philosopher John Dewey (1916, p. 383) put it, to be concerned with education is to be concerned with philosophy: "If we are willing to conceive education as the process of forming fundamental dispositions, intellectual and emotional, toward nature and fellow men, philosophy may even be defined as *the general theory of education*."

Philosophy is also important to schools. Most schools have a statement of philosophy that serves to focus the efforts of teachers, administrators, students, and parents in a desired direction. A school's philosophy is actually a public statement of school values, a description of the educational goals it seeks to attain. So important is a school's philosophy that school accrediting agencies evaluate schools partially on the basis of whether they achieve the goals set forth in their statements of philosophy.

WHAT IS THE NATURE OF PHILOSOPHY?

Philosophy is concerned with identifying the basic truths about being, knowledge, and conduct. While the religions of the world arrive at these truths based on supernatural revelations, philosophers use their reasoning powers to search for answers to the fundamental questions of life. Philosophers use a careful, step-by-step, question-and-answer technique to extend their understanding of the world. Through very exacting use of language and techniques of linguistic and conceptual analysis, philosophers attempt to describe the world in which we live.

The word *philosophy* may be literally translated from the original Greek as "love of wisdom." In particular, a philosophy is a set of ideas formulated to comprehend the world. Among the world's great philosophers have been Socrates, Plato, Aristotle, Saint Thomas Aquinas, Réné Descartes, John Locke, David Hume, Jean-Jacques Rousseau, Immanuel Kant, Georg Hegel, John Stuart Mill, Karl Marx, John Dewey, Jean-Paul Sartre, and Mortimer Adler. They devoted their lives to pondering the significant questions of life: What is truth? What is reality? What life is worth living?

WHAT DETERMINES YOUR EDUCATIONAL PHILOSOPHY?

In simplest terms, your **educational philosophy** consists of what you believe about education—the set of principles that guides your professional action.

Every teacher, whether he or she recognizes it, has a philosophy of education—a set of beliefs about how human beings learn and grow and what one should learn in order to live the good life. Professional teachers recognize that teaching, because it is concerned with *what ought to be*, is basically a philosophical enterprise.

Your behavior as a teacher is strongly connected to your beliefs about teaching and learning, students, knowledge, and what is worth knowing (see Figure 4.1). Regardless of where you stand in regard to these dimensions of teaching, you should be aware of the need to reflect continually on *what* you do believe and *why* you believe it. For example, if your teacher education program is accredited by the National Council for Accreditation of Teacher Education (NCATE) (approximately half of the programs in the nation are), you will be required to learn about educational philosophy in light of the following NCATE standard: "[Teacher candidates] understand and are able to apply knowledge related to the . . . philosophical foundations of education. (National Council for Accreditation of Teacher Education, 2002, p. 196)

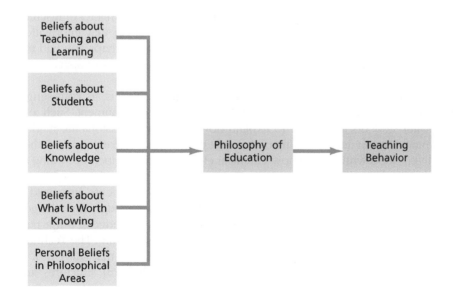

FIGURE 4.1 Educational beliefs and teaching behavior

Beliefs About Teaching and Learning

One of the most important components of your educational philosophy is your belief about teaching and learning. In other words, what will be your primary role as a teacher? Will it be to transmit knowledge to students and then to guide their practice as they develop skills in using that knowledge? Or will it be to develop self-directed learners by building on students' interests, prior experiences, and current understandings? The first view emphasizes *transmission* of knowledge to students, while the second view emphasizes students' *construction* of knowledge.

The transmission view emphasizes changes in students' behavior. Learning involves making associations between various stimuli and responses. In other words, learning results from forces that are *external* to the individual. The constructivist view, on the other hand, emphasizes the individual student's experiences and cognitions. Learning occurs when personal experiences lead to changes in thoughts or actions. That is, learning is largely the result of *internal* forces within the individual. To assess your current beliefs about teaching and learning, complete the activity presented in Figure 4.2.

Beliefs About Students

Your beliefs about students will have a great influence on how you teach. Every teacher formulates an image in his or her mind about what students are like—their dispositions, skills, motivation levels, and expectations. What you believe students are like is based on your unique life experiences, particularly your observations of young people and your knowledge of human growth and development.

Negative views of students may promote teacher-student relationships based on fear and coercion rather than on trust and helpfulness. Extremely positive views may risk not providing students with sufficient structure and direction and not communicating sufficiently high expectations. In the final analysis, the truly professional teacher—the one who has a carefully thought-out educational philosophy—recognizes that, although children differ in their predispositions to learn and grow, they all *can* learn. In regard to beliefs about students, it is important that teachers convey positive attitudes toward their students and a belief that they *can* learn.

Beliefs About Knowledge

How teachers view knowledge is directly related to how they go about teaching. If teachers view knowledge as the sum total of small bits of subject matter or discrete facts, students will most likely spend a great deal of time learning that information in a straightforward, rote manner. Recall your own school days; perhaps you had to memorize the capitals of the fifty states, definitions for the eight parts of speech, the periodic table in chemistry, and so on.

Other teachers view knowledge more conceptually, that is, as consisting of the big ideas that enable us to understand and influence our environment. Such a teacher would want students to be able to explain how legislative decisions are made in the state capital, how an understanding of the eight parts of speech can empower the writer and enliven one's writing, and how chemical elements are grouped according to their atomic numbers.

Finally, teachers differ in their beliefs about whether students' increased understanding of their own experiences is a legitimate form of knowledge. Knowledge of self and one's experiences in the world is not the same as knowledge about a particular subject, yet personal knowledge is essential for a full, satisfying life. The Technology in Action feature for this chapter profiles a teacher who believes that study of a foreign language should go beyond knowledge of correct grammatical structures and rote

124

For each pair of statements about the teacher's role, circle the response that most closely reflects where you stand regarding the two perspectives. Remember, there are no correct responses, and neither perspective is better than the other.

Constructivist Perspective		Transmission Perspective
"I mainly see my role as a facilitator. I try to provide opportunities and resources for my students to discover or construct concepts for themselves."	*vs.*	"That's all nice, but students really won't learn the subject unless you go over the material in a structured way. It's my job to explain, to show students how to do the work, and to assign specific practice."

Definitely Prefer	Tend to Prefer	Cannot Decide	Tend to Prefer	Definitely Prefer

Constructivist Perspective		Transmission Perspective
"It is a good idea to have all sorts of activities going on in the classroom. Some students might produce a scene from a play they read. Others might create a miniature version of the set. It's hard to get the logistics right, but the successes are so much more important than the failures."	*vs.*	"It's more practical to give the whole class the same assignment, one that has clear directions, and one that can be done in short intervals that match students' attention spans and the daily class schedule."

Definitely Prefer	Tend to Prefer	Cannot Decide	Tend to Prefer	Definitely Prefer

Constructivist Perspective		Transmission Perspective
"The most important part of instruction is that it encourage 'sense-making' or thinking among students. Content is secondary."	*vs.*	"The most important part of instruction is the content of the curriculum. That content is the community's judgment about what children need to be able to know and do."

Definitely Prefer	Tend to Prefer	Cannot Decide	Tend to Prefer	Definitely Prefer

Constructivist Perspective		Transmission Perspective
"It is critical for students to become interested in doing academic work—interest and effort are more important than the particular subject-matter they are working on."	*vs.*	"While student motivation is certainly useful, it should not drive what students study. It is more important that students learn the history, science, math, and language skills in their textbooks."

Definitely Prefer	Tend to Prefer	Cannot Decide	Tend to Prefer	Definitely Prefer

FIGURE 4.2 Where do you stand?

Source: Adapted from Jason L. Ravitz, Henry Jay Becker, and Yan Tien Wong. Constructivist-Compatible Beliefs and Practices Among U.S. Teachers. *Center for Research on Information Technology and Organizations, University of California, Irvine; and University of Minnesota, July 2000.*

memorization of vocabulary words. For this teacher, the personal knowledge a student gains from cross-national communication is a valid goal for foreign language study.

Beliefs About What Is Worth Knowing

Teachers have different ideas about what should be taught. One teacher, who tends to prefer a transmission view of teaching, believes it is most important that students learn the basic skills of reading, writing, computation, and oral communication. These are the

TECHNOLOGY in *ACTION*

Web Conferencing in 11th-Grade Chinese Language Class

Louise Zhao has taught Advanced Chinese at Lincoln High School for the past 5 years. Her approach is part presentation and lots and lots of practice. Whenever possible, she tries to bring in native Chinese speakers to speak to her class, but this usually takes the form of a presentation. However, the presentation did not give her students what she was really after—to have her students engage in extensive one-on-one conversations with Chinese speakers.

Mrs. Zhao was born in Shanghai and still has family living there. She communicates with them often using various online communication tools, but it was not until she walked in on her 13-year-old son carrying on a video phone call with his cousin living in Shanghai that she realized she had the solution to her classroom dilemma. The next day she went to her principal and presented her idea. He agreed and she began to develop her lesson plan.

Through her family connections, she made contact with a high school teacher in Shanghai, Mr. Lee. He teaches English to Chinese students. The two teachers agreed that they would have their students meet once each week, for one hour, via Elluminate. Elluminate is web conferencing software that allows individuals or groups to conference via text, audio, and/or graphics online. The local community college had just purchased an Elluminate web conferencing license. As part of its community outreach, the community college allowed the local school district in its service area to use the tool. Each student in Mrs. Zhao's class would be paired with a student in Mr. Lee's class. During their one-hour Elluminate session, they would speak Chinese for the first 30 minutes and then speak English for the next 30 minutes. The session would also be recorded so Mr. Lee and Mrs. Zhao could review the individual conversations at a later time and provide feedback to their students.

To make this happen, however, Mrs. Zhao realized she had a lot to do. She had to schedule the weekly events—adjusting for time-zone differences. She had to pair the students, ensure that the students stayed on task, and create a setting conducive for one-on-one conversation.

Luckily for Mrs. Zhao, the school's computer lab was quite modern, and each computer in the lab had been fitted with microphone headsets. The headset speakers would keep out external noise so that her 20-plus students seated in the computer lab could chat away and not disturb their neighbors. With the setting and technology taken care of, the next thing she had to deal with was timing. There was no way that she could make the timing of this event coincide within the hours of the standard school day. What she decided to do was make these events voluntary. To her surprise, all of her students agreed to attend the first session. At 4:00 P.M. each Thursday, her students would meet in the computer lab, click on their Elluminate session proposal, and connect with their counterparts in Shanghai, who were seated at their computers at 7:00 A.M. the next day, their time. This novelty was the first thing the students discussed. Although they are only halfway through the semester, the students appear each week for their conversations with their friends on the other side of the world.

WEB CONFERENCING: Web conferencing allows individuals or groups to connect on the Web via video and/or audio. This is usually a synchronous or live session in which individuals are seated at their computers and interact with others. Participants can be in the same building or in another country. To participate in a web videoconference, you will need a USB video input, a microphone, appropriate computer sound and video cards, the video conferencing software or plugin, and an Internet connection robust enough to handle a web conference.

VISIT: http://thinkofit.com/webconf/index.htm

This website offers thorough reviews of many web conferencing options.

POSSIBLE USES: Teachers have used web conferencing for tutoring sessions, meeting with parents, bringing outside speakers into their classroom, pursuing professional development opportunities, and connecting with colleagues around the country.

TRY IT OUT: There are many options to choose from if you would like to have your students participate in a web videoconference. If you visit the site listed above, you will have the opportunity to try many of them on a temporary basis for free. One easy web conferencing solution is Windows Messenger. Just open Messenger and click on Start Video Conversation. Type in the e-mail address of the person you want to conference with and you are connected.

skills they will need to be successful in their chosen occupations, and it is the school's responsibility to prepare students for the world of work. Another teacher believes that the most worthwhile content is to be found in the classics, or the Great Books. Through mastering the great ideas from the sciences, mathematics, literature, and history, students will be well prepared to deal with the world of the future. Still another teacher, one who tends toward a constructivist view of teaching, is most concerned with students learning how to reason, communicate effectively, and solve problems. Students who master these cognitive processes will have learned how to learn—and this is the most realistic preparation for an unknown future. And finally, another teacher is concerned with developing the whole child, teaching students to become self-actualizing persons. Thus, the content of the curriculum should be meaningful to the student, contributing as much as possible to the student's efforts to become a mature, well-integrated person. As you can see, there are no easy answers to the question, What knowledge is of most worth? Your beliefs about teaching and learning, students, knowledge, and what knowledge is worth knowing thus are the foundation of your educational philosophy. To reflect further on these beliefs, go to MyEducationLab and examine a "subtraction story" a young child wrote to show what she knows about numbers. Based on this example, what do you think this child's teacher believes about teaching and learning, students, knowledge, and what knowledge is worth knowing?

PEARSON
myeducationlab

Go to MyEducationLab, select Chapter 4 and then Activities and Applications to analyze the artifact Write a Subtraction Story.

WHAT ARE THE BRANCHES OF PHILOSOPHY?

To provide you with additional tools to use in formulating and clarifying your educational philosophy, this section presents brief overviews of six areas of philosophy that are of central concern to teachers: metaphysics, epistemology, axiology, ethics, aesthetics, and logic. Each of these areas focuses on one of the questions that have concerned the world's greatest philosophers for centuries: What is the nature of reality? What is the nature of knowledge and is truth ever attainable? According to what values should one live life? What is good and what is evil? What is the nature of beauty and excellence? And finally, What processes of reasoning will yield consistently valid results?

Metaphysics

Metaphysics is concerned with explaining, as rationally and as comprehensively as possible, the nature of reality (in contrast to how reality *appears*). What is reality? What is the world made of? These are metaphysical questions. Metaphysics is also concerned with the nature of being and explores questions such as, What does it mean to exist? What is humankind's place in the scheme of things? Metaphysical questions such as these are at the very heart of educational philosophy. As one educational philosopher put it, "nothing short of the fullest awareness possible of 'man's place in the cosmos' is the constant problem of the philosopher of education" (Bertocci, 1956, p. 158). Or as two educational philosophers put it: "Our ultimate preoccupation in educational theory is with the most primary of all philosophic problems: metaphysics, the study of ultimate reality" (Morris & Pai, 1994, p. 28).

Metaphysics has important implications for education because the school curriculum is based on what we know about reality. And what we know about reality is driven by the kinds of questions we ask about the world. In fact, any position regarding what the schools should teach has behind it a particular view of reality, a particular set of responses to metaphysical questions.

Epistemology

The next major set of philosophical questions that concerns teachers is called **epistemology.** These questions all focus on knowledge: What knowledge is true? How does knowing take place? How do we know that we know? How do we decide between opposing views of knowledge? Is truth constant, or does it change from situation to situation? And finally, What knowledge is of most worth?

How you answer the epistemological questions that confront all teachers will have significant implications for your teaching. First, you will need to determine what is true about the content you will teach, then you must decide on the most appropriate means of teaching this content to students. Even a casual consideration of epistemological questions reveals that there are many ways of knowing about the world, at least five of which are of interest to teachers.

1. **Knowing based on authority**—for example, knowledge from the sage, the poet, the priest, or the ruler. In schools, the textbook, the teacher, and the administrator are the sources of authority for students. In everyday conversations, we refer to unnamed experts as sources of authoritative knowledge: "*They* say we'll have a manned flight to Mars by the middle of the century."

2. **Knowing based on divine revelation**—for example, knowledge in the form of supernatural revelations from the sun god of early peoples, the many gods of the ancient Greeks, or the Judeo-Christian god.

3. **Knowing based on empiricism (experience)**—for example, knowledge acquired through the senses, the informally gathered empirical data that direct most of our daily behavior. When we state that experience is the best teacher, we refer to this mode of knowing.

4. **Knowing based on reason and logical analysis**—for example, knowledge inferred from the process of thinking logically. In schools, students learn to apply rational thought to tasks such as solving mathematical problems, distinguishing facts from opinions, or defending or refuting a particular argument. Many students also learn a method of reasoning and analyzing empirical data known as the scientific method. Through this method, a problem is identified, relevant data are gathered, a hypothesis is formulated based on these data, and the hypothesis is empirically tested.

5. **Knowing based on intuition**—for example, knowledge arrived at without the use of rational thought. Intuition draws from our prior knowledge and experience and gives us an immediate understanding of the situation at hand. Our intuition convinces us that we know something, but we don't know how we know.

Axiology

The next set of philosophical problems concerns values. Teachers are concerned with values "because school is not a neutral activity. The very idea of school expresses a set of values" (Nelson, Carlson, & Palonsky, 2000, p. 304).

Among the axiological questions teachers must answer for themselves are: What values should teachers encourage students to adopt? What values raise humanity to our highest expressions of humaneness? What values does a truly educated person hold?

Axiology highlights the fact that the teacher has an interest not only in the *quantity* of knowledge that students acquire but also in the *quality* of life that becomes possible because of that knowledge. Extensive knowledge may not benefit the individual if he or she is unable to put that knowledge to good use. This point raises additional questions: How do we define quality of life? What curricular experiences contribute most to that quality of life? All teachers must deal with the issues raised by these questions.

Ethics

While axiology addresses the question, What is valuable? **ethics** focuses on, What is good and evil, right and wrong, just and unjust?

Knowledge of ethics can help the teacher solve many of the dilemmas that arise in the classroom. Frequently, teachers must take action in situations where they are unable to gather all the relevant facts and where no single course of action is totally right or wrong. For example, a student whose previous work was above average plagiarizes a term paper: Should the teacher fail the student for the course if the example of swift, decisive punishment will likely prevent other students from plagiarizing? Or should the teacher, following her hunches about what would be in the student's long-term interest, have the student redo the term paper and risk the possibility that other students might get the mistaken notion that plagiarism has no negative consequences? Another ethical dilemma: Is an elementary mathematics teacher justified in trying to increase achievement for the whole class by separating two disruptive girls and placing one in a mathematics group beneath her level of ability?

Ethics can provide the teacher with ways of thinking about problems where it is difficult to determine the right course of action. Ethics also helps teachers to understand that "ethical thinking and decision making are not just following the rules" (Strike & Soltis, 1985, p. 3). This chapter's Teachers' Voices: Research to Reality feature illustrates the lessons learned by one teacher after grappling with an ethical dilemma.

Aesthetics

The branch of axiology known as **aesthetics** is concerned with values related to beauty and art. Although we expect that teachers of music, art, drama, literature, and writing regularly have students make judgments about the quality of works of art, we can easily overlook the role that aesthetics ought to play in *all* areas of the curriculum. Harry Broudy, a well-known educational philosopher, said that the arts are necessary, not "just nice" (1979, pp. 347–350). Through the heightening of their aesthetic perceptions, students can find increased meaning in all aspects of life.

Aesthetics can also help the teacher increase his or her effectiveness. Because it may be viewed as a form of artistic expression, teaching can be judged according to artistic standards of beauty and quality. In this regard, the teacher is an artist whose medium of expression is the spontaneous, unrehearsed, and creative encounter between teacher and student.

Logic

Logic is the area of philosophy that deals with the process of reasoning and identifies rules that will enable the thinker to reach valid conclusions. The public is nearly unanimous in its belief that a key goal of education is to teach students how to think. The two kinds of logical thinking processes that teachers most frequently have students master are *deductive* and *inductive* thinking. The deductive approach requires the thinker to move from a general principle or proposition to a specific conclusion that is valid. By contrast, inductive reasoning moves from the specific to the general. Here, the student begins by examining particular examples that eventually lead to the acceptance of a general proposition. Inductive teaching is often referred to as discovery teaching—by which students discover, or create, their own knowledge of a topic.

Perhaps the best-known teacher to use the inductive approach to teaching was the Greek philosopher Socrates (ca. 470–399 B.C.). His method of teaching, known today as

How might this teacher be helping his students develop their logical thinking skills? With reference to the level and subject area for which you are preparing to teach, what activities can help students develop their ability to think logically?

TEACHERS' VOICES RESEARCH TO REALITY

Marcus Goodyear
DOLLARS AND POINTS

Teacher Marcus Goodyear faced a dilemma after giving a student a grade of 50 for her final research paper because half of it was plagiarized. The research paper grade gave the student a six-weeks' grade of 69 (one point short of a passing grade of 70). The failing grade made the girl ineligible to compete in athletics. However, the teacher reflects on whether he made the "right" decision after meeting with the girl's upset parents and learning that the father has serious health problems.

After almost a week, I asked my principal for advice. What would he do? I asked my department head. Miraculously neither of them had ever become cynical, and so I trusted them. "Give her the point," they said. "It isn't worth it to hold the line. They'll drag you to the school board. They'll make you look like the villain. They'll examine every minor grade under a microscope. Just give her the point and let her have a seventy."

On the grade change form I checked "teacher error." The student became eligible. She went on to the state competition that year. "What will you say to the people you beat?" I wanted to ask her. "What will you say to the students who had enough honor not to plagiarize their research papers?" But I swallowed my pride. I swallowed some of my moral self-righteousness. I even swallowed my anger at parents who will bully their way through teachers and administrators and anyone else standing between them and their entitlements. Because I hadn't known about her dad's health problems. If the girl had just told me that she thought her father might die, I would have given her extra time on the paper. I would have allowed more makeup work. I would have helped her. I should have helped her.

Part of me still felt like I was compromising academics for athletics. Part of me wanted to punish the student for the actions of her parents. But I learned an important lesson: Always err on the side of the student.

Because I do make mistakes, of course. I made a big mistake with that plagiarized paper—I assumed the worst of my student. I should have given the girl a chance to confess and rewrite the paper. Now I know to reward students for what they do well, rather than punish students for what they do poorly. Some students will need to face

consequences for their mistakes, but that can never become my focus as a teacher. It would destroy me. It would make me shrivel up into bitterness and indignation that the students, the teachers, the whole educational system was just going to hell. Everyone makes mistakes in the classroom, even me. That is what the classroom is for. And those mistakes will only make me worthless and vindictive if I remain proud and absolute. Like some one-room schoolhouse tyrant. Or like the cynics down the hall.

During that conference [with the girl's parents] I also realized that no amount of points brings value to a student's education. Passing my class, passing the state achievement test, even passing the Advanced Placement test were all based on an economic view of the world. These things reduce human actions and feelings to a few numbers—either test scores or the price of a college class. These things work as external rewards, but the biggest rewards are always internal. In addition to points, I can give my students respect and trust and confidence and faith. They need to become adults; they need me to treat them like adults.

Why would I treat them any other way?

Above all I finally realized that I teach for the students. Not their parents. Not my peers. Not even for myself or the paycheck at the end of every month. I teach for my students to rise above their mistakes.

And the mistakes of their teachers.

Some of them will. I know it.

QUESTIONS

1. Based on his account of the plagiarism incident, what are Goodyear's views about the following elements of educational philosophy: Beliefs about teaching and learning? Beliefs about students? Beliefs about knowledge? Beliefs about what is worth knowing?

2. Why does Goodyear decide to change his student's grade? Do you agree or disagree with his decision? Why?

3. What ethical dilemmas might you encounter when you begin to teach? How will you resolve those ethical dilemmas?

Marcus Goodyear teaches at O'Connor High School in San Antonio, Texas. The preceding is excerpted from his chapter that appears in Molly Hoekstra (ed.), *Am I Teaching Yet? Stories from the Teacher-Training Trenches*, Portsmouth, NH: Heinemann, 2002, pp. 70–75.

the Socratic method, consisted of holding philosophical conversations (dialectics) with his pupils. **Socratic questioning** is a discussion that is characterized by the following:

- The discussion leader only asks questions.
- The discussion is systematic (not a free-for-all).
- The leader's questions direct the discussion.
- Everyone participates in an effort to "go beneath the surface" and to explore the complexities of the topic or issue under discussion.

The legacy of Socrates lives in all teachers who use Socratic questioning to encourage students to think for themselves. Figure 4.3 presents "The Art of Socratic Questioning Checklist."

The next section examines philosophical orientations to teaching that have been developed in response to the branches of philosophy we have just examined.

The following list can be used to foster disciplined questioning on the part of students. Students might take turns leading Socratic discussions in groups. During the process, some students might be asked to observe the students leading the discussion, and then afterward provide feedback using the following guidelines (which all students should have a copy of during the discussion).

1. Did the questioner respond to all answers with another question?

2. Did the questioner make the *goal* of the discussion clear?
   (What is the goal of this discussion? What are we trying to accomplish?)

3. Did the questioner pursue relevant *information*?
   (What information are you basing that comment on? What experience convinced you of that?)

4. Did the questioner question *inferences,* interpretations, and conclusions where appropriate or significant?
   (How did you reach that conclusion? Could you explain your reasoning? Is there another possible interpretation?)

5. Did the questioner focus on key ideas or *concepts*?
   (What is the main idea you are putting forth? Could you explain that idea?)

6. Did the questioner note questionable *assumptions*?
   (What exactly are you taking for granted here? Why are you assuming that?)

7. Did the questioner question *implications* and consequences?
   (What are you implying when you say . . . ? Are you implying that . . . ? If people accepted your conclusion and then acted on it, what implications might follow?)

8. Did the questioner call attention to the *point of view* inherent in various answers?
   (From what point of view are you looking at this? Is there another point of view we should consider?)

9. Did the questioner keep the central *question* in focus?
   (I am not sure exactly what question you are raising. Could you explain it? Remember that the question we are dealing with is . . . .)

10. Did the questioner call for a clarification of *context*, when necessary?
    (Tell us more about the situation that has given rise to this problem. What was going on in this situation?)

FIGURE 4.3 The art of Socratic questioning checklist
Source: Richard Paul and Linda L. Elder. (2006). The Thinker's Guide to the Art of Socratic Questioning. Dillon Beach, CA: Foundation for Critical Thinking, p. 10.

WHAT ARE FIVE MODERN PHILOSOPHICAL ORIENTATIONS TO TEACHING?

Five major coherent philosophical orientations to teaching have been developed in response to the questions concerning metaphysics, epistemology, axiology, ethics, aesthetics, and logic, with which all teachers must grapple. These orientations, or schools of thought, are perennialism, essentialism, progressivism, existentialism, and social reconstructionism. The following sections present a brief description of each of these orientations, moving from those that are teacher-centered to those that are student-centered (see Figure 4.4). Each description concludes with a sample portrait of a teacher whose behavior illustrates that philosophical orientation in action.

Perennialism

As the term implies, **perennialism** views truth as constant, or perennial. The aim of education, according to perennialist thinking, is to ensure that students acquire knowledge of these unchanging principles or great ideas. Perennialists also believe that the natural world and human nature have remained basically unchanged over the centuries; thus, the great ideas continue to have the most potential for solving the problems of any era. Furthermore, the perennialist philosophy emphasizes the rational thinking abilities of human beings; it is the cultivation of the intellect that makes human beings truly human and differentiates them from other animals.

The curriculum, according to perennialists, should stress students' intellectual growth in the arts and sciences. To become culturally literate, students should encounter in these areas the best, most significant works that humans have created. In regard to any area of the curriculum, only one question needs to be asked: Are students acquiring content that represents humankind's most lofty accomplishments in that area? Thus, a high school English teacher would require students to read Melville's *Moby Dick* or any of Shakespeare's plays rather than a novel on the current best-seller list. Similarly, science students would learn about the three laws of motion or the three laws of thermodynamics rather than build a model of the space shuttle.

Perennialist Educational Philosophers

Two of the best known advocates of the perennialist philosophy have been Robert Maynard Hutchins (1899–1977) and Mortimer Adler (1902–2001). As president of the University of Chicago, Hutchins (1963) developed an undergraduate curriculum based on the study of the Great Books and discussions of these classics in small seminars. Hutchins's perennialist curriculum was based on three assumptions about education:

1. Education must promote humankind's continuing search for truth. Whatever is true will always, and everywhere, be true; in short, truth is universal and timeless.

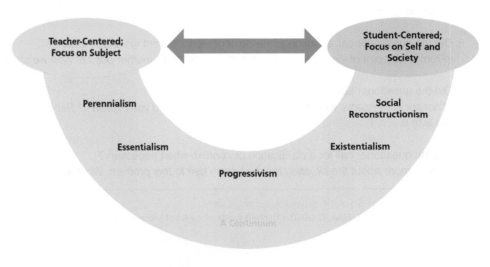

FIGURE 4.4 Five philosophical orientations to teaching

2. Because the mind's work is intellectual and focuses on ideas, education must also focus on ideas. The cultivation of human rationality is the essential function of education.

3. Education should stimulate students to think thoughtfully about significant ideas. Teachers should use correct and critical thinking as their primary method, and they should require the same of students.

Noted educational philosopher Mortimer Adler, along with Hutchins, was instrumental in organizing the Great Books of the Western World curriculum. Through the study of over 100 enduring classics, from Plato to Einstein, the Great Books approach aims at the major perennialist goal of teaching students to become independent and critical thinkers. It is a demanding curriculum, and it focuses on the enduring disciplines of knowledge rather than on current events or student interests.

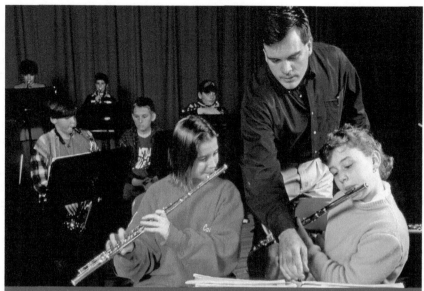

Perennialist teachers often inspire students to seek truth, discover universalities in human experience, and celebrate the achievement of human civilization. How might this music lesson reflect perennialist ideas? How might the lesson be different if it were based on the essentialist educational philosophy?

Portrait of a Perennialist Teacher

Mrs. Bernstein has been teaching English at the high school since the mid-1980s. Among students and teachers as well, she has a reputation for demanding a lot. As one student put it, "You don't waste time in Mrs. Bernstein's classes."

During the early 1990s, she had a difficult time dealing with students who aggressively insisted on being taught subjects that they called relevant. As a graduate of a top-notch university in the East, where she received a classical, liberal education, Mrs. Bernstein refused to lessen the emphasis in her classes on great works of literature that she felt students needed to know, such as *Beowulf* and the works of Chaucer, Dickens, and Shakespeare.

As far as her approach to classroom management is concerned, one student sums it up this way: "She doesn't let you get by with a thing; she never slacks off on the pressure. She lets you know that she's there to teach and you're there to learn." Mrs. Bernstein believes that hard work and effort are necessary if one is to get a good education. As a result, she gives students very few opportunities to misbehave, and she appears to be immune to the grumblings of students who do complain openly about the workload.

She becomes very animated when she talks about the value of the classics to students who are preparing to live as adults in the 21st century:

> The classics are unequaled in terms of the insights they can give students into the major problems that they will have to deal with during their lifetimes. Though our civilization has made impressive technological advances during the last two centuries, we have not really progressed that much in terms of improving the quality of our lives as human beings. The observations of a Shakespeare or a Dickens on the human condition are just as relevant today as they were when they were alive.

Essentialism

Essentialism, which has some similarities to perennialism, is a conservative philosophy of education originally formulated as a criticism of progressive trends in schools by William C. Bagley (1874–1946), a professor of education at Teachers College,

Columbia University. Bagley founded the Essentialistic Education Society and, to promote the society's views, the educational journal *School and Society*.

Essentialism holds that our culture has a core of common knowledge that the schools are obligated to transmit to students in a systematic, disciplined way. Unlike perennialists, who emphasize a set of external truths, essentialists stress what they believe to be the essential knowledge and skills (often termed "the basics") that productive members of our society need to know.

According to essentialist philosophy, schooling should be practical and provide children with sound instruction that prepares them for life; schools should not try to influence or set social policies. Critics of essentialism, however, charge that such a tradition-bound orientation to schooling will indoctrinate students and rule out the possibility of change. Essentialists respond that, without an essentialist approach, students will be indoctrinated in humanistic and/or behavioral curricula that run counter to society's accepted standards and need for order.

Portrait of an Essentialist Teacher

Mr. Samuels teaches mathematics at a junior high school in a poor section of a major urban area. Prior to coming to this school six years ago, he taught at a rural elementary school.

Middle-aged and highly energetic, Mr. Samuels is known around the school as a hardworking, dedicated teacher. His commitment to children is especially evident when he talks about preparing "his" children for life in high school and beyond. "A lot of teachers nowadays have given up on kids," he says with a touch of sadness to his voice. "They don't demand much of them. If we don't push kids now to get the knowledge and skills they're going to need later in life, we've failed them. My main purpose here is to see that my kids get the basics they're going to need."

Mr. Samuels has made it known that he does not approve of the methods used by some of the younger, more humanistic-oriented teachers in the school. At a recent faculty meeting, for example, he was openly critical of some teachers' tendency to "let students do their own thing" and spend time "expressing their feelings." He called for all teachers to focus their energies on getting students to master subject-matter content, "the things kids will need to know," rather than on helping students adjust to the interpersonal aspects of school life. He also reminded everyone that "kids come to school to learn." All students would learn, he pointed out, if "teachers based their methods on good, sound approaches that have always worked—not on the so-called innovative approaches that are based on fads and frills."

Mr. Samuels's students have accepted his no-nonsense approach to teaching. With few exceptions, his classes are orderly and businesslike. Each class period follows a standard routine. Students enter the room quietly and take their seats with a minimum of the foolishness and horseplay that mark the start of many other classes in the school. As the first order of business, the previous day's homework is returned and reviewed. Following this, Mr. Samuels presents the day's lesson, usually a 15- to 20-minute explanation of how to solve a particular kind of math problem. His minilectures are lively, and his wide-ranging tone of voice and animated, spontaneous delivery convey his excitement about the material and his belief that students can learn. During large-group instruction, Mr. Samuels also makes ample use of a whiteboard, software such as Geometer's Sketchpad, and manipulatives such as a large abacus and colored blocks of different sizes and shapes.

Progressivism

Progressivism is based on the belief that education should be child-centered rather than focused on the teacher or the content area. The writing of John Dewey (1859–1952) in the 1920s and 1930s contributed a great deal to the spread of progressive ideas. Briefly, Deweyan progressivism is based on the following three central assumptions:

1. The content of the curriculum ought to be derived from students' interests rather than from the academic disciplines.

2. Effective teaching takes into account the whole child and his or her interests and needs in relation to cognitive, affective, and psychomotor areas.

3. Learning is essentially active rather than passive.

Progressive Strategies

The progressive philosophy also contends that knowledge that is true in the present may not be true in the future. Hence, the best way to prepare students for an unknown future is to equip them with problem-solving strategies that will enable them to discover meaningful knowledge at various stages of their lives. Teachers with a progressive orientation give students a considerable amount of freedom in determining their school experiences. Contrary to the perceptions of many, however, progressive education does not mean that teachers do not provide structure or that students are free to do whatever they wish. Progressive teachers begin with where students are and, through the daily give-and-take of the classroom, lead students to see that the subject to be learned can enhance their lives.

In a progressively oriented classroom, the teacher serves as a guide or resource person whose primary responsibility is to facilitate student learning. The teacher helps students learn what is important to them rather than passing on a set of so-called enduring truths. Toward this end, the progressive teacher tries to provide students with experiences that replicate everyday life as much as possible. Students have many opportunities to work cooperatively in groups, often solving problems that the group, not the teacher, has identified as important. To understand how a progressive teaching philosophy emphasizes students' interests, go to MyEducationLab and examine a young student's attempt to write the Pledge of Allegiance from memory. How might an assignment related to the Pledge of Allegiance look different if it was developed by a teacher with a progressive educational philosophy?

myeducationlab

Go to MyEducationLab, select Chapter 4 and then Activities and Applications to analyze the artifact Pledge of Allegiance (Language Arts 3–5).

Portrait of a Progressive Teacher

Mr. Barkan teaches social studies at a middle school in a well-to-do part of the city. Boyishly handsome and in his mid-thirties, Mr. Barkan usually works in casual attire—khaki pants, soft-soled shoes, and a sports shirt. He seems to get along well with students. Mr. Barkan likes to give students as much freedom of choice in the classroom as possible. Accordingly, his room is divided into interest and activity centers, and much of the time students are free to choose where they want to spend their time. One corner at the back of the room has a library collection of paperback and hardcover books, an easy chair, and an area rug; the other back corner of the room is set up as a project area and has a worktable on which are several globes, maps, large sheets of newsprint, and assorted drawing materials. At the front of the room in one corner is a small media center with a computer and flat-screen monitor, laser printer, and DVD/VCR.

Mr. Barkan makes it a point to establish warm, supportive relationships with his students. He is proud of the fact that he is a friend to his

What hallmarks of progressive education are evident in this photograph of one of the first classrooms in the country operated according to Dewey's philosophy? What would a progressive classroom look like today?

students. "I really like the kids I teach," he says in a soft, gentle voice. "They're basically good kids, and they really want to learn if we teachers, I mean, can just keep their curiosity alive and not try to force them to learn. It's up to us as teachers to capitalize on their interests."

The visitor to Mr. Barkan's class today can sense his obvious regard for students. He is genuinely concerned about the growth and nurturance of each one. As his students spend most of their time working in small groups at the various activity centers in the room, Mr. Barkan divides his time among the groups. He moves from group to group and seems to immerse himself as an equal participant in each group's task. One group, for example, has been working on making a papier-mâché globe. Several students are explaining animatedly to him how they plan to transfer the flat map of the world they have drawn to the smooth sphere they have fashioned out of the papier-mâché. Mr. Barkan listens carefully to what his students have to say and then congratulates the group on how cleverly they have engineered the project. When he speaks to his students, he does so in a matter-of-fact, conversational tone, as though speaking to other adults.

As much as possible he likes to bring textbook knowledge to life by providing his students with appropriate experiences—field trips, small-group projects, simulation activities, role-playing, Internet explorations, and so on. Mr. Barkan believes that his primary function as a teacher is to prepare his students for an unknown future. Learning to solve problems at an early age is the best preparation for this future, he feels.

> The increase in the amount of knowledge each decade is absolutely astounding. What we teach students as true today will most likely not be true tomorrow. Therefore, students have to learn how to learn and become active problem-solvers. In addition, students need to learn how to identify problems that are meaningful to them. It doesn't make much sense to learn to solve problems that belong to someone else. To accomplish these things in the classroom, teachers have to be willing to take the lead from the students themselves—to use their lives as a point of departure for learning about the subject. What this requires of the teacher is that he or she be willing to set up the classroom along the lines of a democracy, a close community of learners whose major purpose for being there is to learn. You can't create that kind of classroom atmosphere by being a taskmaster and trying to force kids to learn. If you can trust them and let them set their own directions, they'll respond.

Existentialism

PEARSON
myeducationlab

Go to MyEducationLab, select Chapter 4 and then Activities and Applications to analyze the artifact Why We Study History (Social Studies 3–5).

Existential philosophy is unique because it focuses on the experiences of the individual. Other philosophies are concerned with developing systems of thought for identifying and understanding what is common to *all* reality, human existence, and values. **Existentialism,** on the other hand, offers the individual a way of thinking about *my* life, what has meaning for *me*, what is true for *me*. In general, existentialism emphasizes creative choice, the subjectivity of human experiences, and concrete acts of human existence over any rational scheme for human nature or reality. To understand how existentialism can influence teaching, go to MyEducationLab and examine a teacher's assignment that gives students a variety of options to show their knowledge of a book they have read. In what ways does this assignment reflect an existential approach to teaching?

The writings of Jean-Paul Sartre (1905–1980), well-known French philosopher, novelist, and playwright, have been most responsible for the widespread dissemination of existential ideas. According to Sartre (1972), every individual first exists, and then he or she must decide what that existence is to mean. The task of assigning meaning to that existence is the individual's alone; no preformulated philosophical belief system can tell one who one is. It is up to each of us to decide who we are. According to Sartre, "Existence precedes essence. . . . First of all, man exists, turns up, appears on the scene, and, only afterwards, defines himself" (1972, p. 98).

Life, according to existential thought, has no meaning, and the universe is indifferent to the situation humankind finds itself in. Moreover, "existentialists [believe] that too many people wrongly emphasize the optimistic, the good, and the beautiful—all of which create a false impression of existence" (Ozmon & Craver, 2007). With the freedom that we have, however, each of us must commit ourselves to assign meaning to his or her *own* life. As Maxine Greene, who has been described as "the preeminent American philosopher of education today" (Ayers & Miller, 1998, p. 4), "We have to know about our lives, clarify our situations if we are to understand the world from our shared standpoints" (1995, p. 21). The human enterprise that can be most helpful in promoting this personal quest for meaning is the educative process. Therefore, teachers must allow students freedom of choice and provide them with experiences that will help them find the meaning of their lives. This approach, contrary to the belief of many, does not mean that students may do whatever they please; logic indicates that freedom has rules, and respect for the freedom of others is essential.

Existentialists judge the curriculum according to whether it contributes to the individual's quest for meaning and results in a level of personal awareness that Greene terms wide-awakeness. As Greene (1995b, pp. 149–150) suggests, the ideal curriculum is one that provides students with extensive individual freedom and requires them to ask their own questions, conduct their own inquiries, and draw their own conclusions: "To feel oneself en route, to feel oneself in a place where there are always possibilities of clearings, of new openings, this is what we must communicate to the young if we want to awaken them to their situation and enable them to make sense of and to name their worlds." The Teaching on Your Feet feature in this chapter illustrates how one teacher with an existential point of view enabled a student to become more "wide awake" and to find meaning in his life.

Existentialism and Postmodernism

A philosophical orientation that has received increased attention since the 1980s, **postmodernism** has many similarities with existentialism. Postmodern thinking influences the curriculum content and instructional strategies some teachers use.

Postmodernists challenge the metaphysical views—or explanations of "reality"—that are presented in many textbooks. These books, they claim, present a "historically constructed" view of reality that gives advantages to some persons and groups in our society (white males, for example), while it marginalizes others (people of color, women, and unskilled workers, for example).

Postmodernist educators are critical of school curricula that advance the perspectives of dominant groups and ignore other "voices." They point out, for example, that some history books, written from a Eurocentric perspective, state that Columbus "discovered" a "New World." The people who lived in what is now the United States centuries before the arrival of Columbus, of course, have a very different perspective because their native cultures endured disease, genocide, and forced assimilation at the hands of the Europeans.

Similarly, English teachers with a postmodern orientation point out that most of the literature students are required to read has been written by "dead white males" (Shakespeare, Melville, and Hawthorne, for example). Students seldom have opportunities to read the "voices" of authors who represent women, people of color, and writers from developing countries.

In general, postmodernists believe there are no absolute truths. Postmodernism disputes the certainty of scientific, or objective, explanations of reality. In addition, postmodernism is skeptical of explanations that claim to be true for all groups, cultures, traditions, or races. Similar to existentialists, postmodernists emphasize what is true for the individual. Reality is based on our interpretations of what the world means to us individually. Postmodernism emphasizes concrete experience over abstract principles.

Postmodernism is "post" because it rejects the "modern" belief that there are scientific, philosophical, and religious truths. Postmodernists believe there are many truths, and many different voices that need to be heard.

TEACHING ON YOUR FEET

OPENING THE GATES

Reading the world precedes reading the word.
—Paulo Freire and Donaldo Macedo
Literacy: Reading the Word and the World (1987)

It is said that mathematics, and especially algebra, is the greatest of gatekeepers. Indeed, it is the subject that prevents most students from aspiring to higher education. I teach mathematics at a school that is mostly comprised of students of color (75 percent Hispanic, 8 percent African American). Here, roughly 50 to 60 percent of the students will manage to graduate within their four years. Furthermore, less than 20 percent of those that do graduate go on to pursue a four-year college degree. Needless to say, as a teacher of Mexican descent, my teaching and the learning of mathematics is a personal endeavor.

A few years ago, I took my geometry class on an excursion throughout our campus. We were studying shapes and their angles. Students sketched and described the geometrical relationships of the school's buildings and their features. My objective for my students was to allow them to discover not only the usefulness of mathematics but its liberating power to those who can maneuver through it and make it their own. I wanted to empower them to move past academic barriers to a life with more choices. As my students scattered to explore and investigate the architectural geometry that is our school, two boys asked me if they could simply go back to the classroom. They saw no point in the activity. They were bored.

Rather than have them meander back to our classroom and cause any disruptions, I asked them what is it that they saw besides a cluster of impersonal and innate objects such as buildings. They looked dumbfounded at my odd question. "What do you mean?" they asked me. "Look around you. Who is always cleaning the trash and filth that the students carelessly leave behind after lunch? And now think who is in the office making decisions about your education?" I did not have to say much after that. The point of my questions was clear to the boys as they saw men who looked like them cleaning the campus.

ANALYSIS

As teachers, it is difficult to see if we have made a difference in the young minds that are entrusted to us. We may plant seeds that never flower but we may also one day, in the distant future, see the blossom of that seed. Years later, one of the boys who had seen no point in school came back to visit me. He was a freshman at Cal Poly University in Pomona. As we talked, our conversation traveled back to that one day when the class was exploring the geometry of the school. He asked me if I remembered what I had told him. I recounted the basic story but I was surprised when he quoted me: "There are two kinds of people in this world: those who own the building and those who clean it. Your education will determine who you become." Even though I had forgotten I had said those specific words to him, he had obviously internalized them. As he left, a wide grin on his face, he said: "I want to use my body from the neck up rather than from the neck down."

I guess those seeds we plant can sometimes take root and eventually build the foundation of our students' character. It is that tender hope in this truth that gives life to our teacher's heart . . . our spirit. As we come to believe in this, we become the guardians of our students' hope and dreams.

REFLECTION

- What are some other gate-keeping academic subjects that may limit students' life choices if they do not master them?
- How could a teacher who is not of Mexican descent handle a similar situation without offending the students?
- What guest speakers could a teacher invite to motivate students to persist through studies that currently seem meaningless to them?

Sergio Mora
Montclair High School

PEARSON **myeducationlab** *To answer these questions online, go to MyEducationLab at www. myeducationlab.com, select the Activities and Application section, and click on this chapter's Teaching on Your Feet.*

Postmodernists maintain that knowledge is invented or constructed in the minds of people, not discovered as modernists claim. Thus, the knowledge that teachers teach and students learn does not necessarily correspond to reality. Instead, that knowledge is a human construction. Knowledge, ideas, and language are created by people, not because they are true but because they are useful.

According to postmodernists, reality is a story. Reality exists only in the minds of those who perceive it. As a result, no version of reality can claim to be the truth because versions of reality are merely human creations.

Portrait of an Existentialist Teacher

After he started teaching English eight years ago at a suburban high school, Fred Winston began to have doubts about the value of what he was teaching students. Although he could see a limited, practical use for the knowledge and skills he was teaching, he felt he was doing little to help his students answer the most pressing questions of their lives. Also, Fred had to admit to himself that he had grown somewhat bored with following the narrow, unimaginative Board of Education curriculum guides.

During the next eight years, Fred gradually developed a style of teaching that placed emphasis on students finding out who they are. He continued to teach the knowledge covered on the achievement test mandated by his state, but he made it clear that what students learned from him, they should use to answer questions that were important to them. Now, for example, he often gives writing assignments that encourage students to look within in order to develop greater self-knowledge. He often uses assigned literature as a springboard for values clarification discussions. And whenever possible, he gives his students the freedom to pursue individual reading and writing projects. His only requirement is that students be meaningfully involved in whatever they do.

Fred is also keenly aware of how the questions his students are just beginning to grapple with are questions that he is still, even in his mid-thirties, trying to answer for himself. Thoughtfully and with obvious care for selecting the correct words, he sums up the goals that he has for his students:

> I think kids should realize that the really important questions in life are beyond definitive answers, and they should be very suspicious of anyone—teacher, philosopher, or member of organized religion—who purports to have the answers. As human beings, each of us faces the central task of finding *our own* answers to such questions. My students know that I'm wrestling with the same questions they're working on. But I think I've taught them well enough so that they know that my answers can't be their answers.

Fred's approach to teaching is perhaps summed up by the bumper sticker on the sports car he drives: "Question authority." Unlike many of his fellow teachers, he wants his students to react critically and skeptically to what he teaches them. He also presses them to think thoughtfully and courageously about the meaning of life, beauty, love, and death. He judges his effectiveness by the extent to which students are able and willing to become more aware of the choices that are open to them.

Social Reconstructionism

As the term implies, **social reconstructionism** holds that schools should take the lead in changing or reconstructing the current social order. Theodore Brameld (1904–1987), acknowledged as the founder of social reconstructionism, based his philosophy on two fundamental premises about the post–World War II era: (1) We live in a period of great crisis, most evident in the fact that humans now have the capability of destroying civilization overnight, and (2) humankind also has the intellectual, technological, and moral potential to create a world civilization of "abundance, health, and humane capacity" (Brameld, 1959, p. 19). In this time of great need, then, the schools should become the primary agent for planning and directing social change. In short, schools should not only *transmit* knowledge about the existing social order; they should seek to *reconstruct* it as well.

Social Reconstructionism and Progressivism

Social reconstructionism has clear ties to progressive educational philosophy. Both provide opportunities for extensive interaction between teacher and students and among students themselves. Furthermore, both place a premium on bringing the community, if not the entire world, into the classroom. Student experiences often include field trips, community-based projects of various sorts, and opportunities to interact with persons beyond the four walls of the classroom.

A social reconstructionist curriculum is arranged to highlight the need for various social reforms and, whenever possible, allow students to have firsthand experiences in reform activities. Teachers realize that they can play a significant role in the control and resolution of these problems, that they and their students need not be buffeted about like pawns by these crises.

According to Brameld and social reconstructionists such as George Counts, who wrote *Dare the School Build a New Social Order?* (1932), schools should provide students with methods for dealing with the significant crises that confront the world: war, economic depression, international terrorism, hunger, natural disasters, inflation, and ever-accelerating technological advances. The logical outcome of such education would be the eventual realization of a worldwide democracy (Brameld, 1956). Unless we actively seek to create this kind of world through the intelligent application of present knowledge, we run the risk that the destructive forces of the world will determine the conditions under which humans will live in the future.

Portrait of a Social Reconstructionist Teacher

At the urban high school where she teaches social studies and history, Martha Perkins has the reputation for being a social activist. On first meeting her, she presents a casual and laid-back demeanor. Her soft voice and warm smile belie the intensity of her convictions about pressing world issues, from international terrorism and hunger to peaceful uses of space and the need for all humans to work toward a global community.

During the early 1970s, Martha participated as a high school student in several protests against the war in Vietnam. This also marked the beginning of her increased awareness of the need for social justice in society. Like many young people of that era, Martha vigorously supported a curriculum that focused on students understanding these inequities and identifying resources that might eliminate them from society. Before she graduated from high school, Martha had formulated a vision of a healthier, more just society, and she vowed to do what she could to make that vision become a reality during her lifetime.

Martha feels strongly about the importance of having students learn about social problems as well as discovering what they can do about them. "It's really almost immoral if I confront my students with a social problem and then we fail to do anything about it," she says. "Part of my responsibility as a teacher is to raise the consciousness level of my students in regard to the problems that confront all human beings. I want them to leave my class with the realization that they can make a difference when it comes to making the world a more humane place."

For Martha to achieve her goals as a teacher, she frequently has to tackle controversial issues—issues that many of her colleagues avoid in the classroom. She feels that students would not learn how to cope with problems or controversy if she were to avoid them.

> I'm not afraid of controversy. When confronted with controversy, some teachers do retreat to the safety of the more "neutral" academic discipline. However, I try to get my students to see how they can use the knowledge of the discipline to work for social justice. So far, I've gotten good support from the principal. She's backed me up on several controversial issues that we've looked at in class: the nuclear energy plant that was to be built here in this county, the right to die, and absentee landlords who own property in the poorer sections of the city.

Two additional philosophical orientations may be placed under the broad umbrella of social reconstructionism—critical pedagogy and feminist pedagogy. These orientations have a significant influence on the curriculum content some teachers emphasize and the instructional strategies they use. The following sections provide brief descriptions of these orientations.

Critical Pedagogy

Much like social reconstructionsim, **critical pedagogy** focuses on how education can promote **social justice,** especially for those who do not enjoy positions of power and influence in society. Critical pedagogy teaches students how to identify and to understand the complexities of social injustice. It gives them "the tools to better themselves and strengthen democracy, to create a more egalitarian and just society, and thus to deploy education in a process of progressive social change" (Kellner, 2000).

One educator who advocated critical pedagogy was Paulo Freire (1921–1997). He spent his childhood in the comfort of the Brazilian middle class. However, he encountered poverty when his father lost his job as a military officer during the economic crisis of 1929 (Smith & Smith, 1994). That experience "led him to make a vow, at age eleven, to dedicate his life to the struggle against hunger, so that other children would not have to know the agony he was then experiencing." It also led him to understand what he described as "'the culture of silence' of the dispossessed" (Freire, 1970, p. 10). The difficulty poor people encountered when they tried to improve the quality of their lives he attributed to the physical conditions of poverty and to a deep sense that they were not entitled to move beyond their plight. Freire also believed that paternalism embedded in the political and educational systems led to inequality of opportunity. "Rather than being encouraged and equipped to know and respond to the concrete realities of their world, they (poor students) were kept 'submerged' in a situation in which such critical awareness and response were practically impossible" (Freire, 1970, p. 11).

Freire regarded education, and particularly literacy, as the best way to improve the quality of one's life. Influenced by numerous philosophers, psychologists, and political thinkers, including Sartre, Mahatma Gandhi, and Martin Luther King, Jr., he developed a philosophy of education for his doctoral dissertation in 1959. His dissertation provided the basis for his now internationally famous book, *Pedagogy of the Oppressed.* The key premise of his book is that "human interaction rarely escapes oppression of one kind or another; by reason of class, race, or gender, people tend to be victims and/or perpetrators of oppression" (Torres, 1994, p. 181). His approach to education "calls for dialogue and ultimately conscientization—critical consciousness or awareness—as a way to overcome relationships of domination and oppression" (Torres, 1994, p. 187).

Freire contrasted his pedagogy with what he described as a "banking" concept of education—teachers "deposit" their knowledge into empty "accounts" (their students). Freire's success in working with poor, illiterate adults in Northern Brazil was so great that he was regarded as a threat to the existing political order. He was imprisoned and eventually exiled.

Feminist Pedagogy

According to an advocate of **feminist pedagogy** and a teacher at an elementary school in Indiana, schools "serve the power of dominant ideologies and beliefs" (Scering, 1997, p. 62). To ensure the growth and well-being of *all* students in a society dominated by the beliefs and perspectives of white males, then, "feminist pedagogy challenges the emphasis on efficiency and objectivity that perpetuate the domination of masculine rationality. . . . The role of schools in perpetuating unequal social, cultural, political, and economic realities is a central theme of [feminist pedagogy]"(Scering, 1997, p. 62). Thus, the goal of feminist pedagogy is to create caring communities of engaged learners who respect differences and work collaboratively to make democracy a reality for all classes of people.

A leading advocate for feminist pedagogy is bell hooks (she does not use capital letters in her name). According to hooks,

> Feminist education—the feminist classroom—is and should be a place where there is a sense of struggle, where there is a visible acknowledgment of the union of theory and practice, where we work together as teachers and students to overcome the estrangement and alienation that have become so much the norm. . . . Most importantly, feminist pedagogy should engage students in a learning process that makes the world "more real than less real." (hooks, 1989, p. 51)

In *Teaching to Transgress: Education as the Practice of Freedom*, hooks (1994, p. 12) states that education should be viewed as "the practice of freedom, [and] more than ever before . . . educators are compelled to confront the biases that have shaped teaching practices in our society and to create new ways of knowing, different strategies for the sharing of knowledge." hooks (2003, p. xv) also maintains that the classroom should be "a place that is life-sustaining and mind-expanding, a place of liberating mutuality where teacher and student together work in partnership."

Advocates of feminist pedagogy point out that different voices and different ways of knowing tend not to be acknowledged in classrooms dominated by Eurocentric, patriarchal curricula. hooks (2003, p. 3), for example, calls for the "decolonisation of ways of knowing."

Another well-known advocate of feminist pedagogy and a scholar instrumental in developing the legal definition of sexual harassment, Catharine MacKinnon (1994), explains how what is viewed as *the truth* in our society is determined by those in positions of power: "Having power means, among other things, that when someone says, 'this is how it is,' it is taken as being that way. . . . Powerlessness means that when you say, 'this is how it is,' it is not taken as being that way. This makes articulating silence, perceiving the presence of absence, believing those who have been socially stripped of credibility, critically contextualizing what passes for simple fact, necessary to the epistemology of a politics of the powerless."

WHAT PSYCHOLOGICAL ORIENTATIONS HAVE INFLUENCED TEACHING PHILOSOPHIES?

In addition to the five philosophical orientations to teaching described in previous sections of this chapter, several schools of psychological thought have formed the basis for teaching philosophies. These psychological theories are comprehensive worldviews that serve as the basis for the way many teachers approach teaching practice. Psychological orientations to teaching are concerned primarily with understanding the conditions that are associated with effective learning. In other words, what motivates students to learn? What environments are most conducive to learning? Chief among the psychological orientations that have influenced teaching philosophies are humanistic psychology, behaviorism, and constructivism.

Humanistic Psychology

Humanistic psychology emphasizes personal freedom, choice, awareness, and personal responsibility. As the term implies, it also focuses on the achievements, motivation, feelings, actions, and needs of human beings. The goal of education, according to this orientation, is individual self-actualization.

Humanistic psychology is derived from the philosophy of **humanism,** which developed during the European Renaissance and Protestant Reformation and is based on the belief that individuals control their own destinies through the application of their intelligence and learning. People "make themselves." The term *secular humanism* refers to the closely related belief that the conditions of human existence relate to human nature and human actions rather than to predestination or divine intervention.

In the 1950s and 1960s, humanistic psychology became the basis of educational reforms that sought to enhance students' achievement of their full potential through self-actualization (Maslow, 1954, 1962; Rogers, 1961). According to this psychological orientation, teachers should not force students to learn; instead, they should create a climate of trust and respect that allows students to decide what and how they learn, to question authority, and to take initiative in "making themselves." Teachers should be what noted psychologist Carl Rogers calls facilitators, and the classroom should be a place "in which curiosity and the natural desire to learn can be nourished and enhanced" (1982, p. 31). Through their nonjudgmental understanding of students, humanist teachers encourage students to learn and grow.

Portrait of a Humanist Teacher

Ten years ago, Carol Alexander began teaching at a small rural middle school—a position she enjoys because the school's small size enables her to develop close relationships with her students and their families. Her teaching style is based on humane, open interpersonal relationships with her students, and she takes pride in the fact that students trust her and frequently ask her advice on problems common to children in early adolescence. The positive rapport Carol has developed with her students is reflected in the regularity with which former students return to visit or to seek her advice.

Carol is also committed to empowering her students, to giving them opportunities to shape their learning experiences. As she puts it: "I encourage students to give me feedback about how they feel in my classroom. They have to feel good about themselves before they can learn. Also, I've come to realize that students should help us (teachers) plan. I've learned to ask them what they're interested in. 'What do you want to do?' 'How do you want to do it?'"

Much of Carol's teaching is based on classroom discussions in which she encourages students to share openly their ideas and feelings about the subject at hand. Carol's interactions with students reveal her skill at creating a conversational environment that makes students feel safe and willing to contribute. During discussions, Carol listens attentively to students and frequently paraphrases their ideas in a way that acknowledges their contributions. She frequently responds with short phrases that indicate support and encourage the student to continue the discussion, such as the following: "I see. Would you say more about that?" "That is an interesting idea; tell us more."

When Carol is not facilitating a whole-group discussion, she is more than likely moving among the small cooperative-learning groups she has set up. Each group decided how to organize itself to accomplish a particular learning task—developing a strategy for responding to a threat to the environment or analyzing a poem about brotherhood, for example. "I think it's important for students to learn to work together, to help one another, and to accept different points of view," says Carol.

Behaviorism

Behaviorism is based on the principle that desirable human behavior can be the product of design rather than accident. According to behaviorists, it is an illusion to say that humans have a free will. Although we may act as if we are free, our behavior is really determined by forces in the environment that shape our behavior. "We are what we are and we do what we do, not because of any mysterious power of human volition, but because outside forces over which we lack any semblance of control have us caught in an inflexible web. Whatever else we may be, we are not the captains of our fate or the masters of our soul" (Power, 1982, p. 168).

Founders of Behavioristic Psychology

John B. Watson (1878–1958) was the principal originator of behavioristic psychology and B. F. Skinner (1904–1990) its best-known promoter. Watson first claimed that human behavior consisted of specific stimuli that resulted in certain responses. In part, he based this new conception of learning on the classic experiment conducted by Russian

143

psychologist Ivan Pavlov (1849–1936). Pavlov had noticed that a dog he was working with would salivate when it was about to be given food. By introducing the sound of a bell when food was offered and repeating this several times, Pavlov discovered that the sound of the bell alone (a conditioned stimulus) would make the dog salivate (a conditioned response). Watson was so confident that all learning conformed to this basic stimulus-response model (now termed classical or type S conditioning) that he once boasted, "Give me a dozen healthy infants, well-formed, and my own specified world to bring them up in, and I'll guarantee to take any one at random and train him to become any type of specialist I might select—doctor, lawyer, artist, merchant-chief and, yes, even beggarman and thief, regardless of his talents, penchants, tendencies, abilities, vocations, and race of his ancestors" (Watson, 1925, p. 82).

Skinner went beyond Watson's basic stimulus-response model and developed a more comprehensive view of conditioning known as operant (or type R) conditioning. Operant conditioning is based on the idea that satisfying responses are conditioned, unsatisfying ones are not. In other words, "The things we call pleasant have an energizing or strengthening effect on our behaviour" (Skinner, 1972, p. 74). Thus, the teacher can create learners who exhibit desired behaviors by following four steps:

1. Identify desired behaviors in concrete (observable and measurable) terms.
2. Establish a procedure for recording specific behaviors and counting their frequencies.
3. For each behavior, identify an appropriate reinforcer.
4. Ensure that students receive the reinforcer as soon as possible after displaying a desired behavior.

Portrait of a Behaviorist Teacher

Jane Day teaches fourth grade at a school with an enrollment of about 500 in a small midwestern town. Now in her fifth year at the school, Jane has spent the last three years developing and refining a systematic approach to teaching. Last year, the success of her methods was confirmed when her students received the highest scores on the state's annual basic skills test.

Her primary method is individualized instruction, wherein students proceed at their own pace through modules she has put together. The modules cover five major areas: reading, writing, mathematics, general science, and spelling. She is working on a sixth module, geography, but it won't be ready until next year. She has developed a complex point system to keep track of students' progress and to motivate them to higher levels of achievement. The points students accumulate entitle them to participate in various in-class activities: free reading, playing with the many games and puzzles in the room, drawing or painting in the art corner, or playing videogames on one of the two personal computers in the room.

Jane has tried to convert several other teachers at the school to her behavioristic approach, and she is eager to talk to anyone who will listen about the effectiveness of her systematic approach to instruction. When addressing this topic, her exuberance is truly exceptional: "It's really quite simple. Students just do much better if you tell them exactly what you want them to know and then reward them for learning it."

In regard to the methods employed by some of her colleagues, Jane can be rather critical. She knows some teachers in the school who teach by a trial-and-error method and "aren't clear about where they're going." She is also impatient with those who talk about the "art" of teaching; in contrast, everything that she does as a teacher is done with precision and a clear sense of purpose. "Through careful design and management of the learning environment," she says, "a teacher can get the results that he or she wants."

Constructivism

In contrast to behaviorism, constructivism focuses on processes of learning rather than on learning behavior. According to **constructivism,** students use cognitive processes to *construct* understanding of the material to be learned—in contrast to the view that they *receive* information transmitted by the teacher. Constructivist approaches support student-centered rather than teacher-centered curriculum and instruction. The student is the key to learning.

Unlike behaviorists who concentrate on directly observable behavior, constructivists focus on the mental processes and strategies that students use to learn. Our understanding of learning has been extended as a result of advances in **cognitive science**— the study of the mental processes students use in thinking and remembering. By drawing from research in linguistics, psychology, anthropology, neurophysiology, and computer science, cognitive scientists are developing new models for how people think and learn.

Teachers who base classroom activities on constructivism know that learning is an active, meaning-making process, that learners are not passive recipients of information. In fact, students are continually involved in making sense out of activities around them. Thus, the teacher must *understand students' understanding* and realize that students' learning is influenced by prior knowledge, experience, attitudes, and social interactions.

These children are active learners in a real or relevant context, constructing their own meanings through direct experience. How might this lesson be seen as an eclectic blend of progressive, existential, and constructivist ideals?

Portrait of a Constructivist Teacher

Lisa Sanchez teaches English at a middle school in a large midwestern city. The walls of her classroom are decorated with students' work—poetry, drawings, and students' writing reflecting various stages of the writing process: prewriting, revising, and final drafts.

Working in five groups, four students in each group, Lisa's eighth-grade students are translating *Romeo and Juliet* into modern English. Each group is translating a different act. Later, each group of students will choose a scene to enact, after designing a set and contemporary costumes. Lisa points out that her students will have to make decisions regarding the most appropriate costumes for each character based on their understanding of Shakespeare's play. "I want them to understand how Romeo and Juliet is relevant even today."

As students discuss the most appropriate translation line by line, Lisa moves from group to group. She asks clarifying questions and provides encouragement as students work to understand the meaning of Shakespeare's words.

At the end of class, Lisa explains her approach to teaching: "My teaching is definitely student-centered. I try to create a democratic classroom environment. My students are actively involved in creating meaning and knowledge for themselves. They do a lot of work in small groups, and they learn to question, investigate, hypothesize, and invent. They have to make connections between what they already know and new knowledge."

HOW CAN YOU DEVELOP YOUR EDUCATIONAL PHILOSOPHY?

As you read the preceding brief descriptions of five educational philosophies and three psychological orientations to teaching, perhaps you felt that no single philosophy fit perfectly with your idea of the kind of teacher you want to become. Or there may have been some element of each approach that seemed compatible with your

TEACHERS' VOICES
Walk in My Shoes

Phil Kuras, a ninth- to eleventh-grade history and literature teacher at Red Rock High School in Sedona, Arizona, appreciates his colleagues and credits them with his comfort level in his first year of teaching. While working on a master's degree in education at Northern Arizona University, he did his practicum at Red Rock in the fall of 2004, working at the school under the tutelage of a carefully selected veteran teacher. Phil observed for a while and eventually began teaching lessons. He did so well that when a teacher needed to take a leave of absence in the spring, the principal asked Phil if he would fill in as a long-term substitute teacher. Phil agreed and was able to combine that position with his student teaching. Being responsible for everything from day one was a "baptism by fire" to Phil, and he explains that he could not have done it without the mutual cooperation and support of his colleagues.

"If you respect your students, they will respect you."

A rich background of experience contributed to Phil's ability to teach well under unique circumstances. Before attending college, Phil had served in the U.S. Army for eight years, where he learned Russian and spent two tours of duty in Germany. When he left the service, he attended the University of Arizona under the G.I. Bill, receiving a B.A. in anthropology. In traveling across five continents exploring the world, Phil developed a sense of curiosity about the world that informs his teaching and that he hopes to instill in his students.

When he returned to the United States, Phil decided to seek a master's degree in education. It was not an easy decision because it meant two more years of school and absorbing student loans. But he decided to "go for it" and describes the step as "a leap of faith." When asked why he wanted to teach, Phil simply says, "My parents and other people have asked me that, too. I don't know what to tell them. It just feels right. Teaching is not so much what I do as it is who I am. I've known for several years that I wanted to teach."

Now with only half a year of teaching under his belt, Phil is fully aware of how busy even a new teacher can be. In addition to his classes, he continues with his studies at Northern Arizona University, working part-time on an M.A.

in history. He has also stepped in as the freshman boy's basketball coach and was selected to be the junior class sponsor. The latter means overseeing the junior prom. "It's like planning a wedding!" he exclaims. And as the "father of the bride," his biggest challenge is fundraising and managing the money for the event.

Phil's main advice for new teachers is to become as familiar as possible with instructional methodologies and assessment practices that address the needs of ELLs (English language learners). "I have no greater challenge in the classroom than effectively addressing the needs of these students. The trick is to teach both content and language while keeping them engaged in all classroom activities."

Phil encourages new teachers to respect students. "If you respect your students, they will respect you. All that a good teacher does is based on that premise."

His final advice for new teachers is to see themselves as teachers of reading and writing, regardless of content area, a message drilled into him by his master's professors. A current goal for Phil is to find ways to teach writing more effectively. He wants students in his literature class to read for content, but he also wants them to look at the writing itself and consider it from the author's perspective in order to improve their own.

As Phil prepared for his first full year of teaching, he drew on concepts he learned in several books from his master's program, including *The First Days of School: How to Be an Effective Teacher* by Harry K. Wong and Rosemary T. Wong, *After The End* by Barry Lane, and *Preparing to Teach Writing* by James Williams. He also looks forward to again participating in the school's Critical Friends Group, a monthly gathering of six to twelve teachers who discuss their teaching problems and efforts to improve student learning. The spirit of collaboration and support that emanates from this group and the rest of the faculty at Red Rock High School have been critical to Phil's early success in the classroom.

Phil Kuras

own emerging philosophy of education. In either case, don't feel that you need to identify a single educational philosophy around which you will build your teaching career. In reality, few teachers follow only one educational philosophy, and as Figure 4.1 shows, educational philosophy is only one determinant of the professional goals a teacher sets. These goals are influenced by factors such as political dynamics, social forces, the expectations of one's immediate family or community, and economic conditions. For example, the Teachers' Voices: Walk in My Shoes for this chapter profiles Phil Kuras and explains how his life experiences, including extensive world travel, influenced his approach to teaching.

Most teachers develop an *eclectic* philosophy of education, which means they develop their own unique blending of two or more philosophies. To help you identify the philosophies most consistent with your beliefs and values about educational goals, curriculum, and teachers' and students' roles in learning, complete the following philosophic inventory in Figure 4.5. The self-knowledge you glean from completing the inventory and the philosophical constructs presented in this chapter provide a useful framework for studying the historical development of U.S. schools presented in the next chapter. For example, you will be able to see how philosophical orientations to education waxed and waned during each period—whether it was the perennialism and essentialism that characterized colonial schools, the progressivism of the 1920s and 1930s, the essentialism of the 1950s and 1980s, the humanism and social reconstructionism of the 1960s, or the constructivism of the 1990s and the first decade of the new century.

The following inventory is to help identify your educational philosophy. Respond to the statements on the scale from 5, "Strongly Agree," to 1, "Strongly Disagree," by circling the number that most closely fits your perspective.

	Strongly Agree				Strongly Disagree
1. The curriculum should emphasize essential knowledge, *not* students' personal interests.	5	4	3	2	1
2. All learning results from rewards controlled by the external environment.	5	4	3	2	1
3. Teachers should emphasize interdisciplinary subject matter that encourages project-oriented, democratic classrooms.	5	4	3	2	1
4. Education should emphasize the search for personal meaning, *not a* fixed body of knowledge.	5	4	3	2	1
5. The ultimate aim of education is constant, absolute, and universal: to develop the rational person and cultivate the intellect.	5	4	3	2	1
6. Schools should actively involve students in social change to reform society.	5	4	3	2	1
7. Schools should teach basic skills, *not* humanistic ideals.	5	4	3	2	1

FIGURE 4.5 Philosophic inventory

(continues)

	Strongly Agree				Strongly Disagree
8. Eventually, human behavior will be explained by scientific laws, proving there is no free will.	5	4	3	2	1
9. Teachers should be facilitators and resources who guide student inquiry; they should *not* be managers of behavior.	5	4	3	2	1
10. The best teachers encourage personal responses and develop self-awareness in their students.	5	4	3	2	1
11. The curriculum should be the same for everyone: the collective wisdom of Western culture delivered through lecture and discussion.	5	4	3	2	1
12. Schools should lead society toward radical social change, *not* transmit traditional values.	5	4	3	2	1
13. The purpose of schools is to ensure practical preparation for life and work, *not* to encourage personal development.	5	4	3	2	1
14. Good teaching establishes an environment to control student behavior and to measure learning of prescribed objectives.	5	4	3	2	1
15. Curriculum should emerge from students' needs and interests: therefore, it *should not* be prescribed in advance.	5	4	3	2	1
16. Helping students develop personal values is more important than transmitting traditional values.	5	4	3	2	1
17. The best education consists primarily of exposure to great works in the humanities.	5	4	3	2	1
18. It is more important for teachers to involve students in activities to criticize and transform society than to teach the Great Books.	5	4	3	2	1
19. Schools should emphasize discipline, hard work, and respect for authority, *not* encourage free choice.	5	4	3	2	1

FIGURE 4.5 Philosophic inventory *(continued)*

	Strongly Agree				Strongly Disagree
20. Human learning can be controlled: Anyone can be taught to be a scientist or a thief; therefore, personal choice is a myth.	5	4	3	2	1
21. Education should enhance personal growth through problem solving in the present, *not* emphasize preparation for a distant future.	5	4	3	2	1
22. Because we are born with an unformed personality, personal growth should be the focus of education.	5	4	3	2	1
23. Human nature is constant—its most distinctive quality is the ability to reason. Therefore, the intellect should be the focus of education.	5	4	3	2	1
24. Schools perpetuate racism and sexism camouflaged as traditional values.	5	4	3	2	1
25. Teachers should efficiently transmit a common core of knowledge, *not* experiment with curriculum.	5	4	3	2	1
26. Teaching is primarily management of student behavior to achieve the teacher's objectives.	5	4	3	2	1
27. Education should involve students in democratic activities and reflective thinking.	5	4	3	2	1
28. Students should have significant involvement in choosing what and how they learn.	5	4	3	2	1
29. Teachers should promote the permanency of the classics.	5	4	3	2	1
30. Learning should lead students to involvement in social reform.	5	4	3	2	1
31. On the whole, school should and must indoctrinate students with traditional values.	5	4	3	2	1
32. If ideas cannot be proved by science, they should be ignored as superstition and nonsense.	5	4	3	2	1
33. The major goal for teachers is to create an environment where students can learn on their own by guided reflection on their experiences.	5	4	3	2	1

FIGURE 4.5 *(continued)*

(continues)

	Strongly Agree				Strongly Disagree
34. Teachers should create opportunities for students to make personal choices, *not* shape their behavior.	5	4	3	2	1
35. The aim of education should be the same in every age and society, *not* differ from teacher to teacher.	5	4	3	2	1
36. Education should lead society toward social betterment, *not* confine itself to essential skills.	5	4	3	2	1

Philosophic Inventory Score Sheet

In the space available, record the number you circled for each statement (1–36) from the inventory. Total the number horizontally and record it in the space on the far right of the score sheet. The highest total indicates your educational philosophy.

Essentialism

Essentialism was a response to progressivism and advocates a conservative philosophic perspective. The emphasis is on intellectual and moral standards that should be transmitted by the schools. The core of the curriculum should be essential knowledge and skills. Schooling should be practical and not influence social policy. It is a back-to-basics movement that emphasizes facts. Students should be taught discipline, hard work, and respect for authority. Influential essentialists include William C. Bagley, H. G. Rickover, Arthur Bestor, and William Bennett; E. D. Hirsch's *Cultural Literacy* could fit this category.

```
_____  +  _____  +  _____  +  _____  +  _____  +  _____  =  _____
   1          7          13         19         25         31       Total
```

Behaviorism

Behaviorism denies free will and maintains that behavior is the result of external forces that cause humans to behave in predictable ways. It is linked with empiricism, which stresses scientific experiment and observation; behaviorists are skeptical about metaphysical claims. Behaviorists look for laws governing human behavior the way natural scientists look for empirical laws governing natural events. The role of the teacher is to identify behavioral goals and establish reinforcers to achieve goals. Influential behaviorists include B. F. Skinner, Ivan Pavlov, J. B. Watson, and Benjamin Bloom.

```
_____  +  _____  +  _____  +  _____  +  _____  +  _____  =  _____
   2          8          14         20         26         32       Total
```

FIGURE 4.5 Philosophic inventory *(continued)*

Progressivism

Progressivism focuses on the child rather than the subject matter. The students' interests are important; integrating thinking, feeling, and doing is important. Learners should be active and learn to solve problems by reflecting on their experiences. The school should help students develop personal and social values. Because society is always changing, new ideas are important to make the future better than the past. Influential progressivists include John Dewey and Francis Parker.

_____ + _____ + _____ + _____ + _____ + _____ = _____
  3   9   15   21   27   33   Total

Existentialism

Existentialism is a highly subjective philosophy that stresses the importance of the individual and emotional commitment to living authentically. It emphasizes individual choice over the importance of rational theories. Jean Paul Sartre, the French philosopher, claimed that "existence precedes essence." People are born, and each person must define him- or herself through choices in life. Influential existentialists include Jean Paul Sartre, Soren Kierkegaard, Martin Heidegger, Gabriel Marcel, Albert Camus, Carl Rogers, A. S. Neill, and Maxine Greene.

_____ + _____ + _____ + _____ + _____ + _____ = _____
  4   10   16   22   28   34   Total

Perennialism

The aim of education is to ensure that students acquire knowledge about the great ideas of Western culture. Human beings are rational, and this capacity needs to be developed. Cultivation of the intellect is the highest priority of an education worth having. The highest level of knowledge in each field should be the focus of curriculum. Influential perennialists include Robert Maynard Hutchins, Mortimer Adler, and Allan Bloom.

_____ + _____ + _____ + _____ + _____ + _____ = _____
  5   11   17   23   29   35   Total

Reconstructionism

Reconstructionists advocate that schools should take the lead to reconstruct society. Schools have more than a responsibility to transmit knowledge: They have the mission to transform society as well. Reconstructionists go beyond progressivists in advocating social activism. Influential reconstructionists include Theodore Brameld, Paulo Freire, and Henry Giroux.

_____ + _____ + _____ + _____ + _____ + _____ = _____
  6   12   18   24   30   36   Total

Source: Prepared by Robert Leahy for Becoming a Teacher, *Third Edition, 1995. Used by permission of the author.*

FIGURE 4.5 *(continued)*

SUMMARY

Why Is Philosophy Important to Teachers?

- Knowledge of educational philosophy enables teachers to understand the complex political forces that influence schools, to evaluate more effectively current proposals for change, and to grow professionally. Professional teachers continually strive for a clearer, more comprehensive answer to basic philosophical questions.
- Most schools have a statement of philosophy that describes educational values and goals.

What Is the Nature of Philosophy?

- Philosophy, which means "love of wisdom," is concerned with pondering the fundamental questions of life: What is truth? What is reality? What life is worth living?

What Determines Your Educational Philosophy?

- An educational philosophy is a set of beliefs about education, a set of principles to guide professional action.
- A teacher's educational philosophy is made up of personal beliefs about teaching and learning, students, knowledge, and what is worth knowing.

What Are the Branches of Philosophy?

- The branches of philosophy and the questions they address are (1) metaphysics (What is the nature of reality?), (2) epistemology (What is the nature of knowledge and is truth attainable?), (3) axiology (What values should one live by?), (4) ethics (What is good and evil, right and wrong?), (5) aesthetics (What is beautiful?), and (6) logic (What reasoning processes yield valid conclusions?).

What Are Five Modern Philosophical Orientations to Teaching?

- *Progressivism*—The aim of education should be based on the needs and interests of students.

- *Perennialism*—Students should acquire knowledge of enduring great ideas.
- *Essentialism*—Schools should teach students, in a disciplined and systematic way, a core of "essential" knowledge and skills.
- *Existentialism*—In the face of an indifferent universe, students should acquire an education that will enable them to assign meaning to their lives. Postmodernism, which is similar to existentialism, maintains that there are no absolute truths and disputes the certainty of scientific, or objective, explanations of reality.
- *Social reconstructionism*—In response to the significant social problems of the day, schools should take the lead in creating a new social order. Critical pedagogy, much like social reconstructionism, focuses on how education can promote social justice, especially for those who do not enjoy positions of power and influence in society. Feminist pedagogy, also similar to social reconstructionism, maintains that different voices and different ways of knowing tend not to be acknowledged in classrooms that are dominated by Eurocentric, patriarchal curricula.

What Psychological Orientations Have Influenced Teaching Philosophies?

- *Humanism*—Children are innately good, and education should focus on individual needs, personal freedom, and self-actualization.
- *Behaviorism*—By careful control of the educational environment and with appropriate reinforcement techniques, teachers can cause students to exhibit desired behaviors.
- *Constructivism*—Teachers should "understand students' understanding" and view learning as an active process in which learners construct meaning.

How Can You Develop Your Educational Philosophy?

- Instead of basing their teaching on only one educational philosophy, most teachers develop an eclectic educational philosophy.
- Professional teachers continually strive for a clearer, more comprehensive answer to basic philosophical questions.

PROFESSIONAL REFLECTIONS AND ACTIVITIES

Teacher's Journal

1. Recall one of your favorite teachers at the elementary, middle, or high school levels. Which of the educational philosophies or psychological orientations to teaching described in this chapter best capture that teacher's approach to teaching? Write a descriptive sketch of that teacher in action. How has this teacher influenced your educational philosophy?

2. This chapter refers to the work of several educational philosophers. After researching further, select one of them and write a journal entry in which you describe how that person's work has influenced your educational philosophy.

Teacher's Research

1. Numerous organizations influence educational policy and practice in the United States. Visit the websites of two or more of the following organizations and compare the educational philosophies that are reflected in their goals, position statements, and political activities with regard to education:
Alternative Public Schools Inc. (APS)
American Federation of Teachers (AFT)
National Education Association (NEA)
Chicago Teachers Union (or other municipal teachers' organization)
National Congress of Parents and Teachers (PTA)
Parents as Teachers (PAT)
Texas State Teachers Association (or other state teachers' organization)

2. Beginning at the home page of the American Philosophical Association (APA), NOESIS Philosophical Research Online, EpistemeLinks: Philosophical Resources on the Internet, or Guide to Philosophy on the Internet, compile a list of online publications, associations, and reference materials that you could use in developing further your educational philosophy.

Observations and Interviews

1. Interview two teachers to determine how they answer the questions posed at the beginning of this chapter:

What should the purpose(s) of education be? What knowledge is of most worth? What values should teachers encourage their students to develop? How should learning be evaluated? What similarities and differences do you note in the answers given by the two teachers?

2. Have a group of teachers at a local school complete the philosophic inventory presented in Figure 4.5. How do the teachers' responses compare to your responses on the inventory?

---

myeducationlab To complete additional observations and interviews, go to MyEducationLab at www.myeducationlab.com, select the Virtual Field Experience section, and click on this chapter's Observations and Interviews.

Professional Portfolio

Each month, prepare a written (or videotaped) statement in which you explain one of the following key elements of your educational philosophy (see Figure 4.1). At the end of five months, you should have a statement for each set of beliefs.

- Beliefs about teaching and learning
- Beliefs about students
- Beliefs about knowledge
- Beliefs about what is worth knowing
- Personal beliefs in philosophical areas

As appropriate, revise your belief statements throughout the course and during the remainder of your teacher education program. On completion of your teacher education program, review your portfolio entry and make any appropriate revisions. The ability to provide a full explanation of your philosophy of education will be a definite advantage when you begin to look for your first job as a teacher.

---

myeducationlab Now go to MyEducationLab at www.myeducationlab.com to test your understanding of chapter content by completing this chapter's Study Plan.

Historical Foundations of U.S. Education

7

Historical Foundations of U.S. Education

> *The true business of the schoolroom connects itself, and becomes identical, with the great interests of society.*
>
> Horace Mann,
> *Twelfth Report, 1848*

CLASSROOM CASE
The Realities of Teaching

THE CHALLENGE: Understanding how historical events have influenced teaching in today's schools.

During your first year of teaching, you are talking with other teachers in the faculty lounge about high-stakes testing and teacher accountability. The discussion was sparked by a televised presidential address the night before, during which the president stressed the importance of education and America's future.

"I think the president understands the challenges we face as teachers," one teacher says.

"Right, it was good to see a positive, honest portrayal of teachers," another offers. "The message seemed to be 'Let's get behind our teachers and support them more. The work they do is important to America.'" Two of the teachers nod their heads in agreement.

A third teacher looks up from the papers he is grading. "Exactly," he says, "I think people are beginning to see that problems in the schools are not the fault of the schools themselves. They just reflect what's happened in society over the years." Two of the teachers murmur their agreement.

Then a teacher who plans to retire at the end of the year begins to speak. She is seated on the other end of the couch on which you're sitting. Everyone listens carefully, perhaps to convey to her that her opinion is especially valued.

"I've been teaching for more than 25 years," she says, "When I started teaching we didn't have the emphasis on accountability like we have today. We had a job to do, and that was to teach kids. We were there to teach, and the kids, believe it or not, were there to learn."

Before she continues, she closes her teacher's record book into which she had been entering students' scores on last month's state-mandated achievement test. "Then, about ten years ago, the federal government started really getting involved. Teaching is so different today; we're constantly thinking about the next test and how well our kids are going to do. The feds have mandated statewide tests, and thousands of kids across the country are being held back. I can't think of any real good that has come out of the federal government's involvement in education."

"What has the federal government done to make things better for teachers like us?" she asks.

What do you say?

FOCUS QUESTIONS

1. Why is educational history important?
2. What were teaching and schools like in the American colonies (1620–1750)?
3. What were the goals of education during the Revolutionary period (1750–1820)?
4. How was the struggle won for state-supported common schools (1820–1865)?
5. How did compulsory education change schools and the teaching profession (1865–1920)?
6. What were the aims of education during the Progressive Era (1920–1945)?
7. How did education change during the modern postwar era (1945 to the present)?

WHY IS EDUCATIONAL HISTORY IMPORTANT?

In *The Life of Reason*, George Santayana said, "Those who cannot remember the past are condemned to repeat it." Similarly, Adlai Stevenson, presidential candidate in 1952 and 1956, said, "We can chart our future clearly and wisely only when we know the path which has led us to the present." For teachers, the implication of these statements is clear—the past has an impact on teaching and schools today. Accomplished teachers learn from our nation's educational past. They know that educational practices from the past have not disappeared—they continue to evolve, and they shape the present, as well as the future. We cannot understand schools today without a look at what they were yesterday. Today's teachers must be students of our educational past so that they may provide leadership to improve our educational future. For an example of one way to learn about schooling in the past, go to MyEducationLab and examine an assignment given to fourth-grade students to interview their parents and grandparents about their experiences in school. What do you think your parents and grandparents would say about their schooling experiences?

The current system of public and private education in the United States is an ongoing reflection of its historical foundations and of the aspirations and values brought to this country by its founders and generations of settlers. Thus, it is impossible to understand schools today without a look at what they were yesterday. Becoming familiar with events that have shaped education in the United States is an important part of your education as a professional.

Still, you may wonder, what is the value of knowing about the history of U.S. education? Will that knowledge help you to be a better teacher? First, knowledge of the events that have influenced our schools will help you evaluate more effectively current proposals for change. You will be in a better position to evaluate changes if you understand how schools have developed and how current proposals might relate to previous change efforts. Second, awareness of events that have influenced teaching is a hallmark of professionalism in education.

Just as an effective democracy demands enlightened, aware citizens, so, too, does a profession require knowledgeable professionals. Camille Beliveau, profiled in the Teachers' Voices feature for this chapter, knows that the study of history is an important part of professional knowledge.

This chapter presents a brief overview of six periods of education in the United States. Each section examines the social forces, events, and persons that, in the author's judgment, have had the greatest impact on schools in our country.

Go to MyEducationLab, select Chapter 5 and then Activities and Applications to analyze the artifact Why We Study History (Social Studies 3–5).

WHAT WERE TEACHING AND SCHOOLS LIKE IN THE AMERICAN COLONIES (1620–1750)?

Education in colonial America had its primary roots in English culture. The settlers of our country initially tried to develop a system of schooling that paralleled the British two-track system. If students from the lower classes attended school at all, it was at the elementary level for the purpose of studying an essentialist

TEACHERS' VOICES
Walk in My Shoes

Camille Beliveau credits her love of history and the decision to become a history teacher to the "phenomenal" history teacher she had in high school, her father. During summers he took Camille to "every Civil War battlefield on the East Coast," and in one class he assigned the reading of *The Killer Angels,* Michael Saaran's Pulitzer Prize–winning historical novel about the Battle of Gettysburg. It became one of her favorite books. That her father never seemed to get old was another reason Camille wanted to become a teacher. "The kids kept him young and gave him energy and a sense of humor."

Camille studied to be a teacher at the University of New Hampshire in a five-year program that concluded with a master's thesis and full-year internship. In their sophomore year, students were required to spend two weeks observing in schools to determine early if their desires to teach were based on reality. Camille was grateful that she participated in the full-year internship because during that time she learned to create assessment tools, discovered teaching methodologies not presented in classes, and recognized the importance of paperwork, such as the significance of the attendance record in a court of law.

She spent her first four years teaching at Colebrook Academy, a small school in New Hampshire. Later, her husband's graduate studies took them from New England to Norfolk, Virginia. After a week as a "bad waitress," Camille found a teaching position at Norview High School, an ethnically diverse urban school whose student majority is African American. Now in her fifth year at Norview High, Camille loves the school, her students, and the classes she teaches—U.S. history, world history, government, and advanced placement U.S. history.

The school transition for her meant that she needed to start all over to rebuild her reputation and gain trust from students and colleagues. Over the years, Camille moved naturally into leadership roles, mentoring new teachers and serving as the adviser for school clubs, in-

cluding the National Honor Society and Kiwanis Service Key Club. She was also selected to participate in the American History Teacher Scholars Program, a three-year collaborative project in which outstanding history teachers in the school district pair up with college professors at Tidewater Community College to explore local history and design curricula to integrate it into the required history standards of learning.

Camille offers a few tips to new teachers. First, upon entering teaching, Camille wished that she had known more content: She discovered that it is not until you teach something that you realize how much content you need to know. "Knowing your content, the history behind it, and how to teach it is the key to classroom management. If you don't know your content, the students won't respect you," she advises.

Second, because teaching can be stressful, Camille suggests that each weekend teachers take at least one day off from school. "Don't grade a paper; don't open the computer; just step back and gain perspective." She warns new teachers that their lives should not be all about their jobs and that they should not neglect their own learning.

Camille remains a teacher "not to be rich but to be enriched." She loves her students and values the connections she has with them, some of whom face major challenges in their lives. In her time with them, she tries to change their focus and to help them learn something, while helping them laugh, feel safe, and escape whatever it is that makes them sad. She celebrates the times when she sees her love of history sparked in them. At minimum, her hope is that at some point in the future, when her students are driving through Pennsylvania with their kids in the car, they will decide to stop to visit Gettysburg. There, they might pass on to their children the love of history Camille's father shared with her.

Camille Beliveau

> *"Knowing your content, the history behind it, and how to teach it is the key to classroom management."*

What textbooks might students have used in this early American classroom? What educational beliefs and values were reflected in the curriculum and instruction of this period?

curriculum of reading, writing, and computation and receiving religious instruction. Students from the upper classes had the opportunity to attend Latin grammar schools, where they were given a college-preparatory education that focused on perennialist subjects such as Latin and Greek classics.

Above all, the colonial curriculum stressed religious objectives. Generally, no distinction was made between secular and religious life in the colonies. The religious motives that impelled the Puritans to endure the hardships of settling in a new land were reflected in the schools' curricula. The primary objective of elementary schooling was to learn to read so that one might read the Bible and religious catechisms and thereby receive salvation.

The Status of Teachers

Because those who taught in colonial schools could do so with minimal qualifications—and for little pay—their status was relatively low. Respect increased with grade level and the amount of education required for the position. Elementary school teachers, the majority of whom had no more than an elementary education themselves, were given the least respect, and teachers in the few secondary schools were accorded the highest status.

Colonial teachers were "special but shadowed" according to Dan Lortie (1975). Because teachers, and members of the clergy, were educated, they were "special" and expected to have high moral character. On the other hand, teachers were "shadowed" because they were subordinate to the clergy, the power elite in the community. Teachers' extra duties reflected their marginal status: "Teachers rang the church bells, . . . swept up . . . taught Bible lessons, and occasionally substituted for the ailing pastor. Those who wished to teach had to accept stern inspection of their moral behavior" (Lortie, 1975, p. 11).

Teaching was also shadowed by what was seen as the "real" work of the community—farming. "Farming was the vital preoccupation. And though males were preferred as teachers, in the summer months, when men were needed to work the land, women were recruited to take their places" (Lightfoot, 1978, p. 47).

Colonial Schools

myeducationlab

Go to MyEducationLab, select Chapter 5 and then Activities and Applications to anlyze the artifact Colonial Village Setup (Social Studies 6–8).

In the New England colonies (Massachusetts Bay, New Hampshire, and Connecticut), there was a general consensus that church, state, and schools were interrelated. As a result, town schools were created throughout these colonies to teach children the basics of reading and writing so they could learn the scriptures. These schools were heavily influenced by the Puritans, a group of Protestants who believed in strict religious discipline and simplified religious ceremonies. To reflect further on the nature of colonial schools, go to MyEducationLab and examine a student's drawing of a map of a colonial village, including a colonial school. What does the location of the school suggest about the importance of schools in colonial communities?

The Puritan view of the child included the belief that people are inherently sinful. Even natural childhood play was seen as devil-inspired idleness. The path to redemption lay in learning to curb one's natural instincts and behave like an adult as quickly as possible.

To bring about this premature growth, the teacher had to correct the child constantly and try to curb his or her natural instincts. As one historian put it, "In colonial New England the whole idea of education presumed that children were miniature adults possessed of human degeneracy. The daily school routine was characterized by harshness and dogmatism. Discipline was strict, and disobedience and infractions of rules were often met with severe penalties meted out by quick-tempered, poorly qualified instructors" (Rippa, 1997, p. 30).

The middle colonies (New York, New Jersey, Pennsylvania, and Delaware) were more diverse, and groups such as the Irish, Scots, Swedes, Danes, Dutch, and Germans established **parochial schools** based on their religious beliefs. Anglicans, Lutherans, Quakers, Jews, Catholics, Presbyterians, and Mennonites in the middle colonies tended to establish their own schools. In the largely Protestant southern colonies (Virginia, Maryland, Georgia, and North and South Carolina), wealthy plantation owners believed the primary purpose of education was to promote religion and to prepare their children to attend colleges and universities in Europe. The vast majority of small farmers received no formal schooling, and the children of African slaves received only the training they needed to serve their masters.

No one type of schooling was common to all the colonies. The most common types, however, were the dame schools, the reading and writing schools, and the Latin grammar schools.

The Dame Schools

Dame schools provided initial instruction for boys and often the only schooling for girls. These schools were run by widows or housewives in their homes and supported by modest fees from parents. At **dame schools,** classes were usually held in the kitchen, where children learned only the barest essentials of reading, writing, and arithmetic during instruction lasting for a few weeks to one year. Females might also be taught sewing and basic home-making skills. Students often began by learning the alphabet from a horn book. Developed in medieval Europe, the **horn book** was a copy of the alphabet covered by a thin transparent sheet made from a cow's horn. "The layer of horn protected the parchment from the wear and tear and smudges of little hands" (Urban & Wagner, 2004, p. 43). The alphabet and the horn covering were attached to a paddle-shaped piece of wood. Students often hung their hornbooks around their necks with a leather cord threaded through a hole in the paddle.

Reading and Writing Schools

At **reading and writing schools,** boys received an education that went beyond what their parents could teach them at home or what they could learn at a dame school. Reading lessons were based on the Bible, various religious catechisms, and the New England Primer, first printed in 1690. The Primer introduced children to the letters of the alphabet through the use of illustrative woodcuts and rhymed couplets. The first couplet began with the pronouncement that

> In Adam's fall
> We sinned all.

And the final one noted that

> Zaccheus he
> Did climb the Tree
> His Lord to see.

The Primer also presented children with large doses of stern religious warnings about the proper conduct of life.

Latin Grammar Schools

The Boston Latin School was founded in 1635 to provide a precollege education for the new country's future leaders. At a mass meeting that April, the residents of Boston decided that "our brother Philemon Pormont shall be entreated to become schoolmaster, for the teaching and nurturing of children with us" (Button & Provenzo, 1983, p. 17). The **Latin grammar school,** comparable to today's secondary school, was patterned after the classical schools of Europe. Boys enrolled in the Latin grammar schools at the age of seven or eight, whereupon they began to prepare to enter Harvard College (established in 1636). Following graduation from Harvard, they would assume leadership roles in the church.

At first, grammar schools were seven-year schools; later, they were made into four-year schools. The quality of teaching in the Latin grammar schools was higher than that found in the dame schools or reading and writing schools. In addition, grammar school teachers assumed that students had learned to read and write, either at home or in dame schools.

Latin and Greek were the principal studies in these schools, though arithmetic was introduced in 1745. Students were required to read Latin authors and to speak Latin in poetry and prose as well as conjugate Greek verbs. As the following description indicates, both the curriculum and the mode of instruction were rigorous:

> In most of the Latin schools, the course of study lasted for seven years. Apparently school was in session six days a week and continued throughout the winter and summer. The school day was usually from six to eleven o'clock in the morning and from one to four or five o'clock in the afternoon. The boys sat on benches for long hours. Great faith was placed in the *memoriter* method of drill and rote learning. Through repeated recitations the students were conditioned to respond with a definite answer to a particular question. Class discussions were not permitted. The Latin schools inherited the English tradition of severe discipline. It was not unusual for a quick-tempered schoolmaster to hit a pupil for an unsatisfactory recitation. School regulations designated the punishments which should be meted out for fighting, lying, cursing, and playing cards or dice. (Rippa, 1984, p. 43)

Contrast how students were treated in Latin grammar schools during the colonial era with how the teacher profiled in this chapter's Teaching on Your Feet feature treats her unmotivated, emotionally troubled student, Frank.

The Origins of Mandated Education

As today's citizens know, compulsory education laws require that parents, or those who have custody of children between certain ages, send their children to school. During the colonial era, however, this was not the case.

Universal compulsory education had its origins in the **Massachusetts Act of 1642,** viewed by some as the first school law in the colonies (Urban & Wagoner, 2004). Prior to this date, parents could decide whether they wished their children to be educated at home or at a school. Church and civic leaders in the colonies, however, decided that education could no longer remain voluntary. They saw that many children were receiving inadequate occupational training. Moreover, they realized that organized schools would serve to strengthen and preserve Puritan religious beliefs.

The Puritans decided to make education a civil responsibility of the state. The Massachusetts General Court passed a law in 1642 that required each town to determine whether young people could read and write. Parents and apprentices' masters whose children were unable "to read and understand the principles of religion and the capital laws of the country" (Rippa, 1997, p. 36) could be fined and possibly lose custody of their children.

Although the Massachusetts Act of 1642 did not mandate the establishment of schools, it did make it clear that the education of children was a direct concern of the local citizenry. In 1648, the court revised the 1642 law, reminding town leaders that "the good education of children is of singular behoof and benefit to any commonwealth" and that some parents and masters were still "too indulgent and negligent of their duty" (Cohen, 1974, pp. 394–395). As the first educational law in this country, the Massachusetts Act of 1642 was a landmark.

TEACHING ON YOUR FEET

WORTH THE STRUGGLE

"If there is no struggle, there is no progress." Frederick Douglass's words apply not only to history but also to teaching. When I first became a teacher, I thought I would enter the classroom and instantly inspire all of my students to fall in love with American History. Although I have been fortunate enough to teach many students who make progress and eventually come to appreciate history, I have also struggled with student issues that transcend academic subject matter; indeed, the biggest challenge most teachers encounter are unmotivated students.

I remember one unmotivated student especially well. Frank (not his real name) arrived in the middle of the year, when my classroom was running smoothly and all of my students were accustomed to my classroom policies and procedures. Frank had long hair that nearly covered his face, kept his head down, and rarely looked me in the eye. I quickly realized that Frank was not just unmotivated but was also emotionally troubled. He was moody and frequently missed school, and when I asked him a question, he would usually shrug his shoulders and whisper, "I don't care." He was falling behind in his schoolwork and was unresponsive to the motivational speeches I often gave when students failed to turn in a homework assignment. Despite his behavior, I wanted to help Frank. I offered him individual attention through after-school tutoring.

To ensure that Frank received proper help, I shared my concerns with the school psychologist. She met with Frank and suggested that I could best help Frank by listening to him and showing a genuine interest in him and his life. I decided to ignore his antisocial behavior and treat him as if he were the most interesting student in class.

The tutoring sessions turned out to be the perfect environment to get to know Frank well. Initially, Frank was very quiet and withdrawn. The first few tutoring sessions were very mechanical: I reviewed a lesson with him then he would work on the homework. During lessons, I tried to relate the material to his life. I tried to connect history with his life in the here and now. Although it took some time, he slowly began to open up and talk to me about his life and family. I took this time to listen and relate his experiences to a lesson.

After two months of tutoring sessions, I began to see an improvement in Frank's mood. He was still shy, but he started answering questions in class and showing an interest in American History. At the end of the school year, Frank participated in the eighth-grade promotion ceremony. Afterward, to my surprise, he handed me a card. I read the card later that evening. It was a simple message thanking me for being kind to him.

ANALYSIS

I originally thought I had helped Frank academically, but I came to realize that I had helped him personally, too. What meant more to Frank than any mere history lesson was the attention and kindness shown to him by a teacher. As teachers, we must always remember that students are people first and that personal kindness can make kids want to succeed. Having an unmotivated student is a struggle, but the progress you can make in a student's life by caring is worth it.

REFLECTION

- Why was contacting the school psychologist a wise step?
- What other strategies can teachers use to connect with discouraged or antisocial students?
- How can middle and high school teachers compliment their students without bringing ridicule on them from their peers?

Elizabeth Gubbons
Las Palmas Middle School

PEARSON myeducationlab *To answer these questions online, go to MyEducationLab at www.myeducationlab.com, select the Activities and Application section, and click on this chapter's Teaching on Your Feet.*

The **Massachusetts Act of 1647,** often referred to as the Old Deluder Satan Act (because education was seen as the best protection against the wiles of the devil), mandated the establishment and support of schools. In particular, towns of fifty households or more were to appoint a person to instruct "all such children as shall resort to him to write and read." Teachers were to "be paid either by the parents or masters of such children, or by the inhabitants in general" (Rippa, 1997, p. 36). This act also required towns of 100 households or more to establish a Latin grammar school to prepare students for Harvard College. A town that failed to satisfy this law could be assessed a fine of five pounds.

Support for mandated education was later expanded by passage of the Northwest Ordinance in 1785, which gave federal land to the states for educational purposes. The Ordinance divided the Northwest Territories (now Illinois, Indiana, Michigan, Ohio, Wisconsin, and part of Minnesota) into 36-square-mile sections, with the sixteenth square mile designated for public schools.

Education for African Americans and Native Americans

At the close of the American Revolution, nearly all of the half million African Americans were slaves who could neither read nor write (Button & Provenzo, 1989). In most cases, those who were literate had been taught by their masters or through small, church-affiliated programs. Literate Native Americans and Mexican Americans usually had received their training at the hands of missionaries. One of the first schools for African Americans was started by Elias Neau in New York City in 1704. Sponsored by the Church of England, Neau's school taught African and Native Americans how to read as part of the church's efforts to convert students.

Other schools for African and Native Americans were started by the Quakers, who regarded slavery as a moral evil. Though Quaker schools for African Americans existed as early as 1700, one of the best known was founded in Philadelphia in 1770 by Anthony Benezet, who believed that African Americans were "generously sensible, humane, and sociable, and that their capacity is as good, and as capable of improvement as that of white people" (Button & Provenzo, 1989, p. 45). Schools modeled on the Philadelphia African School opened elsewhere in the Northeast, and so-called Indian schools were also founded as philanthropic enterprises.

The Quakers also founded Indian schools as philanthropic enterprises. In 1819, federal funds for reservation schools were first granted through the newly created Office of Indian Affairs. Federal involvement brought little improvement in programs and enrollments, however. In 1901, for instance, only 300 of the 4,000 to 5,000 school-age Navajos attended school (Button & Provenzo, 1989, p. 276).

From the 17th to the late 20th centuries, schools were segregated by race. The first recorded official ground for school segregation dates back to a decision of the Massachusetts Supreme Court in 1850. When the Roberts family sought to send their daughter Sarah to a white school in Boston, the court ruled that "equal, but separate" schools were being provided and that the Roberts therefore could not claim an injustice (*Roberts v. City of Boston,* 1850). From the beginning, however, schools were not equal, and students did not have equal educational opportunity.

As the nation moved toward civil war, positions on the institution of slavery and the education of slaves hardened. While abolitionists established schools for free and escaped blacks, some southern states made the teaching of reading and writing to slaves a crime. After the Civil War and emancipation, schools for former slaves were opened throughout the South through the **Freedman's Bureau,** but racial segregation and discrimination remained a central feature of the American way of life.

WHAT WERE THE GOALS OF EDUCATION DURING THE REVOLUTIONARY PERIOD (1750–1820)?

Education in the United States during the Revolutionary period was characterized by a general waning of European influences on schools. Though religious traditions that had their origins in Europe continued to affect the curriculum, the young country's need to develop agriculture, shipping, and commerce also exerted its influence on the curriculum. By this time, the original settlers who had emigrated from Europe had been replaced by a new generation whose most immediate roots were in the new soil of the United States. This new, exclusively American identity was also enhanced by the rise of civil town governments, the great increase in books and newspapers that addressed life in the new country, and a turning away from Europe toward the unsettled west. The colonies' break with Europe was most potently demonstrated in the American Revolution of 1776.

Following independence, many leaders were concerned that new disturbances from within could threaten the well-being of the new nation. Among these leaders were Benjamin Franklin, Sarah Pierce, Thomas Jefferson, and Noah Webster. To preserve the freedoms that had been fought for, a system of education became essential. Through education, people would become intelligent, participating citizens of a constitutional democracy.

Benjamin Franklin's Academy

Benjamin Franklin (1706–1790) designed and promoted the Philadelphia Academy, a private secondary school, which opened in 1751. This school, which replaced the old Latin grammar school, had a curriculum that was broader and more practical and also focused on the English language rather than Latin. The academy was also a more democratically run institution than previous schools had been. Though **academies** were largely privately controlled and privately financed, they were secular and often supported by public funds. Most academies were public because anyone who could pay tuition could attend, regardless of church affiliation (Rippa, 1997, p. 65).

In his Proposals *Relating to the Education of Youth in Pennsylvania,* written in 1749, Franklin noted that "the good Education of youth has been esteemed by wise men in all ages, as the surest foundation of the happiness both of private families and of commonwealths" (Franklin, 1931, p. 151).

Franklin's proposals for educating youth called for a wide range of subjects that reflected perennialist and essentialist philosophical orientations: English grammar, composition, and literature; classical and modern foreign languages; science; writing and drawing; rhetoric and oratory; geography; various kinds of history; agriculture and gardening; arithmetic and accounting; and mechanics.

Sarah Pierce's Female Academy

English academies, often called people's colleges, multiplied across the country, reaching a peak of 6,185 in 1855, with an enrollment of 263,096 (Spring, 1997, p. 22). Usually, these academies served male students only; a notable exception was Sarah Pierce's Litchfield Female Academy in Litchfield, Connecticut. Pierce (1767–1852) began her academy in the dining room of her home with two students; eventually, the academy grew to 140 female students from nearly every state and from Canada (Button & Provenzo, 1989, p. 87).

For the most part, however, girls received little formal education in the 17th and 18th centuries and were educated for entirely different purposes than were boys. As the following mission statement for Pierce's Academy suggests, an essentialist rather than perennialist curriculum was appropriate for girls:

> Our object has been, not to make learned ladies, or skillful metaphysical reasoners, or deep read scholars in physical science: there is a more useful, tho' less exalted and less brilliant station that woman must occupy, there are duties of incalculable importance that she must perform: that station is home; these duties are the alleviation of the trials of her parents; the soothing of the labours & fatigues of her partner; & the education for time and eternity of the next generation of immortal beings. (Button & Provenzo, 1989, p. 88)

Some women enrolled in **female seminaries,** first established in the early 19th century to train women for higher education and public service outside the home. Educational opportunities for women expanded in conjunction with social reform movements that gradually led to greater political equality for women, including the right to vote in the 20th century. For example, Troy Seminary, founded in 1821 by educator and poet Emma Willard (1787–1870), became one of the first women's colleges in the country.

Thomas Jefferson's Philosophy

Thomas Jefferson (1743–1826), author of the Declaration of Independence, viewed the education of common people as the most effective means of preserving liberty. As historian S. Alexander Rippa put it, "Few statesmen in American history have so vigorously strived for an ideal; perhaps none has so consistently viewed public education as the indispensable cornerstone of freedom" (1997, p. 55).

Jefferson was born at Shadwell, Virginia, to a father who was a member of Virginia's landed gentry. Educated at the College of William and Mary, the second college to open in America, Jefferson went on to become one of this country's most influential leaders. Author of the Declaration of Independence at age 33, he also served the public as a member of the Virginia legislature, governor of Virginia, minister to France, secretary of state, vice president, and two-term president of the United States. His life demonstrated his wholehearted dedication to education. He was fluent in Latin, Greek, and many modern languages. He was strongly influenced by the work of the English philosopher John Locke, various British ideas on constitutional law, and the writings of French educators.

Jefferson was dedicated to human freedom and repulsed by any form of tyranny or absolutism. "I have sworn," he once said, "upon the altar of God, eternal hostility against every form of tyranny over the mind of man" (Rippa, 1984, p. 68). Toward this end, Jefferson was decidedly influential in the intellectual and educational circles of his day. He was a member of the American Academy of Arts and Sciences and president of the American Philosophical Society.

For a society to remain free, Jefferson felt, it must support a continuous system of public education. He proposed to the Virginia legislature in 1779 his Bill for the More General Diffusion of Knowledge. This plan called for state-controlled elementary schools that would teach, with no cost to parents, three years of reading, writing, and arithmetic to all white children. In addition, 20 state grammar schools would be created in which selected poor students would be taught free for a maximum period of six years. Jefferson's plan departed somewhat from the practical orientation of Franklin because the grammar schools would teach boys a more academic curriculum: English grammar, Greek, Latin, geography, and advanced arithmetic.

Jefferson was unsuccessful in his attempt to convince the Virginia House of Burgesses of the need for a uniform system of public schools as outlined in his bill. Jefferson was able to implement many of his educational ideas, however, through his efforts to found the University of Virginia. He devoted the last years of his life to developing the university, and he lived to see the university open with 40 students in March 1824, one month before his 81st birthday.

Noah Webster's Speller

In the years following the Revolution, several textbooks were printed in the United States. Writers and publishers saw the textbook as an appropriate vehicle for promoting democratic ideals and cultural independence from England. Toward this end, U.S. textbooks were filled with patriotic and moralistic maxims. Among the most widely circulated books of this type were Noah Webster's *Elementary Spelling Book* and *The American Dictionary*.

Born in Connecticut, Noah Webster (1758–1843) had successful careers as a lawyer, writer, politician, and schoolmaster. He first introduced his speller in 1783 under the cumbersome title, *A Grammatical Institute of the English Language*. Later versions were titled the *American Spelling Book* and the *Elementary Spelling Book*. Webster's speller earned the nickname "the old blue-back" because early copies of the book were covered in light blue paper and later editions covered with bright blue paper.

In the introduction to his speller, Webster declared that its purpose was to help teachers instill in students "the first rudiments of the language, some just ideas of religion, morals and domestic economy" (Button & Provenzo, 1989, p. 65). Throughout, the little book emphasized patriotic and moralistic virtues. Short, easy-to-remember maxims taught pupils to be content with their lot in life, to work hard, and to respect the property of others. Readers were cautioned to "prefer solid sense to vain wit" and to "let no jest intrude to violate good manners." Webster also gave readers extensive instructions on how to behave in school:

> He that speaks loud in school will not learn his own book well, nor let the rest learn theirs; but those that make no noise will soon be wise, and gain much love and good will.

> Shun the boy that tells lies, or speaks bad words; for he would soon bring thee to shame. (Commager, 1962, pp. 61–63)

Webster's speller was so popular that it eventually sold over 24 million copies. Historian Henry Steele Commager said of the book, "The demand was insatiable. . . . No other secular book had ever spread so wide, penetrated so deep, lasted so long" (1958, p. 12). It has been estimated that more than 1 billion people have read Webster's book.

Webster's speller addressed so many topics that it has been called one of the first curriculum guides for the elementary grades (Johanningmeier, 1980, p. 65). Webster was a post-Revolutionary educational leader who had a profound impact on the American language, and he "did much to help define the new nation" (Urban & Wagoner, 2004, p. 79).

HOW WAS THE STRUGGLE WON FOR STATE-SUPPORTED COMMON SCHOOLS (1820–1865)?

The first state-supported high school in the United States was the Boston English Classical School, established in 1821. The opening of this school, renamed English High School in 1824, marked the beginning of a long, slow struggle for state-supported **common schools** in this country. Those in favor of free common schools tended to be city residents and nontaxpayers, democratic leaders, philanthropists and humanitarians, members of various school societies, and working people. Those opposed were rural residents and taxpayers, members of old aristocratic and conservative groups, owners of private schools, members of conservative religious sects, Southerners, and non-English-speaking residents. By far the most eloquent and effective spokesperson for the common school was Horace Mann.

Horace Mann's Contributions

Horace Mann (1796–1859) was a lawyer, Massachusetts senator, and the first secretary of a state board of education. He is best known as the champion of the common school movement, which has led to the free, public, locally controlled elementary schools we know today. Mann worked tirelessly to convince people that their interests would be well served by a system of universal free schools for all:

> [A free school system] knows no distinction of rich and poor, of bond and free, or between those, who, in the imperfect light of this world, are seeking, through different avenues, to reach the gate of heaven. Without money and without price, it throws open its doors, and spreads the table of its bounty, for all the children of the State. (Mann, 1868, p. 754)

Improving Schools

In 1837, Mann accepted the position of Secretary of the Massachusetts State Board of Education. At the time, conditions in Massachusetts schools were deplorable, and Mann immediately began to use his new post to improve the quality of schools. Through the twelve annual reports he submitted while secretary and through *The Common School Journal*, which he founded and edited, Mann's educational ideas became widely known in this country and abroad.

In his widely publicized *Fifth Report* (published in 1841), Mann told the moneyed conservative classes that support of common public schools would provide them "the cheapest means of self-protection and insurance." Where could they find, Mann asked, "any police so vigilant and effective, for the protection of all the rights of person, property and character, as such a sound and comprehensive education and training, as our system of Common Schools could be made to impart?" (Rippa, 1997, p. 95).

In his *Seventh Report* (published 1843), Mann extolled the virtues of schools he had visited in Prussia that implemented the humanistic approaches of noted Swiss educator Johann Heinrich Pestalozzi (1746–1827). "I heard no child ridiculed, sneered at, or scolded, for making a mistake," Mann wrote (Rippa, 1997, p. 96).

The Normal School

During the late 1830s, Mann put forth a proposal that today we take for granted. Teachers, he felt, needed more than a high school education to teach; they should be trained in professional programs. The French had established the *école normale* for preparing teachers, and Mann and other influential educators of the period, such as Catherine Beecher (1800–1878), whose sister, Harriet Beecher Stowe (1811–1896), wrote *Uncle Tom's Cabin*, believed that a similar program was needed in the United States. Through her campaign to ensure that women had access to an education equal to that of men and her drive to recruit women into the teaching profession, Beecher contributed significantly to the development of publicly funded schools for training teachers (Holmes & Weiss, 1995).

The first public **normal school** in the United States opened in Lexington, Massachusetts, on July 3, 1839. The curriculum consisted of general knowledge courses plus courses in pedagogy (or teaching) and practice teaching in a model school affiliated with the normal school. In 1849, Electa Lincoln Walton (1824–1908), an 1843 graduate of the normal school, became acting head administrator and the first woman to administer a state normal school. Walton was energetic and determined to succeed, as her journal reveals:

> Many people think women can't do much. I'd like to show them that they can keep a Normal School and keep it well too. . . . I will succeed. . . . I will never be pointed at as an example of the incompetency of woman to conduct a large establishment well." (Holmes & Weiss, 1995, p. 42)

When Mann resigned as secretary in 1848, his imprint on education in the United States was broad and deep. As a result of his unflagging belief that education was the "great equalizer of the conditions of men—the balance wheel of the social machinery" (Mann, 1957, p. 87), Massachusetts had a firmly established system of common schools and led the way for other states to establish free public schools.

Reverend W. H. McGuffey's Readers

Reverend William Holmes McGuffey (1800–1873) had perhaps the greatest impact on what children learned in the new school. Far exceeding Noah Webster's speller in sales were the famous **McGuffey readers.** It has been estimated that 122 million copies of the six-volume series were sold after 1836. The six readers ranged in difficulty from the first-grade level to the sixth-grade level. Through such stories as "The Wolf," "Meddlesome Matty," and "A Kind Brother," the readers emphasized virtues such as hard work, honesty, truth, charity, and obedience.

Absent from the McGuffey readers were the dour, pessimistic views of childhood so characteristic of earlier primers. Nevertheless, they had a religious, moral, and ethical influence over millions of American readers. Through their reading of the "Dignity of Labor," "The Village Blacksmith," and "The Rich Man's Son," for example, readers learned that contentment outweighs riches in this world. In addition to providing explicit instructions on right living, the McGuffey readers also taught countless children and adults how to read and study.

Justin Morrill's Land-Grant Schools

The common school movement and the continuing settlement of the West stimulated the development of public higher education. In 1862, the **Morrill Land-Grant Act,** sponsored by Congressman Justin S. Morrill (1810–1898) of Vermont, provided federal land for states either to sell or to rent in order to raise funds for the establishment of colleges of agriculture and mechanical arts. Each state was given a land subsidy of 30,000 acres for each representative and senator in its congressional delegation.

Eventually, $7.5 million from the sale of over 17 million acres was given to land-grant colleges and state universities. The Morrill Act of 1862 set a precedent for the federal government to take an active role in shaping higher education in the United States. A second Morrill Act in 1890 provided even more federal funds for land-grant colleges.

OF THE ECLECTIC SEREIS.   15

LESSON VIII.

his	this	bite	keep	wants
can	four	play	moon	watch
hog	cow	kind	sheep	stands
how	dark	most	chase	shines

SEE how this dog stands on his feet. He wants to play with John.

A dog has four feet. A dog and a cat can see in the dark.

Dogs keep watch at night, and bark. They bark most when the moon shines.

A dog will chase a sheep, or a hog, or a cow, and bite it. If you are kind to the dog, he will not bite you.

What did children learn from typical lessons in 19th century textbooks like this one, the story of "The Boy and Dog" from McGuffey's *The Eclectic First Reader*?

HOW DID COMPULSORY EDUCATION CHANGE SCHOOLS AND THE TEACHING PROFESSION (1865–1920)?

From the end of the Civil War to the end of World War I, publicly supported common schools steadily spread westward and southward from New England and the Middle Atlantic states. Beginning with Massachusetts in 1852, compulsory education laws were passed in 32 states by 1900 and in all states by 1930.

Because of compulsory attendance laws, an ever-increasing proportion of children attended school. In 1869–70, only 64.7 percent of 5- to 17-year-olds attended public school. By 1919–20, this proportion had risen to 78.3 percent; and in 2004–05, it was 91.7 percent (National Center for Education Statistics, March 25, 2008). The growth in enrollment on the high school level was exceptional. Historical data from the National Center for Education Statistics (March 25, 2008) enable us to determine that between 1880 and 1920, the population in the United States increased 108 percent, and high school enrollment increased 1,900 percent!

As common schools spread, school systems began to take on organizational features associated with today's schools: centralized control; increasing authority for state, county, and city superintendencies; and a division of labor among teachers and administrators at the individual school site. Influenced by the work of Frederick W. Taylor (1856–1915), an engineer and the founder of **scientific management,** school officials undertook reforms based on management principles and techniques from big business. For example, they believed that top-down management techniques should be applied to schools as well as factories.

Higher Education for African Americans

In *Up from Slavery*, Booker T. Washington (1856–1915) recounts how he walked part of the 500 miles from his home in West Virginia to attend the Hampton Normal and Agricultural Institute of Virginia, one of the country's first institutions of higher education for African Americans. Four years after graduating from Hampton, Washington returned to be the school's first African American instructor.

Washington had a steadfast belief that education could improve the lives of African Americans, just as it had for white people: "Poverty and ignorance have affected the black man just as they affect the white man. But the day is breaking, and education will bring the complete light" (Rippa, 1997, p. 122). In 1880, Washington helped to found the Tuskegee Institute, an industrial school for African Americans in rural Alabama. According to Washington, the institute would play a key role in bringing about racial equality:

> The Tuskegee idea is that correct education begins at the bottom, and expands naturally as the necessities of the people expand. As the race grows in knowledge, experience, culture, taste, and wealth, its wants are bound to become more and more diverse; and to satisfy these wants there will be gradually developed within our ranks—as already has been true of the whites—a constantly increasing variety of professional and business men and women. (Button & Provenzo, 1989, p. 274)

Not all African Americans shared Washington's philosophy and goals. William E. Burghardt DuBois (1868–1963), the first African American to be awarded a Ph.D. and one of the founders of the National Association for the Advancement of Colored People (NAACP), challenged Booker T. Washington's views on education. In his book *The Souls of Black Folks*, DuBois criticized educational programs that seemed to imply that African Americans should accept inferior status and develop manual skills. DuBois called for the education of the most "talented tenth" of the African American population to equip them for leadership positions in society as a whole.

The Kindergarten

Early childhood education also spread following the Civil War. Patterned after the progressive, humanistic theories of the German educator Friedrich Froebel (1782–1852), the **kindergarten,** or "garden where children grow," stressed the motor development and self-activity of children before they began formal schooling at the elementary level. Through play, games, stories, music, and language activities, a foundation beneficial to the child's later educational and social development would be laid. After founding the first kindergarten in 1837, Froebel developed child-centered curriculum materials that were used in kindergartens in the United States and throughout the world.

Margarethe Schurz (1832–1876), a student of Froebel, opened the first U.S. kindergarten in her home at Watertown, Wisconsin, in 1855. Her small neighborhood class was conducted in German. In 1860, Elizabeth Palmer Peabody (1804–1891), sister-in-law of Horace Mann and the American writer Nathaniel Hawthorne, opened the first private English-speaking kindergarten in this country in Boston.

Initially, kindergartens were privately supported, but in St. Louis in 1873, Susan Blow (1843–1916) established what is commonly recognized as the first successful public kindergarten in the United States. She patterned her kindergarten after one she visited while in Germany. So successful was her program that by 1879, a total of 131 teachers were working in 53 kindergarten classes (Button & Provenzo, 1989, p. 169).

The U.S. Bureau of Education recorded a total of twelve kindergartens in the country in 1873, with 72 teachers and 1,252 students. By 2006, enrollments had mushroomed to 2,599,000 in public kindergartens and 353,000 in private kindergartens (National Center for Education Statistics, March 25, 2008).

The Professionalization of Teaching

During the later 1800s, professional teacher organizations began to have a great influence on the development of schools in America. The National Education Association (NEA), founded in 1857, and the American Federation of Teachers (AFT), founded in 1916, labored diligently to professionalize teaching and to increase teachers' salaries and benefits. The NEA also appointed its Committee of Ten in 1892 and its Committee of Fifteen in 1893 to make recommendations for secondary and elementary curricula, respectively. In 1913, the NEA appointed the Commission on the Reorganization of Secondary Education to reexamine the secondary curriculum in regard to students' individual differences.

Committee of Ten

During 1892–1893, the directors of the National Education Association appropriated $2,500 for a **Committee of Ten** to hold nine conferences that focused on the following subjects in the high school curriculum: (1) Latin; (2) Greek; (3) English; (4) other modern languages; (5) mathematics; (6) physics, astronomy, and chemistry; (7) natural history (biology, botany, and zoology), (8) history, civil government, and political science; and (9) geography (physical geography, geology, and meteorology). The group's members decided that the primary function of high schools was to take intellectually elite students and prepare them for life. Their recommendations stressed mental discipline in the humanities, languages, and science.

Committee of Fifteen

The report of the Committee of Ten sparked such discussion that in 1893 the National Education Association appointed the **Committee of Fifteen** to examine the elementary curriculum. In keeping with the view that high schools were college preparatory institutions, the committee's report, published in 1895, called for the introduction of Latin, the modern languages, and algebra into the elementary curriculum. In addition, the curriculum was to be organized around five basic subjects: grammar, literature, arithmetic, geography, and history.

Reorganization of Secondary Education

In 1913 the National Education Association appointed the **Commission on the Reorganization of Secondary Education.** The commission's report, *Cardinal Principles of Secondary Education*, was released in 1918 and called for a high school curriculum designed to accommodate individual differences in scholastic ability. Seven educational goals, or "cardinal principles," were to provide the focus for schooling at all levels: health, command of fundamental processes (reading, writing, and computation), worthy home membership, vocation, citizenship, worthy use of leisure time, and ethical character.

Women's Influence on Teaching

By the early 1900s, the demand for teachers had grown dramatically. Because of greater demand for teachers, greater job mobility, and more and more women becoming teachers, the character of teaching changed. Both respected and regarded with suspicion, teachers became distanced from the communities they served. In his classic book *The Sociology of Teaching,* Willard Waller (1932) refers to this distancing as an "impenetrable veil" between the teacher and the rest of the community. Nevertheless, "women, as . . . vessels of virtue, were considered the ideal teachers for a system of schooling that emphasized moral development" (Spring, 2005, p. 145).

In spite of their "second-class citizenship" (Spring, 2005, p. 145), women became influential in shaping educational policies during the early 1900s, in part through the women's suffrage movement that led to the right to vote. Women such as Ella Flagg Young (1845–1918), superintendent of Chicago schools from 1909 to 1915, and Catherine Goggin and Margaret Haley, leaders of the Chicago Teachers Federation, played important roles in the governance of Chicago schools (Spring, 2005). Another Chicagoan and visionary educational leader, Jane Addams (1860–1935), founded Hull House, a social and educational center for poor immigrants. In *Democracy and Social Ethics* (published in 1902), Addams drew from her training as a social worker and developed a philosophy of socialized education that linked schools with other social service agencies and institutions in the city. At the ceremony to present her the Nobel Peace Prize in 1931, Addams was described as "the foremost woman of her nation" (Rippa, 1997, p. 142).

WHAT WERE THE AIMS OF EDUCATION DURING THE PROGRESSIVE ERA (1920–1945)?

From the end of World War I to the end of World War II, education in the United States was influenced significantly by the philosophy of progressivism.

Progressivism is a philosophical orientation based on the belief that life is evolving in a positive direction, that people may be trusted to act in their own best interest, and that education should focus on children's interests and practical needs.

During the late 19th and early 20th centuries, supporters of the progressive movement were intent on social reform to improve the quality of American life. In 1919, the Progressive Education Association was founded and went on to devote the next two decades to implementing progressive theories in the classroom that they believed would lead to the improvement of society.

Progressives were not united by a single educational philosophy. For the most part, they were opposed to autocratic teaching methods; teaching styles that relied almost exclusively on textbooks, recitations, and rote memorization; the relative isolation of the classroom from the real world; and classroom discipline based on fear or physical punishment.

Teachers in progressive schools functioned as guides rather than taskmasters. They first engaged students through providing activities related to their natural interests, and then they moved students to higher levels of understanding. To teach in this manner was demanding: "Teachers in a progressive school had to be extraordinarily talented and well educated; they needed both a perceptive understanding of children and a wide knowledge of the disciplines in order to recognize when the child was ready to move through an experience to a new understanding, be it in history or science or mathematics or the arts" (Ravitch, 1983, p. 47).

John Dewey's Laboratory School

Progressive educational theories were synthesized most effectively and eloquently by John Dewey (1859–1952). Born in the year that Darwin's *Origin of Species* was published, Dewey graduated from the University of Vermont when he was 20. He later earned a doctorate at Johns Hopkins University, where his thinking was strongly influenced by the psychologist William James.

From 1894 to 1904, Dewey served as head of the departments of philosophy, psychology, and pedagogy at the University of Chicago. From 1904 until he retired in 1930, Dewey was a professor of philosophy at Columbia University. Dewey's numerous writings have had a profound impact on U.S. schools. In his best-known works, *The School and Society* (1900) and *The Child and the Curriculum* (1902), Dewey states that school and society are connected and that teachers must begin with an understanding of the child's world, the psychological dimension, and then progress to the logical dimension represented by the accumulated knowledge of the human race.

While at the University of Chicago, Dewey and his wife, Alice, established the Laboratory School for testing progressive principles in the classroom. The school opened in 1896 with two instructors and 16 students and, by 1902, had grown to 140 students with 23 teachers and 10 university graduate students as assistants. The children, 4 to 14 years old, learned traditional subjects by working cooperatively in small groups of 8 to 10 on projects such as cooking, weaving, carpentry, sewing, and metalwork (Rippa, 1997).

With Dewey as director and his wife as principal, the school became a virtual laboratory for testing Dewey's ideas. The school was so unique that historian Lawrence Cremin referred to it as "the most interesting experimental venture in American education" (1961, p. 136). In addition to giving students a meaningful, relevant education, Dewey's school had two purposes: "(1) to exhibit, test, verify, and criticize [Dewey's] theoretical statements and principles; and (2) to add to the sum of facts and principles in its special line with question marks, rather than fixed rules" (Mayhew & Edwards, 1936, p. 3).

What made Dewey's Laboratory School unique was that it was thoroughly child-centered. The curriculum was a natural outgrowth of the children's interests. The faculty was committed to following the lead set by students. For example, "a student or students might express an interest in milk. The teacher would guide the students to sources of the production, chemistry, and distribution of milk. Groups of students might visit the local dairy and develop a group project on milk for the classroom. During this group study of milk, students might learn chemistry, economics, arithmetic, social history, and cooperation" (Spring, 2008, pp. 300–301).

Maria Montessori's Method

While Dewey's ideas provided the basis for the development of progressive education in the United States, progressive educators in Europe were similarly developing new approaches that would also affect U.S. education. Chief among these was Maria Montessori (1870–1952), an Italian physician who was influenced by Rousseau and believed that children's mental, physical, and spiritual development could be enhanced by providing them with developmentally appropriate educational activities.

At Montessori's school for poor preschool-age children in Rome, teachers created learning environments based on students' levels of development and readiness to learn new material. According to the **Montessori method,**

> [C]hildren pass through "sensitive periods" for particular intellectual, social, and moral awakenings. These are sensitive periods for language, movement, music, order, and so on. The central role of the adult . . . is to recognize these sensitive periods and direct the child to work designed to foster those awakenings. (Cossentino & Whitcomb, 2007, p. 117)

Montessori teachers use prescribed sets of materials and physical exercises to develop students' knowledge and skills, and students are allowed to use or not use the materials as they see fit. The materials arouse students' interest, and the interest motivates them to learn. Through highly individualized instruction, students develop self-discipline and self-confidence. Montessori's ideas spread throughout the world; by 1915, almost 100 Montessori schools were operating in the United States (Webb, Metha, & Jordan, 1999). Today, Montessorian materials and activities are a standard part of the early childhood and elementary curricula in public schools throughout the nation.

The Decline of Progressive Education

By the start of World War II, the progressive education movement, faced with rising public criticism, began a rapid decline. "All sorts of people seemed to believe that the U.S. system of public education was woefully out of step with the needs of the nation. As a result, an undifferentiated fury was directed at progressive education" (Hartman, 2008, p. 1). Many of the schools' deficiencies were blamed on progressive approaches that were seen as soft and lacking the structure and discipline children needed. In 1955, the Progressive Education Association ceased operation. Patricia A. Graham (1967, p. 145) has observed that when the association began in 1919, "progressive education meant all that was good in education; 35 years later nearly all the ills in American education were blamed on it."

In spite of its short life, the progressive education movement had an unmistakable impact on American education. Many current practices in schools have their origins in the experimentation of the progressive era: inquiry or discovery learning, self-paced instructional approaches, field trips, flexible scheduling, open-concept classrooms, nongraded schools, small-group activities, and school-based counseling programs, to name a few.

Education of Immigrants and Minorities

The diversity of America's school population increased dramatically during the late nineteenth and early twentieth centuries. Latin Americans, Eastern Europeans, and southern Europeans followed earlier waves of Western and northern European immigrants such as the Irish and Germans. As with Native American education, the goal of immigrant education was rapid assimilation into an English-speaking Anglo-European society that did not welcome racially or ethnically different newcomers.

Also at stake was the preservation or loss of traditional culture. In some areas, school policies included the punishment of Cuban and Puerto Rican children, for example, for speaking Spanish in school, and children learned to mock their unassimilated parents. In other areas, efforts were made to exclude certain groups, such as Asians, and ethnic enclaves established separate schools for the purpose of preserving, for example, traditional Chinese culture.

By the time Native Americans were granted U.S. citizenship in 1924, confinement on reservations and decades of forced assimilation had devastated Native American cultures and provided few successful educational programs. "The federal government forcibly placed tribal children in the harsh, military-like institutions in an effort to assimilate them into the dominant culture" (King, February 3, 2008). Boarding school children who spoke their native language were beaten with a strap, while other children were forced to watch. By the early 1930s, an estimated two-thirds of Native Americans had attended boarding schools. The emotional scars from the boarding school experience continue into the present, and the national Boarding School Healing Project was launched in South Dakota in 2002 by Indians from various states (King, February 3, 2008). To reflect further on the cultural genocide against Native Americans, go to MyEducationLab and watch a video in which two experts share their ideas related to the cultural genocide that began in America in 1492.

In 1928, a landmark report titled *The Problem of Indian Administration* recommended that Native American education be restructured. Recommendations included building day schools in Native American communities and the reform of boarding schools for Native American children. In addition, the report recommended that school curricula be revised to reflect tribal cultures and the needs of local tribal communities. In the Teachers' Voices feature for this chapter, a Native American teacher stresses the importance of curricula that affirm the identity of Native American students.

An early champion of the educational rights of African Americans was Mary McLeod Bethune (1875–1955). The fifteenth child of former slaves in South Carolina, Bethune attended a school operated by the Presbyterian Board of Missions for Freedmen and Barber-Scotia College in Concord, North Carolina. She then went on to study at the Moody Bible Institute in Chicago. She went to Daytona Beach in 1904 where, with only $1.50 in savings, she founded the Daytona Normal and Industrial School for Training Negro Girls.

The school was in a rundown building Bethune rented. At first, she had only six students, including her son. To keep the school open, Bethune and her students sold sweet

myeducationlab

Go to MyEducationLab, select Chapter 5 and then Activities and Applications to watch the video Genocide Impact.

American Indian children who attended boarding schools were not allowed to speak their native languages. Why is it important for school curricula to reflect and honor students' cultural backgrounds?

TEACHERS' VOICES RESEARCH TO REALITY

Kristine Shotley

NATIVE AMERICAN TEACHERS NEED SUPPORT

When I was studying to be a teacher, a white female student in the same program asked me what I thought my chances were of finding a job after graduation. I replied that, because I am Native American, and a woman, I thought I would have excellent opportunities for immediate employment. "How nice," she said, "to turn two negatives into two positives!" I was taken aback. It had not occurred to me that in this day and age, I would still have to defend my identity.

In the United States, most Native American children are still taught by non-Native teachers. There are fewer than 18,000 Native American teachers working today.

To recruit more teachers, we need to develop curricula that affirm our Native American identity. For example, elementary school kids need to learn an accurate and truthful account of American history. How many times do we have to reiterate that Christopher Columbus did not "discover" America?

When I was growing up, Native American history was not taught. I endured the appalled looks of my white classmates when our teachers presented a one-sided account of American history. I felt apologetic for my ancestors who tried to defend their lands from white settlers.

The United States [must address] the lack of Native American teachers. I want my son and other Native American sons and daughters to realize they can become anything they choose because they have the educational background they need.

QUESTIONS

1. Shotley says teachers should develop curricula that "affirm" Native American identity. What are the characteristics of curricula that "affirm" the diverse identities of today's students?
2. What should a teacher do if the only instructional materials available present outdated, perhaps even distorted, interpretations of American history?

Kristine Shotley is a member of the Fond Du Lac Tribe of Ojibwe in Minnesota, and she writes for *The Circle*, a Native American news and arts paper published in Minneapolis. This article is from Progressive Media Project, January 12, 2000.

---

potato pies and fried fish and gave concerts in nearby resort hotels. In 1923, the school merged with a boys' school in Jacksonville, Florida, and became Bethune-Cookman College a year later.

Bethune was an eloquent spokesperson for the educational rights of African American youth. During the Great Depression of the 1930s, she was appointed to the Advisory Board of the National Youth Administration (NYA). That year, almost 24 percent of the 21 million youth between 16 and 24 years of age were out of school and jobless. When Bethune spoke eloquently about the needs of African American youth, President Franklin Roosevelt added an office of minority affairs to the NYA and asked Bethune to direct it.

The level of Bethune's commitment to education is reflected in a comment she made in the *Journal of Negro Education* (Collier-Thomas, Summer 1982): "I cannot rest while there is a single Negro boy or girl lacking a chance to prove his worth." As director of the NYA, she made it possible for 150,000 African American young people to attend high school and for 60,000 to graduate from college.

World War II and Increasing Federal Involvement in Education

World War II created conditions in this country that led the federal government to fund several educational programs. One of these, the **Lanham Act** (1941), provided funding for (1) the training of workers in war plants by U.S. Office of Education personnel, (2) the construction of schools in areas where military personnel and workers on federal projects resided, and (3) the provision of child care for the children of working parents.

Another influential and extensive federal program in support of education was the Servicemen's Readjustment Act, popularly known as the **G.I. Bill of Rights.** Signed into law by President Franklin D. Roosevelt in 1944, the G.I. bill has provided millions of veterans with payments for tuition and room and board at colleges and universities and at special schools. Similar legislation was later passed to grant educational benefits to veterans of the Korean and Vietnam conflicts. Not only did the G.I. bill stimulate the growth of American colleges and universities, it also changed the character of the higher education student population. Generally, the returning veterans were older and more serious than students who had not served in the military.

HOW DID EDUCATION CHANGE DURING THE MODERN POSTWAR ERA (1945 TO THE PRESENT)?

Throughout the 20th century and into the new century, many long-standing trends in U.S. education continued. These trends may be grouped and summarized in terms of three general patterns, shown in Figure 5.1. At the same time, the decades since the end of World War II have seen a series of profound changes in U.S. education. These changes have addressed three as yet unanswered questions: (1) How can full and equal educational opportunity be extended to all groups in our culturally pluralistic society? (2) What knowledge and skills should be taught in our nation's schools? (3) How should knowledge and skills be taught?

The 1950s: Defense Education and School Desegregation

Teachers and education were put in the spotlight in 1957 when the Soviet Union launched the first satellite, *Sputnik*, into space. Stunned U.S. leaders immediately blamed the space lag on inadequacies in the education system. The Soviet Union was first into space, they maintained, "because the schools had long been under the sway

FIGURE 5.1 Three general patterns of trends in U.S. education

Americanization
- Americanizing of European educational institutions and instructional models
- Americanizing of English language textbooks and curriculum
- Cultural assimilation of immigrants and others through education
- Aims of education based on moral didacticism and pragmatism
- Aims of education relating to child development and child welfare
- Aims of education relating to success in a society based on capitalism
- Aims of education relating to citizenship in a democracy

Democratization
- Steady growth of compulsory, free, secular, publicly funded education
- Preservation of state, local, and parental control of schooling and schools
- Protection of teachers' and students' rights under the U.S. Constitution
- Shifts in educational reform initiatives that reflect a two-party electoral system
- Continual expansion of early childhood education
- Continual expansion of opportunities for higher education and adult education
- Traumatic periodic extensions of educational opportunity to "other" Americans (women; racial, ethnic, and language minorities; people with disabilities)

Professionalization
- Professionalizing of teaching as an occupation
- Professionalizing of teacher organizations and associations
- Growth in scientific and bureaucratic models for the management of schools
- Rising standards for qualifications to teach
- Continual development of institutions and programs for teacher education
- Greater application of theory and research on teaching and learning
- Generally rising status and salaries for teachers as members of a profession

of progressive education, which de-emphasized intellectual values" (Hartman, 2008, p. 176). U.S. students, for example, were taught less science and mathematics, and fewer foreign languages than their European counterparts.

From our perspective today, "the 1950s can be characterized as a war between U.S. and Soviet school systems—each trying to educate the best scientists and engineers for development of military technology" (Spring, 2008, p. 221). In the public's mind, the ability of America to defend itself was directly related to the quality of its schools. As Vice Admiral H. G. Rickover put it in his 1959 book *Education and Freedom,* "education is our first line of defense" (1959).

The federal government appropriated millions of dollars over the next decade for educational reforms that reflected the essentialist educational philosophy. Through provisions of the **National Defense Education Act of 1958,** the U.S. Office of Education sponsored research and innovation in science, mathematics, modern foreign languages, and guidance. Out of their work came the new math; new science programs; an integration of anthropology, economics, political science, and sociology into new social studies programs; and renewed interest and innovations in foreign language instruction. Teachers were trained in the use of new methods and materials at summer workshops, schools were given funds for new equipment, and research centers were established. In 1964, Congress extended the act for three years and expanded Title III of the act to include money for improving instruction in reading, English, geography, history, and civics.

During the reform activity of the 1960s, public school enrollments rose dramatically. In 1950, about 25 million children were enrolled; in 1960, about 36 million; and in 1970, about 50 million. As a result of a decline in births, however, this trend stopped abruptly in the late 1970s. In the fall of 1979, for example, 41.5 million students were enrolled in K–12 classes, a decrease of 1,069,000, or 2.5 percent, from the year before (Rippa, 1984).

The curriculum reform movement of the 1960s did not bear the positive results that its supporters hoped for. The benefits of the new federally funded programs reached only a small percentage of teachers. In regard to some of the new materials—those related to the new math, for example—teachers complained that the recommended approaches failed to take into account the realities of classroom life. Many of the materials, it turned out, were developed by persons who had little or no classroom experience. Thus, many teachers of the 1960s ignored the innovations and continued teaching as they had always done. In fact, this tendency for teachers to resist many educational reforms has continued into the present. As Diane Ravitch points out,

> A teacher whose career began in 1960 has lived through an era of failed revolutions. One movement after another arrived, peaked, and dispersed. Having observed the curriculum reform movement, the free school movement, the minimum competency movement, and, more recently, the back-to-basics movement, a veteran teacher may be excused for secretly thinking, when confronted by the next campaign to "save" the schools, "This too shall pass." (1985, p. 303)

The end of World War II also saw the beginning of school **desegregation.** On May 17, 1954, the U.S. Supreme Court rejected the "separate but equal" doctrine that had been used since 1850 as a justification for excluding African Americans from attending school with whites. In response to a suit filed by the NAACP on behalf of a Kansas family, Chief Justice Earl Warren declared that to segregate school children "from others of similar age and qualifications solely because of their race generates a feeling of inferiority as to their status in the community that may affect their hearts and minds in a way unlikely ever to be undone" (***Brown v. Board of Education of Topeka,* 1954**).

The Supreme Court's decision did not bring an immediate end to segregated schools. Though the court one year later

When African American students desegregated Little Rock Central High School in 1957, they were protected by the National Guard. What is the legacy of school desegregation today?

177

ordered that desegregation proceed with "all deliberate speed," opposition to school integration arose in school districts across the country. Some districts, whose leaders modeled restraint and a spirit of cooperation, desegregated peacefully. Other districts became battlegrounds, characterized by boycotts, rallies, and violence.

The 1960s: The War on Poverty and the Great Society

The 1960s, hallmarked by the Kennedy administration's spirit of action and high hopes, provided a climate that supported change. Classrooms were often places of pedagogical experimentation and creativity reminiscent of the progressive era. The open-education movement, team teaching, individualized instruction, the integrated-day concept, flexible scheduling, and nongraded schools were some of the innovations that teachers were asked to implement. These structural, methodological, and curricular changes implied the belief that teachers were capable professionals.

The image of teachers in the 1960s was enhanced by the publication of several books by educators who were influenced by the progressivist educational philosophy and humanistic psychology. A. S. Neill's *Summerhill* (1960), Sylvia Ashton-Warner's *Teacher* (1963), John Holt's *How Children Fail* (1964), Herbert Kohl's *36 Children* (1967), James Herndon's *The Way It Spozed to Be* (1969), and Jonathan Kozol's *Death at an Early Age* (1967)—a few of the books that appeared at the time—gave readers inside views of teachers at work and teachers' perceptions of how students learn.

The administrations of Presidents Kennedy and Johnson funneled massive amounts of money into a War on Poverty. Education was seen as the key to breaking the transmission of poverty from generation to generation. The War on Poverty developed methods, materials, and programs such as subsidized breakfast and lunch programs, Head Start, Upward Bound, and the Job Corps that would be appropriate to children who had been disadvantaged due to poverty.

The War on Poverty has proved much more difficult to win than imagined, and the results of such programs 40 years later have been mixed. The 3- to 6-year-olds who participated in Head Start did much better when they entered public schools; however, academic gains appeared to dissolve over time. Although the Job Corps enabled scores of youth to avoid a lifetime of unemployment, many graduates returned to the streets where they eventually became statistics in unemployment and crime records. The education of low-income children received a boost in April 1965 when Congress passed the **Elementary and Secondary Education Act.** As part of President Johnson's Great Society program, the act allocated funds on the basis of the number of poor children in school districts. Thus, schools in poverty areas that frequently had to cope with problems such as low achievement, poor discipline, truancy, and high teacher turnover rates received much needed assistance in addressing their problems.

In 1968, the Elementary and Secondary Education Act was amended with Title VII, the Bilingual Education Act. This act provided federal aid to low-income children "of limited English-speaking ability." The act did not spell out clearly what bilingual education might mean other than to say that it provided money for local school districts to "develop and carry out new and imaginative elementary and secondary school programs" to meet the needs of non-English-speaking children. Since the passing of Title VII, debate over the ultimate goal of bilingual education has been intense: Should it help students make the transition to regular English-speaking classrooms, or should it help such students maintain their non-English language and culture? Chapter 8 examines both sides of this debate.

The 1970s: Accountability and Equal Opportunity

The 1970s saw drops in enrollment, test scores, and public confidence in our nation's schools. At the same time, new educational policies called for equality of education for all in the United States. Troubled by the continued low academic performance of many

U.S. students, parents, citizens groups, and policymakers initiated a back-to-basics movement and called for increased teacher accountability.

Many school systems had to cope with financial crises during the 1970s. Public and private elementary school enrollments, instead of increasing as they had since 1940, declined by nearly 5 million during the 1970s (National Center for Education Statistics, March 25, 2008). As a result of declining enrollments, schools received less state aid. Moreover, voters frequently failed to support referendums to increase school funding because they lacked confidence in the schools.

Many parents responded to the crisis by becoming education activists, seeking or establishing alternative schools, or joining the home education movement led by John Holt, who by then had given up on reforming schools. These parents believed they could provide a better education for their children than public school teachers. Those who kept their children in the public schools demanded teacher **accountability,** which limited teachers' instructional flexibility and extended their evaluation paperwork. Basal readers and teacher-proof curricular packages descended on teachers, spelling out with their cookbook directions the deeper message that teachers were not to be trusted to teach on their own. Confidence in teachers reached a low point.

In addition, during the late 1960s and early 1970s, increasing numbers of young people questioned what the schools were teaching and how they were teaching it. Thousands of them mobilized in protest against an establishment that, in their view, supported an immoral, undeclared war in Vietnam and was unconcerned with the oppression of minorities at home. In their search for reasons why these and other social injustices were allowed to exist, many militant youth groups singled out the schools' curricula. From their perspective, the schools taught subjects irrelevant to finding solutions to pressing problems.

Responding in good faith to their critics' accusations, schools greatly expanded their curricular offerings and instituted a wide variety of instructional strategies. In making these changes, however, school personnel gradually realized that they were alienating other groups: taxpayers who accused schools of extravagant spending; religious sects who questioned the values that children were being taught; **back-to-basics** advocates who charged that students were not learning how to read, write, and compute; and citizens who were alarmed at steadily rising school crime, drugs, and violence.

Despite the siege on teachers and schools, however, the reforms of the 1960s and 1970s did result in a number of improvements that have lasted into the present. More young people graduate from high school now than in previous decades, more teachers have advanced training, school buildings are better equipped, and instructional methods and materials are both more relevant to learners and more diverse.

For those people who had been marginalized by the educational system, the federal acts that were passed in the 1970s brought success and encouragement: the Title IX Education Amendment prohibiting sex discrimination (1972), the Indian Education Act (1972), the Education for All Handicapped Children Act (1975), and the Indochina Migration and Refugee Assistance Act (1975).

Title IX of the Education Amendments Act, which took effect in 1975, stated that "no person in the United States shall, on the basis of sex, be excluded from participation in, be denied the benefits of, or be subjected to discrimination under any education program or activity receiving Federal financial assistance."

The **Education for All Handicapped Children Act (Public Law 94–142),** passed by Congress in 1975, extended greater educational opportunities to children with disabilities.

What impact has Title IX had on the education of females? What does *equal educational opportunity* for female and male students really mean?

This act (often referred to as the **mainstreaming** law) specifies extensive due process procedures to guarantee that children with special needs will receive a free, appropriate education in the least restrictive educational environment. Through the act's provisions, parents are involved in planning educational programs for their children.

The 1980s: A Great Debate

The first half of the 1980s saw a continuation, perhaps even an escalation, of the criticisms aimed at the schools during the two previous decades. In fact, Lee Shulman (1987) characterized much of the 1980s as an era of "teacher bashing." With the publication in 1983 of the report by the National Commission on Excellence in Education, *A Nation at Risk: The Imperative for Educational Reform,* a great national debate was begun on how to improve the quality of schools. *A Nation at Risk* and dozens of other national reports on U.S. schools gave evidence to some that the schools were failing miserably to achieve their goals. The following excerpt from the first paragraph of *A Nation at Risk* exemplifies the tone of many of these reports:

> Our Nation is at risk. Our once unchallenged preeminence in commerce, industry, science, and technological innovation is being overtaken by competitors throughout the world . . . the educational foundations of our society are presently being eroded by a rising tide of mediocrity that threatens our very future as a Nation and a people. (National Commission on Excellence in Education, 1983)

Responses included more proposals for curriculum reform. Mortimer Adler's ***Paideia Proposal*** (1982) called for a perennialist core curriculum based on the Great Books. ***High School: A Report on Secondary Education in America*** (1983), written by Ernest Boyer (1928–1995) for the Carnegie Foundation for the Advancement of Teaching, suggested strengthening the academic core curriculum in high schools, a recommendation that was widely adopted. In 1986, former secretary of the U.S. Department of Education William Bennett advocated a perennialist high school curriculum that he described in *James Madison High* (1987). Educators at the middle school level began to create small learning communities, eliminate tracking, and develop new ways to enhance student self-esteem as a result of the Carnegie Council on Adolescent Development report *Turning Points: Preparing American Youth for the 21st Century* (1989). These and other reform reports that swept the nation during the 1980s made a lasting imprint on education in the United States.

The 1990s: Teacher Leadership

The push to reform schools begun in the 1980s continued throughout the 1990s, and teaching was transformed in dramatic ways. In response to challenges such as greater diversity, greater international competition, less support for public education, and decentralization and deregulation of schools, innovative approaches to teaching and learning were developed throughout the United States (see Figure 5.2). Teachers went beyond the classroom and assumed leadership roles in school restructuring and educational reform. Through collaborative relationships with students, principals, parents, and the private sector, teachers changed the nature of their profession. As one high school teacher said in the

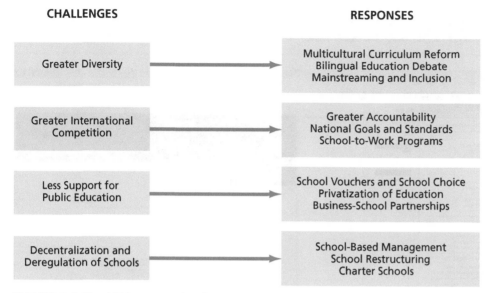

CHALLENGES

RESPONSES

Greater Diversity → Multicultural Curriculum Reform / Bilingual Education Debate / Mainstreaming and Inclusion

Greater International Competition → Greater Accountability / National Goals and Standards / School-to-Work Programs

Less Support for Public Education → School Vouchers and School Choice / Privatization of Education / Business-School Partnerships

Decentralization and Deregulation of Schools → School-Based Management / School Restructuring / Charter Schools

FIGURE 5.2 The 1990s: A sample of trends in education

late 1990s: "I see it [change] happening. Not overnight, but I think it's going to. When I first started teaching in the early sixties, I would never have envisioned things changing as much as they have" (Grant & Murray 1999, p. 212).

The New Century: Equity, Excellence, and Accountability

An excerpt from the mission statement of the International Centre for Educational Change at the Ontario Institute for Studies in Education captures well the world of teaching during the second decade of the new century—it is a "a world of intensifying and rapid change . . . [characterized by] new technologies, greater cultural diversity, restructured approaches to administration and management, and a more sophisticated knowledge-base about teaching and learning." The Technology in Action feature for this chapter illustrates the technologically rich, complex teaching environment referenced in the Ontario Institute mission statement.

When you become a teacher, your work will be enhanced if you understand and appreciate the historical context for U.S. education, as presented in Figure 5.3. The left-hand column of the timeline identifies three themes that will continue to be educational priorities during the decades to come: *equity* for all students, *excellence* and high standards, and *accountability* for schools and teachers.

The United States has set for itself an education mission of truly ambitious proportions. To realize fully this mission during the decades to come will be difficult, but an examination of our history shows that it is not impossible. In little more than 380 years, our education system has grown from one that provided only a minimal education to an advantaged minority to one that now provides maximal educational opportunity to the majority. Clearly, the first decade of the new century provides ample evidence that our nation will not waver from its long-standing commitment to ensuring that all children have equal access to educational excellence.

TECHNOLOGY in *ACTION*

Screen Capture in 12th-Grade Calculus

At any given moment, a student struggles in Mr. DeWilt's 12th-grade calculus class. The textbook, his instruction, and the text's website were good, but he needed something more. Mr. DeWilt needed something directly related to his lessons. He needed additional support to build on his previous discussions with students, but also something flexible and personal. Most of his students understood the class material most of the time. However, if you did the "math" over the course of the school year, a number of students "did not get it."

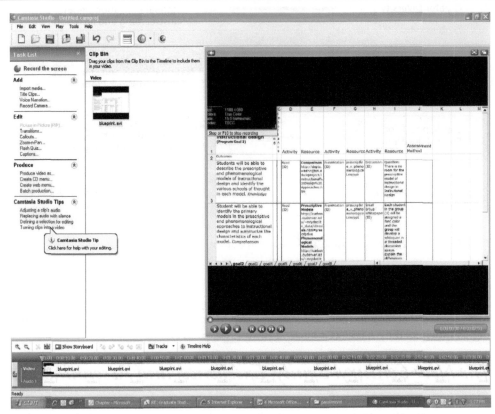

Source: Techsmith Corporation. http://www.techsmith.com (accessed July 6, 2008). Used by permission.

The textbook he used had a supplemental DVD where his students can view video examples of calculus problems and their solutions—in his opinion, these were very effective. During a Web search for additional educational support, Mr. DeWilt located a free Web-based calculus tool. The tool allows students to plug in a problem and complete the equation. However, this free tool was not user-friendly and had little technical help and documentation. He was spending more time explaining how to use the tool than on the calculus concepts he wanted his students to learn. He needed something that the students could access any time they ran into trouble, something they could go back to again and again.

At first, he tried videotaping his work on the computer screen, but that did not work. The audio was poor and the image quality was worse. Also, it was extremely time-consuming to set up the video equipment for each student issue.

Frustrated, Mr. DeWilt sent an e-mail to the textbook's publisher asking how the computer screen recordings on the

DVD were so clear. He learned that the publisher used a screen capture software called Camtasias.

After a brief conversation with Jenny Seasam, the building instructional technology (IT) person, Mr. DeWilt had a copy loaded to his office computer. Now, when a student comes to him with a calculus problem, he opens the free Web-based calculus tool, puts on his headset microphone, launches Camtasia, and walks the student through the application. When he finishes, he saves the file as a Web file and publishes it on his class website. Students can access it any time, anywhere. This solution not only helps his students with their technical issues, but also helps reinforce the calculus concepts addressed in Mr. DeWilt's classroom.

SCREEN CAPTURE: Screen capture is a tool that allows you to record your movements on a computer screen while adding voice, text, and graphics. This is an easy-to-use, cost-effective way to create custom, just-in-time tutorials, examples, and navigation on your computer screen. To use this tool, you will need at least 1 GB of RAM, a sound card, a video card, microphone, and speakers.

VISIT: http://www.techsmith.com/products.asp. The Techsmith website offers several variations of its screen capture software. There are other free tools available to you as an educator. The easiest way to find free tools is to Google "screen capture, free software."

POSSIBLE USES: Screen capture software can be used to record website navigation, software tutorials, or any other computer-based activity that you want to demonstrate to an audience. Teachers have used screen capture software to help students understand how to navigate a complex website. Teachers have also used screen capture software to develop tutorials to help their students use a specific piece of software. For example, see the Try It Out section of this feature below. Instead of presenting this to you in text, I could use the software tool to capture the instructions I present below that allow you to visually watch me navigate the Camtasia software.

TRY IT OUT: You have several screen capture options available to you as an educator. The tool spotlighted in this feature is just one example that you can use. If you want to demo Camtasia, you can download a free trial version from the Techsmith website (listed above). Once you have downloaded the software and installed it, merely click on the Camtasia icon on your desktop or the Camtasia link in your Start Menu. After that initial click, you will be prompted to open an existing project or start a new one.

Let's start a new one. As you set up your project, you will need to make some decisions. First, will you record a region of your computer screen, a specific window, or the entire screen? The answer will depend on the project you want to create. You will also need to determine the size of your video image. Larger images are easier to watch, but they result in a larger file size, which can be problematic for Web delivery of the screen capture. After you determine the type of audio for the project, you are ready to continue.

Now, click on the part of your computer screen you want to capture—a highlighted box will surround the section that will be recorded. If the highlighted section is accurate, click "Record" from your Camtasia Recorder prompt. From this point everything you do on your computer will be captured. When you are done recording, hit "Stop Recording" and save the file. If you like what you did, you can render (recreate) the file to an appropriate file format, like Quicktime or Flash. If you do not like it, place your unrendered file on the editing timeline, edit it, and then render.

Religious Emphasis	1620	1620 — Emphasis on basic skills needed to learn religious catechisms and read prayers. Curriculum also includes surveying, navigation, and bookkeeping. Education primarily for the elite.
	1640	1636 — Latin grammar (college-prep) schools established and, like Harvard and Yale Colleges, emphasize Latin, Greek, theology, and philosophy for those preparing to enter law or religion.
	1660	1647 — Massachusetts Law of 1647 mandates a reading and writing teacher for towns of 50 or more families; a Latin teacher for towns of 100 or more. Females taught basics to enable them to carry out religious and family responsibilities.
	1680	
	1700	1700s — Public schools teach reading, writing, and basic mathematics (counting, adding, and subtracting) to prepare students for jobs and apprenticeships.
	1720	
	1740	
Political Emphasis	1760 / 1780	Early 1750s — Academies teach secondary students a practical curriculum (drawing, surveying, navigation, merchant's accounting, etc.) to become tradesmen and workers.
	1800 / 1820 / 1840	1821 — First public high school teaches basic skills and history, geography, health, and physical training.
Utilitarian Emphasis	1860	1860 — First English-speaking kindergarten emphasizes growth, activity, play, songs, and stories.
		1874 — Free public schooling now includes high schools that place strong emphasis on vocational education and reading, writing, and mathematics.
Education for Masses	1880	1893 — Committee of Ten asserts that high schools are for college-bound and curriculum should emphasize mental disciplines in humanities, language, and science.
	1900	1918 — Commission on Reorganization of Secondary Education focuses on individual differences. Curriculum to stress Seven Cardinal Principles.
	1920	1930s & 1940s — Progressive education movement stresses curriculum based on student's needs and Interests. Home economics, health, family living, citizenship, and woodshop added to the curriculum.
	1940	1957 — Soviet *Sputnik* sparks emphasis on science, mathematics, and languages.
The Excellence Movement	1960	1960s — Calls for relevancy result in expanded course offerings and electives.
		Mid 1970s — Back-to-basics movement emphasizes reading, writing, mathematics, and oral communication.
	1980	1983 — *Nation at Risk* report calls for "five new basics"—English, mathematics, science, social studies, and computer science.
		1985 — Rigorous core curricula advocated at all levels in an effort to increase standards and to ensure quality.
		1989 — The Carnegie Council on Adolescent Development report, *Turning Points,* recommends the creation of learning communities and a core academic program for middle-level students. President George H. W. Bush convenes education summit meeting for 50 state governors.
		1990 — President George H. W. Bush unveils Goals 2000, identifying six educational goals: readiness for school; high school completion; student achievement and citizenship: science and mathematics; adult literacy and lifelong learning; and safe, disciplined, and drug-free schools.
		1994 — President Bill Clinton signs into law Goals 2000: Educate America Act.
		1995 — President Bill Clinton creates the National Information Infrastructure (NII) to encourage schools to become connected to the "information superhighway."
		1996 — President Bill Clinton launches the President's Educational Technology Initiative.
	2000	1999 — President Bill Clinton signs into law the Educational Excellence for All Children Act, reauthorizing the Elementary and Secondary Education Act.
High-Stakes Testing; School and Teacher Accountability		2002 — President George W. Bush signs into law the No Child Left Behind Act of 2001.
	2010	2013 — By 2013–14, public schools must guarantee that all students can pass state-proficiency tests.

FIGURE 5.3 Historical timeline for U.S. education

SUMMARY

Why Is Educational History Important?

- An understanding of educational history is necessary so teachers can provide leadership to improve our educational future.
- Educational history is an important part of professional knowledge.

What Were Teaching and Schools Like in the American Colonies (1620–1750)?

- Colonial education was patterned after the British two-track system, and its primary objective was to promote religion.
- Colonial teachers had low status, though respect increased with grade level.
- Puritans believed children were naturally corrupt and sinful and should be disciplined sternly at the dame schools, reading and writing schools, and Latin grammar schools common to the colonies.
- Mandated education in the United States had its origins in two colonial laws: the Massachusetts Acts of 1642 and 1647.
- At the end of the American Revolution, the few African and Native Americans who were literate were taught at church-sponsored schools that were segregated by race.

What Were the Goals of Education During the Revolutionary Period (1750–1820)?

- During the Revolutionary period, characterized by a declining European influence on American education, education in the new democracy was shaped by the ideas of Benjamin Franklin, Thomas Jefferson, and Noah Webster.
- Educational opportunities for women were often limited to preparing them for family life.

How Was the Struggle Won for State-Supported Common Schools (1820–1865)?

- Horace Mann, a strong advocate for state-supported, free common schools, believed that teachers should receive postsecondary training in normal schools.
- The six-volume McGuffey reader, with its moral lessons and emphasis on virtue, determined much of what children learned at school.
- The Morrill Land-Grant Act, passed in 1862, provided federal land for colleges and set a precedent for federal involvement in education.

How Did Compulsory Education Change Schools and the Teaching Profession (1865–1920)?

- The spread of common schools and dramatic increases in their enrollments led to the use of scientific management techniques for their operation.
- Booker T. Washington, founder of the Tuskegee Institute, believed education could prepare African Americans to live peaceably with whites, while W. E. B. DuBois believed African Americans should educate themselves for leadership positions and not accept inferior status.
- Kindergartens became common and used child-centered curricula patterned after German educator Friedrich Froebel's ideas.
- The National Education Association (NEA) and the American Federation of Teachers (AFT) were founded to professionalize teaching and increase teachers' salaries and benefits.
- The NEA appointed the Committee of Ten and the Committee of Fifteen to make recommendations for the secondary and elementary school curricula, respectively.
- The Commission on the Reorganization of Secondary Education, appointed by the NEA to reexamine the secondary curriculum in regard to students' individual differences, developed "seven cardinal principles" for

schooling at all levels: health, command of fundamental processes (reading, writing, and computation), worthy home membership, vocation, citizenship, worthy use of leisure time, and ethical character.

What Were the Aims of Education During the Progressive Era (1920–1945)?

- John Dewey's Laboratory School at the University of Chicago, a model of progressive education, offered a curriculum based on children's interests and needs.
- Progressive educator Maria Montessori developed age-appropriate materials and teaching strategies that were implemented in the United States and throughout the world.
- Public criticism of progressive education led to its decline at the start of World War II.
- School enrollments became increasingly diverse as a result of immigration, and a goal of education was the rapid assimilation of all groups into an English-speaking Anglo-European culture.

How Did Education Change During the Modern Postwar Era (1945 to the Present)?

- The Soviet Union's launching of Sputnik in 1957 sparked educational reform, particularly in science,

mathematics, and foreign language education. Schools were ordered to desegregate with "all deliberate speed" as a result of a 1954 decision by the Supreme Court in Brown v. Board of Education of Topeka.
- Innovative curricula and instructional strategies were used in many classrooms of the 1960s. The Elementary and Secondary Education Act of 1965, part of President Johnson's Great Society and War on Poverty programs, provided federal money to improve the education of poor children.
- Alarmed by declining test scores, the public became critical of schools during the 1970s and demanded accountability. An array of federal legislation was passed to provide equal educational opportunity for all students.
- A Nation at Risk and other reports during the 1980s addressed weaknesses in U.S. schools and sparked debate on how to improve U.S. education.
- In response to continuing challenges to education today, teachers are taking leadership roles in school restructuring, school governance, curriculum change, and other aspects of educational reform.
- Three themes will continue to be educational priorities during the decades to come: equity for all students, excellence and high standards, and accountability for schools and teachers.

PROFESSIONAL REFLECTIONS AND ACTIVITIES

Teacher's Journal

1. Benjamin Franklin suggested that education is "the surest foundation" for happiness. To what extent do you agree or disagree with Franklin's statement?
2. Based on what you have read in this chapter, identify several broad or long-term trends in the development of U.S. education that continue today. How are those trends reflected in educational policies and practices through the decades? How are these trends evident at different points in the past and now? How might these trends be manifested in the future?

Teacher's Research

1. Identify a trend or issue in education and then use the Internet to gather information about its roots in the past and effects on teaching today. Consider, for

example, the debate about the use of corporal punishment in the schools. Other areas to research include:

tax-supported schools
school desegregation
progressive education
higher education
early childhood education
equal educational opportunity for women
immigrant education
teacher education
educational technology
literacy

As your information accumulates, identify specific links between the past and present. Transcribe your notes into a brief narrative report and pool your findings with those of classmates.

2. Use online references to research in greater detail the contributions of a pioneer in education whose work is summarized in this chapter.

Observations and Interviews

1. Interview veteran teachers and administrators at a local school and ask them to comment on the changes in education that they have observed and experienced during their careers. In particular, compare their remarks to this chapter's discussion of education during the post–World War II era, using this chapter's descriptions of the era to guide your questions. What events do respondents identify as having had the greatest impact on their teaching?
2. Visit a museum in your area for the purpose of examining some artifacts from early U.S. educational history. Take notes on what you find and describe several of the artifacts to the rest of your class.

myeducationlab To complete additional observations and interviews, go to MyEducationLab at www.myeducationlab.com, select the Virtual Field Experience section, and click on this chapter's Observations and Interviews.

Professional Portfolio

Prepare a videotaped oral history that focuses on the changes that have occurred over the years in local schools or an interest of local concern. You may decide to interview experienced teachers, administrators, or school board members, or you may decide to interview older members of the community.

Prior to conducting your interviews, prepare several interview questions that focus on your area of interest. At the conclusion of each interview, invite the interviewee to provide any other relevant information he or she might have.

myeducationlab Now go to MyEducationLab at www.myeducationlab.com to test your understanding of chapter content by completing this chapter's Study Plan.

Governance and Finance of U.S. Schools

8

From Chapter 6 of *Becoming a Teacher*, 8/e. Forrest W. Parkay. Beverly Hardcastle Stanford.

Governance and Finance
of U.S. Schools

CLASSROOM CASE
The Realities of Teaching

THE CHALLENGE: Understanding how educational politics influence teachers and schools.

You just entered the teachers' lounge during your planning period. At once, you know the four teachers in the lounge are having a heated discussion.

"Look at No Child Left Behind. That shows how the federal government is a pawn of big business," says Cheng-Yi, a physical education (PE) teacher. "Big business controls the schools."

"I don't see how you can say that," says Alex, a science teacher.

"Well, high-tech industries are worried about international competition," Cheng-Yi continues. "So they exert political pressure on the feds. Then the feds lean on us to teach the skills industry needs to be competitive."

"That sounds far-fetched, almost like a conspiracy," says Alex, breaking into a smile.

"Yeah, what does No Child Left Behind have to do with big business?" asks Kim, an English teacher, before taking a sip of her water.

"No Child Left Behind mandates testing in math and reading," Cheng-Yi continues. "It doesn't say art and music, does it? What about literature and history? Those subjects won't make us competitive in the global marketplace."

"Cheng-Yi has got a point," adds Anita, one of the school's four master teachers and chair of the site-based council. "Big business has a lot of political clout when it comes to schools. Believe me, when a businessperson on the site-based council talks, we listen."

"That's the way it is," says Cheng-Yi, nodding his head.

"Remember when the president of the chamber of commerce came to our September in-service and talked about how the schools produce a product?" asks Anita. "In her eyes, the 'product' we produce is workers with basic skills."

"Exactly," Cheng-Yi says with enthusiasm. "Education in this country is really controlled by big business."

"Come on," Kim sighs. "You two have got to politicize everything when it comes to education. Alex is right, there's no business-sector agenda that's being played out in the schools."

"Right," Alex says. "Remember, No Child Left Behind was developed by politicians, and we elected them—that sounds pretty democratic to me. I mean . . . 'we the people' control the schools."

"Wait a minute," Cheng-Yi says. "No Child Left Behind is really being pushed by big business."

191

"Yeah, think about the ultimate aim of No Child Left Behind. Is it really to produce citizens for democracy?" Anita interjects. "No, the real aim is to produce good workers, good consumers—people who strengthen the economy."

"Right," Cheng-Yi says.

"Well, I still think you're stretching things," says Kim. "Why don't we ask the new teacher here. What do you think?"

The four teachers look at you, awaiting your response. What do you say?

FOCUS QUESTIONS

1. Why do you need to understand educational politics?
2. How does the local community influence schools?
3. What powers and influence do states have in governing schools?
4. How do regional education agencies assist schools?
5. How does the federal government influence education?
6. How are schools financed in the United States?
7. What are some trends in funding for equity and excellence?
8. How will the privatization movement affect equity and excellence in education?

WHY DO YOU NEED TO UNDERSTAND EDUCATIONAL POLITICS?

At this point in your teacher education program, you are probably most concerned about the challenges of teaching—creating a positive classroom climate; ensuring that all students learn; and learning to work with teachers, administrators, and parents, for example. Compared to meeting these challenges, understanding how educational politics influence school governance may not seem important. However, "it is important for all citizens, including teachers, students, school administrators, and elected officials, to understand the deep-rooted controversies surrounding the functioning of public schools" (Spring, 2008, p. 10).

Perhaps you think that politics and teaching should remain separate. However, education is not (and never will be) apolitical. It is a fact of life that school policies are developed in a political milieu, and "reforming schools is essentially a series of political acts, not technical solutions to problems" (Cuban, 2003, p. 59).

Many complex political forces currently influence school governance in the United States (see Figure 6.1), as the opening classroom case for this chapter illustrated. In general, *politics* refers to how people use power, influence, and authority within an organization to persuade others to act in desired ways. **Educational politics** refers to how people use power, influence, and authority to affect instructional and curricular practices within a school or school system. Clearly, you will have much to gain from becoming politically astute and involved. For instance, the following examples illustrate how several teachers benefited from their knowledge of educational politics:

- Two teachers, members of the local school council (LSC) for a school in a poor urban area, organized a group of parent volunteers who eventually helped reduce student truancy and improve students' attitudes toward school.
- Three high school English teachers received a state grant to develop a humanities program—their grant application included letters of support from the president of the board of education and the superintendent.
- A group of teachers went door to door passing out information about a much-needed remodeling and expansion project at their school; two months later, voters approved funding for the project.

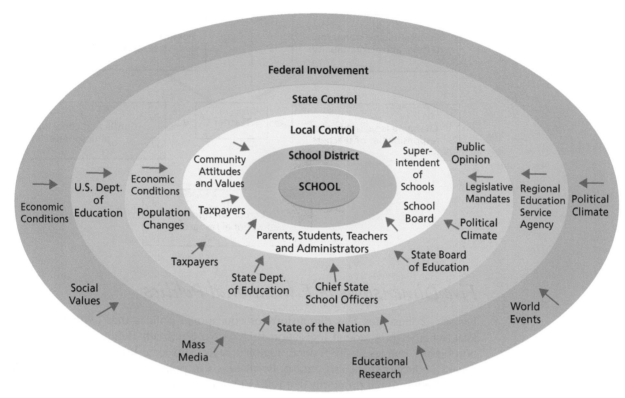

FIGURE 6.1 Political influences on the schools

Among the groups who will compete to shape educational policies during your teaching career, at least 10 can be identified:

1. **Parents**—concerned with controlling local schools so that quality educational programs are available to their children.
2. **Students**—concerned with policies related to freedom of expression, dress, behavior, and curricular offerings.
3. **Teachers**—concerned with their role in school reform, improving working conditions, terms of employment, and other professional issues.
4. **Administrators**—concerned with providing leadership so that various interest groups, including teachers, participate in the shared governance of schools and the development of quality educational programs.
5. **Taxpayers**—concerned with maintaining an appropriate formula for determining local, state, and federal financial support of schools.
6. **Federal, state, and local authorities**—concerned with the implementation of court orders, guidelines, and legislative mandates related to the operation of schools.
7. **Ethnic and racial groups**—concerned with the availability of equal educational opportunity for all and with legal issues surrounding administrative certification, terms of employment, and evaluation.
8. **Educational theorists and researchers**—concerned with using theoretical and research-based insights as the bases for improving schools at all levels.
9. **Corporate sector**—concerned with receiving from the schools graduates who have the knowledge, skills, attitudes, and values to help an organization realize its goals.
10. **Special interest groups**—concerned with advancing educational reforms that reflect particular religious, philosophical, and economic points of view.

FIGURE 6.2 Five dimensions of educational politics that influence teachers

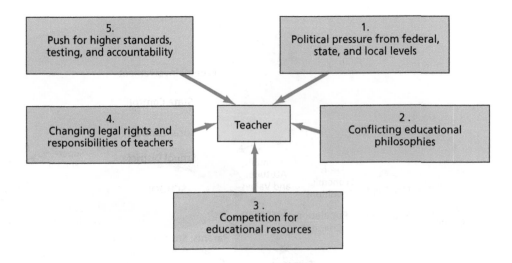

FIGURE 6.2 Five dimensions of educational politics that influence teachers

Five Dimensions of Educational Politics

Figure 6.2 illustrates five dimensions of educational politics that influence teachers. First, whether it is federal legislation such as No Child Left Behind or a local school bond issue, politics at the federal, regional, state, and local levels influence teachers. Second, educators, citizens, and policymakers use politics to lobby for the development of educational programs that reflect their educational philosophies. Third, the allocation of resources to schools can easily become a political issue in a community, as anyone who has voted on a school bond issue knows. Fourth, the legal rights and responsibilities of teachers and students are continuously changing, often as a result of conflicting political views about education. And fifth, one of the "hottest," politically charged issues in education today involves the push for higher standards; mandated testing to ensure that students have mastered those standards; and calls for **accountability** to ensure that schools, teachers, and administrators produce results.

Indeed, it is no exaggeration to say that educational politics can place a teacher "in the line of fire." This chapter's Teachers' Voices: Research to Reality feature, for example, describes how one teacher came into "the line of fire" after publicly expressing his disagreement with an educational reform mandated by his school board.

The next four sections of this chapter examine how educational politics at the local, state, regional, and national levels influence schools and teachers.

HOW DOES THE LOCAL COMMUNITY INFLUENCE SCHOOLS?

While the Constitution does not address public education, the Tenth Amendment is used as the basis for giving states the legal authority to create and manage school systems. In addition, as illustrated in Figure 6.1, various individuals and groups, though not legally empowered, compete vigorously to influence those legally entitled to operate the schools.

The Tenth Amendment gives to the states all powers not reserved for the federal government and not prohibited to the states. The states, in turn, have created local school districts, giving them responsibility for the daily operation of public schools. As a result of efforts to consolidate districts, the number of local public school districts has declined from 117,108 in 1939–40 to 14,166 in 2005–06 (National Center for Education Statistics, March 25, 2008).

Local School District

Local school districts vary greatly in regard to demographics such as number of school-age children; educational, occupational, and income levels of parents;

TEACHERS' VOICES RESEARCH TO REALITY

John Flickinger
THROWN TO THE WOLVES

January 6, 2003. I was excited to get back to my students after the Christmas break, and especially happy to be starting my yearly exploration of the mind of Henry David Thoreau. We began with *Civil Disobedience*.

Soon, my students' hatred for Thoreau's verbose nineteenth-century style gave way to amazement at his brilliant intellect and his wonderful ideas. By the end of the week, fine young minds were interpreting the transcendental concepts of Henry David Thoreau, showing me things I had never thought of in all my years of teaching.

Then along came A-B block scheduling. Instead of seeing our students every day for 50 minutes, we would see them every other day for 90. Two teachers surveyed the faculty: 149 against, 13 for. We took the results and a stack of research showing the folly of block scheduling to the school board. Their reaction was a "so what" shrug. "We are placing you on block scheduling. End of discussion."

The next day, the teachers wore black ribbons mourning the death of site-based management. It was decisions made by people in the trenches that made Montwood a national Blue Ribbon school. And site-based management is mandated by our state education department. But A-B scheduling was a done deal.

My students asked, "What should we do?" Being a teacher, I answered their question with a question. "What does Thoreau say?" They dug into *Civil Disobedience*. "It's not only our right but our responsibility to make our feelings known," they said. I was so proud of them.

Students and parents organized to express their opinions. Two meetings were called by the district and abruptly canceled. Then I heard rumors of a student walkout. I wrote on my board, "No Walk-Out." The next morning, 1,000 students gathered in front of the school. They chanted and waved placards, peacefully expressing their dissatisfaction. Panic stricken, the district called the police. A hundred riot-gear-clad, helmet-wearing officers turned a peaceful protest into a riot. The smell of mace hung in the clear January air. Afterward, the superintendent told us this riot was "entirely the teachers' fault." The next morning, I sent an e-mail praising the actions of 99.9 percent of our students. I blamed the incident on arrogant district officials. Security showed up at my door. I was told to report to the principal's office. I was suspended for improper use of district e-mail. National attention was now focused on our school.

That night, I was ambushed on my porch by a local TV station with ties to the district. I refused to speak. On the 10 o'clock news, there I was peeking out of my front door. "The teacher rumored to have incited the riot refused to speak to us." My e-mail was read, edited to sound like support for the riot and an appeal for more violence.

Then e-mails began to arrive from places like Stanford, MIT, Columbia, and Notre Dame, from my former students. "Emerson and Thoreau and their life-changing philosophy are the reason I am here today," they said.

At the next board meeting, a parent delivered a stack of letters testifying to the influence of my teaching. Parents and students held signs: "Give us back our teacher." I tried to hold back the tears. I failed.

When I am 80 years old and someone asks me what I did in life, I will remember those students holding those signs. I will straighten up and proudly say, "I was a teacher."

The powers that be threw two of us to the wolves. I was out in the cold among the hungry lupus. I survived because of my defenders. My first stop was the campus rep of the Texas State Teachers Association. A lawyer in Austin jumped on a plane and arrived in El Paso just in time to take notes quietly at the Friday night district meeting. He was noticed. At every meeting, people were there to support me. When I walked into a potential ambush by district officials, I was accompanied by two union representatives who have spent a lifetime protecting teachers. And today, I am back in the classroom teaching the lessons of the last month.

QUESTIONS

1. If the majority of teachers in a school or district are opposed to a reform mandated by their school board, what should they do?

2. Why do you think the school board decided to mandate block scheduling, in spite of the teachers' 149–13 vote against the change?

3. In what ways does this case support the observation that "politics . . . is typically informal, often clandestine, and frequently illegitimate. It is illegitimate because it is behavior usually designed to benefit the individual or group at the expense of the organization" (Hoy & Miskel, 2001, p. 28)?

John Flickinger teaches English at Montwood High School in El Paso, Texas. The preceding is excerpted from his article that appeared in *NEA Today: The Magazine of the National Education Association*, May 2003, p. 7.

operating budget; number of teachers; economic resources; and number of school buildings. Some serve extremely wealthy communities, others serve impoverished ghetto neighborhoods or rural areas. Their operations include 335 one-teacher elementary schools in this country (National Center for Education Statistics, March 25, 2008) as well as scores of modern, multibuilding campuses in heavily populated areas.

The largest school districts are exceedingly complex operations. The largest—the New York City school system—has almost 1 million pupils (from 190 countries), almost 66,000 teachers (a number that exceeds the number of students in Cincinnati; Minneapolis; Portland, Oregon; Sacramento; Seattle; and St. Louis), over 1,200 schools, and total annual expenditures of more than $12 billion. The New York system, overseen by a schools chancellor, consists of 32 community school districts, each with its own superintendent. Table 6.1 shows selected statistics for the 10 largest school districts in the United States and jurisdictions for the 2004–05 school year.

The organizational structures of school districts also differ. Large urban systems, which may contain several districts, tend to have a more complex distribution of roles and responsibilities than do smaller districts. Figure 6.3 shows the organizational chart for a school district of about 20,000 pupils.

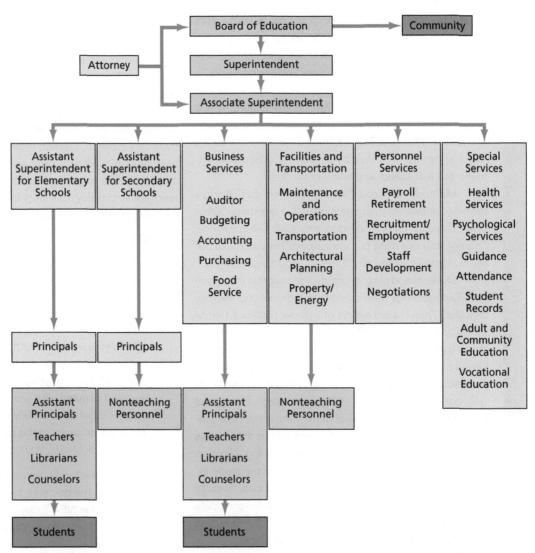

FIGURE 6.3 Typical organizational structure for a medium-size school district (20,000 pupils)

TABLE 6.1 Selected statistics for the 10 largest school districts in the United States and jurisdictions, by school district: school year 2004–05

Name of reporting district	City	State	County	Number of students[1]	Number of full-time equivalent (FTE) teachers[2]	Number of 2003–04 completers[3]	Number of schools[4]
Reporting districts[3]	†	†	†	11,270,624	614,484	520,117	16,328
New York City Public Schools	Brooklyn	NY	Kings	986,967	65,803*	39,539*	1,205
Los Angeles Unified	Los Angeles	CA	Los Angeles	741,367	35,186	29,621	721
Puerto Rico Department of Education	San Juan	PR	San Juan	575,648	43,054	31,946	1,523
City of Chicago School District	Chicago	IL	Cook	426,812	25,260	16,745	634
Dade County School District	Miami	FL	Miami-Dade	368,933	20,086	18,599	381
Clark County School District	Las Vegas	NV	Clark	283,221	14,222	11,389	307
Broward County School District	Fort Lauderdale	FL	Broward	274,591	15,271	14,192	272
Houston Independent School District	Houston	TX	Harris	208,945	12,009	8,520	304
Hillsborough County School District	Tampa	FL	Hillsborough	189,469	11,975	9,380	257
Philadelphia City School District	Philadelphia	PA	Philadelphia	187,547	9,838	10,331	270

*Data from 2001–02

---

†Not applicable.

[1]Full-time equivalent (FTE) is the amount of time required to perform an assignment stated as a proportion of a full-time position. It is computed by dividing the amount of time employed by the amount of time normally required for a full-time position. FTE is not a head count, for example, 2 half-time employees represent 1 FTE.

[2]Includes high school diploma recipients as well as other high school completers (e.g., certificates of attendance), but not high school equivalencies (e.g., GEDs).

[3]Totals for number of schools may differ from published estimates because they exclude closed, inactive, and future schools.

[4]Totals do not include districts where data were not available.

[5]Data from 2001–02.

Note: Data include all 50 states, the District of Columbia, Puerto Rico, four outlying areas (American Samoa, Guam, the Commonwealth of the Northern Mariana Islands, and the U.S. Virgin Islands), the Bureau of Indian Education, and the Department of Defense dependents schools (overseas and domestic).
Source: National Center for Education Statistics. (April 2008). Characteristics of the 100 Largest Public Elementary and Secondary School Districts in the United States: 2004–05, pp. A-4, A-5.

School Board

A **school board,** acting as a state agent, is responsible for the following: approving the teachers, administrators, and other school personnel hired by the superintendent; developing organizational and educational policies; and determining procedures for evaluating programs and personnel.

In most communities, school board members are elected in general elections. In some urban areas, however, board members are selected by the mayor. Board members typically serve a minimum of three to five years, and their terms of office are usually staggered. School boards usually range from five to fifteen members, with five or seven frequently suggested as the optimum size. Board members in urban areas usually are paid, but in most other areas they are not.

A survey of urban school boards found that 52 percent were women and 48 percent were men. In addition, urban school board membership does not reflect the growing diversity of students enrolled in urban schools—57 percent of board members were White, 30 percent were African American, and 4 percent were Asian or other backgrounds. The survey also revealed that urban school board members differ from the general population: almost 15 percent were business leaders, 9 percent were attorneys, almost 7 percent were entrepreneurs, and more than 1 percent were physicians (Council of Great City Schools, October 2005).

Nearly all school board meetings are open to the public; in fact, many communities even provide radio and television coverage. Open meetings allow parents and interested citizens an opportunity to express their concerns and to get more information about problems in the district.

School boards play a critical role in the U.S. education system. However, school boards have been criticized for not educating themselves about educational issues, being reluctant to seek input from their communities, not communicating a vision of educational excellence to their communities, and not developing positive relationships with superintendents.

Some states have taken steps to reform school boards. For example, Arkansas provides board members with training in developing partnerships with their communities, creating a vision of educational excellence, and team building. West Virginia restructured school boards, and board members must complete training that focuses on "boardmanship and governing effectiveness." One study of school boards found that effective boards

- focus on student achievement,
- allocate resources to needs,
- watch the return on investment,
- use data, and
- engage the communities they serve (Ward & Griffin, March 21, 2006).

Superintendent of Schools

Though school boards operate very differently, the **superintendent** is the key figure in determining a district's educational policy. Though the board of education delegates broad powers to the superintendent, his or her policies require board approval. The specific responsibilities of the superintendent are many. Among the most important are the following:

- To serve as professional adviser to the board of education and to make policy recommendations for improving curricular and instructional programs.
- To act as employer and supervisor of professional and nonteaching personnel (janitors, cafeteria workers, etc.).
- To represent the schools in their relations with the community and to explain board of education policies to the community.
- To develop policies for the placement and transportation of students within the district.
- To prepare an annual school budget and adhere to the budget adopted by the school board.

How the superintendent and his or her board work together is related to the size of the school district, with superintendents and school boards in larger districts more likely to be in conflict. School boards in smaller districts are more effective, however, when they do oppose the superintendent. In large districts, the board's own divisiveness makes it less likely that the board will successfully oppose the superintendent (Wirt & Kirst, 1997).

Superintendents must have great skill to respond appropriately to the many external political forces that demand their attention, and conflict is inevitable. Effective superintendents demonstrate that they are able to play three roles simultaneously: politician, manager, and teacher. It is a demanding position, and turnover is high; for example, between 1980 and 1995, the New York City school system had ten chancellors (Hurwitz, 1999).

The Role of Parents

Parents may not be involved legally in the governance of schools, but they do play an important role in education. One characteristic of successful schools is that they have developed close working relationships with parents. Children whose parents or guardians support and encourage school activities have a definite advantage in school. The Teaching on Your Feet feature in this chapter, for example, describes a classroom discipline problem that almost led a teacher to contact the parents of several students who were bullying a special education student. Fortunately, the teacher was able to resolve the situation without contacting the parents.

Through participation on school advisory and site-based councils, parents are making an important contribution to restructuring and school reform efforts around the country. In addition, groups such as the parent-teacher association (PTA), parent-teacher organization (PTO), or parent advisory council (PAC) give parents the opportunity to communicate with teachers on matters of interest and importance to them. Through these groups, parents can become involved in the life of the school in a variety of ways—from making recommendations regarding school policies to providing much-needed volunteer services, or to initiating school-improvement activities such as fundraising drives. For an example of how parents can serve as advocates for their children's education, go to MyEducationLab and watch a video that shows how family members advocate for a student with special needs.

Many parents are also influencing the character of education through their involvement with the growing number of private, parochial, for-profit, and charter schools. In addition, many parents are activists in promoting school choice, voucher systems, and the home schooling movement.

Some parents even join well-funded conservative think tanks that launch sophisticated national campaigns to remove from public schools practices and materials that they find objectionable. People for the American Way (May 25, 2008) reported that, between 1990 and 2000, there were 6,364 censorship challenges, 71 percent of which were to materials in schools or school libraries. The basis of challenge are detailed below:

- 1,607 were challenges to "sexually explicit" material
- 1,427 were challenges to material considered to use "offensive language"
- 1,256 were challenges to material considered non-age-appropriate or "unsuited to age group"
- 842 were challenges to material with an "occult theme or promoting the occult or Satanism"
- 737 were challenges to material considered to be "violent"
- 515 were challenges to material with a homosexual theme or "promoting homosexuality"
- 419 were challenges to material "promoting a religious viewpoint"
- 317 challenges to materials that included "nudity"

School Restructuring

At many schools across the country, exciting changes are taking place in how schools are controlled locally. To improve the performance of schools, to decentralize the system of governance, and to enhance the professional status of teachers, some districts are **restructuring** their school systems. Restructuring goes by several names: shared governance, administrative decentralization, teacher empowerment, professionalization,

myeducationlab

Go to MyEducationLab, select Chapter 6 and then Activities and Applications, and watch the video Parents as Child Advocates.

TEACHING ON YOUR FEET

"THE SOBS COULD BE HEARD . . ."

The sobs could be heard down the long hallway, intensifying as I drew closer to Room 18. Along with the sobs were the usual noises of students bustling to class—poking one another, laughing, and talking loudly. Angel was the last student to enter the classroom. Sniffling, and with halting speech, he told me that he had once again been teased on the playground for being in special education. "Special Eder" was the moniker his classmates had given him. My heart raced and the blood rushed to my cheeks as I took on the stance of "Mother Bear," wanting to protect this special needs student from cruel remarks.

"Who was it this time?" I asked. Angel responded with the names he had given so many times: Matthew, Raul, and Randy. Often, I had talked to these three fifth-graders, first kindly, and then, upon repeated offenses, not so pleasantly. Each time, I asked "How would you feel if you were in Angel's shoes?" and "How could you?" They gave me the answers I wanted to hear, but then did nothing to change their behavior. Repeatedly, Angel's cries preceded him into the classroom—his retreat.

As I pondered my next step, several options seemed workable:

- Confront the perpetrators again.
- Talk to Angel privately to reassure him.
- Call the boys' parents.

Then, just as I opened the window to bring in some fresh air, a fresh idea surfaced: Why not give Angel strategies for handling these verbal attacks? Why hadn't this occurred to me before? Perhaps I wanted to be the person to make everything okay for my students. This was admirable, but I was going about it the wrong way. If I taught Angel some coping strategies, he could probably end the bullying; plus, he would have the skills to solve future problems.

My first job was to make Angel understand that the teasing he experienced on the playground was intended to upset him. If he got upset, his "enemies" had won. This was not an easy lesson to convey to Angel. However, by having other members of the class role play his tormentors, we slowly chipped away at those hurt feelings and started restoring Angel's confidence. The strategies I taught the children to use whenever they were faced with rude remarks included:

- Return taunts with humor.
- Say nothing, smile and walk away.
- Repeat, "Wow" after each rude remark.

Each strategy was intended to defuse an instance of bullying by other students and enable Angel to become the "winner."

Now, I would like to say it went smoothly and the conflict ended right away. However, this wasn't the case. Angel was a good sport and, initially, his use of the strategies caught the playground bullies off-guard. They kept up their bullying, but Angel was consistent with his broken-record technique of, "Wow."

Then, one day weeks later, he came into the classroom and stated that he had had "the perfect recess." As Angel shared his experience with the entire class, his classmates were encouraging and supportive. They, too, admitted to being teased at different times and said that they might try a little "Wow" in their defense strategies.

ANALYSIS

I learned a valuable lesson through all of this. It is important to teach students strategies for dealing with teasing. Teaching students to mediate their own conflicts provides them with a valuable, lifelong skill. Now, whenever I feel that Mother Bear mode kicking in, I know it is time to teach, or re-teach, the valuable lesson of standing up for oneself.

Teaching offers opportunities to teach some of life's most important lessons. I am constantly grateful to students like Angel who provide me with such opportunities.

REFLECTION

- When students bully their classmates, what should guide teachers in deciding whether they should intervene?
- How else can teachers teach children to stand up for themselves?
- What strategies can be used to counter bullying and to promote kindness among children?

Betsy McIntire
Special Education Teacher
Barranca Elementary School

PEARSON **myeducationlab** To answer these questions online, go to MyEducationLab at www.myeducationlab.com, select the Activities and Application section, and click on this chapter's Teaching on Your Feet.

bottom-up policymaking, school-based planning, school-based management, distributed leadership, and shared decision making. What all these approaches have in common is allowing those who know students best—teachers, principals, aides, custodians, librarians, secretaries, and parents—greater freedom in deciding how to meet students' needs.

The *Handbook on Restructuring and Substantial School Improvement,* developed by The Academic Development Institute with support from the U.S. Department of Education, includes the following among the "indicators" at successfully restructured schools:

- A team structure is officially incorporated into the school improvement plan and school governance policy.

- A leadership team consisting of the principal, teachers who lead the instructional teams, and other key professional staff meets regularly (twice a month or more for an hour each meeting).

- The leadership team regularly looks at school performance data and aggregated classroom observation data and uses that data to make decisions about school improvement and professional development needs.

- Professional development of individual teachers includes an emphasis on indicators of effective teaching.

- Parent policies, activities, and programs cultivate the "curriculum of the home."

- The school maintains a central database that includes each student's test scores, placement information, demographic information, attendance, behavior indicators, and other variables useful to teachers (Walberg, 2007, pp. 119–120, 122–123, 127).

The Technology in Action feature for this chapter describes how a leadership team of teachers increased students' access to the latest technology by working with their principal to purchase a Second Life "island," a 3D virtual world where students can interact with other students and build virtual environments.

School-Based Management

A frequently used approach to restructuring schools is **school-based management (SBM).** Most SBM programs have three components in common:

1. Power and decisions formerly made by the superintendent and school board are delegated to teachers, principals, parents, community members, and students at local schools. At SBM schools, teachers can become involved directly in decisions about curriculum, textbooks, standards for student behavior, staff development, promotion and retention policies, teacher evaluation, school budgets, and the selection of teachers and administrators.

2. At each school, a decision-making body (known as a board, cabinet, site-based team, or council)—made up of teachers, the principal, and parents—implements the SBM plan.

3. SBM programs operate with the full support of the superintendent of schools.

What are the goals of school restructuring? In school-based management, who participates in the governance and management of schools? How is school-based management different from the school board model of local governance?

TECHNOLOGY in *ACTION*

Virtual Worlds in a Seventh-Grade Combined Classroom

Candis Randall knew her students loved videogames. In fact she had incorporated some videogame instruction into her history classroom already and her students really enjoyed it. However, the free and less expensive videogame instruction she could access was quite prescriptive. That is, the variables programmed into the game allowed only for specific action and reaction. This was fine for basic and procedural lessons, but she had a hard time finding applications that addressed more in-depth concepts and that allowed for flexible critical thinking. As she researched, she found an alternative approach, something different than a videogame—virtual worlds. These virtual worlds allowed students to explore interesting places alone or in groups; to interact with other students; and to build structures, environments, and/or organisms.

Virtual world video games enable students to explore places alone or in groups and build structures, environments, and organisms. Students cover concepts and learning outcomes that are usually addressed in their regular classes. The social connection provided by virtual worlds has great potential to have a positive impact on education.

She set up her avatar (a 3D representation of herself) and began to explore Second Life, an online, 3D virtual world. She found a number of islands that she could use in her lessons, but the real benefit occurred after she demonstrated Second Life (SL) to her fellow teachers. After the demo and a series of in-depth conversations, the teachers convinced their principal to purchase an island for the school. They also decided that the English teacher, Mr. Lee; the math teacher, Mrs. Sanchez; the art teacher, Mr. Hummer; the technology teacher, Ms. Sushak; and Ms. Randall would participate in a pilot activity.

The Teachers' Voices: Walk in My Shoes feature in this chapter profiles Gil Navarro, a first-year teacher who provided leadership for his school's site-based council and other improvement-oriented committees at his school.

Chicago School Reform

A pioneer in school-based management has been the City of Chicago Public Schools. For years, the Chicago Public School System faced an array of problems: low student achievement, periodic teacher strikes, budget crises, a top-heavy central bureaucracy, and schools in the decaying inner city that seemed beyond most improvement efforts. In response to these problems, a 55-member committee of business, education, and community leaders developed a school reform proposal. Among the group's recommendations was the creation of a **local school council (LSC)** for each of the city's more than 550 schools, with the majority of council members being parents of schoolchildren.

They all agreed that they would spend the next month using Second Life as their virtual classroom. They and their students would participate in Second Life activities that would cover the concepts and learning outcomes normally addressed for that month in each of their classes. They created a new form of combined or blended classroom, which allows individual teachers to address specific academic disciplines using connected subject matter or a common theme.

The teachers agreed that the first activity would be a lesson on Medieval England. The students in Mrs. Sanchez's math class were asked to build a castle on the school's Second Life island. Mr. Hummer's students created thematic graphics, such as family crests, portraits, and landscapes. Mr. Lee's student set prose requirements on the island; that is, students could not speak to one another unless they "speaketh correctly." Ms. Randall's students researched the type of activities that might take place around a medieval castle.

Then they set up a series of roles that individual students would assume. There were a lord and his lady, groomsmen, knights, a constable, and more. Each student was assigned a role to play and was required to interact appropriately.

The activity was a tremendous success. As word got out about the fun these students were having in math, history, English, and art, other students and teachers in the school began visiting the school's medieval community. A rumor supposedly started that a student from a neighboring middle school had heard about the activities taking place and was trying to raise an army to storm the castle.

VIRTUAL WORLDS: Virtual worlds, such as Second Life, are online, three-dimensional spaces in which participants can explore, interact, and create. In addition to their stunning visual effect, the social connection provided by these worlds makes their potential impact on education quite promising. Think of a videogame on an X-box or Play Station and then take out all of the variables of the game—no objective, no action/reaction programmed into it. Now, you create the rules and objectives, and you create some of the buildings. You determine what you look like and how you will communicate.

VISIT: http://secondlife.com. On this site, you can read about the product, learn how others are using Second Life, and download the player.

POSSIBLE USES: Teachers have successfully used virtual worlds to help their students visit active volcanoes, experience schizophrenia, walk through the scene of a Van Gogh painting, and explore the solar system. Students have experienced life in a post–Civil War western town, experienced and responded to a natural disaster as a medical provider, seen artificial intelligence at work, and been granted citizenship in Athens.

TRY IT OUT: The most popular virtual world at the time of this publication is Second Life. To try it out, visit the website listed above and download the software. You will create a user account that will eventually become a 3D representation of yourself, known as an avatar. Choose your name carefully because it will stick with you for all time in SL. Once you have your name, decide what you will look like—your gender, race, body type, hair (or no), clothing, and gestures. Once your avatar is complete, you will walk through a tutorial, where you learn how to walk, shop, fly, and talk. Once the tutorial is completed, you are free to live your second life.

■ ■ ■ ■ ■ ■ ■ ■

In December 1988, the Illinois state legislature passed the Chicago School Reform Act, "a series of bold, original reforms [that] attracted intense nationwide interest, particularly because many of the problems faced by Chicago's schools are shared by schools throughout the nation" (Russo, 2004, p. v). Among the provisions of the act were the following:

- School budgets would be controlled by a local school council made up of six parents, two community members, two school employees, and the principal.
- The council had the authority to hire and fire the principal.
- The council, with input from teachers and the principal, had the authority to develop an improvement plan for the local school.
- New teachers would be hired on the basis of merit, not seniority.
- Principals could remove teachers 45 days after serving them official notice of unsatisfactory performance.

TEACHERS' VOICES
Walk in My Shoes

Gil Navarro was in the middle of obtaining a doctoral degree and teaching a class at a nearby university when he was activated in the U.S. Marine Corps Reserve to serve in Iraq. He was also in his eighth and ninth years of teaching fourth and fifth grade.

While in Iraq, Gil noticed that some of his fellow Marines did not receive mail or e-mails from home, so he asked his students and supporters for help. One friend posted the pictures of Gil's Marine Corps Unit in her university classroom, and her graduate students, all teachers as well, signed up to have their classes adopt one of the soldiers. The children's e-mails, letters, and care packages made a difference for the Marines Gil sought to help. Such leadership and eagerness to help people connect has been a common thread throughout Gil's teaching career.

Like more and more people today, Gil Navarro discovered his call to education after first trying another career. After earning a degree in business administration and working in private business for four years, Gil realized that he enjoyed some aspects of his work, but it left him drained. Around that same time, California had instituted a class-size reduction initiative that left schools with a serious teacher shortage. When a friend invited him to speak with her principal about a possible teaching position, Gil was drawn to the opportunity because he had enjoyed previous work in a university summer program for eighth-grade potential dropouts. "I enjoyed these types of jobs, helping students become better," Gil explains, and so he sought and obtained a teaching position.

Gil loved the work: "It was too much fun to be a career, and the rewards made up for the long hours that

"... the rewards made up for the long hours that teachers work."

teachers work." While teaching, Gil took courses to earn his teaching credential and master's degree.

Gil's inclination toward leadership was evident from the beginning of his teaching career. In his first year, Gil became treasurer of the parent teacher association and used his business background to set up a budget program for the group. He mentored the parents who assumed the treasurer's role after him, guiding them to become more technically skilled. In the process, he believes, parents discovered that "school was not a scary place to be." Gil also became involved with various committees at the school, including the school's site council committee, the technology committee, and the conflict resolution committee.

Gil continued his studies to learn as much as possible about his new profession, and his studies in education eventually led to a doctoral degree, enhanced his teaching, and opened new career paths for him. They enabled Gil to teach at the university level, sharing his knowledge and experience with students preparing to teach. His exceptional and outstanding teaching career thus far illustrates some of the profession's realities and possibilities.

Gil advises new teachers to take on new challenges each year and to learn how "to work smarter rather than harder." He encourages teachers to study more about emotional intelligence. "I wish someone had told me how important the emotional piece is." He recommends Daniel Goleman's book, *Emotional Intelligence: Why It Can Matter More Than I.Q.* Being tuned to children's emotions, just as being tuned to the emotional needs of his colleagues in the Marines, is a strength that Gil shares with others.

Gil Navarro

- A professional personnel advisory committee of teachers would have advisory responsibility for curriculum and instruction.

The first six years of the Chicago Reform Act produced few concrete improvements. In 1995, frustrated with the district's chronic fiscal problems and inability to increase student achievement, the Illinois legislature gave Mayor Richard M. Daley control over Chicago's schools. Daley created a five-member "reform board of trustees" and appointed a chief executive officer (CEO) who advocated "a balance between local control and central-office control" (Hendrie, 1999).

By many accounts, the Chicago reform efforts were a continuing "struggle about how to improve an urban school system" (Hendrie, 1999). Friction between the mayor's management team and the parent-dominated LSCs intensified with each report that an LSC member had abused his or her authority.

In spite of conflicts over the governance of Chicago schools, the program resulted in modest increases in student achievement. In 1990, less than one-quarter of the city's third- through eighth-graders read at the national norm; by 2000, more than one-third (36.4 percent) did so (Hess, 2000). Mathematics scores improved even more—from just over one-quarter of elementary students at the national norm in 1990 to just under half in 2000 (Hess, 2000). At the high school level, graduation rates for 19-year-olds increased slightly, and dropout rates for 19-year-olds decreased slightly (Miller, Allensworth, & Kochanek, 2002).

The preceding gains, however, were not uniform in schools across the city; for example, the city's lowest-performing schools showed little improvement (Rosenkranz, 2002). In addition, the Chicago Reform Act's goal for Chicago schools to reach national norms within five years was not reached.

In spite of modest results, however, the Chicago experiment is clearly one of the more dramatic efforts to empower parents and make them full partners in school governance. In reflecting on the accomplishments of the Chicago Reform Act, the chief academic officer during many years of the reform observed:

> There were three major accomplishments. The first was fiscal stability, being able to run a school system without worrying about funding. Fiscal stability led to union stability, which was number two, because we had contracts, no strikes, we knew that the schools were going to open each year, and people had confidence in the system. And the third was that we had an overarching academic program that addressed the needs of the students. (Buckney, 2004, p. 159)

WHAT POWERS AND INFLUENCE DO STATES HAVE IN GOVERNING SCHOOLS?

Above the level of local control, states have a great influence on schools. Since the 1990s, the influence of the state on educational policy has increased steadily.

For example, every state (except Iowa) has statewide academic standards, and every state has mandated a standardized test to assess students' mastery of academic standards. Currently, 22 states require students to attain minimum scores on state assessments to graduate from high school. An additional four states will implement exit exams by 2012 (Education Commission of the States, April 20, 2007). In addition, more than 20 states give state boards of education the authority to intervene in academically "bankrupt" schools whose students score too low as a group.

In response to criticisms of U.S. education, many states launched extensive initiatives to improve education, such as the following:

- Increased academic standards
- Greater accountability for teachers
- Testing students in teacher education programs prior to graduation
- Frequent assessments of students' mastery of basic skills
- Professional development as a criterion for continued employment of teachers
- Recertification of experienced teachers

As mentioned previously, the Tenth Amendment to the Constitution allows the states to organize and to administer education within their boundaries. To meet the responsibility of maintaining and supporting schools, the states have assumed several powers:

- The power to levy taxes for the support of schools and to determine state aid to local school districts

- The power to set the curriculum and, in some states, to identify approved textbooks
- The power to determine minimum standards for teacher certification
- The power to establish standards for accrediting schools
- The power to pass legislation necessary for the proper maintenance and support of schools

To carry out the tasks implied by these powers, the states have adopted a number of different organizational structures. Most states, however, have adopted a hierarchical structure similar to that presented in Figure 6.4.

The Roles of State Government in Education

Various people and agencies play a role in operating the educational system within each state. Though state governments differ, the state legislature, the state courts, and the governor have a direct, critical impact on education in each state.

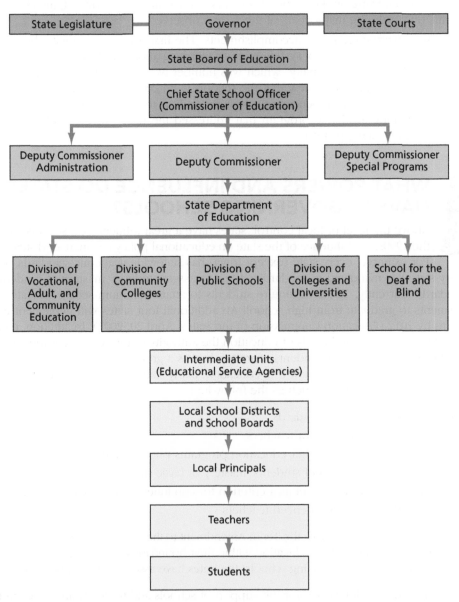

FIGURE 6.4 Organizational structure of a typical state school system

The Legislature

In nearly every state, the legislature is responsible for establishing and maintaining public schools and for determining basic educational policies within the state. Among the policies that the state legislature may determine are the following:

- How the state boards of education will be selected and what their responsibilities will be
- How the chief state school officer will be selected and what his or her duties will be
- How the state department of education will function
- How the state will be divided into local and regional districts
- How higher education will be organized and financed
- How local school boards will be selected and what their powers will be

In addition, the legislature may determine how taxes will be used to support schools, what will or will not be taught, the length of the school day and school year, how many years of compulsory education will be required, and whether or not the state will have community colleges and/or vocational/technical schools. Legislatures may also make policies that apply to matters such as pupil attendance, admission, promotion, teacher certification, teacher tenure and retirement, and collective bargaining.

Other policies developed by the state legislature may also apply to nonpublic schools in the state—policies related to health services, building construction, safety, school lunch services, textbooks, and testing of pupils, for example. In general, state legislatures may pass laws that provide for the reasonable supervision of nonpublic educational institutions.

The State Courts

From time to time, state courts are called on to uphold the power of the legislature to develop laws that apply to schools. The state courts must determine, however, that this power does not conflict with the state constitution or the U.S. Constitution. It is important to remember, too, that the role of state courts is not to develop laws but to rule on the reasonableness of laws that apply to specific educational situations.

Perhaps no state court has had a greater impact on education than the Kentucky Supreme Court. In 1989, the court ruled that the state's entire school system was "inadequate." Naming the state superintendent and the state education agency as part of the problem and pointing out that Kentucky schools were ineffective and inequitable, the court labeled the school system "unconstitutional." The court called on the governor and the legislature to develop an entirely new system of education for the state. A 22-member task force, appointed by the governor and the legislature, then developed the 906-page **Kentucky Education Reform Act (KERA)** passed in 1990. KERA required each school to form a school-based management council by 1996 with authority to set policy in eight areas: curriculum, staff time, student assignment, schedule, school space, instructional issues, discipline, and extracurricular activities. Three teachers, two parents (elected by their peers), and the principal comprised each council.

KERA dramatically equalized funding across the state, and some school districts made substantial gains in funding for students. "Districts with low incomes or little property value per student [were] just as likely to have high educational spending as are wealthy districts" (Hoyt, 1999, p. 36). In addition, teacher salaries and student/teacher ratios improved compared to national averages. However, student achievement, as measured by test score gains or graduation rates, did not improve (The Kentucky Institute for Education Research, 2001).

The Governor

Although the powers of governors vary greatly from state to state, a governor can, if he or she chooses, have a great impact on education within the state. The governor may appoint and/or remove educators at the state level, and in some states the governor may even appoint the chief state school officer. Furthermore, in every state except North Carolina, the governor may use his or her veto power to influence the legislature to pass certain laws related to education.

Governors are also extremely influential because they make educational budget recommendations to legislatures and, in many states, they may elect to use any accumulated balances in the state treasury for education. Governors can also have a significant impact on matters related to curriculum and instruction within the state and, indeed, across the nation. For example, Roy Romer, former governor of Colorado, was instrumental in organizing ACHIEVE, an effort by U.S. governors and corporate leaders to raise academic standards and develop accountability systems for schools. In addition, the **National Governors' Association (NGA)** is active in teacher education and school reforms.

State Takeover of Schools

Since passage of the No Child Left Behind Act of 2001, **state takeover** is an intervention that can be applied to chronically low-achieving schools and districts. The School District of Philadelphia has been the site of the nation's largest takeover of schools. In 2002, the state of Pennsylvania, frustrated by years of low achievement and a decade of budget crises in the School District of Philadelphia, took charge of the city's 200,000-pupil system. The state replaced Philadelphia's nine-member school board with an appointed school reform commission (SRC) composed of three members appointed by the governor and two appointed by the city's mayor. The SRC then hired a new CEO who immediately instituted sweeping changes, including the implementation of districtwide common curricula and a system of frequent benchmark assessments to be used for diagnostic purposes.

More controversially, the SRC adopted a "diverse provider" model as it turned over management of 45 of the district's lowest-performing elementary and middle schools to seven for-profit and nonprofit organizations, including two local universities. The private managers were given additional per-pupil funding to support their work.

During 2002–2006, achievement gains at Philadelphia schools managed privately did not exceed achievement gains at students in the rest of the district. "With respect to state takeover, results are ambiguous: Subsequent to the state's takeover of the district, proficiency percentages increased district-wide, but the total increase over four years was not substantially greater than the increase of other low-achieving schools in the state, in most cases" (Gill, Zimmer, Christman, & Blanc, 2007).

State Board of Education

The **state board of education,** acting under the authority of the state legislature, is the highest educational agency in a state. Every state, with the exception of Wisconsin, has a state board of education. Most states have two separate boards, one responsible for elementary through secondary education, the other for higher education.

The method of determining board members varies from state to state. In some states, the governor appoints members of the state board; in other states, members are selected through general elections. People disagree on which is better: electing or appointing board members. Some believe that election to the state board may cause members to be more concerned with politics than with education. Others argue that elected board members are more aware of the wishes of the public, whom the schools are supposed to serve. People in favor of appointing members to the state board suggest that appointment increases the likelihood that individuals will be chosen on the basis of merit rather than politics.

The regulatory and advisory functions generally held by state boards are as follows:

- Ensuring that local school districts adhere to legislated educational policies, rules, and regulations
- Setting standards for issuing and revoking teaching and administrative certificates
- Establishing standards for accrediting schools
- Managing state monies appropriated for education

- Developing and implementing a system for collecting educational data needed for reporting and program evaluation
- Advising the governor and/or the state legislature on educational issues
- Identifying both short- and long-range educational needs in the state and developing plans to meet those needs
- Hearing all disputes arising from the implementation of its educational policies

In addition, a few state boards of education have instituted a statewide textbook adoption system. In the adoption system, boards choose a small number of titles for each subject area and grade level for all the state's schools. Individual schools and teachers then select their textbooks from this list. North Carolina, for example, has created a 23-member textbook commission made up of teachers, principals, parents, and a local superintendent. Textbooks are evaluated using criteria based on the North Carolina Standard Course of Study, and adopted textbooks are placed on the statewide textbook list for five years.

State Department of Education

The educational program of each state is implemented by the state's department of education, under the leadership of the chief state school officer. State departments of education have a broad set of responsibilities, and they affect literally every school, school district, and teacher education program in a state. In general, the state board of education is concerned with policymaking, the **state department of education** with the day-to-day implementation of those policies.

A great boost for the development of state departments of education came with the federal government's Elementary and Secondary Education Act of 1965 (see Chapter 5). This act and its subsequent amendments required that local applications for federal funds to be used for innovative programs and for the education of disadvantaged, disabled, bilingual, and migrant students first receive approval from state departments of education.

Today, the responsibilities of state departments of education include (1) certifying teachers, (2) distributing state and federal funds to school districts, (3) reporting to the public the condition of education within the state, (4) ensuring that school districts adhere to state and federal guidelines, (5) accrediting schools, (6) monitoring student transportation and safety, and (7) sponsoring research and evaluation projects to improve education within the state.

Perhaps the most significant index of the steady increase in state control since the 1980s is the fact that the states now supply the majority of funding for schools. Clearly, the power and influence of state departments of education will continue to be extensive.

Chief State School Officer

The **chief state school officer** (known as the commissioner of education or superintendent of public instruction in many states) is the chief administrator of the state department of education and the head of the state board of education. In 25 states, the state board of education appoints the chief state school officer; in 15 states, the office is filled through a general election; and in the remaining 10, the governor appoints an individual to that position (Council of Chief State School Officers, May 26, 2008).

Although the specific responsibilities of the chief state school officer vary from state to state, most individuals in this position hold several responsibilities in common:

1. Serving as chief administrator of the state department of education and state board of education
2. Selecting state department of education personnel
3. Recommending educational policies and budgets to the state board
4. Interpreting state school laws and state board of education policies
5. Ensuring compliance with state school laws and policies

209

6. Mediating controversies involving the operation of schools within the state
7. Arranging for studies, committees, and task forces to address educational problems and recommend solutions
8. Reporting on the status of education to the governor, legislature, state board, and public

HOW DO REGIONAL EDUCATION AGENCIES ASSIST SCHOOLS?

When you think about how schools are governed and the sources of political pressure applied to them, you probably think of influences originating at three levels: local, state, and federal. There is, however, an additional source of control—the regional, or intermediate, unit. The intermediate unit of educational administration, or the **regional educational service agency (RESA),** is the least understood branch of the state public school system. Through the intermediate unit, local school districts can receive supportive services that, economically and logistically, they could not provide for themselves.

Today, about half of the states have some form of intermediate or regional unit. The average unit is made up of 20 to 30 local school districts and covers a 50-square-mile area. The intermediate or regional unit has many different names: educational service district (in Washington), county education office (in California), education service center (in Texas), intermediate school district (in Michigan), multicounty educational service unit (in Nebraska), and board of cooperative educational services (in New York).

The primary role of the intermediate unit is to provide assistance directly to districts in the areas of staff development, curriculum development, instructional media, and program evaluation. Intermediate or regional units also help school districts with their school improvement efforts in targeted areas such as bilingual education, vocational education, educational technology, and the education of gifted and talented students and students with disabilities. Although intermediate units monitor local school districts to see that they follow state educational guidelines, local districts, in fact, exert great influence over RESAs by identifying district-level needs that can be met by the intermediate unit.

HOW DOES THE FEDERAL GOVERNMENT INFLUENCE EDUCATION?

Since the birth of the United States, the federal government has played a major role in shaping the character of schools. This branch of government has always recognized that the strength and well-being of the country are directly related to the quality of its schools. The importance of a quality education, for example, has been highlighted by many U.S. Supreme Court rulings supporting the free speech rights of teachers and students under the First Amendment and the right of all citizens to equal educational opportunity under the Fourteenth Amendment.

Federal Initiatives

The federal government has taken aggressive initiatives to influence education at several points in U.S. history, such as the allocation of federal money to improve science, mathematics, and foreign language education after the former Soviet Union launched *Sputnik,* the world's first satellite. During World War II, the federal government funded several new educational programs. One of these, the Lanham Act (1941), provided funding for (1) the training of workers in war plants by U.S. Office of Education personnel, (2) the construction of schools in areas where military personnel and workers on federal projects resided, and (3) the provision of child care for the children of working parents.

Another influential and extensive federal program in support of education was the Servicemen's Readjustment Act, popularly known as the **G.I. Bill of Rights.** Signed into law by President Franklin D. Roosevelt in 1944, the G.I. bill has provided millions of veterans with payments for tuition and room and board at colleges and universities and at technical schools. Similar legislation was later passed to grant educational benefits to veterans of the Korean and Vietnam conflicts. Not only did the G.I. bill stimulate the growth of colleges and universities in the United States, it also opened higher education to an older and nontraditional student population.

The executive, legislative, and judicial branches of the federal government influence education in four ways:

1. **Exert moral suasion**—develop a vision and promote educational goals for the nation; for example, to honor public and private K–12 schools that are either academically superior in their states or that demonstrate dramatic gains in student achievement, Rod Paige, former secretary of education under the George W. Bush administration, launched the No Child Left Behind—Blue Ribbon Schools Program (U.S. Department of Education, 2002b).

2. **Provide categorical aid**—assist school systems with funding if they adopt federally endorsed programs, methods, or curricula.

3. **Regulate**—withhold federal funds if a school system fails to follow legal statutes related to equal educational opportunity.

4. **Fund educational research**—identify and then fund research projects related to federal goals for education.

The Impact of Presidential Policies

Presidential platforms on education can have a profound effect on education. Presidents Reagan and George H. W. Bush, for example, scaled back federal involvement in education. President Clinton's administration, on the other hand, assumed a more active role in ensuring equal educational opportunity. And the No Child Left Behind Act developed and implemented during President George W. Bush's two terms will have a significant impact on our nation's schools for some time to come.

Midway through the 2008 presidential primaries, the three leading candidates recognized the importance of clarifying to the electorate their positions regarding education. Their comments regarding No Child Left Behind and teacher pay are presented below:

Clinton

We can do better than No Child Left Behind. This law is not working for our teachers, our parents, and, most importantly, our kids.

We have a teacher shortage because we have a respect shortage. I believe we need to raise base teacher pay and provide . . . incentives for teachers who teach in high-need schools.

Obama

[Teachers] feel betrayed and frustrated by No Child Left Behind. We shouldn't reauthorize it without changing it fundamentally. We left the money behind for [NCLB].

We can find new ways to increase pay that are developed with teachers, not imposed on them and not based on some arbitrary test score. That's how we're going to close the achievement gap.

McCain

No Child Left Behind was a good beginning. We now, after a number of years of examination and practice with it, know there are some things that badly need fixing.

Education is often at the center of the issues during election campaigns. Why is education such an important focal point for candidates and communities alike?

Choice and competition is the key to success in education in America. That means . . . rewarding good teachers and finding bad teachers another line of work. (Hawkins-Simons, May 8, 2008)

Advice to the President

One indicator of how a president can influence education is reflected in *Letters to the Next President: What We Can Do About the Real Crisis in Public Education* (Glickman, 2004), a book that appeared just prior to the 2004 presidential election. The editor introduces the set of more than 35 letters from students, accomplished teachers, principals, parents, education scholars, and policymakers by making the following comments to the next president:

> MR. OR MS. NEXT PRESIDENT, read these letters while waking up in the morning, riding planes during the day to your next campaign stop, and in the quiet moments. Be thoughtful, be pragmatic, but please stand up and be articulate and committed to what must be an important part of your agenda—an education for each of our children that equips them to sit as equals at the table of American democracy. (Glickman, 2004, p. 6)

In the prologue he wrote for the same book, entertainer Bill Cosby, who received his doctorate in education from the University of Massachusetts, was more frank:

> I'm assuming that the President of the United States probably never went to a poor and neglected public school—where books have missing pages, walls have peeling paint, children have nothing to draw or write with, and where there is no library for reading a story or doing homework. These are the junkiest rooms: the poorest public schools where every year there are more cutbacks; where there's less money all the time.
>
> This time, on top of the mess is a new mess—a slew of new directives stretching budgets for more tests, more requirements, more unfunded programs—creating even more gaps in the education given to our wealthiest kids compared to our poorest kids.
>
> Wealthy people drive by the junky school and comfort themselves that money is not the issue. But nothing that is dear to America was ever maintained without it, from our nation's security to our communications systems, from our airlines to our highways. Believe this: the poor performance of schools and the lack of achievement among many of our students is indeed about money. We need money to secure great teachers, money to update teaching methods, money for technology and supplies, and money for time. Time is a precious commodity and teachers need it to meet and plan with students, parents, principals, and citizens about how to take back their schools so that they can teach and kids can learn.
>
> . . . . [W]e can sweep up all of this mess and get back to what education comes down to: caring, intelligent, trustworthy, and knowledgeable adults who will ensure that every student can learn. (Cosby, 2004, pp. xii–xiii)

U.S. Department of Education

In addition to supporting educational research, disseminating the results of research, and administering federal grants, the U.S. Department of Education advises the president on setting a platform for national education policy. For example, during 2008, U.S. Secretary of Education Margaret Spellings called for legislation to strengthen NCLB and summarized the impact of that legislation: "Thanks to No Child Left Behind, we are finally taking an honest look at our schools . . . and realizing just how far we have to go. No Child Left Behind has identified about 2,300 out of nearly 100,000 schools nationwide that have missed annual targets for 5 or more years running" (U.S. Department of Education, April 22, 2008).

HOW ARE SCHOOLS FINANCED IN THE UNITED STATES?

To provide free public education to all school-age children in the United States is a costly, complex undertaking. Today's school districts are big-business enterprises and must provide services and facilities to students from many ethnic, racial, social, cultural, linguistic, and individual backgrounds. Thus, "public school finance is, and will be for the foreseeable future, a massive industry . . . in the United States" (Baker, Green, & Richards, 2008, p. v).

Expenditures for educational services and facilities have been rising rapidly and are expected to continue rising through 2016 (see Figure 6.5). Total expenditures for public elementary and secondary schools in 2006 were $449.6 billion, and the total **expenditure per pupil** was $9,154 (National Center for Education Statistics, April 2008). Figure 6.6 shows how the education dollar for public schools is allocated.

The Challenge of Equitable Funding

Financing an enterprise as vast and ambitious as the U.S. system of free public schools has not been easy. It has proved difficult both to devise a system that equitably distributes the tax burden for supporting schools and to provide equal educational services and facilities for all students.

An additional funding challenge is that "rather than one national education system [in the United States], there are 50 state systems that raise revenues from local, state, and federal sources." Dollars are distributed quite unequally across the states, districts, and schools. And as Figure 6.6 shows, about 71 percent of education dollars is available for instruction and student support services, while a significant proportion (about 29 percent) goes to operations and administration.

Moreover, financial support of schools tends to be outpaced by factors that continually increase the cost of operating schools—inflation, rising enrollments, and the need to update aging facilities, for example. Not surprisingly, "lack of financial support/funding/money" was seen as the number 1 problem confronting local schools for four consecutive years (2004–2007) according to Gallup polls of the public's attitudes toward the public schools.

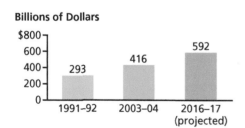

FIGURE 6.5 Actual and projected numbers for current expenditures in public elementary and secondary schools in 2004–05 dollars: selected years, 1991–92 through 2016–17

Source: Projection of Education Statistics to 2016, Figure L. *Washington, DC: National Center for Education Statistics, December 2007.*

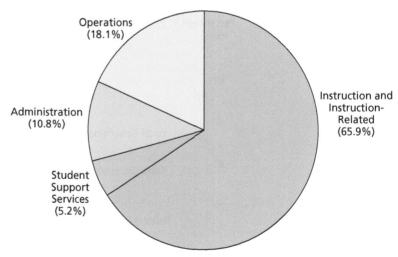

FIGURE 6.6 Percentage distribution of current expenditures for public elementary and secondary education in the United States, by function: fiscal year 2006

Source: Revenues and Expenditures for Public Elementary and Secondary Education, School Year 2005–06 (Fiscal Year 2006). *Washington, DC: National Center for Education Statistics, April 2008, Figure 3.*

Sources of Funding

A combination of revenues from local, state, and federal sources is used to finance public elementary and secondary schools in the United States. As Figure 6.7 shows, schools received 44.0 percent of 2004–05 funding from the state, 46.9 percent from local and other sources, and 9.2 percent from the federal government. Since 1980, schools have received almost equal funding from local and state sources. Prior to that date, however, schools received most of their revenues from local sources, and early in the 20th century, nearly all school revenues were generated from local property taxes.

Revenues for education are influenced by many factors, including the apportionment of taxes among the local, state, and federal levels; the size of the tax base at each level; and competing demands for allocating funds at each level. In addition, funding for education is influenced by the following factors:

- The rate of inflation
- The health of the national economy
- The size of the national budget deficit
- Taxpayer revolts to limit the use of property taxes to raise money, such as Proposition 13 in California and Oregon's property tax limitation
- Changes in the size and distribution of the population
- School-financed lawsuits to equalize funding and ensure educational opportunity

Local Funding

At the local level, most funding for schools comes from **property taxes,** which are determined by the value of property in the school district. Property taxes are assessed against real estate and, in some districts, also against personal property such as cars, household furniture and appliances, and stocks and bonds. Increasing taxes to meet the rising costs of operating local schools or to fund needed improvements is often a heated issue in many communities.

Although property taxes provide a steady source of revenue for local school districts, there are inequities in how taxes are determined. By locating in areas where taxes are lowest, for example, businesses and industries often avoid paying higher taxes while continuing to draw on local resources and services. In addition, the fair market

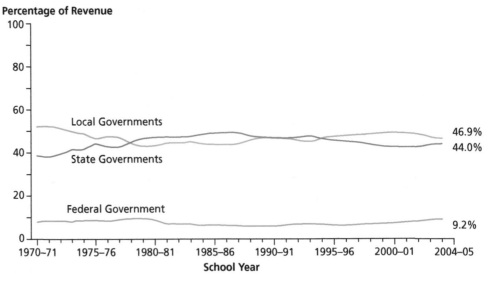

FIGURE 6.7 Percentage of revenue for public elementary and secondary schools, by source of funds: 1970–71 through 2004–05

Source: Digest of Education Statistics: 2007. Figure 9 and Table 162. Washington, DC: National Center for Education Statistics, March 2008.

value of property is often difficult to assess, and groups within a community sometimes pressure assessors to keep taxes on their property as low as possible. Most states specify by law the minimum property tax rate for local school districts to set. In many districts, an increase in the tax rate must have the approval of voters. Some states place no cap, or upper limit, on tax rates, and other states set a maximum limit.

State Funding

Most state revenues for education come from sales taxes and income taxes. Sales taxes are added to the cost of items such as general goods, gasoline, amusements, alcohol, and insurance. Income taxes are placed on individuals (in many states) and on business and industry. To reflect further on state funding for education, go to MyEducationLab and examine a student's illustration of how the state funds public education. Does the illustration accurately depict funding for education in your state?

As mentioned previously, states contribute nearly 50 percent of the resources needed to operate the public schools. The money that a state gives to its cities and towns is known as **state aid.** Table 6.2 compares selected states on the percentage of

About 50 percent of funding for schools comes from the state level. What steps have citizens in your state taken to increase state funding for education? How successful have those steps been?

myeducationlab

Go to MyEducationLab, select Chapter 6 and then Activities and Application to analyze the artifact Purpose of the State Government (Social Studies).

TABLE 6.2 Revenues and percentage distribution of revenues for public elementary and secondary education, by source and state or jurisdiction: fiscal year 2006

State or Jurisdiction	Revenues (in thousands of dollars)				Percentage distribution		
	Total	Local[1]	State	Federal	Local[1]	State	Federal
United States[2]	$520,643,954	$230,939,051	$242,151,076	$47,553,827	44.4	46.5	9.1
Alaska	1,712,601	416,227	1,005,181	291,193	24.3	58.7	17.0
California	63,785,872	19,048,880	37,847,078	6,889,913	29.9	59.3	10.8
District of Columbia[3]	1,201,091	1,054,392	†	146,698	87.8	†	12.2
Florida	24,816,807	12,518,858	9,795,679	2,502,270	50.4	39.5	10.1
Massachusetts	13,850,962	6,571,045	6,507,612	772,305	47.4	47.0	5.6
Michigan	18,978,793	6,158,717	11,259,666	1,560,410	32.5	59.3	8.2
Nevada	3,696,968	2,474,464	958,743	263,761	66.9	25.9	7.1
New York	46,776,452	23,533,105	19,859,481	3,383,866	50.3	42.5	7.2
Ohio	21,106,426	10,285,836	9,217,115	1,603,474	48.7	43.7	7.6
Texas	39,691,436	21,496,767	13,421,855	4,772,813	54.2	33.8	12.0
Washington	9,759,939	2,948,407	5,933,610	877,922	30.2	60.8	9.0
Wisconsin	9,726,952	4,053,773	5,086,692	586,486	41.7	52.3	6.0

†Not applicable.
[1]Local revenues include intermediate revenues.
[2]U.S. totals include the 50 states and the District of Columbia.
[3]The District of Columbia has only one school district; therefore, it is not comparable to other states.

Note: Detail may not sum to totals because of rounding.

Source: Revenues and Expenditures for Public Elementary and Secondary Education, School Year 2005–06 (Fiscal Year 2006). Washington, DC: National Center for Education Statistics, April 2008, Table 1.

education funds received from local, state, and federal sources in relation to total expenditures for fiscal year 2006.

Federal Funding

The role of the federal government in providing resources for education has been limited. As shown in Figure 6.7, the federal share of funding for public elementary and secondary schools peaked in 1979–80 at 9.8 percent and had declined to 6.1 percent by 1989–90. Prior to 1980, the federal government had in effect bypassed the states and provided funding for local programs that were administered through various federal agencies, such as the Office of Economic Opportunity (Head Start, migrant education, and Follow Through) and the Department of Labor (Job Corps and the Comprehensive Employment Training Act [CETA]).

Since the Reagan administration (1980–1988), federal aid has increasingly been given directly to the states in the form of **block grants,** which a state or local education agency may spend as it wishes, with few limitations. The 1981 **Education Consolidation and Improvement Act (ECIA)** gave the states a broad range of choices in spending federal money. The ECIA significantly reduced federal aid to education, however, thus making state aid to education even more critical.

Although a small proportion of the funds for schools comes from the federal level, the federal government has enacted supplemental programs to help meet the educational needs of special student populations. Such programs are often referred to collectively as **entitlements.** The most significant entitlement is the Elementary and Secondary Education Act of 1965, which President George W. Bush reauthorized in 2002 as the No Child Left Behind Act. Title I of the act allocates $1 billion annually to school districts with large numbers of students from low-income families. Among the other funded entitlement programs are the Vocational Education Act (1963), the Manpower Development and Training Act (1963), the Economic Opportunity Act (1964), the Bilingual Education Act (1968), the Indian Education Act (1972), and the Education for All Handicapped Children Act (1975).

The federal government also provides funding for preschool programs such as Project Head Start. Originally started under the Economic Opportunity Act of 1964 to provide preschool experiences to poor children, Head Start was later made available to children whose parents were above the poverty level. Funding for Head Start was $4.66 billion in 1999. Reauthorized by Congress in 1998, Head Start served an estimated 830,000 children and their families that year. The Head Start Act Amendments of 1994 also established the Early Head Start program, designed to serve pregnant women and children under age 3 from low-income families.

WHAT ARE SOME TRENDS IN FUNDING FOR EQUITY AND EXCELLENCE?

The fact that schools rely heavily on property taxes for support has resulted in fiscal inequities for schools. Districts with higher property wealth can generate more money per pupil than can districts with lower property values. The degree of inequity between the wealthiest and the poorest districts, therefore, can be quite large. In some states, the ability of one district to generate local property tax revenues may be several times greater than another district's. In addition, "[W]ealthy African Americans, whites, Asians, and Hispanics can choose to live in school districts with adequate and exceptional public schools" (Spring, 2008, p. 95), while poor families do not have that option. Therefore, students from poor families are less likely to have access to educational opportunities and resources such as the following:

- Preschool programs
- High-quality teachers
- Challenging curricula
- High standards

- Up-to-date technology
- Modern facilities (Spring, 2008, pp. 95–96)

In *The Shame of the Nation: The Restoration of Apartheid Schooling in America*, Jonathan Kozol (2005) presents a compelling analysis of inequities in school funding. For example, the following compares per-pupil spending in five major U.S. cities with spending in wealthy nearby suburbs (black and Hispanic enrollments ranged from 72 to 95 percent in the cities and 8 to 20 percent in the suburbs):

- Chicago ($8,483) . . . . Highland Park and Deerfield, IL ($17,291)
- Philadelphia ($9,299) . . . . Lower Merion, PA ($17,261)
- New York City ($11,627) . . Manhasset, NY ($22,311)
- Detroit ($9,576) . . . . Bloomfield Hills, MI ($12,825)
- Milwaukee ($10,874) . . . . . Maple Dale–Indian Hill, WI ($13,955) (Kozol, 2005, pp. 321–324)

Such discrepancies in per-pupil funding led Joel Spring to assert that "[S]tatistics on school spending demonstrate a virulent form of institutional racism" (Spring, 2008a, p. 94).

Tax Reform and Redistricting

To correct funding inequities, several court suits were initiated during the 1970s. In the 1971 *Serrano v. Priest* case in California, it was successfully argued that the relationship between spending and property wealth violated the state's obligation to provide equal protection and education. The California Supreme Court ruled that the quality of a child's education should not depend on the "wealth of his parents and neighbors." The court also recognized that communities with a poor tax base could not be expected to generate the revenues of more affluent districts. Nevertheless, the court did not forbid the use of property taxes to fund education.

Then, in 1973, the U.S. Supreme Court decided in *San Antonio Independent School District v. Rodriguez* that fiscal inequities stemming from unequal tax bases did not violate the Constitution. That Court's decision reversed a lower court's ruling claiming that school financing on the basis of local property taxes was unconstitutional.

Regardless of the mixed outcomes of court challenges, many state legislatures have enacted school finance equity reforms during the last 15 years. Some states (California, Hawaii, New Mexico, Washington, and West Virginia, for example) have **full-funding programs** in which the state sets the same per-pupil expenditure level for all schools and districts.

Other states have adopted new funding formulas to broaden their revenue base. Level funding augmented by sales taxes, cigarette taxes, state lottery revenues, property taxes on second homes, and school-choice plans are among the solutions tried. One of the most dramatic changes in educational funding occurred in Michigan in 1993 with the passage of Proposal A, a plan that greatly reduced school funding from local property taxes and increased funding from the state's sales tax.

Because each state has been free to determine the number of districts within its boundaries, a common approach to achieving equal funding is **redistricting,** redrawing school district boundaries to reduce the range of variation in the ability of school districts to finance education. Redistricting not only equalizes funding; it can also reduce the cost of maintaining and operating schools if smaller districts are combined. The per-pupil cost of instruction, supplies, and equipment is usually lower in large districts. In addition, greater resources often allow larger districts to offer a broader curriculum and higher salaries to attract more qualified teachers.

Vertical Equity

Other states have developed various mechanisms to provide **vertical equity,** that is, allocating funds according to legitimate educational needs. Thus, additional support is given to programs that serve students from low-income backgrounds; those with limited English proficiency, or special gifts and talents; and those who need special education or vocational programs. Vertical equity is based on the assumption that "some 'unequal' students should have access to 'unequal' levels of resources" (Baker, Green, & Richards, 2008, p. 98).

Additional state-appropriated funds to cover the costs of educating students with special needs are known as **categorical aid.** Funding adjustments are also made to compensate for differences in costs within a state—higher expenses due to rural isolation or the higher cost of living in urban areas, for example. Some states even conduct periodic regional cost of living analyses, which are then used to determine adjustments in per-pupil funding.

School Choice

One of the most bitter struggles for control of schools in the United States is centered around **school choice,** the practice of allowing parents to choose the schools their children attend. The issue is especially heated for choice programs that would allow parents to choose a private school, with the public paying all or part of the tuition. According to the 2007 Phi Delta Kappa/Gallup poll of the public's attitudes toward the public schools, 67 percent opposed, and 33 percent favored, such school choice programs if the government paid *all* of the tuition. If the government paid *part* of the tuition, 48 percent opposed, and 51 percent approved (Rose & Gallup, 2007).

Debate continues about whether school choice programs will, in fact, promote equity and excellence. Advocates of school choice believe that giving parents more options will force public schools to adjust to free-market pressures—low-performing schools would have to improve or shut down. They also contend that parents whose children must now attend inferior, and sometimes dangerous, inner-city schools would be able to send their children elsewhere. In addition, some supporters see choice as a way to reduce the influence of top-heavy school bureaucracies and teachers' unions.

On the other hand, opponents believe that school choice would have disastrous consequences for public schools and lead to students being sorted by race, income, and religion. School choice, they argue, would subsidize the wealthy by siphoning money away from the public schools and further widen the gap between rich and poor districts.

Other critics contend that school choice could lead to the creation of segregated schools and schools that would be more committed to competing for education dollars and the most able, manageable students. A study of the impact of competition on three urban school systems concluded that "competition did not force [the districts] to substantially alter system, governance, management, or operations." And in the words of an observer at two schools, "teachers have thirty kids in their classroom just like they did last year, just like they did ten years ago. They still teach the same way. [Vouchers] haven't affected what they do" (Hess, 2002, p. 198).

Voucher Systems

One approach to providing educational equity that has generated considerable controversy is the **voucher system** of distributing educational funds. According to voucher plans, parents would be given government-funded vouchers to purchase educational services at the schools of their choice.

Voucher systems were first suggested more than 50 years ago by Milton Friedman, a well-known conservative economist and Nobel laureate. Friedman believes that schools would be much better if they were operated by private businesses rather than the government. "If we had a system of free choice we would also have a system of competition, innovation, which would change the character of education. . . . Reform has to come through competition from the outside, and the only way you can get competition is by making it possible for parents to have the ability to choose" (Friedman, 2003).

The most controversial voucher proposals would allow parents to choose from among public as well as private (secular, parochial, for-profit, and charter) schools; others would limit parents' choice to public schools. Voucher programs require that parents and guardians reflect on the kind of educational experiences they want for their children.

Debates about vouchers regularly make the national news. In 1999, Florida became the first state to offer state-paid tuition to children in failing public schools to attend a public, private, or religious school of choice; however, a Florida judge ruled in 2006 that the program violated the Florida constitution because it gave tax money to religious schools (*Bush v. Holmes*, 2006). However, in 2002, the Supreme Court ruled that a school voucher program in Cleveland did not infringe on the constitutional separation of church and state (*Zelman v. Simmons-Harris*, 2002). The Court majority said that the parents had a sufficient range of choices among secular and religious schools, and that the voucher plan did not violate the First Amendment prohibition against the establishment of religion.

Evaluation of Voucher Programs

Approximately a dozen different voucher programs exist in various states. Each program has different rules and regulations controlling its size and scope and the terms of participation. Because "distinguishing those voucher programs that are designed to be large, generous, and inclusive from those that are small, stingy, and restrictive sometimes requires wading through technical legal and regulatory documents" (Enlow, 2004, pp. 1–2), the Milton and Rose D. Friedman Foundation released *Grading Vouchers: Ranking America's School Choice Programs* in 2004.

The report evaluates and ranks the nation's school voucher programs on three criteria: how many students are eligible to receive a voucher (Student Eligibility), how much money the voucher is worth (Purchasing Power), and how many and what type of private schools parents can choose (School Eligibility). For each category, the program is assigned a letter grade, and the final ranking is based on the average of the three. The criteria reflect Friedman's vision of a voucher system of education in which "all students, regardless of income or any other criteria, are able to use 100 percent of the state and local funds to attend public and private schools that are largely free from government interference" (Enlow, 2004, p. 2).

According to the report, the best voucher program is Florida's McKay Scholarship, with a 3.6 GPA, or A−, while the lowest scoring voucher program is the Iowa Personal Tax Credit, with a 1.76 GPA, or C−. Milwaukee's voucher program, the nation's oldest program for low-income families, receives a grade of C, while Colorado's program, one of the newest, gets a B−. (In 2003, a Denver district court judge struck down Colorado's voucher legislation.)

Another study, the longest voucher study in the country (Metcalf, 2003), has evaluated the Cleveland voucher program since 1998. The longitudinal study is following a group of 1,000 Cleveland voucher students from the first grade to determine if they are doing better in private schools compared to their public school peers. The voucher students are being compared with 5,000 public school students. The public school students are divided into four groups: (1) those who applied for vouchers but weren't accepted into the program, (2) those who were awarded vouchers but didn't use them, (3) those who used vouchers for one or more years but returned to public school, and (4) those who chose never to apply for the voucher program.

How does the voucher system for education work? Why are vouchers controversial, and why are many people against a voucher system?

The following are among the findings for the Cleveland voucher program:

- During the first three years of school, public school students, on average, made larger academic gains than students in the voucher program. After the first three years, however, there were no consistent or statistically significant differences in academic achievement as a result of vouchers.

- Many low-income families eligible to participate in the voucher program declined to do so because the cost to attend private school, even with a voucher, was too high. In addition, the limited number and range of participating private schools further discouraged families from using vouchers.

- When low-income families declined to participate, their unused vouchers were likely to be used by students who are not minority, who are more affluent, and who are already enrolled in a private school (Metcalf, 2003).

It is clear that the debate over school choice will continue for the foreseeable future. Gradually, support for school choice appears to be increasing—currently, almost half of the states allow some form of "interdistrict" transfer, which allows students to attend public schools outside their home district. In fact, Grant and Murray (1999, p. 235) suggest that "it is conceivable that by 2020 as many as a quarter of all students could be enrolled in some 'school of choice,' whether private or public."

Education-Business Coalitions

To develop additional sources of funding for equity and excellence, many local school districts have established coalitions with the private sector. Businesses may contribute funds or materials needed by a school; sponsor sports teams; award scholarships; provide cash grants for pilot projects and teacher development; provide mentors, volunteers, or expertise; and even construct school buildings. Among the types of education-business coalitions are the National Alliance of State Science and Mathematics Coalitions (NASSMC), the largest network of state-level education-business coalitions in the country; the Business Roundtable, a group of CEOs of leading U.S. companies; and partnerships with chambers of commerce. Private support for K–12 education, including the corporate sector, totals about $3.6 billion annually (Hills & Hirschhorn, May 2007). Figure 6.8 shows that the "partnership outcome" of greatest interest to education-business coalitions is workforce preparedness.

One example of an education-business partnership is GE's College Bound initiative, a five-year $100 million program with three targeted U.S. school districts, which focuses on reducing the achievement gap and increasing the number of low-income students who attend college. In its partnership with Jefferson County, Kentucky, schools, "GE makes extensive use of company volunteers for the following: to convene teachers, union representatives, consultants and district staff; to build an educational advisory council with outside education experts; and to help build capacity for the district through consulting on human resources, management, IT, security, and other services" (Hills & Hirschhorn, May 2007, p. 15).

FIGURE 6.8 Partnership outcomes of greatest interest to business coalitions

Source: Business Coalition Leaders Speak Out on Education. Charlotte, NC: DeHavilland Associates, June 2007, p. 4. Survey conducted during May 2–18, 2007, of 529 business coalitions working at the local, state, regional, and national levels.

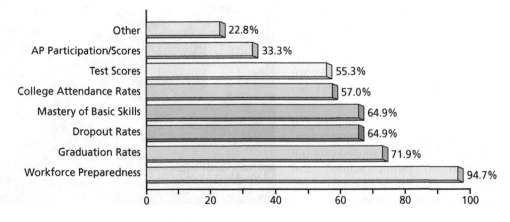

The largest amount of private support for education in the United States comes from the Bill and Melinda Gates Foundation. The Foundation has spent more than $1 billion on more than 1,500 partnerships with our nation's schools. Chicago has opened 100 new schools with the help of Gates Foundation money, and New York City has opened 200. A priority for the Foundation is the reform of high schools in urban areas and helping schools develop more academically rigorous curricula. The foundation awarded the Chicago Public Schools $21 million to develop new curricula and to make classes more rigorous (Hills & Hirschhorn, 2007). An open letter from Bill and Melinda Gates (May 28, 2008) stresses the important role that education-business coalitions can play in improving high schools in poor communities throughout the United States:

> Here in the United States, only one-third of the students who start the ninth grade will graduate from high school with the skills they need to succeed in college and work. A disproportionate number of those who fall behind will be African American and Hispanic.
>
> Our work with high schools in the United States . . . involves dozens of partners, from grass-roots community organizations all the way up to national policymakers. Changing high schools will require the efforts of parents, teachers, school administrators, school districts, a range of organizations devoted to school reform, and government leaders at every level. We need this kind of coordinated approach to make sure we prepare every child for college, work, and citizenship.

If schools in the United States are to succeed in meeting the challenges of the future, they will need to be funded at a level that provides quality educational experiences to students from a diverse array of backgrounds. Though innovative approaches to school funding have been developed, much remains to be done before both excellence and equity characterize all schools in the United States.

HOW WILL THE PRIVATIZATION MOVEMENT AFFECT EQUITY AND EXCELLENCE IN EDUCATION?

One of the most dramatic reforms in U.S. education during the last decade has been the development of charter schools and for-profit schools, both of which were developed to provide an alternative to the perceived inadequacies of the public schools. On many different levels—governance, staffing, curricula, funding, and accountability—the **privatization movement** is a radical departure from schools as most people have known them. Between 1998 and 2004, the number of private companies operating public schools increased from 13 to 53, and the number of privately managed schools increased from 135 to 463 (Molnar, Wilson, & Allen, 2004, p. 9).

Charter Schools

In 1991, Minnesota passed the nation's first charter school legislation calling for up to eight teacher-created and -operated, outcome-based schools that would be free of most state and local rules and regulations. When the St. Paul City Academy opened its doors in September 1992, it became the nation's first charter school. Since then, the charter school movement has grown to almost 4,000 schools operating nationwide in 2007 and serving over 1,500,000 students (Center for Educational Reform, April 2007).

Charter schools are independent, innovative, outcome-based, public schools. As *Education Week* (2005) put it: "The basic charter concept is simple: Allow a group of teachers or other would-be educators to apply for permission to open a school. Give them dollar for dollar what a public school gets for each student. Free them from the bureaucracy that cripples learning and stifles innovation at so many public schools."

To open a charter school, an original charter (or agreement) is signed by the school's founders and a sponsor (usually the local school board). The charter specifies the learning outcomes that students will master before they continue their studies. Charter schools, which usually operate in the manner of autonomous school districts (a feature that distinguishes them from the alternative schools that many school districts operate), are public schools and must teach all students. If admission requests for a charter school exceed the number of available openings, students are selected by drawing.

According to U.S. Charter Schools (May 28, 2008), the purpose of most charter schools is to:

- Increase opportunities for learning and access to quality education for all students
- Create choice for parents and students within the public school system
- Provide a system of accountability for results in public education
- Encourage innovative teaching practices
- Create new professional opportunities for teachers
- Encourage community and parent involvement in public education
- Leverage improved public education broadly

Because charter schools are designed to promote the development of new teaching strategies that can be used at other public schools, they can prove to be an effective tool for promoting educational reform and the professionalization of teaching in the future. Charter schools also give teachers unprecedented leadership opportunities and the ability to respond quickly to students' needs:

Research on Charter Schools

In a report titled *Do Charter Schools Measure Up? The Charter School Experiment After 10 Years,* the American Federation of Teachers (AFT) suggested that, by mid-2002, charter schools had not lived up to the claims of their advocates. The following are among the shortcomings of charter schools, according to the AFT report:

- Charter schools contribute to the racial and ethnic isolation of students.
- Charter school teachers are less experienced and lower paid than teachers in other public schools.
- Charter school students generally score no better (and often do worse) on student achievement tests than other comparable public school students.
- Charter schools have not been held to the "bargain" they made—trading freedom from rules for increased accountability.
- Charter schools were supposed to experiment with new curricula and classroom practices, but they have proven no more innovative than other public schools (American Federation of Teachers, 2002, pp. 5–6).

Another study of charter schools compared reading and mathematics scores on the 2003 National Assessment of Educational Progress (NAEP) for fourth-grade students at 150 charter schools with those of students in other public schools. Results indicated that underprivileged students in charter schools do worse in reading and mathematics than students in other schools. However, students of the same race or ethnicity scored as well in either type of school. Overall, the NAEP assessment found that less than one-third of students, regardless of the type of school they attended, were "proficient" in mathematics or reading, according to federal standards (U.S. Department of Education, Institute for Education Sciences, 2004).

On the other hand, another 2004 research report indicated that charter school students outperformed students in comparable traditional public schools in reading and mathematics (Hoxby, 2004). The researcher compared the achievement of 99 percent of all elementary students enrolled in charter schools with that of students in neighboring public schools with similar racial compositions. Results indicated that charter school students were 5.2 percent more likely to be proficient in reading and 3.2 percent more likely to be proficient in mathematics on their state's exam.

Regardless of the mixed results on the effectiveness of charter schools, few charter schools have been closed because of failure to meet academic outcomes. Instead, charter school closings are related to "low enrollment, facility problems, financial improprieties, or mismanagement" (Hess, 2004, p. 509). By 2002, 194 (6.95 percent) of the nation's 2,790 charter schools had been closed, but only 0.005 percent were closed for failure to meet academic outcomes (Hess, 2004).

For-Profit Schools

One of the hottest educational issues today is the practice of turning the operation of public schools over to private, for-profit companies. Advocates of privatization believe privately operated schools are more efficient; they reduce costs and maximize "production"—that is, student achievement. Opponents, however, are concerned that profit, rather than increasing student achievement, is the real driving force behind **for-profit schools.** For-profit education companies focusing on the pre-K to 12 level had revenues of $58 billion in 2001 (Eduventures, 2003). Critics of for-profit schools are also concerned that school districts may not be vigilant enough in monitoring the performance of private education companies.

Edison Schools, Inc.

Concerned about the slow pace of educational reform in the United States, Christopher Whittle, the originator of Channel One, launched the $3 billion Edison Project in 1992—an ambitious plan to develop a national network of more than 1,000 for-profit secondary schools by 2010. As of 2001–02, the Edison Project, now named Edison Schools, Inc., had become the largest company involved in the for-profit management of K–12 schools, and it served 74,000 students in 133 schools located in 22 states and the District of Columbia (Edison Schools, Inc., 2004).

In 1999, Edison Schools, Inc., reported that achievement was steadily moving upward at the "vast majority" of Edison schools. At 17 of the Edison schools that had been able to establish achievement trends, 14 had records the company labeled "positive" or "strongly positive," and 3 had records that were labeled "weak" (Walsh, 1999b).

However, in a report analyzing the results reported by Edison the previous year, the American Federation of Teachers claimed that the company exaggerated achievement gains at many schools and downplayed negative results at others. "On the whole, Edison results were mediocre," the report claimed (American Federation of Teachers, 1998, p. 10).

Teacher-Owned Schools?

An innovative approach to for-profit schools has been suggested by Richard K. Vedder (2003) in his book *Can Teachers Own Their Own Schools? New Strategies for Educational Excellence.* Vedder believes that for-profit public schools would benefit from competition and develop cost-effective ways to achieve educational quality. In addition, such schools would attract additional funding and expertise needed to revolutionize school systems.

Vedder's approach is patterned after Margaret Thatcher's privatization of government council housing in England, privatization reforms in Latin America, and the employee stock ownership plan (ESOP) movement in the United States. He suggests that teachers, administrators, and other educational stakeholders become the owners of schools, thus acquiring an attractive financial stake in the process. Such privatization reforms could pave the way for new, cost-effective means of improving education for all students. Vedder believes that schools in which teachers, administrators, and parents have a significant financial stake would foster vibrant school communities with increased parental involvement and the innovation and efficiency essential to produce educational excellence.

One example of a teacher-owned school is the George Washington Community School, a college-prep high school serving 9th- to 12th-grade students in Northern Virginia. The mission of the school is "the development and implementation of a holistic educational program which will develop and optimize the giftedness and intelligence of each student in an in-depth, enriched, and technically advanced college preparatory environment that emphasizes authentic application of knowledge, not merely assimilation of information." Teachers at the school have flexibility over the curriculum and teaching methods. As a result, classes like "Conspiracy Theories," "Political Geography," and "Sea Adventures" are offered in addition to traditional courses.

SUMMARY

Why Do You Need to Understand Educational Politics?

- Understanding educational politics is an important form of professional knowledge.
- Parents; students; teachers; administrators; taxpayers; federal, state, and local authorities; ethnic and racial groups; educational theorists and researchers; the corporate sector; and special interest groups exert political influence on education.
- *Politics* refer to how people use power, influence, and authority within an organization to persuade others to act in desired ways.
- Educators use within-school politics to influence instructional and curricular practices within a school.
- Five dimensions of educational politics influence teachers: (1) political pressure from federal, state, and local levels; (2) conflicting educational philosophies; (3) competition for educational resources; (4) changing legal rights and responsibilities of teachers; and (5) the push for higher standards, testing, and accountability.

How Does the Local Community Influence Schools?

- Local school districts, which vary greatly in size, locale, organizational structure, demographics, and wealth, are responsible for the management and operation of schools.
- Local school boards, whose members are usually elected, set educational policies for a district; however, many people believe that boards should be reformed to be better informed and more responsive.
- The superintendent, the chief administrator of a local district, has a complex array of responsibilities and must work cooperatively with the school board and others in an environment that is often politically turbulent.
- Through groups like the PTA or PTO, some parents are involved in local school activities and reform efforts; others are involved with private schools; and some actively promote alternative approaches to

education such as school choice, voucher systems, and home schooling.

What Powers and Influence Do States Have in Governing Schools?

- The state legislature, state courts, and the governor significantly influence education by setting policies related to the management and operation of schools within a state; many states have even passed legislation allowing them to take over academically failing school districts or individual schools.
- The state board of education, the highest educational agency in a state, regulates education and advises the governor and others on important educational policies.
- The state department of education implements policies related to teacher certification, allocation of state and federal funds, enforcement of state and federal guidelines, school accreditation, and research and evaluation projects to improve education.
- The chief state school officer oversees education within a state and, in collaboration with the governor, legislature, state board of education, and the public, provides leadership to improve education.

How Do Regional Education Agencies Assist Schools?

- The regional educational service agency (RESA), an intermediate unit of educational administration in about half of the states, provides assistance to two or more school districts for staff development, curriculum development, instructional media, and program evaluation.

How Does the Federal Government Influence Education?

- The federal government influences education at the state level through funding general and categorical programs, establishing and enforcing standards and regulations, conducting and disseminating educational research, providing technical assistance to improve education, and encouraging equity and excellence for the nation's schools.

- The national legislature, federal and state supreme courts, and the president significantly influence education by exerting moral suasion for the improvement of schools, providing categorical aid for federal programs, ensuring that school systems follow legal statutes, and funding educational research.
- The U.S. Department of Education supports and disseminates educational research, administers federal grants in education, and assists the president in developing and promoting a national agenda for education.
- At times, the roles of the federal, state, and local governments in education are in conflict.

How Are Schools Financed in the United States?

- Schools are supported with revenues from the local, state, and federal levels, with most funding now coming from the state level. Local funding is provided through property taxes, which in many instances results in inequitable funding for schools located in areas with an insufficient tax base.
- One challenge to financing schools has been the development of an equitable means of taxation for the support of education.

What Are Some Trends in Funding for Equity and Excellence?

- Inequities among school districts often reflect differences in the value of property that can be taxed for the support of schools.
- Many state legislatures have enacted tax reforms, including full-funding programs, that set the same per-pupil expenditures for all schools and districts. Some states have achieved greater equity through redistricting—redrawing district boundaries to reduce funding inequities.
- Some states achieve vertical equity by providing additional funding, or categorical aid, to educate students with special needs. Also, many local districts and schools receive additional funding through partnerships with the private sector and/or community groups.
- School choice and voucher programs are two controversial approaches to providing parents the freedom to select the schools their children attend.

How Will the Privatization Movement Affect Equity and Excellence in Education?

- Charter schools and for-profit schools, both part of the privatization movement, were developed in response to perceived inadequacies of the public schools.
- Charter schools are independent, innovative, outcome-based public schools started by a group of teachers, parents, or others who obtain a charter from a local school district, a state, or the federal government.
- Research on charter schools is mixed—some studies show that charter school students outperform students at other schools, while other studies show the opposite.
- Very few charter schools have been closed because of failure to meet academic outcomes; about 7 percent have been closed because of low enrollment, facility problems, financial improprieties, or mismanagement.
- Edison Schools, Inc. (formerly the Edison Project) is an example of for-profit schools operated by private corporations.
- For-profit schools owned by teachers, administrators, and other stakeholders have been suggested as one way to improve the quality of schools.

PROFESSIONAL REFLECTIONS AND ACTIVITIES

Teacher's Journal

1. As this chapter points out, many individuals and groups believe that they should play an important role in school governance. Rank order (from *greatest influence* to *least influence*) the extent to which you think each of the following individuals or groups *should* control schools: students, teachers, administrators, parents, the school board, the local school district, the state government, and the federal government. Are there certain areas of schooling that should be controlled by these individuals and groups? Compare your rankings with those of your classmates. What differences do you note?

2. Imagine that you are going to open a charter school. How would this school differ from the schools in your community? What would you say to parents to convince them to send their children to your school?

Teacher's Research

1. Use your favorite search engine to visit the websites for several charter schools. What do these schools have in common? How are they different?
2. Visit the U.S. Department of Education's charter school website and click on the State Policies for Charter Schools link. How do the states' charter school policies differ? How are they similar?

Observations and Interviews

1. Using Figure 6.2 as a guide, interview a teacher in a local school about his or her perceptions of the political influences on teachers. Ask the teacher to select one influence and describe how it currently affects the school where the teacher works.
2. Interview a teacher and ask him or her to rank order (from *greatest influence* to *least influence*) the extent to which each of the following individuals or groups *should* control schools: students, teachers, administrators, parents, the school board, the local school district, the state government, and the federal government. How do the teacher's beliefs compare with your own?

---

myeducationlab To complete additional observations and interviews, go to MyEducationLab at www.myeducationlab.com, select the Virtual Field Experience section, and click on this chapter's Observations and Interviews.

Professional Portfolio

Think of businesses and groups in your community that may make good candidates for a partnership with a school. Select one of them and develop a proposal outlining the nature, activities, and benefits of the partnership you envision.

---

myeducationlab Now go to MyEducationLab at www.myeducationlab.com to test your understanding of chapter content by completing this chapter's Study Plan.

Ethical and Legal Issues in U.S. Education

9

Ethical and Legal Issues
in U.S. Education

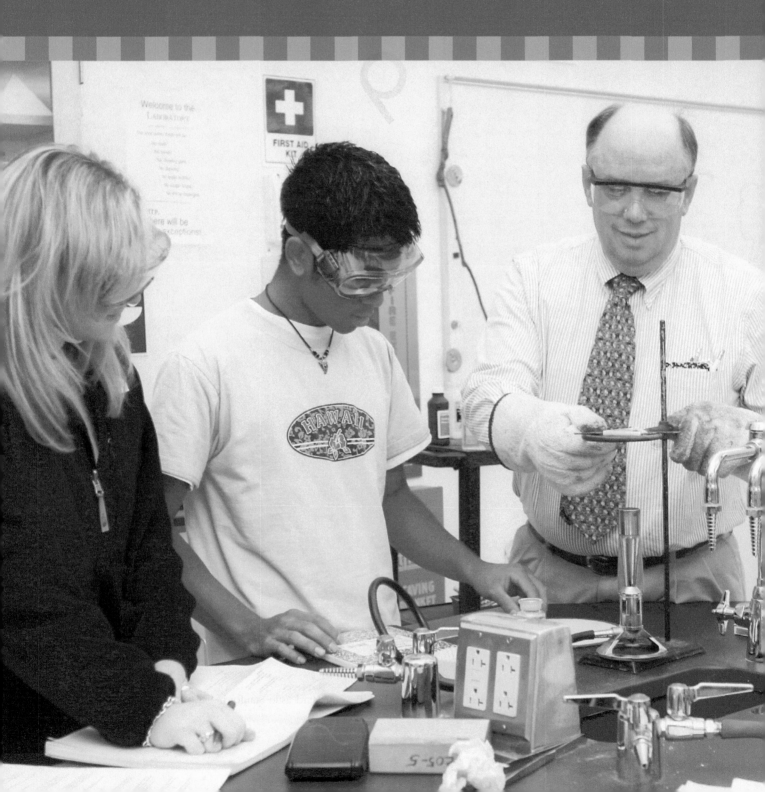

CLASSROOM CASE
The Realities of Teaching

THE CHALLENGE: Understanding the legal rights of students related to dress and appearance.

Manda, a student in your middle-school class, idolizes gothic rock stars and has begun to dress like them. Her once-pretty long black hair is now cut short except for several random strands that hang down to her shoulders. Lately, she's been applying a sweet-smelling, gooey, pink gel to her hair, which seems to be changing gradually from black to red.

Today, she is wearing black-checked stockings and an old evening dress that she bought at a local secondhand clothing store. The heavy makeup that encircles her brown eyes and the ruby red lipstick applied recklessly to her thin lips give her face a hardened, almost grotesque look.

Since she began dressing like this, other students have started to tease her. She's resilient and seems to be handling the situation well enough, but she has created a commotion in your class that gets worse by the day.

A few other girls have started to copy her style. Today, you notice that Janna is dressed in a similar manner. Her short blond hair is slicked back, as though she just stepped out of the shower. She is wearing a tight black skirt that is several inches above the knee and a bright green polyester blouse that looks as though it might glow in the dark.

Janna strolls around the room, taking her time, and, if her smile is any indication, delighting in the fact that everyone's eyes are on her. Several students laugh at her hysterically and point. Janna stares menacingly at them and finally slides into the seat behind Manda. Their classmates continue to giggle and squirm in their seats.

"All right, class," you begin. "Let's settle down. Take out the homework you did last night."

But it's more difficult than usual to get your students' attention this Monday. It's obvious that Manda's and Janna's appearance has unsettled the whole class.

As you continue with the lesson, you wonder if you have the right to speak to Manda and Janna and request that they change their appearance. Or do they have the right to wear whatever they want to school?

FOCUS QUESTIONS

1. Why do you need to know about education and the law?
2. Why do you need a professional code of ethics?
3. What are your legal rights as a teacher?

229

4. Do student teachers have the same rights as teachers do?

5. What are your legal responsibilities as a teacher?

6. What are the legal rights of students and parents?

7. What are some issues in the legal rights of school districts?

The case above is similar to that of a Kentucky middle school student who was not allowed to wear blue jeans to school. The girl's father filed suit, claiming that the school's dress code violated his daughter's right to freedom of expression and his right to control the dress of his children. The case eventually worked its way to the U.S. Court of Appeals. The court ruled that the student's right to wear blue jeans is not "a fundamental right entitled to heightened protection." In addition, the plaintiff failed to demonstrate that the school district lacked a rational basis for the dress code. The court concluded that the student's claim demonstrated nothing more than a "generalized and vague desire to express her middle-school individuality" (*Blau v. Fort Thomas Public School District*, 2005).

WHY DO YOU NEED TO KNOW ABOUT EDUCATION AND THE LAW?

At this point in your teacher education program, understanding how the law influences schools and teachers may not seem important. However, federal and state legislation and court decisions will affect your life as a teacher. What are your legal responsibilities when you take students on a field trip? Are you responsible if a student is injured during your class? Can a parent prevent you from using curriculum materials that the parent finds offensive? What guidelines must you follow when photocopying instructional materials from books and magazines? How can you copyright-protect materials you and your students publish on the Internet? These are just a few legal issues you might encounter as a teacher. Without knowledge of the legal dimensions of such issues, you will be ill-equipped to protect your rights and the rights of your students. This chapter examines ethical and legal issues that affect the rights and responsibilities of teachers, administrators, students, and parents.

WHY DO YOU NEED A PROFESSIONAL CODE OF ETHICS?

Your actions as a teacher will be determined not only by what is legally required of you but also by what you know you *ought* to do. You must do what is legally right, and you must *do the right thing*. A specific set of values will guide you. A deep and lasting commitment to professional practice should characterize your role as a teacher. You will need to adopt a high standard of professional ethics and model behaviors that are in accord with that code of ethics.

At present, the teaching profession does not have a uniform **code of ethics** similar to the Hippocratic oath, which all doctors are legally required to take when they begin practice. However, the largest professional organization for teachers, the National Education Association (NEA), has a code of ethics for members that includes the following statement: "The educator accepts the responsibility to adhere to the highest ethical standards."

Ethical Teaching Attitudes and Practices

Teaching is an ethical enterprise; that is, a teacher has an obligation to act ethically, to follow what he or she knows to be the most appropriate professional action to take.

The best interests of students, not the teacher, provide the rule of thumb for determining what is ethical and what is not. Behaving ethically is more than a matter of following the rules or not breaking the law—it means acting in a way that promotes the learning and growth of students and helps them realize their potential. The Teaching on Your Feet feature for this chapter illustrates how one teacher modified his behavior to promote the learning and growth of a "problem" student.

Unethical acts break the trust and respect on which good teacher-student relationships are based. Examples of unethical conduct would be to use grades as a form of punishment, express rage in the classroom, or intentionally trick students on tests. You can no doubt think of other examples from your own experience as a student.

Ethical Dilemmas in the Classroom and School

As a teacher, you will probably encounter **ethical dilemmas** in the classroom and in the school. You will have to take action in situations in which all the facts are not known or for which no single course of action can be called right or wrong. At these times, it can be quite difficult to decide what an ethical response might be. Dealing satisfactorily with ethical dilemmas in teaching often requires the ability to see beyond short-range consequences to consider long-range consequences.

An important part of responding to an ethical dilemma is identifying possible consequences of one's actions. Consider, for example, the following three questions based on actual case studies. On the basis of the information given, how would you respond to each situation? What might be the consequences of your actions?

1. Should the sponsor of the high school literary magazine refuse to print a well-written story by a budding writer if the piece appears to satirize a teacher and a student?

2. Is a reading teacher justified in trying to increase achievement for an entire class by separating two disruptive students and placing one in a reading group beneath his reading level?

3. Should a chemistry teacher punish a student (on the basis of circumstantial, inconclusive evidence) for a laboratory explosion if the example of decisive, swift punishment will likely prevent the recurrence of a similar event and thereby ensure the safety of all students?

There are no "right" answers to the above questions. To the extent possible, you want to make the "best" decision in each case. A noted scholar of professional ethics, Kenneth A. Strike, suggests the following characteristics of a "good," ethical decision:

1. The decision is supported by evidence. This evidence supports the claim that acting on this decision is more likely to achieve desired ends at an appropriate cost than other courses of action that might be taken.

2. The ends aimed at by the decision are the ends that ought to be aimed at.

3. The decision can be implemented morally.

4. The decision has been legitimately achieved (Strike, 2007, p. 113).

What ethical dilemmas might this experiment pose for a teacher? How might you respond? On what moral or ethical grounds would you base your response?

TEACHING ON YOUR FEET

SOME STUDENTS DESERVE A BREAK

Mark Twain once said, "I could live two months on one good compliment." That statement also holds true for most students in today's classrooms. When all else fails, give students a "break." Try to make something positive out of something that otherwise might be viewed as disrespectful and/or defiant. Doing so might make your school year (and life) easier and much more productive.

When I was a beginning teacher, I asked several of the veteran teachers at my school for advice before my first day of teaching. To my surprise, they all had the same thing to say: "Don't smile until Christmas!" That bit of advice was not very reassuring, especially since it does not fit my personality. Although they didn't mean it literally, they felt strongly about being strict and not building friendships with students. After my first few weeks of teaching, I understood exactly what they meant, even if I did not totally agree with their philosophy.

I started off the first week by making sure that my students understood the rules and expectations for my class. Common in many junior high classes, I was met with rolling eyes and witty remarks from a select few in each class. I put on my strictest face and made sure that those students knew that I meant business. After addressing those students in class, there was only one who continued to fight me on it. I'll call him Johnny.

Throughout the next couple of months, Johnny and I disagreed on several different occasions. Johnny was the student who demanded attention; he had a comment for everything that occurred in class. He would not take "no" for an answer, and he had a history of defiance. Every time we had a disagreement, I sent him to the guidance office, called his parents, and hoped for the best. But the next day I would be met with even more resistance and negative attitude. I repeated this process several times before I decided I needed to change my strategy. Why was this student giving me such a hard time? What was I doing wrong? I thought being strict and firm was the way to start off the school year but, to be honest, it consumed all of my energy in and out of class. It was time to find a better way to reach Johnny.

After speaking to the administration and some of Johnny's other teachers, I realized that I was not alone. With one exception, they all had problems with him. To my surprise, the exception was a beginning teacher like myself. I had to know her secret. When I asked her how she "handled" Johnny, she simply said, "Some students deserve a break." She explained that there are some students who respond to consequences and others who don't. Johnny was one who did not. He needed a "break" to be successful.

WHAT ARE YOUR LEGAL RIGHTS AS A TEACHER?

With each freedom that we have comes a corresponding responsibility to others and to the community in which we live. As long as there is more than one individual on this planet, there is a need for laws to clarify individual rights and responsibilities. This necessary balance between rights and responsibilities is perhaps more critical to teaching than to any other profession. Teachers have the same rights as other citizens; however, teachers must "operate within the legal boundaries of the U.S. Constitution, their respective state constitutions, and case law as well as statutory law at both state and federal levels" (Essex, 2008, p. xi). The primary legal rights of teachers are illustrated in Figure 7.1.

While schools do have limited power over teachers, teachers' rights to **due process** cannot be violated. Like all citizens, teachers are protected from being treated arbitrarily by those in authority. A principal who disagrees with a teacher's methods cannot suddenly fire that teacher. A school board cannot ask a teacher to resign merely

TEACHING ON YOUR FEET

The next day, I called Johnny out of class to speak to him one on one. I reassured him that he wasn't in trouble and that all I wanted to do was talk to him. I asked him what it is about me that he didn't like, and he responded, "You treat me like all of the others (teachers) do." When I asked him how he wanted to be treated, he said, "I don't know . . . with respect." I proceeded to tell him that in order to receive respect, you have to give it. Then he said something that surprised me. "You need to take some of your own advice." In that moment, my two-month career as a schoolteacher flashed before my eyes. I was speechless. After an awkward silence, I sent him back to class. I thought long and hard about how I was coming across to my students and came to the conclusion that, while being strict and firm (without cracking a smile) worked for the majority of my students, I was at times being disrespectful to a select few—Johnny in particular.

Following class the next day, I thanked Johnny for our conversation. He seemed surprised by my reaction. I joked with him, telling him that he could make big money for his advice and offered him my apologies for the way I had been treating him in front of the class. I told him that he was a born leader and that students in the class looked up to him. I assured him that he could use his pull with the students to do good things and to persuade them to act appropriately. I could tell that those words meant a lot to him. From that day forward, Johnny and I had a mutually respectful relationship. And, most important, I had an influential student who supported my approach to classroom management.

ANALYSIS

Classroom management cannot be learned entirely through a textbook. It must also be learned through experience. There is no single approach to classroom management that suits all students in a classroom. Each class has students who respond differently to a teacher's approach to classroom management. If you empower a student to be a leader in your classroom and go about it in the right way, you can gain support for your approach to classroom management.

REFLECTION

- What are the pros and cons of taking the advice of other teachers regarding classroom management?
- List the characteristics of a student who might be a "red flag" for classroom misbehavior.
- What are other strategies a teacher can use to have a positive influence on students who chronically misbehave?
- Is there a universally effective approach to classroom management? Explain.

Julius Dichosa
Eighth-Grade Physical Science, Department Chair, Las Palmas Middle School

PEARSON myeducationlab *To answer these questions online, go to MyEducationLab at www.myeducationlab.com, select the Activities and Application section, and click on this chapter's Teaching on Your Feet.*

---

by claiming that the teacher's political activities outside school are "disruptive" to the educational process. A teacher cannot be dismissed for "poor" performance without ample documentation that the performance was, in fact, poor and without sufficient time to meet clearly stated performance evaluation criteria.

Certification

Suppose, for example, that Peggy Hernandez is a junior high school English teacher and lives in a state with a law specifying that a teacher must show proof of five years of successful teaching experience for a teaching certificate to be renewed. Last year was Peggy's fifth year of teaching, and her principal gave her an unsatisfactory performance rating. Peggy's principal told her that her teaching certificate cannot be renewed. Is the principal correct?

Peggy's principal is mistaken about the grounds for nonrenewal of a teaching certificate. According to the state's law, unsuccessful performance, or a failure to complete the

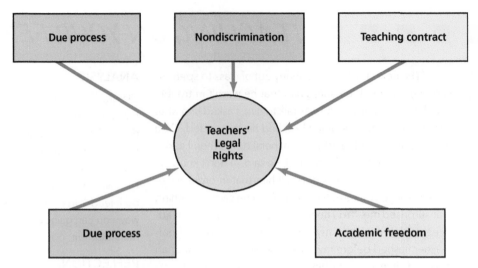

FIGURE 7.1 Teachers' legal rights

school year, is grounds for nonrenewal of a certificate—not performance that is judged to be unsatisfactory. Because state laws vary and unsuccessful performance is defined differently in different states, however, Peggy's principal might have been correct if she taught in another state. The Teacher's Voices: Walk in My Shoes feature for this chapter profiles a teacher who completed her teacher education program in Louisiana and then went on to meet the requirements for teacher certification in California.

No teacher who meets all of a state's requirements for initial certification can arbitrarily be denied a certificate. "However, obtaining a certificate does not guarantee the right to retain it" (Imber & van Geel, 2005, p. 212). For a certificate to be revoked, the reason must be job-related and demonstrably impair the teacher's ability to perform satisfactorily. In this regard, the case of a California teacher whose certificate was revoked because someone admitted to having a homosexual relationship with the teacher is often cited. The court determined that the teacher's homosexual conduct was not an impairment to the teacher's performance and ordered the certificate restored (*Morrison v. State Board of Education,* 1969).

When courts have upheld the refusal to hire and the right to terminate homosexual teachers, these decisions have been influenced by factors such as sexual involvement with students or public acts of indecency (Imber & van Geel, 2005). Fourteen states and the District of Columbia have laws that prohibit discrimination on the basis of sexual orientation in regard to employment (LaMorte, 2008, p. 246). Today, it is "difficult, if not impossible, for local school systems to deny employment or dismiss homosexuals on the basis of their sexual orientation" (LaMorte, 2008, p. 247).

Teachers' Rights to Nondiscrimination

George, who pled guilty to possession of marijuana and cocaine in a criminal trial, was not reinstated in his teaching position after his criminal record was expunged. George claims that he is being discriminated against because of his past. Is he right?

States may impose certain limitations on initial certification as long as those limitations are not discriminatory with regard to race, religion, ethnic origin, sex, or age. Nearly all the states, for example, require that applicants for a teaching certificate pass a test that covers basic skills, professional knowledge, or academic subject areas. Qualifications for initial certification may also legally include certain personal qualities. George's case for example, is based on a Louisiana case involving a man who was not reinstated in his teaching position, even though his criminal record had been expunged. The court maintained that he had committed the act, and that expunging the record did not erase

TEACHERS' VOICES
Walk in My Shoes

Frannie Knobloch Finley embarked on a life-changing adventure when she took a summer job as a waitress on Catalina Island, off the coast of California. She fell in love with lush flora, ocean sunsets, relaxed lifestyle, absence of automobiles, and friendliness of the small community of island residents. By the end of the summer, she knew she would return.

That fall, she went back to Louisiana State University and finished her senior year of college, where she was an education major. She had begun there as a premed major but discovered that she "hated reading biology books." She took a career discovery test in the university's Career Center and scored highest on teaching. She switched her major to education and decided to become a math teacher. She did her student teaching in Louisiana and graduated, and then returned to Catalina to find a teaching job.

Her first year back on the island, she substitute-taught often and embarked on the additional tests and training the state of California required of teachers seeking to obtain the state teaching credential. Frannie knew these legal hurdles were worth her time and effort to reach her goal.

Once hired full-time three years ago, she quickly became successful and appreciated. She teaches both middle and high school students. She is also an Advancement Via Individual Determination (AVID) teacher in a program to help mid-achieving students gain the knowledge and skills to enter and graduate from a four-year college.

Her principal reports that Frannie's students did well in the Standardized Testing and Reporting (STAR) tests, and "all three of her Advanced Placement students passed the AP exam. Our AP Calculus enrollment tripled this year. Our other advanced math classes have increased in enrollment because of her effectiveness, I believe." Frannie was elected chair of the math department.

The AVID elective class is a favorite for Frannie. Designed for students with a 2.5 to 3.5 grade point average, the program "goes over study skills, college research, [and] college admissions research, and refines their writing." The class meets the first 45 minutes of every day and has tutorials twice a week. For the latter, students work in small groups focusing on a question each member brings—something they have been taught or asked to do that they don't understand. Students help each other in the group first, but then older students can step in to help. Usually schools have university students assist in the program, but without a college on the island, upper classmen play that helping role.

Her advice for people preparing to teach is "to be consistent, not be afraid to ask for help, and find someone who is good at classroom management and observe them. Then create your own."

The decision Frannie made four years ago has clearly assisted her school, the math department, and students, but it has also enriched her life. She enjoys nature, running, hiking, and kayaking and living in a walking community. Coaching the school's cross-country team is also a treat for her. But most of all, she appreciates bonding with the students: "I love the connection with kids—they keep me young."

"I love the connection with kids—they keep me young"

Frannie Knobloch Finley
Avalon High School

that fact, nor did it erase the "moral turpitude" of the teacher's conduct (*Dubuclet v. Home Insurance Company*, 1995).

The right to **nondiscrimination** in regard to employment is protected by Title VII of the Civil Rights Act of 1964, which states:

> It shall be an unlawful employment practice for an employer (1) to fail or refuse to hire or to discharge any individual, or otherwise to discriminate against any individual with respect to his compensation, terms, conditions, or privileges of employment, because of such individual's race, color, religion, sex, or national origin; or (2) to limit, segregate, or classify his employees or applicants

for employment in any way which would deprive or tend to deprive any individual of employment opportunities or otherwise adversely affect his status as an employee, because of such individual's race, color, religion, sex, or national origin.

Teaching Contracts

A **teaching contract** represents an agreement between the teacher and a board of education. For a contract to be valid, it must contain these five basic elements:

1. **Offer and acceptance**—The school board has made a formal offer, and the employee has accepted the contract terms.
2. **Competent parties**—The school board is not exceeding the authority granted to it by the state, and the teacher meets the criteria for employment.
3. **Consideration**—Remuneration is promised to the teacher.
4. **Legal subject matter**—The contract terms are neither illegal nor against public policy.
5. **Proper form**—The contract adheres to state contract laws.

Before signing a teaching contract, read it carefully and be certain that it is signed by the appropriate member(s) of the board of education or board of trustees. Ask for clarification of any sections you don't understand. Any additional nonteaching duties should be spelled out in writing rather than left to an oral agreement. Because all board of education policies and regulations will be part of your contract, you should also read any available teacher handbook or school policy handbook.

The importance of carefully reading a contract and asking for clarification is illustrated in the following case:

> Victor Ming had just begun his first year as an English teacher at a high school in a city of about 300,000. Victor became quite upset when he learned that he had been assigned by his principal to sponsor the poetry club. The club was to meet once a week after school. Victor refused to sponsor the club, saying that the contract he had signed referred only to his teaching duties during regular school hours. Could Victor be compelled to sponsor the club?

Certain assignments, though not specified in a contract, may be required of teachers in addition to their regular teaching load, as long as there is a reasonable relationship between the teacher's classroom duties and the additional assignment. Such assignments can also include supervision of school events on weekends. Although Victor's contract did not make specific reference to club sponsorship, such a duty would be a reasonable addition to his regular teaching assignment.

When school authorities have assigned teachers to additional duties not reasonably related to their teaching, the courts have tended to rule in favor of teachers who file suit. For example, a school's directive to a tenured teacher of American history to assume the additional role of basketball coach was not upheld by a court of appeals (*Unified School District No. 241 v. Swanson,* 1986).

Due Process in Tenure and Dismissal

Tenure is a policy that provides the individual teacher with job security by (1) preventing his or her dismissal on insufficient grounds and (2) providing him or her with due process in the event of dismissal. Tenure is granted to teachers by the local school district after a period of satisfactory teaching, usually two to five years. In most cases, tenure may not be transferred from one school district to another.

The following case highlights the importance of tenure to a teacher's professional career:

> A teacher was dismissed from his teaching position by the school board after it learned that the teacher was a homosexual. The teacher filed suit in

court, claiming that his firing was arbitrary and violated the provisions of tenure that he had been granted. The school board, on the other hand, maintained that his conduct was inappropriate for a teacher. Was the school board justified in dismissing the teacher?

The events in this case were actually heard by a court, which ruled that the teacher was unfairly dismissed (*Burton v. Cascade School District Union High School No. 5,* 1975). The court said that the board violated the teacher's rights as a tenured employee by failing to show "good and just cause" for dismissal. The teacher was awarded the balance due under his contract and an additional one-half year's salary. In a similar case, however, a court upheld the dismissal of a teacher whose sexual orientation was the target of parents' complaints and students' comments. The court ruled that the teacher could no longer effectively carry out his teaching duties (*Gaylord v. Tacoma School District No. 10,* 1977).

The practice of providing teachers with tenure is not without controversy. Some critics point out that tenure policies make it too difficult to dismiss incompetent teachers and that performance standards are high in many other fields that do not provide employees with job security. Generally, however, the courts have held the position that tenure insulates teachers from "special-interest groups and political factions, thereby enabling them to perform their professional duties without undue interference. When this occurs, the educational system is improved and students derive the benefits of quality education" (Essex, 2008, p. 271).

Just about every state today has a tenure law that specifies that a teacher may be dismissed with good cause. What counts as a good cause varies from state to state, however. The courts have ruled on a variety of reasons for **dismissal:** (1) insubordination, (2) incompetence or inefficiency, (3) neglect of duty, (4) conduct unbecoming a teacher, (5) subversive activities, (6) retrenchment or decreased need for services, (7) physical and/or mental health, (8) age, (9) causing or encouraging disruption, (10) engaging in illegal activities, (11) using offensive language, (12) personal appearance, (13) sex-related activities, (14) political activities, and (15) use of drugs or intoxicants.

For a tenured teacher to be dismissed, a systematic series of steps must be followed so that the teacher receives due process and his or her constitutionally guaranteed rights are not violated. Due process involves a careful, step-by-step examination of the charges brought against a teacher. Most states have outlined procedures that adhere to the following nine steps:

1. The teacher must be notified of the list of charges.
2. Adequate time must be provided for the teacher to prepare a rebuttal to the charges.
3. The teacher must be given the names of witnesses and access to evidence.
4. The hearing must be conducted before an impartial tribunal.
5. The teacher has the right to representation by legal counsel.
6. The teacher (or legal counsel) can introduce evidence and cross-examine adverse witnesses.
7. The school board's decision must be based on the evidence and findings of the hearing.
8. A transcript or record must be maintained of the hearing.
9. The teacher has the right to appeal an adverse decision.

These steps notwithstanding, it should be noted that due process is "a dynamic concept . . . and depends largely on a combination of the specifics in a situation, the law governing the situation, the particular time in history in which judgment is being rendered, and the predilections of the individual judge(s) rendering the decision" (LaMorte, 2008, p. 7). The following case illustrates these points:

Near the start of his fifth year of teaching at an elementary school in a small city, and two years after earning tenure, Mr. Mitchell went through a sudden and painful divorce. A few months later, a woman whom he had met around the time of his divorce moved into the house he was renting.

For the remainder of the school year he and the woman lived together. During this time, he received no indication that his lifestyle was professionally unacceptable, and his teaching performance remained satisfactory.

At the end of the year, however, Mr. Mitchell was notified that he was being dismissed because of immoral conduct; that is, he was living with a woman he was not married to. The school board called for a hearing and Mr. Mitchell presented his side of the case. The board, nevertheless, decided to follow through with its decision to dismiss him. Was the school board justified in dismissing Mr. Mitchell?

Though at one time teachers could readily be dismissed for living, unmarried, with a member of the opposite sex, "in today's environment, dismissal of adulterous teachers, unmarried and pregnant teachers, or an unmarried teacher living with a person of the opposite sex is rarely brought before the courts" (LaMorte, 2008, p. 240). Because the board had not shown that Mr. Mitchell's alleged immoral conduct had a negative effect on his teaching, his dismissal would probably not hold up in court unless the community as a whole was upset by his behavior. Moreover, Mr. Mitchell could charge that his right to privacy as guaranteed by the Ninth Amendment to the Constitution had been violated. Overall, it appears that the decision to dismiss Mr. Mitchell was arbitrary and based on the collective bias of the board. Nevertheless, teachers should be aware that courts frequently hold that teachers are role models, and the local community determines "acceptable" behavior both in school and out of school.

Teachers also have the right to organize and to join teacher organizations without fear of dismissal. In addition, most states have passed **collective bargaining** laws that require school boards to negotiate contracts with teacher organizations. Usually, the teacher organization with the most members in a district is given the right to represent teachers in the collective bargaining process.

An important part of most collective bargaining agreements is the right of a teacher to file a **grievance,** a formal complaint against his or her employer. A teacher may not be dismissed for filing a grievance, and he or she is entitled to have the grievance heard by a neutral third party. Often, the teachers' union or professional association that negotiated the collective bargaining agreement will provide free legal counsel for a teacher who has filed a grievance.

One right that teachers are not granted by collective bargaining agreements is the right to strike. Like other public employees, teachers do not have the legal right to strike in most states. Teachers who do strike run the risk of dismissal (*Hortonville Joint School District No. 1 v. Hortonville Education Association,* 1976); however, when teacher strikes occur, a school board cannot possibly replace all the striking teachers.

Academic Freedom

A teacher of at-risk students at an alternative high school used a classroom management/motivational technique called Learnball. The teacher divided the class into teams, allowed students to elect team leaders and determine class rules and grading exercises, and developed a system of rewards that included listening to the radio and shooting baskets with a foam ball in the classroom. The school board ordered the teacher not to use the Learnball approach. Did the teacher have the right to continue using this teaching method?

This case is based on actual events involving a teacher in Pittsburgh. The teacher brought suit against the board to prevent it from imposing a policy that banned Learnball in the classroom. The teacher cited the principle of **academic freedom** and claimed that teachers have a right to use teaching methods and materials to which school officials might object. A U.S. District Court, however, upheld the school board policy against Learnball (*Murray v. Pittsburgh Board of Public Education,* 1996).

Although the courts have held that teachers have the right to academic freedom, it is not absolute and must be balanced against the interests of society. In fact, education law expert Michael LaMorte (2008, p. 223) suggests that the concept of academic freedom "is no longer as strong a defense as it once was for teachers." For this defense to prevail, "it must be shown that the teacher did not defy legitimate state and local curriculum directives; followed accepted professional norms for that grade level and subject matter; discussed matters which were of public concern; and acted professionally and in good faith when there was no precedent or policy" (p. 223).

Famous Cases

A landmark case involving academic freedom focused on John Scopes, a biology teacher who challenged a Tennessee law in 1925 that made it illegal to teach in a public school "any theory which denies the story of the Divine Creation of man as taught in the Bible, and to teach instead that man is descended from a lower order of animals." Scopes maintained that Darwin's theory about human origins had scientific merit and that the state's requirement that he teach the biblical account of creation violated his academic freedom.

Scopes's trial, which came to be known as the monkey trial, attracted national attention. Prosecuting Scopes was the "silver-tongued" William Jennings Bryan, a famous lawyer, politician, and presidential candidate. The defending attorney was Clarence Darrow.

Scopes believed strongly in academic freedom and his students' right to know about scientific theories. He expressed his views in his memoirs, *Center of the Storm*:

> Especially repulsive are laws restricting the constitutional freedom of teachers. The mere presence of such a law is a club held over the heads of the timid. Legislation that tampers with academic freedom is not protecting society, as its authors piously proclaim. By limiting freedom they are helping to make robot factories out of schools; ultimately, this produces non-thinking robots rather than the individualistic citizens we desperately need—now more than ever before. (1966, p. 277)

The monkey trial ended after eleven days of heated, eloquent testimony. Scopes was found guilty of violating the Butler Act and was fined $100. The decision was later reversed by the Tennessee Supreme Court on a technicality.

Since the Scopes trial, controversy has continued to surround the teaching of evolution. In many states during the 1980s, for example, religious fundamentalists won rulings that required science teachers to give equal time to both creationism and evolution in the classroom. The Supreme Court, however, in *Edwards v. Aguillard* (1987) ruled that such "balanced treatment" laws were unconstitutional. In the words of the Court: "Because the primary purpose of the [Louisiana] Creationism Act is to advance a particular religious belief, the Act endorses religion in violation of the First Amendment."

In 1999, controversy over evolution again emerged when the Kansas State Board of Education removed the teaching of evolution and discussion of the origin of the universe from state science standards. A newly elected Kansas Board of Education voted to restore evolution to state science standards in 2001, however. Similarly, evolution became a topic of public debate in Ohio during 2006, when the Ohio State Board of Education voted to eliminate from state science curriculum standards a statement that encouraged students to "critically analyze" evolution.

Another case suggesting that a teacher's right to academic freedom is narrow and limited is *Krizek v. Cicero-Stickney Township High School District No. 201* (1989). In this instance, a district court ruled against a teacher whose contract was not renewed because she showed her students an R-rated film (*About Last Night*) as an example of a modern-day parallel to Thornton Wilder's play *Our Town*. Although the teacher told her students that they would be excused from viewing the film if they or their parents objected, she did not communicate directly with their parents. The teacher's attempt to consider the objections of students and parents notwithstanding, the court concluded that the length of the film indicates that its showing was more than an inadvertent mistake or a mere slip of the tongue, but rather was a planned event, and thus indicated that the teacher's approach to teaching was problematic.

Though concerned more with the right of a school to establish a curriculum than with the academic freedom of teachers per se, other cases have focused on the teacher's use of instructional materials. In *Mozert v. Hawkins County Board of Education* (1987, 1988), for example, a group of Tennessee parents objected to "secular humanist" materials used by their children's teachers. In *Smith v. Board of School Commissioners of Mobile County* (1987), 624 parents and teachers initiated a court suit alleging that 44 history, social studies, and home economics texts used in the Mobile County, Alabama, public schools encouraged immorality, undermined parental authority, and were imbued with the "humanist" faith. In both cases, the courts supported the right of schools to establish a curriculum even in the face of parental disapproval. In *Smith v. Board of School Commissioners of Mobile County* (1987), the Eleventh Circuit Court stated that "[i]ndeed, given the diversity of religious views in this country, if the standard were merely inconsistency with the beliefs of a particular religion there would be very little that could be taught in the public schools."

States' Rights and Academic Freedom

The above cases notwithstanding, the courts have not set guidelines for situations when the teacher's freedom conflicts with the state's right to require teachers to follow certain curriculum guidelines. The same federal court, for example, heard a similar case regarding a high school teacher who wrote a vulgar word for sexual intercourse on the blackboard during a discussion of socially taboo words. The court sidestepped the issue of academic freedom and ruled instead that the regulations authorizing teacher discipline were unconstitutionally vague and, therefore, the teacher could not be dismissed. The court did observe, however, that a public school teacher's right to traditional academic freedom is "qualified," at best, and the "teacher's right must yield to compelling public interests of greater constitutional significance."

In reviewing its decision, the court also said, "Nothing herein suggests that school authorities are not free after they have learned that the teacher is using a teaching method of which they disapprove, and which is not appropriate to the proper teaching of the subject, to suspend him [or her] until he [or she] agrees to cease using the method" (*Mailloux v. Kiley*, 1971).

Although some teachers have been successful in citing academic freedom as the basis for teaching controversial subjects, others have not. Teachers have been dismissed for ignoring directives regarding the teaching of controversial topics related to sex, polygamy, race, and religion. Though the courts have not been able to clarify just where academic freedom begins and ends, they have made it clear that the state does have a legitimate interest in what is taught to impressionable children.

Do Student Teachers Have the Same Rights as Teachers Do?

Do student teachers have the same legal status as certified teachers? Read the following case:

> Meg Grant looked forward to the eight weeks she would spend as a student teacher in Mrs. Walker's high school English classes. Meg knew that Mrs. Walker was one of the best supervising teachers she might have been paired with, and she was anxious to do her best.
>
> In Mrs. Walker's senior class, Meg planned to teach *Brave New World*. Mrs. Walker pointed out to Meg that this book was controversial and some parents might object. She asked Meg to think about selecting an additional title that students could read if their parents objected to *Brave New World*. Meg felt that Mrs. Walker was bowing to pressure from conservative parents, so she decided to go ahead and teach the book.

Two weeks later Meg was called down to the principal's office where she was confronted by an angry father who said, "You have no right to be teaching my daughter this communist trash; you're just a student teacher." What should Meg do? Does she have the same rights as a fully certified teacher?

In some states, a student teacher such as Meg might have the same rights and responsibilities as a fully certified teacher; in others, her legal status might be that of an unlicensed visitor. The most prudent action for Meg to take would be to apologize to the father and assure him that if any controversial books are assigned in the future, alternative titles would be provided. In addition, Meg should learn how important it is for a student teacher to take the advice of his or her supervising teacher.

"The legal status of the student teacher is a perennial question with both student teachers and cooperating teachers" (Wentz, 2001, p. 55). One study found that the authority of student teachers to teach was established by law in only 40 states, and no state had a statutory provision regulating the dismissal of a student teacher, the assignment of a student teacher, or the denial of the right to student-teach (Morris & Curtis, 1983). Nevertheless, student teachers should be aware that a potential for liability exists with them just as it does with certified teachers.

One area of debate regarding student teachers is whether they can act as substitutes for their cooperating teachers or even other teachers in a school building. Unfortunately, many school districts have no policy regarding this practice. Depending on statutes in a particular state, however, a student teacher may substitute under the following conditions:

- A substitute teacher is not immediately available.
- The student teacher has been in that student-teaching assignment for a specified minimum number of school days.
- The supervising teacher, the principal of the school, and the university supervisor agree that the student teacher is capable of successfully handling the teaching responsibilities.
- A certified classroom teacher in an adjacent room or a member of the same teaching team as the student teacher is aware of the absence and agrees to assist the student teacher if needed.
- The principal of the school or the principal's representative is readily available in the building.
- The student teacher is not paid for any substitute service (this matter is negotiable in some jurisdictions) (Dunklee & Shoop, 2002, pp. 89–90).

Given the ambiguous status of student teachers, it is important that you begin your student-teaching assignment with knowledge of the legal aspects of teaching and a clear idea of your rights and responsibilities. Follow the recommendations in Figure 7.2 made by school law experts Julie Mead and Julie Underwood.

FIGURE 7.2 Legal advice for student teachers
Source: Julie Mead and Julie Underwood, "A Legal Primer for Student Teachers," in Gloria Slick (ed.), Emerging Trends in Teacher Preparation: The Future of Field Experience. Thousand Oaks, CA: Corwin Press, 1995, pp. 49–50.

Legal Advice for Student Teachers

1. Read the teacher's handbook, if one is available, and discuss its contents with the cooperating teacher. Be sure you understand its requirements and prohibitions.
2. Thoroughly discuss school safety rules and regulations. Be certain you know what to do in case of emergency, before assuming complete control of the classroom.
3. Be aware of the potential hazards associated with any activity and act accordingly to protect children from those dangers.
4. Be certain you know what controls the district has placed on the curriculum you will be teaching. Are there specific texts and/or methodologies that district policy requires or prohibits?
5. Be certain that student records are used to enhance and inform your teaching. Make certain that strict confidentiality is respected.
6. Document any problems you have with students, when you are a student teacher *and* when you are working in a paid position, in case you are called on to relate details at a later time.

WHAT ARE YOUR LEGAL RESPONSIBILITIES AS A TEACHER?

Teachers are responsible, of course, for meeting the terms of their teaching contracts. As noted previously, teachers are responsible for duties not covered in the contract if they are reasonably related to teaching. Among these duties may be club sponsorship; lunchroom, study hall, or playground duty; academic counseling of students; and record keeping.

Teachers are also legally responsible for the safety and well-being of students assigned to them. Although it is not expected that a teacher be able to control completely the behavior of young, energetic students, a teacher can be held liable for any injury to a student if it is shown that the teacher's negligence contributed to the injury. The Teachers' Voices: Research to Reality feature for this chapter illustrates one teacher's concern about the safety and well-being of her students during a field trip.

Avoiding Tort Liability

An eighth-grade science teacher in Louisiana left her class for a few moments to go to the school office to pick up some forms. While she was gone, her students continued to do some laboratory work that involved the use of alcohol-burning devices. Unfortunately, one girl was injured when she tried to relight a defective burner. Could the teacher be held liable for the girl's injuries?

The events described above actually occurred (*Station v. Travelers Insurance Co.,* 1974). The court that heard the case determined that the teacher failed to provide adequate supervision while the students were exposed to dangerous conditions. Considerable care is required, the court observed, when students handle inherently dangerous objects, and the need for this care is magnified when students are exposed to dangers they don't appreciate.

At times, teachers may have concerns about their liability for damages as a result of their actions. The branch of law concerned with compensating an individual who suffers losses resulting from another's negligence is known as tort law. "Tort law deals with . . . negligent behavior that results in an injury, intentional injuries, libel and slander, and injuries resulting from defects in buildings or land" (Imber & van Geel, 2005, p. 5).

According to **tort liability** law, an individual who is negligent and at fault in the exercise of his or her legal duty may be required to pay monetary damages to an injured party. Generally, the standard of behavior applied by the courts is that "of a reasonable person acting prudently in light of the circumstances" (Imber & van Geel, 2005, p. 268). However, teachers are held to a higher standard than ordinary citizens, and certain teachers (e.g., physical education, chemistry, and shop teachers) are held to an even higher standard because of the increased risk of injury involved in the classes they teach. Table 7.1 presents several examples of cases in which students were injured and educators were found to have breached their duty of care.

Negligence

In contrast to the decision reached by the Louisiana court mentioned earlier, the courts have made it clear that there are many accidents that teachers cannot reasonably foresee that do result in student injuries. For example, a teacher on playground duty was found not to be negligent when a student threw a rock that struck another student in the eye. After the teacher walked past a group of boys, one boy threw a small rock that hit a larger rock on the ground and then bounced up to hit the other boy in the eye. The court ruled that "[w]here the time between an act of a student and injury to a fellow student is so short that the teacher had no opportunity to prevent injury, it cannot be said that negligence of the teacher is a proximate cause of the injury" (*Fagen v. Summers,* 1972). In another case, the court ruled that a New York teacher could not have anticipated that the paper bag she asked a student to pick up contained a broken bottle that cut the student (*West v. Board of Education of City of New York,* 1959). In two almost identical cases, the courts ruled that a teacher of a class with a good behavior record could not reasonably be expected

TEACHERS' VOICES RESEARCH TO REALITY

Mary Hanson
OPENING THE DOOR TO POSSIBILITIES

As a third-grade teacher in a metropolitan city in southern California, I have made efforts to be more than just "the teacher" or *la maestra* to my students—I have tried to be a mentor who provides more than reading, writing, and math lessons. Most of my students come from low-income families, where their view of their place in the community has been defined not only by their economic status, but also by the fact that extracurricular activities are limited and their exposure to many things we take for granted (like "take your daughter to work" day) are practically non-existent. So I seize any opportunity to bring community members to my classroom to share their experiences with my third graders.

This year, I was fortunate enough to have a Junior Achievement (JA) volunteer teach four lessons on business: the business of running a city, a bank, a newspaper, and a restaurant. The students were so engaged by this last unit that we became immersed in the business of being restaurateurs. The JA volunteer arranged for us to visit a local Italian restaurant, Bucca di Beppo, in Old Town. This was going to be the chance for them to see how a real restaurant works!

I must admit I had reservations about this trip. Our volunteer was so confident, and here I was thinking about things like 40 busy little hands near boiling kettles and sharp objects, or someone blurting out some embarrassing remark, but I just put in my paperwork to district transportation and kept my fingers crossed. I gave the students firm reminders to wash their hands and mind their manners. I reminded them that they were representing our school.

At the restaurant, Mr. Chavez, the sous chef, greeted us at the door. Walking inside the closed restaurant (they are open only for dinner), each child was wide-eyed. The restaurant, famous for its photo-covered walls, was mesmerizing. There were hundreds upon hundreds of pictures, each conveying some aspect of Italian culture: families eating mounds of spaghetti, pictures of the pope, the statues and fountains of Rome. After the initial shock wore off, the students passed through the kitchens and were seated in the largest seating area in the restaurant. Like magic, they transformed into curious little restaurant specialists.

Too soon, [our visit ended] and we had to return to the bus. Mr. Chavez was sad to see us go because there were so many more questions. He called to a worker in the kitchen, "Make those pizzas *to go!*" The next thing I knew, we were back on the bus and I was carrying a gift from the restaurant for each child and pizza for 20. Tired, I slumped in the front seat, realizing we had gotten through this with no mishaps, no burned fingers, no embarrassing comments, and I was prouder than I ever thought I could be.

After we wolfed down the pizza and drank half my case of bottled water, we debriefed. We talked about what we'd learned. The third graders talked about figuring out how to make a profit if you prepare a meal. They talked about the *cold* freezer and how buying one costs a lot of money. They talked about a lot of things that they saw, including the pictures on the walls. But the part I liked most was that they started to talk about the possibilities. I can't count how many times before this field trip I had heard these low-income kids, whose parents are working at low-paying, dead-end jobs, talk about the low-paying, dead-end jobs they would take when they turn 18. At least four kids have continued to talk about going to cooking school, and two more thought it would be cool going to restaurants and fixing the refrigerators and freezers. Brenda, who had told me more than once that when she grew up she was going to clean houses like her mom, told me that when she was 18, she was going to go to Bucca di Beppo and ask for a job as a pasta chef. "I'd have to start as a helper, I think," she said with serious eyes, "but I could get better!" She smiled and ran out to recess.

PERSONAL REFLECTION

1. Despite the potential liability issues, how did Ms. Hanson's students benefit from the experience?
2. Assume that one of Ms. Hanson's students was cut by a sharp object while in the restaurant's kitchen. Under what circumstances would Ms. Hanson not be liable for the student's injury? Under what circumstances would Ms. Hanson be liable for the student's injury?
3. When arranging field trips, what steps can a teacher take to minimize the possibility of being liable for a student's injury?

Mary Hanson is a National Board Certified Teacher in the Pasadena Unified School District, Pasadena, CA. This feature is excerpted from her contribution to Adrienne Mack-Krisher's *Powerful Classroom Stories from Accomplished Teachers*, Thousand Oaks, CA: Corwin Press, 2004, pp. 156–159.

TABLE 7.1 Selected court decisions in which school personnel were found negligent for failure to meet a "standard of care"

1. A woodworking instructor allowed a student to operate a table saw without the use of a safeguard, which resulted in serious damage to his proximal interphalangeal joint *Borbin v. State,* 506 So, 2d 888 (La. App. 1987).
2. A student dislocated his shoulder during an intramural football game, when the school provided no protective equipment and improper supervision of the game. *Locilento v. John A. Coleman Catholic High School,* 525 N.Y.S.2d 198 (A.D. 3d Dept. 1987).
3. An eleven-year-old student suffered serious head injuries from a blow in the head during a kick game and was without medical attention for more than an hour. The one-hour delay caused a hematoma to grow from the size of a walnut to that of an orange. *Barth v. Board of Education,* 490 N.E.2d 77 (Ill. App. 1st Dist. 1986).
4. An eight-year-old girl was seriously burned when her costume caught fire from a lighted candle on her teacher's desk. *Smith v. Archbishop of St. Louis,* 632 S.W.2d 516 (Mo. App. 1982).
5. A twelve-year-old boy was killed when he fell through a skylight at school while retrieving a ball. *Stabl v. Cocolico School District,* 534 A.2d 1141 (Pa. Cmwith. 1987).
6. A boy was seriously injured while playing on school grounds when he fell into a hole filled with glass, trash, and other debris, due to the absence of school officials to warn him of the dangerous condition. *Dean v. Board of Education,* 523 A.2d 1059 (Md. App. 1987).
7. A female student was en route to class when she pushed her hand through a glass panel in a smoke-colored door, causing severe and permanent damage. *Bielaska v. Town of Waterford,* 491 A.2d 1071 (Conn. 1985).
8. A high school student was seriously injured when he was tackled and thrown to the ground during a touch football game in gym class that was inadequately supervised and the players began to use excessive force. *Hyman v. Green,* 403 N.W.2d 597 (Mich. App. 1987).

Source: Adapted from Nathan L. Essex. School Law and the Public Schools: A Practical Guide for Educational Leaders. Boston: Allyn and Bacon, 1999, pp. 100, 126. Copyright © by Allyn and Bacon. Reprinted by permission.

to anticipate that a student would be injured by a pencil thrown by a classmate while the teacher was momentarily out of the room attending to her usual duties (*Ohman v. Board of Education,* 1950; *Simonetti v. School District of Philadelphia,* 1982).

When a court considers a case involving tort liability, evidence is examined to determine whether the responsible party (the school district, the administrator, or the teacher) acted negligently. For a school official to be considered liable, the following must be shown to be present:

1. A legal duty.
2. A breach of duty.
3. A causal connection, often referred to as "proximate cause," between the conduct and the resultant injury.
4. Actual loss or damage (LaMorte, 2008, p. 423).

As a teacher, you should be alert to conditions that might lead to accidental injury of one or more students. You will have a duty to your pupils, and you could be held liable for injuries that students incur as a result of your **negligence.** However, your liability extends only to injuries your students might suffer if you fail to provide the degree of care for pupils that a reasonable person would. A review of court cases involving the tort liability of teachers suggests that most cases involve at least one of the following:

- Inadequate supervision
- Inadequate instruction
- Lack of or improper medical treatment of pupils
- Improper disclosure of defamatory information concerning pupils—for example, release of school records that contain negative statements about a student

Teachers' concern about their potential liability for failing to prevent injury to students has been lessened by the availability of liability insurance. Many professional teacher organizations offer liability coverage as part of their membership benefits. Teachers may also purchase individual liability insurance policies. In addition, school districts in approximately half of the states have immunity from liability for torts committed by district employees (LaMorte, 2008, p. 425).

Educational Malpractice

Since the mid-1970s, several plaintiffs have charged in their **educational malpractice** suits that schools should be responsible for a pupil whose failure to achieve is significant. In the first of such cases, the parents of Peter W. Doe charged that the San Francisco Unified School District was negligent because it allowed him to graduate from high school with a fifth-grade reading level and this handicap would not enable him to function in adult society. In particular, they charged that the "defendant school district, its agents and employees, negligently and carelessly failed to provide plaintiff with adequate instruction, guidance, counseling and/or supervision in basic academic skills such as reading and writing, although said school district had the authority, responsibility, and ability [to do so]." They sought $500,000 for the negligent work of the teachers who taught Peter.

In evaluating the claim of Peter and his parents, the court pointed out that the alleged injury was not within the realm of tort law and that many factors beyond a school's responsibility or control can account for lack of achievement. The court did not hold the school responsible for Peter's lack of achievement and made it clear that to do so would be to set a precedent with potentially drastic consequences: "To hold [schools] to an actionable duty of care, in the discharge of their academic functions, would expose them to the tort claims—real or imagined—of disaffected students and parents in countless numbers. . . . The ultimate consequences, in terms of public time and money, would burden them—and society—beyond calculation" (*Peter Doe v. San Francisco Unified School District,* 1976).

Reporting Child Abuse

Teachers are required by law to report suspected child abuse. Local, state, and federal child welfare agencies encourage teachers to be observant of children's appearance and behavior that might indicate symptoms of physical, emotional, or sexual abuse. Table 7.2 presents a list of physical and behavioral indicators of potential child abuse. Many communities, through their police departments or other public and private agencies, provide programs adapted for children to educate them about child abuse and to show them how to obtain help.

The Fourth Amendment guarantees protection against unlawful search and seizure, and on occasion, parents and guardians have alleged a Fourth Amendment violation, claiming that school personnel should not have questioned or examined a student to determine if child abuse had occurred. In a Pennsylvania case, the court concluded that the Fourth Amendment had not been violated as a result of school personnel questioning a student about suspected abuse. According to the court, Pennsylvania's Child Protective Services Law required teachers and administrators to determine if there was "reason to believe" that a student had been abused (*Picarella v. Terrizzi,* 1995).

Schools usually have a process for dealing with suspected abuse cases that involves the school principal, a nurse, and the reporting teacher. Because a child's welfare may be further endangered when abuse is reported, caution and sensitivity are required. To examine a diary note written by a child whose father physically abused him, go to MyEducationLab. What steps should the child's teacher have taken in this instance?

Observing Copyright Laws

The continuing development of information technology has resulted in a new set of responsibilities for teachers regarding copyright laws pertaining to the use of photocopies, videotapes, and computer software. Congress revised the Copyright Act in 1976 by adding

PEARSON
myeducationlab

Go to MyEducationLab, select Chapter 7 and then Activities and Applications to analyze the artifact Dear Diary-Bar (Language Arts 3–5).

TABLE 7.2 Physical and behavioral indicators of child abuse and neglect

Signs of Physical Abuse

Physical Indicators

- Unexplained bruises and welts on the face, throat, upper arms, buttocks, thighs, or lower back in unusual patterns or shapes that suggest the use of an instrument (belt buckle, electrical cord) on an infant in various stages of healing and that regularly appear after an absence, the weekend, or a vacation.
- Unexplained burns or cigarette burns, especially found on the palms, the soles of feet, abdomen, buttocks; immersion burns producing "stocking" or "glove" demarcations on hands and feet; doughnut-shaped burns on buttocks or genital area.
- Rope burns.
- Infected burns indicating delay in treatment; burns in the shape of common household utensils or appliances.

Behavioral Indicators

- Behavioral extremes (withdrawal, aggression, regression, depression).
- Inappropriate or excessive fear of parent or caretaker.
- Antisocial behavior such as substance abuse, truancy, running away, fear of going home.
- Unbelievable or inconsistent explanation for injuries.
- Lies unusually still while surveying surroundings (for infants).
- Unusual shyness; wariness of physical contact.

Signs of Sexual Abuse

Physical Indicators

- Torn, stained, or bloody underclothes.
- Frequent, unexplained sore throats; yeast or urinary infections.
- Somatic complaints, including pain and irritation of the genitals.
- Sexually transmitted diseases.
- Bruises or bleeding from external genitalia, vagina, or anal region.
- Pregnancy.

Behavioral Indicators

- The victim's disclosure of sexual abuse.
- Regressive behaviors (thumb sucking, bed-wetting, fear of the dark).
- Promiscuity or seductive behaviors.
- Disturbed sleep patterns (recurring nightmares).
- Unusual and age-inappropriate interest in sexual matters.
- Avoidance of undressing or wearing extra layers of clothes.
- Sudden decline in school performance; truancy.
- Difficulty in walking or sitting.

Signs of Emotional Abuse

Physical Indicators

- Eating disorders, including obesity or anorexia.
- Speech disorders (stuttering, stammering).
- Developmental delays in the acquisition of speech or motor skills.
- Weight or height substantially below norm.
- Flat or bald spots on head (infants).
- Nervous disorders (rashes, hives, facial tics, stomachaches).

Behavioral Indicators

- Habit disorders (biting, rocking, head banging).
- Cruel behavior; seeming to get pleasure from hurting children, adults, or animals; seeming to get pleasure from being mistreated.
- Age-inappropriate behaviors (bed-wetting, wetting, soiling).
- Behavioral extremes: overly compliant–demanding; withdrawn–aggressive; listless–excitable.

TABLE 7.2 (*continued*)

Signs of Neglect
Physical Indicators

- Poor hygiene, including lice, scabies, severe or untreated diaper rash, bedsores, body odor.
- Squinting.
- Unsuitable clothing; missing key articles of clothing (underwear, socks, shoes); overdressed or underdressed for climate conditions.
- Untreated injury or illness.
- Lack of immunizations.
- Indicators of prolonged exposure to elements (excessive sunburn, insect bites, colds).
- Height and weight significantly below age level.

Behavioral Indicators

- Unusual school attendance.
- Chronic absenteeism.
- Chronic hunger, tiredness, or lethargy.
- Begging or collecting leftovers.
- Assuming adult responsibilities.
- Reporting no caretaker at home.

Source: Adapted from Childabuse.com. (2008). Anchorage, AK: Arctic Originals, Inc. Retrieved from: http://www.childabuse.com/help.htm.

the doctrine of fair use. Although the fair use doctrine cannot be precisely defined, it is generally interpreted as it was in *Marcus v. Rowley* (1983)—that is, one may "use the copyrighted material in a reasonable manner without [the copyright holder's] consent" as long as that use does not reduce the demand for the work or the author's income.

To "move the nation's copyright law into the digital age," the **Digital Millennium Copyright Act (DMCA)** amended the Copyright Act in 1998. The DMCA makes it illegal to circumvent copy-blocking measures (encryption and encoding, for example) that control access to copyrighted works. However, according to the statute, educational institutions may circumvent access control measures "solely for the purpose of making a good faith determination as to whether they wish to obtain authorized access to the work."

With the vast amount of material (in text, audio, video, and graphic formats) available over the Internet, teachers must consider copyright laws and restrictions that apply to this material. Unfortunately, the Copyright Act does not provide guidelines for the use of intellectual property found on the Internet. In any case, teachers should understand that content they view on the Internet is published material, and the doctrine of fair use applies to the use of such materials.

Photocopies

To clarify the fair use doctrine as it pertained to teachers photocopying instructional materials from books and magazines, Congress endorsed a set of guidelines developed by educators, authors, and publishers. These guidelines allow teachers to make single copies of copyrighted material for teaching or research, but they are more restrictive regarding the use of multiple copies. The use of multiple copies of a work must meet the tests of brevity, spontaneity, and cumulative effect.

- Brevity means that short works can be copied. Poems or excerpts cannot be longer than 250 words, and copies of longer works cannot exceed 1,000 words or 10 percent of the work (whichever is less). Only one chart or drawing can be reproduced from a book or an article.
- The criterion of spontaneity means that the teacher doing the copying would not have time to request permission from the copyright holder.
- The criterion of cumulative effect limits the use of copies to one course and limits the material copied from the same author, book, or magazine during the semester. Also, no more than nine instances of multiple copying per class are allowed during a semester.

Videotapes

Guidelines for the use of videotapes made by teachers of television broadcasts were issued by Congress in 1981. Videotaped material may be used in the classroom only once by the teacher within the first 10 days of taping. Additional use is limited to reinforcing instruction or evaluation of student learning, and the tape must be erased within 45 days.

Computer Software

With the explosion of computer-based technology in schools, teachers face a new ethical and legal issue—adhering to copyright laws as they relate to computer software. Making an illegal copy of software on a computer hard drive—in effect, stealing another person's intellectual property—is quite easy. "It is very common for otherwise ethical and moral people to ask for and/or offer illegal copies of software to one another" (Schwartz & Beichner, 1999, p. 193). It is important therefore that, as a teacher, you be an exemplar of ethical behavior regarding copyrighted computer software. Just as you would not allow students to plagiarize written material or submit work that was not their own, you should follow the same standard of behavior regarding the use of computer software.

Software publishers have become concerned about the abuse of their copyrighted material. Limited school budgets and the high cost of software have led to the unauthorized reproduction of software. To address the problem, the Copyright Act was amended in 1980 to apply the fair use doctrine to software. Accordingly, as a teacher, you may now make one backup copy of a program. If you were to make multiple copies of software, the fair use doctrine would be violated because the software is readily accessible for purchase and making multiple copies would substantially reduce the market for the software. Software publishers have several different options for licensing their software to schools, and you should be aware of the type of license that has been purchased with each software program you use.

The increased practice of networking computer programs—that is, storing a copy of a computer program on a network file server and serving the program to a computer on the network—is also of concern to software publishers. The practice has not yet been tested in the courts. As more public schools develop computer networks, however, the issue of networked software will most likely be debated in the courts.

Currently, the Copyright Act is being revised to reflect how the doctrine of fair use should be applied to digital data. Two questions currently not answered by copyright law as it pertains to the educational use of computer software are the legality of (1) installing a single program on several computers in a laboratory and (2) modifying the program for use in a computer network. The Copyright Act specifies four factors for determining whether use of copyrighted material constitutes fair use or an infringement: (1) the purpose and character of the use, including whether such use is of a commercial nature or is for nonprofit educational purposes; (2) the nature of the copyrighted work; (3) the amount and substantiality of the portion used in relation to the copyrighted work as a whole; and (4) the effect of the use on the potential market for or value of the copyrighted work.

E-Mail and the Internet

With the huge increase in the transmission of documents via e-mail, copyright laws have been extended to cyberspace. Material published online may include a statement by the author(s) that the material is copyright-protected and may not be duplicated without permission. In other cases, the material may include a statement such as the following: "Permission is granted to distribute this material freely through electronic or by other means, provided it remains completely intact and unaltered, the source is acknowledged, and no fee is charged for it." If the material is published without restrictions on the Internet, one may assume that the author waives copyright privileges; however, proper credit and a citation should accompany the material if it is reproduced. The Technology in Action feature in this chapter explains how virtual labs can help students understand academic areas such as biology, astronomy, chemistry, and physics. If students use material from such sites in written papers and reports, they should be sure to cite the source of their information.

TECHNOLOGY in *ACTION*

Virtual Labs in a Ninth-Grade Biology Classroom

Copyright © 1994–2005 by Berkeley Lab. Used by permission of the Lawrence Berkeley National Lab

At this time each year, Mrs. Rajid's students start to squirm. She teaches introductory ninth-grade science, and the class will be dissecting frogs during the coming weeks. Also at this time each year, many of her students bring in notes from their parents excusing them from the lesson. Mrs. Rajid has evidence of a direct correlation between those students who do not participate in the frog-dissecting activity and their gradual poor performance in science over their time in high school science. She needed something to help her students understand the concepts of the lesson and at the same time disassociate themselves from the grossness of cutting open a frog.

So Mrs. Rajid went on a dissecting frogs WebQuest and found several options; one was quite user-friendly, accessible on the Web, and free. She decided to use the virtual lab (a software program that replicates the activities in a physical lab) in her next lesson, before the permission slips went home. The next day, she took her students into the computer lab, had them open a Web browser, and navigate to the dissecting frog website. She then asked them to dissect their virtual frogs. A few students made comments like "Yuck" and "Gross," but the students performed quite well. They each had a frog preserved in formaldehyde, dissected it, and were able to identify the appropriate organs and structure.

The next week, when it was time to send home the permission slips for dissecting the real frog, she found that a much higher percentage of her students were planning to participate. She also found that her students were much bettered prepared to perform the real activity. They knew what to do, how to do it, and what the expectations of the activity were. She thought that some day this virtual lab might indeed replace the need for the actual experience—at much less cost and with no formaldehyde smell.

VIRTUAL LABS: Virtual labs replicate the activities that take place in a physical lab and deliver basic desired learning outcomes without the need for equipment, supplies, and dangerous materials. Although the effectiveness of virtual labs is debated among practitioners, there is no doubt that their growing popularity, combined with the technology enhancements of the industry, is a promising development for teachers. These labs usually take the form of interactive animation in which the student makes decisions, performs actions, and selects tools, and the animation program responds appropriately. Some virtual labs use video, graphics, and audio to supplement the learning materials.

VISIT: http://www.sciencecentral.com/. This site is updated continually with new tools and user ratings.

POSSIBLE USES: Teachers have successfully used virtual labs to help students understand biology, physics, astronomy, and chemistry. Some virtual labs allow students to practice appropriate stream restoration techniques, explore a human cadaver and perform an autopsy, and mix complex combinations of elements to see how those elements interact with one another.

TRY IT OUT: Open a Web browser and visit http://www.sciencecentral.com/. Click on the Biology link. Then enter "virtual frog" in the internal search engine. Several options will come up; pick the one that looks most appealing.

The following are guidelines for determining how much of a certain medium is considered fair to use without obtaining permission from the copyright holder:

- **Motion media**—Up to 10 percent or three minutes, whichever is less.
- **Text**—10 percent or 1,000 words, whichever is less.
- **Poems**—An entire poem up to 250 words may be used, but no more than three poems by one poet or five poems by different poets from any anthology. For longer poems, 250 words may be used.
- **Music, lyrics, and music video**—Up to 10 percent but no more than 30 seconds. Any alterations shall not change the basic melody or the character of the work.
- **Illustrations and photography**—No more than five images by an artist or a photographer.
- **Numerical data sets**—Up to 10 percent or 2,500 cell entries, whichever is less (Green, Brown, & Robinson, 2008, p. 120).

Publishing on the Internet

Thousands of teachers and their students around the globe are publishing material on their home pages on the Internet. Teacher- and student-produced materials can be copyright-protected by including a statement that the materials may not be duplicated without permission. In addition, teachers should be careful not to include information that would enable someone to identify children in a class. Children's last names should never be published, nor should photos of children be published with any identifying information.

WHAT ARE THE LEGAL RIGHTS OF STUDENTS AND PARENTS?

myeducationlab

Go to MyEducationLab, select Chapter 7 and Activities and Applications to analyze the artifact Schoolwide Standards.

As a prospective teacher, you have an obligation to become familiar with the rights of students. Since the 1960s, students have confronted teachers and school districts more often with what they perceive to be illegal restrictions on their behavior. To examine a set of schoolwide standards one high school has for students, go to MyEducationLab. This section presents brief summaries of selected major court decisions that clarify students' rights related to freedom of expression, suspension and expulsion, search and seizure, privacy, and nondiscrimination.

Freedom of Expression

The case of *Tinker v. Des Moines Independent Community School District* (1969) is perhaps the most frequently cited case concerning students' **freedom of expression.** The Supreme Court ruled in *Tinker* that three students, ages 13, 15, and 16, had been denied their First Amendment freedom of expression when they were suspended from school for wearing black armbands to protest the Vietnam War. The court ruled that neither teachers nor students "shed their rights to freedom of speech or expression at the schoolhouse gate." In addition, the Court found no evidence that the exercise of such a right interfered with the school's operation.

Censorship

One area of student expression that has generated frequent controversy is that of student publications. Prior to 1988, the courts generally made it clear that student literature enjoyed constitutional protection and that it could be regulated only if it posed a substantial threat of school disruption, if it was libelous, or if it was judged vulgar or obscene after publication. However, school officials could use "prior **censorship**" and require students to submit literature before publication if such controls were necessary to maintain order in the school.

Within these guidelines, students frequently defended successfully their right to freedom of expression. For example, the right of high school students to place in the school newspaper an advertisement against the war in Vietnam was upheld (*Zucker v.*

Panitz, 1969). Students' right to distribute information on birth control and on laws regarding marijuana were also upheld in *Shanley v. Northeast Independent School District* (1972). And other cases upheld the right of students to publish literature that was critical of teachers, administrators, and other school personnel (*Scoville v. Board of Education of Joliet Township High School District 204,* 1970, 1971; *Sullivan v. Houston Independent School District,* 1969).

In January 1988, however, the Supreme Court, in a 5–3 ruling in *Hazelwood School District v. Kuhlmeier,* departed from the earlier *Tinker* decision and gave public school officials considerable authority to censor school-sponsored student publications. The case involved a Missouri high school principal's censorship of articles in the school newspaper, the *Spectrum,* on teenage pregnancy and the impact of divorce on students. The principal believed the articles were inappropriate because they might identify pregnant students and because references to sexual activity and birth control were inappropriate for younger students. Several students on the newspaper staff distributed copies of the articles on their own and later sued the school district, claiming that their First Amendment rights had been violated.

Writing for the majority in *Hazelwood School District v. Kuhlmeier,* Justice Byron White (who had voted with the majority in *Tinker*) said school officials could bar "speech that is ungrammatical, poorly written, inadequately researched, biased or prejudiced, vulgar or profane, or unsuitable for immature audiences." White also pointed out that *Tinker* focused on a student's right of "personal expression," and the Missouri case dealt with school-sponsored publications that were part of the curriculum and bore the "imprimatur of the school." According to White, "Educators do not offend the First Amendment by exercising editorial control over the style and content of student speech in school-sponsored expressive activities so long as their actions are reasonably related to legitimate pedagogical concerns."

A case involving an attempt to regulate an underground student newspaper entitled *Bad Astra,* however, had a different outcome. Five high school students in Renton, Washington, produced a four-page newspaper at their expense, off school property, and without the knowledge of school authorities. *Bad Astra* contained articles that criticized school policies, a mock poll evaluating teachers, and several poetry selections. The students distributed 350 copies of the paper at a senior class barbecue held on school grounds.

After the paper was distributed, the principal placed letters of reprimand in the five students' files, and the district established a new policy whereby student-written, non-school-sponsored materials with an intended distribution of more than 10 were subject to predistribution review. The students filed suit in federal district court, claiming a violation of their First Amendment rights. The court ruled, however, that the new policy was "substantially constitutional." Maintaining that the policy was unconstitutional, the students filed an appeal in 1988 in the Ninth Circuit Court and won. The court ruled that *Bad Astra* was not "within the purview of the school's exercise of reasonable editorial control" (*Burch v. Barker,* 1987, 1988).

Dress Codes

Few issues related to the rights of students have generated as many court cases as have dress codes and hairstyles. The demand on the courts to hear such cases prompted Supreme Court Justice Hugo L. Black to observe that he did not believe "the federal Constitution imposed on the United States Courts the burden of supervising the length of hair that public school students should wear" (*Karr v. Schmidt,* 1972). In line with Justice Black's observation, the Supreme Court has repeatedly refused to review the decisions reached by the lower courts.

In general, the courts have suggested that schools may have dress codes as long as such codes are clear and reasonable, and students are notified. However, when the legality of such codes has been challenged, the rulings have largely indicated that schools may not control what students wear unless it is immodest or is disruptive of the educational process.

Students in private schools, however, do not have First Amendment protections provided by *Tinker v. Des Moines Independent Community School District* because private schools are not state affiliated. As a result, students at private schools can be required to wear uniforms, and "[d]isagreements over 'student rights' . . . are generally resolved by applying contract law to the agreement governing the student's attendance" (LaMorte, 2008, p. 117).

At one time, educators' concerns about student appearance may have been limited to hairstyles and immodest dress; however, today's educators, as Michael LaMorte (2008, p. 175) points out, may be concerned about "T-shirts depicting violence, drugs (e.g., marijuana [leaves]), racial epithets, or characters such as Bart Simpson; ripped, baggy, or saggy pants or jeans; sneakers with lights; colored bandanas; baseball or other hats; words shaved into scalps, brightly colored hair, distinctive haircuts or hairstyles, or ponytails for males; exposed underwear; Malcolm X symbols; Walkmans, cellular phones, or beepers; backpacks; tattoos, unusual-colored lipsticks, pierced noses, or earrings; and decorative dental caps."

Because gangs, hate groups, and violence in and around public schools have become more prevalent during the last decade, rulings that favor schools are becoming more common when the courts "balance the First Amendment rights of students to express themselves against the legitimate right of school authorities to maintain a safe and disruption-free environment" (LaMorte, 2008, p. 175). This balance is clearly illustrated in *Jeglin v. San Jacinto Unified School District* (1993). In this instance, a school's dress code prohibiting the wearing of clothing with writing, pictures, or insignia of professional or college athletic teams was challenged on the grounds that it violated students' freedom of expression. The court acknowledged that the code violated the rights of elementary and middle school students, but not those of high school students. Gangs, known to be present at the high school, had intimidated students and faculty in connection with the sports-oriented clothing. The court ruled that the curtailment of students' rights did not "demand a certainty that disruption will occur, but only the existence of facts which might reasonably lead school officials to forecast substantial disruption."

After the 1999 Columbine High School shootings in Littleton, Colorado, which left fourteen students and a teacher dead—including the two gunmen, who were members of a clique called the Trench Coat Mafia—many school districts made their rules for student dress more restrictive. Ten days after the shootings, a federal judge who upheld a school's decision to suspend a student for wearing a T-shirt that said "Vegan" (a vegetarian who doesn't eat animal products), said "gang attire has become particularly troubling since two students wore trench coats in the Colorado shooting." And in Jonesboro, Arkansas, where four students and a teacher were shot and killed the previous year, a group of boys and girls identifying themselves as the Blazer Mafia were suspended for ten days (Portner, 1999).

To reduce disruption and violence in schools, some school districts now require younger students to wear uniforms. In 1994, the 90,000-student Long Beach, California, school system became the first in the nation to require K–8 students to wear uniforms. Currently, the Birmingham, Alabama; Chicago; Dayton, Ohio; Oakland, California; and San Antonio public schools require elementary-age students to wear uniforms. At the beginning of the 2002–03 school year, Memphis took steps to become the nation's first large urban district to require all students to wear uniforms when school commissioners voted 8–1 to implement a school uniform policy for the district's 175 schools (Richard, 2002b).

Currently, half the states have school districts with mandatory school uniform requirements, and "estimates suggest that over the next several years, one in four public school students may be wearing uniforms" (LaMorte, 2008, p. 178). Courts have upheld mandatory school uniform policies. For example, a court ruled against a parent who challenged New York City's school uniform policy for pre-K through eighth-grade students. The parent claimed that the opt-out provision would make his daughter stick out, while the New York City Board of Education stated that the policy would "promote a more effective learning climate; foster school unity and pride; improve student performance; foster self-esteem; eliminate label competition; simplify dressing and minimize costs to parents; teach children appropriate dress and decorum in the 'workplace'; and help to improve student conduct and discipline" (*Lipsman v. New York City Board of Education*, 1999).

ETHICAL AND LEGAL ISSUES IN U.S. EDUCATION

Due Process in Suspension and Expulsion

In February and March 1971, a total of nine students received ten-day suspensions from the Columbus, Ohio, public school system during a period of citywide unrest. One student, in the presence of his principal, physically attacked a police officer who was trying to remove a disruptive student from a high school auditorium. Four others were suspended for similar conduct. Another student was suspended for his involvement in a lunchroom disturbance that resulted in damage to school property. All nine students were suspended in accordance with Ohio law. Some of the students and their parents were offered the opportunity to attend conferences prior to the start of the suspensions, but none of the nine was given a hearing. Asserting that their constitutional rights had been denied, all nine students brought suit against the school system.

In a sharply divided 5–4 decision, the Supreme Court ruled that the students had a legal right to an education, and that this "property right" could be removed only through the application of procedural due process. The Court maintained that suspension is a "serious event" in the life of a suspended child and may not be imposed by the school in an arbitrary manner (*Goss v. Lopez*, 1975).

As a result of cases such as *Goss v. Lopez*, every state has outlined procedures for school officials to follow in the suspension and expulsion of students. In cases of short-term suspension (defined by the courts as exclusion from school for 10 days or less), the due process steps are somewhat flexible and determined by the nature of the infraction and the length of the suspension. As Figure 7.3 shows, however, long-term suspension (more than 10 days) and expulsion require a more extensive due process procedure. The disciplinary transfer of a disruptive student to an alternative school, designed to meet his or her needs, is not considered an expulsion (Alexander & Alexander, 2009; LaMorte, 2008).

In response to an increase of unruly students who disrupt the learning of others, a few districts and states have granted teachers the authority to suspend students for up to 10 days. Teachers in Cincinnati, Ohio, and Dade County, Florida, for example, have negotiated contracts that give them authority to remove disruptive students from their classrooms; however, district administrators decide how the students will be disciplined. In 1995, Indiana became the first state to grant teachers the power to suspend students, and the following year, New York's governor proposed legislation to allow teachers to remove students from their classrooms for up to 10 days for "committing an act of violence against a student, teacher, or school district employee; possessing or threatening to use a gun, knife, or other dangerous weapon; damaging or destroying school district property; damaging the personal property of teachers or other employees; or defying an order from a teacher or administrator to stop disruptive behavior" (Lindsay, 1996, p. 24).

Reasonable Search and Seizure

You have reason to believe that a student has drugs, and possibly a dangerous weapon, in his locker. Do you, as a teacher, have the right to search the student's locker and seize any illegal or dangerous items?

According to the Fourth Amendment, citizens are protected from search and seizure conducted without a search warrant. With the escalation of drug use in schools and school-related violence, however, cases involving the legality of **search and seizure** in schools have increased. These cases suggest guidelines that you can follow if confronted with a situation such as that described here.

The case of *New Jersey v. T.L.O.* (1985) involved a 14-year-old student (T.L.O.) whom a teacher found smoking a cigarette in a restroom. The teacher took the student to the principal's office, whereupon the principal asked to see the contents of her purse. On opening the purse, the principal found a pack of cigarettes and what appeared to be drug paraphernalia and a list titled "People who owe me money." T.L.O. was arrested and later found guilty of delinquency charges.

After being sentenced to one year's probation, T.L.O. appealed, claiming that the evidence found in her purse was obtained in violation of the Fourth Amendment and

Due Process in Suspension and Expulsion

Suspension

1. Adequate notice must be provided to students and parents regarding the existence of rules governing student behavior. These should be clearly communicated to all affected by their implementation.
2. A record should be compiled that includes the following information:
   a. The infraction allegedly committed.
   b. The time of the alleged infraction.
   c. The place the alleged infraction occurred.
   d. Those person(s) who witnessed the alleged act.
   e. Previous efforts made to remedy the alleged misbehavior.
3. Students facing suspension should, at minimum, be provided some type of notice followed by a brief informal hearing.
4. Students should be provided either oral or written notice of charges against them, the evidence school authorities have to support the charges, and an opportunity to refute the charges.
5. Because permanent removal is not intended, no delay is necessary between the time notice is given and the time of the actual hearing. In most instances, school officials may informally discuss alleged misconduct with students immediately after it is reported.
6. During the hearing, the school official should listen to all sides of the issue. There should be adequate time provided for students to present their side of the issue without interruption.
7. Parents or guardians should be informed of the hearing and provided written notification of the action that results from the hearing. At a minimum, the written notice should include:
   a. The charge(s) brought against the student.
   b. A description of the evidence used to support the charge(s).
   c. The number of days suspended.
   d. A determination of whether suspension is an in-school or out-of-school suspension.
   e. A list of other conditions that must be met before the student returns to school (e.g., a conference with parent or guardian).
   f. A statement that informs parents or guardians that the suspension can be appealed to the district's pupil personnel director or a designee.
8. Parents or guardians should be informed by phone of the suspension, followed by written notification, which should be promptly mailed, preferably by registered mail on the day of the hearing.

Expulsion

1. Students, parents, or legal guardians should be informed based on school or district policy of specific infractions that may result in expulsion. They should also be informed of their Fourteenth Amendment rights regarding substantive and procedural due process.
2. In cases of serious misconduct for which serious disciplinary measures may be imposed, the student is entitled to written notice of the charges and has the right to a fair hearing. Written notice must be furnished to the student and parent or guardian well in advance of the actual hearing.
3. At a minimum, the following procedural steps should be considered:
   a. Written notice of charges.
   b. Right to a fair hearing.
   c. Right to inspect evidence.
   d. Right to present evidence on student's behalf.
   e. Right to legal counsel.
   f. Right to call witnesses.
   g. Right to cross-examination and to confrontation.
   h. Right against self-incrimination.
   i. Right to appeal.

Source: Adapted from Nathan L. Essex. (2008). *School Law and the Public Schools: A Practical Guide for Educational Leaders.* Boston: Pearson, pp. 87–88, 91.

FIGURE 7.3 Due process in suspension and expulsion

that her confession to selling marijuana was tainted by an illegal search. The U.S. Supreme Court found that the search had been reasonable. The Court also developed a two-pronged test of "reasonableness" for searches: (1) a school official must have a reasonable suspicion that a student has violated a law or school policy, and (2) the search must be conducted using methods that are reasonable in scope.

Another case focused on the use of trained dogs to conduct searches of 2,780 junior and senior high school students in Highland, Indiana. During a 2½ to 3-hour period, six teams with trained German shepherds sniffed the students. The dogs alerted their handlers a total of 50 times. Seventeen of the searches initiated by the dogs turned up beer, drug paraphernalia, or marijuana.

What are students' rights with regard to their persons, lockers, personal property, and records in school and on school grounds? How are school districts' rights of search and seizure decided? In what ways have students' rights to privacy been upheld?

Another 11 students, including 13-year-old Diane Doe, singled out by the dogs were strip-searched in the nurse's office. It turned out that Diane had played with her dog, who was in heat, that morning and that the police dog had responded to the smell of the other dog on Diane's clothing.

Diane's parents later filed suit, charging that their daughter was searched illegally. The court ruled that the use of dogs did not constitute an unreasonable search, nor did holding students in their homerooms constitute a mass detention in violation of the Fourth Amendment. The court did hold, however, that the strip searches of the students were unreasonable. The court pointed out that the school personnel did not have any evidence to suggest that Diane possessed contraband because she had emptied her pockets as requested prior to the strip search. Diane was awarded $7,500 in damages (*Doe v. Renfrow,* 1980, 1981).

Court cases involving search and seizure in school settings have maintained that school lockers are the property of the schools, not students, and may be searched by school authorities if reasonable cause exists. In addition, students may be sniffed by police dogs if school authorities have a reasonable suspicion that illegal or dangerous items may be found. Last, courts "have increasingly upheld teachers who had engaged in strip searches, especially if it involved younger students. . . . however, individualized suspicion is required to conduct an intrusive search" (LaMorte, 2008, p. 171).

In general, the courts have tried to balance the school's need to obtain information and the student's right to privacy. To protect themselves from legal challenges related to searches, educators should follow guidelines that have been suggested by school law experts:

- Inform students and parents at the start of the school year of the procedures for conducting locker and personal searches.
- Base any search on "reasonable suspicion."
- Conduct any search with another staff member present.
- Avoid strip searches or mass searches of groups of students.
- Require that police obtain a search warrant before conducting a search in the school.

Some schools use drug testing as a requirement for either attendance or interscholastic participation, including sports competition, or as a means of discipline. A 1988 court case upheld a urinalysis drug test for randomly selected student athletes because those whose tests were positive were suspended only from participating in sports for a period of time and no disciplinary or academic penalties were imposed (*Schaill v. Tippecanoe School Corp.,* 1988). Similarly, the U.S. Supreme Court reversed a lower court's ruling and stated that a school district's desire to reduce drug use justified the degree of intrusion required by random tests of student athletes' urine (*Acton v. Vernonia School District,* 1995). A few school districts have attempted to implement mandatory drug testing of teachers. So far the courts have upheld the decision rendered in *Patchogue-Medford Congress of Teachers v. Board of Education of Patchogue-Medford Union Free School District* (1987) that drug testing of teachers violates the Fourth Amendment's prohibition of unreasonable searches.

Privacy

Prior to 1974, students and parents were not allowed to examine school records. On November 19, 1974, Congress passed the Family Educational Rights and Privacy Act (FERPA), which gave parents of students under 18 and students 18 and older the right to examine their school records. Every public or private educational institution must adhere to the law, known as the **Buckley Amendment,** or lose federal money.

Under the Buckley Amendment, schools must do the following:

1. Inform parents and students of their rights.
2. Provide information to parents and students about the type of educational records available and how to obtain access to them.
3. Allow parents or students to review records; request changes; request a hearing if changes are not allowed; and, if necessary, add their own explanation about the records.
4. Not give out personally identifiable information without prior written, informed consent of a parent or students.
5. Allow parents and students to see the school's record of disclosures.

The Buckley Amendment actually sets forth the minimum requirements that schools must adhere to, and many states and school districts have gone beyond these minimum guidelines in granting students access to their records. Most high schools, for example, now grant students under age 18 access to their educational records, and all students in Virginia, elementary through secondary, are guaranteed access to their records.

Exceptions

Several exceptions are allowed by the Buckley Amendment. The teacher's gradebook, psychiatric or treatment records, notes or records written by the teacher for his or her exclusive use or to be shared with a substitute teacher, or the private notes of school law enforcement units, for example, are not normally subject to examination.

The provisions of FERPA came to the nation's attention in 2000 when Kristja Falvo challenged the practice of having students grade one another's papers (peer grading) on the grounds that it was embarrassing to her three children and resulted in grading errors. A district court disagreed and ruled in favor of the school district, maintaining that peer grading is a common school practice. However, the Tenth Circuit Court of Appeals reversed that decision and ruled that the practice of peer grading violated students' privacy because grades are entered into teachers' gradebooks and thus fit the definition of "educational records" (*Falvo v. Owasso Independent School District,* 2000). Eventually, however, the case reached the Supreme Court, which ruled 9–0 that the privacy law was not intended to protect grades on day-to-day classroom assignments and that students could grade one another's work (*Owasso Independent School District v. Falvo,* 2002).

Cameras in Classrooms

Another privacy-related issue emerged in 2003 when schools in Biloxi, Mississippi, became the first in the nation to use cameras to monitor activities in classrooms. Previously, some schools used cameras to monitor hallways, cafeterias, auditoriums, and parking lots.

Some observers worry that cameras in classrooms will interfere with learning activities and could be misused. Others contend that teachers' and students' privacy is violated by the use of cameras. Nevertheless, regarding the presence of five hundred cameras in classrooms at the start of the school year, a Biloxi School District official pointed out: "Students, parents and teachers don't mind them at all" (Lewis, 2003).

Students' Rights to Nondiscrimination

Schools are legally bound to avoid discriminating against students on the basis of race, sex, religion, disability, sexual orientation, marital status, or infection with a disease such as HIV/AIDS that poses no threat to students. One trend that has confronted schools with the need to develop more thoughtful and fair policies has been the epidemic in teenage pregnancies.

In regard to students who are married, pregnant, or parents, the courts have been quite clear: Students in these categories may not be treated differently. A 1966 case in Texas involving a 16-year-old mother established that schools may provide separate classes or alternative schools on a voluntary basis for married and/or pregnant students. However, the district may not require such students to attend separate schools, nor may they be required to attend adult or evening schools (*Alvin Independent School District v. Cooper,* 1966).

The courts have made an about-face in their positions on whether students who are married, pregnant, or parents can participate in extracurricular activities. Prior to 1972, participation in these activities was considered a privilege rather than a right, and restrictions on those who could participate were upheld. In 1972, however, cases in Tennessee, Ohio, Montana, and Texas established the right of married students (and, in one case, a divorced student) to participate (*Holt v. Sheldon,* 1972; *Davis v. Meek,* 1972; *Moran v. School District No. 7,* 1972; and *Romans v. Crenshaw,* 1972). Since then, restrictions applicable to extracurricular activities have been universally struck down.

During the 1980s, many school districts became embroiled in controversy over the issue of how to provide for the schooling of young people with HIV/AIDS and whether school employees with HIV/AIDS should be allowed to continue working. In rulings on HIV/AIDS-related cases since then, the courts have sided with the overwhelming medical evidence that students with AIDS pose no "significant risk" of spreading the disease. "To date, courts have revealed a high degree of sensitivity to students with HIV or AIDS and to their being included in the public school mainstream" (LaMorte, 2008, p. 362). In 1987, for example, a judge prevented a Florida school district from requiring that three hemophiliac brothers who were exposed to HIV/AIDS through transfusions be restricted to homebound instruction (*Ray v. School District of DeSoto County,* 1987).

To stem the spread of HIV/AIDS, school systems in many large cities—New York, Los Angeles, San Francisco, and Seattle, to name a few—have initiated programs to distribute condoms to high school students. New York's condom-distribution program, which initially did not require parental consent, was challenged in 1993 (*Alfonso v. Fernandez*). The court ruled that the program was a "health issue" and that the district could not dispense condoms without prior parental approval. The court maintained that the program violated parents' due process rights under the Fourteenth Amendment to raise their children as they see fit; however, the program did not violate parents' or students' freedom of religion. Three years later, however, the U.S. Supreme Court declined to review a Massachusetts high court ruling that upheld a school board's decision to place condom machines in high school restrooms and allow junior- and senior-level students to request condoms from the school nurse (*Curtis v. School Committee of Falmouth,* 1995, 1996).

WHAT ARE SOME ISSUES IN THE LEGAL RIGHTS OF SCHOOL DISTRICTS?

Clearly, the law touches just about every aspect of education in the United States today. The media remind us daily that ours is an age of litigation; no longer are school districts as protected as they once were from legal problems.

Corporal punishment, sexual harassment, religious expression, and home schooling are among the issues in the legal rights of school districts.

Corporal Punishment

The practice of **corporal punishment** has had a long and controversial history in education in the United States. Currently, policies regarding the use of corporal punishment vary widely from state to state, and even from district to district.

Critics believe that corporal punishment "is neither a necessary nor an effective response to misbehavior in school" (Slavin, 2000, p. 391), and some believe that the practice is "archaic, cruel, and inhuman and an unjustifiable act on the part of the state" (LaMorte, 2008, p. 154). In spite of such arguments against its effectiveness, corporal punishment continues to be widespread. Nevertheless, almost half of the states and many school districts currently ban corporal punishment, and many others restrict its use (Alexander & Alexander, 2009; LaMorte, 2008).

The most influential Supreme Court case involving corporal punishment is *Ingraham v. Wright*, decided in 1977. In Dade County, Florida, in October 1970, junior high school students James Ingraham and Roosevelt Andrews were paddled with a wooden paddle. Both students received injuries as a result of the paddlings, with Ingraham's being the more severe. Ingraham, who was being punished for being slow to respond to a teacher's directions, refused to assume the "paddling position" and had to be held over a desk by two assistant principals while the principal administered twenty "licks." As a result, Ingraham "suffered a hematoma requiring medical attention and keeping him out of school for several days."

The Court had two significant questions to rule on in *Ingraham*: Does the Eighth Amendment's prohibition of cruel and unusual punishment apply to corporal punishment in the schools? Second, if it does not, should the due process clause of the Fourteenth Amendment provide any protection to students before punishment is administered? In regard to the first question, the Court, in a sharply divided 5–4 decision, ruled that the Eighth Amendment was not applicable to students being disciplined in school, only to persons convicted of crimes. On the question of due process, the Court said, "We conclude that the Due Process clause does not require notice and a hearing prior to the imposition of corporal punishment in the public schools, as that practice is authorized and limited by the common law." The Court also commented on the severity of the paddlings in *Ingraham* and said that, in such cases, school personnel "may be held liable in damages to the child and, if malice is shown, they may be subject to criminal penalties."

Though the Supreme Court has upheld the constitutionality of corporal punishment, many districts around the country have instituted policies banning its use. Where corporal punishment is used, school personnel are careful to see that it meets criteria that have emerged from other court cases involving corporal punishment:

- Specific warning is given about what behavior may result in corporal punishment.
- Evidence exists that other measures attempted failed to bring about the desired change in behavior.
- Administration of corporal punishment takes place in the presence of a second school official.
- On request, a written statement is provided to parents explaining the reasons for the punishment and the names of all witnesses.
- [The punishment meets] the reasonableness standard—punishment must be within the bounds of reason and humanity.
- [The punishment meets] the good faith standard—the person administering the punishment is not motivated by malice and does not inflict punishment wantonly or excessively. (Dunklee & Shoop, 2002, p. 127)

258

Sexual Harassment

Though few victims report it, 80 percent of students in a national survey reported that they had been sexually harassed, and one in three said they experienced it "often" (American Association of University Women, 2002, p. III-2). Another survey found that 64 percent of lesbian, gay, bisexual, or transgender (LGBT) students fear for their safety while at school, and about two-thirds were sexually harassed (Kosciw & Diaz, 2006). Currently, nine states have antibullying policies that specifically mention sexual orientation (Robinson, February/March 2008, p. 58).

In addition to harassment by the opposite sex, same-sex harassment, usually against **LGBT students,** is a problem at some schools. Since the mid-1990s, several school districts have faced lawsuits filed by gay and lesbian students who claimed that school officials failed to protect them from verbal and physical antigay harassment.

In *Flores v. Morgan Hill Unified School District* (2003), several students claimed their school did not respond adequately to a seven-year period of antihomosexual harassment they endured. In its ruling that teachers and administrators failed to enforce the school district's antiharassment and antidiscrimination policies, the Court stated, "The record contains sufficient evidence for a jury to conclude that the defendants intentionally discriminated against the plaintiffs in violation of the Equal Protection Clause." The school district eventually agreed to pay $1.1 million to six of the students.

On the other hand, the courts have been reluctant to hold school districts liable unless the harassment was foreseeable and preventable, and they deliberately failed to intervene. School districts were not found liable for damages in the following cases: Student aides videotaped the girls' locker room and bathrooms over a two-year period (*Harry A. v. Duncan*, 2005); a student received a punch intended for another student (*Mohammed ex rel. Mohammed v. School District of Philadelphia,* 2005); a student was verbally harassed due to ancestry and race (*Yap v. Oceanside Union Free School District*, 2004).

Regarding sexual harassment of students by educators, the courts have generally ruled that school districts may be held liable if the district knew or should have known of the harassment. In one case, *Franklin v. Gwinnett County Public Schools* (1992), the Supreme Court found a school district liable because district administrators knew that a teacher had repeatedly sexually abused a student and took no steps to stop the harassment. The Court ruled that the student could collect damages for sexual harassment under Title IX of the Education Act of 1972. In *Gebser v. Lago Vista Independent School District* (1998), however, the Supreme Court ruled that a school district was not liable for damages resulting from teacher-to-student harassment, unless a school official with "authority to institute corrective measures on the district's behalf has actual notice of, and is deliberately indifferent to, the teacher's misconduct."

Increased reports of sexual harassment of students by educators are causing some teachers to be apprehensive about working closely with students, and a small number of teachers even report that they fear being falsely accused by angry, disgruntled students. As a school superintendent put it, "There's no question but that the attitudes of personnel in schools are changing because of the many cases [of sexual harassment] that have come up across the country. I think all of us are being extremely cautious in how we handle students and in what we say and do with students and employees" (*Spokesman Review*, 1993, p. 1A). To address the problem, many school districts have suggested guidelines that teachers can follow to show concern for students, offer them encouragement, and congratulate them for their successes.

Religious Expression

Conflicts over the proper role of religion in schools are among the most heated in the continuing debate about the character and purposes of education in the United States. Numerous school districts have found themselves embroiled in legal issues related to school prayer, Bible reading, textbooks, creationism, intelligent design, singing of

Christmas carols, distribution of religious literature, New Age beliefs, secular humanism, religious holidays, use of school buildings for religious meetings, and the role of religion in moral education, to name a few. On the one hand, conservative religious groups wish to restore prayer and Christian religious practices in the public schools; on the other, secular liberals see religion as irrelevant to school curricula and maintain that public schools should not promote religion. In addition, somewhere between these two positions are those who believe that, while schools should not be involved in the *teaching of* religion, they should *teach about* religion.

Evolution Versus Creationism and Intelligent Design

Issues related to religious expression in the schools have been most heated in regard to the teaching of evolution in science classes. School law experts Kern Alexander and M. David Alexander (2009, p. 390) explain how efforts to diminish the teaching of evolution and advance the teaching of creationism in schools have changed over the years:

> The efforts of Christian Fundamentalists to insert the biblical Book of Genesis' explanation into the teaching of science in the public school classrooms evolved in stages from direct state prohibitions to teaching Darwinian evolution, to teaching creation as a science, to balanced treatment of both creationism and evolution, and finally to the latest intelligent design movement (IDM).

Legal Rulings

Scores of court cases have addressed school activities related to the First Amendment principle of separation of church and state. As Michael Imber and Tyll van Geel put it: "By far the most common constitutional objection raised against a school program is that it fails to respect the wall of separation between church and state" (2005, p. 21). In one of these landmark cases (*Engel v. Vitale*, 1962), the U.S. Supreme Court ruled that recitation of a prayer said in the presence of a teacher at the beginning of each school day was unconstitutional and violated the First Amendment, which states: "Congress shall make no law respecting an establishment of religion, or prohibiting the free exercise thereof." Justice Hugo Black, who delivered the opinion of the Court, stated, "[I]t is no part of the business of government to compose official prayers for any group of the American people to recite as a part of a religious program carried on by government."

The following year, the U.S. Supreme Court ruled that Bible reading and reciting the Lord's Prayer in school were unconstitutional (*School District of Abington Township v. Schempp*, 1963). In response to the district's claim that unless these religious activities were permitted, a "religion of secularism" would be established, the Court stated, "[W]e agree of course that the State may not establish a 'religion of secularism' in the sense of affirmatively opposing or showing hostility to religion, thus 'preferring those who believe in no religion over those who do believe.' We do not agree, however, that this decision in any sense has that effect."

To determine whether a state has violated the separation of church and state principle, the courts refer to the decision rendered in *Lemon v. Kurtzman* (1971). In this instance, the U.S. Supreme Court struck down an attempt by the Rhode Island legislature to provide a 15 percent salary supplement to teachers of secular subjects in nonpublic schools and Pennsylvania legislation to provide financial supplements to nonpublic schools through reimbursement for teachers' salaries, texts, and instructional materials in certain secular subjects. According to the three-part test enunciated in *Lemon v. Kurtzman*, governmental practices "must (1) have a secular legislative purpose; (2) have a principal or primary effect that neither advances nor inhibits religion; and (3) not foster an excessive entanglement with religion" (LaMorte, 2008, p. 42). Though criticized vigorously by several Supreme Court justices since 1971, the so-called **Lemon test** has not been overruled. Table 7.3 presents additional selected U.S. Supreme Court cases related to religion and schools.

Since the mid-1990s, lower courts have heard several cases addressing the question of whether parents' right to direct their children's upbringing meant they could demand curricula and learning activities that were compatible with their religious beliefs.

TABLE 7.3 Selected U.S. Supreme Court cases related to religion and schools (listed in chronological order)

Epperson v. Arkansas (1968): Court overturned the state's anti-evolution statute on the grounds that a state may not deny students access to scientific information because of religious convictions.

Wisconsin v. Yoder (1972): Court decision exempted Amish children from mandatory school attendance beyond the eighth grade if the Amish provided a structured vocational training program for their children.

Mueller v. Allen (1983): Court upheld Minnesota's tax deductions for expenses incurred while sending children to secular elementary or secondary schools.

Wallace v. Jaffree (1985): Court invalidated Alabama's school-sponsored moment of silence in Mobile, Alabama.

Edwards v. Aguillard (1987): Court overturned Louisiana's requirement that equal time be devoted to evolution and creationism.

Stone v. Graham (1990): Court ruled that a Kentucky law mandating the posting of the Ten Commandments in public school classrooms was designed to advance a particular faith, thus violating the First Amendment's establishment of religion clause.

Board of Education of Westside Community Schools v. Mergens (1990): Court upheld the legality of the Equal Access Act (1984), which allowed student religious groups to meet in public secondary schools during noninstructional time.

Zobrest v. Catalina Foothills School District (1993): Court ruled that parochial school sign-language interpreters paid with public funds did not violate the First Amendment.

Agostini v. Felton (1997): Decision overturned the *Aguilar v. Felton* (1985) ruling that prohibited public school employees from providing remedial instruction in sectarian institutions. The *Agostini* ruling focused on Title I of the Elementary and Secondary Education Act of 1965, which required that comparable services be offered to parochial school pupils.

Mitchell v. Helms (2000): Court allowed the use of government funds to provide instructional materials to religious schools.

Santa Fe Independent School District v. Jane Doe (2000): Court ruled that a Texas school district's policy of allowing voluntary student-initiated and -led invocations before football games violated the establishment clause of the First Amendment.

Good News Club v. Milford Central School (2001): Court ruled that a public school could not deny a Christian group from meeting in the school after hours; if a district allows community groups to use the school, it cannot deny use to religious groups.

Without exception, the courts have rejected parent-rights cases against the schools. Those rights, according to a U.S. Court of Appeals ruling in support of a schoolwide assembly on HIV/AIDS, "do not encompass a broad-based right to restrict the flow of information in the public schools" (*Brown v. Hot, Sexy and Safer Productions, Inc.*, 1996). In a similar case, parents objected to a Massachusetts school district's policy of distributing condoms to junior and senior high school students who requested them. The state's Supreme Judicial Court rejected the parent-rights argument and their argument that the program infringed on their First Amendment right to free exercise of religion: "Parents have no right to tailor public school programs to meet their individual religious or moral preferences" (*Curtis v. School Committee of Falmouth*, 1995).

Efforts to replace teaching of creationism in science classrooms with intelligent design (ID) theory have been similarly rejected by the courts. In a case that received nationwide attention, *Kitzmiller v. Dover Area School District* (2005), a federal court struck down an attempt by the Dover, Pennsylvania, School Board to insert the teaching of intelligent design in the classroom. The court concluded that ID is not science:

> We find that ID fails on three different levels, any one of which is sufficient to preclude a determination that ID is science. They are (1) ID violates centuries-old ground rules of science by invoking and permitting supernatural causation; (2) the argument of irreducible complexity, central to ID, employs the

Today's students come from families with diverse religious backgrounds. What challenges do schools face in educating students from diverse religious backgrounds? How can teachers be sure they do not discriminate against students from religious backgrounds that differ from their own?

same flawed and illogical contrived dualism that doomed creation science in the 1980s; and (3) ID's negative attacks on evolution have been refuted by the scientific community.

Guidelines for Religious Activities in Schools

In 2003, the U.S. Department of Education issued federal guidelines requiring school districts to allow students and teachers to engage in religious activities, including prayer, at school. Districts that violate the rules—or fail to promise in writing that they will comply with the guidelines—risk the loss of federal education funds. The following points are included in the guidelines:

- Students may "read their Bibles or other scriptures, say grace before meals, and pray or study religious materials with fellow students during recess, the lunch hour or other non-instructional time."

- Teachers should not discriminate against students who "express their beliefs about religion in homework, artwork, and other written and oral assignments."

- In certain circumstances, schools may have to grant parental requests to "excus[e] students from class" for religious reasons.

- Teachers and other school employees, "when acting in their official capacities as representatives of the state," cannot encourage or participate in prayer activities with students. Before school or during lunch, however, school employees are free to meet with other employees for prayer or Bible study (*NEA Today,* 2003, p. 13).

Homeschooling

One spin-off of the public's heightened awareness of the problems that schools face has been the decision by some parents to educate their children in the home. While most homeschoolers view homeschooling as an opportunity to provide their children with a curriculum based on religious values, many homeschoolers are motivated not by religious doctrine but by concern about issues such as school violence, poor academic quality, or peer pressure. It is estimated that over 2 million students are currently homeschooled, and the number increases by about 12 percent each year (LaMorte, 2008, pp. 27–28).

Home schooling is legal in all the states and the District of Columbia; however, how it is regulated, and whether resources are allocated, vary greatly. In most states, homeschoolers must demonstrate that their instruction is "equivalent" to that offered in the public schools, a standard set in *New Jersey v. Massa* (1967). Additional requirements may include participation in standardized testing, a minimum number of hours of instruction, submission of attendance records and lesson plans, adherence to a minimum curriculum, and minimum academic credentials for parents or guardians (LaMorte, 2008, p. 28).

Legal support for homeschooling has been mixed. In 1998, a Massachusetts court ruled that home visits by a local superintendent were not a valid requirement for approval by school officials of a homeschooling program (*Brunelle v. Lynn Public Schools,* 1998). In 1993 and 1994, legislation to require homeschool teachers to be state certified were defeated in South Dakota and Kansas, and similar laws were overturned in Iowa and North Dakota. However, a federal district court upheld a West Virginia statute making children ineligible for homeschooling if their standardized test scores fell below the 40th percentile (*Null v. Board of Education,* 1993). In Iowa, mandatory homeschooling reports to the state were upheld in *State v. Rivera* (1993); homeschoolers in that state must submit course outlines and weekly lesson plans, and provide the amount of time spent on areas of the curriculum. A Maryland law requiring the state's monitoring of homeschooling was upheld despite a parent's claim that the state's curriculum promoted atheism, paganism, and evolution (*Battles v. Anne Arundel County Board of Education,* 1996). And courts have not been sympathetic to homeschoolers who would like to have their children participate in extracurricular activities or other after-school activities (for example, *Swanson v. Guthrie Independent School District No. 1,* 1998).

As the preceding cases related to homeschooling show, school law is not static—instead, it is continually evolving and changing. The legal issues examined in this chapter make it clear that the law touches just about every aspect of the teacher's professional life. Ours is an age of litigation, and the teacher is no longer quite as free as in the past to determine what happens behind the closed classroom door.

While the review of school law in this chapter has answered some of the more common questions teacher education students have about their rights and responsibilities as a teacher, it may have made you aware of other questions for which you need answers. Because school law is constantly changing and laws pertaining to education vary from state to state, you may wish to consult current publications on school law in your state.

SUMMARY

Why Do You Need to Know About Education and the Law?

- Federal and state legislation and court decisions affect the daily lives of teachers, and teachers must have knowledge of school law to protect their rights and the rights of students.

Why Do You Need a Professional Code of Ethics as Teachers Do?

- A professional code of ethics guides teachers' actions, helps them see beyond the short-range consequences of their actions to the long-range consequences, and helps them respond appropriately to ethical dilemmas in the classroom.
- Ethical decisions (1) are supported by evidence, (2) aim at ends that ought to be aimed at, (3) can be implemented morally, and (4) are legitimately achieved.

What Are Your Legal Rights as a Teacher?

- The right to due process protects teachers from arbitrary treatment by school districts and education

officials regarding certification, nondiscrimination, contracts, tenure, dismissal, and academic freedom.
- The constitutional rights of teachers must be balanced against a school's need to promote its educational goals.

Do Student Teachers Have the Same Rights as Teachers Do?

- Student teachers should be aware that a potential for liability exists for them just as it does with certified teachers, and they should clarify their rights and responsibilities prior to beginning student teaching.

What Are Your Legal Responsibilities as a Teacher?

- Teachers are responsible for meeting the terms of their teaching contracts, including providing for their students' safety and well-being.
- Three legal responsibilities that concern teachers are avoiding tort liability, recognizing the physical and behavioral indicators of child abuse and then reporting suspected instances of such abuse, and observing copyright laws for instructional materials used in the classroom.

What Are the Legal Rights of Students and Parents?

- Generally, students' freedom of expression can be limited if it is disruptive of the educational process or incongruent with the school's mission.
- Students can be neither suspended nor expelled without due process.
- Courts have developed a two-pronged test for search and seizure actions involving students: (1) School officials must have "reasonable" suspicion that a student has violated a law or school policy, and (2) the search must be done using methods that are reasonable and appropriate given the nature of the infraction.
- Under the Buckley Amendment, students have the right to examine their school records, and schools may not give third parties information about students without the students' prior written consent.
- Schools may not discriminate against students on the basis of race, sex, religion, disability, marital status, or infection with a noncommunicable disease such as HIV/AIDS.

What Are Some Issues in the Legal Rights of School Districts?

- Some states and school districts allow the use of corporal punishment if it meets criteria that have emerged from other court cases involving corporal punishment.
- School officials can be held responsible if they fail to act on reports of sexual harassment of students by their peers or by professional staff. School officials also can be held responsible if they fail to take steps to protect gay and lesbian students from antigay harassment.
- The First Amendment principle of separation of church and state has been applied to numerous court cases involving religious expression in the public schools. In 2003, the U.S. Department of Education issued guidelines outlining religious activities that are allowed at school.
- Homeschooling is legal in all states, though most require homeschoolers to demonstrate that their instruction is equivalent to that in public schools.

PROFESSIONAL REFLECTIONS AND ACTIVITIES

Teacher's Journal

1. Read the National Education Association's Code of Ethics for Teachers, which is available on the Internet. Regarding Principle I, a teacher's commitment to students, describe a situation you have observed or experienced in which you think a teacher may have violated this principle. Regarding Principle II, a teacher's commitment to the profession, describe a situation in which a teacher might have violated that principle. What are your goals for ethical conduct as a teacher?

2. How can you accommodate students in your classroom who may come from backgrounds with worldviews that differ from Christianity—for example, Islam, Judaism, Buddhism, or a naturalistic worldview that is free of supernatural and mystical elements?

Teacher's Research

1. Go to the American Bar Association's website, where you can access its journal, a database of court decisions, and analyses of many of those decisions. Read the complete court decision for one or more legal cases mentioned in this chapter. After reading the case, do you agree with the court's decision? Why or why not?

2. Go to the websites for the National Education Association and the American Federation of Teachers. What legal information related to the legal issues discussed in this chapter do these sites provide for teachers?

Observations and Interviews

1. Interview an experienced teacher about the legal rights of teachers. Ask this teacher for examples of situations for which it was important that he or she (or another teacher) was familiar with the legal rights of teachers.

2. Interview another experienced teacher about the legal responsibilities of teachers. Ask this teacher for examples of situations in which it was important that he or she (or another teacher) was familiar with the legal responsibilities of teachers.

PEARSON **myeducationlab** To complete additional observations and interviews, go to MyEducationLab at www.myeducationlab.com, select the Virtual Field Experience section, and click on this chapter's Observations and Interviews.

Professional Portfolio

Survey a group of students, teachers, and/or parents regarding a legal issue in education. Among the legal issues and questions you might address are the following:

- Should tenure for teachers be abolished? Does tenure improve the quality of the education that students receive?
- Under what circumstances should restrictions be placed on what teachers teach and how they teach?
- Should parents be allowed to provide homeschooling for their children?
- Are parents justified in filing educational malpractice suits if their children fail to achieve in school?
- Under what circumstances should restrictions be placed on students' freedom of expression?
- Should schools have the right to implement dress codes? Guidelines for students' hairstyles? School uniforms?
- Should corporal punishment be banned? If not, under what circumstances should it be used?
- How should schools combat the problem of sexual harassment?

- To combat drug abuse, should schools implement mandatory drug testing of students? Of teachers?
- Should students have access to their educational records? Should their parents or guardians?
- As part of an HIV/AIDS prevention program, should condoms be distributed to high school students? Should parental approval be required for participation?

The report summarizing the results of your survey should include demographic information such as the following for your sample of respondents: gender, age, whether they have children in school, level of education, and so on. When you analyze the results, look for differences related to these variables.

PEARSON myeducationlab Now go to MyEducationLab at www.myeducationlab.com to test your understanding of chapter content by completing this chapter's Study Plan.

Foundations of Teaching: Florida-Specific Resources

Objectives:

- Identify the major influences, issues, ideologies, and individuals in the history of Florida education.
- Describe how the prominent philosophies of education affect teaching and learning in Florida.
- Evaluate how socioeconomic status and race affect students in Florida.
- Describe how laws affect Florida schools, teachers, and students.
- Explain the management structure of Florida schools.
- Describe how Florida schools are financed.

FEAP Competencies:

Assessment (FEAP #1): The preprofessional teacher collects and uses data gathered from a variety of sources. These sources include both traditional and alternate assessment strategies. Furthermore, the teacher can identify and match the students' instructional plans with their cognitive, social, linguistic, cultural, emotional, and physical needs.

Continuous Improvement (FEAP #3): The preprofessional student realizes that she/he is in the initial stages of a lifelong learning process and that self-reflection is one of the key components of that process. While his/her concentration is, of necessity, inward and personal, the role of colleagues and school-based improvement activities increases as time passes. The preprofessional student's continued professional improvement is characterized by self-reflection, working with immediate colleagues and teammates, and meeting the goals of a personal professional development plan.

Diversity (FEAP #5): The preprofessional teacher establishes a comfortable environment which accepts and fosters diversity. The teacher must demonstrate knowledge and awareness of varied cultures and linguistic backgrounds. The teacher creates a climate of openness, inquiry, and support by practicing strategies such as acceptance, tolerance, resolution, and mediation.

Ethics **(FEAP #6)** adheres to the Code of Ethics and Principles of Professional Conduct of the Education Profession in Florida.

Human Development and Learning Drawing (FEAP #7): The preprofessional teacher draws upon well established human development/learning theories and concepts and a variety of information about students, the preprofessional teacher plans instructional activities.

Learning Environments (**FEAP #9**): The preprofessional teacher understands the importance of setting up effective learning environments and has techniques and strategies to use to do so, including some that provide opportunities for student input into the processes. The teacher understands that she/he will need a variety of techniques and work to increase his/her knowledge and skills.

Role of the Teacher (FEAP #11): The preprofessional teacher communicates and works cooperatively with families and colleagues to improve the educational experiences at the school.

Important Concepts

- History of schooling
- Teacher preparation
- Philosophy
- Metaphysics
- Epistemology
- Axiology
- Logic
- Socioeconomic status
- At-risk
- Ethics
- Federal funding
- Site-based management
- Expenditure per pupil

Activities

Objective 1: Identify the major influences, issues, ideologies, and individuals in the history of Florida education.

The history of education in Florida mirrors that of much of the country and can be illustrated with highlights of past events—key examples from one school district. During the late 1800s in Pasco County, Florida, most schools were built of wood and contained one or two rooms, and one teacher taught first through sixth or eighth grade and had as many as thirty students.

In 1887 teacher salaries ranged from twenty dollars a month to as much as forty-five, and schools were open for three months a year, from October through December.

In a 1908 report to the state, the school superintendent of Pasco County reported that many schools were operating for a term of eight months, and he also reported that there were five black schools in the county, each operating for a term of four months.

In a 1916 report, the superintendent mentioned uniform county examinations of all students in seventh and eighth grades.

In the 1920s and 1930s some schools operated as "strawberry schools." At these schools children went to school during the summer and took the winter months off to help their parents with the strawberry harvest.

In 1939, the Dade City Banner reported, "Quite a sizable deficit still existed and the board was confronted with the question of a reduction in teachers' pay." A few months later the Pasco County Teachers' Association was organized.

In a 2005 obituary in the Tampa Tribune, Pasco County School Superintendent Chester Taylor was honored as the school leader who helped end school segregation in the 1960s. In an earlier interview, the superintendent told of meeting members of the Ku Klux Klan to explain the desegregation plan. He told Klan members that their children and black children were going to attend school together, and it didn't matter whether they liked it.

Questions for Reflection

1. School history in Florida's Pasco County has been captured and is available on the Internet via a series of reports from various school superintendents. http://fivay.org/education.html . Choose a time period and read through the articles. Summarize one. Did you find it interesting? Why or why not?
2. Beginning with the report from 1900, read through the years and see what you notice. In 1900, for example, the superintendent was pleased to report that the "deportment of children" was improved. Teachers were qualified because they graduated from the local high school. Describe one or two interesting facts that you notice. How do these items differ from what we see in today's classrooms?
3. Choose an individual school from the list. How has it changed over the years?

Objective 2: Describe how the prominent philosophies of education affect teaching and learning in Florida.

According to Florida's Bureau of School Improvement, the mission of Florida's K–20 Education system is "to allow its students to increase their proficiency by allowing them the opportunity to expand their knowledge and skills through rigorous and relevant learning opportunities in accordance with the mission statement and accountability requirements" of Florida law. Florida statute identifies the process for establishing state and sector-specific standards and measures that are focused on student success, addressable through policy and program changes, efficient and of high quality, measurable over time, simple to explain and display to the public, and aligned with other measures and other sectors to support a coordinated K–20 education system.

Each school district in Florida is required to submit a School Improvement Plan to the Bureau of School Improvement.

Questions for Reflection

1. Select a Florida county and school, and locate its School Improvement Plan at http://www.flbsi.org/0809_sip_template/login.aspx?AspxAutoDetectCookieSupport=1 (Choose the Read-Only file.). Summarize the school's mission statement.
2. Summarize the school's vision and belief statements, too.
3. How would you categorize this particular school's philosophy?

Objective 3: Evaluate how socioeconomic status and race affect students in Florida.

Florida is a state struggling to meet problems resulting from enormous challenges. In terms of divorce, for example, in 2006 the Florida Department of Health's Office of Vital Statistics reported over 85,000 divorces, or about 4.7 divorces per 1,000 couples. By comparison, the national rate that year was 3.6 divorces per 1,000 couples. The Centers for Disease Control and Prevention's National Center for Health Statistics ranked Florida's divorce rate as the tenth highest in the nation.

In terms of poverty, given the rapid growth and development of Florida's population and its tourist-related economy, Florida has a higher poverty rate than the American average. According to the Research Institute of Social and Economic Policy, Florida has an unusually high percentage of low-wage jobs and more children live in poverty, especially African Americans and Hispanics. More than a quarter of all Florida households could not afford adequate housing in 2002, and only half of private sector employers in Florida offer health insurance to employees. Of the fifty states, Florida has the lowest rate of employer-provided pensions.

For the children in Florida's schools, the children whose families struggle, such statistics put them at risk for school failure.

According to a study conducted by the Urban Institute, Florida has a proportionally larger minority population than the United States as a whole. The state has an equal percentage of blacks and Hispanics. More than 90 percent of Floridians reside in metropolitan areas, which is a considerably greater percentage than in the nation as a whole. Florida is growing much faster than the rest of the country. The teen birth rate is somewhat higher and the overall birth rate somewhat lower than the rates for the United States as a whole, while the percent of births to unmarried women and unmarried teens is higher than the national averages.

Visit the Florida Education and Community Data Profiles at http://www.fldoe.org/eias/eiaspubs/pdf/fecdp0506.pdf .

Questions for Reflection

1. Read through the information regarding socioeconomic status on pages 9-12 of the data profiles above. What are some important trends that you see reflected in this data?
2. With what socioeconomic status (SES) group(s) are you most familiar? How did your own SES affect your school days?
3. What are some ways that you plan to reach out to students from different SES group(s)? How will you meet the needs of students from low-income families?

Objective 4: Describe how laws affect Florida schools, teachers, and students.

In Florida, school laws are established by elected officials who meet regularly in Tallahassee. Ultimately it is the Florida legislature that establishes, by statute, educational policies and procedures. The Florida Department of Education then provides technical assistance to the state's 67 school districts to help implement the laws.

Making amendments to existing laws and establishing statutes for new legislation, the Florida legislature sets state policies for schools K–12. Policies include a vast range of topics, including requirements for school guidance programs, dropout reentry requirements, and religious observances.

When elected officials vote on educational issues, they do so on the advice of concerned citizens and business leaders. Many nonprofit groups have been formed to serve as advocates for educational policy, and several groups are leaders in Florida.

The Florida Education Policy Foundation is one such organization. It "serves as the catalyst that promotes excellence for Florida's elementary, secondary and post-secondary education by fostering the development of community and private sector resources."

Questions for Reflection

1. Visit the Florida Education Policy Foundation. What are some programs they support? Why do you think they support these particular programs?
2. How does this organization secure its funding? Describe some ways that you could get involved in this or other organizations as you progress in your career.

3. Describe some ways that citizen groups and elected officials impact the educational process. How will you get involved in this process in the future?

Objective 5: Explain the management structure of Florida schools.

The state governor appoints the State Board of Education and the Commissioner of Education. The mission of the State Board of Education, according to their Website, is to "increase the proficiency of all students within one seamless, efficient system, by providing them with the opportunity to expand their knowledge and skills through learning opportunities and research valued by students, parents, and communities, and to maintain an accountability system that measures student progress toward the following goals."

The Commissioner of Education acts as adviser to the governor and state legislators for topics relating to Florida education.

In addition, the Governmental Relations Office, a body of the Florida Department of Education is responsible for championing and advocating education policies set by the governor, the State Board of Education, and the commissioner of education, before the Florida legislature. Educational policies and funding are determined and set by the Florida Legislature.

Although each of Florida's school districts is comprised of a superintendent, a local school board, and the district staff who work to implement programs and policies across all schools in the given district, differences exist. For example, as stated in the text, school districts can differ dramatically in size, some relatively small with 300 or fewer students and those that enroll as many as 1,000 students per year.

Questions for Reflection

1. The Florida Department of Education provides data on each of the state's school districts. Visit the state list and select a district that interests you. If you need to do so, you can also search by using the state map. What kind of data is available for your district?
2. Compare your chosen district's data to that of Miami-Dade. How is it similar? How is it different?
3. Now compare your chosen district's data to that of Jefferson County. How does it compare?

Objective 6: Describe how Florida schools are financed.

School funding is a large portion of the Florida state budget every year. In fact, the governor's proposed education budget for 2007 was $33.4 BILLION dollars! This is a 4% increase from the previous year's budget.

Where does the money come from? Many of the funds come from property tax dollars. However, in 1987, Floridians voted in favor of using proceeds from the Florida Lottery to fund public education. Since then, the Florida Department of Education has produced an annual publication of Education Appropriations funded by the Florida lottery. The document includes a history of appropriated lottery funds since the beginning of the Florida Lottery. Education's share of the lottery funds, about a billion dollars each year, is deposited in the Educational Enhancement Trust Fund, and the legislature determines which education programs will be funded.

Questions for Reflection

1. How do you feel about public education funds coming from a lottery system? What are the benefits and drawbacks of this kind of system?
2. Consider the most recent report of Education Appropriations funded by the Florida lottery. What are some areas funded by Florida's lottery money?
3. What surprises you about the use of lottery money?

Important Sources

Selecting Schools – A Florida Department of Education Resource
http://www.fldoe.org/eias/flmove/default.asp
"Parents who are moving to Florida or are moving to a new school district should spend some time researching the school district and schools their children will attend. Initially, parents should determine which characteristics of a school and school district are most important for meeting the needs of their children. For instance, parents may be interested in the academic performance of students at the school, test scores, programs for special needs of students, courses offered, teacher turnover rates, the availability of special resources, the size of the school population, the number of students per class, dropout rates, graduation rates, and other information. Parents may also want to know how the school is regarded by parents whose students attend the school and how the school is regarded in the community."

Florida Education Association
http://www.coe.ufl.edu/FEA/
This state affiliate of the National Education Association (NEA) dates back to 1886 with the formation of the first professional educators' organization in the state, later becoming known as the teachers' union.

The Code of Ethics and the Principles of Professional Conduct of the Education Profession in Florida
http://www.fldoe.org/asp/pdf/ethics.pdf
Subtitled "Professionalism through integrity," this document defines the State Board of Education Rule (6B-1.006 FAC) and outlines the professional obligations of educators, particularly to "a high moral standard." According to the Code developed by the Florida

Education Standards Commission, "The educator's primary professional concern will always be for the student and for the development of the student's potential."

American Civil Liberties Union of Florida
http://www.aclufl.org/issues/students/studentrightshandbook.cfm
This site is from the American Civil Liberties Union of Florida, and provides a link to a free downloadable copy of a student rights handbook entitled Know Your Rights: A Handbook for Public School Students in Florida.

Office of K–20 Budget Management
http://www.fldoe.org/budget/strategy.asp
Within the Florida Department of Education, the Office of K–20 Budget Management "provides for the development and use of strategic management information for the preparation of long and short-range plans, budgets for public schools, community colleges, colleges and universities, and related education activities."

Florida State Certification Exam Practice Questions

Directions: The following are 10 multiple-choice questions. Each question prompt is followed by 4 answer choices. Select the response that BEST answers the question.

Question #1
What is the most important reason for why a teacher should align learning standards and the curricular process before beginning instruction?

   (A)   Learning standards describe the manner in which learners will be assessed
   (B)   Learning standards prescribe specific activities for each content standard
   (C)   Learning standards design scope and sequence for the course curriculum
   (D)   Learning standards list the topics required by the curriculum

Question #2
Which of these would be an example of how student diversity affects motivational strategies?

   (A)   Classroom teachers have different criteria for success.
   (B)   Diverse students require different forms of praise and recognition.
   (C)   Classroom teachers give and receive criticism differently.
   (D)   Diverse students need individualized behavior management plans.

Question #3

Which of the following provisions is included in IDEA?

(A) Students may opt out of the tests.
(B) Student scores are calculated using different norms.
(C) Time limits for assessments are waved for the students.
(D) Accommodations may be provided to the students.

Question #4

Elementary school students want to use the computer to find images on the Internet to create a report on Florida history. Mrs. Keathley agrees and says that students will need to identify the Web site from which the images came. Which of these tasks best describes why the teacher requested this task of her students?

(A) It will allow others to find the Web sites the students used.
(B) It will encourage the need to cite references in work.
(C) It will create a resource for students to use in the future.
(D) It will allow the teacher to test Florida technology standards.

Question #5

Mr. Hartley, in preparing for parent-teacher conferences, reviewed the Florida ethical and legal requirements he is required to follow regarding grading. Which of the following would be inappropriate during meetings with students and their parents?

(A) Emphasizing final products over the learning process.
(B) Discussing grades of one student with another parent.
(C) Stating a student will get a poor grade if work doesn't improve.
(D) Evaluating students on teacher expectations for performance.

The following scenario should be used in answering questions #15, #16, and #17.

Ms. Cascade teaches Science to inclusive classes of eighth-grade students. Her typical class has 50% ESL students. One student in each class has an IEP and is reading below grade level. One student in each class is academically advanced and may be identified as gifted and talented. One student in her fifth-period class was retained due to an existing health problem.

Before the school year began, Ms. Cascade reflected on how the previous year went. She identified goals for this new school year:

- Focus on students' communication skills (both in writing and oral presentations).
- Encourage cooperative learning and teamwork through large and small group activities.
- Enhance students' reading and writing skills in content area of Science.

Question #6

One of the first assignments of the school year is to have students working in pairs. Ms. Cascade wants students to informally interview a classmate, share their interests in science, and then formally introduce their partners to the rest of the class. Which activity best meets her goals and her students' needs?

(A) Provide handouts with a sample interview and a introduction for all students to use as a guide.

(B) Give students a list of interview questions and tell students the type of information to present in the introductions.

(C) Allow students to talk amongst themselves about the assignment until all the directions are made clear.

(D) Present a rubric for completing the assignment, identifying how the interview and the introduction will be evaluated.

Question #7

Ms. Cascade wanted to assess her students' writing abilities at the beginning of the year. She asked students to write about where they traveled on their summer vacations. Tomas said he did not take a vacation, but played video games at home. Which response will most likely motivate Thomas to complete the lesson?

(A) Ask Thomas what task he would like to complete instead.

(B) Encourage Thomas to create a fictional vacation story.

(C) Tell Tomas to work with another student who took a vacation.

(D) Give Tomas alternative topics for writing the paper.

Question #8

"I don't know what is going on. I can't seem to follow your directions." Miguel told Ms. Cascade. Miguel was a student in her class that had an IEP, stating he should be able to write his own notes about the lecture or lesson. Puzzled, Ms. Cascade looked to see what additional scaffolding she could provide to assist Miguel.

Which of the following would be the best strategy to use?

(A) Have Miguel audio tape the lecture, reviewing the tape to ensure his notes are accurate.

(B) Give Miguel an outline of the lecture with blanks to insert his notes into the lecture.

(C) Have Miguel take notes during the lecture and have Ms. Cascade review them at the end of class.

(D) Give Miguel a seat near a student he likes so he can ask questions about the lecture.

Question #9

Teachers have been discussing the connection between peer pressure and negative responses to school. Identify the plan that will best negate the influence of peer pressure.

(A) Discuss the issue openly with the students.
(B) Encourage achievement among at-risk students.
(C) Allow students to role-play their feelings about school.
(D) Hold a parent-teacher conference with concerned parents.

Question #10

Mr. Tsung overhears two of his best students talking about the fact that they couldn't start their homework until 7 or 8 at night, due to chores and family obligations. Later that day, he receives a phone call from one of the student's parents, expressing concern about the balance between school and family responsibilities. What is the best way for Mr. Tsung to respond?

(A) Schedule an appointment with the parent to discuss family support and counseling options.
(B) Discuss options with the parent and student to balance school and home responsibilities.
(C) Assure the parent that steps will be taken at school to accommodate for this situation.
(D) Compare the amount of homework he requires to that assigned by other teachers.

ANSWER KEY

Question Number	Key
1	C
2	B
3	D
4	B
5	B
6	A
7	D
8	B
9	A
10	B

Today's Students

11

Today's Students

CLASSROOM CASE
The Realities of Teaching

THE CHALLENGE: Developing a classroom climate that encourages students to see themselves as one cohesive group rather than several small groups formed according to race.

It is the first day of school, and students are just now entering your classroom. There is a lot of talking, joking, and good-natured horseplay.

This year, you have set up your classroom for cooperative learning. Five octagonal tables are distributed evenly around the room. Students at each table will make up a team. Though students will work in teams, you plan to de-emphasize competition among the teams. Instead, you want the entire class to see itself, eventually, as one unified group.

As the students select tables at which to sit, you notice that they are clustering themselves into four distinct racial groups. The Anglo-European American students are seated at two tables; the African American, Latino, and Asian American students are seated, separately, at the remaining three tables.

"Welcome to my class," you begin. "We are going to have a great year together!"

The students gradually quiet down and give you their attention. You continue with a brief overview of what students will learn in your class that year. Following the overview, you ask each student to introduce himself or herself to the class.

As students introduce themselves, you are thinking about how students have obviously used race as a criterion for choosing a table at which to sit. Your preference is for students to choose work tables for the year. You realize that assigning tables might minimize the tendency of students to cluster by race, however, that would work against the democratic classroom climate you hope to create. Also, your hunch is that interaction among students would still reflect racial group membership, regardless of assigned seats.

You are well aware that during the next few days you will set the tone for the new school year. What can you do during that time to encourage students to interact as much as possible across racial groups? What can you do throughout the school year to encourage cohesiveness in your diverse classroom?

FOCUS QUESTIONS

1. How is diversity reflected in the culture of the United States?
2. What does equal educational opportunity mean?

281

3. What is meant by bilingual education?

4. What is multicultural education?

5. How is gender a dimension of multicultural education?

The opening classroom case illustrates how important it is for teachers to be aware of diversity in the classroom. As a teacher, you will need to communicate effectively with students from diverse populations and cultural backgrounds. You will have students from families that differ from the idealized traditional family. Some of your students may be from biracial families, adoptive families, stepfamilies, gay families, or immigrant families. "About half of today's children will spend some portion of childhood in a single-parent family, and more than a third will live with a stepparent. Over half of marriages end in divorce, and two-thirds of divorced women and three-quarters of divorced men will remarry" (Heilman, 2008, p. 9).

It would be impossible to develop a different curriculum for each group of students in your multicultural classroom—that would place undue emphasis on differences among students. Instead, you can develop a curriculum that affirms each student's culture and increases their awareness and appreciation of the rich diversity in U.S. culture.

This chapter looks at cultural diversity in the United States and the challenges of equalizing educational opportunity for all students. A goal for your professional development as a teacher, then, is to see cultural diversity as an asset to be preserved and valued, not a liability. The United States has always derived strength from the diversity of its people, and all students should receive a high-quality education so that they may make their unique contributions to society.

HOW IS DIVERSITY REFLECTED IN THE CULTURE OF THE UNITED STATES?

The percentage of ethnic minorities in the United States has been growing steadily since the end of World War II. As Figure 8.1 shows, 37.9 million immigrants lived in the United States in 2007. According to the Center for Immigration Studies (2007), immigrants account for one in eight U.S. residents, and between 1.5 and 1.6 million immigrants arrive in the United States each year. The Center (2007) describes the challenge of providing equal educational opportunity to the growing U.S. immigrant population:

> Immigrants and their young children (under 18) now account for one-fifth of the school-age population, one-fourth of those in poverty, and nearly one-third of those without health insurance, creating enormous challenges for the nation's schools. . . . The low educational attainment of many immigrants, 31 percent of whom have not completed high school, is the primary reason so many live in poverty, use welfare programs, or lack health insurance, not their legal status or an unwillingness to work.

In addition, the Census Bureau estimates that by 2025, half of U.S. youth will be white and half minority, and by 2050, no single group will be a majority among adults.

Increasing diversity in the United States is reflected, of course, in the nation's schools. In 2007, 41.3 percent of public school students were considered to be part of a minority group, an increase of more than 19 percentage points from 1972 (National Center for Education Statistics, September 2007). This increase was largely due to the growth in the proportion of Latino students. In 2007, Latino students accounted for 19.2 percent of the public school enrollment, up by more than 13 percentage points from 1972. African Americans were 17.3 percent of the public school enrollment in 2007, up

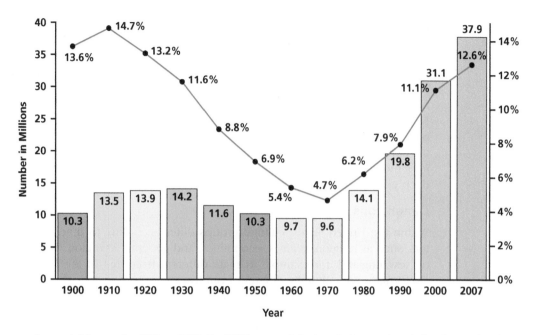

Decennial Census for 1900 to 2000. For 2007 we used the March Current Population Survey (CPS), which does not include those in group quarters. The 600,000 immigrants in group quarters have been added to the 2007 CPS to make it comparable with the historic censuses.

FIGURE 8.1 Immigrants in the United States: Number and percentage, 1990–2007

Source: Center for Immigration Studies. (2007). Immigrants in the United States, 2007: A Profile of America's Foreign-Born Population. *Washington, DC: Author. Retrieved on June 8, 2008, from http://www.cis.org/articles/2007/back1007.html#author.*

by more than 2 percentage points from 1972. The percentage of students from other racial and ethnic minority groups also increased, from 1 percent in 1972 to 5.7 percent in 2007 (National Center for Education Statistics, September 2007).

Changes in the racial and ethnic composition of student enrollments are expanding the array of languages and cultures found in the nation's public schools. Differences in student backgrounds offer opportunities to enhance the learning environment; however, these differences also raise challenges for schools. For example, there is an increased demand for bilingual programs and teachers in many parts of the country. All but a few school districts face a critical shortage of minority teachers. And there is a need to develop curricula and strategies that address the needs and backgrounds of all students—regardless of their social class; gender; sexual orientation; or ethnic, racial, or cultural identity.

The Meaning of Culture

One mission of schools is to maintain the culture of the United States. But what is the U.S. culture? Is there a single culture to which everyone in the country belongs? Before answering that question, we must define the term *culture.* Simply put,

Today's classrooms are becoming increasingly diverse. What knowledge and skills will help to meet the learning needs of students from racial/ethnic, cultural, and linguistic backgrounds that are different from yours?

283

culture is the way of life common to a group of people. It consists of the values, attitudes, and beliefs that influence their traditions and behavior. It is also a way of interacting with and looking at the world. At one time, it was believed that the United States was like a melting pot in which ethnic cultures would melt into one; however, ethnic and cultural differences have remained very much a part of life in the United States. A salad-bowl analogy captures more accurately the **cultural pluralism** of U.S. society. That is, the distinguishing characteristics of cultures are to be preserved rather than blended into a single culture. Or, as one columnist observed regarding the continuing increase in people of mixed race identity in the United States: "America's melting pot isn't going to create a bland, homogenous porridge so much as a deeply flavored, spicy stew" (Stuckey, May 28, 2008).

Dimensions of Culture

Within the United States, cultural groups differ according to other distinguishing factors, such as religion, politics, economics, and geographic region. The regional culture of New England, for example, is quite different from that of the Southeast. Similarly, Californians are culturally different from Iowans.

However, everyone in the United States does share some common dimensions of culture. James Banks, an authority on multicultural education, has termed this shared culture the "national macroculture" (2008). In addition to being members of the national macroculture, people in the United States are members of ethnic groups. An **ethnic group** is made up of individuals within a larger culture who share a self-defined racial or cultural identity and a set of beliefs, attitudes, and values. Members of an ethnic group distinguish themselves from others in the society by physical and social attributes. You should be aware also that the composition of ethnic groups can change over time, and that there is often as much variability within groups as between them.

Cultural Identity

In addition to membership in the national macroculture, each individual participates in an array of subcultures, each with its customs and beliefs. Collectively, these subcultures determine an individual's **cultural identity,** an overall sense of who one is. Other possible elements that might shape a person's cultural identity include age, racial identity, exceptionalities, language, gender, sexual orientation, income level, and beliefs and values. The importance of these elements differs among people. For some, their cultural identity is most strongly determined by their occupations; for others, it is determined by their ethnicity; and for others, by their religious beliefs.

Remember that your future students will have their own complex cultural identities, which are no less valid for being different. For some of them, these identities may make them feel disconnected from the attitudes, expectations, and values conveyed by the school. You will be challenged as a teacher to understand the subtle differences in cultural identities among your students. You will need to create a learning environment that enables all students to feel connected to their school experiences.

Some of your students may have cultural backgrounds that are individualistic, while the backgrounds of others may be collectivistic. **Individualistic cultures** tend to emphasize the individual and his or her success and achievement. **Collectivistic cultures,** on the other hand, tend to emphasize group membership and a sense of "we," rather than "I" (Greenfield, 1994; Hofstede, 2001; Rothstein-Fisch & Trumbull, 2008; Triandis, 1989). "While self-realization is the ideal with many individualistic cultures, in the collectivist model, individuals must fit into the group, and group realization is the ideal" (Waltman & Bush-Bacelis, 1995, pp. 66–67). Figure 8.2 presents a comparison of individualistic and collectivistic cultures that can be helpful in understanding how students from different cultural backgrounds view life in classrooms. Remember, though, that everyone has values and points of view that are both individualistic and collectivistic. The two types of cultures represent "general tendencies that may emerge when the members of . . . [a] culture are considered as a whole" (Markus & Kitayama, 1991, p. 225).

Individualist Cultures	Collectivistic Cultures
(*United States, Canada, Western Europe, Australia*)	(*Many Asian, African, and South American Cultures*)
Individual uniqueness, self-determination	Loyalty to group and family
Independence, self-reliance, and individual achievement	Interdependence, cooperation, and group success
Self-expression	Adherence to group norms
Individual choice	Group consensus
Equality of relationships	Hierarchical relationships
Task orientation	Group orientation
Individual well-being	Group well-being
Self-esteem	Modesty

FIGURE 8.2 Individualistic and collectivistic cultures: A comparison

Language and Culture

Culture is embedded in language, a fact that has resulted in conflict among different groups in our society. Some groups support the preservation of ethnic cultures, yet they believe that members of non-English-speaking groups must learn English if they are to function in U.S. society. Those who wish to preserve linguistic diversity are also in conflict with those who wish to establish English as a national language.

Much of the debate has focused on **bilingual education**—using two languages as the medium of instruction. Bilingual education is designed to help students maintain their ethnic identity and become proficient in both English and the language of the home, to encourage assimilation into the mainstream culture and integrate the home language and culture with a new one. Some people are strongly opposed to any form of bilingual education, and others support it as a short-term way to teach English to students.

Clearly, language diversity is an important dimension of U.S. cultural diversity. Many students come from homes where English is not spoken. About 5.1 million **limited English proficient (LEP)** students attended public schools in 2005–06, or about 9.7 percent of the total enrollment (National Clearinghouse for English Language Acquisition, 2008). LEP students have limited ability to understand, read, or speak English, and they have a first language other than English. The number of LEP students increased by more than 57 percent between 1995–96 and 2005–06 (National Clearinghouse for English Language Acquisition, 2008). Among the states, California has the most public school LEP students (24.9 percent), followed by Arizona (16 percent), Texas (15.7 percent), Florida (8.3 percent), and New York (6.9 percent) (National Center for Education Statistics, October 2006). States report over 400 languages spoken by LEP students nationwide, with 76 percent claiming Spanish as their native language. Although certain areas of the country report particularly high numbers of LEP students, Figure 8.3 indicates that the continued increase in the number of LEP students is being felt throughout the United States. The Technology in Action feature in this chapter explains how one teacher uses a text-to-speech (TTS) program to teach her LEP students.

Students' language patterns became a topic of national debate in late 1996 when the Oakland, California, school district passed a resolution on ebonics (a blend of the words *ebony* and *phonics*), also known as black English. The resolution, which recognized ebonics as the primary language of many of the district's 28,000 African American students, called for them to be taught in their primary language and suggested that some students might be eligible for state and federal bilingual education or ESL money.

Critics of the resolution pointed out that black English is a nonstandard form of English or a dialect of English—not a foreign language. Other critics were concerned that students and teachers would be taught ebonics. In the midst of intense national debate, the district revised the resolution so that it no longer called for students to be taught in their primary language (or dialect of English). Instead, the district would implement new programs to move students from the language patterns they bring to school toward proficiency in standard English. Other dialects of English and their use

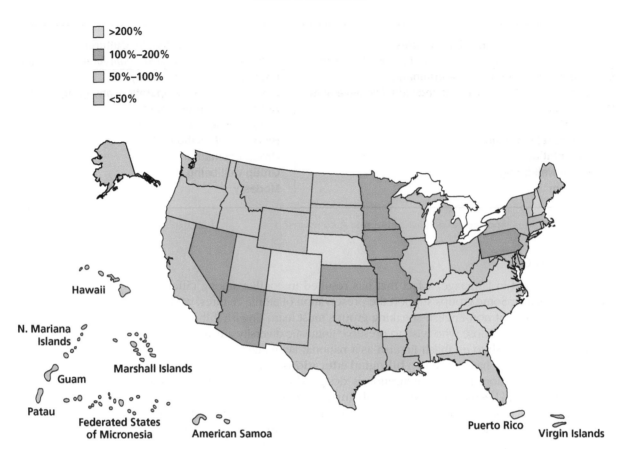

FIGURE 8.3 The growing number of limited English proficient (LEP) students, 1995–2006

Source: National Clearinghouse for English Language Acquisition. (2008). The growing numbers of limited English proficient students: 1995/96–2005/06. Washington, DC: Author. Retrieved from http://www.ncela.gwu.edu/policy/states/reports/statedata/200rLEP/GrowingLEP_0506.pdf.

in the classroom have been debated from time to time—for example, Chicano English, Cajun English, or Hawaiian Creole English (more popularly known as pidgin English).

The Concept of Multiculturalism

Multiculturalism stresses the importance of seeing the world from different cultural frames of reference, and recognizing and valuing the rich array of cultures within a nation and within the global community. **Multiculturalism** affirms the need to create schools where differences related to race, ethnicity, gender, sexual orientation, disability, and social class are acknowledged and all students are viewed as valuable resources for enriching the teaching–learning process. Furthermore, a central purpose of multiculturalism is to prepare students to live in a culturally pluralistic world. This worldview "contrasts sharply with cultural assimilation, or 'melting pot' images, where ethnic minorities are expected to give up their traditions and blend in or be absorbed by the mainstream society or predominant culture" (Bennett, 2007, p. 4).

For teachers, multiculturalism also means actively seeking out experiences within other cultures that lead to increased understanding of and appreciation for those ways of life. To provide such cross-cultural experiences for their students, some teacher education programs have developed cultural immersion experiences that enable prospective teachers to live in their students' neighborhoods and communities while student teaching. The University of Alaska-Fairbanks Future Teachers of Alaska Program, for example, enables students to live in remote Alaskan Native villages during their year-long student teaching experience. Students at Indiana University can participate in the Cultural Immersion Projects program, including an Overseas Practicum and the Native American Reservation Project. Through student teaching on a reservation, in another country, or on the Rio Grande border, students have a life-altering cultural immersion experience. As Marisa

TECHNOLOGY in *ACTION*

Using Text-to-Speech in a Third-Grade Reading Class

Mrs. Kelly teaches English as a Second Language at Wilson Elementary. Although she understands the importance of one-on-one instruction in any classroom, she found that the English proficiency of her students in her ESL classes was so diverse it was impossible to sit with individual students for any extended period of time. She would have preferred to work individually with each student, helping him or her pronounce each word, reading along with the student and helping when he or she encountered a word they did not understand. The problem with this approach was the time required to instruct each student—there were only so many hours in a day.

Mrs. Kelly knew that it was important for her ESL students to hear the words they were reading. She would stand at the front of her classroom and read to the students as they followed along in their copy of the book. The problem was that each student was at a different level of English proficiency. If students did speak up when they had difficulty (which was rare due to the large class setting), she found that the more proficient speakers were impatient as she worked to instruct the student who was having difficulty.

To solve this problem, Mrs. Kelly introduced a text-to-speech (TTS) program in her class. (TTS uses a synthesized computer voice to read text on a computer screen or in an electronic file.) Students now sit at the computer and read along with the TTS program as it highlights the text that is being spoken. With this program, students can select an appealing voice: male or female, older or younger, softer or more authoritative.

Mrs. Kelly finds that the text-to-speech program provides the individual instruction that her students need, and it has improved their reading ability, vocabulary retention, and pronunciation. For example, when she listens to her students read, she identifies words that are difficult for a particular student to pronounce, and she writes a list of these words for each student. The student then plugs those words into the TTS program and listens to the correct pronunciation of the word. Each student can listen to the word as many times as needed. Her students see the TTS program as a second teacher and now identify difficult pronunciations before they read for Mrs. Kelly.

TEXT-TO-SPEECH: Text-to-speech is the process of converting electronic text to digital audio. The TTS program reads the text and then speaks the words for the listener. There are two approaches for converting text to speech. The first is user-directed, the other is author-directed. The user-directed application requires that the user of TTS identify the text to be converted. This can be done by highlighting the identified text or uploading an electronic file of the text to the TTS program. The author-directed application requires the author of the website, videogame, or text file to identify the text to be spoken. Several text-to-speech programs are available today. The most popular programs present a realistic human voice.

VISIT: http://www.naturalreaders.com/. The NaturalReaders website allows users to download a free version of its TTS software and view an applications demonstration.

POSSIBLE USES: Teachers have used text-to-speech programs to proofread student writing, listen to term papers on their iPod during their commute to and from work, help students with reading or vision difficulties, create e-books for their students, and improve English as a second language instruction.

TRY IT OUT: Three of the most popular text-to-speech products are NeoSpeech, TextAloud, and NaturalReader. All of these products have demonstrations on their websites. For example, the NaturalReader website allows users to click on an application demonstration that presents TTS in e-mail, PDF, Word, and a Web browser. Although there are several variation of TTS, a visit to most TTS websites will provide a good introduction to text-to-speech.

■ ■ ■ ■ ■ ■ ■ ■ ■

Churchill, a Native American Reservation Project participant and student teacher at a school on the Navajo Indian Reservation in Pinon, Arizona, put it: "The thing I love most about being on the reservation is the students. They're so fun, and they love coming and hanging out and learning, and they're just fun to talk to. They teach you so much about their culture and living out on the reservation, and just their perspective on life is a lot different" (Indiana University, March 14, 2008). Churchill stayed on as a teacher at the school after her student-teaching assignment ended.

PEARSON
myeducationlab

Go to MyEducationLab, select Chapter 8 and then Activities and Applications to watch the video Ethnic Diversity.

Ethnicity and Race

Understanding the distinction between ethnicity and race will enable you to provide students with educational experiences that reflect ethnic and racial diversity in meaningful ways. **Ethnicity** refers to a "shared sense of peoplehood, culture, identity, and shared language and dialects." (Banks, 2009, p. 16). To further consider the meaning of ethnicity, go to MyEducationLab and watch a video that examines ethnic identity.

On the other hand, **race** is a subjective concept that is used to distinguish among human beings on the basis of biological traits. However, anthropologists "reject the concept of race as a scientifically valid biological category and . . . argue instead that 'race' is a socially constructed category" (Mukhopadhyay & Henze, 2003, p. 670).

Numerous racial categories have been proposed, but because of the diversity among humans and the mixing of genes that has taken place over time, no single set of racial categories is universally accepted. Because many genetic factors are invisible to the naked eye (DNA, for example), noted anthropologist Ashley Montagu has suggested that there could be as few as three "races" (Negroid, Caucasoid, and Mongoloid) or as many as 300, depending on the kind and number of genetic features chosen for measurement. In his classic book, *Man's Most Dangerous Myth: The Fallacy of Race*, Montagu pointed out:

> It is impossible to make the sort of racial classification which some anthropologists and others have attempted. The fact is that all human beings are so . . . mixed with regard to origin that between different groups of individuals . . . "overlapping" of physical traits is the rule. (1974, p. 7)

Mixed-Race Identity

To reflect the realities of racial identities in the United States, the questionnaire for Census 2000 was changed so that people with a mixed-race background could select "one or more races" for their racial identity. In addition, the "Spanish/Hispanic/Latino" category allowed respondents to choose among the following: Mexican, Mexican American, and Chicano; Puerto Rican; Cuban; and "other" Spanish/Hispanic/Latino. Similarly, respondents who self-identified as "Asian or Pacific Islander" had the following choices: Asian Indian, Chinese, Filipino, Japanese, Korean, Vietnamese, "other" Asian, Native Hawaiian, Guamanian or Chamorro, Samoan, and "other" Pacific Islander.

The 2000 Census counted 3.1 million interracial couples, or about 6 percent of married couples. About 7.3 million Americans, or 3 percent of the population, identified themselves as being two or more races. Forty-one percent of the mixed-race population was under age 18 (Navarro, March 31, 2008). It is estimated that the number of multiracial Americans is increasing at 10 times the rate of the white population (Stuckey, May 28, 2008). For people of mixed race, decisions about how to identify themselves are influenced by how and where they were raised, how others perceive them, what they look like, and the cultural identity with which they most strongly identify.

People with a mixed-race identity received more attention when Senator Barack Obama, who has a white mother from Kansas and a black father from Kenya, was selected by the Democratic Party to be its candidate for the 2008 presidential election. As an educator who identifies herself as African American, American Indian, and white said, "I think Barack Obama [brought] these deeply American stories to the forefront. Maybe we'll get a little bit further in the dialogue on race" (Navarro, March 31, 2008).

It is also clear that racial and ethnic identities in the United States are becoming more complex. We now know that "racial and ethnic identities derive their meanings from social and historical circumstances, that they can vary over time, and that they can sometimes even be slipped on and off like a change of clothing" (Coughlin, 1993). For example, a third-generation descendent of a Japanese immigrant may choose to refer to himself or herself as a Japanese American, an American, or an Asian American. Furthermore, it is evident that "specific racial categories acquire and lose meaning over time" (Coughlin, 1993), and the use of ethnic and racial labels and expressions of group membership is largely self-selected and arbitrary.

There are many ethnic groups in U.S. society, and everyone belongs to at least one. However, as James Banks points out:

> An individual is ethnic to the extent that he or she shares the values, behavioral patterns, cultural traits, and identification with a specific ethnic group. Many individuals have multiple ethnic attachments; others consider themselves "American" rather than ethnic. An individual's identity with his or her ethnic group varies significantly with the period of life, economic and social status, and situations or settings. (2009, p. 16)

The Concept of Minorities

To understand the important concept of **minorities,** it may help to remember that even though the term *minority* technically refers to any group numbering less than half of the total population, in certain parts of the country "minorities" are actually the majority. More important than the numbers themselves, however, is an appreciation of how many groups of people have continuously struggled to obtain full educational, economic, political, and social opportunities in society. Along with minority racial and ethnic groups, others who have traditionally lacked power in U.S. public life are immigrants; the poor; children and the elderly; non-English speakers; members of minority religions; women; and people who are gay, lesbian, bisexual, or transgender. Groups who have been most frequently discriminated against in terms of the quality of education they have received include African Americans, Spanish-speaking Americans, Native Americans, Asian Americans, exceptional learners, people with disabilities, and females. There is mounting evidence that many students from these groups continue to receive a substandard education that does not meet their needs or empower them to participate fully and equally in life in the United States.

Minority Groups and Academic Achievement

Minority-group students are disproportionately represented among students who have failed to master minimum competencies in reading, writing, and mathematics. It has been estimated that ethnic minority students are two to four times more likely than others to drop out of high school. In addition, "in many schools across the nation, racial and language minority students are over-represented in special education and experience disproportionately high rates of suspension and expulsion" (Bennett, 2003, p. 18).

From 1999 to 2005, the number of students taking advanced placement (AP) exams increased by a larger percentage among minority students than among White students (National Center for Education Statistics, September 2007). In addition, the number of minority students who complete high school and continue their education in college continues to increase. Despite these gains, progress is uneven, and an **achievement gap** exists between White students and Hispanic, Black, and American Indian/Alaska Native students on many measures of educational achievement. For example, on the 2005 National Assessment of Educational Progress (NAEP) reading assessment, higher percentages of Asian/Pacific Islander and White fourth-graders and eighth-graders scored at or above "Proficient" than did American Indian/Alaska Native, Black, and Hispanic students at the same grade levels (National Center for Education Statistics, September 2007).

When we consider the lower achievement levels of minority students, it is important to note the much higher incidence of poverty among minority families and the research showing that socioeconomic status—not race, language, or culture—contributes most strongly to students' achievement in school (Coleman et al., 1966; Jencks et al., 1972; Jencks & Phillips 1998; National Center for Education Statistics, 1980). It is understandably difficult for poor children to learn well if they endure the stress of living in crime-ridden neighborhoods, dwelling in dilapidated homes, or going to school hungry.

Stereotyping and Racism

While teachers should expand their knowledge of and appreciation for the diverse cultural backgrounds of their students, they should also guard against forming stereotypes or overgeneralizations about those cultures. **Stereotyping** is the process of attributing behavioral characteristics to all members of a group. In some cases, stereotypes are formed on the basis of limited experiences with and information about the group being stereotyped, and the validity of these stereotypes is not questioned.

Within any cultural group that shares a broad cultural heritage, however, considerable diversity exists. For example, two Puerto Rican children who live in the same community and attend the same school may appear alike to their teachers when, in reality, they are very different. One may come from a home where Spanish is spoken and Puerto Rican holidays are observed; the other child may know only a few words of Spanish and observe only the holidays of the majority culture.

In addition to being alert for stereotypes they and others may hold, teachers should learn to recognize **individual racism,** the prejudicial belief that one's ethnic or racial group is superior to others. An obvious feature of racism in the United States "is that many whites see themselves as better than persons and groups of color, and as a result exercise their power to prevent people of color from securing the prestige, power, and privilege held by them" (Gollnick & Chinn, 2009, p. 63). Teachers should also be able to recognize **institutional racism,** which occurs when institutions "behave in ways that are overtly racist (i.e., specifically excluding people-of-color from services) or inherently racist (i.e., adopting policies that while not specifically directed at excluding people-of-color, nevertheless result in their exclusion)" (Randall, 2001).

In light of the arbitrariness of the concept of race, James A. Banks points out, "In most societies, *the social significance of race is much more important than the presumed physical differences among groups*" (2009, p. 71, italics in original). Unfortunately, many people attach great importance to the concept of race. If you believe "that human groups can be validly grouped on the basis of their biological traits and that these identifiable groups inherit certain mental, personality, and cultural characteristics that determine their behavior" (Banks, 2009, p. 72) then you hold racist beliefs. When people use such beliefs as a rationale for oppressing other groups, they are practicing racism.

As a teacher, you will not be able to eliminate stereotypic thinking or racism in society. However, you have an obligation to all your students to see that your curriculum and instruction are free of any forms of stereotyping or racism. You need to assess your own cultural attitudes and values and determine whether you have stereotypes about other cultural groups.

Class and Socioeconomic Status

"One of the most critical issues that educators routinely face is that of social class and poverty" (Gollnick & Chinn, 2009, p. 339). About 18 percent of children in the United States today live in poverty (Cauthen & Fass, 2007). Nearly 13 million children live in families with incomes below the federal poverty level—$21,200 a year for a family of four (National Center for Children in Poverty, 2008). It is generally acknowledged, however, that families need an income about twice the federal poverty level to make ends meet. Families with incomes at this level are referred to as *low income.* Thirty-nine percent of children, about 28 million, in the United States, live in low-income families (National Center for Children in Poverty, 2008).

The percentage of children living at or below the federal poverty level varies greatly from state to state. As Figure 8.4 shows, child poverty ranges from 6 percent in New Hampshire to 29 percent in Mississippi. The percentage of children in poverty also varies greatly by race/ethnicity. For example, the left-hand side of Figure 8.5 shows that 40 percent of American Indian children live in poverty, while 10 percent of White children live in poverty. However, the right-hand side of the figure shows that White children comprise the largest group of poor children in the United States.

Teachers in inner-city schools or schools in poor rural communities may find that nearly all their students are from families who live in poverty. For children, poverty can contribute to depression, lower levels of sociability and/or initiative, problematic peer

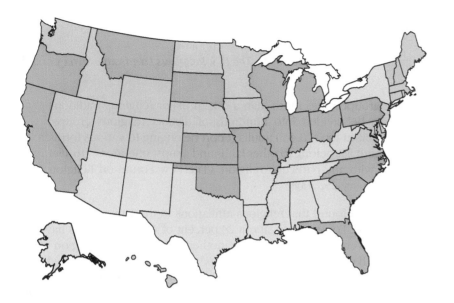

FIGURE 8.4 Child poverty rates across the states and the District of Columbia, 2006
Source: Sarah Fass and Nancy K. Gauthen, Who Are America's Poor Children? The Official Story, November 2007, National Center for Children in Poverty. New York: Columbia University—Mailman School of Public Health, p. 2.

- 20% or more (13 states): AL, AR, AZ, DC, GA, KY, LA, MS, NM, NY, TN, TX, WV
- 15–19% (17 states): CA, FL, IL, IN, KS, MI, MO, MT, NC, OH, OK, OR, PA, RI, SC, SD, WI
- 10–14% (19 states): AK, CO, CT, DE, HI, ID, IA, ME, MD, MA, MN, NE, NV, NJ, ND, UT, VA, WA, WY
- Under 10% (2 states): NH, VT

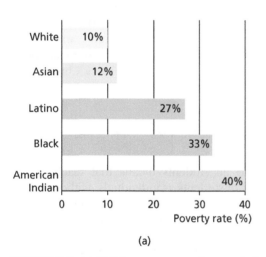

(a)

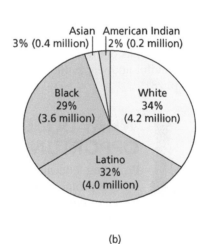

(b)

FIGURE 8.5 (a) Child poverty rates by race/ethnicity, 2006; (b) poor children by race/ethnicity, 2006

Source: Sarah Fass and Nancy K. Cauthen, Who Are America's Poor Children? The Official Story, November 2007. National Center for Children in Poverty. New York: Columbia University—Mailman School of Public Health, p. 2.

relations, and disruptive classroom behavior (Eamon, July 2001). Poverty can impede children's ability to learn and contribute to social, emotional, and behavioral problems.

A classic book by Michael Harrington (1962), *The Other America: Poverty in the United States*, suggested that there is a *culture of poverty*. Harrington's book encouraged Presidents Kennedy and Johnson to launch the War on Poverty. According to Harrington, this culture of poverty tends to be passed from generation to generation. As a result, it becomes increasingly difficult for children from poor families to receive an adequate education. "Poverty is passed on from generation to generation because of the increasing difficulty for children of the poor to receive adequate education and job training" (Spring, 2008b, p. 405).

Religious Pluralism

Today's schools are religiously pluralistic. As *The U.S. Religious Landscape Survey* noted, the U.S. population

> can be usefully grouped into more than a dozen major religious traditions that, in turn, can be divided into hundreds of distinct religious groups. Overall, nearly eight-in-ten (78.4%) adults report belonging to various forms of Christianity, about 5% belong to other faiths and almost one-in-six (16.1%) are not affiliated with any particular religion. (The Pew Forum on Religion & Public Life, February 25, 2008)

The *Landscape Survey* also found that religious affiliations in the United States are not only diverse, they are fluid. For example, about 28 percent of American adults have left the faith in which they were raised in favor of another religion, or no religion at all. The survey also found that the number of people who say they are unaffiliated with any particular faith today (16.1%) is more than double the number who say they were not affiliated with any particular religion as children. The survey also found that the United States "is on the verge of becoming a minority Protestant country." Barely 51 percent of Americans report that they are members of Protestant denominations. Figure 8.6 illustrates the religious diversity, by race, in the United States.

Different religious groups in America can have different expectations of the schools. Depending on the religious makeup of a local community, areas such as the following can emerge as points of conflict between the community and the school: sex education, teaching of evolution and/or intelligent design, and liberal points of view in textbooks. In a religiously pluralistic society such as the United States, "educators would do well to inform themselves of the religious groups in their community and in their school. In doing so, they greatly enhance their ability to function in the classroom, mindful and respectful of the religious rights of all students" (Gollnick & Chinn, 2009, p. 281).

WHAT DOES EQUAL EDUCATIONAL OPPORTUNITY MEAN?

Providing educational opportunity to all students means that teachers and schools promote the full development of students as individuals, without regard for race, ethnicity, gender, sexual orientation, socioeconomic status, religion, abilities, or disabilities. More specifically, educators fulfill this important mission by continually evaluating the appropriateness of the curricular and instructional experiences they provide to each student. The Teachers' Voices: Research to Reality feature in this chapter, by first-year teacher Chrysta Bakstad, describes how an inquiry group of teachers at her school accomplished that mission.

The following sections review the progress that has been made to provide students from diverse groups with equal educational opportunity and present strategies for teaching in diverse classrooms. Strategies for each group draw from research that suggests that particular learning styles may be associated with specific ethnic groups in U.S. society (Bennett, 2007; Hale-Benson, 1986; Shade, 1982). These strategies should not lead you to assume, however, that all students from a certain group learn in a particular way. As Christine I. Bennett, an expert on multicultural education, points out:

> The notion that certain learning styles are associated with different ethnic groups is both promising and dangerous. Promise lies in the realization that low academic achievement among some ethnic minorities may sometimes be attributed to conflicts between styles of teaching and learning, not low intelligence. This leads to the possibility that teachers will alter their own instructional styles to be more responsive to the learning needs of students. Danger lies in the possibility that new ethnic stereotypes will develop while

	Non-Hispanic				Latino	Number
	White	Black	Asian	Other/Mixed		
	%	%	%	%	%	
Total population	71	11	3	3	12	35,101,000
Total Protestants	74	16	1	3	5	18,753,000
Members of evangelical Protestant churches	81	6	2	4	7	9,380,000
Members of mainline Protestant churches	91	2	1	3	3	7,383,000
Members of historically Black Protestant churches	2	92	0	1	4	1,990,000
Catholic	65	2	2	2	29	7,987,000
Mormon	86	3	1	3	7	571,000
Church of Jesus Christ of Latter-day Saints	87	2	1	3	7	547,000
Jehovah's Witness	48	22	0	5	24	212,000
Orthodox	87	6	2	3	1	358,000
Greek Orthodox	95	3	0	1	2	167,000
Other Christian	77	11	0	8	4	126,000
Jewish	95	1	0	2	3	671,000
Reform	95	0	1	1	3	309,000
Conservative	96	1	0	1	2	218,000
Muslim*	37	24	20	15	4	1,030,000
Buddhist	53	4	32	5	6	405,000
Hindu	5	1	88	4	2	255,000
Other faiths	80	2	1	13	5	436,000
Unitarian and other liberal faiths	88	2	2	5	4	291,000
New Age	84	1	0	10	5	113,000
Unaffiliated	73	8	4	4	11	4,955,000
Atheist	86	3	4	2	5	499,000
Agnostic	84	2	4	4	6	817,000
Secular, unaffiliated	79	5	4	4	8	1,971,000
Religious, unaffiliated	60	16	2	5	17	1,668,000

*From "Muslim Americans: Middle Class and Mostly Mainstream," Pew Research Center, 2007
Due to rounding, rows may not add to 100.
Question: Are you, yourself, of Hispanic origin or descent, such as Mexican, Puerto Rican, Cuban, or some other Spanish background? [IF HISPANIC ASK:] Are you white Hispanic, black Hispanic, or some other race? [IF NON-HISPANIC ASK:] What is your race? Are you white, black, Asian, or some other?

FIGURE 8.6 Religious diversity and race in the United States
Source: The Pew Forum on Religion & Public Life. (February 25, 2008). The U.S. Religious Landscape Survey. Washington, DC.: Author, p. 44.

old ones are reinforced, as in "Blacks learn aurally," "Asians excel in math," "Mexican American males can't learn from female peer tutors," and "Navajos won't ask a question or participate in a discussion." (2007, p. 69)

Anglo-European Americans are omitted from our review, not because students from this very diverse group have always had equal educational opportunities but because this group represents the historically dominant culture. To a great extent, it has determined the curricular and instructional practices found in schools.

TEACHERS' VOICES RESEARCH TO REALITY

Chrysta Bakstad
EQUAL EDUCATIONAL OPPORTUNITY FOR ALL STUDENTS

Participating in an "inquiry group" has provided an opportunity for me to reflect with other staff members. I am part of the "Wednesday Inquiry Group" that meets every other Wednesday, from 12:15 P.M. until 3:00 P.M. During this time an "Inquiry Sub," trained in the arts, teaches my class. My group consists of seven teachers, the school nurse, and a site coordinator The teachers involved represent all grade levels, kindergarten through fifth, and special education and bilingual teachers. The teaching experience of group members ranges from first-year teacher to those who have taught over ten years. The site coordinator is an "external critical friend" to the school who participates in all three inquiry group sessions and serves as the facilitator for the group.

Inquiry has allowed me to reflect on my teaching practices with a group of teachers with whom I typically would not have the opportunity to sit and talk. Topics of discussion centered around our school's two "essential questions": (1) "What can I do to ensure that the inequitable pattern of student achievement no longer exists?" and (2) "What can I do to ensure that there is student and parent voice in my classroom?" Still, the topics of discussion are extremely diverse: racial and ethnic issues, creating and sustaining a learning community, critical pedagogy, teaching tolerance, discipline, the school structure, parent involvement, and teaching "growth and development." The group also reads and discusses professional articles and books and agrees to take action as a result of these discussions. For example, at one meeting we agreed to pay attention to how we used "choice" in the classroom. At another meeting, we agreed to pay attention to how we call on students in class. After every

agreement [on what the group will observe] we report back our findings at the following meeting. The results create a new springboard for discussion.

As the youngest member of the group, I am in no way made to feel like I am the least experienced. My opinions and viewpoints are listened to and validated. I feel safe expressing my views, even if I think that they will not be embraced by all of the members of the group. Because this is my first year in the school community as a credentialed teacher, inquiry is a good place for me to express my opinions. I am much more comfortable talking in small, intimate settings. This experience has given me an opportunity in a safe setting to reflect and find my "voice."

When I contribute to my inquiry group, I bring with me the experiences of my recent courses saturated in theory. This theoretical grounding has positively influenced my development as a reflective professional because I am able to approach and evaluate my classroom practice from a multitude of perspectives. I have had the opportunity to share books, articles, and my research papers with the group. The positive reaction and interest expressed in my contributions have enhanced my comfort and feeling of inclusion.

PERSONAL REFLECTION

1. When you think about the diverse students whom you will teach, what are your concerns?
2. What knowledge and abilities do you now have that will enable you to meet the learning needs of diverse students in your classroom?
3. What additional knowledge and abilities do you plan to develop? How will you develop those?

Chrysta Bakstad is a first-year teacher, kindergarten and grades 1 and 2. She contributed the preceding to *Teaching to Change the World*, 3rd Edition, by Jeannie Oakes and Martin Lipton. Boston: McGraw-Hill, 2007, pp. 372–373.

Like the groups we discuss, however, "Anglo-European American" is not a single, monolithic culture. Americans whose ethnic heritage is English, Polish, German, Italian, Irish, Slovakian, Russian, or Swedish, for example, often differ greatly in religious and political traditions, beliefs, and values. Their individual ethnic identity may or may not be strengthened by recent immigrants from their country of origin. European ethnics have nevertheless assimilated into the mainstream U.S. society more completely than others.

Education and African Americans

Of the more than 301 million persons living in the United States, nearly 39 million are African Americans (U.S. Census Bureau, 2007 Population Estimates). According to U.S. Census Bureau projections, the African American population in the United States is expected to increase to 61.4 million (14.6 percent of the total) in 2050. The incidence of social problems such as unemployment, crime, drug abuse, poverty, inadequate housing, and dropping out of school is proportionally greater for African Americans than for Whites. The struggle of African Americans to improve their quality of life after the end of slavery has been hampered for generations by persistent racism, discrimination, poverty, crime, unemployment, and underemployment.

The civil rights movement of the 1960s and 1970s made it clear that African Americans had been denied full access to many aspects of U.S. life, including the right to a good education. A 1976 report by the United States Commission on Civil Rights, for example, revealed that a southern school district in the 1930s spent nearly 18 times as much for the education of White pupils as it did for the education of African Americans.

The Desegregation Era

Perhaps the most blatant form of discrimination against African Americans has been school segregation and unequal educational opportunity. As you may have learned, an attempt was made to justify segregation with the idea of separate but equal schools. It was not until the National Association for the Advancement of Colored People (NAACP) brought suit on behalf of a Kansas family (*Brown v. Board of Education of Topeka, Kansas*) in 1954 that the concept of separate but equal schools was decidedly struck down.

The parents of Linda Brown felt that the education their fourth-grader was receiving in the segregated Topeka schools was inferior. When their request that she be transferred to a White school was turned down, they filed suit. In a landmark decision, the U.S. Supreme Court ruled that segregated schools are "inherently unequal" and violate the equal protection clause of the Fourteenth Amendment. U.S. citizens, the justices asserted, have a right to receive an equal opportunity for education.

As a result of opportunities created during the civil rights movement, a substantial number of African Americans are now members of the middle class. Affirmative action programs have enabled many African Americans to attain high-ranking positions in the business, medical, legal, and educational professions. For example, the U.S. Census Bureau reported the following in 2007:

- 1.3 million African Americans, 25 and older, held advanced degrees (i.e., master's, doctorate, medical, or law); in 1996, 683,000 African Americans had this level of education
- 2.3 million African Americans attended college in the fall of 2005, an increase of about 1 million from 15 years earlier
- 26 percent of African Americans work in management, professional, and related occupations; there are 44,900 African American physicians and surgeons, 80,000 postsecondary teachers, 48,300 lawyers, and 52,400 chief executives

Resegregation of Schools in the United States

As the United States continues to become more ethnically and racially diverse, there is evidence that schools have been resegregating since 1990, according to *Resegregation in American Schools*, a Harvard University report (Orfield & Yun, 1999). The report included the following findings:

- Latinos attend the most severely segregated schools.
- Since the late 1980s, schools in the South have been resegregating.
- As African Americans and Latinos move to the suburbs, they are attending segregated schools, especially in urban areas.

- States with a high proportion of African American students made progress toward desegregation in the 1970s; however, all showed increases in school segregation between 1980 and 1996.
- Segregated schools, with the exception of those for White students, tend to have a high concentration of poverty, which has a negative influence on student achievement.

One reason for the trend back to resegregation has been Supreme Court rulings that removed judicial supervision of school districts' efforts to desegregate—for example, *Board of Education of Oklahoma City Public Schools v. Dowell* (1991), *Freeman v. Pitts* (1992), and *Brown v. Unified School District No. 501* (1999). In addition, the Supreme Court ruled in *Missouri v. Jenkins* (1995) that Kansas City schools did not have to maintain desegregation through a magnet school approach until actual benefits for African American students were shown. Such rulings by the Supreme Court prompted the filing of many lawsuits to end desegregation in several large school districts.

The Learning Needs of African American Students

Research on factors related to students' success in school suggests that schools are monoethnic and do not take into account the diverse needs of ethnic minority-group students (Banks, 2009; Bennett, 2007). In the case of African American students, the failure of the school curriculum to address their learning needs may contribute to high dropout rates and below-average achievement. For example, research indicates that teaching strategies that emphasize cooperation—not competition—often result in higher achievement among African American (and Mexican American) students (Aronson & Gonzalez, 1988). In addition, it has been suggested that because many African Americans have grown up in an oral tradition; they may learn better through oral/aural activities—for example, reading aloud and listening to audiotapes (Bennett, 2006). However, one should not assume that all African Americans learn better aurally.

The following case illustrates how Steven, a 12-year-old African American student who was having difficulty learning math and developing his reading skills, benefited from teachers who were sensitive to his learning needs. After Steven's school failed to make adequate yearly progress (AYP) as required by No Child Left Behind, teachers began to receive in-service training to meet the instructional needs of students from culturally diverse backgrounds. The school principal also started after-school tutoring programs.

> Steven participated in the after-school tutoring program, where he received direct instruction in reading and mathematics. Teachers learned that he had an interest in astronomy, and textbooks and supplemental materials on astronomy were presented to him at his readability levels. Math across the curriculum was implemented, and he saw a direct benefit from instruction in math. As a result, Steven was able to see the utility of math in several different contexts. For example, teachers participating in the after-school tutoring program created math problems around the astronomy subject matter. After several months of direct instruction . . . Steven's reading comprehension and word recall improved. (Obiakor, 2007, p. 36)

Afrocentric Schools

To address the educational inequities that African American and other minority-group students may experience as a result of segregation, many communities have tried to create more ethnically and racially diverse classrooms through the controversial practice of busing students to attend schools in other neighborhoods. Also, some African Americans have recently begun to call for **Afrocentric schools**— schools that focus on African American history and cultures for African American pupils. Proponents believe that the educational needs of African American students can be met more effectively in schools that offer Afrocentric curricula and build on the strengths of the African American community.

296

Private Afrocentric schools, or Black academies, have sprung up across the country in recent years, many supported by the growing number of African Americans who practice Islam. Curricula in these schools emphasize the people and cultures of Africa and the history and achievements of African Americans. Teaching methods are often designed for culture-based learning styles, such as choral response, learning through movement, and sociability. One Afrocentric school is the Betty Shabbaz International Charter School, a K–8 school in Chicago. Students at the school, three-quarters of whom are from families in poverty, perform better than the district average on state tests, and more than twice as many Shabbaz students passed the state test in 2004 than in 2000 (Heffter, August 27, 2007).

At another Afrocentric school, the elementary-level African American Academy in Seattle, a teacher uses African drums to help students learn geography. The following serves as the mission statement of the academy: "The mission of the African American Academy is to meet the needs of African American and all children, providing them with an academic and African-centered education: nurturing them, in order to meet their emotional needs, while helping them to develop positive social and cultural skills which will enable them to become leaders of tomorrow" (June 9, 2008).

Education and Latino and Hispanic Americans

Hispanic Americans, the fastest growing minority group in the United States, account for about 14.8 percent of the population, and it has been estimated that an additional 5 million illegal aliens who speak Spanish may be in the country. By 2050, the Hispanic population is expected to be 24.4 percent, or more than 100 million.

Included in the category of Hispanic Americans are people who call themselves Latinos and Chicanos and who report their ancestry as Mexican, Puerto Rican, Cuban, Central American, or South American. Five states have populations that are more than 10 percent Hispanic: California, Texas, New Mexico, Arizona, and Colorado. Many states have passed English-only laws and made efforts to restrict Hispanic immigrants' access to education. Prior to 1983, six states had English-language laws; however, efforts by political action groups such as U.S. English, founded by the late Senator S. I. Hayakawa of California in 1983, were instrumental in getting English-only laws passed in 30 states by 2008 (U.S. English, 2008). U.S. English has also lobbied periodically the U.S. Congress to pass legislation to make English the official language of the United States. Most recently, the English as the Official Language Act of 2008 was introduced to the House of Representatives in April 2008.

Socioeconomic Factors

Although some Spanish-speaking immigrants come to the United States hoping to escape a life of poverty in their home country, many others come because they have relatives in the United States or they wish to take advantage of business opportunities in this country. For those Spanish-speaking immigrants who lack job skills and have little education, however, adjusting to the complexities and demands of life in the United States may be difficult.

Socioeconomic factors affect the education of some Hispanics, such as the children of migrant farm workers. Among the estimated 1 million or so migrant farm workers in this country, more than 70 percent are Spanish-speaking. The dropout rate among all migrant workers is 90 percent, and 50 percent leave school before finishing the ninth grade (Bennett, 2007). Migrant children are handicapped by the language barrier, deprivation resulting from poverty, and irregular school attendance. Some states have educational intervention programs in place for reaching this group.

What effects has the growing Hispanic population in the U.S. had on schools both throughout the country and in some states in particular? Why might some Hispanic Americans prefer assimilation over bilingual education for their children?

The Learning Needs of Spanish-Speaking Students

What can easily happen to Spanish-speaking learners if they are taught by teachers who are not sensitive to their learning needs is illustrated in Christine I. Bennett's portrait of Jesús, an LEP student:

> Jesús Martinez was a bright, fine-looking six-year-old when he migrated with his family from Puerto Rico to New York City. At a time when he was ready to learn to read and write his mother tongue, Jesús was instead suddenly thrust into an English-only classroom where the only tool he possessed for oral communication (the Spanish language) was completely useless to him. Jesús and his teacher could not communicate with each other because each spoke a different language and neither spoke the language of the other. Jesús felt stupid, or retarded; his teacher perceived him to be culturally disadvantaged and beyond her help. However, she and the school officials agreed to allow him to "sit there" because the law required that he be in school. (2007, p. 6)

Bennett also captures well the dilemma that many Spanish-speaking LEP students find themselves in: "Students with limited English proficiency are often caught up in conflicts between personal language needs—for example, the need to consolidate cognitive skills in the native language—and a sociopolitical climate that views standard English as most desirable and prestigious" (2003, p. 271).

The degree to which students from Spanish-speaking backgrounds are motivated to learn English varies from group to group. Mexican American students who live in the Southwest may retain the Spanish language to maintain ties with family and friends in Mexico. Recently arrived Cubans, on the other hand, may have a stronger motivation to learn the language of their new country. In regard to what they wish to learn, children take their cues from the adults around them. If their parents or guardians, friends, and relatives have learned English and are bilingual, then they will be similarly motivated. Many Hispanic Americans who value assimilation over their traditional culture favor English-only education.

However, the limited English proficiencies of many children raised in native Spanish-speaking families contribute significantly to the difficulties they have in school. To address the needs of these students, federally funded bilingual-bicultural programs encourage teachers to view bicultural knowledge as a bridge to the school's curriculum. Bilingual education is examined in detail later in this chapter.

Education and Asian Americans and Pacific Islanders

Asian Americans and Pacific Islanders represent about 4.4 percent, or 14 million, of the total population of the United States. The U.S. Census Bureau estimates that the Asian and Pacific Islander population in the United States will increase to 18 million (5.4 percent of the total), and then to 33 million (8.0 percent of the total) in 2050 (U.S. Census Bureau, 2008). This group, comprising at least 34 ethnic groups who speak more than 300 languages and dialects (Asian Americans/Pacific Islanders in Philanthropy, 1997), is tremendously diverse and includes people from South Asia, primarily Bangladesh, India, and Pakistan; Southeast Asia, including Indochina (Laos, Thailand, Indonesia, Malaysia, and Vietnam) and the Philippines; East Asia, including China, Hong Kong, Japan, Korea, and Taiwan; and the Pacific Islands, including Hawaii, Guam, and Samoa. About 51 percent of the total Asian American and Pacific Islander population lives in the western United States (U.S. Census Bureau, 2008).

Historical, Cultural, and Socioeconomic Factors

The three largest Asian American groups are Chinese (22.6 percent of Asian Americans), Filipinos (18.3 percent), and Japanese (7.8 percent) (Le, 2008). Although these groups differ significantly, each "came to the United States seeking the American dream, satisfied important labor needs, and became victims of an anti-Asian movement designed to prevent their further immigration to the United States. [They] also experienced tremendous economic, educational, and social mobility and success in U.S. society" (Banks, 2009, p. 398).

The California gold rush of 1849 brought the first immigrants from Asia, Chinese men who worked in mines, on railroads, and on farms, and who planned to return to their families and homeland. Early Chinese immigrants encountered widespread discrimination in their new country, with anti-Chinese riots occurring in San Francisco, Los Angeles, and Denver between 1869 and 1880. In 1882, Congress passed the Immigration Act, which ended Chinese immigration until 1902. The Chinese were oriented toward maintaining their traditional language and religion and established tight-knit urban communities, or Chinatowns. Recently, many upwardly mobile, professional Chinese Americans have been assimilated into suburban communities, while newly arrived, working-class immigrants from China and Hong Kong are settling in redeveloped Chinatowns.

Japanese immigrants began to arrive in Hawaii and the U.S. mainland in the late 1800s; most worked in agriculture, fisheries, the railroads, or industry and assimilated rapidly despite racial discrimination. The San Francisco Board of Education, for example, began to segregate all Japanese students in 1906, and the Immigration Act of 1924 ended Japanese immigration until 1952. During World War II, the United States was at war with Japan. In response to war hysteria over the "yellow peril," the United States government interned 110,000 Japanese Americans, most of them American-born, in 10 detention camps from 1942 to 1946. Since World War II, Japan has developed into one of the world's leading economic and technological powers—an accomplishment that has contributed, no doubt, to a recent decline in Japanese immigration to the United States.

Filipinos began to immigrate to Hawaii and the mainland as field laborers during the 1920s. They, too, encountered racism; in 1934, Congress passed the Tydings-McDuffie Act, which limited Filipino immigration to the United States to 50 persons annually. The following year, President Franklin Roosevelt signed the Repatriation Act, which provided free transportation to Filipinos willing to return to the Philippines. While most early Filipino immigrants had little education and low income, recent immigrants have tended to be professional, technical workers who hope to obtain employment in the United States more suitable for their education and training than they could in the Philippines (Banks, 2009).

Teachers' Concerns About Asian American Students

Asian Americans are frequently stereotyped as hard-working, conscientious, and respectful of authority, what many people view as a so-called model minority (Fong, 2007). In fact, 42.9 percent of Asian Americans 25 years and over have a bachelor's degree or more, compared to 25.3 percent of the White population (Le, 2008). The unreliability of such stereotypes notwithstanding, Asian American parents do tend to require their children to respect authority and value education. However, "for many Asian American students, this image is a destructive myth," according to a report titled *An Invisible Crisis: The Educational Needs of Asian Pacific American Youth*. "As their schools fail them, these children become increasingly likely to graduate with rudimentary language skills, to drop out of school, to join gangs, or to find themselves in the low-paying occupations and on the margins of American life" (Asian Americans/Pacific Islanders in Philanthropy, 1997). Families often pressure children to be successful academically through sacrifice and hard work. At the same time, there has been an increase in the number of Asian American youth who are in conflict with their parents' way of life. Leaders in Asian American communities have expressed concern about increases in dropout rates, school violence, and declining achievement. Some Indochinese Americans, for example, face deep cultural conflict in schools. Values and practices that are accepted in U.S. culture, such as dating and glorification of the individual, are sources of conflict between many Indochinese students and their parents (Fong, 2007).

Teachers need to be sensitive to cultural conflicts that may contribute to problems in school adjustment and achievement for Asian American students and realize that

> [s]tereotypes about Asian "whiz kids" and jealousy over the relatively high percentages of Asian Americans in the nation's colleges and universities may blind some non-Asian parents, fellow students, and teachers to the deep cultural conflict many Southeast Asian Americans face in our schools. (Bennett, 2007, p. 173)

To help Asian American students adjust to the U.S. culture, Qiu Liang offers teachers the following advice based on his school experiences as a Chinese immigrant:

> They [teachers] should be more patient [with an immigrant child] because it is very difficult for a person to be in a new country and learn a new language. Have patience. If the teacher feels there is no hope in an immigrant child, then the child will think, "Well, if the teacher who's helping me thinks that I can't go anywhere, then I might as well give up myself." (Igoa, 1995, pp. 99–100)

Similarly, Dung Yoong offers these recommendations based on her educational experiences as a Vietnamese immigrant:

> Try to get them to talk to you. Not just everyday conversation, but what they feel inside. Try to get them to get that out, because it's hard for kids. They don't trust—I had a hard time trusting and I was really insecure because of that.
>
> [P]utting an immigrant child who doesn't speak English into a classroom, a regular classroom with American students, is not very good. It scares [them] because it is so different. [Teachers] should start [them] slowly and have special classes where the child could adapt and learn a little bit about American society and customs. (Igoa, 1995, p. 103)

Education and Native Americans and Alaskan Natives

Native Americans and Alaskan Natives peopled the Western Hemisphere more than 12,000 years ago. Today, they represent about 1.5 percent of the total U.S. population, or about 2.9 million people (U.S. Census Bureau, 2008). This group consists of 517 federally recognized and 365 state-recognized tribes, each with its own language, religious beliefs, and way of life. The six largest groups are the Cherokee Nation, over 729,533 members; the Navajo Nation, 298,197; the Latin American Indian, 180,940; the Choctaw Nation, 158,774; the Sioux Nation, 153,360; and the Chippewa Nation, 149,669 (U.S. Census Bureau, 2008).

Approximately 538,300 Native Americans live on 275 reservations located primarily in the West. In rank order, the five states with the largest number of Native Americans and Alaskan Natives are California, Oklahoma, Arizona, Texas, and New Mexico (U.S. Census Bureau, 2008). Though most Native Americans live in cities, many are establishing connections with reservation Indians as a means of strengthening their cultural identities.

Native Americans are an example of the increasing ambiguity of racial and ethnic identities in the United States. For example, controversy exists over who is Native American. "Some full-blooded native people do not regard a person with one-quarter native heritage as qualifying, while others accept $\frac{1}{128}$" (Bennett, 2007, p. 152). While most Native Americans consider a person with one-quarter or more tribal heritage to be a member, the U.S. Census Bureau considers anyone who claims native identity to be a member. An expert on Native Americans and Alaskan Natives, Arlene Hirschfelder (1986), points out that 52 legal definitions of Native Americans have been identified. Native Americans were declared U.S. citizens in 1924, and Native American nations have been recognized as independent, self-governing territories since the 1930s.

Historical, Cultural, and Socioeconomic Factors

Perhaps more than any other minority group, Native Americans have endured systematic long-term attempts to eradicate their languages and cultures. Disease, genocide, confinement on reservations, and decades of forced assimilation have devastated Native American cultures. It was not until 2000 that the U.S. government officially apologized for the Bureau of Indian Affairs' "legacy of racism and inhumanity that included massacres, forced relocation of tribes and attempts to wipe out Indian languages and cultures" (Kelley, 2000, p. 1).

In 1492, Native American people used 2 billion acres of land; currently, they own about 94 million acres of land, or about 5 percent of U.S. territory (Bennett, 2006). Today, the rates of unemployment, poverty, and lack of educational attainment among Native Americans are among the nation's highest. Since the 1970s, however, there has been a resurgence of interest in preserving or restoring traditional languages, skills, and land claims.

There are hundreds of Native American languages, which anthropologists have attempted to categorize into six major language families (Banks, 2008). Older tribal members fluent in the original tribal language and younger members often speak a form of so-called reservation English. The challenge of educating Native Americans from diverse language backgrounds is further complicated by the difference in size of various Native American populations. These range from the more than 700,000 Cherokee to the 200 or so Supai of Arizona. As a result of the extreme diversity among Native Americans, it has even been suggested that "There is no such thing as an 'Indian' heritage, culture, or value system. [N]avajo, Cherokee, Sioux, and Aleut children are as different from each other in geographic and cultural backgrounds as they are from children growing up in New York City or Los Angeles" (Gipp, 1979, p. 19).

Education for Native American children living on reservations is currently administered by the federal government's Bureau of Indian Affairs (BIA). The **Indian Education Act of 1972 and 1974 Amendments** supplement the BIA's educational programs and provide direct educational assistance to tribes. The act seeks to improve Native American education by providing funds to school districts to meet the special needs of Native American youth, to Indian tribes and state and local education agencies to improve education for youth and adults, to colleges and universities for the purpose of training teachers for Indian schools, and to Native American students to attend college.

Research on Native American Ways of Knowing

Considerable debate has occurred over the best approaches for educating Native Americans. For example, Banks points out that "since the 1920s, educational policy for Native Americans has vacillated between strong assimilationism to self-determination and cultural pluralism" (2006, p. 42). In any case, the culture-based learning styles of many Native Americans and Alaskan Natives differ from that of other students. The traditional upbringing of Native American children generally encourages them to develop a view of the world that is holistic, intimate, and shared. "They approach tasks visually, seem to prefer to learn by careful observation which precedes performance, and seem to learn in their natural settings experientially" (Swisher & Deyhle, 1987, p. 350). Bennett suggests the following guideline to ensure that the school experiences of Native American students are in harmony with their cultural backgrounds: "An effective learning environment for Native Americans is one that does not single out the individual but provides frequent opportunities for the teacher to interact privately with individual children and with small groups, as well as opportunities for quiet, persistent exploration" (2003, p. 212).

Increasingly, Native Americans are designing multicultural programs to preserve their traditional cultures and ways of knowing. Although these programs are sometimes characterized as emphasizing separatism over assimilation, for many Native Americans they are a matter of survival. For example, the Oh Day Aki (Heart of the Earth) Charter School in Minneapolis was created to preserve the languages and cultures of the

What factors contribute to below-average achievement levels of Native American children? How do forces towards assimilation and cultural preservation coexist in the Native American experience?

Northern Plains Indians. Native American teachers at the school provide bilingual instruction in Ojibwe and Dakota. Students are encouraged to wear traditional dress and practice traditional arts, such as drumming and dancing (Oh Day Aki, 2008).

Cultural preservation is also the primary concern at Alaskan Native schools in remote parts of western Alaska and Cherokee schools in the Marietta Independent School District of Stillwell, Oklahoma. In Alaska, elders come into the classroom to teach children how to skin a seal, an education that few Alaskan Native children receive today at home. In an effort to keep the Cherokee language alive, students at the Lost City School near Tulsa, Oklahoma, learn Cherokee, one of the many endangered Native American tongues. In Oklahoma, fewer than 8,000 of the 100,000 Cherokees can speak the language fluently, and most of those are over age 45 (Burns, 2003).

WHAT IS MEANT BY BILINGUAL EDUCATION?

Bilingual education programs are designed to meet the learning needs of students whose first language is not English by providing instruction in two languages. Regardless of the instructional approach used, one outcome for all bilingual programs is for students to become proficient in English. Students are also encouraged to become **bicultural,** that is, able to function effectively in two or more linguistic and cultural groups.

In 1968, Congress passed the Bilingual Education Act, which required that language-minority students be taught in both their native language and English. In response to the act, school districts implemented an array of bilingual programs that varied greatly in quality and effectiveness. As a result, many parents filed lawsuits, claiming that bilingual programs were not meeting their children's needs.

In 1974, the Supreme Court heard a class action suit (*Lau v. Nichols*) filed by 1,800 Chinese students in San Francisco who charged that they were failing to learn because they could not understand English. The students were enrolled in all-English classes and received no special assistance in learning English. In a unanimous ruling, the Court asserted that federally funded schools must "rectify the language deficiency" of students who "are certain to find their classroom experiences wholly incomprehensible." That same year, Congress adopted the Equal Educational Opportunity Act (EEOA), which stated in part that a school district must "take appropriate action to overcome language barriers that impede equal participation by its students in its instructional programs."

While most bilingual programs serve Latino and Hispanic American students, there is an increasing need for bilingual teachers who are proficient in a variety of second languages. In fact, many school districts are offering salary bonuses for bilingual teachers.

Bilingual programs are tremendously varied. In fact, "any discussion about bilingual education should begin with the understanding that bilingual education is neither a single program nor a consistent 'methodology' for teaching language minority students" (Ovando, Combs, & Collier, 2006, p. 8). Generally, however, four types of bilingual education programs are currently available to provide special assistance to the 5.1 million language-minority students in the United States (see Figure 8.7).

Four Types of Bilingual Education Programs

Immersion programs: Students learn English and other subjects in classrooms where only English is spoken. Aides who speak the first language of students are sometimes available, or students may also listen to equivalent audiotape lessons in their first language.

Transition programs: Students receive reading lessons in their first language and lessons in English as a second language (ESL). Once they sufficiently master English, students are placed in classrooms where English is spoken and their first language is discontinued.

Pullout programs: On a regular basis, students are separated from English-speaking students so that they may receive lessons in English or reading lessons in their first language. These are sometimes called sheltered English programs.

Maintenance programs: To maintain the student's native language and culture, instruction in English and instruction in the native language are provided from kindergarten through 12th grade. Students become literate.

FIGURE 8.7 Four types of bilingual education programs

Research and Debate on Bilingual Programs

Research on the effectiveness of bilingual programs is mixed (Golnick & Chinn, 2009). Some who have examined the research conclude that bilingual programs have little effect on achievement (American Institutes of Research, 2003; Hakuta, 2001a, 2001b). Others have found that well-designed bilingual programs do increase students' achievement and are superior to monolingual programs (Crawford, 2004, 2007; Krashen & Mc-Field, 2005; Nieto, 2002).

Considerable debate surrounds bilingual programs in the United States. Those in favor of bilingual education make the following points:

- Students are better able to learn English if they are taught to read and write in their native language.
- Bilingual programs allow students to learn content in their native language rather than delaying that learning until they master English.
- Further developing competencies in students' native languages provides important cognitive foundations for learning English and academic content.
- Second-language learning is a positive value and should be as valid for a Spanish-speaker learning English as for an English-speaker learning Spanish.
- Bilingual programs support students' cultural identity, social context, and self-esteem.

On the other hand, those opposed to bilingual programs make the following points:

- Public schools should not be expected to provide instruction in all the first languages spoken by their students, nor can schools afford to pay a teacher who might teach only a few students.
- The cost of bilingual education is high. Bilingual programs divert staff and resources away from English-speaking students.
- If students spend more time exposed to English, they will learn English more quickly.
- Bilingual programs emphasize differences among and barriers between groups; they encourage separateness rather than assimilation and unity.
- Bilingual education is a threat to English as the nation's first language.

Advice for Monolingual Teachers

Although the future of bilingual education in the United States is uncertain, teachers must continue to meet the needs of language-minority students. These needs are best met by teachers who speak their native language as well as English (Snipes, Soga, & Uro, 2007). This is often not possible, however, and monolingual teachers will find increasing numbers of LEP students in their classrooms. The following classroom strategies are useful for both monolingual and bilingual teachers:

- Be aware of each student's language abilities.
- Make sure appropriate cultural experiences are reflected in the material.
- Document the success of selected materials.
- Experiment with the materials until you find the most appropriate for your particular student.
- Make a smooth transition into the new material.
- Be sure to become knowledgeable about the cultures and heritages of your students to ensure appropriateness and compatibility of the material (Ariza, 2006, pp. 110–111).

Additional tips for adapting material for LEP students are:

- Develop your own supplemental materials.
- Tape-record directions for the material so students can replay them for clarity.
- Provide alternatives to responding verbally to questions (e.g., use prearranged signals, give students a card to hold up, a flag, or any indicator they can use instead of speaking).
- Rewrite sections of the text to condense the reading for those with lower proficiency levels.
- Outline the material for the students before they read.
- Teach students the meaning of using bold headings, italicized words, subheadings, and transition words (*first, last, however, although,* etc.).
- Reduce the number of pages or items to be completed by the student.
- Break tasks into smaller subtasks.
- Substitute a similar, less complex task.
- Develop study guides for all students (Ariza, 2006, p. 110).

 ## WHAT IS MULTICULTURAL EDUCATION?

Multicultural education is committed to the goal of providing all students—regardless of socioeconomic status; gender; sexual orientation; or ethnic, racial, or cultural backgrounds—with equal opportunities to learn in school. Multicultural education is also based on the fact that students do not learn in a vacuum—their culture predisposes them to learn in certain ways. And finally, multicultural education recognizes that current school practices have provided—and continue to provide—some students with greater opportunities for learning than students who belong to other groups. The suggestions presented in the preceding section are examples of multicultural education in practice. The Teachers' Voices: Walk in My Shoes feature in this chapter profiles Lenora Mar, an award-winning special education teacher who has a gift for bringing out the potential in each student.

As multiculturalism has become more pervasive in U.S. schools, controversy over the need for multicultural education and its purposes has emerged. "Multicultural education is sometimes criticized as focusing on differences rather than similarities among groups. On the other side, it is criticized for not adequately addressing issues of power and oppression that keep a number of groups from participating equitably in society" (Gollnick & Chinn, 2009, p. 8). Though multicultural education is being challenged by some, public dialogue and debate about how schools can address diversity more effectively is healthy—an indicator that our society is making real progress toward creating a culture that incorporates the values of diverse groups.

Dimensions of Multicultural Education

According to James A. Banks, "Multicultural education is a way of viewing reality and a way of thinking, and not just content about various ethnic, racial, and cultural groups" (Banks, 2006, p. 8). More specifically, Banks suggests that multicultural education be conceptualized as consisting of five dimensions: (1) content integration, (2) the knowledge construction process, (3) prejudice reduction, (4) an equity pedagogy, and (5) an empowering school culture and social structure (see Figure 8.8). As you progress through your teacher-education program and eventually begin to prepare curriculum materials and instructional strategies for your multicultural classroom, remember that integrating content from a variety of cultural groups is just one dimension of multicultural education.

Multicultural education promotes students' positive self-identity and pride in their heritage, acceptance of people from diverse backgrounds, and critical self-assessment. In addition, multicultural education can prompt students, perhaps with guidance from their teachers, to promote social justice and to take action against prejudice and discrimination

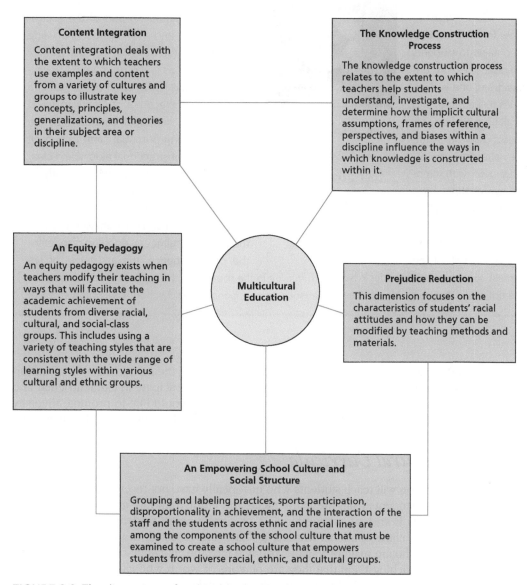

FIGURE 8.8 The dimensions of multicultural education

Source: Reprinted with the permission of James A. Banks, from James A. Banks, *An Introduction to Multicultural Education* (4th edition), 2008. Boston: Allyn & Bacon, p. 32.

TEACHERS' VOICES
Walk in My Shoes

Lenora Mar, a 30-year veteran special education teacher and a 2008 Los Angeles County Teacher of the Year, is an inspiration. Her principal describes her as:

An exemplary teacher who undertakes dealing with students with various learning disabilities and disorders like it is no different than teaching the average child. She is unflappable, inspiring, and treasured by the parents and staff. She manages the most troubling and challenging students with respect and finesse.

Her special day class for third- to fifth-grade students in 2008 contains 16 students who have a wide range of disabilities: "A couple are on the autism spectrum; one is deaf; one has other health issues related to eating or chewing; and almost all have auditory, visual, sensory-motor processing deficits. Additionally, over half have attention deficit-hyperactivity, one is diagnosed with emotional disturbances, and two or three have emotional issues that require counseling."

Asked to describe two special education cases, one especially challenging and one hopeful and uplifting, Lenora tells of Joe and Rita (not their real names). Joe, a new third-grader in her class, was diagnosed as emotionally disturbed. He was eas-

"She is unflappable, inspiring, and treasured by the parents and staff."

ily frustrated and upset, and his anger could quickly escalate to an outburst. Lenora explains, "Learning to read and interpret facial cues, body language, or tension can be one way to prevent an outburst. In addition, frequent reminders of upcoming changes to our routine or giving Joe a preview of new skills he'll be learning helps him anticipate change and prevent negative reactions." Working with him was a delicate matter, however; "Twice this year he has taken apart my classroom, throwing things down, turning furniture over, screaming, yelling angrily, and kicking."

In the beginning part of the escalation, Lenora and her instructional aide would ignore the behavior as much as they could as long as it was not harmful to others. Not taking her eyes off of Joe, Lenora would signal the other students to leave him alone. If his anger escalated to the point of causing potential harm to himself or others, the instructional aide would clear the classroom, and Lenora would gently try "to contain the child, calm him, and eventually debrief with him."

Such challenging behavior requires the teacher's calmness, ongoing respect for the child, patience, the assistance of another adult in the room, and the support of school personnel such as the principal and school psychologist. Over

---

my education lab
Go to MyEducationLab, select the topic Diversity and Multiculturalism, and view the video What Is Diversity?

within their school. For example, students might reduce the marginalization of minority-group students in their school by inviting them to participate in extracurricular and after-school activities. To get an idea of how students would like to promote diversity at their school, go to MyEducationLab and watch the video titled What Is Diversity?

Multicultural Curricula

As a teacher, you will teach students who historically have not received full educational opportunity—students from the many racial and ethnic minority groups in the United States; students from low-income families or communities; students with exceptional abilities or disabilities; students who are lesbian, gay, bisexual, or transgender (LGBT); and students who are male or female. You will face the challenge of reaching out to all students and teaching them that they are persons of worth who can learn. The following case about 12-year-old Yvette illustrates that challenge.

Yvette is 12 years old and lives with her older brother and younger sister in an apartment in the city. Yvette and her brother were born in Puerto Rico,

time, with Lenora's gifted teaching and the assistance of others, Joe is likely to make great strides.

Rita is a success story. She started in Lenora's special day class as a third-grader and remained with her until fifth grade. "She came in diagnosed as a high-functioning individual who exhibited characteristics typical of a student with autism." She was reading at grade level, her math skills were a year or two behind, and she had a lot of weaknesses in social situations. Her teachers in the regular classroom were concerned because she was a loner in the classroom and on the playground.

In the special day class, Lenora encouraged Rita to be actively involved and praised her each time she contributed to class. "I gave her a risk-free place to grow in her self-confidence, and she grew socially." She started to organize things on her own, preparing a get-well card for a classmate and a birthday card for Lenora that she had the other students sign. Rita asked to teach an art lesson to the class and auditioned for a speaking part in a play that all the fifth-grade classes performed for parents. Rita's recent triennial battery of tests indicated that she "no longer exhibits characteristics typical of a student with autism, and she has been re-diagnosed with just learning disabilities. We recommended transitioning her from a special day class to a less restrictive environment!"

For people preparing to be teachers in regular classrooms, Lenora advises that they should "be organized, well-prepared, flexible, versatile, open-minded, and have more than one strategy or activity in their repertoire. They should definitely have a strong behavior management system."

For future special education teachers, Lenora recommends that they should also "have a predictable, structured program, pile on the praises and positive comments, and establish a risk-free atmosphere where children can rebuild their self-esteem, their self-confidence, and believe in themselves again. That way, they can learn the skills they need to be as successful as they can be at their level of ability." Respect is also a key for Lenora. "I bring respect to the students and I expect them to respect me and each other."

She offers special education teachers wise advice: "I feel it is important to build trust and rapport with the student and especially with the parents. Developing an open, ongoing communication system between home and school is essential. Coming prepared and informed to the annual Individualized Educational Plan (IEP) meetings facilitates the meetings and reflects your professionalism."

It is easy to see why Lenora is an award-winning teacher and someone highly valued by parents, colleagues, and her administration. Her regard for and belief in all children and their potential to learn are treasured gifts for those committed to her care.

Lenora Mar
Cullen Elementary School

and her sister was born in the United States. Yvette's mother and father brought the family to the mainland two years ago.

Three months ago, Yvette transferred into your class. It appears that the transition is difficult for her. Her work would improve if she got more involved, you think. However, she seems afraid to risk making mistakes, especially in reading and language arts.

Yvette seems to trust you, so you've decided to talk to her after school today. She usually waits in your classroom until her brother Juan arrives to walk her home.

You begin by asking, "How is school going?"

As she speaks, timidly at first and then more openly and naturally, you realize that Yvette is still struggling to adjust to the challenges of living on the mainland. She misses her grandmother, who lived with the family in Puerto Rico. She also says she does not speak English well enough. She is worried that the other children will tease her if she speaks out in class. You also learn that Yvette has missed school frequently because of bad headaches and stomach problems. When you ask Yvette if her parents are coming to the next PTA meeting, Yvette tells you they probably will not come because they do not speak English.

How can you get Yvette more involved in classroom activities? What strategies could you use to help her to increase her reading, speaking, and writing skills? How might you make Yvette's parents feel welcome and comfortable at the school?

As a teacher, you will develop a curriculum that increases students' awareness and appreciation of the rich diversity in U.S. culture. A **multicultural curriculum** addresses the needs and backgrounds of all students regardless of their cultural identity. As Banks suggests, the multicultural curriculum "enable[s] students to derive valid generalizations and theories about the characteristics of ethnic groups and to learn how they are alike and different, in both their past and present experiences. . . . [It] focus[es] on a range of groups that differ in their racial characteristics, cultural experiences, languages, histories, values, and current problems" (2009, p. 16). Teachers who provide multicultural education hold the following beliefs:

- Cultural differences have strength and value.
- Schools should be models for the expression of human rights and respect for cultural and group differences.
- Social justice and equality for all people should be of paramount importance in the design and delivery of curricula.
- Attitudes and values necessary for the continuation of a democratic society can be promoted in schools.
- Schooling can provide the knowledge, skills, and dispositions (i.e., values, attitudes, and commitments) to help students from diverse groups learn.
- Educators working with families and communities can create an environment that is supportive of multiculturalism (Gollnick & Chinn, 2009, p. 4).

In developing a multicultural curriculum, you should be sensitive to how your instructional materials and strategies can be made more inclusive so that they reflect cultural perspectives, or "voices," that previously have been silent or marginalized in discussions about what should be taught in schools and how it should be taught. Effective teachers attend to these previously unheard voices, not as an act of tokenism but with a genuine desire to make the curriculum more inclusive. The Teaching on Your Feet feature in this chapter describes how Romaine Washington was able to relate curriculum content to her students' cultural backgrounds.

Multicultural Instructional Materials and Strategies

To create classrooms that are truly multicultural, teachers must select instructional materials that are sensitive, accurately portray the contributions of ethnic groups, and reflect diverse points of view. Teachers must also recognize that "[s]ome of the books and other materials on ethnic groups published each year are insensitive, inaccurate, and written from mainstream and insensitive perspectives and points of view" (Banks, 2009, p. 108). Some guidelines for selecting multicultural instructional materials follow:

- Books and other materials should accurately portray the perspectives, attitudes, and feelings of ethnic groups.
- Fictional works should have strong ethnic characters.
- Books should describe settings and experiences with which all students can identify and yet should accurately reflect ethnic cultures and lifestyles.
- The protagonists in books with ethnic themes should have ethnic characteristics but should face conflicts and problems that are universal.
- The illustrations in books should be accurate, ethnically sensitive, and technically well done.

TEACHING ON YOUR FEET

¡SÍ SE PUEDE! (IT CAN BE DONE!)

What do you do when multiculturalism gets shaved down to biculturalism and students ask why more groups are not represented in the literature? From Puritanism to the Slave Narrative, from Transcendentalism to the Harlem Renaissance, Modernists, Beat Poets, Post-Modernists, and the Black Arts Movement, students are presented with myriad voices and views of American life. Mario asked one day, "Why is everything black and white?" Melissa followed his question with, "Where are Mexicans in these stories? Weren't they around? Why don't we read about them?"

The questions Mario and Melissa raised were on my mind as I prepared to teach the poignant, readily accessible novel Of Mice and Men. From previous experience, I knew that students would love Lennie and hate Curly. We would identify the themes of loneliness and alienation. We would explore the concept of the American dream, as told by George. We would have a mock trial, and the jury would decide whether euthanasia is pardonable under certain circumstances. Yet when it is all said and done, we would still be left with the Mexican migrant worker waiting at the roadside for his story to be told.

This year my English class would be half Latino, with quite a few English language learners. I longed to engage them on another level. I recalled the legacy of Cesar Chavez, which would provide the cultural, historical, and literary connection I needed. Although he was not an activist at the time in which Of Mice and Men takes place, he was a child during that time period. He had a difficult time in school because he was the child of migrant workers who had moved more than 35 times. In addition, he spoke only Spanish. Children at his school would be hit on the knuckles when they did not speak English. I inform my students that, despite those challenges, Chavez became a great orator and activist for migrant workers.

We speculate about the difference his presence might have made if he had been an activist during the time period of the novel. We read some of his quotes and relate them to the novel's characters and conflicts. Finally, we deconstruct a collage picture of Cesar Chavez in which his face, clothes, and the background are made up of migrant workers in the fields and holding peaceful demonstrations. All of the images in the collage symbolize important aspects of Chavez's life. I ask students to write about what they see and what they think it symbolizes. Detail by detail, they embrace the lesson. Phillip asks, "Can I have the picture we are writing about? I really like it." I respond using the slogan of the UFW (United Food Workers), "¡Sí se puede!"

ANALYSIS

Because of time constraints and limited resources, what should be a multicultural education often ends up being marginal and bicultural. It is impossible to teach about all cultures, but it is imperative that we at least try to include the cultures represented in our classrooms. Incorporating the lesson on Cesar Chavez broadened the class's cultural boundaries and validated the observation and request made by the students. This will serve to encourage them to speak up in the future when they feel underrepresented.

REFLECTION

- How can teachers create a supportive environment where students feel comfortable discussing concerns about culture in the curriculum?
- What are other ways teachers can incorporate multicultural context and content into the curriculum if resources are not readily made available?

Romaine Washington
English Teacher
Los Osos High School

PEARSON **myeducationlab** To answer these questions online, go to MyEducation-Lab at www.myeducationlab.com, select the Activities and Application section, and click on this chapter's Teaching on Your Feet.

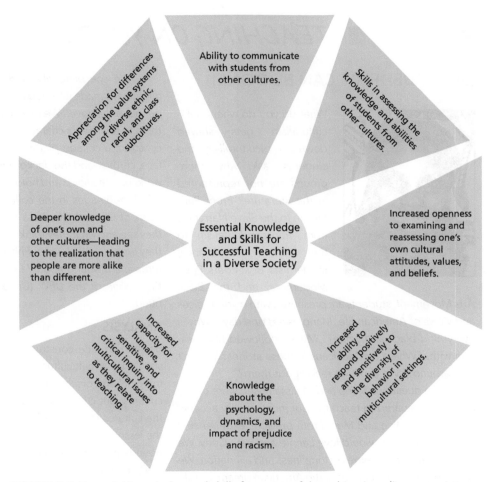

Ability to communicate with students from other cultures.

Skills in assessing the knowledge and abilities of students from other cultures.

Appreciation for differences among the value systems of diverse ethnic, racial, and class subcultures.

Increased openness to examining and reassessing one's own cultural attitudes, values, and beliefs.

Deeper knowledge of one's own and other cultures—leading to the realization that people are more alike than different.

Essential Knowledge and Skills for Successful Teaching in a Diverse Society

Increased capacity for humane, sensitive, and critical inquiry into multicultural issues as they relate to teaching.

Increased ability to respond positively and sensitively to the diversity of behavior in multicultural settings.

Knowledge about the psychology, dynamics, and impact of prejudice and racism.

FIGURE 8.9 Essential knowledge and skills for successful teaching in a diverse society
Source: Adapted from Forrest W. Parkay and Henry T. Fillmer, "Improving Teachers' Attitudes Toward Minority-Group Students: An Experimental Approach to Multicultural Inservice," New Horizons Journal of Education, November 1984, pp. 178–179.

- Ethnic materials should not contain racist concepts, clichés, phrases, or words.
- Factual materials should be historically accurate.
- Multiethnic resources and basal textbooks should discuss major events and documents related to ethnic history (Banks, 2009, pp. 109–110).

Yvonne Wilson, a first-grade teacher in Talmoon, Minnesota, and an Ojibwe Indian, points out that a teacher's willingness to learn about other cultures is very important to students and their parents:

> People in the community know if you are trying to understand their culture. Students also see it. Becoming involved—going to a powwow or participating in other cultural events—shows people that here is a teacher who is trying to learn about our culture.

myeducationlab

Go to MyEducationLab, select Chapter 8 and Activities and Applications to watch the video Multicultural Perspectives in the Curriculum.

Participating wholeheartedly in cross-cultural experiences will help you to grow in the eight areas outlined in Figure 8.9 as essential for successful teaching in a diverse society. By developing knowledge and skills in these eight areas, you will be well prepared to meet the educational needs of all your students. To reflect further on multicultural curricula, go to MyEducationLab to watch a teacher talk with a Native American parent about including multicultural perspectives in the curriculum.

HOW IS GENDER A DIMENSION OF MULTICULTURAL EDUCATION?

Although it may be evident that gender affects students' learning in many ways, it may not be evident that gender is an important dimension of multicultural education. However, "culturally democratic classrooms also consider gender differences" (Oakes & Lipton, 2007, p. 277). For example, the following comments by a first-year high school science teacher stress the importance of gender differences in the classroom.

> I have high expectations for all of my students, not just the boys. If I challenge a boy to figure out the answer to a scientifically engaging problem for himself, and then go and give the answer to a girl, I send an unconscious message that I do not think my female student can figure it out by herself. I encourage the girls' active participation when it is easy for them to be drowned out by the louder and more aggressive boys. I encourage girls to ask questions and help them use scientific methodology to find answers. I challenge them to think about why there are more men who do science than women. (Oakes & Lipton, 2007, p. 278)

Gender Differences

Cultural differences between males and females are partially shaped by society's traditional expectations of them. Through **sex role stereotyping,** families, the media, the schools, and other powerful social forces condition boys and girls to act in certain ways regardless of abilities or interests. As mentioned in Chapter 3, one of the aims of schools is to socialize students to participate in society. One dimension of the **sex role socialization** process conveys to students certain expectations about the way boys and girls are "supposed" to act. Girls are supposed to play with dolls, boys to play with trucks. Girls are supposed to be passive; boys are supposed to be active. Girls are supposed to express their feelings and emotions when in pain; boys are supposed to repress their feelings and deny pain.

Students may be socialized into particular gender-specific roles as a result of the curriculum materials they use at school. By portraying males in more dominant, assertive ways and portraying females in ways that suggest that they are passive and helpless, textbooks can subtly reinforce expectations about the way girls and boys "should" behave. Within the last few decades, however, publishers of curriculum materials have become more vigilant about avoiding these stereotypes.

Gender and Education

It was not until Title IX of the Education Amendments Act was passed in 1972 that women were guaranteed equality of educational opportunity in educational programs receiving federal assistance. Title IX has had the greatest impact on athletic programs in schools. The law requires that both sexes have equal opportunities to participate in and benefit from the availability of coaches, sports equipment, resources, and facilities. For contact sports such as football, wrestling, and boxing, sports that were not open to women, separate teams are allowed.

The right of females to equal educational opportunity was further enhanced with the passage of the **Women's Educational Equity Act (WEEA)** of 1974. This act provides the following opportunities:

- Expanded math, science, and technology programs for females
- Programs to reduce sex role stereotyping in curriculum materials
- Programs to increase the number of female educational administrators

What impact has the Women's Education Equity Act (WEEA) of 1974 had on the education of females? Why and in what ways does gender bias, for both girls and boys, persist in many U.S. classrooms and schools?

- Special programs to extend educational and career opportunities to minority, disabled, and rural women
- Programs to help school personnel increase educational opportunities and career aspirations for females
- Encouragement for more females to participate in athletics

Despite reforms stemming from WEEA, several reports in the early 1990s criticized schools for subtly discriminating against girls in tests, textbooks, and teaching methods. Research on teacher interactions in the classroom seemed to point to widespread unintentional gender bias against girls. Two of these studies, *Shortchanging Girls, Shortchanging America* (1991) and *How Schools Shortchange Girls* (1992), both commissioned by the American Association of University Women (AAUW), claimed that girls were not encouraged in math and science and that teachers favored boys' intellectual growth over that of girls.

In the mid-1990s, however, some gender equity studies had more mixed findings. In their analysis of data on achievement and engagement of 9,000 eighth-grade boys and girls, University of Michigan researchers Valerie Lee, Xianglei Chen, and Becky A. Smerdon (1996) concluded that "the pattern of gender differences is inconsistent. In some cases, females are favored; in others males are favored." Similarly, University of Chicago researchers Larry Hedges and Amy Nowell found in their study of 32 years of mental tests given to boys and girls that, while boys do better than girls in science and mathematics, they were "at a rather profound disadvantage" in writing and scored below girls in reading comprehension (Hedges, 1996, p. 3).

Additional research and closer analyses of earlier reports on gender bias in education were beginning to suggest that boys, not girls, were most shortchanged by the schools (Gurian, 2007; Sommers, 1996, 2000). Numerous articles, as well as a PBS series that began with a program titled "The War on Boys," challenged the conclusions of the earlier AAUW report, *How Schools Shortchange Girls.* Other commentary discounted gender bias in the schools as a fabrication of radical feminism; among the first to put forth this view was Christina Hoff Sommers's (1994) controversial book, *Who Stole Feminism? How Women Have Betrayed Women*; Judith Kleinfeld (1998) followed with *The Myth That Schools Shortchange Girls: Social Science in the Service of Deception*, as did Cathy Young (1999) with *Ceasefire! Why Women and Men Must Join Forces to Achieve True Equality.*

What some people had come to call the gender wars took another turn when the AAUW released *Where the Girls Are: The Facts About Gender Equity in Education* in 2008. The report, which examined trends in standardized test scores by gender, race, ethnicity, and family income during the past 35 years, found that family income, not gender, is most closely associated with academic success. The analysis of scores on tests such as the SAT and ACT college entrance exams led the AAUW to conclude:

> The overarching message of this report is one of good news. Overall and within racial/ethnic groups and family income levels, girls and boys are improving by most measures of educational achievement, and most achievement gaps are narrowing. The past few decades have seen remarkable gains for girls and boys in education, and no evidence indicates a crisis for boys in particular. If a crisis exists, it is a crisis for African American and Hispanic students and students from lower-income families—both girls and boys. (American Association of University Women, May 2008, p. 68)

Figure 8.10 presents the AAUW's findings for SAT performance by gender and race/ethnicity from 1994 to 2004.

Lesbian, Gay, Bisexual, and Transgender (LGBT) Students

In addition to gender bias, some students experience discrimination on the basis of their sexual orientation. To help all students realize their full potential, teachers should ac-

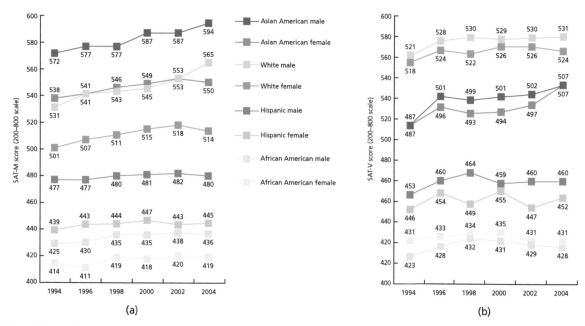

FIGURE 8.10 (a) SAT mathematics mean score, by gender and race/ethnicity, 1994–2004; (b) SAT verbal/critical reading mean score, by gender and race/ethnicity, 1994–2004

Source: Adapted from AAUW Educational Foundation analysis of unpublished data provided by the College Board; Where the Girls Are: The Facts About Gender Equity in Education. American Association of University Women. (2008), pp. 40–41, Figures 16 and 17. Washington, DC: Author.

knowledge the special needs of gay, lesbian, and bisexual students because "there is an invisible gay and lesbian minority in every school, and the needs of these students [a]re often unknown and unmet" (Besner & Spungin, 1995, p. xi). One study of 120 gay and lesbian students ages 14 to 21 found that only one-fourth said that they were able to discuss their sexual orientation with school counselors, and less than one in five said they could identify someone who had been supportive of them (Tellijohann & Price, 1993). Moreover, a similar study of lesbian and gay youth reported that 80 percent of participants believed their teachers had negative attitudes about homosexuality (Sears, 1991).

Based on estimates that as much as 10 percent of society may be homosexual, a high school with an enrollment of 1,500 might have as many as 150 gay, lesbian, and bisexual students (Besner & Spungin, 1995; Stover, 1992). The National Education Association, the American Federation of Teachers, and several professional organizations have passed resolutions urging members and school districts to acknowledge the special needs of these students.

The nation's first dropout prevention program targeting gay, lesbian, and bisexual students was implemented in the Los Angeles school system. Known as Project 10, the program focuses on education, suicide prevention, dropout prevention, creating a safe environment for homosexual students, and HIV/AIDS education (Uribe & Harbeck, 1991). In 1993, Massachusetts became the first state to adopt an educational policy prohibiting discrimination against gay and lesbian students and teachers. At one Massachusetts high school, gay and straight students created the Gay-Straight Alliance (GSA), a school-sanctioned student organization that gives students a safe place to discuss sexual orientation issues (Bennett, 1997).

In 2003, about 100 students enrolled in the Harvey Milk School, the nation's first public high school for gay, lesbian, bisexual, and transgender students. Housed in an office building in New York City, the school is named after California's first elected gay official—a member of the board of supervisors in San Francisco—who was assassinated after less than a year in office. New York City also cosponsors after-school programs, such as art and music, and counseling and support services for as many as 2,000 gay and lesbian students (Ferguson, 2003).

Homosexual students can experience school-related problems and safety risks. The hostility that gay, lesbian, and bisexual youth can encounter may cause them to

313

feel confused, isolated, and self-destructive. Teachers and other school personnel can provide much needed support. Informed, sensitive, and caring teachers can play an important role in helping all students develop to their full potential. Such teachers realize the importance of recognizing diverse perspectives, and they create inclusive classroom environments that encourage students to respect differences among themselves and others and to see the contributions that persons from all groups have made to society.

Gender-Fair Classrooms and Curricula

Although research and debate about the bias boys and girls encounter in school will no doubt continue, it is clear that teachers must encourage girls and boys to develop to the full extent of their capabilities and provide them an education that is free from **gender bias**—subtle favoritism or discrimination on the basis of gender.

Following is a list of basic guidelines for creating a **gender-fair classroom.** Adherence to these guidelines will help teachers "address the inequities institutionalized in the organizational structure of schools, the curriculum selected to be taught, the learning strategies employed, and their ongoing instructional and informal interactions with students" (Stanford, 1992, p. 88).

- Become aware of differences in interactions with girls and boys.
- Promote boys' achievement in reading and writing and girls' achievement in mathematics and science.
- Reduce young children's self-imposed sexism.
- Teach about sexism and sex role stereotyping.
- Foster an atmosphere of collaboration between girls and boys.

SUMMARY

How Is Diversity Reflected in the Culture of the United States?

- The percentage of ethnic minorities in the United States has been growing steadily since World War II. By 2025, half of U.S. youth will be White and half minority; by 2050, no single group will be a majority among adults. Currently, the majority of students in several states and many urban districts are from groups traditionally thought of as minority.
- Culture is defined as the way of life common to a group of people, including beliefs, attitudes, habits, values, and practices.
- Ethnicity refers to a commonly shared racial or cultural identity and a set of beliefs, values, and attitudes. The concept of race is used to distinguish among people on the basis of biological traits and characteristics. A minority group is a group of people who share certain characteristics and are fewer in number than the majority of a population.
- The increase of people who identify themselves as mixed race is one indication that racial and ethnic

identities in the United States are becoming more complex.
- The lower achievement levels of certain minority-group students compared to those of their Anglo-European American and Asian American counterparts reflect the strong connection between socioeconomic status and achievement.
- Stereotyping is the process of attributing certain behavioral characteristics to all members of a group, often on the basis of limited experiences with and information about the group being stereotyped. Individual racism is the prejudicial belief that one's own ethnic or racial group is superior to others, and institutional racism refers to laws, customs, and practices that lead to racial inequalities.

What Does Equal Educational Opportunity Mean?

- Equal educational opportunity means that teachers promote the full development of students without regard for race, ethnicity, gender, sexual orientation, socioeconomic status, abilities, or disabilities.

- Teachers can meet the needs of minority students by becoming familiar with their cultural and linguistic backgrounds and learning styles.
- In spite of increasing diversity in the United States, there has been a trend since 1990 for schools to resegregate.

What Is Meant by Bilingual Education?

- Bilingual education programs provide instruction in a student's first language and English. The goal of bilingual programs is for students to function effectively in two or more linguistic/cultural groups. Four approaches to bilingual education are immersion, maintenance, pullout, and transition programs.

What Is Multicultural Education?

- Five dimensions of multicultural education have been suggested: content integration, the knowledge construction process, prejudice reduction, an equity pedagogy, and an empowering school culture and social structure.
- Effective multicultural materials and instructional strategies include the contributions of ethnic groups and reflect diverse points of view, or "voices," that previously may have been silenced or marginalized in society.

How Is Gender a Dimension of Multicultural Education?

- The behavior of boys and girls in our society is influenced by sexism, sex role socialization, and sex role stereotyping.
- The latest research indicates that family income, not gender, is most closely associated with academic achievement.
- Teachers can provide an education free of gender bias by creating gender-fair classrooms and curricula and providing students with safe, supportive learning environments.

PROFESSIONAL REFLECTIONS AND ACTIVITIES

Teacher's Journal

1. What are the characteristics of those who are effective in teaching students from cultural backgrounds other than their own? Which of these characteristics can be acquired or developed further through education or training experiences?
2. What is your cultural identity? To what subcultures do you belong, and how do these contribute to your cultural identity?

Teacher's Research

1. Gather data from the National Center for Education Statistics regarding trends in achievement levels, educational attainment, and dropout rates for one of the following groups of which you are not a member: African Americans, Latino and Hispanic Americans, Asian Americans and Pacific Islanders, and Native Americans and Alaskan Natives. To what extent are achievement levels and educational attainment increasing? To what extent are dropout rates decreasing?
2. Go to the website for the American Association of University Women (AAUW) and download the 2008 report, *Where the Girls Are: The Facts About Gender Equity in Education*. The report presents achievement data by gender, race, ethnicity, and family income. What are some implications these data have for teachers?

Observations and Interviews

1. If possible, visit a school that has an enrollment of students whose cultural or socioeconomic backgrounds differ from your own. What feelings and questions about these students emerge as a result of your observations? How might your feelings affect your teaching and teaching effectiveness? How can you research answers to your questions?
2. Interview a teacher at the school identified in the above activity. What special satisfactions does he or she experience from teaching at the school? What significant problems relating to diversity does he or she encounter, and how are they dealt with?

PEARSON myeducationlab To complete additional observations and interviews, go to MyEducationLab at www.myeducationlab.com, select the Virtual Field Experience section, and click on this chapter's Observations and Interviews.

Professional Portfolio

Prepare an annotated directory of local resources for teaching students about diversity, implementing multicultural curricula, and promoting harmony or equity among diverse groups. For each entry, include an annotation—that is, a brief description of the resource materials and their availability. Resources for your personalized directory should be available through local sources such as your university library, public library, community agencies, and so on. Among the types of resources you might include are the following:

- Films, videos, audiocassettes, books, and journal articles

- Simulation games designed to improve participants' attitudes toward diversity
- Motivational guest speakers from the community
- Ethnic museums and cultural centers
- Community groups and agencies dedicated to promoting understanding among diverse groups
- Training and workshops in the area of diversity

---

myeducation**lab** Now go to MyEducationLab at www.myeducationlab.com to test your understanding of chapter content by completing this chapter's Study Plan.

Addressing Learners' Individual Needs

12

Addressing Learners' Individual Needs

*I love the kids. They are so charming and fun,
and when they learn—it's amazing.*

A teacher quoted in *What Only Teachers*
Know *About Education* (Babbage, 2008, p. 150)

CLASSROOM CASE
The Realities of Teaching

THE CHALLENGE: Motivating a gifted student to work up to her or his potential.

You are concerned about the poor performance of Ricardo, a student in your eighth-period high school class. Ricardo is undeniably bright. When he was 10, he had an IQ of 145 on the Stanford-Binet. Last year, when he was 16, he scored 142. Ricardo's father is a physician, and his mother is a professor. Both parents clearly value learning and are willing to give Ricardo any needed encouragement and help.

Throughout elementary school, Ricardo had an outstanding record. His teachers reported that he was brilliant and very meticulous in completing his assignments. He entered high school amid expectations by his parents and teachers that he would continue his outstanding performance. However, during his first two years of high school, Ricardo never seemed to live up to his promise. Now, halfway through his junior year, Ricardo is failing English and geometry. Ricardo seems to be well adjusted to the social side of school. He has a lot of friends and says that he likes school.

Today, you are meeting with Ricardo to find out why he is failing two of his classes. You begin the conversation with a few comments about last night's basketball game and mention that you saw Ricardo at the game.

After those comments, you change the focus of the conversation. "So, Ricardo, tell me about English and geometry. It looks like you may not pass those courses."

"I just don't like to study," Ricardo says, sliding down in his chair as he tries to convey a nonchalant attitude. "Besides, studying doesn't get you anywhere around here."

"What do you mean, 'doesn't get you anywhere around here'?" you ask.

"When I first got here, kids would say I was 'frantic,' you know. 'Cause I'd finish all my work in class. I felt funny about it, 'cause here I am trying to do all my work to try and get an 'A.' I'm really working, and they're always putting me down 'cause I try. Well, I just got tired of that."

FOCUS QUESTIONS

1. How do students' needs change as they develop?
2. How do students vary in intelligence?
3. How do students vary in ability and disability?
4. What are special education, mainstreaming, and inclusion?
5. How can you teach all learners in your inclusive classroom?

As the preceding classroom case about Ricardo suggests, when you become a teacher you must understand and appreciate students' unique learning and developmental needs. You must be willing to learn about students' abilities and disabilities and to explore the special issues and concerns of students at three broad developmental levels—childhood, early adolescence, and late adolescence. Learning about the intellectual and psychological growth of students at the age level you plan to teach is essential, as the following comment by a student suggests:

> To me what makes a good teacher is someone who understands the students. If the teacher knows how the students are thinking, you can teach a class more easily. I mean, if you see the kids are dead, common sense will tell you you better change your strategy, you know? If all these kids are looking at you like a bunch of zombies, common sense will tell you you're doing something wrong. (Michie, 1999, pp. 143–144)

Understanding how students' interests, questions, and problems will change throughout their school years will help you serve them in the present. This chapter examines how students' needs change as they develop and how their needs reflect various intelligences, abilities, and disabilities.

HOW DO STUDENTS' NEEDS CHANGE AS THEY DEVELOP?

Development refers to the predictable changes that all human beings undergo as they progress through the life span—from conception to death. It is important to remember that students develop at different rates. Within a given classroom, for example, some students will be larger and physically more mature than others, some will be socially more sophisticated, and some will be able to think at a higher level of abstraction.

As humans progress through different stages of development, they mature and learn to perform the tasks that are a necessary part of daily living. There are several different types of human development. For example, as children develop physically, their bodies undergo numerous changes. As they develop cognitively, their mental capabilities expand so that they can use language and other symbol systems to solve problems. As they develop socially, they learn to interact more effectively with other people—as individuals and in groups. And as they develop morally, their actions come to reflect a greater appreciation of principles such as equity, justice, fairness, and altruism.

Because no two students progress through the stages of cognitive, social, and moral development in quite the same way, teachers need perspectives on these three types of development that are flexible, dynamic, and, above all, useful. By becoming familiar with models of cognitive, social, and moral development, teachers at all levels, from preschool through college, can better serve their students. Three such models are Piaget's theory of **cognitive development,** Erikson's stages of **psychosocial development,** and Kohlberg's stages of **moral reasoning.**

Piaget's Model of Cognitive Development

Jean Piaget (1896–1980), the noted Swiss biologist and philosopher, made extensive observational studies of children. He concluded that children reason differently from adults and even have different perceptions of the world. Piaget surmised that children learn through actively interacting with their environments, much as scientists do, and proposed that a child's thinking progresses through a sequence of four cognitive stages. According to Piaget's theory of cognitive development, the rate of progress through the four stages varies from individual to individual.

During the school years, students move through the **preoperational stage,** the **concrete operations stage,** and the **formal operations stage;** however, because of individual interaction with the total environment, each student's perceptions and learning will be unique. According to Piaget:

> The principal goal of education is to create [learners] who are capable of doing new things, not simply repeating what other generations have done—[learners] who are creative, inventive, and discoverers. [We] need pupils who are active, who learn early to find out by themselves, partly by their own spontaneous activity and partly through material we set up for them; who learn early to tell what is verifiable and what is simply the first idea to come to them. (quoted in Ripple & Rockcastle, 1964, p. 5)

Figure 9.1, based on Piaget's work and more recent research, shows the progression of logical thinking and appropriate teaching strategies as thinking abilities develop.

Erikson's Model of Psychosocial Development

Erik Erikson's (1902–1994) model of psychosocial development delineates eight stages, from infancy to old age (see Table 9.1). For each stage, a **psychosocial crisis** is central in the individual's emotional and social growth. Erikson expresses these crises in polar terms; for instance, in the first stage, that of infancy, the psychosocial crisis is trust versus mistrust. Erikson explains that the major psychosocial task for the infant is to develop a sense of trust in the world but not to give up totally a sense of distrust. In the tension between the poles of trust and mistrust, a greater pull toward the more positive pole is considered healthy and is accompanied by a virtue. In this case, if trust prevails, the virtue is hope.

Shortly before his death in 1994 at the age of 91, Erikson postulated a ninth stage in the human life cycle, *gerotranscendence,* during which some people mentally transcend the reality of their deteriorating bodies and faculties. In the final chapter of an extended version of Erikson's *The Life Cycle Completed,* first published in 1982, his wife and lifelong colleague, Joan M. Erikson (1901–1997), described the challenge of the ninth stage:

> Despair, which haunts the eighth stage, is a close companion in the ninth, because it is almost impossible to know what emergencies and losses of physical ability are imminent. As independence and control are challenged, self-esteem and confidence weaken. Hope and trust, which once provided firm support, are no longer the sturdy props of former days. To face down despair with faith and appropriate humility is perhaps the wisest course. (1997, pp. 105–106)

When we examine the issues and concerns of students in childhood and early and late adolescence later in this chapter, we will return to Erikson's model of psychosocial development. For further information on this significant and useful theory of development, you may wish to read Erikson's first book, *Childhood and Society* (1963).

Kohlberg's Model of Moral Development

According to Lawrence Kohlberg (1927–1987), the reasoning process people use to decide what is right and wrong evolves through three levels of development. Within each level, Kohlberg has identified two stages. Figure 9.2 shows that at Level I, the preconventional level, the individual decides what is right on the basis of personal needs and rules developed by others. At Level II, the conventional level, moral decisions reflect a desire for the approval of others and a willingness to conform to the expectations of family, community, and country. At Level III, the postconventional level, the individual has developed values and principles that are based on rational, personal choices that can be separated from conventional values.

Kohlberg suggests that "over 50 percent of late adolescents and adults are capable of full formal reasoning [i.e., they can use their intelligence to reason abstractly, form hypotheses, and test these hypotheses against reality], but only 10 percent of these adults dis-

Grade Level	Age-Typical Characteristics	Suggested Strategies
K–2	• Emergence of class inclusion • Emergence of conservation in simple tasks (e.g., conservation of liquid and number) • Increasing ability to explain and justify conclusions about logical reasoning tasks	• Use concrete manipulatives and experiences to illustrate concepts and ideas. • Provide practice in classifying objects in multiple ways—for instance, by shape, size, color, and texture. • In early arithmetic lessons, determine whether children have achieved conservation of number—for instance, by asking them whether a set of objects you have just rearranged has more or fewer objects than it had previously.
3–5	• Emergence of conservation in more challenging tasks (e.g., conservation of weight) • Occasional abstract and hypothetical thinking • Ability to understand simple fractions (e.g., $\frac{1}{3}$, $\frac{1}{6}$, $\frac{1}{8}$) that can be related to concrete objects	• Supplement verbal explanations with concrete examples, pictures, and hands-on activities. • Have students engage in simple scientific investigations, focusing on familiar objects and phenomena. • Introduce simple fractions by relating them to everyday objects (e.g., pizza slices, kitchen measuring cups).
6–8	• Increasing ability to reason logically about abstract, hypothetical, and contrary-to-fact situations • Some ability to test hypotheses and to separate and control variables, especially when an adult provides hints about how to proceed • Increasing ability to understand and work with proportions • Some ability to interpret proverbs, figures of speech, and other forms of figurative language	• Present abstract concepts and principles central to various academic disciplines, but make them concrete in some way (e.g., relate *gravity* to everyday experiences, show a diagram of an *atom*). • Assign mathematics problems that require use of simple fractions, ratios, or decimals. • Ask students to speculate on the meanings of well-known proverbs (e.g., "Two heads are better than one," "A stitch in time saves nine").
9–12	• Greater ability to think abstractly in math and science than in the social sciences • Increasing proficiency in aspects of the scientific method (e.g., formulation and testing of hypotheses, separation and control of variables) • Greater proficiency in interpreting figurative language • Idealistic (but not always realistic) views about how government, social policy, and other aspects of society should be changed	• Study particular topics in depth; introduce complex and abstract explantions and theories. • Have students design some of their own experiments in science labs and science fair projects. • Ask students to speculate on the meanings of unfamiliar proverbs (e.g., "As you sow, so shall you reap," "Discretion is the better part of valor"). • Encourage discussions about social, political, and ethical issues; elicit multiple perspectives on these issues.

FIGURE 9.1 Logical thinking abilities at different grade levels

Source: From Jeanne E. Ormrod. Essentials of Educational Psychology, 1e. Published by Merrill, an imprint of Pearson Education. Copyright 2009 by Pearson Education. Reprinted by permission. All rights reserved.

play principled (Stages 5 and 6) moral reasoning" (2006, p. 139). In addition, Kohlberg found that maturity of moral judgment is not highly related to IQ or verbal intelligence.

Kohlberg's model has been criticized because it focuses on moral reasoning rather than actual behavior, and it tends to look at moral development from a male perspective. Carol Gilligan, for example, suggests that male moral reasoning tends to address the rights of the individual, while female moral reasoning addresses the individual's responsibility to other people. In her book *In a Different Voice: Psychological Theory and*

TABLE 9.1 Erikson's eight stages of psychosocial development

Stage	Approximate Age	Psychosocial "Crisis"	Description	"Basic Strength" (Positive Result if Crisis Is Adequately Resolved)
1. Infancy	Birth to 18 months	Trust versus basic mistrust	Infant needs to be nurtured and loved; if not, he or she becomes insecure and mistrustful.	Drive and hope
2. Early childhood	18 months to 3 years	Autonomy versus shame	Child focuses on developing physical skills—toilet training, walking, talking, feeding self; inadequate resolution of crisis leads to feelings of shame and doubt.	Self-control, courage, and will
3. Play age	3 to 6 years	Initiative versus guilt	Child learns to develop skills through play and cooperation; inadequate resolution of crisis leads to sense of guilt and fearfulness.	Purpose and direction
4. School age	6 to 12 years	Industry versus inferiority	Child acquires new skills, knowledge; develops sense of achievement; inadequate resolution of crisis leaves child feeling inadequate and inferior.	Competence and method
5. Adolescence	12 to 20 years	Identity versus role confusion, identity diffusion	Adolescent focuses on clarifying identity, developing social relationships with peers and others, and grappling with moral issues; inadequate resolution of crisis leads to self-doubt and self-consciousness.	Fidelity and devotion
6. Young adulthood	20 to 35 years	Intimacy versus isolation	Young adult seeks companionship and love through relationships with friends and becoming intimate with a "significant other"; inadequate resolution of crisis leads to feelings of isolation and distance from others.	Love and affiliation
7. Middle adulthood	35 to 65	Generativity versus self-absorption or stagnation	Adult focuses on family relationships, parenting, and creative and meaningful work; inadequate resolution of crisis leads to feelings of stagnation and alienation.	Care and production
8. Late adulthood	65 to death	Integrity versus despair	Adult focuses on meaning and purpose in one's life, lifetime accomplishments and contributions, acceptance of oneself and fulfillment; inadequate resolution of crisis leads to feelings of failure, disdain for world, and fear of death.	Wisdom and acceptance

I. Preconventional Level of Moral Reasoning

Child is responsive to cultural rules and labels of good and bad, right or wrong, but interprets these in terms of consequences of action (punishment, reward, exchanges of favors).

Stage 1:   *Punishment-and-obedience orientation*
Physical consequences of action determine its goodness or badness.
Avoidance of punishment and deference to power are valued.

Stage 2:   *The instrumental-relativist orientation*
Right action consists of that which satisfies one's own needs and occasionally the needs of others. Reciprocity is a matter of "you scratch my back and I'll scratch yours."

II. Conventional Level of Moral Reasoning

Maintaining the expectations of the individual's family, group, or nation is perceived as valuable, regardless of consequences.

Stage 3:   *The interpersonal concordance or "good boy–nice girl" orientation*
Good behavior is that which pleases or helps others and is approved by them.

Stage 4:   *The "law and order" orientation*
Orientation toward fixed rules and the maintenance of the social order. Right behavior consists of doing one's duty and showing respect for authority.

III. Postconventional, Autonomous, or Principled Level of Moral Reasoning

Effort to define moral principles that have validity and application apart from the authority of groups.

Stage 5:   *The social-contract, legalistic orientation*
Right action defined in terms of rights and standards that have been agreed on by the whole society. This is the "official" morality of the U.S. government and Constitution.

Stage 6:   *The universal-ethical-principle orientation*
Right is defined by conscience in accord with self-chosen ethical principles appealing to logic and universality.

FIGURE 9.2 Kohlberg's theory of moral reasoning

Source: Adapted from Lawrence Kohlberg, "The Cognitive-Developmental Approach to Moral Education," in Forrest W. Parkay, Eric J. Anctil, and Glen Hass (Eds.), Curriculum Planning: A Contemporary Approach, 8th Edition. Boston: Allyn and Bacon, 2006, p. 138. The original version appeared in Journal of Philosophy, 70(18), 1973, 631–632.

Women's Development (1993), Gilligan refers to women's principal moral voice as the "ethics of care," which emphasizes care of others over the more male-oriented "ethics of justice." Thus, when confronted with a moral dilemma, females tend to suggest solutions based more on altruism and self-sacrifice than on rights and rules (Gilligan, 1993).

The question remains: Can moral reasoning be taught? Can you help students develop so that they live according to principles of equity, justice, caring, and empathy? Kohlberg suggests the following three conditions that can help children internalize moral principles:

1. Exposure to the next higher stage of reasoning
2. Exposure to situations posing problems and contradictions for the child's current moral structure, leading to dissatisfaction with his [her] current level
3. An atmosphere of interchange and dialogue combining the first two conditions, in which conflicting moral views are compared in an open manner (Kohlberg, 2006, p. 145).

One approach to teaching values and moral reasoning is known as **character education,** a movement that "promotes the teaching of core values that can be taught directly through course curricula, especially in literature, social studies, and social science classes" (Power et al., 2008, p. xxxvi). There is no single way for teachers to develop students' character; however, in comments made shortly after the shooting deaths of 14 students and a teacher at Columbine High School in Colorado, well-known sociologist and organizer of several White House conferences on character education Amitai Etzioni

(1999) said, "What schools should help youngsters develop—if schools are going to help lower the likelihood of more Columbines—are two crucial behavior characteristics: the capacity to channel impulses into prosocial outlets, and empathy with others." Figure 9.3 illustrates a 12-point strategy teachers can use to create moral classroom communities.

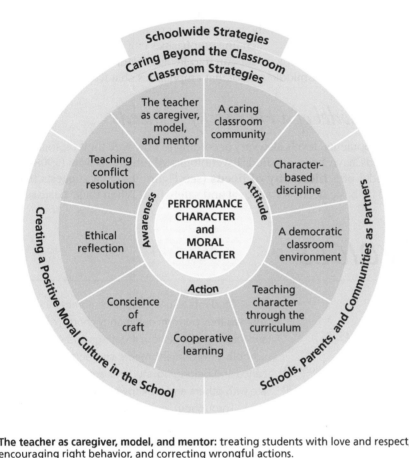

FIGURE 9.3 A 12-point comprehensive approach to character education
Source: Thomas Lickona. Center for the 4th and 5th Rs. (2008). Cortland, NY: SUNY Cortland School of Education. Retrieved from http:// www.cortland.edu/character/ 12pts.asp.

1. **The teacher as caregiver, model, and mentor:** treating students with love and respect, encouraging right behavior, and correcting wrongful actions.

2. **A caring classroom community:** teaching students to respect and care about each other.

3. **Character-based discipline:** using rules and consequences to develop moral reasoning, self-control, and a generalized respect for others.

4. **A democratic classroom environment:** using the class meeting to engage students in shared decision making and in taking responsibility for making the classroom the best it can be.

5. **Teaching character through the curriculum:** using the ethically rich content of academic subjects as vehicles for values teaching.

6. **Cooperative learning:** fostering students' ability to work with and appreciate others.

7. **Conscience of craft:** developing students' sense of academic responsibility and the habit of doing their work well.

8. **Ethical reflection:** developing the cognitive side of character through reading, research, writing, and discussion.

9. **Teaching conflict resolution:** teaching students how to solve conflicts fairly, without intimidation or violence.

10. **Caring beyond the classroom:** using role models to inspire altruistic behavior and providing opportunities for school and community service.

11. **Creating a positive moral culture in the school:** developing a caring school community that promotes the core virtues.

12. **School, parents, and communities as partners:** helping parents and the whole community join the schools in a cooperative effort to build good character.

Many schools, such as the Hyde Schools in Bath, Maine, and Woodstock, Connecticut, emphasize specific moral values in their curricula. The character-based educational program at the Hyde Schools focuses on five words: *curiosity, courage, concern, leadership,* and *integrity* (Stengel & Tom, 2006). Kennedy Middle School in Eugene, Oregon, implemented the Second Step program, described by a teacher as "a school-wide curriculum that teaches students skills such as how to communicate, problem-solve, and work together in a community. They learn the importance of responsibility and honesty . . . [and] a large section at the beginning of each unit emphasizes empathy" (DeRoche & Williams, 2001, p. 163). The Teachers' Voices: Research to Reality feature in this chapter describes the River School, a charter middle school that emphasizes character education.

Maslow's Model of a Hierarchy of Needs

Students' developmental levels also vary according to how well their biological and psychological needs have been satisfied. Psychologist Abraham Maslow (1908–1970) formulated a model of a **hierarchy of needs** (see Figure 9.4) that suggests that people are motivated by basic needs for survival and safety first. When these basic needs have

TEACHERS' VOICES RESEARCH TO REALITY

Linda Inlay
VALUES: THE IMPLICIT CURRICULUM

Whether teachers intend to or not, they teach values. A school's culture communicates values through the ways in which faculty, parents, and students treat one another and through school policies on issues such as discipline and decision making. At River School, a charter middle school of approximately 160 students, we work hard to develop an entire school culture that teaches character through the explicit curriculum of reading, writing, and arithmetic and through an implicit curriculum of values.

At River School, we rarely talk about character—nor do we have posters or pencils that trumpet values—because we know that the most effective character education is to model the values that we want to see in our students. We attempt to align every part of our school—from assessment to awards, from decision making to discipline—to encourage and foster students' character development.

The middle school years are about testing limits and shedding the old skin of the elementary school years, and we expect our students to cross boundaries as a way to learn about choice, consequences, freedom, and responsibility. Students say that they notice that our discipline system is different because we treat them like adults, even when they don't act like adults. We trust in our students' innate ability to make good decisions for themselves—with practice over time.

Students also learn that the community depends on them as they perform community chores, offer community service, and plan school meetings and events. When the school's environment meets students' needs for significance and belonging, students are more likely to cooperate with others and look toward the common good.

Throughout our school, the implicit message is clear: We deeply respect our students, not just because they are our students, but because all human beings have the right to be respected in these ways. The seminal ideas of our program are not new. We have simply translated them into practical, day-to-day applications embedded in the school setting so that the entire school's culture becomes our implicit curriculum. Everything that we do and say teaches character.

PERSONAL REFLECTION

1. What examples can you cite to support Inlay's assertion that "whether teachers intend to or not, they teach values"?
2. Reflect on the schools you have attended. What values did you learn while attending those schools?

Linda Inlay is director of the River School in Napa, California. The preceding is excerpted from her article, "Values: The Implicit Curriculum," in *Educational Leadership* 60, No. 6 (March 2003): 69–71.

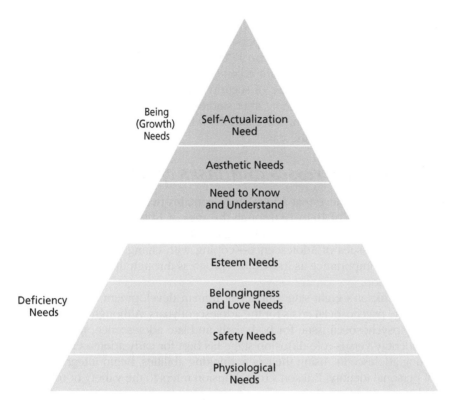

FIGURE 9.4 Maslow's hierarchy of needs

Note: The four lower-level needs are called deficiency needs *because the motivation to satisfy them decreases when they are met. On the other hand, when* being (growth) *needs are met, motivation to fulfill them increases.*

Source: Based on Abraham H. Maslow, Toward a Psychology of Being, *3rd Edition. New York: John Wiley & Sons, 1959; and* Motivation and Personality, *3rd Edition. Boston: Addison-Wesley, 1987.*

been met sufficiently, people naturally seek to satisfy higher needs, the highest of which is self-actualization—the desire to use one's talents, abilities, and potentialities to the fullest. Students whose needs for safety have been fairly well satisfied will discover strong needs for friendship, affection, and love, for example. If efforts to satisfy the various needs are thwarted, the result can be maladjustment and interruption or delay in the individual's full and healthy development.

Students differ markedly in terms of where they are on Maslow's hierarchy of needs. Many families lack the resources to provide adequately for children's basic needs. Children from families that are concerned with day-to-day survival may not receive the support that could help them succeed in school. They come to school tired and hungry and may have trouble paying attention in class. Others may be well fed and clothed but feel unsafe, alien, or unloved; they may seek to protect themselves by withdrawing emotionally from activities around them.

Developmental Stresses and Tasks of Childhood

During Erikson's school-age stage, children strive for a sense of industry and struggle against feelings of inferiority. If successful, they gain the virtue of competence, believing in their abilities to do things. If children find evidence that they are inferior to others, if they experience failure when they try new tasks, and if they struggle without ever gaining a sense of mastery, then they feel incompetent.

Children gain the sense of industry needed at this age by playing seriously, mastering new skills, producing products, and being workers. When they first go to school, they are oriented toward accomplishing new things. (Some kindergartners expect to learn to read on their first day of school and are disappointed when they don't!) For young schoolchildren, the idea of work is attractive; it means that they are doing something grown-up.

Is childhood a time of carefree play or a period of stress? Certainly the answer depends on the life circumstances and personality of the individual child. In a study of stressful events in the lives of more than 1,700 children in the second through the ninth grades in six countries, Karou Yamamoto and his associates found that the most stressful events "threaten[ed] one's sense of security and occasion[ed] personal denigration and embarrassment" (1996, p. 139). Other studies have shown that serious stress is experienced by latchkey children, for example, who are left on their own or in each other's care for part or all of the day.

Developmental Stresses and Tasks of Adolescence

Many psychologists believe that adolescence contains two distinct stages: an early period covering the ages of 10 to 12 through the ages of 14 to 16, and a late period from approximately 15 to 16 through 19. Although continuity exists in each individual's life, the psychosocial issues of adolescence—coping with change and seeking identity—vary in form and importance as individuals progress through the transition from childhood to adulthood.

In Erik Erikson's eight-stage model of human development, identity versus role diffusion is the psychosocial crisis for the adolescent years. Although the quest for identity is a key psychosocial issue for both early and late adolescence, many believe that Erikson's identity-versus-role-diffusion stage fits best for early adolescence. During this time, young adolescents, using their new thinking abilities, begin integrating a clearer sense of personal identity. Erikson's role diffusion refers to the variety of roles that adolescents have available to them.

According to Erikson's theory, when adolescents identify themselves with a peer group, with a school, or with a cause, their sense of fidelity—the virtue of this stage—is clear and strong. At this stage, adolescents are loyal and committed, sometimes to people or ideas that may dismay or alarm their parents, sometimes to high ideals and dreams.

In late adolescence, the quest for identity shifts from relying on others to self-reliance. Young people continue to work on strengthening their sense of identity in late adolescence, but as they do so, they draw less on the reactions of their peers and more on their own regard for what matters. Although late adolescents possess an array of interests, talents, and goals in life, they share a desire to achieve independence. More like adults than children, late adolescents are anxious to use newly acquired strengths, skills, and knowledge to achieve their own purposes, whether through marriage, parenthood, full-time employment, education beyond high school, a career, or military service.

The vulnerability of today's adolescents is evident in the results of a survey of 1 million students based on 40 "developmental assets" (positive relationships, opportunities, skills, and values) adolescents need to become healthy, mature adults: "[O]n average, youth have less than half of the 40 assets they need to grow up healthy, caring, and responsible. . . . [T]his statistic remains relatively consistent among urban, rural, and suburban communities" (Search Institute, 2002). Moreover, "a solid majority of American adults—two thirds—spontaneously describe adolescents in starkly negative terms: *wild, rude, irresponsible*. Half give

What developmental task do these two middle school students need to accomplish as part of their psychosocial development? How can their teacher help with those developmental tasks?

those descriptions even to younger children" (Scales, 2001, p. 64). The list of alarming concerns in adolescence includes academic failure and retention, accidents, assaultive behavior, criminal activity, cultism, depression, discipline problems, dropping out, drug abuse, eating disorders, homicides, incest, prostitution, running away, school absenteeism, suicide, teenage pregnancy, vandalism, and the contraction of sexually transmitted diseases.

As a teacher, what can you do to help children and adolescents develop to their full potential? To help prevent the problems that place them at risk, an energetic, creative, and multifaceted approach is necessary. Figure 9.5 presents several strategies for helping students develop competence, positive self-concepts, and high esteem and for intervening to prevent or address problems that place them at risk.

HOW DO STUDENTS VARY IN INTELLIGENCE?

In addition to developmental differences, students differ in terms of their intellectual capacity. Unfortunately, test scores, and sometimes intelligence quotient (IQ) scores, are treated as accurate measurements of students' intellectual ability because of their convenience and long-time use. What is intelligence, and how has it been redefined to account for the many ways in which it is expressed?

---

1. **Provide opportunities and encouragement for students to develop competence.**
   - Provide a learning environment in which students can risk making mistakes.
   - Assign work that students can perform successfully and still be challenged.
   - Have realistic but high expectations for students.
   - Express belief in students' ability to succeed.
   - Encourage industry by letting students work on goals or projects of their choosing.
   - Provide opportunities for students to take special responsibility.
   - Assign older students to work with younger ones.
   - Reward industry and competence.

2. **Promote the development of positive self-concept and high self-esteem.**
   - Give praise more than criticism.
   - Take students and their work seriously.
   - Respect students' dignity.
   - Plan individual and group activities that boost morale.
   - Provide opportunities for students to interact and work cooperatively.
   - Teach and model acceptance of human diversity and individuality.
   - Develop systems for the recognition and reward of individual and group achievement.
   - Support students' efforts to achieve and appropriately express independence.

3. **Intervene to prevent or address problems that place students at risk.**
   - Provide a safe and structured learning environment where students feel secure.
   - Practice effective leadership and classroom management.
   - Provide opportunities to discuss preferences, values, morals, goals, and consequences.
   - Teach and model critical thinking, decision making, and problem solving.
   - Teach and model prosocial attitudes and behaviors and conflict resolution strategies.
   - Provide information on subjects of special concern to students and parents.
   - Cultivate family involvement.
   - Collaborate, consult, network, and refer on behalf of students.

FIGURE 9.5 What teachers can do to help children and adolescents develop

Though many definitions of **intelligence** have been proposed, the term has yet to be completely defined. One view is that intelligence is the ability to learn. As David Wechsler, the developer of the most widely used intelligence scales for children and adults, said: "Intelligence, operationally defined, is the aggregate or global capacity to act purposefully, to think rationally, and to deal effectively with the environment" (1958, p. 7). Other perspectives on intelligence include the following:

- It is *adaptive*. It involves modifying and adjusting one's behavior to accomplish new tasks successfully.
- It is related to *learning ability.* Intelligent people learn information more quickly and easily than less intelligent people.
- It involves the *use of prior knowledge* to analyze and understand new situations effectively.
- It involves the complex interaction and coordination of *many different thinking and reasoning processes*.
- It is *culture-specific.* What is "intelligent" behavior in one culture is not necessarily intelligent behavior in another culture (Ormrod, 2006, p. 153).

Intelligence Testing

The intelligence tests that we now use can be traced to the 1905 Metrical Scale of Intelligence designed by French psychologists Alfred Binet and Theodore Simon, who were part of a Paris-based commission that wanted a way to identify children who would need special help with their learning. Binet revised the scale in 1908, which was adapted for American children in 1916 by Lewis Terman, a psychologist at Stanford University. Terman's test was further adapted, especially by the U.S. Army, which transformed it into a paper-and-pencil test that could be administered to large groups. The use of such intelligence tests has continued throughout the years. Approximately 67 percent of the population have an IQ between 85 and 115—the range of normal intelligence.

Individual intelligence tests are presently valued by psychologists and those in the field of special education because they can be helpful in diagnosing a student's strengths and weaknesses. However, group intelligence tests given for the purpose of classifying students into like-score groups have received an increasing amount of criticism.

Group IQ tests have been criticized because test items and tasks are culturally biased, drawn mostly from White middle-class experience. Thus, the tests are more assessments of how informed students are about features in a specific class or culture than of how intelligent they are in general. This complaint became a formal, legal challenge when, on the basis of their IQ test scores, a group of African American children were put into special classes for mentally retarded children. Their parents brought the complaint to the courts in 1971 and persisted with it all the way to the federal appellate court, where a decision was eventually made in their favor in 1984. In that well-known case, *Larry P. v. Riles* (1984), the court decided that IQ tests were discriminatory and culturally biased. However, in another case, *PASE v. Hannon* (1980), an Illinois district court ruled that when IQ tests were used in conjunction with other forms of assessment, such as teacher observation, they were not discriminatory for placement purposes. Although the criticism continues, psychometricians are attempting to design culture-free intelligence tests.

Multiple Intelligences

Many theorists believe that intelligence is a basic ability that enables one to perform mental operations in the following areas: logical reasoning, spatial reasoning, number ability, and verbal meaning. However, other theorists believe "that conventional notions of intelligence are incomplete and hence inadequate. [One's] ability to achieve success depends on capitalizing on one's strengths and correcting or compensating for one's weaknesses through a balance of analytical, creative, and practical abilities" (Sternberg, 2002, pp. 447–448). For example, Howard Gardner believes that human beings possess at least eight separate forms of intelligence; "each intelligence reflects the potential to solve problems or to fashion products that are valued in one or more cultural settings. [Each] features its own distinctive form of mental representation" (1999, pp. 71–72). Drawing on the theories of others and research findings on savants, prodigies, and other exceptional individuals, Gardner originally suggested in *Frames of Mind* (1983) that human beings possessed seven human intelligences: logical-mathematical, linguistic, musical, spatial, bodily-kinesthetic, interpersonal, and intrapersonal. In the mid-1990s, he identified an eighth intelligence, that of the naturalist. In *The Disciplined Mind* (Gardner, 1999, p. 72), he suggests that "it is possible that human beings also exhibit a ninth, existential intelligence—the proclivity to pose (and ponder) questions about life, death, and ultimate realities" and a tenth, spiritual intelligence. According to Gardner, every person possesses at least the eight intelligences (see Figure 9.6), yet each person has his or her particular blend of the intelligences.

Logical-mathematical intelligences enables individuals to use and appreciate abstract relations. Scientists, mathematicians, and philosophers all rely on this intelligence. So do the students who "live" baseball statistics or who carefully analyze the components of problems—either personal or school-related—before systematically testing solutions.

Linguistic intelligence allows individuals to communicate and make sense of the world through language. Poets exemplify this intelligence in its mature form. Students who enjoy playing with rhymes, who pun, who always have a story to tell, who quickly acquire other languages—including sign language—all exhibit linguistic intelligence.

Musical intelligence allows people to create, communicate, and understand meanings made out of sound. While composers and instrumentalists clearly exhibit this intelligence, so do the students who seem particularly attracted by the birds singing outside the classroom window or who constantly tap out intricate rhythms on the desk with their pencils.

Spatial intelligence makes it possible for people to perceive visual or spatial information, to transform this information, and to re-create visual images from memory. Well-developed spatial capacities are needed for the work of architects, sculptors, and engineers. The students who turn first to the graphs, charts, and pictures in their textbooks, who like to "web" their ideas before writing a paper, and who fill the blank space around their notes with intricate patterns are also using their spatial intelligence.

Bodily-kinesthetic intelligence allows individuals to use all or part of the body to create products or solve problems. Athletes, surgeons, dancers, choreographers, and craftspeople all use bodily-kinesthetic intelligence. The capacity is also evident in students who relish gym class and school dances, who prefer to carry out class projects by making models rather than writing reports, and who toss crumpled paper with frequency and accuracy into wastebaskets across the room.

Interpersonal intelligence enables individuals to recognize and make distinctions about others' feelings and intentions. Teachers, parents, politicians, psychologists, and salespeople rely on interpersonal intelligence. Students exhibit this intelligence when they thrive on small-group work, when they notice and react to the moods of their friends and classmates, and when they tactfully convince the teacher of their need for extra time to complete the homework assignment.

Intrapersonal intelligence helps individuals to distinguish among their own feelings, to build accurate mental models of themselves, and to draw on these models to make decisions about their lives. Although it is difficult to assess who has this capacity and to what degree, evidence can be sought in students' uses of their other intelligences—how well they seem to be capitalizing on their strengths, how cognizant they are of their weaknesses, and how thoughtful they are about the decisions and choices they make.

Naturalist intelligence allows people to distinguish among, classify, and use features of the environment. Farmers, gardeners, botanists, geologists, florists, and archaeologists all exhibit this intelligence, as do students who can name and describe the features of every make of car around them.

FIGURE 9.6 The eight intelligences

Gardner's theory of **multiple intelligences** is valuable for teachers. As Robert Slavin suggests, "Teachers must avoid thinking about children as smart or not smart because there are many ways to be smart" (2000, p. 130). Some students are talented in terms of their interpersonal relations and exhibit natural leadership abilities. Others seem to have a high degree of what some researchers have termed **emotional intelligence**—awareness of and ability to manage their feelings (Salovey & Feldman-Barrett, 2002; Salovey, Mayer, & Caruso, 2002; Salovey & Sluyter, 1997). Differences in musical, athletic, and mechanical abilities can be recognized by even the minimally informed observer. Because these intelligences are not tested or highlighted, they may go unnoticed and possibly wasted.

However, keep in mind Gardner's "reflections" 14 years after the publication of *Frames of Mind:*

> MI [multiple intelligences] may be appealing, but it is not for the faint-hearted, nor for those in search of a quick fix. After initial experimentation with the ideas and practices of MI, practitioners realize that MI is not an end in itself. To say that one has an MI classroom or an MI school is not meaningful—one has to ask "MI for what?" (1997, p. 20)

Learning Styles

Students vary greatly in regard to **learning styles,** the approaches to learning that work best for them. These differences have also been called *learning style preferences* or *cognitive styles.* The National Task Force on Learning Style and Brain Behavior suggests that there is a "consistent pattern of behavior and performance by which an individual approaches educational experiences. It is the composite of characteristic cognitive, affective, and physiological behaviors that serve as relatively stable indicators of how a learner perceives, interacts with, and responds to the learning environment." (cited in Bennett, 1990, p. 94)

Students' learning styles are determined by a combination of hereditary and environmental influences. Some more quickly learn things they hear; others learn faster when they see material in writing. Some need a lot of structure; others learn best when they can be independent and follow their desires. Some learn best in formal settings; others learn best in informal, relaxed environments. Some need almost total silence to concentrate; others learn well in noisy, active environments. Some are intuitive learners; some prefer to learn by following logical, sequential steps.

There is no one "correct" view of learning styles to guide teachers in their daily decision making. Culture-based differences in learning styles are subtle, variable, and difficult to describe (Zhang & Sternberg, 2001), and learning styles change as the individual matures. Moreover, critics maintain that there is little evidence to support the validity of dozens of conceptual models for learning styles and accompanying assessment instruments. Nevertheless, you should be aware of the concept of learning styles and realize that any given classroom activity may be more effective for some students than for others. Knowledge of your own and your students' learning styles will help you to individualize instruction and motivate your students. To keep track of information related to students' learning styles, academic progress, and individual learning needs, some teachers use a learning management system (LMS), such as the one described in the Technology in Action feaure in this chapter.

As a teacher, you will quickly learn that no one instructional approach matches the learning styles and needs of every child. How can you gather information about your students' preferred approaches to learning?

Learning With Style

An example of how one school modified its educational programs is Libertyville High School in Libertyville, Illinois. All Libertyville freshmen take a five-week course called Learning

With Style during the second half of their lunch period. At the beginning of the course, students complete the Learning Preference Inventory (Hanson & Silver, 2000) to help the students and their teachers understand their personal learning styles.

During the course, students learn about different approaches to learning, and they begin to reflect on their own learning behaviors. With the help of teachers, guidance counselors, and parents, each student develops a set of skills and learning strategies that matches his or her interests.

Students also learn about the strengths and weaknesses of each style. Students develop "personal growth plans" and explore careers that fit their learning styles. Students map out their high school careers, meeting regularly with their guidance counselors to discuss and revise their goals in light of new learning and experiences.

All teachers at the high school are trained in learning styles. They work closely with the teacher of the Learning With Style course and the guidance counselors. Parents are also encouraged to attend an adult version of the learning style course at night. Parents then help their children and the school make the best decisions about the child's education and future career.

During the adult learning style course, the teacher reviews student profiles and explains to parents how their children learn, what they need to be successful, and what areas may need special attention. Parents learn about how a student's learning style can influence decisions about college, vocation, and becoming a lifelong learner. The teacher of the learning style course sums up how knowledge of students' learning styles can help teachers establish authentic learning communities in their classrooms: "It keeps the learning environment fresh by helping us to remember that every student has unique interests, talents, and needs and that as an educational institution, we really can treat all our students to the personalized learning program they need and deserve" (Strong, Silver, & Perini, 2001, pp. 92–93).

HOW DO STUDENTS VARY IN ABILITY AND DISABILITY?

Students also differ according to their special needs and talents. Some enter the world with exceptional abilities or disabilities, others encounter life experiences that change their capabilities significantly, and still others struggle with conditions that medical scientists have yet to understand. To the fullest extent possible, all children and youth with exceptionalities are given a public education in the United States. The Teachers' Voices: Walk in My Shoes feature in this chapter profiles Michael Kremer, a high school teacher who is committed to meeting the learning needs of all his students—from advanced placement students to students with autism.

Exceptional Learners

Children "who require special education and related services if they are to realize their full human potential" (Hallahan & Kauffman, 2006, p. 8) are referred to as **exceptional learners.** They are taught by special education teachers and by regular teachers into whose classrooms they have been integrated or included. Among the many exceptional children that teachers may encounter in the classroom are students who have physical, mental, or emotional disabilities and students who are gifted or talented.

Special needs students are often referred to synonymously as *handicapped* or *disabled.* However, it is important for teachers to understand the following:

> Many individuals with disabilities believe that the terms *disability* and *handicap* have very different meanings and interpretations. They are convinced that it is because of their *disabilities* (e.g., conditions and impairments) that society *handicaps* them (e.g., presents challenges and barriers). . . . Thus the ways in which people are treated by society and by other individuals are what present the real barriers that influence people's outcomes. Difficult situations occur not because of a condition or disability

TECHNOLOGY in *ACTION*

Learning Management Systems in the Classroom

Mr. Roper knew he would be traveling a lot this coming fall. His principal had found a competent substitute to fill in when he was out. However, Mr. Roper found that he wasted time trying to catch up after being gone: retrieving lost assignments, reviewing student progress, receiving updates on classroom discussion, and falling behind in grading coursework. Mr. Roper decided he would try the school's newly adopted learning management system (LMS), Moodle. (An LMS is an online course management website.) The LMS would allow him to organize his learning resources, student assessments, discussions, and activity schedule all in one place. And only his students would have access to the course materials because the site was password-protected. Only his students could participate in the discussions and review his comments on their work.

Mr. Roper realized that building a course in Moodle would take some effort. He started working early in the summer. He began by creating a course calendar that contained all the activities and assignments for the coming term. He created PowerPoint files for all his lectures and then narrated them in PowerPoint. He created detailed assignment instructions, resources, and grading criteria. He linked each assignment to a discussion topic and provided specific performance criteria for each discussion. He then uploaded these files into Moodle. He created an assignment dropbox—a place where his students could upload their assignments into Moodle. Thus, Mr. Roper could access the assignments any place he could connect his laptop to the Internet. He could open the assignments, review them, grade them, and return them to the students anywhere, anytime. His students could then review Mr. Roper's comments and view their grades. They could also ask for clarification on comments made by Mr. Roper—all online.

When the fall semester began, Mr. Roper took his class on a tour of the course Moodle site. He instructed his students about how to use the discussion, the assignment dropbox, the calendar, and other components of the course site. He made the Moodle site part of his daily activities, whether he was in the classroom or not.

When the semester was over, he found that he never lost an assignment—they were all saved online. He was part of the online discussion even when he was on the road. He could access the threaded discussion from home to comment on student postings. And so could his students.

One of the unforeseen benefits that Mr. Roper loved about the LMS was the course tracking system. He could see who logged in, where they went, how long they stayed, and what they did. This allowed him to assess each student's classroom participation. Another positive benefit for his student assessment was the text-based online course discussions. All discussions were archived, which allowed Mr. Roper to accurately assess a student's discussion performance. The asynchronous discussions were also appealing to students. They commented that the self-paced aspect of the online discussion gave them time to reflect on other student's comments and then post something thoughtful, as opposed to spontaneous.

LEARNING MANAGEMENT SYSTEM (LMS): An LMS, or content management system (CMS), is a set of linked software tools that allows teachers to manage student activities, create learning communities through an array of communication tools, assess student performance with automatically graded tests or quizzes, upload assignments, and track navigation. The LMS is an online course website that is password-protected.

VISIT: http://www.moodle.org. The Moodle site will help you understand the requirements to becoming a Moodle user. On the site, you can download a variety of free Moodle versions; read, watch, and listen to Moodle support materials; take part in the Moodle community discussion; and explore various examples, tips, and advice for teachers interested in using Moodle in their classrooms.

POSSIBLE USES: Teachers have used learning management systems to coordinate student activities, allow students to upload assignments from their home computers, and participate in discussions with other students any place and any time.

TRY IT OUT: The best way to experience Moodle is through the Demo Course link at www.moodle.org. You will find several options on the demonstration site. You also have the option to download a free version of the Moodle program, which you can run from your own computer. Before you can do any of this, however, you need to become a member. Just click on the Create New Account link and follow the instructions.

 # TEACHERS' VOICES
Walk in My Shoes

Michael Kremer's 38-year career in teaching has been filled with successful experiences teaching a wide variety of students and courses and working in unique situations and leadership roles. He values students and believes that a key to addressing their individual needs is to teach the *whole* person.

Michael began teaching in the California Institution for Women, a correctional facility in Corona, California. He taught reading, English, and literature classes for half a day and was the prison librarian the other half. Some of his students were working on their General Educational Development (GED) to complete their high school work. Some came to class for the sense of freedom it provided, some came to learn, some realized they would get nowhere without learning how to read. Teaching at the prison was a major learning experience for Michael, who was then 23 and had been fairly sheltered. His students there taught him "a great deal about being a teacher and the needs that people have."

The career that followed is varied. He has taught high school English, drama, computer programming, humanities, and college English and drama. He was the English Department Chair at Montclair High School for 5 years, coached football for 18 years and the academic decathlon team for 5 years, and directed over 100 plays. He has been teaching drama full-time for the past 20 years and has a program "big enough to have 2 full-time drama teachers." His current program has over 350 students.

He taught 18 years at Montclair High School, 13 years at Etiwanda High School, and has been teaching at Los Osos High School since it opened in 2002. Under Michael's leadership, the Drama Department became one of the very best in southern California, winning prestigious awards and recognitions.

Michael's passion for teaching is obvious. Regarding the subjects he has taught and leadership roles he has had, he says, "At the time I loved everything; each new experience was fun. At this stage, I love teaching drama because it benefits students in so many ways."

For a drama teacher, addressing individual learners' needs is a necessity. "I'll have in my classes everything from the number-one advanced placement (AP) student to

"Each student is a rare example of humanity . . . You can become an important facet in his or her development."

students with autism whose parents are shocked that they'll get up in front of anybody and do a play." He uses small groups, works individually with students, and assigns partners, "making sure that kids are working with a variety of other kids and abilities. Addressing individual learners' needs is really built in; I'm extraordinarily lucky."

Michael believes that drama should be an emotionally safe place for all students. "Being in the audience, students have to respect the abilities of others, have to respect the work they do, and have to cheer them on." Stage fright happens to all types of students. "We need to provide a safe environment where they can try new things without fear of condemnation."

Michael's advice for new teachers is "to take the time to get to know the kids." His words reflect what his high school English teacher told him when he hired Michael to return to teach at his alma mater: "The kids here are not English teachers' students; you need to get out of the classroom and see them in other classes. You need to go to their football games and other performances."

He believes that "when students see you're interested in them as people, not just because they're part of your English class, they start to look at you as not just one of their six teachers—and you start to build trust. The comfort level starts when you show an interest in the whole person." The number and variety of students Michael draws to the stage and the growth of his drama programs confirm the soundness of his advice.

Michael's abilities help explain the outstanding reputation of his award-winning school. Most important to Michael are the opportunities he has to enrich the lives of students. He writes, "you are not working with a product that can be easily forced into shape; you are helping living, thinking, emotional beings whose lives are unique and whose needs force the teacher to ad lib and improvise. . . . each student is a rare example of humanity for whom you can become an important facet of his or her development."

Michael Kremer
Los Osos High School

but, rather, because people with disabilities are denied full participation in society as a consequence of their minority status. (Smith, 2007, pp. 9–10)

For example, Stephen W. Hawking, a gifted physicist, has amyotrophic lateral sclerosis (also known as Lou Gehrig's disease), which requires him to use a wheelchair for mobility and a speech synthesizer to communicate. If Hawking had to enter a building accessible only by stairs, or if a computer virus infected his speech synthesizer program, his disability would then become a handicap. As Hawking pointed out in his widely read book *A Brief History of Time: From the Big Bang to Black Holes* (1988), "I was fortunate that I choose theoretical physics, because it is all in the mind. So my disability has not been a serious handicap."

In addition, as a teacher you should know that current language use emphasizes the concept of "people first." In other words, a disabling condition should not be used as an adjective to describe a person. Thus, you should say "a child with a visual impairment," not a "blind child" or even a "visually impaired child."

You should also realize that the definitions for disabilities are generalized, open to change, and significantly influenced by the current cultural perception of normality. For example, the American Association on Mental Retardation (AAMR) has changed its definition of mental retardation seven times since 1950 to reflect shifting views of people with cognitive disabilities.

Cautions about labeling should also apply to gifted and talented students. Unfortunately, people commonly have a negative view of gifted and talented youngsters. Like many ethnic groups, gifted students are "different" and thus have been the target of many myths and stereotypes. However, a landmark study of 1,528 gifted males and females begun by Lewis Terman (Terman, Baldwin, & Bronson 1925; Terman & Oden, 1947, 1959) in 1926 and to continue until 2010 has "exploded the myth that high-IQ individuals [are] brainy but physically and socially inept. In fact, Terman found that children with outstanding IQs were larger, stronger, and better coordinated than other children and became better adjusted and more emotionally stable adults" (Slavin, 2003, p. 429).

Students With Disabilities

Table 9.2 shows that the percentage of all students participating in federally supported education programs for students with disabilities increased from 8.3 percent in 1976–77 to 13.5 percent in 2006–07. Nearly 6.7 million students participated in these programs in 2008 (National Center for Education Statistics, May 29, 2008).

Various tests and other forms of assessment are used to identify persons in various categories of disability. The following brief definitional characteristics are based on the Individuals with Disabilities Education Act (IDEA) and definitions used by professional organizations dedicated to meeting the needs of persons in each category.

1. **Specific learning disabilities (LD)**— learning is significantly hindered by difficulty in listening, speaking, reading, writing, reasoning, or computing
2. **Speech or language impairments**— significant difficulty in communicating with others as a result of speech or language disorders
3. **Mental retardation**— significant limitations in cognitive ability
4. **Serious emotional disturbance (SED)**— social and/or emotional maladjustment that significantly reduces the ability to learn
5. **Hearing impairments**— permanent or fluctuating mild to profound hearing loss in one or both ears
6. **Orthopedic impairments**— physically disabling conditions that affect locomotion or motor functions
7. **Other health impairments**— limited strength, vitality, or alertness caused by chronic or acute health problems
8. **Visual impairments**— vision loss that significantly inhibits learning
9. **Multiple disabilities**— two or more interrelated disabilities

TABLE 9.2 Percentage of children and youth ages 3–21 served under the Individuals with Disabilities Education Act (IDEA), by disability: Selected years, 1976–77 through 2006–07

Age and disability	1976 –77	1980 –81	1990 –91	1994 –95	1996 –97	1998 –99	2000 –01	2002 –03	2004 –05	2006 –07
All disabilities	8.3	10.1	11.4	12.2	12.6	13.0	13.3	13.5	13.8	13.5
Specific learning disabilities[1]	1.8	3.6	5.2	5.6	5.8	6.0	6.1	5.9	5.7	5.4
Speech or language impairments	2.9	2.9	2.4	2.3	2.3	2.3	3.0	2.9	3.0	3.0
Mental retardation	2.2	2.0	1.3	1.3	1.3	1.3	1.3	1.2	1.2	1.1
Emotional disturbance	0.6	0.8	0.9	1.0	1.0	1.0	1.0	1.0	1.0	0.9
Hearing impairments	0.2	0.2	0.1	0.1	0.1	0.2	0.2	0.2	0.2	0.2
Orthopedic impairments	0.2	0.1	0.1	0.1	0.1	0.1	0.2	0.2	0.2	0.1
Other health impairments	0.3	0.2	0.1	0.2	0.4	0.5	0.6	0.8	1.1	1.2
Visual impairments	0.1	0.1	0.1	0.1	0.1	0.1	0.1	0.1	0.1	0.1
Multiple disabilities	—	0.2	0.2	0.2	0.2	0.2	0.3	0.3	0.3	0.3
Deaf-blindness	—	#	#	#	#	#	#	#	#	#
Autism	—	—	—	#	0.1	0.1	0.2	0.3	0.4	0.5
Traumatic brain injury	—	—	—	#	#	#	#	#	#	0.1
Developmental delay	—	—	—	—	—	#	0.4	0.6	0.7	0.7
Preschool-age with disability[2]	†	†	0.9	1.2	1.2	1.2	†	†	†	†

— Not available.

† Not applicable.

Rounds to zero.

[1] A disorder in one or more of the basic psychological processes involved in understanding or in using language, spoken or written, that may manifest itself in an imperfect ability to listen, think, speak, read, write, spell, or to do mathematical calculations, including conditions such as perceptual disabilities, brain injury, minimal brain dysfunction, dyslexia, and developmental aphasia.

[2] Beginning in 1976, data were collected for preschool-aged children by disability type; those data are combined above with data for youth ages 6–21. However, the 1986 Amendments to the Education of the Handicapped Act (now known as IDEA) mandated that data not be collected by disability for students ages 3–5. Accordingly, those data are reported as a separate row for years 1990–91 through 1999–2000. Beginning in 2000–01, states were again required to report preschool children by disability.

Note: Detail may not sum to totals because of rounding. Special education services through the Individuals with Disabilities Education Act (IDEA) are available for eligible youth identified by a team of qualified professionals as having a disability that adversely affects academic performance and as in need of special education and related services. The total includes youth receiving special education services through IDEA in early education centers and elementary and secondary schools in the 50 states and the District of Columbia and in Bureau of Indian Affairs (BIA) schools through 1993–94. Beginning in 1994–95, estimates exclude BIA schools.

Source: National Center for Education Statistics. (2008). The Condition of Education 2008. Washington, DC: Author. Retrieved from http://nces.ed.gov/programs/coe/2008/section1/table.asp?tableID=868.

10. **Deaf-blindness**— vision and hearing disability that severely limits communication
11. **Autism and other**— significantly impaired communication, learning, and reciprocal social interactions

Of the 6.7 million children in special education, nearly half are identified as having a specific learning disability (National Center for Education Statistics, September 2007). Since the term **learning disability (LD)** was first introduced in the early 1960s, there has been no universally accepted definition. The National Joint Committee on Learning Disabilities (2008) states:

> A learning disability is a neurological disorder. In simple terms, a learning disability results from a difference in the way a person's brain is "wired." Children with learning disabilities are as smart or smarter than their peers. But they may have difficulty reading, writing, spelling, reasoning, recalling and/or organizing information if left to figure things out by themselves or if taught in conventional ways.

Some students have trouble remembering verbal instructions or recognizing words in print (*dyslexia*), while others have trouble working with numbers (*dyscalulia*). A learning disability can't be cured or fixed; it is a lifelong issue. With the right support and intervention, however, children with learning disabilities can succeed in school and go on to successful, often distinguished careers later in life. Parents can help children with learning disabilities achieve such success by encouraging their strengths, knowing their weaknesses, understanding the educational system, working with professionals, and learning about strategies for dealing with specific difficulties. The Teaching on Your Feet feature in this chapter profiles Rhoda Silverberg, who learned how to meet the needs of her students with learning disabilities.

Imagine that you are concerned about two of your new students—Mary and Bill. Mary has an adequate vocabulary and doesn't hesitate to express herself, but her achievement in reading and mathematics doesn't add up to what you believe she can do. Often, when you give the class instructions, Mary seems to get confused about what to do. In working with her one on one, you've noticed that she often reverses letters and numbers the way much younger children do—she sees a *b* for a *d* or a *6* for a *9*. Mary may have a learning disability, causing problems in taking in, organizing, remembering, and expressing information. Like Mary, students with learning disabilities often show a significant difference between their estimated intelligence and their actual achievement in the classroom.

Bill presents you with a different set of challenges. He is obviously bright, but he frequently seems to be out of sync with classroom activities. He gets frustrated when he has to wait for his turn. He sometimes blurts out answers before you've even asked a question. He can't seem to stop wiggling his toes and tapping his pencil, and he often comes to school without his backpack and homework. Bill may have **attention deficit hyperactivity disorder (ADHD),** one of the most commonly diagnosed disabilities among children. It is estimated that between 3 and 5 percent of children have ADHD in the United States. In a classroom of 25 to 30 students, at least one will probably have ADHD. Students with an **attention deficit disorder (ADD)** have difficulty focusing their attention long enough to learn well. Children with ADD/ADHD do not qualify for special education unless they also have another disability in a federally defined category.

Treatment for students with ADD/ADHD includes behavior modification and medication. Since the early 1980s, Ritalin has become the most commonly prescribed drug for ADD/ADHD, and more than 1 million American children are currently estimated to take Ritalin to increase their impulse control and attention span.

Teachers can help in the early identification of students with learning disabilities so they can receive the instructional adaptations or special education services they need by being alert for students who exhibit several of the following academic and behavioral characteristics:

- **Significant discrepancy between potential and achievement**
- **Inability to problem-solve**
- Substantial delay in academic achievement

TEACHING ON YOUR FEET

FINDING THE SECRET

"I now can see—and measure—progress with my students."

Despite years of teaching reading to special needs students, I always felt as if I didn't know what I was doing. Imagine the frustration. As a resource language arts teacher, I thought that everyone else knew the secret to teaching reading and that I was the only one who didn't. I worked with my students using lots of good literature, having them make predictions about what would happen next, having them use the beginning sound and the context to guess a word if they didn't know it. I had them memorize spelling lists. They might know the words for that week, but not much longer. At the end of the year I would inform the parents that Scott, John, or Heather was making good progress. But how did I know that? I had no proof.

One year I shared my classroom with a tutor who needed space to work with her student who had characteristics of dyslexia. She spoke highly of the program she used, an Orton-Gillingham-based program that was a research-based, sequential, structured phonics program. After observing the progress her student was making, two colleagues and I begged our administration to let us train in this program. After an exacting year of training—a 2-day overview, 5 seminars throughout the year, and 60 lessons working with a student one on one—I knew I had the secret! Eleven years later, I no longer experience that frustration I felt back then. I now can see—and measure—progress with my students. Being able to share with the students and their parents the measurable progress via pretests and posttests brings pleasure to all of us.

But oh, for the Scotts and Heathers I worked with many years ago! How I wish that I had had that training from the very beginning of my teaching career and that I could have seen that pleasure on their faces as they decoded and spelled increasingly difficult words. I try not to beat myself up about it, but I have a new motto: If you don't have the tools, find them!

ANALYSIS

Teaching well means seeking the best for students and continually learning new approaches, strategies, and programs to assist them. It means trying one method after another until the "secret" is found—and then advocating for the needed training and resources. And, as Silverberg's comments in this feature illustrate, it also means committing time and energy to gain new knowledge and skills.

REFLECTION

- In what ways can teachers continue to learn after they complete their teacher credential programs?
- What professional skills most call for ongoing teacher learning?

Rhoda Silverberg
Dyslexia Specialist
West Ridge Middle School

PEARSON myeducationlab To answer these questions online, go to MyEducatioLab at www.myeducationlab.com, select the Activities and Application section, and click on this chapter's Teaching on Your Feet.

- Lack of engagement with learning tasks
- Poor language and/or cognitive development
- Lack of basic reading and decoding skills
- Lack of attention during lectures or class discussion
- Excessive movement, hyperactivity
- Impulsivity
- Poor motor coordination and spatial relation skills
- Poor motivation

To learn about the accommodations that were made for a student with learning disabilities, go to MyEducationLab and watch the video Accommodations for Heather.

PEARSON myeducationlab
Go to MyEducationLab, select Chapter 9 and then Activities and Applications to watch the video Accomodations for Heather.

Students Who Are Gifted and Talented

Gifted and talented students benefit from enriched learning experiences and individualized plans that give them the opportunity to grow at an accelerated rate. What are some forms of enrichment you will offer your students?

Gifted and talented students, those who have demonstrated a high level of attainment in intellectual ability, academic achievement, creativity, or visual and performing arts, are evenly distributed across all ethnic and cultural groups and socioeconomic classes. Although you might think it is easy to meet the needs of gifted and talented students, you will find that this is not always the case. "Students with special gifts or talents often challenge the system of school, and they can be verbally caustic. Their superior abilities and unusual or advanced interests demand teachers who are highly intelligent, creative, and motivated" (Hallahan & Kauffman, 2000, p. 497). The ability of such students to challenge the system is reflected in a recent U.S. Department of Education study that found that gifted and talented elementary schoolchildren have mastered 35 percent to 50 percent of the grade curriculum in five basic subject areas before starting the school year.

Giftedness may take many forms. Joseph S. Renzulli (1998), director of the National Research Center on the Gifted and Talented at the University of Connecticut, for example, suggests two kinds of giftedness: "schoolhouse giftedness [which] might also be called test-taking or lesson-learning giftedness" and "creative-productive giftedness." The trend during the last few decades has been to broaden our view of what characterizes giftedness.

Variations in criteria used to identify gifted and talented students are especially evident in the reported incidence of giftedness from state to state; for example, Massachusetts and Vermont identify only 0.8 percent of their students as gifted and talented, while Oklahoma identifies 14.0 percent (National Center for Education Statistics, May 2007). Depending on the criteria used, estimates of the number of gifted and talented students range from 3 to 5 percent of the total population. Among the characteristics of the gifted are the following:

- **Precocity**—verbal precocity.
- **Perceptual sensitivity**—good at detecting critically relevant, salient cues; notices what others fail to notice.
- **Persistent concentration**—ability to attend to a task intensively, without being distracted by noise in the environment.
- **Superior memory**—may be restricted to domain(s) of excellence.
- **Efficient coordination**—ability to coordinate two or more tasks.
- **Curtailed learning and reasoning**—ability to "intuit" solutions without following step-by-step procedures; solves problems by making "intuitive leaps."
- **Flexible thinking**—knowing when to call upon inner resources and deciding which resources to apply for the best result.
- **Metacognitive awareness**—awareness of one's own thinking; keeping track of one's understanding of a problem.
- **Speedy processing**—ability to process information quickly.
- **Philosophical thinking**—concern with "larger questions" that focus on, for example, the future of humankind or the cosmos. (Hoh, 2008, pp. 57–83)

Effective teachers of the gifted and talented have many of the same characteristics as their students. "Characteristics that reoccur across the studies of exemplary teachers of the gifted include: intellectualism, subject matter expertise, a personal rapport with high-ability learners, and enjoyment in teaching them" (Robinson, 2008, p. 676). Four innovative approaches for meeting the educational needs of gifted students are acceleration, self-directed or independent study, individual education programs (IEPs), and alternative or magnet schools.

Acceleration

The effectiveness of accelerated programs for intellectually precocious students is "striking" (Gross, 2008, p. 248). For example, in a review of hundreds of research findings in education, Kulik was "not able to find any educational treatment that consistently yielded higher effect size (i.e., positive results) than [acceleration]" (2004, p. 20). The following acceleration options have proven to be the most beneficial at different grade levels:

- **Elementary school**—early entrance, grade skipping, nongraded classes, and curriculum compacting (modifying the curriculum to present it at a faster pace).
- **Junior high school**—grade skipping, grade telescoping (shortening the amount of time to complete a grade level), concurrent enrollment in a high school or college, subject acceleration, and curriculum compacting.
- **Senior high school**—concurrent enrollment, subject acceleration, advanced placement (AP) classes, mentorships, credit by examination, and early admission to college.

One example of acceleration is a suburban Chicago alternative school where high-potential at-risk students work at their own pace in high-tech classrooms. They engage in integrative accelerative learning, which offers advanced curricula and encourages individual creativity, positive reinforcement, and relaxation. At the National Research Center on Gifted and Talented Education, teachers in experimental classrooms practice thematic curriculum compacting, which encourages brighter students to forge ahead in the regular curriculum while all students work to their strengths, and less able students still get the time and attention they need. Also, many colleges and universities now participate in accelerated programs whereby gifted youth who have outgrown the high school curriculum may enroll in college courses.

Self-Directed or Independent Study

For some time, self-directed or independent study has been recognized as an appropriate way for teachers to maintain the interest of gifted students in their classes. Gifted students usually have the academic backgrounds and motivation to do well without constant supervision and the threat or reward of grades.

Individual Education Programs (IEPs)

Since the passage of PL 94-142 and the mandating of individual education programs (IEPs) for special education students, IEPs have been promoted as an appropriate means for educating gifted students. Most IEPs for gifted students involve various enrichment experiences; self-directed study; and special, concentrated instruction given to individuals or small groups in pullout programs. For example, at Columbia Teachers College in New York, economically disadvantaged students identified as gifted participate in Project Synergy, which pairs students with mentors who nurture their talents and guide them through advanced academic content.

Alternative or Magnet Schools

Several large-city school systems have developed magnet schools organized around specific disciplines, such as science, mathematics, fine arts, basic skills, and so on. The excellent programs at these schools are designed to attract superior students from all parts of the district. Many of these schools offer outstanding programs for gifted and talented youth.

WHAT ARE SPECIAL EDUCATION, MAINSTREAMING, AND INCLUSION?

Prior to the 20th century, children with disabilities were usually segregated from regular classrooms and taught by teachers in state-run and private schools. Today, an array of programs and services in general and special education classrooms is aimed at developing the potential of exceptional students. Three critical concepts to promote the growth, talents, and productivity of exceptional students are special education, mainstreaming, and inclusion.

Special education refers to "specially designed instruction that meets the unusual needs of an exceptional student" (Hallahan & Kauffman, 2006, p. 13). Teachers who are trained in special education become familiar with special materials, techniques, equipment, and facilities for students with disabilities. For example, children with visual impairment may require reading materials in large print or Braille; students with hearing impairment may require hearing aids and/or instruction in sign language; those with physical disabilities may need special equipment; those with emotional disturbances may need smaller and more highly structured classes; children with special gifts or talents may require access to working professionals. "Related services—special transportation, psychological assessment, physical and occupational therapy, medical treatment, and counseling—may be necessary if special education is to be effective" (Hallahan & Kauffman, 2006, p. 13).

Special Education Laws

Until 1975, the needs of students with disabilities were primarily met through self-contained special education classes within regular schools. That year, however, Congress passed the **Education for All Handicapped Children Act (Public Law 94-142).** This act guaranteed to all children with disabilities a free and appropriate public education. The law, which applied to every teacher and every school in the country, outlined extensive procedures to ensure that exceptional students between the ages of 3 and 18 were granted due process in regard to identification, placement, and educational services received. As a result of PL 94-142, the participation of students with disabilities in all classrooms and school programs became routine.

In 1990, PL 94-142 was replaced by the **Individuals with Disabilities Education Act (IDEA).** IDEA included the major provisions of PL 94-142 and extended the availability of a free, appropriate education to youth with disabilities between the ages of 3 and 21. IDEA, which is one of the most important and far-reaching pieces of educational legislation ever passed in this country, has several provisions with which all teachers should be familiar. In 1997, the **Amendments to the Individuals with Disabilities Education Act (IDEA 97)** were passed. IDEA 97, and its reauthorization in 2004, went beyond IDEA's focus on public school *access* for students with disabilities to emphasize educational *outcomes*, modified eligibility requirements, IEP guidelines, public and private placements, student discipline guidelines, and procedural safeguards.

IDEA requires that all children with disabilities be educated in the **least restrictive environment.** In other words, a student must be mainstreamed into a general education classroom whenever such integration is feasible and appropriate and the child would receive educational benefit from such placement. Figure 9.7 shows the educational service options for students with disabilities, from the least restrictive to the most restrictive. Among schools with high-incidence disabilities (those with a child count over 100,000), students with speech or language impairments and specific learning disabilities are served in the regular classroom for most of the school day. Students with emotional disturbance, mental retardation, and multiple disabilities typically receive services outside the regular classroom for more than 60 percent of the school day (President's Commission on Excellence in Special Education, 2002).

Individualized Education Program

Every child with a disability must have a written **individualized education program (IEP)** that meets the child's needs and specifies educational goals, methods for achieving those goals, and the number and quality of special educational services to be provided. The IEP must be reviewed annually by five parties: (1) a parent or guardian, (2) the child, (3) a teacher, (4) a professional who has recently evaluated the child, and (5) others, usually the principal or a special education resource person from the school district. Figure 9.8 presents an example of an individualized education plan (IEP).

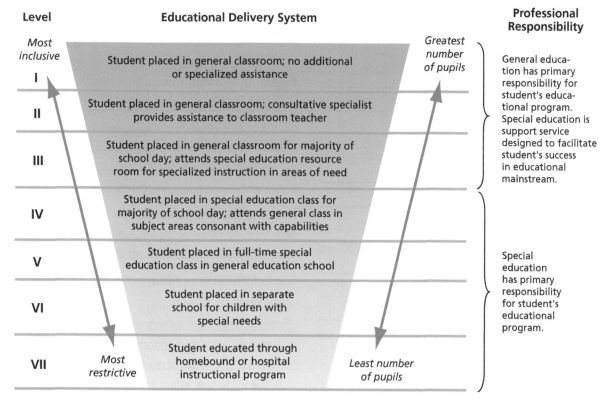

FIGURE 9.7 Educational service options for students with disabilities

Source: Michael L. Hardman, Clifford J. Drew, and M. Winston Egan, *Human Exceptionality: Society, School, and Family,* 7th ed. Boston: Allyn and Bacon, 2002, p. 29. Copyright © 2002 by Allyn and Bacon. Reprinted by permission.

Related Services

IDEA 97 ensures that students with disabilities receive any related services, including "transportation, and such developmental, corrective, and other supportive services as may be required to assist a child with a disability to benefit from special education" (Amendments to IDEA 97).

Confidentiality of Records

IDEA also ensures that records on a child are kept confidential. Parental permission is required before any official may look at a child's records. Parents can amend a child's records if they feel information in it is misleading, inaccurate, or violates the child's rights.

Due Process

IDEA gives parents the right to disagree with an IEP or an evaluation of their child's abilities. If a disagreement arises, it is settled through an impartial due process hearing presided over by an officer appointed by the state. At the hearing, parents may be represented by a lawyer, give evidence, and cross-examine, and are entitled to receive a transcript of the hearing and a written decision on the case. If either the parents or the school district disagrees with the outcome, the case may then be taken to the civil courts.

Meeting the Mainstreaming Challenge

To help you satisfy the provisions of IDEA, you will probably have opportunities as a teacher to participate in in-service programs designed to acquaint classroom teachers with the unique needs of students with disabilities. In addition, your teacher education program may require a course on teaching students with special educational needs.

The guidelines for IDEA suggest that schools must make a significant effort to include, or mainstream, all children in the classroom. However, it is not clear how

Student's Primary Classification: <u>Serious Emotional Disturbance</u>
Secondary Classification: <u>None</u>

Student Name <u>Diane</u>

Date of Birth <u>5-3-96</u>

Primary Language:

HOME <u>English</u> Student <u>English</u>

Date of IEP Meeting <u>April, 27, 2009</u>

Entry Date to Program <u>April, 27, 2009</u>

Projected Duration of Services <u>One school year</u>

Services Required <u>Specify amount of time in educational and/or related services per day or week</u>

General Education Class <u>4–5 hours p/day</u>

Resource Room <u>1–2 hours p/day</u>

Special Education Consultation in General Education Classroom

<u>Coteaching and consultation with general education teacher in the areas of academic and adaptive skills as indicated in annual goals and short-term objectives</u>

Self-Contained <u>None</u>

Related Services <u>Group counseling sessions twice weekly with guidance counselor. Counseling to focus on adaptive skill development as described in annual goals and short-term objectives</u>

Recreational Program <u>45 min. daily in general ed PE class with support from adapted PE teacher as necessary</u>

Assessment

Intellectual <u>WISC-R</u>

Educational <u>Key Math Woodcock Reading</u>

Behavioral/Adaptive <u>Burks</u>

Speech/Language _____

Other _____

Vision <u>Within normal limits</u>

Hearing <u>Within normal limits</u>

Classroom Observation Done

Dates <u>1/15–2/25/09</u>

Personnel Conducting Observation <u>School Psychologist, Special Education Teacher, General Education Teacher</u>

Present Level of Performance Strengths:

<u>1) Polite to teachers and peers</u>

<u>2) Helpful and cooperative in the classroom</u>

<u>3) Good grooming skills</u>

<u>4) Good in sports activities</u>

Access to General Education Curriculum

<u>Diane will participate in all content areas within the general education curriculum. Special education supports and services will be provided in the areas of math and reading.</u>

Effect of Disability on Access to General Education Curriculum

<u>Emotional disabilities make it difficult for Diane to achieve at expected grade level performance in general education curriculum in the areas of reading and math. It is expected that this will further affect her access to the general education curriculum in other content areas (such as history, biology, English) as she enters junior high school.</u>

Participation in Statewide or District Assessments

<u>Diane will participate in all state- and districtwide assessments of achievement. No adaptations or modifications required for participation.</u>

Justification for Removal From General Education Classroom:

<u>Diane's objectives require that she be placed in a general education classroom with support from a special education teacher for the majority of the school day. Based on adaptive behavior assessment and observations, Diane will receive instruction in a resource room for approximately one to two hours per day in the areas of social skill development.</u>

Reports to Parents on Progress Toward Annual Goals:

<u>Parents will be informed of Diane's progress through weekly reports of progress on short-term goals; monthly phone calls from general education teachers, special education teachers, and school psychologist; and regularly scheduled report cards at the end of each term.</u>

FIGURE 9.8 A sample individualized education plan (IEP)

Source: Adapted from Michael L. Hardman, Clifford J. Drew, and M. Winston Egan, Human Exceptionality: Society, School, and Family, 7th ed. Boston, Allyn and Bacon, 2002, pp. 123–125. Copyright © 2002 by Allyn and Bacon. Used with permission.

Areas Needing Specialized Instruction and Support

1. Adaptive Skills

   - Limited interaction skills with peers and adults
   - Excessive facial tics and grimaces
   - Difficulty staying on task in content subjects, especially reading and math.
   - Difficulty expressing feelings, needs, and interests

2. Academic Skills

   - Significantly below grade level in math—3.9
   - Significantly below grade level in reading—4.3

Annual Review: Date: _____

Comments/Recommendations

_____

_____

_____

_____

_____

Team Signatures   IEP Review Date _____

LEA Rep. _____

Parent _____

Sp Ed Teacher _____

Gen Ed Teacher _____

School Psych _____

Student (as appropriate) _____

Related Services Personnel (as appropriate) _____

Objective Criteria and Evaluation Procedures _____

IEP–Annual Goals and Short-Term Objectives	Persons Responsible	Objective Criteria and Evaluation Procedures
#1 ANNUAL GOAL: Diane will improve her interaction skills with peers and adults. S.T. OBJ. Diane will initiate conversation with peers during an unstructured setting twice daily. S.T. OBJ. When in need of assistance, Diane will raise her hand and verbalize her needs to teachers or peers without prompting 80% of the time.	General education teacher and special education teacher (resource room) School psychologist consultation	Classroom observations and documented data on target behavior
#2 ANNUAL GOAL: Diane will increase her ability to control hand and facial movements. S.T. OBJ. During academic work, Diane will keep her hands in an appropriate place and use writing materials correctly 80% of the time. S.T. OBJ. Diane will maintain a relaxed facial expression with teacher prompt 80% of the time. Teacher prompt will be faded over time.	General education teacher and special education teacher (resource room) School psychologist consultation	Classroom observations and documented data on target behavior
#3 ANNUAL GOAL: Diane will improve her ability to remain on task during academic work. S.T. OBJ. Diane will work independently on an assigned task with teacher prompt 80% of the time. S.T. OBJ. Diane will complete academic work as assigned 90% of the time.	General education teacher and special education teacher (resource room) School psychologist consultation	Classroom observations and documented data on target behavior

(continues)

FIGURE 9.8 continued

IEP—Annual Goals and Short-Term Objectives	Persons Responsible	Objective Criteria and Evaluation Procedures
#4 ANNUAL GOAL: <u>Diane will improve her ability to express her feelings.</u> **S.T. OBJ.** <u>When asked how she feels, Diane will give an adequate verbal description of her feelings or moods with teacher prompting at least 80% of the time.</u> **S.T. OBJ.** <u>Given a conflict or problem situation, Diane will state her feelings to teachers and peers 80% of the time.</u>	General education teacher and special education teacher (resource room) School psychologist consultation	Classroom observations and documented data on target behavior
#5 ANNUAL GOAL: <u>Diane will improve math skills one grade level.</u> **S.T. OBJ.** <u>Diane will improve rate and accuracy in oral 1- and 2- digit division facts to 50 problems per minute without errors.</u> **S.T. OBJ.** <u>Diane will improve her ability to solve word problems involving t—x—v.</u>	Collaboration of general education teacher and special education teacher through coteaching and consultation	Precision teaching Addison Wesley Math Program Scope and Sequence Districtwide Assessment of Academic Achievement
#6 ANNUAL GOAL: <u>Diane will improve reading skills one grade level.</u> **S.T. OBJ.** <u>Diane will answer progressively more difficult comprehension questions in designated reading skills program.</u> **S.T. OBJ.** <u>Diane will increase her rate and accuracy of vocabulary words to 80 wpm without errors.</u>	Collaboration of general education teacher and special education teacher through coteaching and consultation	Precision teaching Barnell & Loft Scope and Sequence Districtwide Assessment of Academic Achievement

FIGURE 9.8 continued

far schools must go to meet this mainstreaming requirement. For example, should children with severe disabilities be included in general education classrooms if they are unable to do the academic work? Recent court cases have ruled that students with severe disabilities must be included if there is a potential benefit for the child, if the class would stimulate the child's language development, or if other students could act as appropriate role models for the child. In one case, the court ordered a school district to place a child with an IQ of 44 in a regular second-grade classroom and rejected as exaggerated the district's claim that the placement would be prohibitively expensive (*Board of Education, Sacramento City Unified School District v. Holland,* 1992). In another case, the court rejected a school district's argument that inclusion of a child with a severe disability would be so disruptive as to significantly impair the learning of the other children (*Oberti v. Board of Education of the Borough of Clementon School District,* 1992).

To meet the mainstreaming challenge, you must have knowledge of various disabilities and the teaching methods and materials appropriate for each. Because teachers with negative attitudes toward students with special needs can convey these feelings to all students in a class and thereby reduce the effectiveness of mainstreaming (Lewis & Doorlag, 2006), as a teacher you must have positive attitudes toward students receiving special education. An accepting, supportive climate can significantly enhance the self-confidence of students with disabilities.

In addition, you should be prepared to participate in the education of exceptional learners. You should be willing to do the following:

1. Make maximum effort to accommodate individual students' needs
2. Evaluate academic abilities and disabilities
3. Refer [students] for evaluation [as appropriate]
4. Participate in eligibility conferences [for special education]
5. Participate in writing individualized education programs
6. Communicate with parents or guardians
7. Participate in due process hearings and negotiations
8. Collaborate with other professionals in identifying and making maximum use of exceptional students' abilities (Hallahan & Kauffman, 2006, pp. 19–20, 22)

The Debate Over Inclusion

While mainstreaming refers to the application of the least restrictive environment clause of PL 94-142, **inclusion** goes beyond mainstreaming to integrate all students with disabilities into general education classes and school life with the active support of special educators and other specialists and service providers, as well as **assistive technology** and adaptive software. Advocates of inclusion believe that "[s]tudents with disabilities are no longer the responsibility of 'someone else,' like the special education teacher, and they are no longer those students who receive their education 'someplace else,' like at the special school. Students with disabilities are the shared responsibility of everyone" (Smith, 2007, p. 33).

Full inclusion goes even further and maintains that "the general education classroom is the most appropriate full-time placement for all students with disabilities—not only those with mild learning and behavior problems, but also those with more severe disabilities" (Lewis & Doorlag, 2006, p. 4). According to the full-inclusion approach, if a child needs support services, these are brought *to the child*; the child does not have to participate in a pullout program to receive support services. Advocates of full inclusion maintain that pullout programs stigmatize participating students because they are separated from their general education classmates, and pullout programs discourage collaboration between general and special education teachers. Those who oppose full inclusion maintain that classroom teachers, who may be burdened with large class sizes and be assigned to schools with inadequate support services, often lack the training and instructional materials to meet the needs of all exceptional students.

In addition, some parents of children with disabilities believe that full inclusion could mean the elimination of special education as we know it, along with the range of services currently guaranteed by federal special education laws. Full inclusion, they reason, would make them depend on individual states, not the federal government, to meet their children's needs. Some parents believe that special education classes provide their children with important benefits.

How do students in general education classrooms feel about their classmates with disabilities? Fifth-grade classmates of Jessica, a student who is nonverbal, nonambulatory, and unable to feed, dress, or care for herself, made these comments (presented in their original form):

- I feel that Jessica has changed my life. How I feel and see handicapped people has really changed. . . . I used to think about handicapped people being really weak and if I would touch her I would hurt her but now I think differently.

- I really like Jessica in my class. Before I met her I never really cared about handycapt people. Jessie is really nice and I like her a lot. Jessica is almost like a sister to me. I like to spend my recess playing with her. I thought a handycaqpt kid would never be part of my life, but now one and alot more are.

- I think it is great that Jessica is in our room. Jessica is very fun. She laughs and smiles a lot. Sometimes she crys but that is OK. I have learned that Handicapped people are just like the others. I used to say "ooh" look at the person but now I don't I have a big fear for handicapped because they are interesting they can do things that other people can't do. I think Jessica has changed because she is with lots of other kids. (Lewis & Doorlag, 2006, p. 12)

Lin Chang, an eighth-grade teacher, addresses the concerns that general education teachers may have about the availability of resources to help them be successful in inclusive classrooms:

At first I was worried that it would all be my responsibility. But after meeting with the special education teacher, I realized that we would work together and I would have additional resources if I needed them. (Vaughn, Bos, & Schumm, 1997, p. 18)

In addition, the following comments by Octavio Gonzalez, a ninth-grade English teacher who has three students with disabilities in two of his five sections of English, express the satisfaction that teachers can experience in inclusive classrooms:

At first I was nervous about having students with disabilities in my class. One of the students has a learning disability, one student has serious motor problems and is in a wheelchair, and the third student has vision problems. Now I have to say the adaptations I make to meet their special learning needs actually help all of the students in my class. I think that I am a better teacher because I think about accommodations now. (Vaughn, et al., 1997, p. 18)

The attitudes of the two teachers quoted above are confirmed in research on teachers' attitudes toward inclusion. Two studies, for example, found that teachers who had experience with inclusion and opportunities for professional development had more positive attitudes toward inclusion and more confidence in their ability to fulfill students' IEPs (Avramidis, Bayliss, & Burden, 2000; Van Reusen, Shoho, & Barker, 2000).

Equal Opportunity for Exceptional Learners

Like many groups in our society, exceptional learners have not often received the kind of education that most effectively meets their needs. Approximately 10 percent of the population age 3 to 21 is classified as exceptional; that is, "they require special education because they are markedly different from most children in one or more of the following ways: They may have mental retardation, learning disabilities, emotional or behavioral disorders, physical disabilities, disorders of communication, autism, traumatic brain injury, impaired hearing, impaired sight, or special gifts or talents" (Hallahan & Kauffman, 2006, p. 8).

Just as there are no easy answers for how teachers should meet the needs of students from diverse cultural backgrounds, there is no single strategy for teachers to follow to ensure that all exceptional students receive an appropriate education. The key, however, lies in not losing sight of the fact that "the most important characteristics of exceptional children are their abilities, not their disabilities" (Hallahan & Kauffman, 2006, p. 7).

To build on students' strengths, classroom teachers must work cooperatively and collaboratively with special education teachers, and students in special education programs must not become isolated from their peers. In addition, teachers must understand how some people can be perceived as "different" and presumed to be "handicapped" because of their appearance or physical condition. Evidence suggests, for example, that people who are short, obese, or unattractive are often victims of discrimination, as are people with conditions such as AIDS, cancer, multiple sclerosis, or epilepsy. It is significant that many individuals with clinically diagnosable and classifiable impairments or disabilities do not perceive themselves as handicapped. The term itself means "permanently unable to be treated equally."

348

Officially labeling students has become a necessity with the passage of laws that provide education and related services for exceptional students. The classification labels help determine which students qualify for the special services, educational programs, and individualized instruction provided by the laws, and they bring to educators' attention many exceptional children and youth whose educational needs could otherwise be overlooked, neglected, or inadequately served. Detrimental aspects include the fact that classification systems are imperfect and have arbitrary cutoff points that sometimes lead to injustices. Also, labels tend to evoke negative expectations, which can cause teachers to avoid and underteach these students, and their peers to isolate or reject them, thereby stigmatizing individuals, sometimes permanently. The most serious detriment, however, is that students so labeled are taught to feel inadequate, inferior, and limited in terms of their options for growth.

HOW CAN YOU TEACH ALL LEARNERS IN YOUR INCLUSIVE CLASSROOM?

Teachers have a responsibility to address all students' developmental, individual, and exceptional learning needs. Although addressing the range of student differences in the inclusive classroom is challenging, it can also be very rewarding. Consider the comments of three teachers who reflect on their experiences teaching diverse learners:

> This is a note I wrote on the bottom of her [final] report card: "Sara is a sweet, bright child. As much as she could be a challenge, she made me a better teacher by keeping me on my toes. I will truly, truly miss her!" (teacher of a student with Turner syndrome)

> It was a gratifying year. I had no idea at the beginning that we would see the progress that we did. . . . Irina came back for a visit today. She ran right up to me and gave me a hug. A year ago, such an obvious display of emotion would have been unthinkable! (teacher of a student with an attachment disorder resulting from a lack of human contact during the years she spent in a Romanian orphanage)

> On complex and difficult days, it sometimes feels like it would be a lot easier not to have children with special needs in my classroom. . . . But, you know, I really mourned having to give Daniel up at the end of the schoolyear. There was a special connection I made with that child, and I wanted to be sure that his next teacher felt the same way. (teacher of a student with Down syndrome) (Kostelnik, Onaga, Rohde, & Whiren, 2002, pp. 55, 92–93, 149)

Attention to three key areas will enable you to create a truly inclusive classroom: collaborative consultation with other professionals, partnerships with parents, and assistive technology for special learners.

Collaborative Consultation With Other Professionals

One approach to meeting the needs of all students is known as **collaborative consultation,** an approach in which a classroom teacher meets with one or more other professionals (a special educator, school psychologist, or resource teacher, for example) to focus on the learning needs of one or more students. Collaborative consultation is based on mutuality and reciprocity (Hallahan & Kauffman, 2006), and participants assume equal responsibility for meeting students' needs. When working with a consultant, general education teachers should "prepare for meetings, be open to the consultant's suggestions, use the consultant's strategies systematically, and document the effectiveness of the ideas [they] try" (Friend & Bursuck, 2002, pp. 95–96). To learn about how a special education teacher has organized her classroom, go to MyEducationLab and watch the video Meet the Teacher, Ms. Trask-Tyler.

myeducationlab

Go to MyEducationLab, select Chapter 9 and then Activities and Applications to watch the video Meet the Teacher, Ms. Trask-Tyler.

To meet the educational goals of a student's IEP, regular education teachers are part of an IEP team that includes special educators, other support personnel, and parents (refer again to Figure 9.8). The following special education professionals are among those who consult with and/or collaborate with regular education teachers:

Consulting teacher—a special educator who provides technical assistance such as arranging the physical setting, helping to plan for instruction, or developing approaches for assessing students' learning

Resource-room teacher—a special educator who provides instruction in a resource room for students with disabilities

School psychologist—consults with the general education teacher and arranges for the administration of appropriate psychological, educational, and behavioral assessment instruments; may observe a student's behavior in the classroom

Speech and language specialist—assesses students' communication abilities and works with general education teachers to develop educational programs for students with speech and/or language disorders

Physical therapist—provides physical therapy for students with physical disabilities

Occupational therapist—instructs students with disabilities to prepare them for everyday living and work-related activities

Partnerships With Parents

In addition to working with education professionals to meet the learning needs of all students, effective teachers develop good working relationships with parents. As the following comment by the mother of a daughter with Rett syndrome makes clear, parents of children with disabilities expect their teachers to be committed to meeting the learning needs of their children: "My child will never be considered a poster child. She does not give professionals the satisfaction of making great progress, nor is she terribly social. But I need the same type of investment by professionals as any other parents of children without disabilities. The most important thing any educator can do for me is to love my Mary" (Howard et al., 2001, p. 123). Parents of exceptional children can be a source of valuable information about the characteristics, abilities, and needs of their children. Also, they can be helpful in securing necessary services for their children, and they can assist you by reviewing skills at home and praising their children for their learning.

The IEP for this student with multiple disabilities provides for assistive technology, which enables him to create and respond to language.

Assistive Technology for Special Learners

The ability of teachers to create inclusive classrooms has increased dramatically as a result of many technological advances that make it easier for exceptional students to learn and communicate. However, no more than 35 percent of students with diagnosed disabilities are receiving assistive technology as part of their federally mandated individualized education plan (IEP) (Bran, Gray, & Silver-Pacuila, June 10, 2008).

The array of assistive technologies for students with disabilities is extensive. For example, personal digital assistants (PDAs), BlackBerrys, and iPhones enable students to access the Internet, send and receive e-mail, and keep track of school assignments. Some devices have wireless capabilities and options for storing and playing digital books, music, and podcasts. Other examples include computer-based word processing and math tutorials that greatly assist students with learning disabilities in acquiring literacy and computational skills. Students with hearing impairments can communicate with other students by using telecommunications equipment, and students with physical disabilities can operate computers through voice commands or with a single switch or key.

Assistive technology also allows persons with disabilities to express themselves in new ways. For example, a young autistic woman posts video on YouTube about her condition. Using a device that enables her to communicate, she explains the thoughts and feelings behind her movements and gestures. Additional recent developments in assistive technology include the following:

- Talking word processor
- Speech synthesizer
- Touch-sensitive computer screens
- Computer screen image enlarger
- Teletypewriter (TTY) (connects to telephone and types a spoken message to another TTY)
- Customized computer keyboards
- Ultrasonic head controls for computers
- Voice-recognition computers
- Television closed captioning
- Kurzweil reading machine (scans print and reads it aloud)

Assistive technology also includes devices to enhance the mobility and everyday activities of people with disabilities (wheelchairs, lifts, adaptive driving controls, scooters, laser canes, feeders). To see how a child with a disability uses an assistive technology software program to learn letter sounds and sound combinations, go to MyEducationLab and watch the video Headsprout Reading.

Many technology-related special education resources and curriculum materials are available on the Internet. One of these sites, The National Center to Improve Practice in Special Education Through Technology, Media, and Materials, at http://www2.edc.org/NCIP, **also maintains discussion forums for teachers of students with disabilities. The dazzling revolution in microelectronics will continue to yield new devices to enhance the learning of all students.**

Go to MyEducationLab, select Chapter 9 and Activities and Applications to watch the video Headsprout Reading.

SUMMARY

How Do Students' Needs Change as They Develop?

- *Development* refers to predictable changes throughout the human life span.
- People move through different stages of cognitive, psychosocial, and moral development throughout their lives.
- Piaget maintains that children pass through four stages of cognitive development as they mature. Effective teachers are aware of the characteristics of

school-age children's thinking during three of these stages: the preoperational stage, the concrete operations stage, and the formal operations stage.

- According to Erikson's model of psychosocial development, people pass through eight stages of emotional and social development throughout their lives. Each stage is characterized by a "crisis" with a positive and negative pole. Healthy development depends on a satisfactory, positive resolution of each crisis.
- Kohlberg believes that moral development, the reasoning people use to decide between right and

wrong, evolves through three levels. Evidence suggests that males and females base their moral reasoning on different factors.

- Character education emphasizes teaching values and moral reasoning.
- Maslow suggests that human growth and development depends on how well the individual's biological and psychological needs have been met.

How Do Students Vary in Intelligence?

- Conflicting definitions of intelligence range from "what IQ tests measure" to "goal-directed adaptive behavior." Some theorists believe intelligence is a single, basic ability, although recent research suggests that there are many forms of intelligence.
- According to Gardner's theory of multiple intelligences, there are at least eight (perhaps 10) human intelligences.
- Although there is conflict about the concept of learning styles, effective teachers are aware of differences among students regarding their preferences for learning activities.

How Do Students Vary in Ability and Disability?

- Some students are called "exceptional" because they have abilities or disabilities that distinguish them from other students. Students with physical, cognitive, or emotional disabilities and students who are gifted and talented have unique learning needs.
- Learning disabilities are the most common disability among students, with attention deficit hyperactivity

disorder (ADHD) and attention deficit disorder (ADD) the most common learning disabilities.

What Are Special Education, Mainstreaming, and Inclusion?

- Special education includes a variety of educational services to meet the needs of exceptional students. Key provisions of the Individuals with Disabilities Education Act (IDEA) include least restrictive environment, individualized education program (IEP), confidentiality of records, and due process.
- Mainstreaming is the process of integrating students with disabilities into regular classrooms.
- Inclusion integrates all students with disabilities into regular classrooms, with the support of special education services as necessary. Full inclusion is the integration of students with disabilities in general education classrooms at all times regardless of the severity of the disability.

How Can You Teach All Learners in Your Inclusive Classroom?

- Through collaborative consultation, an arrangement whereby the regular classroom teacher collaborates with other education professionals, teachers can meet the needs of exceptional students. Collaborative consultation is based on mutuality and reciprocity, and all participants assume responsibility for meeting students' needs.
- An array of assistive technologies and resources is available to help exceptional students learn and communicate in inclusive classrooms.

PROFESSIONAL REFLECTIONS AND ACTIVITIES

Teacher's Journal

1. What are the characteristics of teachers who are successful teachers of students with disabilities? How can you acquire or further develop those characteristics yourself?
2. What are the benefits and limitations of IQ tests? Should teachers know the IQs of their students? If so, how should teachers use that information?

Teacher's Research

1. Using your favorite search engine, search the Internet for resources that a general education teacher might use for exceptional students in her or his classroom.
2. Select two of the major educational journals that focus on the subject area and grade level for which you are preparing to teach. Collect articles that present tips and resources for adapting teaching for students with

special needs. In addition, you may wish to look at journals that focus on special education—for example, *Teaching Exceptional Children*, which focuses on both elementary and secondary education.

Observations and Interviews

1. Interview two or more general education teachers for their ideas about inclusion. If they have had students with special needs in their classrooms, how did they adapt instruction for those students? What do they think are the advantages and disadvantages of inclusion?

2. Visit a local school that provides services for exceptional students. What teams serve students with special needs, and who serves on those teams? How often do they meet, and how do they work with general education teachers? If possible, observe a team meeting. Who are members of the team? To what extent do they have similar recommendations for students' individual education plans? To what extent do they have different recommendations?

PEARSON myeducationlab **MyEducationLab** To complete additional observations and interviews, go to MyEducationLab at www.myeducationlab .com, select the Virtual Field Experience section, and click on this chapter's Observations and Interviews.

Professional Portfolio

Visit Edutopia: What Works in Public Education at the George Lucas Educational Foundation site on the Internet. Gather articles, teaching tips, videos, interviews with practitioners, and other resources related to using assistive technology in the general education classroom.

PEARSON myeducationlab **MyEducationLab** Now go to MyEducationLab at www .myeducationlab.com to test your understanding of chapter content by completing this chapter's Study Plan.

Authentic Instruction and Curricula for Creating a Community of Learners

13

From Chapter 10 of *Becoming a Teacher*, 8/e. Forrest W. Parkay. Beverly Hardcastle Stanford.

Authentic Instruction and Curricula for Creating a Community of Learners

CLASSROOM CASE
The Realities of Teaching

THE CHALLENGE: Creating a positive learning environment in the classroom by having in place a well-planned curriculum *and* effective classroom management practices.

Ms. Cornell received her teaching certificate in May. Soon after, she accepted a position as a fifth-grade teacher at Twin Pines Elementary School. She spent the summer planning her classroom curriculum, identifying her instructional goals for the year, and developing numerous activities to help students achieve those goals. She now feels well prepared for her first year in the classroom.

After the long, hot summer, most of Ms. Cornell's students seem happy to be back at school. On the first day of school, Ms. Cornell jumps headlong into the curriculum she has planned. But three problems quickly present themselves—problems in the form of Eli, Jake, and Vanessa.

These three students seem determined to disrupt the class at every possible opportunity. They move about the room without permission, making a point of annoying others as they walk to the pencil sharpener or wastebasket. They talk out of turn, sometimes being rude and disrespectful to their teacher and classmates and at other times belittling the activities Ms. Cornell has planned so carefully. They rarely complete in-class assignments, preferring instead to engage in horseplay or practical jokes. They seem especially prone to misbehavior during downtimes in the daily schedule—for example, at the beginning and end of the school day, before and after recess and lunch, and on occasions when Ms. Cornell is preoccupied with other students.

Ms. Cornell continues to follow her daily lesson plans, ignoring her problem students and hoping they will begin to shape up. Yet with the three of them egging one another on, the disruptive behavior continues. Furthermore, it begins to spread to other students. By the middle of October, Ms. Cornell's classroom is like a three-ring circus, and instructional objectives are rarely accomplished. The few students who still seem intent on learning something are having a difficult time doing so. (Ormrod, 2006, p. 303)

FOCUS QUESTIONS

1. What determines the culture of the classroom?
2. How can you create a positive learning environment?

3. What are the keys to successful classroom management?
4. What teaching methods do effective teachers use?
5. What is taught in schools?
6. How is the school curriculum developed?

The opening classroom case highlights the importance of organizing the classroom to create a positive learning environment—a cohesive community of learners. Ms. Cornell has planned her curriculum and instructional goals; however, she has not planned how to manage her classroom. Because she has not planned how to keep students engaged and on-task, Eli, Jake, and Vanessa's misbehavior eventually spreads to the rest of the class by October. Ms. Cornell is learning that successful teaching involves knowing both *what* to teach and *how* to teach it.

For teacher education students like you, making the transition between the study of teaching and actual teaching can be a challenge. You will make that transition smoothly, however, if you understand that to create a cohesive community of learners, "teachers must (1) earn the respect and affection of students; (2) be consistent and, therefore, credible and dependable; (3) assume responsibility for seeing that their students learn; and (4) value and enjoy learning and expect students to do so, too" (Good & Brophy, 2008, p. 77). The first two-thirds of this chapter focus on creating a community of learners, and the last third focuses on developing the curriculum.

WHAT DETERMINES THE CULTURE OF THE CLASSROOM?

A community of learners has a strong positive culture. As you learned in Chapter 8, one definition of culture is the way of life common to a group of people. In much the same way, each classroom develops its own culture. Classroom culture is determined by the manner in which teachers and students participate in common activities.

As a teacher, the activities you and your students engage in will be influenced by several factors. You will make countless decisions that will shape the physical and social milieus of your classroom. From seating arrangements, to classroom rules and procedures, to the content and relevance of the curriculum, you will have a strong influence on the culture that emerges in your classroom. You will have many methodological choices to make—when to shift from one activity to another, when to use discussion rather than lecture, how to respond to misbehavior, or whether to make one requirement rather than another.

Classroom Climate

One dimension of classroom culture is **classroom climate**—the atmosphere or quality of life in a classroom. The climate of your classroom will be determined by how you interact with your students and "by the manner and degree to which you exercise authority, show warmth and support, encourage competitiveness or cooperation, and allow for independent judgment and choice" (Borich, 2007, p. 167).

In addition to promoting learning, your classroom climate should convince students that you care about them and believe they can learn, are sensitive to their differing needs and abilities, know the subject matter, and maintain effective classroom discipline. Figure 10.1 shows how important these dimensions of teaching are to a group of roughly 2,000 students and the grades they would give their teachers for each dimension.

The climate of your classroom will be complex and multidimensional; its character will be determined by a wide array of variables, many of which will be beyond your

Question 1: The following is a list of several aspects of teaching. Which one do you think is most important?

Question 2: For each item, how would you grade your teacher?

Base: All students (N = 2,049)

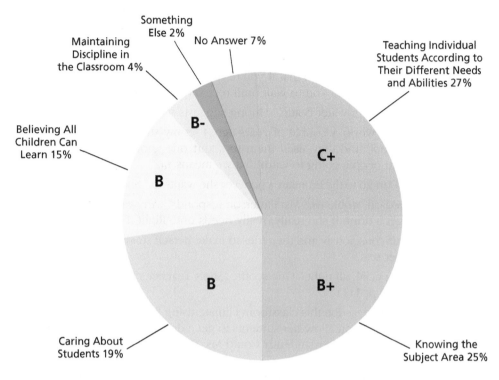

FIGURE 10.1 Most important aspects of teaching and students' ratings

Source: The MetLife Survey of the American Teacher 1001: Key Elements of Quality Schools. *New York: Harris Interactive, Inc., 2001.*

control. However, many classroom variables will be within your control. You can take specific steps to create a classroom climate with the following eight characteristics:

1. A productive, task-oriented focus
2. Group cohesiveness
3. Open, warm relationships between teacher and students
4. Cooperative, respectful interactions among students
5. Low levels of tension, anxiety, and conflict
6. Humor
7. High expectations
8. Frequent opportunities for student input regarding classroom activities

The degree to which these dimensions of classroom climate are present within your classroom will be influenced by your style of communicating and treating students. As the following case illustrates, creating a classroom climate characterized by these eight dimensions is not easy. The moment-to-moment decisions teachers make about how to respond to classroom events can enhance or reduce group cohesiveness and students' motivation to learn.

Dari feels uncomfortable as she makes the seemingly endless trip from her desk to the drinking fountain at the back of the room. If she had a choice, she wouldn't make the trip at all. She is well aware that her classmates resent her being allowed to get a drink whenever she wants to, whereas they have to wait until recess or lunch. They know that the medicine she takes every morning makes her thirsty, but they still tease her about being "Teacher's Pet."

"Why can't the others get drinks when they want to?" she wonders. "It wouldn't be any big deal. Besides, Ms. Patterson is *always* drinking her coffee. She carries that stupid coffee mug around so much that it looks as if it's attached to her body."

"Hey, Ms. Patterson, can I get a drink?" Craig calls out. "It's a really hot day, and I'm thirsty'."

"Of course not, Craig. You know my rule about that." Ms. Patterson is obviously annoyed at his question.

Craig persists. "It's not fair. *You* can drink your coffee whenever you want to."

"I never said life is fair," Ms. Patterson replies. "I'm the teacher, so I have certain privileges. I need to have something to drink because I do most of the talking and my mouth gets dry. Besides, my job is to make sure that you children learn, and I can't do that if you're running to the drinking fountain all the time. It won't kill you to wait until recess to get a drink."

"But we could use a water bottle," Huong suggests.

"No. that won't work. A couple of years ago, I let my students bring water bottles to school, and they used them to squirt one another all the time. When are you people going to learn that *no* means *no*?"

"But you let Dari go to the fountain whenever she wants to," Shelby points out.

"Dari has medical problems," Ms. Patterson responds. "Anyway, I know that she'll only get a drink if she really, really needs one. Right, Dari?"

Dari nods self-consciously and then tries to make herself smaller by scrunching low in her seat.

"Yeah, she's special, all right," Guy scoffs. "She's Teacher's Pet." (Ormrod & McGuire, 2007, p. 111)

How would you describe this classroom climate using the eight dimensions listed earlier? Should Ms. Patterson allow her students to get a drink during class? Is it fair that she drinks coffee in front of her students? Could Ms. Patterson help Dari feel more socially connected to her classmates?

Although how you regard and treat students influences your classroom climate, the instructional decisions you make also influence it. Your decisions can result in three types of relationships among members of the class: cooperative or positive interdependence, competitive or negative interdependence, and individualistic or no interdependence (Johnson & Johnson, 1999). A group project to measure classroom furniture would promote *cooperative interdependence*. A race to be the first student to measure the furniture would call for *competitive interdependence*. And having a student measure the furniture independently would be an example of *no interdependence*. Obviously, you should use strategies that foster all three forms of interactions, depending on your instructional goals. In most cases, though, your primary emphasis will be on furthering cooperative interdependence.

Classroom Dynamics

Interactions between teachers and students are at the very core of teaching. As a teacher, the quality of your interactions with students reveals how you feel about them. If you empathize with students, genuinely respect them, and expect them to learn, you are more likely to develop a classroom climate free of management problems. In classrooms with positive group dynamics, teachers and students work toward a common goal—learning. In classrooms with negative interactions, the energy of teachers and students may be channeled into conflict rather than into learning.

There is no precise formula to guarantee success in the classroom; however, a classroom climate characterized by the following four qualities results in greater student motivation to learn and more positive teacher-student and student-student interactions:

1. Learning activities are well organized, progress smoothly, and are free from distractions or interruptions.
2. The teacher is caring, patient, and supportive, and never ridicules or criticizes students for their efforts to learn.

3. The curriculum is challenging but not so difficult that students become frustrated and decide not to learn.

4. Learning activities are authentic and, to the degree possible, relevant to students' interests and experiences.

Communication Skills

Successful teachers possess effective communication skills. They express themselves verbally and nonverbally (and in writing) in a manner that is clear, concise, and interesting. They "are able to communicate clearly and directly to their students without wandering, speaking above students' levels of comprehension, or using speech patterns that impair their presentation's clarity" (Borich, 2007, p. 10). In addition, they are good listeners. Their students feel that, not only are they heard, they are understood.

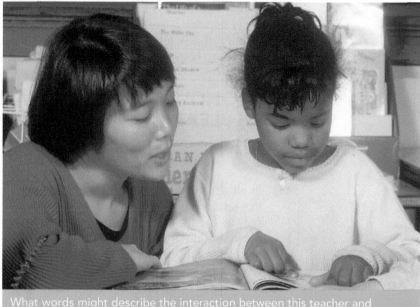

What words might describe the interaction between this teacher and student? What do you think the teacher is saying to her student?

Effective teachers relish the interactive, spontaneous dimensions of classroom discourse. They respond appropriately to events that could sabotage the plans of less effective teachers—a student's misbehavior, announcements on the PA system, interruptions by other teachers or parents, arguments between students, or the mood of the class at a given time.

Interactions Among Students

In addition to engaging in positive, success-oriented interactions with their students, effective teachers foster positive, cooperative interactions among students. As a result, students feel supported by their peers and free to devote their attention to learning. The climate of such a classroom is "mature" and "self-renewing" (Schmuck & Schmuck, 2001). Typically, the classroom climate has evolved through four stages of group development (see Figure 10.2).

During stage 1, students are on their best behavior. Teachers can use this honeymoon period to their advantage. They can discuss classroom rules and procedures, outline learning goals, and clarify expectations. During stage 2, teachers can encourage student participation and communication, while discouraging the formation of cliques.

Groups that have reached stage 2 then move into stage 3, which may last for the remainder of the school year. In stage 3, the group sets clear goals, shares tasks, and agrees on deadlines. A fully evolved group reaches stage 4. In this stage, group members accept responsibility for the quality of life in the group, and they continuously strive to improve it.

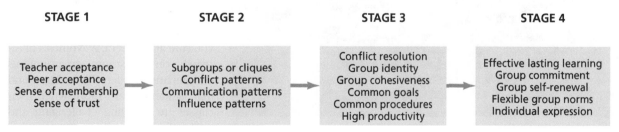

STAGE 1	STAGE 2	STAGE 3	STAGE 4
Teacher acceptance Peer acceptance Sense of membership Sense of trust	Subgroups or cliques Conflict patterns Communication patterns Influence patterns	Conflict resolution Group identity Group cohesiveness Common goals Common procedures High productivity	Effective lasting learning Group commitment Group self-renewal Flexible group norms Individual expression

FIGURE 10.2 Characteristics of groups at four stages of development

Teachers who facilitate group processes in their classrooms recognize that students as well as teachers exert leadership in the classroom. Accomplished teachers identify student leaders and are able to influence these students to use their leadership abilities to help the entire group reach its goals.

HOW CAN YOU CREATE A POSITIVE LEARNING ENVIRONMENT?

A positive classroom climate and positive classroom dynamics are essential for a good learning environment. Developing and then maintaining such an environment is a complex challenge. No single set of strategies will ensure success in all situations. However, educational researchers have identified teacher behaviors that tend to be associated with high levels of student learning. Effective teachers know how to use these behaviors and *for what purposes* they are best suited. The following sections address three important dimensions of positive learning environments: the caring classroom, the physical classroom environment, and classroom organization, including procedures for grouping students for instruction and managing time.

The Caring Classroom

At this point in your preparation to become a teacher, you may doubt your ability to create a positive classroom climate and to orchestrate the complex dynamics of the classroom so that you and your students become a cohesive, productive, and mutually supportive group. In your quest to develop these abilities, remember that an authentic spirit of caring is at the heart of an effective learning environment. *"[C]aring pedagogy* [italics added] can . . . create or restore self-confidence needed for participating in the positive learning opportunities in the classroom. It can also help form the moral foundation of responsible citizenship, productive community membership and leadership, and lifelong engagement in learning" (Paul & Colucci, 2000, p. 45).

How can you establish a **caring classroom**? First, you can demonstrate caring through your efforts to help all students learn to their fullest potential. You can learn as much as you can about your students' abilities and what motivates them to do their best. You should actually become a *student of your students*—as a 10th-grade student states: An effective teacher "[gets] to know all students well" (Harris Interactive, 2001). In addition, as the teacher profiled in the Teachers' Voices: Research to Reality feature in this chapter explains, you can make your classroom a welcoming place for your students' parents and/or guardians.

You should also realize that how you speak and listen to students determines the extent to which they believe you care about them. A synthesis of research on classroom environments that enhance students' learning found that "students learn more when their classes are satisfying, challenging, and

This dynamic kindergarten class exhibits many of the characteristics of a caring classroom climate. Relations are open and trusting; everyone is accepted and actively engaged; a sense of order prevails even in an activity format that calls for self-expression.

TEACHERS' VOICES RESEARCH TO REALITY

Lisa Rieger
A WELCOMING TONE IN THE CLASSROOM

Imagine . . . the first day of school in a first-grade classroom. It is a year full of wondrous expectations for students, parents, and teachers. Often called a magical year, first grade is the time when young children are expected to learn, practice, and independently use specific strategies that will help them become effective communicators, creative problem solvers, and flexible thinkers. As I enthusiastically welcome the many students, parents, and siblings who arrive at my door, I am conscious of the parents' hurrying to get out of my way. I keenly take note of my students' various reactions to this and am not convinced that they agree it is such a prudent idea. Unfortunately, many parents assume that this may be their brief and only opportunity to catch my attention, to relay pertinent information, and personally to chat with me until the first parent-teacher conferences in mid-November. *That is a mind-set worth changing.*

As excited as I am to begin shaping our classroom community of motivated, positive, and determined young children, I believe there is a more pervasive tone worth setting with my students and their families. In many ways, this tone is atypical of the culture of school, where teachers often avoid getting "trapped" by needy or aggressive parents. Often feeling too busy, we begin listening to a parent concern only to find ourselves unable to really do so. The competing internal tick of the school clock prevents us. We dismiss many conversations with a polite request to call and arrange a convenient meeting time or we redirect parents to the school nurse, counselor, or principal. At times, our own discomfort with difference and our overwhelming feelings raise our shoulders to our ears and keep our hands wrapped tightly around the classroom doorknobs. We radiate an anxiety that propels us to close our doors quickly so we can be free of the chaos surrounding our students' lives. We are overeager to begin conforming children to our rules and expectations of school. However, the results can be disastrous for teachers, parents, and students—alienation, unnecessary power struggles, and a general mode of complaining and

unhappiness can soon creep in and take over. The truth is *teachers really do need parents* to help support their children as they transition into early childhood classrooms.

With body language and eye contact, I try to communicate my desire for a different kind of classroom. There will be no shooing parents or family away, especially today. It is important for me to learn their names, shake their hands, smile, and look directly into their eyes, just as I will do with their children. I am reminded that there will be times when I will want and need to ask parents, "How are you?" Many parents will eagerly begin to share some of their lives with me if they sense I am genuinely interested. These kinds of exchanges are enriching and insightful. They can and will happen if parents sense that the classroom climate is safe and free of personal judgment. . . .

Welcoming children and their families into our classrooms requires educators to critically examine the culture and climate in today's schools. I would not be an educator in the pubic school system if I did not believe that there are excellent people, initiatives, programs, and resources in place to serve the needs of today's children. . . . We must welcome our students and families as they are, learn as much as we can from one another, work together, and always create opportunities to celebrate our accomplishments.

PERSONAL REFLECTION

1. With reference to the grade level and subject area for which you are preparing to teach, how can you develop a welcoming tone for all students and their families?
2. What challenges can a teacher face when trying to develop a welcoming tone in his or her classroom? How can a teacher overcome these challenges?

Lisa Rieger is an elementary enrichment teacher with the Binghamton City School District in New York. The preceding is excerpted from a chapter that she wrote for *Other Kinds of Families: Embracing Diversity in Schools.* Reprinted by permission of the publisher. From Tammy Turner-Vorbeck and Monica Miller Marsh (Eds.). *Other Kinds of Families: Embracing Diversity in Schools,* New York: Teachers College Press, Copyright © 2008, pp. 64–80, by Teachers College, Columbia University. All rights reserved.

TABLE 10.1 Fifteen dimensions of classroom environment

Dimension	Learning		Percent Positive Influence on Description
Satisfaction	100%	(17)	Students enjoy classroom work and find it satisfying.
Challenge	87	(16)	Students find the work difficult and challenging.
Cohesiveness	86	(17)	Students know one another well and are helpful and friendly toward one another.
Physical environment	85	(15)	Adequate books, equipment, space, and lighting are available.
Democracy	85	(14)	Students share equally in making decisions that affect the entire class.
Goal direction	73	(15)	Learning goals are clear.
Competition	67	(9)	Competition among students is minimized.
Formality	65	(17)	Class is informal, with few formal rules to guide behavior.
Speed	54	(14)	Students have sufficient time to finish their work.
Diversity	31	(14)	Students' interests differ and are provided for.
Apathy	14	(15)	Students don't care about what the class does.
Favoritism	10	(13)	All students do not enjoy the same privileges; the teacher has favorites.
Cliquishness	8	(13)	Certain students work only with close friends and refuse to interact with others.
Disorganization	6	(17)	Activities are disorganized and confusing, rather than well organized and efficient.
Friction	0	(17)	Tension and quarreling among students characterize the classroom.

Note: Percent indicates the percentage of research studies that reported a positive influence on learning for that dimension; number in parentheses indicates number of research studies that investigated that dimension.

Source: Adapted from Herbert J. Walberg and Rebecca C. Greenberg, "Using the Learning Environment Inventory," *Educational Leadership*, May 1997, p. 47.

friendly and they have a voice in decision making. [When] classes are unfriendly, cliquish, and fragmented, they leave students feeling rejected and therefore impede learning" (Walberg & Greenberg, 1997, p. 46). Table 10.1 is based on this study; it presents 15 dimensions of classroom life and how each influences students' learning at the junior and senior high school levels.

While students learn best in caring classrooms, students must also learn to care for others. Toward this end, Stanford University professor Nel Noddings recommends reorganizing the school curriculum around "themes of care" and suggests that "all students should be engaged in a general education that guides them in caring for self, intimate others, global others, plants, animals, the environment, objects and instruments, and ideas" (2002, p. 99). In addition, Noddings points out that "relations of care and trust should improve (or at least not hurt) achievement, [and] they also might contribute to greater safety, stronger social ties, better citizenship, and greater satisfaction for both teachers and students" (2007, p. 83).

The Physical Environment of the Classroom

When you become a teacher, the physical environment of your school will probably be similar to that of schools you attended. With the help of your students, however, it is possible to improve your surroundings. Fresh air; plants; clean, painted walls; displays of students' work; a comfortable reading or resource area; and a few prints or posters help to create a positive learning environment. Seating arrangements and the placement of other classroom furniture also do much to shape the classroom environment. Although seating by rows may be very appropriate for whole-group instruction or examinations, other arrangements may be more beneficial for other activities. For example, you can enhance small-group activities by moving desks into small clusters in different parts of the room. Figure 10.3 shows the arrangement of a classroom at an exemplary elementary school. The room is designed to encourage students to learn through discovery at learning centers located around the room.

However you design your classroom, be certain that seating arrangements do not reduce the opportunity of some students to learn. For example, students in some classrooms receive more attention if they are seated in the so-called action zone, the middle front-row seats and seats on the middle aisle. Teachers often stand near this area and unknowingly give students seated there more opportunities to speak.

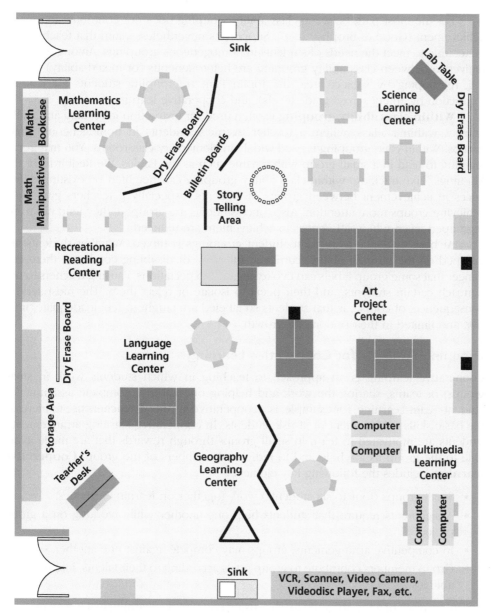

FIGURE 10.3 Learning centers in an elementary classroom

Classroom Organization

A critical factor in creating a positive learning environment is **classroom organization**—how teachers and students are grouped for instruction, how learning tasks are structured, and how other resources are used. The following sections focus on these aspects of classroom organization.

Grouping Students by Ability

Two common approaches for grouping students on the basis of shared characteristics are between-class ability grouping, often called tracking, and within-class ability grouping. Students who attend schools where **between-class ability grouping** is practiced are assigned to classes on the basis of ability or achievement (usually determined by scores on standardized tests). Another form of between-class ability grouping, especially at the high school level, is based on students' goals after graduation. Many high schools, for example, have a college preparatory track, a vocational track, and a business education track.

For the most part, between-class ability grouping does not contribute to greater achievement (Good & Brophy, 2008). Supporters nevertheless claim that teachers are better able to meet the needs of students in homogeneous groupings. Among the alternatives to between-class ability grouping are heterogeneous (or mixed-ability) grouping, regrouping by subject area, the Joplin Plan (regrouping students for reading instruction by ability across grade levels), and cooperative learning.

Within-class ability grouping is often used for instruction in reading and mathematics within a class, where a teacher instructs students in homogeneous, small groups. Within-class grouping is used widely in elementary classrooms. You may recall learning to read in a small group with a name such as the Eagles, the Redbirds, or the Mustangs. Like tracking, within-class ability grouping can heighten preexisting differences in achievement between groups of students, especially if teachers give high-achieving groups more attention. Also, once students are grouped, they tend not to be regrouped, even when differences in achievement are reduced.

At best, evidence to support student groupings is mixed. Whether students are grouped on the basis of ability, curricular interests, or disabling condition, there is a danger that some group labels can evoke negative expectations, causing teachers to underteach certain students, and their peers to isolate or reject them. The most serious consequence, of course, is that students so labeled are taught to feel inadequate, inferior, and limited in their options for growth.

Grouping Students for Cooperative Learning

Cooperative learning is an approach to teaching in which students work in small groups, or teams, sharing the work and helping one another complete assignments. Student-Team-Learning, for example, is a cooperative approach teachers use to increase the basic skills achievement of at-risk students. In cooperative learning arrangements, students are motivated to learn in small groups through rewards that are made available to the group as a whole and to individual members of the group. **Cooperative learning** includes the following key elements:

- Small groups (four to six students) work together on learning activities.
- Assignments require that students help one another while working on a group project.
- In competitive arrangements, groups may compete against one another.
- Group members contribute to group goals according to their talents, interests, and abilities.

Go to MyEducationLab, select Chapter 10 and then Activities and Applications to watch the video Cooperative Learning.

For an example of a fourth-grade teacher using cooperative learning in a lesson on multiplication, go to MyEducationLab.

In addition, cooperative learning is an instructional method that can strengthen students' interpersonal skills. When students from different racial, ethnic, and cultural backgrounds and mainstreamed special-needs students all contribute to a common group goal, friendships increase and group members tend to view one another as more equal in status and worth. The contribution that cooperative learning can make to the culture of the classroom is supported by research that indicates that "students of color and White students have a greater tendency to make cross-racial friendships choices [if] they have participated in interracial learning teams. [Also], the academic achievement of students of color . . . is increased . . . while the academic achievement of White students remains about the same in both cooperative and competitive learning situations" (Banks 2008, p. 99).

Cooperative learning also enables students to learn a variety of roles and responsibilities, as Erik Korporaal, a first-year teacher of grades 4 and 5, explains in the following:

> I began by having my students work on simpler, shorter activities in teams of two. For instance, the small groups worked on math problems that they were already familiar with. I did this so that they could focus on working together rather than struggling to understand the problem. Gradually, I in-

creased the difficulty of the tasks as well as the size of the groups. I reinforced positive behavior and pointed out the types of interactions that led to successful groups. Over time students began to realize the sorts of interactions (e.g., effective communication, listening, delegation of responsibilities, and attention to each member's contributions) that needed to occur in order for their group to succeed. (Oaks & Lipton, 2007, p. 193)

The Technology in Action feature in this chapter describes how a fifth-grade social studies teacher combined cooperative learning and podcasting as a way for her students to study the history of the local community.

Delivering Instruction

The delivery of instruction is a key element in creating positive learning environments. What the teacher and the students do has a powerful influence on learning and on the quality of classroom life. A common activity format in elementary schools consists of students doing seatwork on their own or listening to their teachers and participating in whole-class recitations. In addition, students participate in reading groups, games, and discussions; take tests; check work; view films; give reports; gather information from the Internet; help clean up the classroom; and go on field trips.

As a teacher, you must answer the question, What activity will enable me to accomplish my instructional goals? You should also realize that learning activities should meet students' goals; that is, the activities must be meaningful and authentic for students. **Authentic learning tasks** enable students to see the connections between classroom learning and the world beyond the classroom—both now and in the future. For example, Figure 10.4 presents the work of 12-year-old Mary Lynn when she was given

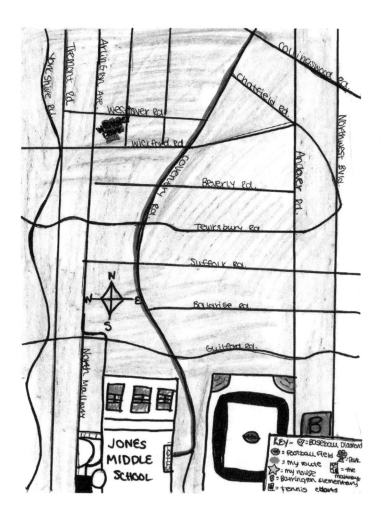

FIGURE 10.4 An authentic mapping activity
Source: From Jeanne E. Ormrod. Essentials of Educational Psychology, 1e. Published by Merrill, an imprint of Pearson Education. Copyright 2006 by Pearson Education. Reprinted by permission. All rights reserved.

TECHNOLOGY in *ACTION*

Podcasting in Fifth-Grade Social Studies

Mrs. Warren teaches fifth-grade social studies at Miliken Elementary School. She is a firm believer in connecting her students to their community. Each year, she has her students research historical and current events from their community and write up the stories they uncover. In the past, she posted these written stories on the school's website, printed them in a newspaper format, or compiled them in a hard-copy book. This year, she decides to try something different: Mrs. Warren wants to podcast her students' stories.

To start, she divided her students into groups of four. Each group was formed around a series of basic skill sets. Each group had a student who was comfortable with podcasting technologies, a student who had strong writing skills, a student who was comfortable speaking into a microphone, and a student who had research skills. The groups were asked to identify an aspect of their community that they wanted to explore. They were also asked to identify one historical event and one current event to report on.

Once Mrs. Warren approved the topics, the students started researching those topics. They developed research notes, a storyboard, and a script for narration. When they had these components, they started creating their audio files. Mrs. Warren allowed the students to either record directly on the computer or use a mobile recording device. Selection of a device depended on the needs of the group. Some groups performed in teams, with one student reading, then another. Some of the groups chose to act out historical events. Members of the group would take on the roles of historical figures from the community, like an old-time radio broadcast. Other groups delivered their podcast as a news report. Some students interviewed members of the community, some acted as news anchors, and others as roving reporters. Mrs. Warren was very impressed with the creativity and accuracy of the reports and the excitement that the activity generated among the students.

What made the activity a true success was Mrs. Warren's approach to publicizing the podcasts. After the first podcast was created, Mrs. Warren made an announcement over the school's public address (PA) system. She alerted the whole school to the availability of the podcasts and where they could get information on accessing the podcasts. Most important, she informed them of a competition. She offered free merchandise at the school store if students answered questions about the stories in the podcasts.

At any moment, walking down the hallway, in the lunchroom, or in class, Mrs. Warren would ask questions. For each correct answer, a student was entered into a drawing. Friday morning of each week, Mrs. Warren would draw a name from the pool of entries and announce the winners over the PA system.

By the second week, students in the school were downloading the podcast to their MP3 players, the computers at school, and—according to parents she spoke with—computers at home. Without a doubt, students were really learning about their community.

PODCASTING: Podcasting is the delivery of audio files over the Internet. What makes podcasting unique is syndication. Syndication allows subscribers to receive, through a Web feed, frequently updated Web content.

VISIT: http://www.mypodcast.com; http://www.podbeam.com. There are several ways to create a podcast and learn about podcasting. The two sites listed here provide free podcasting creation and hosting. They also provide some interesting literature on how, what, and why to podcast.

POSSIBLE USES: Teachers have used podcasts to deliver lecture material to students, to improve their teaching by accessing relevant professional development materials, to improve student reading comprehension, to improve learning through student-generated material, and to update parents on the daily events that transpire in their classrooms.

TRY IT OUT: To create a podcast, you need access to a computer, a microphone, and a Web server. The first step is to create an audio file. You can use any audio recording software to create the file—programs such as Audacity work well. Once the audio file is created, you need to convert it to an MP3 format. Once your audio file is converted to MP3, you need to upload that file, along with a Really Simple Syndication (RSS) file, to a Web server. If you are familiar with basic html, then creating an RSS file is quite simple. If you are not familiar with basic HTML, a quick tutorial will get you ready in a short time. Once the MP3 and RSS file are uploaded to your Web server, the file is ready for prime-time and is accessible to your registered audience.

an authentic assignment to construct a map of the area between her home and school. And the Teaching on Your Feet feature in this chapter describes how one teacher, on the spur of the moment, was able to make the subject matter more meaningful and relevant for his students.

To understand how authentic learning tasks can motivate students to learn, reflect on your own school experiences. Do you recall memorizing facts only because they would appear on a test? Did you ever wonder why a teacher asked you to complete a learning task? Did you ever feel that a teacher asked you to do busywork? What kinds of learning tasks motivated you the most? How often were you involved in authentic learning activities such as the following?

- Giving oral reports based on research you conducted
- Writing an editorial for the school or local newspaper
- Representing the pro or con side in a debate
- Conducting an experiment and then writing the results
- Creating a model to illustrate a process like photosynthesis, a solar eclipse, or combustion in a gasoline engine
- Completing an art project and then participating in an art exhibit for the community
- Tutoring younger children in reading, mathematics, or science
- Developing a website to document an in-class project
- Creating an infomercial using video-editing software and then getting reactions to the infomercial from other classes in your school
- Developing a science webquest and then posting the webquest for evaluation

A comprehensive nationwide study of successfully restructured schools reported that "authentic pedagogy" helps students to (1) "construct knowledge" through the use of higher-order thinking, (2) acquire "deep knowledge" (relatively complex understandings of subject matter), (3) engage in "substantive conversations" with teachers and peers, and (4) make connections between substantive knowledge and the world beyond the classroom (Newmann et al., 1996; Newmann & Wehlage, 1995). In addition, the study found that highly authentic pedagogy classes boost achievement for students at all grade levels.

How Time Is Used

How teachers use time affects student learning. **Allocated time** is the time teachers allocate for instruction in various areas of the curriculum. Teachers vary widely in their instructional use of time. For example, "some students [may receive] as much as four times more instructional time in a given subject than other students in the same grade" (Good & Brophy, 2003, p. 29).

Researchers have shown that time on-task—the amount of time students are actively engaged in learning activities—is directly related to learning. As anyone who has ever daydreamed while appearing to pay attention can confirm, time on task is difficult to measure. In response to this difficulty, researchers have introduced the concept of **academic learning time**—the amount of time a student spends working on academic tasks with a high level of success (80 percent or higher). Not surprisingly, learning time, like allocated time, varies greatly from classroom to classroom. For example, Figure 10.5 shows how the more than 1,000 hours most states mandate for instruction at the elementary level actually result in about 300 hours during which students are truly engaged in meaningful, appropriate tasks.

An additional concept that is proving useful in understanding teachers' use of time in the classroom is known as **opportunity to learn (OTL).** OTL is based on the premise that teachers should use time to provide all students with challenging content through appropriate instruction. Many states are developing OTL standards for how teachers should use time in the classroom.

Claudia Meek, a third-grade teacher in California, points out in her *Phi Delta Kappan* article that state- and district-mandated testing and the time needed to prepare students for testing reduce the amount of instructional time available to teachers. During a 1-year

TEACHING ON YOUR FEET

QUESTIONS AND ANSWERS

I must confess that I was not particularly surprised to see eyes roll as several of my students chimed in and interrupted my heartfelt paean to Shakespeare as they ruefully exclaimed, "Hamlet is way too complicated and confusing!" I suppose they felt that their plaintive cries were necessary at the time to try to curb my rampant enthusiasm before things really got out of hand in my 12th-grade British Literature class.

Struggling to overcome the temptation to launch into a passionate defense of Shakespeare's literary honor, I realized this was probably the best opportunity in recent times to turn that nascent cynicism on its head. So I quickly brought out copies of Tom Stoppard's Rosencrantz & Guildenstern Are Dead—a contemporary, comedic play based on the perspectives of two minor characters from Hamlet—and asked my detractors to read with me. I directed them to the scene where they play Questions and Answers, where words ricochet back and forth in rapid succession as if they were on a tennis court. Rosencrantz and Guildenstern desperately want to extract some answers from Hamlet as they attempt to delve into the cause of his apparent madness, but all they really have are unanswered questions, which ironically become self-reflective as they ponder their own existence and purpose, or lack thereof. I kept pushing the pace of the reading with crisp and emphatic enunciation, and smiles and even wide grins slowly began to break out over their faces as they got caught up in the escalating torrent.

When the exchange finally ended, I deliberately made solid eye contact with my students, and affirmed with complete sincerity that the tough questions that challenge and address the very nature of what we truly are as human beings will always be of great value. We should never be satisfied with oversimplified, pedantic answers when reading a great work of literature such as Hamlet, which deserves the highest respect because, to this very day, it still evokes questions with remarkable power to provoke contemplation of the profound, ironic, and even the absurd.

Almost in unison, my students nodded their heads in agreement. In their eyes, I saw genuine appreciation for the important lesson they had learned that day—not so much about the particular merits of Hamlet per se, but rather that we can and should ascribe value to things that are hard and challenging, because embedded within are the questions that have been and will continue to be meaningful and great.

ANALYSIS

Sometimes, teachers fall into the trap of thinking that all they need is a set process or method to impart some measure of learning. Whether they use videos, study guides, or Socratic circles, sooner or later they realize these techniques can all be suddenly reduced to hollow panaceas because students tend to get bored rather easily, merely go through the motions, or express quite openly their skepticism about the value of the curriculum.

Truly effective teachers must rise to the occasion to surprise and engage their students with fresh perspectives that are innovative and relevant. Although a few talented individuals can accomplish this feat on a fairly impromptu basis, most teachers need to invest careful thought in anticipation of the skeptical student(s), who can be completely turned around if we make ourselves ready for that opportunity when it comes.

REFLECTION

- How can we be better prepared to respond creatively to the skepticism of our students rather than taking a confrontational or argumentative approach?
- What specific materials or resources do we have at our fingertips to extend or enhance the standard curriculum?
- How flexible, adaptable and comfortable should we be with the content we teach? If we feel somewhat limited or lacking, how can we significantly increase the range or scope of our expertise?

Elmer Lee
English Teacher (Grades 9–12)
Eagles Peak Charter School (Renaissance High School Academy)

myeducationlab *To answer these questions online, go to MyEducationLab at www.myeducationlab.com, select the Activities and Application section, and click on this chapter's Teaching on Your Feet.*

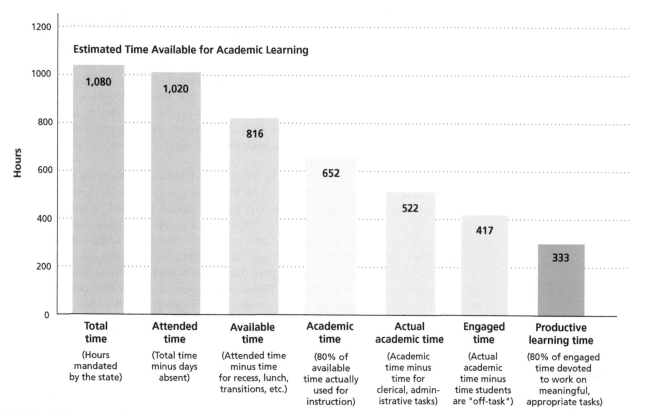

FIGURE 10.5 How much time is there, anyway?

Source: Adapted from Carol Simon Weinstein and Andrew J. Migano Jr. Elementary Classroom Management: Lessons From Research and Practice, 4th ed. Boston: McGraw-Hill, 2007, p. 175. Copyright © 2007 by the McGraw-Hill Companies. Adapted with permission of the McGraw-Hill Companies.

period, approximately 32 hours of her class time were devoted to testing. That same year, 262 hours were devoted to fundraising, disaster preparedness, socialization, holidays, assemblies, regular interruptions, and miscellaneous time losses. Taken together, more than one-third of Meek's classroom time was devoted to these activities. Her observations are based on a large-scale research study conducted by the National Center for Education Statistics and an analysis of data collected from her own classroom (Meek, 2003).

To increase the time available for active learning, many high schools have implemented block scheduling arrangements. **Block scheduling** uses longer blocks of time each class period, with fewer periods each day. Longer blocks of time allow more in-depth coverage of subject matter and lead to deeper understanding and higher-level applications. Block scheduling also gives teachers more time to present complex concepts and students more time to practice applying those concepts to authentic problems.

WHAT ARE THE KEYS TO SUCCESSFUL CLASSROOM MANAGEMENT?

For most new teachers, classroom management is a primary concern. How can you prevent discipline problems from arising and keep students productively engaged in learning activities? Effective **classroom management** cannot be reduced to a cookbook recipe. However, you can take definite steps to create an effective learning environment in your classroom.

Consider the following scenarios of two middle-level classrooms—the same group of students with two different teachers. In which classroom is misbehavior more likely to emerge?

Classroom 1 is a beehive of activity as students continue to study global warming in their science class. Students are working in small groups at four multimedia centers, each with a desktop computer. Each group is developing questions they will post on the class blog for scientists participating on the Andrill Research Immersion for Science

Educators (ARISE) team stationed in Antarctica. "What do you eat in Antarctica?" "How cold is it right now?" "Have you seen any polar bears, seals, penguins, or other wildlife?" The teacher circulates from group to group—listening, asking clarifying questions, and encouraging each group's effort. Some students suggest questions; others clarify the group's thinking—clearly, the students are deeply engaged in the activity.

Classroom 1 is filled with instructional materials. Student work—clay models of igloos, polar bears, and penguins, for example—is on the shelves that line the walls. On the classroom walls are maps of Antarctica drawn by students, color photos of Antarctica printed out on the printer at each learning center, and color printouts of PowerPoint presentations on Antarctica.

Science class is over, and students are now in classroom 2, studying language arts. Students are seated in rows, staring at their literature books while student after student reads two paragraphs from the book. The teacher sits on the desk at the front of the room and occasionally asks a question or makes a comment about the material just read. Several commercially printed posters are on the classroom walls—"Elements of a Novel or Short Story," "Punctuation Rules," and "What Good Readers Do." On one side of the room, beneath the windows, paperback and hardcover books are neatly lined up on the shelves of two bookcases. The room is quiet except for the sound of the student reading, the teacher's occasional comment or question, and the loud ticking of the clock above the classroom door.

The two scenarios above illustrate the fact that good classroom management focuses on "establishing a productive learning environment, rather than control of misbehavior" (Good & Brophy, 2008, p. 77). Sound classroom management techniques are based on the guidelines for creating an effective learning environment presented previously in this chapter—in other words, (1) creating a caring classroom, (2) organizing the physical classroom environment, (3) grouping students for instruction, (4) providing authentic learning tasks, and (5) structuring the use of time to maximize students' learning. Positive leadership and preventive planning thus are central to effective classroom management. To examine an experienced fifth-grade teacher's classroom management plan, go to MyEducationLab.

In addition, you should remember that classroom management refers to how teachers structure their learning environments to prevent, or minimize, behavior problems. *Discipline* refers to the methods teachers use *after* students misbehave. *Classroom management* is prevention-oriented, while discipline is control-oriented. The goal of classroom management is to structure the classroom environment to *maximize student attention* and *minimize disruptive behavior*. The following strategies will help you create a well-managed classroom environment:

- Arrange classroom furniture (desks, tables, and chairs) so that you can easily monitor students' behavior for signs of inattention, boredom, and misbehavior from any point in the room.
- Arrange classroom furniture so that students can move from place to place without disturbing their classmates.
- Keep very interesting instructional materials (for example, a replica of a human skeleton, a model of the solar system, or a large collection of insects) out of sight until you need to use them.
- Separate friends who tend to misbehave and get off-task when they are seated near one another, or separate students who dislike one another and are more likely to misbehave if they are seated close to one another.
- Assign chronically misbehaving students to seats close to your desk.

The Democratic Classroom

Teachers who allow students to participate in making decisions about the physical classroom environment, classroom rules and procedures, modifications to the curriculum, and options for learning activities also have fewer discipline problems. Students in **democratic classrooms** have more power and more responsibility than students in

Go to MyEducationLab, select Chapter 10 and Activities and Applications to analyze the artifact Classroom Management Plan.

conventional classrooms. If students are to live in a democracy, they must learn to manage freedom responsibly; teachers model democracy by giving their students some choices and some control over classroom activities.

William Glasser, well-known psychiatrist and author of *Quality School* (1998a), *The Quality School Teacher* (1998b), *Choice Theory* (1998c), and (with Karen Dotson) *Choice Theory in the Classroom* (1998), recommends that teachers develop "quality" classrooms based on democratic principles. According to Glasser, many teachers struggle with classroom management because their actions are guided by stimulus-response theory. They try to coerce students through rewards or punishment, or what many teachers term logical consequences. Instead, Glasser believes that teachers should establish "quality" environments in the classroom by following choice theory. Choice theory recognizes that human beings make choices that enable them to create "quality worlds" that satisfy four needs: the need to belong, the need for power, the need for freedom, and the need for fun.

From a **choice theory** perspective, misbehavior in the classroom arises when students' learning experiences do not enable them to create quality worlds for themselves. Therefore, teachers "must give up bossing and turn to 'leading'" (Glasser, 1997, p. 600). We follow leaders, Glasser says, because we believe they are concerned about our welfare. To persuade students to do quality schoolwork, teachers must establish warm, non-coercive relationships with students; teach students meaningful skills rather than ask them to memorize information; enable them to experience satisfaction and excitement by working in small teams; and move from teacher evaluation to student self-evaluation. To see a self-evaluation form that a second-grade teacher used to help a student who was having trouble listening, displaying a positive attitude, and staying seated, go to MyEducationLab. The student rated her own behavior three times per day.

Creating a democratic classroom community is not easy; however, the benefits can be significant—as the following comments by Janene Ashford, a first-year teacher of sixth grade, illustrate:

> As the year progressed, my students and I began to realize a democratic classroom community. It was an incredible and sometimes difficult evolution from a teacher-centered and controlled environment to a community created and strengthened by students. "Guess what the teacher wants" (under the guise of democracy) evolved into "What should we do?" under guidelines I determined, and then into "I can't/don't need to do it myself, what do you guys think we should do?" Over the next couple of months, my students and I developed and maintained a wonderfully strong community. (Oakes & Lipton, 2007, p. 284)

Preventive Planning

What other strategies can you use to prevent discipline problems from occurring? The key to prevention is excellent planning and an understanding of life in classrooms. In addition, if you master the essential teaching skills, you will have fewer discipline problems because students will recognize that you are prepared, are well organized, and have a sense of purpose. You will be confident of your ability to teach all students, and your task-oriented manner will tend to discourage misbehavior.

In a seminal study of how teachers prevent discipline problems, Jacob Kounin looked at two sets of teachers: (1) those who managed their classrooms smoothly and productively, with few disruptions, and (2) those who seemed to be plagued with discipline problems and chaotic working conditions. He found that the teachers who managed their classrooms successfully had certain teaching behaviors in common: They (1) displayed the proverbial eyes in the back of the head, a quality of alertness Kounin referred to as *with-it-ness*; (2) used individual students and incidences as models to communicate to the rest of the class their expectations for student conduct—Kounin's *ripple effect*; (3) supervised several situations at once effectively; and (4) were adept at handling transitions smoothly (Kounin, 1970).

In addition to the principles of effective classroom management that Kounin found, two key elements of preventive planning are (1) establishing rules and procedures and

PEARSON
myeducationlab

Go to MyEducationLab, select Chapter 10 and Activities and Applications to analyze the artifact Self-Check.

myeducationlab

Go to MyEducationLab, select Chapter 10 and Activities and Applications to watch the video Low-Profile Classroom Management.

(2) organizing and planning for instruction. For examples of fourth- and seventh-grade teachers responding effectively to various off-task behaviors by students, go to MyEducationLab.

Establishing Rules and Procedures

Successful classroom managers have carefully planned rules and procedures, which they teach early in the year using clear explanations, examples, and practice (Emmer & Evertson, 2009; Evertson & Emmer, 2009; Good & Brophy, 2008). Your classroom rules should be clear, concise, reasonable, and few in number. For example, five general rules for elementary-age students might include: (1) be polite and helpful; (2) respect other people's property; (3) listen quietly while others are speaking; (4) do not hit, shove, or hurt others; and (5) obey all school rules (Evertson & Emmer, 2009). Rules for the secondary level might stipulate the following: (1) bring all needed materials to class, (2) be in your seat and ready to work when the bell rings, (3) respect and be polite to everyone, (4) respect other people's property, (5) listen and stay seated while someone else is speaking, and (6) obey all school rules (Emmer & Evertson, 2009).

It is important to enforce classroom rules consistently and fairly. "Consistency is a key reason why some rules are effective while others are not. Rules that are not enforced or not applied consistently over time result in a loss of prestige and respect for the person who has created the rules and has the responsibility for enforcing them" (Borich, 2007, p. 174).

Procedures—the routines your students follow as they participate in learning activities—are also essential for smooth classroom functioning and minimizing opportunities for misbehavior. How will homework be collected? How will supplies be distributed? How will housekeeping chores be completed? How will attendance be taken? How do students obtain permission to leave the classroom? Part of developing classroom rules and procedures is to decide what to do when students do not follow them. Students must be made aware of the consequences for failing to follow rules or procedures. For example, consequences for rule infractions can range from an expression of teacher disapproval to penalties such as loss of privileges, detention after school, disciplinary conference with a parent or guardian, or temporary separation from the group. To examine a letter one teacher sent home to families to explain classroom rules and procedures, go to MyEducationLab.

myeducationlab

Go to MyEducationLab, select Chapter 10 and Activities and Applications to analyze the artifact Dear Parents.

Organizing and Planning for Instruction

Organizing instructional time, materials, and activities so that classes run smoothly enables you to keep your students engaged in learning, thereby reducing the need for discipline. Time spent planning authentic learning activities that are appropriate for students' needs, interests, and abilities enables you to enjoy the professional satisfaction that comes from having a well-managed classroom.

The following examples illustrate how one eighth-grade teacher began the school year by carefully organizing and planning for instruction. The teacher across the hall, however, was not as well organized; as a consequence, she is more likely to experience misbehavior in her classroom as the year progresses.

Donnell Alexander is waiting at the door for her eighth graders with prepared handouts as students come in the room. She distributes them and says, "Take your seats quickly, please. You'll find your name on the desk. The bell is going to ring in less than a minute and everyone needs to be at his or her desk and quiet when it does. Please read the handout while you're waiting." She is standing at the front of the room, surveying the class as the bell rings. When it stops, she begins, "Good morning, everyone."

Vicki Williams, who also teaches eighth-graders across the hall from Donnell, is organizing her handouts as the students come in the room. Some take their seats while others mill around, talking in small groups. As the bell rings, she looks up and says over the hum of the students. "Everyone take your seats, please. We'll begin in a couple minutes," and she turns back to finish organizing her materials. (Eggen & Kauchak, 2007, p. 380)

Effective Responses to Student Behavior

When students do misbehave, effective teachers draw from a repertoire of problem-solving strategies. These strategies are based on their experience and common sense, their knowledge of students and the teaching–learning process, and their knowledge of human psychology.

There are many structured approaches to classroom management; some are based on psychological theories of human motivation and behavior, while others reflect various philosophical views regarding the purposes of education. None of these approaches, however, is appropriate for all situations, for all teachers, or for all students. The usefulness of a given method depends, in part, on the teacher's individual personality and leadership style and the ability to analyze the complex dynamics of classroom life. In addition, what works should not be the only criterion for evaluating structured or packaged approaches to discipline; what they teach students about their self-worth, acting responsibly, and solving problems is also important (Curwin & Mendler, 1988, p. 1989).

Severity of Misbehavior

Your response to student misbehavior will depend, in part, on whether an infraction is mild, moderate, or severe, and whether it is occurring for the first time or is part of a pattern of chronic misbehaviors. For example, a student who throws a wad of paper at another student might receive a warning for the first infraction. Another student who repeatedly throws objects at other students might receive an after-school detention. Definitions of the severity of misbehavior vary from school to school and from state to state. Figure 10.6 shows the percentage of public schools, categorized by school enrollment size, that reported different types of discipline problems. Notice that smaller schools report significantly fewer discipline problems.

Zero Tolerance

In response to concerns about violence, drugs, and weapons, some schools have implemented zero tolerance policies. The purpose of **zero tolerance policies** is to communicate to students the types of misbehavior that will result in automatic suspension and/or expulsion. Zero tolerance policies are based on the assumption that awareness of automatic, severe consequences for certain types of misbehavior will deter students from those misbehaviors. Evidence indicates, however, that such policies have little effect on students who are inclined to engage in serious misbehavior, and they do not help to create conditions that deter such misbehavior (National Association of School Psychologists, 2008). In light of such evidence, the National Association of School Psychologists has concluded, "Systemic school-wide violence prevention programs, social skills curricula and positive behavioral supports lead to improved learning for all students and safer school communities" (2008, p. 3).

Constructive Assertiveness

The effectiveness of your responses to students' misbehavior depends, in part, on your ability to use constructive assertiveness (Emmer & Evertson, 2009; Evertson & Emmer, 2009). Constructive assertiveness "lies on a continuum of social response between aggressive, overbearing pushiness and timid, ineffectual, or submissive responses that allow some students to trample on the teacher's and other students' rights. Assertiveness skills allow you to communicate to students that you are serious about teaching and about maintaining a classroom in which everyone's rights are respected" (Emmer & Evertson, 2009; Evertson & Emmer, 2009). Communication based on constructive assertiveness is not hostile, sarcastic, defensive, or vindictive; it is clear, firm, and concise. Constructive assertiveness includes three basic elements:

- A direct, clear statement of the problem
- Body language that is unambiguous (e.g., direct eye contact with students, erect posture, and facial expressions that are congruent with the content and tone of corrective statements)
- Firm, unwavering insistence on correct behavior

FIGURE 10.6 Percentage of public schools, categorized by school enrollment size, reporting selected discipline problems that occurred at school: School year 2005–06

Source: U.S. Department of Education and U.S. Department of Justice. (December 2007). Indicators of School Crime and Safety: 2007. Washington, DC: Author, p. 27.

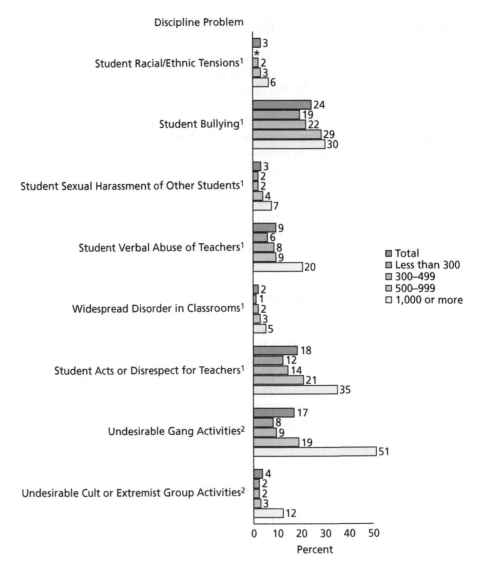

[1] Interpret data with caution.
* Reporting standards not met.
[1] Includes schools that reported the activity happens at least once a week or daily.
[2] Includes schools that reported the activity has happened at all of their schools during the school year.
NOTE: Responses were provided by the principal or the person most knowledgeable about the crime and safety issues at the school. "At school" was defined for respondents to include activities that happen in school buildings, on school grounds, on school buses, and at places that hold school-sponsored events or activities. Respondents were instructed to respond only for those times that were during normal school hours or when school activities or events were in session, unless the survey specified otherwise. Population size is 83,200 public schools.

Lee Cantor developed an approach to discipline based on teacher assertiveness. The approach calls on teachers to establish firm, clear guidelines for student behavior and to follow through with consequences for misbehavior. Cantor (1989, p. 58) comments on how he arrived at the ideas behind assertive discipline: "I found that, above all, the master teachers were assertive; that is, they taught students how to behave. They established clear rules for the classroom, they communicated those rules to the students, and they taught students how to follow them." **Assertive discipline** requires teachers to do the following:

1. Make clear that they will not tolerate anyone preventing them from teaching, stopping learning, or doing anything else that is not in the best interest of the class, the individual, or the teacher.

2. Instruct students clearly and in specific terms about what behaviors are desired and what behaviors are not tolerated.

3. Plan positive and negative consequences for predetermined acceptable or unacceptable behaviors.

4. Plan positive reinforcement for compliance. Reinforcement includes verbal acknowledgment, notes, free time for talking, and, of course, tokens that can be exchanged for appropriate rewards.

5. Plan a sequence of steps to punish noncompliance. These range from writing a youngster's name on the board to sending the student to the principal's office (MacNaughton & Johns, 1991, p. 53).

Figure 10.7 presents the assertive discipline policy in place for grades 6–8 of the Cherokee, Kansas, School District.

Research on the effectiveness of assertive discipline is mixed. "Substantial evidence indicates that giving rewards for good behavior can actually diminish students' intrinsic motivation to learn or to conform to the social norms of the classroom" (Oakes & Lipton, 2007, p. 258). In the following, Javier Espindola, a first-year kindergarten teacher, explains why he eventually decided not to use assertive discipline:

> When my students were sitting quietly and listening to me or when they were on task writing in their journals, I would give them a sticker or happy face to motivate them to continue that behavior. When I saw them talking with peers and not working, I would put their names on the board or give them a sad face.
>
> At first, these strategies worked. Over time, however, I noticed negative effects. Students . . . began to refuse to follow classroom directions, work productively, and respect and listen to their peers and me if they did not receive any rewards.
>
> The first step in removing Assertive Discipline from my classroom was discussing it with my students. I told them that they were no longer going to receive happy faces, stars, stickers, and candies when they were behaving and performing well or consequences such as check marks, sad faces, or names on the board when they were behaving inappropriately. I removed from the chalkboard the chart where I posted check marks when students misbehave and stars when they behave well . . .
>
> I no longer feel the need to have complete control of my students. I have implemented group activities that encourage my students to interact, share experiences, and work with their peers. . . . everyone is capable of improving his or her academic and social skills in a comfortable environment. (Oakes & Lipton, 2007, p. 260)

Teacher Problem Solving

If your efforts to get a student to stop misbehaving are unsuccessful, a problem-solving conference with the student is warranted. A problem-solving conference may give you additional understanding of the situation, thus paving the way for a solution. A conference also helps you and the student understand one another's perspectives better and begin to build a more positive relationship.

The goal of a problem-solving conference is for the student to accept responsibility for his or her behavior and make a commitment to change it. While there is no right way to conduct a problem-solving conference, Glasser's choice theory lends itself to a conferencing procedure that is flexible and appropriate for most situations. Students will usually make good choices (that is, behave in an acceptable manner) if they experience success and know that teachers care about them. The following steps are designed to help misbehaving students see that the choices they make may not lead to the results they want:

1. Have the misbehaving student evaluate and take responsibility for his or her behavior. Often, a good first step is for the teacher to ask, "What are you doing?" and then, "Is it helping you?"

Dear Parents:

To give your child and the students in our classrooms the learning climate that they deserve, we will be initiating the following discipline plan.

Our Philosophy

We believe that all students are capable of behaving appropriately in the classroom. We will not tolerate a student stopping us from teaching and other students from learning.

Classroom Behavior

The students will:

- Follow rules of behavior and instructions the first time they are given.
- Talk only with permission.
- Keep feet, arms, and hands to themselves.
- Stay in their seats except with permission to leave.

Discipline Consequences per Day

If a student chooses to break a rule:

- First—one check—warning
- Second—two checks—30-minute after-school detention
- Third—three checks—60-minute after-school detention
- Fourth—four checks—60-minute after-school detention and sent to principal's office
- ISS (in-school suspension) remainder of day—parents notified

Severe Clause—This goes into effect when there is a severe disruption. Examples: fighting, profane language, severe disobedience/disrespect. Any of these violations will cause a student to be sent to the principal's office immediately.

Positive Behavior—Students may earn rewards for positive behavior. These will be given on an individual and classroom basis. Examples: movies, parties, mini-golf, afternoon recess, etc.

FIGURE 10.7 Assertive discipline policy (grades 6–8)

Source: USD 247 School District; Cherokee, KN. Retrieved on June 29, 2008, from http://www.usd247.com/vnews/display.v/ART/2005/ 03/30/424aebbfa0b08.

2. Have the student make a plan for a more acceptable way of behaving. If necessary, the student and the teacher brainstorm solutions. Agreement is reached on how the student will behave in the future and the consequences for failure to follow through.

3. Require the student to make a commitment to follow the plan.

4. Don't accept excuses for failure to follow the plan.

5. Don't use punishment or react to a misbehaving student in a punitive manner. Instead, point out to the student that there are logical consequences for failure to follow the plan.

6. Don't give up on the student. If necessary, remind the student of his or her commitment to desirable behavior. Periodically ask, "How are things going?"

Developing Your Own Approach to Classroom Management

No approach to classroom management is effective with all students at all times. How you respond to misbehavior in your classroom depends on your personality, value system, and beliefs about children and ranges along a continuum from the minimum power of giving students nonverbal cues to the maximum power of physical intervention.

Classroom management expert Charles Wolfgang points out that teachers usually present one of three philosophies (or attitudes) to students who misbehave:

1. The *relationship-listening* philosophy involves the use of minimum power. This reflects a view that the student has the capabilities to change his or her own behavior, and that if the student is misbehaving, it is because of inner emotional turmoil, flooded behavior, or feelings of inner inadequacy.

2. The *confronting-contracting* philosophy is one of "I am the adult. I know misbehavior when I see it and will confront the student to stop this behavior. I will grant the student the power to decide how he or she will change, and encourage and contract with the student to live up to a mutual agreement for behavioral change."

3. The *rules and consequences* philosophy is one that communicates an attitude of "this is the rule and behavior that I want and I will set out assertively to get this action" (Wolfgang, 2001, pp. 4–5).

In your journey toward becoming a professional teacher, you will develop a repertoire of strategies for classroom management; when you encounter a discipline problem in the classroom, you can analyze the situation and respond with an effective strategy. The ability to do so will give you confidence, like the following beginning teacher:

> I went into the classroom with some confidence and left with lots of confidence. I felt good about what was going on. I established a comfortable rapport with the kids and was more relaxed. Each week I grew more confident. When you first go in, you are not sure how you'll do. When you know you are doing okay, your confidence improves.

WHAT TEACHING METHODS DO EFFECTIVE TEACHERS USE?

Beliefs about teaching and learning, students, knowledge, and what is worth knowing influence the instructional methods a teacher uses. In addition, variables such as the teacher's style, learners' characteristics, the culture of the school and surrounding community, and the resources available all influence the methods you use. All of these components contribute to the model of teaching you use in the classroom. A model of teaching provides you with rules of thumb to follow to create a particular kind of learning environment. As the authors of *Models of Teaching* point out, "models of teaching are really models of *learning*. As we help students acquire information, ideas, skills, values, ways of thinking, and means of expressing themselves, we are also teaching them how to learn" (Joyce, Weil, & Calhoun, 2008, p. 7). Table 10.2 presents brief descriptions of four widely used models of teaching.

Effective teachers use a repertoire of teaching models and assessment strategies, depending on their situations and the goals and objectives they wish to attain. Your teaching strategies in the classroom will most likely be eclectic, that is, a combination of several models and assessment techniques. Also, as you gain classroom experience and acquire new skills and understanding, your personal model of teaching will evolve, enabling you to respond appropriately to a wider range of teaching situations.

Methods Based on Learning New Behaviors

Many teachers use instructional methods that have emerged from our greater understanding of how people acquire or change their behaviors. **Direct instruction,** for example, is a systematic instructional method that focuses on the transmission of knowledge and skills from the teacher (and the curriculum) to the student. Direct instruction is organized on the basis of observable learning behaviors and the actual products of learning. Generally, direct instruction is most appropriate for step-by-step knowledge acquisition and basic skill development, but it is not appropriate for teaching less structured, higher-order skills such as writing, the analysis of social issues, and problem solving. To watch a high school history teacher using the direct instruction model during a lesson on U.S. involvement in the Vietnam War, go to MyEducationLab.

Extensive research was conducted in the 1970s and 1980s on the effectiveness of direct instruction (Gagné, 1974, 1977; Good & Grouws, 1979; Rosenshine, 1988; Rosenshine & Stevens, 1986). The following eight steps represent a synthesis of research on

myeducationlab

Go to MyEducationLab, select Chapter 10 and Activities and Applications to watch the video The Direct Instruction Model.

TABLE 10.2 Four instructional models

	Goals and Rationale	Methods
Cooperative learning	Students can be motivated to learn by working cooperatively in small groups if rewards are made available to the group as a whole and to individual members of the group.	• Small groups (four to six students) work together on learning activities. • Assignments require that students help one another while working on a group project. • In competitive arrangements, groups may compete against one another. • Group members contribute to group goals according to their talents, interests, and abilities.
Theory into practice	Teachers make decisions in three primary areas: content to be taught, how students will learn, and the behaviors the teacher will use in the classroom. The effectiveness of teaching is related to the quality of decisions the teacher makes in these areas.	The teacher follows seven steps in the classroom: 1. Orients students to material to be learned 2. Tells students what they will learn and why it is important 3. Presents new material that consists of knowledge, skills, or processes students are to learn 4. Models what students are expected to do 5. Checks for student understanding 6. Gives students opportunity for practice under the teacher's guidance 7. Makes assignments that give students opportunity to practice what they have learned on their own
Behavior modification	Teachers can shape student learning by using various forms of enforcement. Human behavior is learned, and behaviors that are positively reinforced (rewarded) tend to increase and those that are not reinforced tend to decrease.	• Teacher begins by presenting stimulus in the form of new material. • The behavior of students is observed by the teacher. • Appropriate behaviors are reinforced by the teacher as quickly as possible.
Nondirective teaching	Learning can be facilitated if teachers focus on personal development of students and create opportunities for students to increase their self-understanding and self-concepts. The key to effective teaching is the teacher's ability to understand students and to involve them in a teaching–learning partnership.	• Teacher acts as a facilitator of learning. • Teacher creates learning environments that support personal growth and development. • Teacher acts in the role of a counselor who helps students to understand themselves, clarify their goals, and accept responsibility for their behavior.

direct instruction and may be used with students ranging in age from elementary to senior high school:

1. Orient students to the lesson by telling them what they will learn.
2. Review previously learned skills and concepts related to the new material.
3. Present new material, using examples and demonstrations.
4. Assess students' understanding by asking questions; correct misunderstandings.
5. Allow students to practice new skills or apply new information.
6. Provide feedback and corrections as students practice.
7. Include newly learned material in homework.
8. Review material periodically.

A direct instruction method called **mastery learning** is based on two assumptions about learning: (1) almost all students can learn material if they are given enough time and taught appropriately, and (2) students learn best when they participate in a structured, systematic program of learning that enables them to progress in small, sequenced steps (Bloom, 1981; Carroll, 1963). The following five steps present the mastery learning cycle:

1. Set objectives and standards for mastery.
2. Teach content directly to students.
3. Provide corrective feedback to students on their learning.
4. Provide additional time and help in correcting errors.
5. Follow a cycle of teaching, testing, reteaching, and retesting.

In mastery learning, students take diagnostic tests and then are guided to complete corrective exercises or activities to improve their learning. These may take the form of programmed instruction, workbooks, computer drill and practice, or educational games. After the corrective lessons, students are given another test and are more likely to achieve mastery.

Methods Based on Child Development

Children move through stages of cognitive, psychosocial, and moral development. Effective instruction includes methods that are developmentally appropriate, meet students' diverse learning needs, and recognize the importance of learning that occurs in social contexts. For example, one way that students reach higher levels of development is to observe and then imitate their parents, teachers, and peers, who act as models. "Modeling provides students with specific demonstrations of working with the content. . . . The teacher explicitly demonstrates how the students can be successful in the lesson" (Dell'Olio & Donk, 2007, p. 79).

Effective teachers also use **modeling** by thinking out loud and following three basic steps of mental modeling: (1) demonstrating to students the thinking involved in a task, (2) making students aware of the thinking involved, and (3) focusing students on applying the thinking. In this way, teachers can help students become aware of their learning processes and enhance their ability to learn. "For example, as a teacher demonstrates cutting out a construction paper square to serve as a math manipulative during the next lesson, she might 'think out loud' in class, saying, 'I am cutting this square very carefully because we will be using it today to create fractional shapes. I need the sides of my square to be very neat. My smaller, fraction pieces should be accurate in size'" (Dell'Olio & Donk, 2007, p. 80).

Since the mid-1980s, several educational researchers have examined how learners construct understanding of new material. "Constructivist views of learning, therefore, focus on how learners make sense of new information—how they construct meaning based on what they already know" (Parkay, Anctil, & Hass, 2006, p. 168). Teachers with this constructivist view of learning focus on students' thinking about the material being learned and, through carefully orchestrated cues, prompts, and questions, help students arrive at a deeper understanding of the material. The common elements of **constructivist teaching** include the following:

- The teacher elicits students' prior knowledge of the material and uses this as the starting point for instruction.
- The teacher not only presents material to students but also responds to students' efforts to learn the material. While teaching, the teacher must learn about students' learning.
- Students not only absorb information but also actively use that information to construct meaning.
- The teacher creates a social milieu within the classroom, a community of learners, that allows students to reflect and talk with one another as they construct meaning and solve problems.

These students are building on prior knowledge and using inquiry to acquire new knowledge. What kinds of learning activities require students to use their cognitive abilities in this way?

Constructivist teachers provide students with support, or scaffolding, as they learn new material. By observing the child and listening carefully to what he or she says, the teacher provides **scaffolding** in the form of clues, encouragement, suggestions, or other assistance to guide the student's learning efforts. The teacher varies the amount of support given on the basis of the student's understanding—if the student understands little, the teacher gives more support; conversely, the teacher gives progressively less support as the student's understanding becomes more evident. Overall, the teacher provides just enough scaffolding to enable the student to "discover" the material on his or her own.

The concept of scaffolding is based on the work of L. S. Vygotsky, a well-known Soviet psychologist. Vygotsky (1978, 1986) coined the term *zone of proximal development* to refer to the point at which students need assistance to continue learning. The effective teacher is sensitive to the student's zone of proximal development and ensures that instruction neither exceeds the student's current level of understanding nor underestimates the student's ability.

Methods Based on the Thinking Process

Some teaching methods are derived from the mental processes involved in learning, thinking, remembering, problem solving, and creativity. **Information processing,** for example, is a branch of cognitive science concerned with how people use their long- and short-term memory to access information and solve problems. The computer is often used as an analogy for information-processing views of learning:

> Like the computer, the human mind takes in information, performs operations on it to change its form and content, stores the information, retrieves it when needed, and generates responses to it. Thus, processing involves gathering information and organizing it in relation to what you already know, or *encoding*; holding information, or *storage*; and getting at the information when needed, or *retrieval*. The whole system is guided by *control processes* that determine how and when information will flow through the system. (Woolfolk, 2007, p. 250)

Although several systematic approaches to instruction are based on information processing—teaching students how to memorize, think inductively or deductively, acquire concepts, or use the scientific method, for example—they all focus on how people acquire and use information. Psychologists have identified three types of memory stores used in information processing:

1. **Sensory memory**—information stored briefly until it can be processed by the information-processing system; sensory memory retains information for about one second for vision and two to four seconds for hearing (Leahey & Harris, 2001; Pashler & Carrier, 1996).

2. **Working memory**—holds information while a person processes it; working memory is the conscious part of our information-processing system.

3. **Long-term memory**—a permanent store of information; working memory is limited to about seven items of information for a few seconds; however, long-term memory is vast and may remain for a lifetime (Schunk, 2004).

Table 10.3 presents general teaching guidelines based on these three types of memory stores.

In **inquiry learning** and **discovery learning,** students are given opportunities to inquire into subjects so that they discover knowledge for themselves. When teachers ask students to go beyond information in a text to make inferences, draw conclusions, or form generalizations, and when teachers do not answer students' questions, preferring instead to have students develop their own answers, they are using methods based on inquiry and discovery learning. These methods are best suited for teaching

TABLE 10.3 Applying an understanding of memory stores in your classroom

Sensory Memory

1. To keep students from losing a sensory memory trace, give them a chance to attend to one stimulus before presenting a second one.

   - **Elementary:** A second-grade teacher asks one question at a time and gets an answer before asking a second question.
   - **Middle school:** A pre-algebra teacher displays two problems on the overhead and waits until students have copied them before she starts talking.
   - **High school:** In a geography lesson, a teacher places a map on the overhead and says, "I'll give you a minute to examine the geography of the countries on this map in the front of the room. Then we'll go on."

Working Memory

2. To avoid overloading students' working memories, conduct lessons with questioning.

   - **Elementary:** A first-grade teacher gives students directions for seatwork by presenting them slowly and one at a time. He asks different students to repeat the directions before he has them begin.
   - **Middle school:** A teacher in a woodworking class begins by saying, "The hardness and density of wood from the same kind of tree vary, depending on the amount of rainfall the tree has received and how fast it grows." Then, she waits a moment, holds up two pieces of wood, and says, "Look at these wood pieces. What do you notice about the rings on them?"
   - **High school:** An Algebra II teacher walks students through the solution to problems by having a different student describe each succeeding step to the solution.

3. Provide frequent practice to develop automaticity, and present information in both verbal and visual forms.

   - **Elementary:** A first-grade teacher has his students practice their writing by composing two sentences each day about an event of the previous evening.
   - **Middle school:** To capitalize on the dual-processing capability of working memory, an eighth-grade history teacher prepares a flowchart of the events that led up to the Revolutionary War. As she questions the students about the topic, she refers to the flowchart for each important point and encourages students to use the chart to organize their note taking.
   - **High school:** As a physics teacher discusses the relationship between force and acceleration, he demonstrates by pulling a cart along the desktop with a constant force so the students can see that the cart accelerates.

Long-Term Memory

4. To develop schemas, encourage students to explore relationships between ideas, and between new ideas and prior understanding.

   - **Elementary:** During story time, a second-grade teacher asks students to explain how the events in a story contribute to the conclusion.
   - **Middle school:** In developing the rules for solving equations by substitution, an algebra teacher asks, "How does this process compare to what we did when we solved equations by addition? What do we do differently? Why?"
   - **High school:** To help his students understand cause-and-effect relationships in their study of ancient Greece, a world history teacher asks questions such as: "Why was shipping so important in ancient Greece?" "Why was Troy's location so important, and how does its location relate to the location of today's big cities?" and "Why did Greek city-states exist (instead of larger nation-states)?"

concepts, relationships, and theoretical abstractions, and for having students formulate and test hypotheses. The following example shows how inquiry and discovery learning in a first-grade classroom fostered a high level of student involvement and thinking.

> The children are gathered around a table on which a candle and jar have been placed. The teacher, Jackie Wiseman, lights the candle and, after it has burned brightly for a minute or two, covers it carefully with the jar. The candle grows dim, flickers, and goes out. Then she produces another candle and a larger jar, and the exercise is repeated. The candle goes out, but more slowly. Jackie produces two more candles and jars of different sizes, and the children light the candles, place the jars over them, and the flames slowly go out. "Now we're going to develop some ideas about what has just happened," she says. "I want you to ask me questions about those candles and jars and what you just observed." (Joyce, Weil, & Calhoun, 2004, p. 3)

Methods Based on Peer-Mediated Instruction

Student peer groups can be a deterrent to academic performance (Sternberg, Dornbusch, & Brown, 1996), but they can also motivate students to excel. Because school learning occurs in a social setting, **peer-mediated instruction** provides teachers with options for increasing students' learning. Cooperative learning, described earlier in this chapter, is an example of peer-mediated instruction.

Another example is **group investigation,** in which the teacher's role is to create an environment that allows students to determine what they will study and how. Students are presented with a situation to which they "react and discover basic conflicts among their attitudes, ideas, and modes of perception. On the basis of this information, they identify the problem to be investigated, analyze the roles required to solve it, organize themselves to take these roles, act, report, and evaluate these results" (Thelen, 1960, p. 82).

The teacher's role in group investigation is multifaceted; he or she is an organizer, guide, resource person, counselor, and evaluator. The method is very effective in increasing student achievement (Sharan & Sharan, 1989/1990, pp. 17–21), positive attitudes toward learning, and the cohesiveness of the classroom group. The model also allows students to inquire into problems that interest them and enables each student to make a meaningful, authentic contribution to the group's effort based on his or her experiences, interests, knowledge, and skills.

Other common forms of peer-mediated instruction include peer tutoring and cross-age tutoring. In **peer-tutoring** arrangements, students are tutored by other pupils in the same class or the same grade. **Cross-age tutoring** involves, for example, sixth-grade students tutoring second-grade students in reading. With proper orientation and training, cross-age tutoring can greatly benefit both "teacher" and learner (Henriques, 1997; Schneider & Barone, 1997; Utay & Utay, 1997; Zukowski, 1997). Pilot programs pairing students at risk of dropping out of school with younger children and with special-needs students have proved especially successful.

WHAT IS TAUGHT IN SCHOOLS?

Think back to your experiences as a student at the elementary, middle, junior, and high schools you attended. What did you learn? The curriculum you experienced certainly included reading, computation, penmanship, spelling, geography, and history. In addition to these topics, though, did you learn something about cooperation, competition, stress, football, videogames, computers, popularity, and the opposite sex? Or did you perhaps learn to love chemistry and to hate English grammar?

The countless things you learned in school make up the curriculum that you experienced. Curriculum theorists and researchers have suggested several different definitions for **curriculum,** with no single definition that is universally accepted. Here are some definitions in current use:

1. A course of study, derived from the Latin *currere,* meaning "to run a course"
2. Course content, the information or knowledge that students are to learn
3. Planned learning experiences
4. Intended learning outcomes, the results of instruction as distinguished from the means (activities, materials, etc.) of instruction
5. All the experiences that students have while at school

None of these five is in any sense the right definition. The way we define the word *curriculum* depends on our purposes and the situation we find ourselves in. If, for example, we are advising a high school student on the courses he or she needs to take to prepare for college, our operational definition of curriculum would most likely be "a course of study." However, if we were interviewing sixth-grade students for their views on the K–6 elementary school they had just graduated from, we would probably want to view curriculum as "all the experiences that students have while at school." Let us posit an additional definition of curriculum: *Curriculum refers to the experiences, both planned and unplanned, that enhance (and sometimes impede) the education and growth of students.*

Kinds of Curricula

Elliot Eisner, a noted educational researcher, has said that "schools teach much more—and much less—than they intend to teach. Although much of what is taught is explicit and public, a great deal is not" (2002, p. 87). For this reason, we need to look at the four curricula that all students experience. The more we understand these curricula and how they influence students, the better we will be able to develop educational programs that do, in fact, educate.

Explicit Curriculum

The explicit, or overt, curriculum refers to what a school intends to teach students. This curriculum is made up of several components: (1) the goals, aims, and learning objectives the school has for all students; (2) the actual courses that make up each student's course of study; and (3) the specific knowledge, skills, and attitudes that teachers want students to acquire. If we asked a principal to describe the educational program at his or her school, our question would be in reference to the explicit curriculum. Similarly, if we asked a teacher to describe what he or she wished to accomplish with a particular class, we would be given a description of the explicit curriculum.

In short, the **explicit curriculum** represents the publicly announced expectations the school has for its students. These expectations range from learning how to read, write, and compute to learning to appreciate music, art, and cultures other than one's own. In most instances, the explicit curriculum takes the form of written plans or guides for the education of students. Examples of such written documents are course descriptions, curriculum guides that set forth the goals and learning objectives for a school or district, texts and other commercially prepared learning materials, and teachers' lesson plans. Through the instructional program of a school, then, these curricular materials are brought to life.

Hidden Curriculum

The **hidden curriculum** (also called the *implicit curriculum*) refers to the behaviors, attitudes, and knowledge the culture of the school unintentionally teaches students (Parkay et al., 2006). What students learn via the hidden curriculum can be positive or negative, depending on their day-to-day experiences at school. For example, from teachers who are knowledgeable, well organized, and personable, students are likely to develop positive habits and abilities—cooperating with others, taking responsibility, planning ahead, and forgoing immediate gratification to obtain long-range goals. On the other hand, from teachers who are ill prepared, apathetic, or aloof, students are likely to acquire habits and attitudes that are negative and that discourage personal growth and development—a dislike for learning, the ability to deceive or defy adult authority figures, or a tendency to procrastinate.

In the following examples, four students describe the hidden curricula they experienced in school. In examples 1 and 2, excerpts from letters students wrote to their teachers, the hidden curricula "taught" students to be more confident in their ability to learn. In examples 3 and 4, the hidden curricula undermined the students' confidence and desire to learn.

Example 1

I was in your grade 10 English class. I sure felt safe to take a risk in your class. I actually tried hard, knowing I might fail, but felt safe enough to do so. (Paul, Christensen, & Falk, 2000, p. 23)

Example 2

I was in your grade 9 class and you praised me for my creative writing. Until that time, I had never thought of myself as a very creative person but your faith in me spurred me on to choose English as my major at the university. (Paul et al., 2000, p. 23)

Example 3

The teacher just put [material] on the board and if you don't know how, the teacher get angry. I try to get help but when I come after school, they gotta go somewhere and can't help you . . . like when I ask somebody to help me, just because some other kid won't need help, then they think others won't either; some kids are smarter. (Wilson & Corbett, 2001, p. 38)

Example 4

I was in your 11th grade biology class. I loved science and biology until I took your class. You gave me a great disdain for the subject. Your teaching methods bored the class to tears. We read each chapter out loud at the beginning of the week and spent the rest of the week working quietly on the questions at the end of the chapter along with the endless dittos you passed out. We never discussed anything and you never taught us anything. We were graded on how well we could come up with the answers you thought were right and heaven forbid if we did not head our paper using the "correct" format. I think the only thing I learned in your class was conformity. (Colucci, 2000, p. 38)

As a result of the hidden curriculum of schools, students learn more than their teachers imagine. As a teacher, you will not be aware of all that students are learning through the hidden curriculum of your classroom. However, you can increase the likelihood that what it teaches will be positive. By allowing students to help determine the content of the explicit curriculum, by inviting them to help establish classroom rules, and by providing them with challenges appropriate for their stage of development, teachers can ensure that the outcomes of the hidden curriculum are more positive than negative.

Null Curriculum

Discussing a curriculum that cannot be observed directly is like talking about dark matter or black holes, unseen phenomena in the universe whose existence must be inferred because their incredible denseness and gravitational fields do not allow light to escape. In much the same way, we can consider the curriculum that we do not find in the schools; it may be as important as what we do find. Elliot Eisner has labeled the intellectual processes and content that schools do not teach "the **null curriculum**—the options students are not afforded, the perspectives they may never know about, much less be able to use, the concepts and skills that are not a part of their intellectual repertoire" (2002, pp. 106–107).

386

For example, the kind of thinking that schools foster among students is largely based on manipulations of words and numbers. Thinking that is imaginative, subjective, and poetic is stressed only incidentally. Also, students are seldom taught anthropology, sociology, psychology, law, economics, filmmaking, or architecture.

Eisner points out that "certain subject matters have been traditionally taught in schools not because of a careful analysis of the range of other alternatives that could be offered but rather because they have traditionally been taught. We teach what we teach largely out of habit, and in the process neglect areas of study that could prove to be exceedingly useful to students" (2002, p. 103).

Extracurricular/Cocurricular Programs

The curriculum includes school-sponsored activities—music, drama, special interest clubs, sports, student government, and honor societies, to name a few—that students may pursue in addition to their studies in academic subject areas. When such activities are perceived as additions to the academic curriculum, they are termed *extracurricular*. When these activities are seen as having important educational goals—and not merely as extras added to the academic curriculum—they are termed *cocurricular*. To reflect the fact that these two labels are commonly used for the same activities, we use the term *extracurricular/cocurricular activities*. Though **extracurricular/cocurricular programs** are most extensive at the secondary level, many schools at the elementary, middle, and junior high levels also provide their students with a broad assortment of extracurricular/cocurricular activities. For those students who choose to participate, such activities provide an opportunity to use social and academic skills in many different contexts.

The larger a school is, the less likely it is that a student will take part in extracurricular/cocurricular activities. At the same time, those who do participate tend to have higher self-concepts than those who do not (Coladarci & Cobb, 1996). The actual effects that extracurricular/cocurricular activities have on students' development, however, are not entirely clear.

Students who participate in extracurricular/cocurricular activities tend to receive higher grades than nonparticipants and are more frequently identified as gifted (Gerber, 1996; Jordan & Nettles, 1999; Modi, Konstantopoulos, & Hedges, 1998). However, it is not known whether participation influences achievement, or whether achievement influences participation. Nevertheless, participation has a positive influence on the decision to remain in school (Mahoney & Cairns, 1997), educational aspirations (Modi et al., 1998), and the occupation one aspires to and eventually attains (Brown, Kohrs, & Lanzarro, 1991; Holland & Andre, 1987). Furthermore, students themselves tend to identify extracurricular/cocurricular activities as a high point in their school careers.

It is also clear that students who might benefit the most from participating in extracurricular/cocurricular activities—those below the norm in academic achievement and students at risk—tend not to participate. In addition, students from low socioeconomic backgrounds participate less often (National Center for Education Statistics, 2008).

Curriculum Content

The nation's schools teach what the larger society believes young people should learn. For example, Table 10.4, part A, shows the significant increase—from 1970 to 2006—in the percentage of the public that believes the school curriculum "needs to be changed to meet today's needs." Part B of Table 10.4 similarly shows the increase—from 1979 to 2006—in the percentage of the public that believes public high schools should teach a "wide variety of courses."

The following comments by two parents typify the concern many people have about what is included in the school curriculum:

Education is becoming more about social issues as opposed to reading, writing, and arithmetic. Some of it's fine, but I think schools need to stay with

TABLE 10.4 What should be taught in the schools?

A. Do you think the school curriculum in your community needs to be changed to meet today's needs, or do you think it already meets today's needs?

	National Totals			No Children in School			Public School Parents		
	'06%	'82%	'70%	'06%	'82%	'70%	'06%	'82%	'70%
Needs to be changed	47	36	31	46	33	31	50	42	33
Already meets needs	44	42	46	43	38	36	48	50	59
Don't know	9	22	23	11	29	33	2	8	8

B. Public high schools can offer students a wide variety of courses, or they can concentrate on fewer basic courses, such as English, mathematics, history, and science. Which of these two policies do you think the local high schools should follow in planning their curricula—a wide variety of courses or fewer but more basic courses?

	National Totals			No Children in School			Public School Parents		
	'06%	'01%	'79%	'06%	'01%	'79%	'06%	'01%	'79%
Wide variety of courses	58	54	44	56	50	44	63	64	44
Basic courses	41	44	49	44	48	47	35	35	53
Don't know	1	2	7	*	2	9	2	1	3

*Less than one-half of 1%.

Source: Lowell C. Rose and Alec M. Gallup. (September 2006). The 38th Annual Phi Delta Kappa/Gallup Poll of the Public's Attitudes Toward the Public Schools. Phi Delta Kappan, Vol. 88, No. 1.

the basics. . . . You can't get by in the business world on social issues if you can't add and subtract.

They all talk all the time about this "whole child educational process." . . . It's not your business to make a "whole child." Your business is to teach these students how to read, how to write, and give them the basic skills to balance their checkbook. It's not to make new Emersons out of them. (Johnson & Immerwahr, 1994, p. 13)

HOW IS THE SCHOOL CURRICULUM DEVELOPED?

Although there is no easy-to-follow set of procedures for developing curriculum, Ralph Tyler (1902–1994), a University of Chicago professor instrumental in shaping the Elementary and Secondary Education Act of 1965, has provided four fundamental questions that must be answered in developing any curriculum or plan of instruction. These four questions, known as the **Tyler rationale,** are as follows (Tyler, 1949, p. 1):

1. What educational purposes should the school seek to attain?
2. What educational experiences can be provided that are likely to attain these purposes?
3. How can these educational experiences be effectively organized?
4. How can we determine whether these purposes are being attained?

Some educators believe the Tyler rationale underestimates the complexities of curriculum development because it advocates a straightforward, step-by-step process that is difficult to follow in the real classroom. Nevertheless, Tyler's classic work has been used by a great number of school systems to bring some degree of order and focus to the curriculum development process.

The Focus of Curriculum Planning

In discussing curriculum development, it is helpful to clarify the focus of curriculum planning. Figure 10.8 illustrates two dimensions of this planning process: the focus of curriculum and the time orientation. The focus of curriculum planning may be at the macro- or the micro-level. At the macro-level, decisions about the content of the curriculum apply to large groups of students. The national goals for education and state-level curriculum guidelines are examples of macro-level curricular decisions. At the micro-level, curriculum decisions are made that apply to groups of students in a particular school or classroom. To some extent, you will be a micro-level curriculum developer—that is, you will make numerous decisions about the curricular experiences you provide students in your classroom.

Another dimension of curriculum planning is the time orientation—does the planning focus on the present or the future? In addition to the national goals and state-level curriculum guidelines, the semester-long or monthly plans or unit plans that teachers make are examples of future-oriented curriculum planning. Present-oriented curriculum planning usually occurs at the classroom level and is influenced by the unique needs of specific groups of students. The daily or weekly curriculum decisions and lesson plans that teachers make are examples of present-oriented curriculum planning.

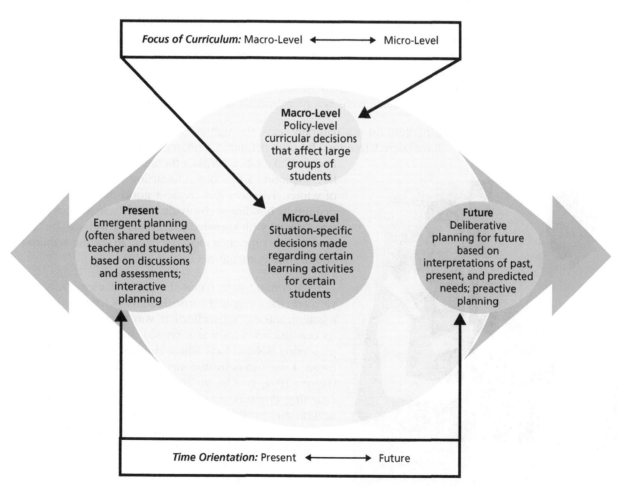

FIGURE 10.8 Two dimensions of curriculum planning: Focus of curriculum and time orientation

Student-Centered Versus Subject-Centered Curricula

A key concern in curriculum development is whether greater emphasis should be given to the requirements of the subject area or to the needs of the students. It is helpful to imagine where a school curriculum might be placed on the following continuum:

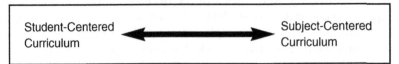

Student-Centered
Curriculum   ⟷   Subject-Centered
Curriculum

Although no course is entirely subject- or student-centered, curricula vary considerably in the degree to which they emphasize one or the other. The **subject-centered curriculum** places primary emphasis on the logical order of the discipline students are to study. The teacher of such a curriculum is a subject-matter expert and is primarily concerned with helping students understand the facts, laws, and principles of the discipline. Subject-centered curricula are more typical of high school education.

Some teachers develop curricula that reflect greater concern for students and their needs. Although teachers of the **student-centered curriculum** also teach content, they emphasize the growth and development of students. This emphasis is generally more typical of elementary school curricula. For a video example of a kindergarten teacher eliciting student ideas and contributions during a lesson on gardening, go to MyEducationLab.

Go to MyEducationLab, select Chapter 10 and Activities and Applications to watch the video Using Student Ideas and Contributions.

The Integrated Curriculum

To provide students with more meaningful learning experiences, you may decide to use an integrated approach to developing the school curriculum. Used most frequently with elementary-age students, the **integrated curriculum** draws from several different subject areas and focuses on a theme or concept rather than on a single subject. Early childhood education expert Suzanne Krogh (2000) suggests that an integrated approach based on thematic webs is a more natural way for children to learn:

> [Children] do not naturally learn through isolating specific subjects. These have been determined by adult definition. Children's natural learning is more likely to take place across a theme of interest: building a fort, exploring a sandbox, interacting with the first snow of winter. Teachers can create a good deal of their curriculum by building webs made up of these themes of interest. Done with knowledge and care, a web can be created that incorporates most, or even all, of the required and desired curriculum. (2000, p. 340)

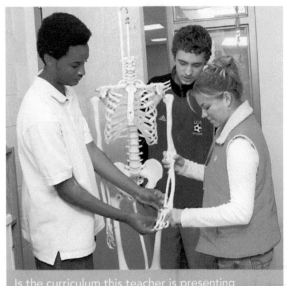

Is the curriculum this teacher is presenting primarily a subject-centered or student-centered curriculum? In what ways might the curriculum be both subject-centered and student-centered?

According to a national survey of elementary teachers' views on the integrated curriculum, 89 percent believed that integration was the "most effective" way to present the curriculum. As one teacher who was surveyed said, "I'm not interested in presenting isolated facts which children seem to memorize and forget. I want to help students put each lesson in perspective" (Boyer, 1995, p. 83). In *The Basic School: A Community for Learning*, Ernest Boyer (1928–1995), a U.S. commissioner of education and president of the Carnegie Foundation for the Advancement of Teaching, suggested that the elementary school curriculum should be integrated according to eight themes or "core commonalities": The Life Cycle, The Use of Symbols, Membership in Groups, A Sense of Time and Space, Response to the Aesthetic, Connections to Nature, Producing and Consuming, and Living with Purpose (Boyer, 1995).

TEACHERS' VOICES
Walk in My Shoes

As the director of choral activities at a K–12 school, Kristina Young stays busy with a large community of learners—202 students in fourth through twelfth grade. She also coaches volleyball, leads her students in performances and competitions, and produces an annual musical adapted from Broadway. In her fourth year of teaching, she recently added to her workload a doctoral degree program, taking courses at an accelerated pace. Kristina makes it all work by drawing on several key principles and incorporating effective teaching, classroom management, and relationship-building strategies to create a strong community of learners.

Kristina first started college pursuing a double music major. In her senior year, her former school asked her to teach there. She accepted, deciding to postpone graduate study in vocal performance. After a year with students, however, she knew she wanted to be a teacher. "I realized that I could do more to impact the lives of others by being a teacher than I could on stage."

Being organized and modeling that organization for students is a principle she finds helpful. Before class she writes on the board what students need to do:

- Step 1: Where to go in the room.
- Step 2: What materials they need.
- Step 3: Time everything needs to be done by.

Create a positive and cohesive community of learners.

The first thing her students do when they walk into her room is look at the board. If the last step does not include a time, "[t]hen they know they have time to chat," Kristina said. "They can get talking out of the way before the lesson begins."

Part of Kristina's organization is establishing routines, but she believes in mixing variety into them to keep things interesting: She'll use different methods to get students' attention and keep them on-task. "Clap once if you can hear me" or "5, 4, 3, 2, 1, clap" and students will join in the clap. She may say, "Signal me if you are ready" and then do something unusual like touching her nose or touching her elbows together. Or she may start singing a note, and students will sing it back. She also uses three small chimes. "I don't want to raise my voice to get their attention."

A third guiding principle is to develop a team of people to assist her and delegate tasks. When Kristina does her annual Broadway musical adaptation, she has a volunteer in charge of lights, another in charge of sound, a fellow teacher to direct the choreography, a staff member to design costumes, and several parents to provide and oversee props. "You can produce something far more incredible if everyone takes a little chunk. I don't need or want to micromanage the whole thing."

In addition to drawing on these principles, Kristina is a successful, professional teacher because of her teaching skills and ability to promote a positive learning environment. Her choir classes are not required, yet her program is growing and receiving recognition beyond the school. In music festivals, her students have been selected as "honor choir," "honor small group," or "honor vocalist" nine times in four years. Kristina continues to keep a positive, creative, and cohesive group. Developing the community begins with a one-day camp in August, before school starts. All choir members and those interested in choir are invited to mingle, participate in games, and learn several songs. On the first day of school, students will already know 80 to 100 other students. Kristina takes groups on field trips throughout the year to reward their hard work.

In class, she finds it effective to plan lessons that get students up and moving and talking to each other. She may teach a concept and then ask students to explain it to a partner, often directing them to pick someone not in their row. "It builds a sense of community, and I am also able to assess if they truly grasp the concept."

Kristina tries to connect students' emotions to music in her music appreciation lessons. She may play a famous piece of music and ask students "to write down words that come to mind when they listen to it or draw pictures." With Camille Saint-Saens's *Carnival of the Animals*, she has students listen for the animals being portrayed in the music.

Her advice for all teachers is to prioritize. Decide on your goals are and then organize your time and efforts accordingly. For future music teachers, she advises that, while you need to be well-versed in subject matter, "[y]ou should realize that some wrong notes or wrong rhythms will happen. Building students' self-efficacy, work ethic, team spirit, and character matters the most."

Clearly, this young teacher has accomplished things expected of gifted teachers with far more experience. She does so by using her intellect and drive, but also by applying sound educational practices to create a positive and cohesive community of learners.

Kristina Young
CCCS of Downey

Who Plans the Curriculum?

Various agencies and people outside the school are involved in curriculum planning. Textbook publishers, for example, influence what is taught because many teachers use textbooks as curriculum guides. The federal government contributes to curriculum planning by setting national education goals, and state departments of education develop both broad aims for school curricula and specific minimum competencies for students to master.

Within a given school, the curriculum-planning team and the classroom teacher plan the curriculum that students actually experience. As a teacher you will draw from a reservoir of curriculum plans prepared by others, thus playing a vital role in the curriculum-planning process. Whenever you make decisions about what material to include in your teaching, how to sequence content, and how much time to spend teaching certain material, you are planning the curriculum.

What Influences Curricular Decisions?

From the earliest colonial schools to schools of the 21st century, curricula have been broadly influenced by a variety of religious, political, and utilitarian agendas. Figure 10.9 illustrates the influence of community pressures, court decisions, students' life situations, testing results, national reports, teachers' professional organizations, research results, and other factors. The inner circle of the figure represents factors that have a more direct influence on curriculum development (such as students' needs and interests, and school policies). The outer circle represents factors that are more removed from the school setting or have less obvious effects on the curriculum. Individual schools respond to all these influences differently, which further affects their curricula. Let us examine some of these influences in greater detail.

Social Issues and Changing Values

Values that affect curriculum planning include prevailing educational theories and teachers' educational philosophies. In addition, curriculum planners respond to social issues and changing values in the wider society. As a result, current social concerns find

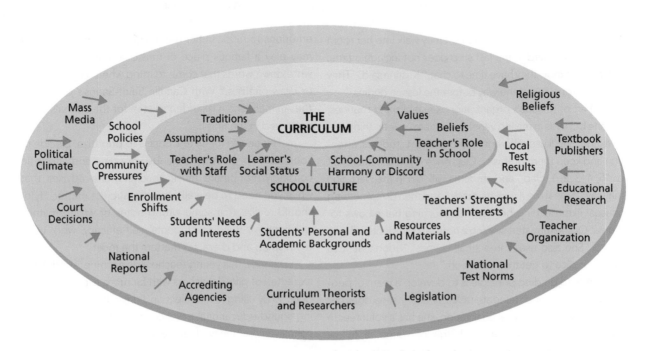

FIGURE 10.9 Influences on the school curriculum

their way into textbooks, teaching aids, and lesson plans. Often curriculum changes are made in the hope that changing what students learn will help solve social problems or achieve local, statewide, or national goals.

Because the United States is so culturally diverse, proposed curriculum changes also reflect divergent interests and values. This divergence then leads to controversies over curriculum content and conflicting calls for reform. Consider, for example, the legal issues surrounding the demands of some groups that Christian teachings and observances be included in the public school curricula or that materials regarded as objectionable on religious grounds be censored or banned; or the trend for states to pass English-only laws and the controversy that erupted in California around the teaching of ebonics, or black English. Additional curriculum controversies have arisen over calls for the elimination of all activities or symbols that have their origins in organized religion, including even secularized or commercialized ones such as Halloween and the Easter bunny. Curriculum changes to promote greater social integration or equity among racial or ethnic groups may draw complaints of irrelevancy or reverse discrimination. Traditionalists may object to curriculum changes that reflect feminist views.

As you can imagine, consensus on many curriculum reform issues is never achieved. Because of their public accountability, however, schools must consider how to respond to those issues. One survey revealed that during a one-year period, half the school districts in Florida received complaints about curriculum content. Included were complaints claiming that the schools were undermining family values, overemphasizing globalism, underemphasizing patriotism, permitting profanity and obscenity, and teaching taboo subjects such as satanism and sex (Sheuerer & Parkay, 1992, pp. 112–118). In the end, the creative and evaluative tasks of choosing and developing curriculum materials are a source of both empowerment and frustration for teachers. Budget constraints, social and legal issues, and state and local curriculum mandates often determine curriculum choices.

Textbook Publishing

Textbooks greatly influence the curriculum. Without a doubt, most teachers base classroom lessons and homework on textbooks. In addition, textbook publishers influence school curricula by providing teaching objectives, learning activities, tests, audiovisual aids, and other supplements to assist their customers.

Like curriculum planners, textbook authors and publishers are influenced by trends in education and by social issues. In response to criticism, for example, publishers now tend to avoid bias in terms of gender, religion, sexual orientation, class, race, and culture. However, because the goal of business is profit, publishers are most responsive to market trends and customer preferences. They are often reluctant to risk losing sales by including subjects that are controversial or that may be offensive to their bigger customers. They may also modify textbooks to appeal to decision makers in populous states that make statewide adoptions of textbooks, such as California and Texas. As an editor at a major publishing house reveals: "When it comes to setting the agenda for textbook publishing, only the 22 states that have a formal adoption process count. The other 28 are irrelevant—even though they include populous giants like New York, Pennsylvania, and Ohio—because they allow all publishers to come in and market programs directly to local school districts" (Ansary, 2004, p. 35). In addition, California and Texas are among several states that systematically review state-approved textbooks for accuracy. Texts with too many errors are dropped from state-approved lists, and publishers are levied fines for failing to correct errors.

Educators have criticized textbooks for inoffensiveness to the point of blandness, for artificially lowered reading levels (called dumbing down), and for pedagogically questionable gimmicks to hold students' attention. Although the publishing industry continually responds to such criticisms, you would be wise to follow systematic guidelines in evaluating and selecting textbooks and other curriculum materials.

SUMMARY

What Determines the Culture of the Classroom?

- From seating arrangements to classroom rules and procedures, to the content and relevance of the curriculum, teachers make many decisions that influence the culture of the classroom.
- Classroom climate refers to the atmosphere or quality of life in a classroom. An important element of a positive learning environment is a caring classroom climate.

How Can You Create a Positive Learning Environment?

- Teachers show care for students by providing support, structure, and appropriate expectations.
- The physical environment of a classroom—seating arrangements and the placement of other classroom furniture, for example—can make a positive contribution to students' learning.
- Classroom organization—how students are grouped for instruction and how time is used—is an important element of the effective learning environment.

What Are the Keys to Successful Classroom Management?

- Teachers who prevent problems before they occur foster effective, harmonious interpersonal interactions; understand how their leadership style influences students; and facilitate the development of the classroom group so that it becomes more cohesive and supportive.
- When management problems occur, effective teachers base their responses on three elements of constructive assertiveness: a clear statement of the problem or concern; unambiguous body language; and a firm, unwavering insistence on appropriate behavior.

What Teaching Methods Do Effective Teachers Use?

- Direst instruction and mastery learning are based on the view that learning is the acquisition of new behaviors.

- Modeling, constructivism, and scaffolding are based primarily on an understanding of how students construct meaning as they learn new material.
- Psychologists have identified three types of memory stores used in information processing: sensory memory, working memory, and long-term memory.
- Peer-mediated instruction, which views learning as taking place in social situations, includes cooperative learning, group investigation, and peer- and cross-age tutoring.

What Is Taught in Schools?

- A general definition of curriculum refers to the experiences, both planned and unplanned, that either enhance or impede the education and growth of students.
- Students experience four types of curricula: what teachers intend to teach (the explicit curriculum), the hidden curriculum, the null curriculum, and extracurricular/cocurricular programs.
- Curriculum content reflects the beliefs of society and what the larger society believes young people should learn.
- Curricula are based on the needs and interests of students and also reflect a variety of professional, commercial, local, state, national, and international pressures.

How Is the School Curriculum Developed?

- Many school systems develop curricula by addressing the four questions in the Tyler rationale: (1) What educational purposes should the school seek to attain? (2) What educational experiences can be provided that are likely to attain these purposes? (3) How can these educational experiences be organized effectively? (4) How can we determine whether these purposes are being attained?
- Curriculum planning focuses on a continuum between the macro-level and the micro-level, and on a continuum between the present and the future.
- Curricula vary in the degree to which they are student-centered or subject-centered.
- The integrated curriculum draws from several different subject areas and focuses on a theme or concept rather than on a single subject.

- Community pressures, court decisions, students' life situations, testing results, national reports, teachers' professional organizations, textbook publishing, and educational research are among the factors that influence the school curriculum.

PROFESSIONAL REFLECTIONS AND ACTIVITIES

Teacher's Journal

1. Recall two of your favorite classes at the elementary through high school levels. Briefly describe each teacher's approach to teaching. How did each teacher usually present new material? Which of the instructional methods discussed in this chapter did the teachers use?
2. With reference to the two teachers you described in number 1, describe their approaches to classroom management. Which of the classroom management strategies discussed in this chapter did they use? How did they typically respond to misbehavior in the classroom?

Teacher's Research

1. Visit the home pages for a few of the following educational research publications on the Internet.
   - *American Educational Research Journal*
   - *Cognition and Instruction*
   - *Contemporary Educational Psychology*
   - *Educational Psychologist*
   - *Educational Psychology Review*
   - *Educational Researcher*
   - *Journal of Educational Psychology*
   - *Journal of Teaching and Teacher Education*
   - *Review of Educational Research*
   - *Review of Research in Education*
   - *Social Psychology of Education*

   Select an article of interest related to increasing student learning. Summarize the article and present a brief oral report to your class. Based on the research findings presented in the article, what are the implications for teaching?
2. Use the Internet to locate websites related to classroom management and discipline. Specifically, locate sites related to topics such as democratic classrooms, choice theory, constructive assertiveness, assertive discipline, caring classrooms, and zero tolerance. Bookmark sites that you find of greatest interest. In addition, visit several school district websites to examine their discipline policies. What similarities and differences do you note among the policies?

Observations and Interviews

1. Spend a half-day observing a classroom at the level you plan to teach and record your impressions regarding that school's hidden curriculum. In addition to the explicit curriculum, what are students learning? If possible, chat briefly with administrators, teachers, and students about your impressions. Share your observations with others in your education class.
2. As a collaborative project with your classmates, conduct an informal survey using the two survey questions presented in Table 10.4. Compare the data you gather with the data presented in the table. What differences do you note? What might account for those differences?

PEARSON myeducationlab Now go to MyEducationLab at www.myeducationlab.com to test your understanding of chapter content by completing this chapter's Study Plan.

Professional Portfolio

Prepare a handout that contains the classroom rules for the subject area and grade level for which you are preparing to teach. You may wish to organize the rules according to the following categories.

- Rules related to academic work
- Rules related to classroom conduct
- Rules that must be communicated on your first teaching day
- Rules that can be communicated later

PEARSON myeducationlab To complete additional observations and interviews, go to MyEducationLab at www.myeducationlab.com, select the Virtual Field Experience section, and click on this chapter's Observations and Interviews.

Curriculum Standards, Assessment, and Student Learning

14

From Chapter 11 of *Becoming a Teacher*, 8/e. Forrest W. Parkay. Beverly Hardcastle Stanford.

Curriculum Standards, Assessment, and Student Learning

CLASSROOM CASE
The Realities of Teaching

THE CHALLENGE: Maintaining a balance between teaching and preparing students to take a state-mandated high-stakes test.

During your second year of teaching, you arrive at school for a 7:30 A.M. meeting of the teacher leadership team (TLT). You were elected to serve on the TLT, which works with the principal and her administrative team to develop the school's academic programs. At its last meeting, the TLT discussed the possibility of a schoolwide approach to prepare students for the state-mandated assessment of student learning (ASL) given in April.

A few minutes before the meeting begins, you visit the classroom of another TLT member. At the last TLT meeting, you both volunteered to search the Internet to find out what the state teachers' association and teachers at other schools in the state think about the ASL. Also, you agreed to find out how schools in the state are preparing students for the ASL.

"What did you find out?" you ask after entering the room. "I was online for about two hours last night. There's a lot of controversy about the ASL."

"I got a few good ideas . . . wasn't able to spend as much time on it as I wanted, however," your friend says. "I've been pulling together resources for the project-based learning activities my kids start next week."

"No problem . . . " you say. "If you ask me, planning for project-based learning is more important than preparing kids for the ASL."

"I promised to give them these handouts today," she continues. "The handout has suggestions for developing a project outline, a timeline, and a PowerPoint project presentation. Plus, I've included an outstanding project report from last year . . . that will let them see what a solid A project report looks like."

Your friend is seated at her desk, stapling handouts for the project-based learning activities. She takes a handout from a neatly crisscrossed stack on top of her desk and staples it. Instead of placing it on a stack of handouts to her left, she hands it to you.

"This looks great," you say, thumbing through the 12-page handout. "A lot of work goes into something like this."

"What did you find out about the ASL?" your friend asks.

"Teachers are really concerned about 'teaching to the test,'" you answer.

"Surprise, surprise," your friend says, the sarcasm evident in her voice. "Tell me more."

"The website for the state teachers' association makes a lot of good points. Basically, teachers should focus on improving student learning, not increasing test scores," you say, your voice emphasizing the two very different views of schooling.

"Yeah, I agree completely," your friend says. "It's like we've lost sight of the fact that the purpose of schooling is to learn, not to get good scores on tests."

"Right," you say. "Also, I got some good information from the National Center for Fair & Open Testing. I got this from their site."

Opening your notebook, you read aloud, "'The National Center for Fair & Open Testing (FairTest) advances quality education and equal opportunity by promoting fair, open, valid, and educationally beneficial evaluations of students, teachers, and schools. FairTest also works to end the misuses and flaws of testing practices that impede those goals. We place special emphasis on eliminating the racial, class, gender, and cultural barriers to equal opportunity posed by standardized tests, and preventing their damage to the quality of education.'"

"Great," your friend says.

"Well, I better get out of here and let you finish your handouts," you say. "We're meeting in about five minutes in the third-floor conference room."

Walking down the hallway to the meeting room, you think about the impact of high-stakes tests on teaching. How much time should teachers spend preparing students to take high-stakes tests? Does test preparation interfere with teaching?

FOCUS QUESTIONS

1. What role will standards play in your classroom?
2. What is standards-based education?
3. What controversies surround the effort to raise standards?
4. What methods can you use to assess student learning?
5. How can you develop high-quality classroom assessments?

As the opening classroom case for this chapter and newspaper headlines remind us, the public is concerned about low test scores, U.S. students' performance on international comparisons of achievement, and our nation's standing in a competitive global economy. Calls from parents, citizen groups, and politicians to hold teachers accountable for student learning have led to higher standards and a search for more effective ways to assess student learning. Clearly, standards and high-stakes tests will be facts of life during your career as a teacher.

Standards and assessments are key elements in the move to hold educators more accountable for student learning. Parents and guardians want to know that schools are educating their children well, and the community wants to know that its investment in school buildings, teachers' salaries, and curricular resources is returning educational dividends.

WHAT ROLE WILL STANDARDS PLAY IN YOUR CLASSROOM?

As adults, we are familiar with standards. To obtain a driver's license, we must demonstrate the knowledge and skills needed to drive a car. At work, we must meet our employer's standards. In this regard, a *standard* refers to a level of knowledge or skill that is generally acknowledged as necessary to perform a specific task or to occupy a particular role in society. In education, for example, standards represent the criteria students must meet to receive a grade of A, to be promoted to the next grade, or to graduate from elementary or high school.

Educational standards take different forms. The type of standards most important to the individual often depends on whether one is a school administrator, teacher, or student. Administrators, for example, are very concerned about standards related to *students' performance on standardized tests of achievement*. In such instances, the administrator (and his or her school board) might focus on a standard such as the following: "During the next five years, the percentage of students scoring above the norm will increase by at least 2 percent each year."

Teachers, of course, are also concerned about standards related to students' performance on standardized tests. In addition, teachers understand that another important standard is their expectations for *student performance and behavior at the classroom level*. Teachers demonstrate their commitment to high standards by giving students intellectually demanding reading and writing assignments; providing extensive, thoughtful feedback on students' work; and presenting intellectually stimulating lessons.

For an example of how one teacher conveys high standards to students, consider Eva Benevento's explanation of how she uses Rigorous Mondays in her sixth-grade classroom:

> Each month I use my Rigorous Mondays to focus on a different kind of product. In September students work on notetaking. Every Monday night they refine and revise their notes to fit our criteria of accuracy, organization, and balance. In October we focus on retellings. November is our author study month. This year we're doing Chekhov and our theme is "Authors as Teachers," so our Monday night essays have focused on what Chekhov is trying to help us see and understand in each of the four stories I read to them. Next Monday they'll select their best essay, read it to a peer-editing group, collect feedback, and revise it for Tuesday. It's all very regular and the predictability helps the students. They know what's expected of them each Monday because they produce the same kind of product four times each month. They can see themselves improve, getting better at producing this kind of writing, or at notetaking. (Strong, Silver, & Perini, 2001, p. 2526)

Students often have yet another perspective on standards; for them, the school curriculum should meet the *standard of being personally relevant, interesting, and meaningful*. The school curriculum should help them meet the developmental challenges of moving from childhood to adulthood. It should help them realize the goals they have set for themselves.

Most teachers and principals believe their school has high academic standards. Figure 11.1, for example, shows that 72 percent of secondary principals and 60 percent of teachers included in a *MetLife Survey of the American Teacher* view their schools as having high standards. However, secondary school students have a different perception of academic standards at their schools; only 38 percent of students surveyed believe standards are high. Many high school students, it seems, would agree with an 11th grade boy quoted in the *MetLife Survey*: "I can't remember the last time I learned something new. . . . I just get sick of the busy work, and usually just end up throwing it aside and not doing it. I want to be LEARNING things" (Harris Interactive, 2001, p. 44).

Administrators, teachers, students, and parents frequently have different perspectives on standards. During the last decade, however, **standards** in education (on occasion called content standards, goals, expectations, learning results, or learning outcomes) have come to be seen primarily as statements that reflect what students should know and be able to do within a particular discipline or at a particular grade level.

WHAT IS STANDARDS-BASED EDUCATION?

Current efforts at educational reform in the United States emphasize **standards-based education (SBE)**—that is, basing curricula, teaching, and assessment of student learning on rigorous, world-class standards. SBE is based on the belief that all students are capable of meeting high standards. In the past, expectations

Secondary School Students

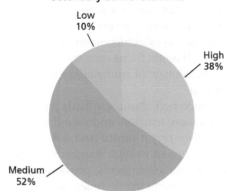

Q240: How would you rate the academic standards at your school?
Base: Secondary school students (N = 2049)
Q305: How would you rate the academic standards at your school?
Base: Secondary school teachers (N = 430)/Secondary school principals (N = 383)

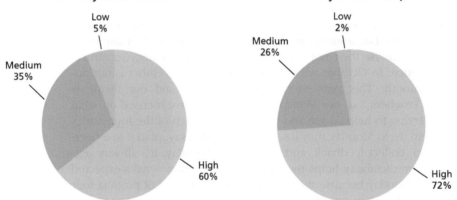

FIGURE 11.1 Academic standards: Students, teachers, and principals

Source: The MetLife Survey of the American Teacher, 2001: Key Elements of Quality Schools. New York: Harris Interactive, 2001, p. 46.

for students from poor families and students who are members of minority groups were sometimes lower than for other students. Today, SBE is seen as a way of ensuring that excellence and equity become part of our nation's public school system. As the 2008 Republican presidential candidate, John McCain, stated: "We can no longer accept low standards for some students and high standards for others. In this age of honest reporting, we finally see what is happening to students who were previously invisible." Similarly, the 2008 Democratic presidential candidate, Barack Obama, emphasized high standards: "Closing the achievement gap that exists in too many cities and rural areas is right. More accountability is right. Higher standards are right" (FairTest, June 2, 2008).

To meet the demand for higher standards, each state has adopted state standards for what students should know and be able to do. For example, here are standards in geometry from three states:

Colorado: Students use geometric concepts, properties, and relationships in problem-solving situations and communicate the reasoning used in solving these problems.

North Dakota: Students understand and apply geometric concepts and spatial relationships to represent and solve problems in mathematical and nonmathematical situations.

Wyoming: Students apply geometric concepts, properties, and relationships in problem-solving situations. Students communicate the reasoning used in solving these problems.

As these examples show, state standards are broad statements of learning outcomes against which student achievement can be measured.

Content and Performance Standards

Standards documents prepared by state education agencies, local school districts, and professional associations typically refer to two types of standards—content standards and performance standards. **Content standards,** as the term implies, refers to the content—or knowledge and skills—students should acquire in various academic disciplines. A common phrase in standards documents is that content standards represent "what students should know and be able to do."

Content standards are often subdivided into benchmarks (frequently called indicators). **Benchmarks** are content standards that are presented as specific statements of what students should understand and be able to do *at specific grade levels or developmental stages*. Here are three statements from the Iowa Core Content Benchmarks:

- **Reading, grades 3–5:** Students can draw conclusions, make inferences, and deduce meaning.
- **Mathematics, grades 6–9:** Students can understand and apply concepts and procedures of algebra.
- **Science, grades 9–12:** Students can understand and apply the processes and skills of scientific inquiry.

In addition, many standards documents refer to performance standards. A **performance standard** specifies "how good is good enough." Performance standards are used to assess the degree to which students have attained standards in an academic area. Performance standards require teacher judgment about the quality of performance or level of proficiency required. Unlike content standards, performance standards reflect levels of proficiency. For example, Iowa performance standards specify the following levels: High Performance Level (Distinguished, Accomplished), Intermediate Performance Level (Skilled, Moderate), and Low Performance Level (Marginal, Weak). Here are samples of Iowa performance standards for reading, mathematics, and science:

Grade 3 Literacy Standards

- *Distinguished:* Understands factual information and new words in context. Can make inferences and interpret either nonliteral language or information in new contexts. Can determine a selection's main ideas and analyze its style and structure.
- *Moderate:* Usually understands factual information and new words in context. Often is able to make inferences and interpret either nonliteral language or information in new contexts. Sometimes can determine a selection's main ideas and analyze its style and structure.
- *Weak:* Seldom understands factual information or new words in context. Rarely is able to make inferences and interpret either nonliteral language or information in new contexts. Seldom can determine a selection's main ideas and analyze aspects of its style and structure.

Grade 8 Mathematics

- *Distinguished:* Understands math concepts and is able to solve word problems. Usually can use estimation methods. Is able to interpret data from graphs and tables.
- *Moderate:* Usually can understand math concepts and sometimes is able to solve word problems. Sometimes can use estimation methods and interpret data from graphs and tables.
- *Weak:* Seldom can understand math concepts or solve word problems. Rarely can use estimation methods or interpret data from graphs and tables.

Grade 11 Science

- *Distinguished:* Makes inferences or predictions from data, judges the relevance and adequacy of information, and recognizes the rationale for and limitations of scientific procedures.

403

- *Moderate:* Sometimes makes inferences or predictions from data, judges the relevance and adequacy of information, and usually recognizes the rationale for and limitations of scientific procedures.
- *Weak:* Seldom makes inferences or predictions from data, sometimes judges the relevance and adequacy of information, and rarely recognizes the rationale for and limitations of scientific procedures.

Standards Developed by Professional Associations

In addition to national, state, and local efforts to raise standards, professional associations are playing a key role in SBE by developing standards in the subject matter disciplines. In many cases, professional associations have developed specific, grade-level **performance expectations**—established levels of achievement, quality of performance, or level of proficiency—for recommended standards as well as classroom activities related to standards.

Standards developed by professional associations are used in the following ways:

- State departments of education, school districts, and schools can use the standards as a guide for developing curricula and assessments of student learning.
- Teachers can use standards to (1) develop goals and objectives for units and courses, (2) evaluate their teaching, and (3) develop ideas for instructional activities and classroom assessments.
- Parents and community members can use standards to assess the quality of education in their local schools and to monitor the achievement levels of their children.

Figure 11.2 presents several professional associations that have recommended curriculum standards in various academic disciplines. You can obtain complete sets of standards from the websites these associations maintain.

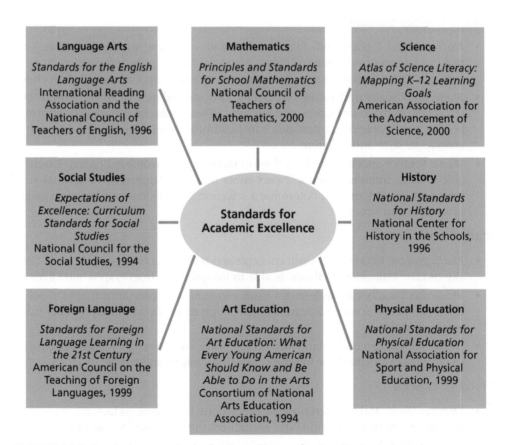

Language Arts

Standards for the English Language Arts
International Reading Association and the National Council of Teachers of English, 1996

Mathematics

Principles and Standards for School Mathematics
National Council of Teachers of Mathematics, 2000

Science

Atlas of Science Literacy: Mapping K–12 Learning Goals
American Association for the Advancement of Science, 2000

Social Studies

Expectations of Excellence: Curriculum Standards for Social Studies
National Council for the Social Studies, 1994

Standards for Academic Excellence

History

National Standards for History
National Center for History in the Schools, 1996

Foreign Language

Standards for Foreign Language Learning in the 21st Century
American Council on the Teaching of Foreign Languages, 1999

Art Education

National Standards for Art Education: What Every Young American Should Know and Be Able to Do in the Arts
Consortium of National Arts Education Association, 1994

Physical Education

National Standards for Physical Education
National Association for Sport and Physical Education, 1999

FIGURE 11.2 Curriculum standards developed by professional associations

Aligning Curricula and Textbooks With Standards and Curriculum Frameworks

An important part of SBE in the United States is aligning curricula and textbooks with national and state standards and curriculum frameworks. **Curriculum alignment** may take two forms. Horizontal alignment occurs when teachers within a specific grade level coordinate instruction across disciplines and examine their school's curriculum to ensure that course content and instruction dovetail across and/or within subject areas. Vertical alignment occurs when subjects are connected across grade levels so that students experience increasingly complex instructional programs as they move through the grades.

A **curriculum framework** is a document, usually published by a state education agency, that provides guidelines, recommended instructional and assessment strategies, suggested resources, and models for teachers to use as they develop curricula that are aligned with national and state standards. Curriculum frameworks are usually written by teams of teachers and state agency personnel, and they serve as a bridge between national and state standards and local curriculum and instructional strategies. In Alaska, for example, curriculum frameworks in CD-ROM format and Frameworks Resource Kits in specific subjects are given to teachers by the Department of Education & Early Development. The CD-ROM provides state-of-the-art information in different formats, including videoclips of educators explaining standards-based curricula. Figure 11.3, taken from the Alaska frameworks, presents English/language arts process skills for writing.

Like teachers, textbook authors and publishers have been influenced significantly by the development of academic standards throughout the nation. Many publishers are revising their textbooks so they are in alignment with state standards and curriculum frameworks, particularly in populous states that make statewide adoptions of textbooks, such as California and Texas.

WHAT CONTROVERSIES SURROUND THE EFFORT TO RAISE STANDARDS?

The push to raise standards has resulted in a widespread, often heated national debate about the role of standards in educational reform. Without a doubt, responses to the call for higher standards have been mixed, and many questions remain unanswered. What are minimum acceptable standards? Who should set those standards? How should students' attainment of those standards be assessed? What should schools do about students who fail to meet those standards? Can standards be raised without increasing dropout rates? Are both excellence and equal opportunity possible if standards are raised? Last, will expanded testing programs based on higher standards discriminate against minority-group students who traditionally score lower on such tests?

Arguments in Support of Raising Standards

"We are moving in this country from a local to a national view of education and we need better arrangements to guide the way." So observed Ernest Boyer (1928–1995) when he was president of the Carnegie Foundation for the Advancement of Teaching. As Boyer's comment implies, the United States, like other nations of the world, needs national goals and standards to motivate its people to excel. Without them, people may become complacent and satisfied with mediocrity. Also, like other countries in our increasingly interdependent world, the United States needs to compare the achievement of its students with those of other countries. Just as a runner will run faster when paced by another, the U.S. educational system can become more effective as a result of comparisons with educational systems in other countries.

One advocate of raising standards and assessing students' attainment of those standards, Diane Ravitch, observed that "[a] failing mark on the state test will be only a

Note: This figure presents graphic explanations of the processes of writing as they have been developed and/or adapted and used by Alaskan educators for the last decade. It is meant to be illustrative rather than prescriptive.

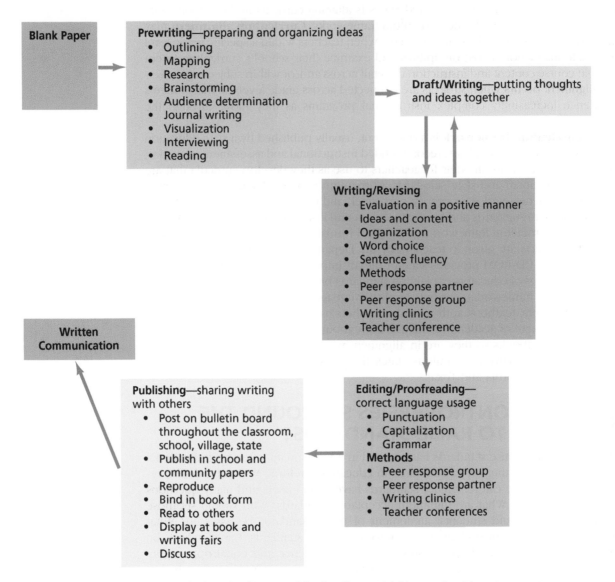

The writing process is recursive thinking leading to writing leading to thinking and writing some more. Not every writer will commit every step in the process to paper. Nor will every idea or piece of writing be carried through the entire process. Only pieces that have completed the process—and not all of those— should be assessed.

FIGURE 11.3 English/language arts process skills

Source: Used with permission of the Alaska Department of Education & Early Development's Curriculum Frameworks Project. Retrieved from www.educ.state .ak.us/tls/frameworks/langarts/30content.htm.

temporary embarrassment, but a poor education will stigmatize for life" (1997, p. 106). In *National Standards in American Education: A Citizen's Guide*, Ravitch outlined several additional arguments in support of the effort to raise standards:

- Standards can improve achievement by clearly defining what is to be taught and what kind of performance is expected.
- Standards (national, state, and local) are necessary for equality of opportunity.
- National standards provide a valuable coordinating function.

- Standards and assessments provide consumer protection by supplying accurate information to students and parents.
- Standards and assessments serve as an important signaling device to students, parents, teachers, employers, and colleges (1996, pp. 134–135).

In addition to the arguments outlined above, it is clear that the United States—as a society rich in ethnicities, religions, nationalities, and language groups—also needs common, rigorous standards for unity. With increasing immigration to the country, which brings diverse groups of people to its urban and suburban neighborhoods and rural areas, schools need to provide a common core knowledge about the democratic heritage of our country and a common curriculum based on high academic standards.

As a mobile society, the United States needs common educational standards so that children from one area will not fall behind when they move to another. Children from a farming community in Minnesota should be able to move to the heart of Dallas without finding themselves behind or ahead of their peers in school. Children from a school in Seattle should be able to transfer to a school in Cincinnati and recognize the curricula studied there.

Concerns About Raising Standards

Opponents of the effort to develop world-class standards as the centerpiece of educational reform point out that the failure of many schools to achieve adequate yearly progress as mandated by No Child Left Behind is evidence that a new approach to educational reform is needed. Instead, they contend, we should become more aware of the lack of uniformity in schools around the country and the needs of the children they serve. As Jonathan Kozol's books *Savage Inequalities* (1991) and *The Shame of the Nation* (2005) vividly illustrate, equal education in the United States is an illusion. To compare the performance of a student in a poor Chicago housing project with that of a student in the same city's wealthy suburbs is to confront the "savage inequalities" found throughout our educational system.

In addition, test score gains attributed to the standards movement have been shown not to reflect real gains in the knowledge and skills the tests were designed to measure. A phenomenon known as score inflation results in students' scores on high-stakes tests rising faster than their scores on other standardized tests given at the same time and measuring the same subjects. Students don't actually know as much as we think they do based only on the high-stakes test scores. Actually, the standards movement may result in test scores that are less accurate than they were prior to the addition of high-stakes assessments (Stecher & Hamilton, 2002).

Also, sanctions imposed on low-performing schools will not ensure that students in those schools are not left behind. The record of success when sanctions such as staff reassignment and school takeover have been imposed is mixed. Students in low-performing schools may not be helped by sanctions, and there is some risk that they will be harmed (Stecher & Hamilton, 2002). Thus, higher standards would further bias educational opportunities in favor of students from advantaged backgrounds, intensify the class-based structure of U.S. society, and increase differences between well-funded and poorly funded schools.

Opponents of efforts to develop world-class standards in U.S. schools have raised numerous additional concerns. The following are among their arguments:

- Raising standards might lead to a national curriculum and an expanded role of the federal government in education.
- The push to raise standards is fueled by conservative interest groups that want to undo educational gains made by traditionally underrepresented groups.
- A focus on higher standards diverts attention from more meaningful educational reform.

- Increased emphasis on tested subjects often results in a decrease in emphasis on subjects not tested.
- World-class standards are often vague and not linked to valid assessments and scoring rubrics.
- Standards frequently describe learning activities, not the knowledge and skills students are expected to learn—for example, "Students will experience various forms of literature."
- The scope and sequence of what students should learn with reference to standards and benchmarks has been unclear; in other words, to what degree and in what order should students learn material?
- Grade-level benchmarks have been created that are unrealistic and developmentally inappropriate for some students; often students are hurried through their learning without sufficient time and instruction to acquire underlying concepts and skills.
- SBE and high-stakes tests based on those standards lead to the practice of teaching to the test, giving priority to academic content covered by the tests and deemphasizing areas of the curriculum not covered. For example, a study of Kentucky's assessment system (Jones & Whitford, 1997) found that test-related sanctions and rewards influenced teachers to "focus on whatever is thought to raise test scores rather than on instruction aimed at addressing individual student needs" (p. 277).

As a teacher, you and your colleagues will no doubt participate in an ongoing dialogue about academic standards at your school. Thus, the role that standards will play in your professional lives will be significant. The following eight questions may help you decide the nature of SBE in your school:

1. Where will we get our standards?
2. Who will set the standards?
3. What types of standards should we include?
4. In what format will the standards be written?
5. At what levels will benchmarks be written?
6. How should benchmarks and standards be assessed?
7. How will student progress be reported?
8. How will we hold students accountable? (Marzano, 1997)

Almost half of the states require students to pass an exit or end-of-course exam before they can graduate. Do you agree with this requirement? What might be some consequences to this requirement?

Standards, Testing, and Accountability

Today's schools and teachers are held accountable for students' mastery of state-mandated educational standards. As part of this push for **accountability,** some states—Florida and South Carolina, for example—rank schools on how well their students learn. In Florida, schools are graded from A through F, and those that receive low grades run the risk of being closed. At the end of the 2001–02 academic year, for example, an elementary school in Pensacola was closed by school officials, though it had managed to move from a grade of F to a D (Sandham, 2002).

In South Carolina, schools are graded good, average, below average, or unsatisfactory. Teachers and principals in high-ranked South Carolina schools receive salary bonuses of up to $1,000 each, while lower-rated schools can face state takeovers or reorganization of their staffs (Richard, 2002a).

Every state has mandated a standardized test to assess students' mastery of academic standards, and most districts are assisting schools in bringing standards-based reform into classrooms. As a result of standards-based reforms at the state level, *how* and *what* teachers teach is changing, and in many cases student achievement is increasing.

High-Stakes Testing

Testing students to assess their learning is not new. However, state-mandated tests often have high-stakes consequences for students, teachers, and administrators. For example, performance on **high-stakes tests** may determine whether a student can participate in extracurricular activities or graduate, or whether teachers and administrators are given merit pay increases.

Twenty-three states require students to pass exit or end-of-course exams in English and math, and in some cases social studies and science, to receive a high school diploma (Lloyd, June 22, 2006). In 15 states, students who do not pass state exit exams can take an alternative route to obtain a standard diploma—for example, presenting a portfolio of their work or filing an appeal.

Consequences of High-Stakes Tests

At the conclusion of the 2003–04 school year, several states withheld thousands of high school diplomas. For example, in Florida, about 12,000 seniors failed the Florida Comprehensive Assessment Test (FCAT), a requirement for graduation. The Florida seniors had several opportunities to take the test, which is first given in the 10th grade (Associated Press, 2004).

In some cases, the large numbers of students who failed the exams prompted states to modify their requirements. New York erased the results of a new math test for juniors and seniors after the passing rate fell much lower than the previous year. Local officials got permission to give diplomas to seniors who failed the exam but passed their math courses. California delayed the consequences of its exit exam from 2004 to 2006 after a study projected that about 20 percent of seniors would be denied diplomas (Feller, 2003).

In Massachusetts, diplomas were withheld from 4,800 seniors in 2003 who failed to pass the Massachusetts Comprehensive Assessment System (MCAS) exam. That year, some students walked out of class and refused to take the test, often with support from parents. The MCAS exam was implemented in 1998, and 2003 was the first year that students were required to pass the exam to graduate. Although 92 percent of seniors statewide passed, some schools graduated a much lower percentage of students. For example, less than 60 percent of the 437 seniors in Lawrence graduated that year (*USA Today,* 2003). Certificates of attainment were available for students who did not pass the exam; however, a high school diploma was still needed for college-bound students and qualification for state and federal financial aid for education beyond high school.

High-Stakes Tests and Educator Accountability

For teachers and administrators, test results are frequently linked to merit rewards, increased funding, or sanctions. Some states and large school districts provide additional funds for high-performing schools or bonuses for educators at those schools. For example, California has several merit-based incentive programs for teachers, schools, and administrators, including the Governor's Performance Awards that give money to schools based on their academic performance index. Similarly, the New York City school system gives bonuses of up to $15,000 to principals and other administrators whose schools show significant gains on test scores. School system administrators group schools into three performance categories—low, middle, and high—taking into account students' economic circumstances. For high schools, factors such as dropout rates are also used.

What type of assessment might this teacher be using?

On the other hand, schools and even entire districts that do poorly on tests can be taken over by the state or in some cases closed. Currently, more than 20 states give state boards of education the authority to intervene in academically bankrupt schools whose students score too low as a group. Of those states, 10 allow students to leave low-performing schools, taking their proportional amount of state funding aid with them. Four of these states directly punish low-performing schools by taking aid away from them. While some states use test scores as one of several accountability indicators, many rely solely on scores.

Testing can also have significant consequences when schools are ranked according to how well they attain a state or district's performance goals. Usually, school rankings are reported in relation to schools of similar size and demographics because test results are closely linked to students' economic backgrounds, with the lowest scores often earned by schools that serve the neediest children (Fetler, 2001; Lindjord, 2000).

High-stakes testing and the push to hold teachers accountable for student learning has led many districts and schools to place great emphasis on preparing students for the tests. In fact, critics assert that the curricular emphasis in schools is shifting from academic content to test preparation. As this chapter's opening classroom case suggests, many teachers feel compelled to teach to the test, or to emphasize item teaching rather than curriculum teaching.

Clearly, the debate over the effectiveness of testing programs based on state-mandated standards will continue for some time. However, professional teachers understand that participating in these programs is only part of their assessment responsibility—they must develop high-quality classroom assessments for day-to-day use in the classroom. The ability to develop and implement high-quality assessments of students' learning is a fundamental part of professional accountability for today's teachers. Teachers must know whether their methods of assessing students' learning are, in fact, enhancing students' ability to learn.

WHAT METHODS CAN YOU USE TO ASSESS STUDENT LEARNING?

myeducationlab

Go to MyEducationLab, select Chapter 11 and then Activities and Applications to analyze the artifact Assessment Methods.

The assessment of student learning will enable you to make judgments about the performance of students and about your performance as a teacher. You will use assessment to evaluate your effectiveness because you recognize that "the best assessments are those that inform instruction" (Wright, 2008, p. 243). To view examples of how teachers assess students' learning to meet the requirements of No Child Left Behind, go to MyEducationLab.

Assessment has been defined as "a process of observing a sample of a student's behavior and drawing inferences about the student's knowledge and abilities" (Ormrod, 2006, p. 338). As a professional teacher, you will work continuously to become aware of the latest approaches to assessing student learning. You will understand the critical role that assessment plays in teaching and the importance of "establishing credible performance standards, communicating these standards to students, and providing feedback to students on their progress" (McMillan, 2001, p. xiii). In addition, the classroom assessments you develop will reflect four guiding principles: "(1) classroom assessments can both *promote* and *verify* student learning, (2) clear and appropriate achievement targets are essential, (3) accurate classroom assessment is essential, and (4) sound assessments require effective communication" (Stiggins, 2005, pp. 21–28).

To assess student learning, you can use both quantitative and qualitative approaches. Quantitative approaches make use of measurement and evaluation techniques—such as teacher-made classroom tests comprised of multiple-choice, true/false, matching, or essay items—or performance-based assessments. **Quantitative assess-**

ments yield numerical scores that teachers use to evaluate student learning as well as the effectiveness of their teaching.

Qualitative approaches may include formal and informal observations of students' performance on various learning tasks, the manner with which they approach those learning tasks, or students' self-reports of their interests and attitudes. For example, teachers routinely assess students' **work habits.** *Work habits* is a term suggested by the Coalition of Essential Schools (see Chapter 13, p. 456) for various dispositions important for effective thinking and learning, including reading with curiosity; reflecting critically on one's own work; developing independence, clarity, and incisiveness of thought; willingness to work hard; an ability to manage time effectively; persistence; accuracy and precision; and working collaboratively. **Qualitative assessments** are more subjective than quantitative assessments. However, quantitative assessments are also subjective because teachers must interpret the meaning of the scores.

Challenges of Assessing Students' Learning

It is difficult to assess what students learn as a result of being taught. The ultimate purpose of teaching is to lead the student to a greater understanding of the things and ideas of this world. But as even the most casual appraisal of human nature will confirm, it is very difficult, perhaps impossible, to determine precisely what another human being does or does not understand. Although the aims or intentions of teaching may be specified with exacting detail, one of the realities of teaching, as the following junior high school teacher points out, is that some of what students learn may be indeterminate and beyond direct measurement:

> There is no clear end result. . . . That frustrates me. I want so badly for my joy [of teaching] to be neatly tied up so that I can look at it admiringly. . . . I want so badly to see my successes—I don't know, give me certificates or badges or jelly beans. Then I can stack them up, count them, and rate myself as a teacher. (Henry et al., 1995, pp. 68–69)

In spite of legislation such as No Child Left Behind that mandates statewide testing in reading and mathematics each year in grades 3–8 and holds schools accountable for students' performance, the conventional wisdom among teachers is that they are often uncertain about just what their students learn. We have miles of computer printouts with test data, but very little knowledge of what lies behind a child's written response, little understanding of how the child experiences the curriculum. As one educational researcher concludes: "The inaccessibility of data is similar both in science and in learning. We cannot directly 'see' subatomic particles, nor can we 'see' the inner-workings of the mind and emotions of the child. Both are inferential: both are subject to human interpretation" (Costa, 1984, p. 202). On the one hand, then, teachers must recognize their limited ability to determine what students actually learn; on the other, they must continuously work to become aware of the latest approaches to assessing students' learning.

Purposes of Classroom Assessment

For most people, the term *classroom assessment* brings to mind a four-step process: (1) the teacher prepares a test (or selects a preexisting test) to cover material that has been taught, (2) students take the test, (3) the teacher corrects the test, and (4) the teacher assigns grades based on how well students performed on the test. Classroom assessment, however, involves more—it provides information that teachers use to (1) determine how well students are learning the material being taught, (2) identify the type of feedback that will enhance student learning, (3) develop strategies for improving their effectiveness as teachers, and (4) determine if students have reached certain levels of performance.

To assess student learning, you will use measurement and evaluation techniques. **Measurement** is the gathering of quantitative data related to the knowledge and skills students have acquired. Measurement yields scores, rankings, or ratings that teachers can use to determine the degree to which students have attained specified standards.

To watch a video of a fourth-grade student taking an informal reading inventory test, the results of which will help his teacher identify his strengths and weaknesses in reading, go to MyEducationLab.

Evaluation involves making judgments about or assigning a value to those measurements. When teachers measure students' attainment of knowledge and skills for the purpose of making decisions about their teaching, they are engaging in **formative evaluation.** For example, Chris Whyte, the middle school science teacher profiled in the Teachers' Voices: Walk in My Shoes feature in this chapter, uses a popular game format to get on-the-spot feedback from students regarding their understanding of material he is teaching.

When teachers use measurements to determine grades at the end of a unit, semester, or year and to decide whether students are ready to proceed to the next phase of their education, they are engaging in **summative evaluation.** Figure 11.4 illustrates the essential elements of effective classroom assessment and the questions that guide teachers' decision making in this important area of teaching.

Standardized Assessments

Standardized assessments (or standardized tests) are pencil-and-paper tests that are taken by large groups of students and scored in a uniform manner. The test items, conditions under which students take the test, how the tests are scored, and how the scores are interpreted are standardized for all who take the test. This standardization enables educators to compare scores for different groups of students in different schools around the country. Standardized assessments are administered at the district, state, and national levels.

The first standardized test in the United States was administered by Horace Mann (1796–1859) in the mid 1800s. Mann wanted to classify students by ability and gather evidence for the effectiveness of the state school system. He hoped to use the results of the state test to further his educational reform efforts. Prior to the use of this standardized test, teachers conducted their own assessments at the individual classroom level.

Current examples of standardized tests are the Iowa Test of Basic Skills, California Achievement Test, Metropolitan Achievement Tests, the Stanford Achievement Test, the Scholastic Assessment Test (SAT), and the ACT Assessment (ACT). In addition, the federal government funds the National Assessment of Educational Progress (NAEP). Periodically, NAEP is used to sample student achievement around the country. On a biannual basis, the performance of national samples of 9-, 13-, and 17-year-olds is assessed. Educational policymakers then use the results—reported by geographic region, gender, and ethnic background—to guide their decision making. First administered in 1969, NAEP has

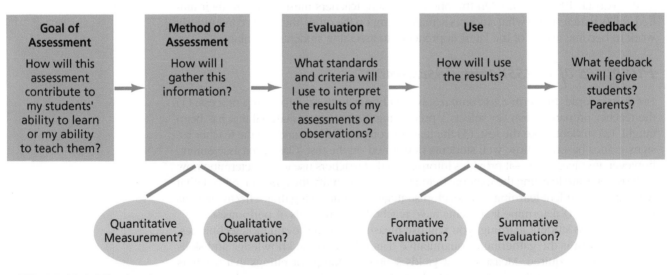

FIGURE 11.4 Effective classroom assessment

 # TEACHERS' VOICES
Walk in My Shoes

Chris Whyte assessed his life and made a major change in his professional journey: He left a military career to become a teacher. A Naval Academy graduate on active duty, Chris realized that what he enjoyed the most about the military was being a trainer and mentor for those he commanded. As a naval officer, he learned systems and how to teach them: "You had to be able to train enlisted personnel pretty quickly." In the past, he had volunteered as a teacher in churches and schools and led youth on mission trips. His heart pulled him toward working with young people, and becoming a teacher was the best way to do that.

His entry into teaching was unique. Without a teaching credential, Chris became a middle school science teacher in a private school. His initial success can be attributed to three factors: the training he had as an officer, his personal spirit and drive, and the supportive school community he joined.

The Naval Academy taught him from early on "to adapt to circumstances and use available resources for support" and instructed him on the basics of teaching. He was assigned a mentor who encouraged him to take advantage of teacher training seminars offered outside school. His drive during this process was toward a worthy goal: "to help students develop a perspective on the world—to see science as more than a rote memory subject but rather as the process of asking questions and seeing the world around them with a critical eye."

Self-Assessment and Assessing Student Learning

Chris describes the school community he joined as "the most supportive professional community I've ever seen." The faculty welcomed him with input, feedback, and supplies. The faculty development director, a teacher/administrator assigned to first-year teachers, visited his classroom two or three times a week and e-mailed him daily sample lessons, useful websites, and announcements of local science events. "Without her I would miss so much!" The school's facilities also supported him. Chris regards the new science center and equipment as "the best possible environment for teaching."

Chris finds teaching to be "probably the most physically taxing thing I've ever done, and that includes the Naval Academy and being on ship in the Middle East." The ongoing need to always be available to students with a wide range of ability and comprehension levels is a challenge. "And you always need to be prepared to teach the topic you're teaching," he added. The pressure is on an emotional level as well: He finds himself needing to be "not just an educator, but also a motivator, a coach and a counselor." However, he adds, "It's never *not* satisfying, as it was in the other job. I'm tired, but it's a good tired."

His assessments of student learning include ways of obtaining on-the-spot feedback from students. His students use small whiteboards to play a *Jeopardy*-style game for speed drills. And "Swat" is the drill his students most enjoy. Chris writes a number of possible answers on the classroom's large whiteboard, divides the class into two teams, and provides each team with a fly swatter. Representatives from each team race each other to swat the right answer when Chris asks a question. He adapts the game for shy students reluctant to race to the board, asking them to reply to questions by writing on their small whiteboards.

Chris's playful spirit and creativity are evident in the favorite lessons he recalls. In a unit on polymers, his students make slime in the lab and then he asks them to explain its properties, why they're seeing what they're seeing, and what's happening at a molecular level. "It's very hands-on, nontoxic slime—really messy. They engage with it and have a lot of fun." Chris also enjoys teaching a thermal energy lab where students make ice cream to understand what is happening from a thermal energy perspective.

Chris offers advice to teachers on two fronts—how to help students learn and how to learn as teachers. For student learning: "Have overarching themes to help students see where you're going with your lessons. Help them understand the important issues by planning a well-organized curriculum that emphasizes the larger topic." For teacher learning: "Be a lifelong learner as a teacher but find someone to help you with that process—someone who can give a listening ear and provide criticism. And attend teacher training seminars and conferences to gain new knowledge and skills."

Chris's reassessment of his professional journey has yielded personal satisfaction for him, but the real beneficiaries are his students and the education community. Chris brings to teaching the integrity, can-do spirit, and resourcefulness of a naval officer, combined with a love of learning and a desire to give students a new perspective on their world.

Chris Whyte
Santa Fe Christian Schools

What might be some of the pressures felt by students and teachers as a result of the increased emphasis on testing?

assessed student learning in all areas of the curriculum.

International Assessments

In 1991, the first **International Assessment of Educational Progress (IAEP)** was conducted, and the achievement of U.S. students was compared to that of students in more than 30 nations. The results indicated that the achievement levels of U.S. students were often below those of students from other countries. The United States also participates in several other international assessments, including the **Trends in International Mathematics and Science Study (TIMSS)** and the **Progress in International Reading Literacy Study (PIRLS)**, both conducted by the International Association for the Evaluation of Educational Achievement (IEA).

PIRLS 2006 results (see Figure 11.5) show that the average reading comprehension score of U.S. fourth-grade students in 2006 was higher than the average score of

Jurisdiction	Average Combined Reading Literacy Score	Jurisdiction	Average Literary Subscale Score	Jurisdiction	Average Informational Subscale Score	
Russian Federation	565	Canada, Alberta	561	Hong Kong, SAR[1]	568	Average is higher than the U.S. average
Hong Kong, SAR[1]	564	Russian Federation	561	Russian Federation	564	
Canada, Alberta	560	Canada, British Columbia	559	Singapore	563	
Canada, British Columbia	558	Hong Kong, SAR[1]	557	Luxembourg	557	Average is not measurably different from the U.S. average
Singapore	558	Hungary	557	Canada, Alberta	556	
Luxembourg	557	Canada, Ontario	555	Canada, British Columbia	554	
Canada, Ontario	555	Luxembourg	555	Canada, Ontario	552	Average is lower than the U.S. average
Hungary	551	Singapore	552	Bulgaria	550	
Italy	551	Italy	551	Italy	549	
Sweden	549	Germany	549	Sweden	549	
Germany	548	Denmark	547	Netherlands[2]	548	
Belgium (Flemish)[2]	547	Sweden	546	Belgium (Flemish)[2]	547	
Bulgaria	547	Netherlands[2]	545	Germany	544	
Netherlands[2]	547	Belgium (Flemish)[2]	544	Denmark	542	

FIGURE 11.5 Average scores for fourth-grade students in participating PIRLS jurisdictions on combined reading literacy scale, literacy subscale, and informational subscale, by jurisdiction: 2006

Source: National Center for Education Statistics, November 2007. The Reading Literacy of U.S. Fourth-Grade Students in an International Context. Washington, DC: Author, p. 7.

Jurisdiction	Average Combined Reading Literacy Score	Jurisdiction	Average Literary Subscale Score	Jurisdiction	Average Informational Subscale Score	
Denmark	546	Canada, Nova Scotia	543	Hungary	541	
Canada, Nova Scotia	542	Bulgaria	542	Latvia	540	
Latvia	541	Lithuania	542	Canada, Nova Scotia	539	
United States[2]	**540**	**United States[2]**	**541**	Chinese Taipei	538	
England	539	England	539	England	537	
Austria	538	Latvia	539	**United States[2]**	**537**	
Lithuania	537	Austria	537	Austria	536	
Chinese Taipei	535	Slovak Republic	533	New Zealand	534	
Canada, Quebec	533	Chinese Taipei	530	Canada, Quebec	533	
New Zealand	532	Canada, Quebec	529	Lithuania	530	
Slovak Republic	531	New Zealand	527	Scotland[2]	527	
Scotland[2]	527	Scotland[2]	527	Slovak Republic	527	
France	522	Poland	523	France	526	
Slovenia	522	Slovenia	519	Slovenia	523	
Poland	519	France	516	Poland	515	
Spain	513	Israel	516	Moldova	508	
Israel	512	Spain	516	Spain	508	
Iceland	511	Iceland	514	Israel	507	
Belgium (French)	500	Norway[1]	501	Iceland	505	
Moldova	500	Belgium (French)	499	Belgium (French)	498	
Norway[1]	498	Romania	493	Norway[1]	494	
Romania	489	Moldova	492	Romania	487	
Georgia	471	Georgia	476	Georgia	465	
Macedonia	442	Macedonia	439	Macedonia	450	
Trinidad and Tobago	436	Trinidad and Tobago	434	Trinidad and Tobago	440	
Iran	421	Iran	426	Iran	420	
Indonesia	405	Indonesia	397	Indonesia	418	
Qatar	353	Qatar	358	Qatar	356	
Kuwait	330	Kuwait	340	Morocco	335	
Morocco	323	Morocco	317	Kuwait	327	
South Africa	302	South Africa	299	South Africa	316	
PIRLS scale average	500	PIRLS scale average	500	PIRLS scale average	500	

[1]Hong Kong, SAR, is a Special Administrative Region (SAR) of the People's Republic of China.
[2]Met guidelines for sample participation rates only after replacement schools were included.
[3]Did not meet guidelines for sample participation rates after replacement schools were included.
Note: Jurisdictions are ordered on the basis of average scores, from highest to lowest. Score differences as noted between the United States and other jurisdictions are statistically significant at the .05 level of statistical significance ($p<.05$).

FIGURE 11.5 continued

students in 22 of the 44 other countries and educational jurisdictions that participated in the PIRLS. Ten countries and educational jurisdictions had average scores higher than the scores of U.S. students; average scores of students in the remaining 12 countries and educational jurisdictions were not significantly different from the scores of U.S. students.

Norm-Referenced Assessments

Some standardized assessments are norm-referenced—that is, students' scores are compared with scores of other students who are similar. The comparison group of students, called the *norm group*, is usually from the same age-group and grade level. An individual student's score is then compared to the average, or mean, score for the total group. Norm-referenced tests are used to determine where a student is compared to the typical performance of other students at the same age and grade level. Thus, **norm-referenced assessments** enable teachers to rank students in terms of their achievement.

To understand the meaning of scores on a norm-referenced assessment, imagine that a student received a total of 75 points on a 100-point norm-referenced assessment. If the mean, or average, score for the comparison group of students was also 75, the student would be at the 50th percentile. That is, 50 percent of the students in the comparison group scored higher, and 50 percent scored lower. However, if the mean score for the comparison group was 90, the student would be in the 30th percentile. That is, 70 percent of the students in the comparison group scored higher, and 30 percent scored lower.

The preceding example can also be used to illustrate how scores on norm-referenced tests should be interpreted carefully. Norm-referenced test scores can be misused. If the student scored in the 30th percentile, it would be a mistake to assume that the score is evidence that the student is doing poorly. The student might not have done well on the material covered by the norm-referenced assessment; however, the student might be doing quite well in other areas not included in the test. Four examples of norm-referenced interpretations of students' performance follow:

1. Alfredo won the one-mile race.
2. On the test of basic skills, Jiling's scores were near the average.
3. On the chemistry test given districtwide, our school had the best scores.
4. On the test of physical fitness, Susan was in the 90th percentile.

Criterion-Referenced Assessments

Other standardized assessments are criterion-referenced—that is, students' learning is compared with clearly defined criteria or standards rather than the performance of other students. **Criterion-referenced assessments** do not indicate what is average or typical for students from the same age-group and grade level. Criterion-referenced assessments indicate what students know and can do within a specific subject area. Students' scores are not compared with the scores of other groups of students.

A teacher might use a criterion-referenced assessment to assess a student's ability to calculate the square root of a number, to write a well-organized paragraph, or to type 60 words per minute on a computer keyboard. In other words, the assessment is made with reference to an instructional objective, rather than the performance of other students on the assessment. Similarly, the student's score is interpreted without reference to how other students performed. Following are four examples of criterion-referenced interpretations of students' performance:

1. In the chemistry lab, Mary can light a Bunsen burner correctly.
2. Juan can identify each element on a periodic table.
3. Yiming can calculate the sine, cosine, and tangent of angles.
4. Using a map of the world, Lashandra can identify the countries that were involved in World War II.

Emerging Trends in Classroom Assessment

As mentioned at the beginning of this chapter, there is a trend to assess student learning with ever-increasing numbers of tests. More recently, however, new forms of assessment are being used. Innovations in assessment are partly in response to criticisms of the fairness and objectivity of standardized tests, such as the Iowa Test of Basic Skills, the Scholastic Assessment Test (SAT), and the American College Test (ACT). Educators and the public have criticized these tests not only for class and gender bias in their content but also for failing to measure accurately students' true knowledge, skills, and levels of achievement. For all these reasons, educators are increasingly going beyond traditional pencil-and-paper tests, oral questioning, and formal and informal observations. In addition, they are using an array of new assessment tools—individual and small-group projects, portfolios of work, exhibitions, videotaped demonstrations of skills, and community-based activities, to name a few.

Increasingly, teachers are using **alternative assessments**—that is, "forms of assessment that require the active construction of meaning rather than the passive regurgitation of isolated facts" (McMillan, 2001, p. 14). The following sections examine several forms of alternative assessments: authentic assessment, portfolio assessment, peer assessment, self-assessment, performance-based assessment, alternate assessment, and project-based learning.

Authentic Assessment

Authentic assessment (sometimes called *alternative assessment*) requires students to use higher-level thinking skills to perform, create, or solve a real-life problem, not just choose one of several designated responses, as on a multiple-choice test item. A teacher might use authentic assessment to evaluate the quality of individual and small-group projects, videotaped demonstrations of skills, or participation in community-based activities. In science, for example, students might design and conduct an experiment to solve a problem and then explain in writing how they solved the problem. To watch a video of a ninth-grade geography teacher assessing her students' higher-order thinking skills, go to MyEducationLab.

Authentic assessments require students to solve problems or to work on tasks that approximate as much as possible those they will encounter beyond the classroom. For example, **authentic assessment** might allow students to select projects on which they will be evaluated, such as writing a brochure, making a map, creating a recipe, writing and directing a play, critiquing a performance, inventing a working machine, producing a video, creating a model, writing a children's book, and so on. In addition, authentic assessment encourages students to develop their own responses to problem situations by allowing them to decide what information is relevant and how that information should be organized and used.

When teachers use authentic assessment to determine what students have learned—and the depth to which they have learned—student achievement and attitudes toward learning improve. For example, a study of eleven pairs of K–12 science and math teachers found that when teachers assess student learning in real-life problem-solving situations, learning and attitudes toward school improve (Appalachia Educational Laboratory, 1993). Similarly, a synthesis of research on successfully restructured schools (Newmann & Wehlage, 1995) revealed that teachers in those schools emphasized authentic assessment. Their assessments focused on students' ability to think; develop in-depth understanding; and apply academic learning to important, realistic problems.

Portfolio Assessment

Portfolio assessment is based on a collection of student work that "tell[s] a story of a learner's growth in proficiency, long-term achievement, and significant accomplishments in a given academic area" (Borich, 2007, p. 428). In short, a portfolio provides examples of important work undertaken by a student, and it represents that student's best work. For example, a high school physics student might include in a portfolio (1) a written report of a physics lab experiment illustrating how vector principles and Newton's laws explain

PEARSON
myeducationlab

Go to MyEducationLab, select Chapter 11 and Activities and Applications to watch the video Assessing Higher-Order Thinking.

the motion of objects in two dimensions, (2) photographs of that experiment in progress, (3) a certificate of merit received at a local science fair, and (4) an annotated list of Internet sites related to vector principles and Newton's laws. For students, an important part of **portfolio assessment** is clarifying the criteria used to select work to be included in the portfolio, and then organizing and presenting that work for the teacher to assess.

Peer Assessment

Peer assessment occurs when students assess one another's work. Typically, peer assessment is done informally during a class session. At times, a student may be more open to accepting critical feedback from a peer than from the teacher. Also, a peer may use a manner of speaking typical of his or her age level (word choice, for example), and it may be easier for another student to understand the feedback. The Teaching on Your Feet feature in this chapter provides an example of how feedback from their peers enabled one teacher's students to understand a concept that they had not understood previously.

Last, as the following teacher indicates, **peer assessment** frees the teacher to observe the peer assessment process and to provide input when necessary:

> We regularly do peer marking—I find this very helpful indeed. A lot of misconceptions come to the fore, and we then discuss these as we are going over the homework. I then go over the peer marking and talk to pupils individually as I go round the room. (Black et al., 2004, p. 14)

Self-Assessment

Self-assessment occurs when students assess their own work and their thought processes while completing that work. It has been suggested that "[self-assessment] is the most underused form of classroom assessment but has the most flexibility and power as a combined assessment and learning tool" (Tileston, 2004, p. 99). When students assess their own work, they become more aware of the factors that promote or hinder their learning. Students may, for example, ask assessment questions such as the following: What have I learned as a result of this activity? What problems did I encounter during my learning? How will I overcome these problems in the future? To view examples of students' comments about the self-assessment process, go to MyEducationLab.

As a teacher, you should help your students, particularly low-achieving students, develop skills of self-assessment. As the following teacher indicates, once students develop self-assessment skills, their learning can improve dramatically:

> The kids are not skilled in what I am trying to get them to do. I think the process is more effective long term. If you invest time in it, it will pay off big dividends, this process of getting the students to be more independent in the way that they learn and to take the responsibility themselves. (Black et al., 2004, p. 14)

Some teachers have taught students how to assess their work using the analogy of a common traffic light. Students label their work green, yellow, or red based on whether they have good, partial, or little understanding, respectively. The teacher then has the "greens" and the "yellows" meet in small groups to help one another, while the teacher meets with the "reds" to address their learning problems.

Performance-Based Assessment

Put simply, **performance-based assessment** is based on observation and judgment (Stiggins, 2005). We observe a student perform a task or review a student-produced product, and we judge its quality. We could observe a student's science experiment and judge the quality of the thinking involved, or we could read a student's research report in history and judge the quality of argumentation and writing. Performance assessment is used to determine what students can do as well as what they know. In some cases, the teacher observes and then evaluates an actual performance or application of a skill; in others, the teacher evaluates a product created by the student.

Performance-based assessment focuses on students' ability to apply knowledge, skills, and work habits through the performance of tasks they find meaningful and en-

Go to MyEducationLab, select Chapter 11 and Activities and Applications to analyze the artifact Self-Assessment Methods.

TEACHING ON YOUR FEET

THE BENEFITS OF PEER ASSESSMENT

Despite my lesson plans, the suggestions I took from the text, and the numerous examples I gave during the day, nothing seemed to work—my sixth-grade class did not understand adjectives. I needed to find a new way to teach my students.

Then it hit me! Have them describe something they see in their bedrooms or on the way home from school each afternoon. So, I changed that night's homework assignment to observing their environment in preparation to write about it the next day. I didn't tell them that I was going to have them share their writing with a classmate.

The next day students came ready to share what they had observed. We did a five-minute brainstorm before they wrote their descriptions. After twenty minutes of nonstop writing, I had the students switch papers with a neighbor. Their neighbor was to draw exactly what the writing described.

I gave them twenty minutes to draw the picture, then hand it back to their neighbor. That's when I heard, "Man, you didn't put any grass in the park. I told you the sun was shining!" "Where's the color? My comforter is blue with white trim. You didn't show that."

Those were the responses I hoped to hear. Because students had not used adjectives, their peers' drawings did not portray what they thought they described. "Ms. Gore, are you saying that using adjectives helps the reader see what I am describing?" asked Melissa. "Now, I get it. Adjectives are colors and sizes. They make things come to life, right? Can we try it again, please?"

Aha! They finally understood adjectives. The assignment for that night was to rewrite their descriptions, which they would again share in class.

The next day, students came in eager to share their writing and then see their classmates' drawings. The results were wonderful—at last, my students understood the importance of using adjectives.

ANALYSIS

Ms. Gore's lesson illustrates how it is sometimes helpful for a teacher to shift a lesson from the abstract to the concrete. When her students did not grasp the abstract concept of adjectives, Ms. Gore made the lesson more concrete—describe something students saw in their bedroom or on their way home from school.

In addition, Ms. Gore made the material to be learned familiar. She personalized the lesson by having students relate it to their own experiences.

And last, Ms. Gore's use of peer assessment enabled her students to get immediate feedback. They could see immediately whether their writing communicated what they intended.

REFLECTION

- How might you personalize a lesson in a subject area you plan to teach?
- What are other methods that provide immediate feedback for students?
- What are other examples of how a teacher might use a concrete approach to teach an abstract concept?

Leslie U. Gore
Literacy Coach
Horace Mann Middle School,

 *To answer these questions online, go to MyEducationLab at www.myeducationlab.com, select the Activities and Application section, and click on this chapter's Teaching on Your Feet.*

gaging. While traditional testing helps teachers answer the question, "Do students know content?" performance-based assessment helps answer the question, "How well can students use what they know?" To view a video that presents a variety of performance tasks that enable students to demonstrate what they know and are able to do, go to MyEducationLab.

Students should find that performance tasks are interesting and relevant to the knowledge, skills, and work habits emphasized in the curriculum. If appropriate, students

Go to MyEducationLab, select Chapter 11 and Activities and Applications to watch the video Performance Assessment.

can help teachers construct performance-based assessments. For example, elementary and high school students helped their teachers construct the following two performance-based assessments, each of which required students to create graphs.

Example 1, Elementary Level—At various times during the school day, students observe and count, at 15-minute intervals, the number of cars and trucks that crossed an intersection without a traffic light near their school. Students also gather the same information for an intersection with a traffic light near the school. Using data for both intersections, students construct graphs to illustrate the results. If the data suggest the need for a light at the intersection without one, the graphs will be sent to the local police department.

As students work on various parts of this performance task, the teacher observes students and makes judgments about the quality of their work. Do the counts of cars and trucks appear to be accurate? Do the graphs illustrate the results clearly? Is the students' decision about the need for a traffic light supported by the data they have gathered?

Example 2, High School Level—Students go online to find data on traffic accidents in their state. Based on the data they locate, students prepare graphs that show, by driver's age, various types of accidents, fatalities, speed at the time of accident, and so on. Exemplary graphs will be displayed in the driver education classroom.

As with the elementary-level example, the teacher makes judgments about the quality of the high school students' work. Naturally, these judgments reflect the teacher's beliefs about the characteristics of exemplary student work at the high school level. Did students visit online sites that have extensive, accurate data on traffic accidents? Were students exhaustive in their online search? Do their graphs show a high degree of technical accuracy? Do the graphs look professional?

Alternate Assessments

Alternate assessments are designed to measure the performance of students who are unable to participate in the traditional large-scale assessments used by districts and states. This approach to assessment emerged as a result of the reference to "alternate assessment" in the 1997 reauthorization of the Individuals with Disabilities Education Act (IDEA), which called for states to have alternate assessments in place by the year 2000. An alternate assessment is an alternative way of gathering data about what a student, regardless of the severity of his or her disability, knows and can do. Alternate strategies for collecting data might consist of observing the student during the school day, asking the student to perform a task and noting the level of performance, or interviewing parents or guardians about the student's activities outside school.

The primary purpose for alternate assessments in state assessment systems is to provide information about how well a school, district, or state is doing in terms of enhancing the performance of *all* students. Gathering data through alternate assessments requires rethinking traditional assessment methods.

An alternate assessment is neither a traditional large-scale assessment nor an individualized diagnostic assessment. For students with disabilities, alternate assessments can be administered to students who have a unique array of educational goals and experiences and who differ greatly in their ability to respond to stimuli, solve problems, and provide responses.

Most states are in the process of developing alternate assessments for students with severe disabilities. The National Center on Educational Outcomes at the University of Minnesota suggests six principles for developing inclusive assessment and accountability systems:

Principle 1. All students with disabilities are included in the assessment system.

Principle 2. Decisions about how students with disabilities participate in the assessment system are the result of clearly articulated participation, accommodation, and alternate assessment decision-making processes.

Principle 3. All students with disabilities are included when student scores are publicly reported, in the same frequency and format as all other students, whether they participate with or without accommodations, or in an alternate assessment.

Principle 4. The assessment performance of students with disabilities has the same impact on the final accountability index as the performance of other students, regardless of how the students participate in the assessment system (i.e., with or without accommodation, or in an alternate assessment).

Principle 5. There is improvement of both the assessment system and the accountability system over time, through the processes of formal monitoring, ongoing evaluation, and systematic training in the context of emerging research and best practice.

Principle 6. Every policy and practice reflects the belief that all students must be included in state and district assessment and accountability systems (Guenemoen, Thompson, Thurlow, & Lehr, 2001).

Project-Based Learning (PBL)

A growing body of research supports the use of project-based learning (PBL) as a way to engage students, cut absenteeism, boost cooperative learning skills, and improve test scores. In **project-based learning (PBL),** students work in teams to explore real-world problems and create presentations to share what they have learned. Compared with learning solely from textbooks, this approach has many benefits for students, including deeper knowledge of subject matter, increased self-direction and motivation, and improved research and problem-solving skills.

Students find PBL very engaging, as George Lucas, founder of the George Lucas Educational Foundation and director of *Star Wars,* points out: "Project learning, student teams working cooperatively, children connecting with passionate experts, and broader forms of assessment can dramatically improve student learning. New digital multimedia and telecommunications can support these practices and engage our students" (George Lucas Educational Foundation, June 2008). As the Technology in Action feature in this chapter illustrates, project-based learning via the Internet is one way teachers can increase their own professional knowledge and skills.

PBL, which transforms teaching from teachers telling to students doing, includes five key elements:

1. Engaging learning experiences that involve students in complex, real-world projects through which they develop and apply skills and knowledge.

2. Recognizing that significant learning taps students' inherent drive to learn, their capability to do important work, and their need to be taken seriously.

3. Learning for which general curricular outcomes can be identified up-front, while specific outcomes of the students' learning are neither predetermined nor fully predictable.

4. Learning that requires students to draw from many information sources and disciplines to solve problems.

5. Experiences through which students learn to manage and allocate resources such as time and materials.

These five key elements are reflected in the following examples of project-based learning.

- At Mountlake Terrace High School in Mountlake Terrace, Washington, teams of students in a high school geometry class design a state-of-the-art high school for the year 2050. The students create a site plan, make simple architectural drawings of rooms and a physical model, plan a budget, and write a narrative report. They present their work to real architects, who judge the projects and "award" the contract.

- At Newsome Park Elementary School in Newport News, Virginia, second-graders curious about the number of medicines a classmate takes and her frequent trips to the doctor investigate—with the classmate's permission—the causes of cystic

TECHNOLOGY in *ACTION*

Fifth-Grade Social Studies Teacher Obtains Online Degree

Ms. Flick is a second-grade teacher at a small rural elementary school. She has taught there for just over three years. By all accounts, she is doing quite well. Her only complaint is the remote location of the school. She likes the quiet of the small town, but she misses the opportunities of a larger urban setting. One of the opportunities she misses is access to higher education because she wants to pursue a master's degree. The problem is that the nearest university is over 100 miles away. If she planned to pursue her master's at this institution, she would either need to take a leave of absence from her teaching duties and relocate to the city where the university is located, or drive several hundred miles each week and take night and summer courses. With her extracurricular responsibilities and her family and community commitments, neither of these options is appealing.

Last year, a colleague of Ms. Flick took an online course in classroom assessment. He had some very positive things to say about the experience.

After a bit of research into online courses and degrees, Ms. Flick was surprised to find so many options available to her. Through the online medium, she now had the option of "attending" a university anywhere in the world, at nationally and internationally recognized institutions, without ever leaving her community.

She found a university that seemed perfect. It offered a graduate degree in a subject area targeted to her professional interests. The tuition was actually less expensive than her local university. What intrigued her most was that the program was described as highly interactive. In other words, this was not a work-at-your-own-pace, all-by-yourself program. According to the program description, the academic rigor was identical to the on-campus experience.

Although unsure of these claims, Ms. Flick enrolled in the program. She started with just one course the first semester—to measure the accuracy of the program descrip-

tion and determine the level of effort needed for success. At first, it was rough going. This style of learning was quite new to her. The most difficult aspect of online learning was carving out time for the coursework. Ms. Flick realized that she would need to create an individual calendar, based on the demands of the course, that would allow her to dedicate time for specific assignments.

As she moved through the semester, Ms. Flick found that the description of the program was very accurate. The courses were highly interactive. She connected with classmates, worked in small groups, developed projects, and made presentations. She was already looking forward to the next semester.

ONLINE DEGREE: Online degrees are one of the fastest growing educational options in the United States. An online degree is an academic degree delivered through an online medium. As with on-campus programs, the student experience depends on the university, the subject matter, and the instructor. Most online degree programs are delivered through a learning management system. In these systems, students interact, submit assignments, make presentations, and follow a guided course experience.

VISIT: http://www.petersons.com. Numerous online degree options are available to you. The site listed here allows you to search for online degrees by level of education, subject matter, or specific institution.

POSSIBLE USES: Teachers have used online courses and degrees to update their résumés, obtain advanced degrees, and improve their teaching without relocating, traveling long distances, or giving up employment.

TRY IT OUT: Most universities that offer online degrees provide opportunities for potential students to take a demo course. At http://petersons.com, visit a university that is of interest to you and look for a demo course link.

fibrosis. They invite experts to tell them about the disease, write their research, use graphs and PowerPoint to tell the story, sell pledges to a cystic fibrosis walkathon, and participate in the walkathon.

- At the Mott Hall School in New York City's Harlem, a fifth-grade project on kites involves using creative-writing skills in poems and stories with kite themes. Students design their own kites on the computer and then make them by hand. They learn about electromagnetism and the principles of ratios and proportions. A casual remark by one student leads to an in-depth study of the role of kites in various cultural celebrations.

The Teachers' Voices: Research to Reality feature in this chapter illustrates how project-based learning is appropriate for students as young as kindergarten age.

HOW CAN YOU DEVELOP HIGH-QUALITY CLASSROOM ASSESSMENTS?

You should use various criteria to grade the assignments students complete and the tests they take. Among the criteria you may consider are effort, neatness, correctness, how well students did compared with other students or with their own past performance, and how long students had been studying the topic. These criteria, of course, focus on what *students* do to demonstrate their learning. To develop high-quality classroom assessments, however, you must focus on what *you* do to ensure that assessments fairly and accurately measure students' knowledge, skills, and levels of achievement. To assess student learning, you should be skilled in the following:

- Choosing and/or developing assessment methods appropriate for attaining instructional goals and objectives
- Administering, scoring, and interpreting the results of both externally produced and teacher-produced assessment methods
- Using assessment results when making decisions about individual students, planning teaching, developing curriculum, and school improvement
- Developing valid grading procedures based on high-quality assessment of student learning
- Communicating assessment results to students, parents, other nonteaching audiences, and other educators
- Recognizing unethical, illegal, and otherwise inappropriate assessment methods and uses of assessment information

To watch a video that shows an example of how a high school world history teacher assesses students' learning while they use online materials, go to MyEducationLab.

Go to MyEducationLab, select Chapter 11 and Activities and Applications to watch the video Assessment Examples Illustrated.

Validity and Reliability

Two important qualities of classroom assessments—whether teacher-made or commercially prepared—are validity and reliability. Because high-quality assessments are directly related to teaching effectiveness, assessments must be valid and reliable. **Validity** refers to the extent to which assessments measure what they are supposed to measure. If assessments fail to do this, they are useless. Valid assessments, however, ensure that what students are asked to do is a direct reflection of stated standards, goals, expectations, and/or targeted learning outcomes. If assessments are valid, teachers can use that information to improve their teaching, and students can use that information to improve their learning.

Surprisingly, perhaps, examples of assessments that lack sufficient validity can be found among state-mandated tests of student learning. For example, Beverly Falk observes:

Numerous accountability systems use tests that have little relation to the standards they are supposed to evaluate. As recently as 1999, at least 25

TEACHERS' VOICES RESEARCH TO REALITY

Mary Russell

PROJECT-BASED LEARNING: BUILDING HOUSES

I just completed a unit on houses with my kindergarten class. . . . By engaging students with a project, in phases, I am able to help them understand the generalizations that frame the unit:

- Houses are built with different kinds of materials.
- Houses come in many shapes and sizes.
- Climate affects the type of house that is built.
- Building a house requires many job skills.
- Design and materials affect the quality of houses. . . .

For the generalization "Design and materials affect the quality of houses" I had them make houses out of marshmallows and toothpicks. We had interesting designs but alas—only certain houses remained standing. We analyzed why, and tried the same theories with block houses.

The preceding activities completed phases one and two of the unit. Phase three was sharing and playing. We shared with parents and other classes. Playing in the house is the reward for all the hard work. [Regarding] insights I . . . have about helping students understand the importance of concepts . . . I think it is the connection to real life. You can find real-life applications of concepts within any theme. Connect students with the real-world applications and let them play the required roles. This is especially true for primary children. Any time a child takes on an adult role, it is important to him or her.

Making the project big in size helps also. I observed the sixth-graders looking at our house. They immediately got in and wanted to play. I began to think about the kind of house they would make and the details they could achieve. I almost wanted to move up a few grades! Teachers need to keep the learning as hands-on as possible. Children will naturally read, write, use mathematics skills, etc., if teachers demand they show their understanding of concepts and generalizations in different ways as they work on a big project.

PERSONAL REFLECTION

1. With reference to the grade level and subject area for which you are preparing to teach, what are some examples of how you might use project-based learning?
2. Project-based learning allows students to study material in greater depth; however, this leaves less time to cover a broader range of material. With respect to the amount of material that can be covered, what do you see as the advantages and disadvantages of project-based learning?

Mary Russell is a teacher at Ponderosa Elementary School, Spokane Valley, Washington. The preceding is excerpted from her contribution to H. Lynn Erickson, *Stirring the Head, Heart, and Soul: Redefining Curriculum, Instruction, and Concept-Based Learning*, 3rd ed. Thousand Oaks, CA: Corwin Press, 2008, pp. 200–201.

states that claimed to be implementing new standards were still using old-style, norm-referenced tests to measure student progress. Although the rhetoric of new and lofty standards is used when discussing what the tests measure, their actual content includes few performance items, and their formats provide scant opportunities for students to demonstrate the higher-order thinking of the new standards. (2002, p. 614)

Reliability refers to the degree to which an assessment provides results that are consistent over time. In other words, an entire test (or individual test item) is considered to be reliable if it yields similar results at different times and under different conditions. For example, imagine that Mr. Hernandez wants to assess his students' multiplication and division skills using whole numbers by giving them a 40-point quiz (20 points for multiplication, 20 points for division). After scoring his students' quizzes, Mr. Hernandez is uncertain about whether he should begin teaching the more complex skills of multiplying and dividing using fractions. He decides to gather more information by giving another quiz three days later on the same multiplication and division skills. The following table presents the scores several students received on both quizzes:

Student	Multiplication		Division	
	Quiz 1	Quiz 2	Quiz 1	Quiz 2
Carlos	20	18	17	9
Kim	14	13	13	17
Shawn	11	11	12	17
Nong	16	17	16	12
Mary	20	19	15	14

The items that assessed students' multiplication skills, Mr. Hernandez notes, are quite consistent (or reliable). On quizzes 1 and 2, all five students received comparable scores, with Carlos and Mary receiving the highest scores on both quizzes, and Shawn and Kim receiving the lowest scores. On the other hand, the items that assessed students' division skills are less consistent (or reliable). On quiz 1, Carlos and Nong received the highest scores on the division items, while Kim and Shawn received the highest scores on the items for quiz 2.

At this point, Mr. Hernandez must make a judgment about the reliability of the information he has gathered. Because the results for the multiplication items are fairly consistent and those for the division items are fairly inconsistent, he decides to spend one more class session instructing students on division using whole numbers before he proceeds to teach multiplication and division using fractions.

Scoring Rubrics

Rubrics are an important element of quality classroom assessments. Sometimes called *scoring guides*, **scoring rubrics** are rating scales that consist of preestablished performance criteria. As a teacher, you can use rubrics to differentiate between levels of student performance on a rating scale, and students can even use them to guide their learning. Rubrics can be used to specify performance criteria for a variety of learning activities—writing an essay, conducting a science experiment, or delivering an informative speech.

Students benefit from seeing examples of excellent work appropriate to their grade and ability levels. "Given clear requirements for success, students are better able to gauge the appropriateness of their own preparation and thus gain control over their own academic well-being. Students who feel in control of their own chances for success are more likely to care and to strive for excellence" (Stiggins, 2005, p. 40).

In addition to developing rubrics, you should collect models of exemplary performances and products by your students. Besides using a scoring rubric to learn about the specific elements that will be used to assess the quality of their work, students must see what quality looks (sounds, feels, smells, or tastes) like. Over time, you should collect sets of excellent work such as graphs, nonfiction writing, solutions to open-ended math problems, and designs for science experiments from students. Less than exemplary work may also be used in the process of teaching students how to use the rubrics.

Rubrics are typically used as scoring instruments when teachers evaluate student performances or products resulting from a performance task. There are two types of rubrics: holistic and analytic. A **holistic rubric** requires the teacher to score the overall process or product as a whole, without judging the component parts separately (Nitko, 2001). Figure 11.6 presents a generic framework for developing a holistic scoring rubric based on a 4-point scale.

As an illustration, a high school English teacher might use the framework presented in Figure 11.6 for holistic assessment of students' ability to write a clear, well-organized essay. A score of 5 would mean the essay reflected characteristics such as clear organization, accurate and precise use of words, adequately developed ideas, insightful analysis of the topic, and effective transitions from paragraph to paragraph. An essay with a score of 3 might have grammatical errors, problems with logic, confusing sentences, and a lack of transitions from paragraph to paragraph. And an essay with a score of 1 might be very confusing and contain only a few sentences that are clear and understandable.

Unlike the holistic scoring rubric, an **analytic rubric** requires that the teacher score separate, individual parts of the product or performance according to prespecified criteria, then add the individual scores to obtain a total score (Moskal, 2000; Nitko, 2001). Figure 11.7 presents a generic framework for developing an analytic scoring rubric based on a 4-point scale.

Let's continue with the example that focuses on teaching essay writing at the high school level. A teacher might evaluate students' essays with reference to the following four criteria, each of which would be evaluated according to the description of performances in Figure 11.7 at the "beginning," "developing," "accomplished," and "highly accomplished" levels:

- Criterion 1: The essay is organized clearly—the introduction sets the stage for what follows and the conclusion summarizes key ideas.
- Criterion 2: The essay is free of grammatical errors.

Score	Description
5	Performance or product reflects complete understanding of the assessment task or problem. The performance or product reflects all requirements of the task or problem.
4	Performance or product reflects considerable understanding of the assessment task or problem. The performance or product reflects all requirements of the task or problem.
3	Performance or product reflects partial understanding of the assessment task or problem. The performance or product reflects nearly all requirements of the task or problem.
2	Performance or product reflects little understanding of the assessment task or problem. Many requirements of the task or problem are missing.
1	Performance or product reflects no understanding of the assessment task or problem.
0	Task or problem not undertaken.

FIGURE 11.6 Generic framework for a holistic scoring rubric

Criterion	Beginning	Developing	Accomplished	Highly Accomplished	Score
Criterion 1	Performance or product reflects beginning level of performance.	Performance or product reflects emerging performance at the mastery level.	Performance or product reflects performance at the mastery level.	Performance or product reflects performance at the highest level of mastery.	
Criterion 2	Performance or product reflects beginning level of performance.	Performance or product reflects emerging performance at the mastery level.	Performance or product reflects performance at the mastery level.	Performance or product reflects performance at the highest level of mastery.	
Criterion 3	Performance or product reflects beginning level of performance.	Performance or product reflects emerging performance at the mastery level.	Performance or product reflects performance at the mastery level.	Performance or product reflects performance at the highest level of mastery.	
Criterion 4	Performance or product reflects beginning level of performance.	Performance or product reflects emerging performance at the mastery level.	Performance or product reflects performance at the mastery level.	Performance or product reflects performance at the highest level of mastery.	

FIGURE 11.7 Generic framework for an analytic rubric

- Criterion 3:   The essay has a unifying idea that is clear and easy to follow.
- Criterion 4:   Effective paragraphing and transitions from one paragraph to the next provide an organizing structure and facilitate movement from one idea to the next.

To help you develop scoring rubrics for eventual use in your classroom, Figure 11.8 presents a step-by-step process for designing holistic and analytic scoring rubrics.

Multiple Measures of Student Learning

There is no single right way to assess student learning. Clearly, it will be important for you to provide your students with multiple opportunities to demonstrate what they know and are able to do. If your students know that they have different ways to demonstrate their success, they will develop more positive views of themselves as learners. They will find learning to be an enjoyable experience.

Students who previously disliked a subject because they associated assessments of learning in that area with failure can develop positive views about a subject if they

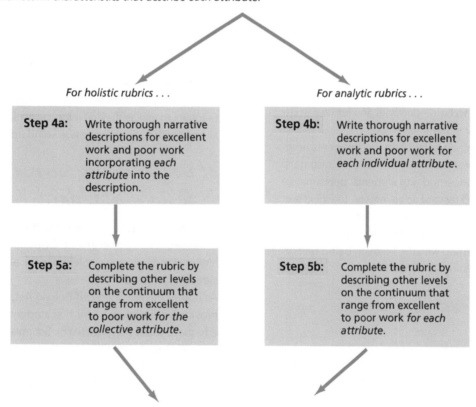

Step 1:   Reexamine the learning objectives to be addressed by the task.

Step 2:   Identify specific observable attributes that you want to see (as well as those you don't want to see) your students demonstrate in their product, process, or performance.

Step 3:   Brainstorm characteristics that describe each attribute.

For holistic rubrics . . .

Step 4a: Write thorough narrative descriptions for excellent work and poor work incorporating *each attribute* into the description.

Step 5a: Complete the rubric by describing other levels on the continuum that range from excellent to poor work *for the collective attribute*.

For analytic rubrics . . .

Step 4b: Write thorough narrative descriptions for excellent work and poor work for *each individual attribute*.

Step 5b: Complete the rubric by describing other levels on the continuum that range from excellent to poor work *for each attribute*.

Step 6:   Collect samples of student work that exemplify each level.

Step 7:   Revise the rubric, as necessary.

FIGURE 11.8 Designing scoring rubrics: A step-by-step procedure

Source: Craig A. Mertler, "Designing Scoring Rubrics for the Classroom," Practical Assessment, Research & Evaluation, 2001, 7 (25). Used with permission.

What are the advantages of using multiple measures to assess students' learning?

know they have different ways to demonstrate their learning—in other words, multiple opportunities to be successful. As assessment expert Rick Stiggins puts it, "We [now] understand how to use classroom assessment to keep students confident that the achievement target is within reach. . . . We must build classroom environments in which students use assessments to understand what success looks like and how to do better next time. . . . If teachers assess accurately and use the results effectively, then students prosper" (Stiggins, 2004, pp. 24–26).

SUMMARY

What Role Will Standards Play in Your Classroom?

- Standards at the state and national levels are part of the movement to hold educators and schools more accountable for student learning.
- School administrators, teachers, and students have different perspectives on standards. Administrators are primarily concerned with students' performance on standardized tests of achievement; teachers are primarily concerned with student performance and behavior at the classroom level; and students are primarily concerned with the learning being personally relevant, interesting, and meaningful.

What Is Standards-Based Education?

- Developing rigorous academic standards, assessing students' mastery of those standards, and holding students and teachers accountable for meeting those standards are key elements of standards-based education.
- Professional associations have developed standards that reflect the knowledge, skills, and attitudes students should develop in the subject matter disciplines.

- A good school curriculum is aligned both horizontally and vertically.
- Curriculum frameworks provide guidelines, recommended instructional and assessment strategies, suggested resources, and models for teachers to use as they develop curricula that are aligned with national and state standards.

What Controversies Surround the Effort to Raise Standards?

- Proponents of higher standards argue that standards increase student achievement. Opponents argue that higher standards may result in decreased emphasis on subjects not tested.
- As part of the No Child Left Behind Act, schools are to provide evidence each year that students are making adequate yearly progress (AYP). Schools that fail to make AYP will be identified as "in need of improvement."
- State-mandated tests often have high-stakes consequences for students, such as determining eligibility to participate in extracurricular activities or to graduate.
- For teachers, administrators, and schools, test results can be linked to merit rewards, increased funding, or sanctions.

What Methods Can You Use to Assess Student Learning?

- Classroom assessment enables teachers to make judgments about the performance of students and about their own performance as teachers.
- To assess student learning, teachers use quantitative and qualitative approaches, measurement and evaluation techniques, and formative and summative evaluation.
- Standardized assessments include norm-referenced assessments and criterion-referenced assessments.
- Among the various types of alternative assessments are authentic assessments, portfolio assessments, peer assessments, self-assessments, performance-based assessments, alternate assessments, and project-based learning.

How Can You Develop High-Quality Classroom Assessments?

- Validity and reliability are two qualities of high-quality classroom assessments.
- Two types of scoring rubrics that can be used to assess students' performance are holistic rubrics and analytic rubrics.
- There is no single right way to assess student learning, and students' views of themselves as learners improve if they know that they have different ways to demonstrate their learning.

PROFESSIONAL REFLECTIONS AND ACTIVITIES

Teacher's Journal

1. Testing is obviously an important part of teaching. To what extent do you think the current emphasis on standardized tests encourages teachers to teach to the test? Is teaching to the test an effective or ineffective way to promote student learning? Explain your answer.

2. Reflect on the many different assessments you experienced when you were a student in K–12 schools. Describe one or two assessments that you felt were accurate assessments of your knowledge and abilities and that motivated you to continue learning. Similarly, describe one or two assessments that you felt were *not* accurate assessments of your knowledge and abilities and that did *not* motivate you to continue learning. What implications do your own experiences have for your future assessment activities as a teacher?

Teacher's Research

1. Go online to your state's department of education home page and find the link to the state's standards. Then compare your state's standards with the standards from another state. How are the two sets of standards similar? How are they different? Is one set of standards clearer than the other?

2. Visit the George Lucas Educational Foundation online (www.glef.org/) and, with reference to the subject matter and grade level for which you are preparing to teach, find two examples of project-based learning activities that are featured at the site. How is student learning assessed in these project-based learning activities? How might you adapt or modify these assessment activities when you become a teacher?

Observations and Interviews

1. Interview at least one teacher at the grade level and in the subject area for which you are preparing to teach for his or her views about standards-based education. Does the teacher believe the effort to raise standards has helped or hurt education?

2. Observe in a classroom at the level you plan to teach. How does the teacher convey to students his or her standards (or expectations) for learning?

---

myeducationlab To complete additional observations and interviews, go to MyEducationLab at www.myeducationlab.com, select the Virtual Field Experience section, and click on this chapter's Observations and Interviews.

Professional Portfolio

Prepare a set of guidelines or strategies for students to follow when they take a standardized test. The strategies might include items such as the following:

- Survey the test, checking for missing pages.
- Read directions carefully.
- Notice use of double negatives.
- Note use of terms such as *always, never, best,* etc.
- Read all choices for multiple-choice test items.
- Check answers.

---

myeducationlab Now go to MyEducationLab at www.myeducationlab.com to test your understanding of chapter content by completing this chapter's Study Plan.

Integrating Technology Into Teaching

15

Integrating Technology
Into Teaching

CLASSROOM CASE
The Realities of Teaching

THE CHALLENGE: Learning how to integrate technology into teaching to engage students fully and to increase their learning.

The teachers at Pierce Junior High School have just participated in an in-service provided by the state education department. The focus of the meeting was the new state technology standards for students. The teachers learned that, in addition to content area standards and grade-level indicators, the state was requiring all teachers to address the technology standards throughout the curriculum. During the workshop, the presenter provided a resource list that included many print and electronic resources teachers could use to help them learn about the technology standards and integrate them into instruction.

Patricia Morello, an eighth-grade English teacher, used technology regularly in her classes, particularly word processing. Her students typed their essays, looked for resources on the Web, and sometimes made graphic organizers to lay out the structure of a text. Patricia felt that she could probably meet the majority of the standards with little change. Just to make sure that she was working in the right direction, she decided to complete the Learning With Technology Profile Tool at www.ncrtec.org/capacity/profile/profwww.htm, which the workshop presenter had highly recommended. When she received her responses in graphical form, she discovered to her dismay that she could do a lot more to use technology to engage learners. She also found that the technology she was using in her classes was neither very challenging nor very functional for students. Patricia understood why the standards should be addressed and decided that she needed to learn more about the use of technology to meet standards, but she was unsure where to begin and how she could fit professional development in technology into her already busy schedule (Egbert, 2009, p. 239).

FOCUS QUESTIONS

1. How is technology transforming teaching and learning?
2. What technologies can be integrated into teaching?
3. To what degree are teachers integrating technology into their teaching?
4. What does research say about technology integration and student learning?
5. What are the challenges of integrating technology into teaching?

Today's teachers face the challenge of engaging tech-savvy students in classroom learning activities. This chapter's classroom case suggests that using technology to engage such students is not a simple matter. Often referred to as digital natives, net-gens, millennials, or generation tech, today's students live in a world that is connected to and continuously transformed by technology. To them, a network password is more important than a social security number.

Today's students are very adept at using various technologies to multitask.

With few exceptions, students are more "wired" than their teachers. Generations ago, students came to school with notebooks, pencils, and pens; today, they come to school with cell phones, laptops, and iPods. In addition, they have grown up in "a techno-drenched atmosphere that has trained them to absorb and process information in fundamentally different ways" (McHugh, 2005). For example, students in grades 3–12 spend an average of 6 hours and 21 minutes each day using some type of media. Because today's students are skilled at multitasking, the figure jumps to about 8½ hours and includes almost 4 hours watching TV and 50 minutes of videogame play. Homework, however, receives only 50 minutes of their time (Rideout, Roberts, & Foehr, 2005). In this chapter's Teachers' Voices: Research to Reality, Merry Herbert describes how awareness of the technology-rich world of her seventh-grade students compelled her to become a skilled blogger, podcaster, and instant messenger, to name just a few of the skills that now enable her to keep up with her millennial students.

HOW IS TECHNOLOGY TRANSFORMING TEACHING AND LEARNING?

For today's students, *anywhere, anytime learning* is a reality. Their learning options include online instruction, various forms of e-learning, and **blended learning**—that is, a blending of traditional face-to-face instruction and online learning. Frequently, all or most of their learning materials and resources are available on the Internet, 24 hours a day, seven days a week.

As the opening quote for this chapter suggests, many schools are behind the times with respect to technology. For example, more than half of high school students are excited about using mobile devices to help them learn; however, only 15 percent of school leaders support this idea (Prensky, 2008, p. 35). Additionally, 65 percent of teachers think educational computer games could help them engage their students, and 46 percent say they would like training on integrating gaming technologies into their teaching, but only 11 percent of teachers actually use them in the classroom. The following statements by students provide additional, compelling evidence that "the traditional classroom lecture creates massive boredom, especially when compared to the vibrancy of [students'] media-saturated, tech-driven world" (Prensky, 2008, p. 33):

- "I'm bored 99 percent of the time." (California)
- "School is really, really boring." (Virginia)
- "Pointless. I'm engaged in two out of my seven classes." (Florida)
- "I'm bored all day because the teachers just talk and talk and talk." (fifth grader)
- "[I wish] teachers would not talk at us, but with us." (West Virgina)
- "She just keeps going on and on." (Detroit)
- "Don't just stand in front and tell." (Albany, NY) (Prensky, 2008, p. 35)

The preceding student comments notwithstanding, technology has transformed teaching and learning. Each day, students communicate via the Internet with other students around the world. Students search the Web for information about whales, the Brazilian rainforest, or the planet Mars. They go to chat rooms for children where they can "talk" to other children in other countries or participate in global networking projects for children. To view a video that illustrates the use of technology to enhance students' learning in a primary grade classroom, go to MyEducationLab.

Technology enables students to experience events or study phenomena that they could not witness firsthand. By integrating technology into various learning tasks and across subject areas, teachers can provide students with learning experiences that would have been impossible a few years ago. Most important, careful and purposeful use of educational technology changes the roles of teachers and students and enhances students' higher-order and problem-solving skills. As you read the following three vignettes, consider how the use of educational technology changes the roles of teachers and students.

myeducationlab

Go to MyEducationLab, select Chapter 12 and then Activities and Applications to watch the video Enhancing Learning Through Technology.

Vignette 1

At first, it may look like they're taking part in a graduation ceremony, but the students who march across the stage at Maine's Falmouth Audubon Society to shake hands with their principal and teachers aren't walking away with diplomas. They're walking away with tangible results of their learning.

In this particular case, the 85 seventh-graders from Helen King Middle School in Portland each received a copy of "Fading Footprints," a CD-ROM they produced about Maine's endangered species. During the ceremony, which included thank-yous to teachers and experts who had helped on the project, some students explained the process. "I made sure all the links worked." Others talked a little about what they learned. "You can ask me anything about the Harlequin duck." Then they all repaired to a courtyard for cake and punch.

"The state's website probably doesn't have as good information as what's in here," says Mark McCollough, a U.S. Fish and Wildlife Service expert on endangered species who had advised the students. "I want to share this with our regional office."

The students are heady with the knowledge that outsiders appreciate their work and that it may be used by professionals. "The hard work that went into it—people are noticing it," beams Amelia, the Harlequin duck expert. "I know I worked a little harder because I knew it was going to be seen," says Miranda, another seventh-grader.

Celebrations with everyone from parents to community members are an important part of the learning process at King, which has adopted the Expeditionary Learning Outward Bound model of personalized, project-based learning. Students stay with the same group of teachers for two years—a practice called looping. At least twice a year, students undertake four- to twelve-week interdisciplinary projects. Besides incorporating such subjects as art, science, and language arts, the projects include well-considered use of computer technology, which has been enhanced by the decision of the state to provide all Maine seventh- and eighth-graders with iBook laptop computers. (George Lucas Educational Foundation, 2004b. ©2004, The George Lucas Educational Foundation. Edutopia.org. All rights reserved.)

Vignette 2

There's no shortage of vivid description in stories from Linda Mitchell's third-grade language arts students at Nuuanu Elementary School in Honolulu. And Mitchell thinks that happy circumstance may have something to do with giving her students a number of ways to come to the writing, including through technology.

Before Tamlyn and Quinn did their descriptive writing, they created storyboards about the action they wanted to represent in an assignment on "expanding the moment"—making the story more intense by describing a

435

TEACHERS' VOICES RESEARCH TO REALITY

Merry Herbert
HALF OF TEACHING IS LEARNING

"You have a screen name?" they query in disbelief. Screen name, IM, blogging, DVD, iPod, podcasts, YouTube, MySpace, HDTV, text messaging, iMac . . . this is the jargon of the *millennials*—my seventh-grade students. Their world is filled with technology; they accept it—and expect it. They use it to communicate, connect, and create. And they use it constantly and confidently.

Yes, I tell them. I have a screen name . . . It's mrsheebz. I blog, instant message (IM), Google, make podcasts, publish on-line books, and text-message. I visit MySpace, Facebook, and YouTube. I use Garageband, Comic Life, iPhoto, iTunes, Frontpage, iMovie, Keynote, and Noteshare. I love the world of technology. Of course, my students think I'm kidding when I tell them I grew up with a rotary phone . . . and a black-and-white TV with three stations of snow. No microwave, no World Wide Web, no cell phones . . . and certainly no computers. But my family did own a typewriter and a complete set of World Book Encyclopedias. I had all the tools necessary to give me an edge in school—then.

Fast-forward 40 years. The 12-year-olds I teach still have the encyclopedia as a wonderful window to the world. But the typewriter is long gone. Instead they possess iMac G4 laptops with the World Book just one of the many promising programs at their fingertips. It's a powerful tool that gives my kids—and me—an edge on learning.

There is no tool that has changed my teaching practice as much as the laptop. All seventh- and eighth-graders in the state of Maine have 24/7 access to their own wireless laptops. In 2001, the Maine Learning and Teaching Initiative (MLTI) was voted and approved; as a result, 1 percent of Maine's educational funds was spent on one-to-one computing—a laptop for every seventh-grader in the state. The following year, the eighth grade was added, for a total of 35,000 laptops. This was a lofty goal aimed at evening the digital divide by providing the World Wide Web to all students in our largely rural state. This was a true democratic ideal: equal opportunity regardless of economic status. At this time, this initiative was the only program of its kind in the world. . . . Teachers spouted clichés like a potato sprouts eyes: a mixed blessing, throwing money in the wind, a two-edged sword, Christmas in July, can't teach an old dog new tricks. The program was embraced by some teachers, scorned by others. I chose to embrace. To learn. Or at least try to learn. For to teach "is to learn twice" (Joseph Joubert). And that has made all the difference in who I am as a teacher.

Using technology has transformed my curriculum and my teaching style. In particular, one-on-one computing has made the single biggest impact on my 27 years of teaching. My entire belief system has been tested and strengthened not only by the advent, but also by the intrusion of the laptop into my classroom. I'm no longer the expert, the disseminator of all-that-needs-to-be-known.

fleeting instant in great detail. From their storyboard, they each created a computer animation of the action. Frame by frame, the animation in turn sparked their imaginations and helped them create word pictures. "It gives you ideas about what you see," says Quinn. HyperStudio and Kid Pix were among the computer programs they used.

"What the animation does is it assists the children in visualizing the action," explains Mitchell, who teaches language arts enrichment classes. "The animation is a way of them developing the picture so they relate that to the writing, to what they hear, what they see, what they feel. Technology gives you one more way of teaching something."

In the library, first-graders are following the progress of Miss Junie 2, an endangered sea turtle they adopted (for 85 cents each) from the Caribbean Conservation Corporation (CCC). Miss Junie 2 started her trip in Tortuguero, Costa Rica, and students regularly click onto the CCC site to check her movements as tracked by satellite and then write about her travels and ocean life in journals. Teacher Erin Okata integrated social studies, language arts, science, math, fine arts, and technology into the project as a way to

I'm a learner, growing along with my students and along with my colleagues. We are a true community of explorers compelled by the MLTI motto: "If you know how to do it, teach someone else. If you don't know how, ask someone else." It's an energizing environment in which to learn: it's the environment of the connected generation.

I teach seventh-grade language arts in a coastal town in southern Maine. The majority of my students come from professional families who have the ability to travel widely, vacation often, own lovely homes, and pay for higher education. It's a homogeneous community, with poor and minority students few and far between. Ninety-two percent of the families in my district had access to the Internet at home when the MLTI program began, so the digital divide was never a huge issue for my students. Yet access to computers at school for word processing and research had always been minimal. Prior to the laptop program, I'd been lucky to obtain an hour a week in the computer lab for my students. Laptops have given us a portable writing lab, instant access to research, and assistive technology.

My teaching philosophy is simple. I strive to create a democratic classroom—an energetic community of caring people engaged in learning. The laptop is a tool, a powerful communication device that has increased my ability to enact democratic ideals on a daily basis. Engagement, energy, and caring: these are more important to me than the content I teach.

The laptop technology has given us multiple ways to create, discover, and explore. Around our school, students are using their laptops to create iMovies about global warming and Civil War enactments. They're using software such as Appleworks to create research brochures about issues, Comic Life to design graphic organizers, Keynote to document learning about famous people and places, and Noteshare to collaborate in a classroom discussion board. They are able to visit online museums and talk with Holocaust survivors via videoconferencing. Field trips and service learning are captured with digital cameras and slide shows. Traditional paper-and-pencil tasks have sprung to life with these various programs that appeal in different ways to students and teachers. In our school, many of us have specialized in particular programs, thereby becoming the "expert down the hall." By learning these programs together and from each other, our learning community has become much more democratic, with interdependence on others for assistance in learning.

PERSONAL REFLECTION

1. What does Herbert mean when she says "half of teaching is learning"? Do you agree?
2. Does the use of technology in schools simplify or complicate teachers' lives? Or both? What examples can you give to support your position?

Merry Herbert teaches seventh-grade language arts at a middle school in Maine. The preceding is excerpted from her contribution to the National Network for Educational Renewal's Teacher Case Story Collection. The Collection is "dedicated to providing a public forum for teachers to share their stories." National Center for Educational Renewal © 2008. Retrieved and adapted from http://www.nnerpartnerships.org/stories/index.html#.

help students develop an awareness of ocean life and to meet specific Hawaii state curriculum standards. (George Lucas Educational Foundation, 2004a. © 2004, The George Lucas Educational Foundation. Edutopia.org. All rights reserved.)

Vignette 3

Ninth- and tenth-grade students are participating in the virtual observatory community that is part of the *Astronomy Village: Investigating the Universe*, developed by the National Aeronautics and Space Administration (NASA). The *Astronomy Village* includes extensive multimedia resources and sophisticated exploration tools and requires that teams of three students select one of the following ten investigations, develop a plan, and carry it out:

- "Search for a Supernova"—Using neutrino data to locate a supernova.
- "Looking for a Stellar Nursery"—Viewing Omega nebula using different wavelengths.
- "Variable Stars"—Identifying a Cepheid variable star in another galaxy.
- "Search for Nearby Stars"—Charting the movement of stars' positions as Earth circles the sun.

- "Extragalactic Zoo"—Exploring different galaxies and clusters.
- "Wedges of the Universe"—Viewing depths of space in two wedges of sky.
- "Search for a Wobbler"—Looking for stars that wobble in their motion.
- "Search for Planetary Building Blocks"—Examining the Orion nebula for proplanetary disks.
- "Search for Earth-Crossing Objects"—Looking for asteroids that cross Earth's path.
- "Observatory Site Selection"—Selecting a site for an observatory. (Jonassen, Howland, Moore, & Marra, 2003, pp. 215–216)

Included as part of the *Astronomy Village* are a star life-cycle simulator, orbital simulator, and 3D star simulator. In addition, the student teams can use the program's digitized video clips; images from the Hubble space telescope and other instruments; audio clips of astronomers discussing their work; and book chapters, NASA publications, and articles from astronomy journals and magazines.

Anywhere, Anytime Learning

As mentioned, anywhere, anytime learning is a reality. Increasingly, teachers are blending online and face-to-face instruction. Depending on the purposes of the lesson, the percentage of time spent online and in the face-to-face classroom varies. The following describes a blended learning experience for fifth-graders:

A group of fifth-graders takes a series of field trips to local water sources where they use handheld computers to gather water samples. When they return to the classroom, they upload their results to a database on the school portal, which aggregates their findings. Then they log onto the project Wiki to document their expedition, allow teachers and administrators to assess their work, read what other classes in the district have found, and share the process with parents and appropriate members of the community.

At the local university, the scientist in charge of the pollution project studies the aggregated findings and decides the data shows the source of pollution is not any one factory but runoff from gardens and driveways adjacent to the river. He sends an instant message to the students, teachers, and administrators thanking them. "Gathering this data would have been impossible without your help," he says. "I simply don't have the staff. But I have the evidence I need now to submit a report to the local government so we can stop this pollution from destroying our rivers."

The students are excited to be part of an effort to save the beach and rivers they love; they don't want to stop there. They set up a blog to publicize their findings. This ultimately leads to a news story, increased local awareness of the pollution problem, a response from the local government, and an eventual reduction in runoff and pollution. The students are galvanized by their success. That they learned a great deal about government, scientific study, and ecosystems is evident from their test scores. And school personnel—even across school boundaries—enjoyed collaborating on the project. (Consortium for School Networking, 2008)

The following are among the advantages that teachers and students realize from such blended learning activities:

- **Virtual field trips**—Students and their teachers can go anywhere in or out of this world.
- **Open discussion**—Online discussions allow for reflection, and archived discussions can be evaluated later.

- **Accessibility**—Students can access learning resources, assignments, and assessment activities from any place that has a computer and an Internet connection.
- **Guest lectures**—Experts from a global community can participate in classroom activities.
- **Vast resources**—Almost limitless resources include data banks, publishers' materials, online labs, and virtual worlds.
- **Accommodation of learning styles**—Online activities allow for audio, video, text, graphics, and interactive animation that appeal to a variety of learning styles.
- **Assessment and tracking**—Most online interactions can be archived and reviewed at any time by teachers.

Technology and the Challenge to Schools

Without a doubt, the Internet, the World Wide Web, and related telecommunications technologies can transform teaching and learning. However, one of the education questions for the future is, How committed are teachers, administrators, policymakers, parents and guardians, and the general public to enabling all students to realize the full impact that technology can have on their learning? As the following statement suggests, the future of schools may depend on educators' response to this challenge:

> The doubling of technological power through the 1990s morphed us into a high-speed, high-tech society. As a result, we are all experiencing accelerated change at a pace never before experienced in human history. Most of us involved in education are simply unprepared for this, and consequently, we have not been able to respond to it as quickly as the world outside of education has. We must quickly catch up or face the unenviable prospect of becoming irrelevant. (McCain & Jukes, 2001, pp. 58–59)

Educators must also develop new assessment techniques to evaluate students' learning that occurs through the use of advanced telecommunications like the Internet and the World Wide Web. The number of correct responses on homework, quizzes, and examinations will no longer suffice to measure students' learning.

E-Learning and Virtual Schools

At Hudson High School in Hudson, Massachusetts, ten students are working at computers in a small room marked "VHS Lab." One of the students is working on an assignment for an online media studies course taught by a teacher in Malaysia. Another student is studying technology and multimedia in a course taught by a teacher in Georgia. Their classmates include students from the United States, Asia, Europe, and South America.

Hudson High School is one of a growing number of high schools in the nation that are using **e-learning,** or online education, to supplement the school curriculum. A small school with an enrollment of 880, Hudson has access to 128 courses online, most of which would not be included in the traditional curriculum. E-learning "broadens the curriculum way beyond what we'd normally be able to offer," says the principal (Trotter, 2002). To view a video of students discussing the benefits and challenges of enrollment in a virtual school, go to MyEducationLab.

Hudson High receives its online courses through the Virtual High School (VHS), a consortium of high schools run by VHS Inc., a nonprofit foundation. The Hudson School District cofounded the program in 1995, along with the Concord Consortium, a nonprofit research and development organization, under a five-year grant from the federal government. The VHS has 200 member schools in 28 states and 8 countries. Each member school must contribute a teacher to teach at least one online class of 20 students.

myeducationlab

Go to MyEducationLab, select Chapter 12 and then Activities and Applications to watch the video Virtual School Advantages.

PEARSON
myeducationlab

Go to MyEducationLab, select Chapter 12 and then Activities and Applications to watch the video Online and Face-to-Face Learning.

The VHS was one of the nation's first two online programs for high schools—the other was the e-school run by the Hawaii Department of Education. Since then, **virtual schools,** in which instruction takes place over the Internet rather than in a traditional classroom, have become increasingly prevalent across the United States. Figure 12.1 shows that more than half of the states had state-established virtual schools or at least one cyber–charter school by 2005. To view a video of the Odyssey Virtual School, a hybrid online school that consists of online learning as well as face-to-face contact with teachers, go to MyEducationLab.

With the spread of virtual schools and courses, some educators, policymakers, and researchers have expressed concern about exaggerated claims for online learning. In addition, they are worried about what is lost when students do not meet face to face with their classmates and teachers. Alan Warhaftig, a Los Angeles high school English teacher who earned certification from the National Board for Professional Teaching Standards (NBPTS), said there is an "overall weakness to that notion that online schools can replace the school environment." He doubts that online classrooms can provide the "looking-in-the-eyes" factor that teachers use to monitor students' understanding of a lesson or how they might be feeling (Trotter, 2002). Similarly, the 2005 Phi Delta Kappan/Gallup Poll (Rose & Gallup, 2005, p. 53) revealed that public school parents disapprove, by 64 percent to 34 percent, of requiring every high school student to take at least one online course while in high school.

The trend toward e-learning and virtual schools no doubt will continue. Meanwhile, several questions need to be addressed to ensure that virtual students have high-quality online learning experiences:

- While online learning may be appropriate for high school students, should online learning be made available to elementary and middle school students?

State has established a virtual school (16)

State has at least one cyber charter school (10)

State has a virtual school and at least one cyber charter school (6)

State has neither (19)

FIGURE 12.1 Cyberschools in the United States

Source: Education Week Research Center, "Technology Counts 2005: Technology Transfer: Moving Technology Dollars in New Directions," Education Week, May 5, 2005, p. 22. Used with permission.

- Should online courses be aligned with state academic standards?
- Who should provide for students' technological needs while they take an online course?
- Are online teachers trained effectively to teach via the Internet?
- Should parent approval be required before a child enrolls in an online course?
- Should students receive the same credit for an online course as they would for an interactive, face-to-face class?
- How can school officials ensure the quality of online courses, especially those offered by teachers in other states or countries?

WHAT TECHNOLOGIES CAN BE INTEGRATED INTO TEACHING?

Today's teachers can integrate a dazzling array of technologies into their teaching. Until the 1970s, the technology available to teachers who wished to use more than the chalkboard was limited to an overhead projector; a 16-mm movie projector; a tape recorder; and, in a few forward-looking school districts, a television set. Today, "new interactive, multimedia, hyperlinked, networked technologies offer myriad possibilities . . . beyond what is possible with traditional materials such as books, paper, and chalkboards" (Wiske, Rennebohm Franz, & Breit, 2005, p. 20). The following sections examine several of the exciting ways that teachers are integrating technology into their teaching.

Online Social Networking

Online social networking refers to an online community of people who share common interests. Participants in **online social networking** can interact in a variety of ways; chat, e-mail, blogging, voice chat, and discussion groups are among the ways group members communicate.

Social networks allow a user to create a profile of himself or herself using text, audio, graphics, video, and pictures; then other individuals or groups can access the profile. As a user's circle of "friends" grows, so does a sense of community. Most social networks have security features that permit users to choose who can view their profile or contact them. Several social networking services are available to teachers and students. The social networking services discussed in the following are but a small sample of those available on the Internet.

FaceBook and MySpace

According to the **FaceBook** website, "FaceBook is a tool that allows individuals or groups to connect with friends, coworkers, classmates, and neighbors. FaceBook allows you to keep up with friends, upload photos, share links and videos, and learn more about the people they meet." Similarly, the **MySpace** website states, "MySpace in an online community that lets you meet your friends' friends. Create a community on MySpace and you can share

Whether in special classes or extracurricular programs, students in today's schools receive a great deal of hands-on involvement with technology. How does this prepare them for post-graduate life?

photos, journals and interests with your growing network of mutual friends!" Teachers have successfully used FaceBook and MySpace to facilitate small-group projects, highlight exemplary work, build a sense of community outside the classroom, and showcase student creative expressions.

As a teacher-user of FaceBook or MySpace, remember that you are in the public eye at all times. Occasionally, there are media reports about teachers being fired or disciplined because of "inappropriate" profiles on FaceBook or MySpace—for example, teachers posting personal opinions about students, uploaded pictures of teachers engaged in activities deemed inappropriate, and inappropriate communication between teachers and students.

YouTube

Another website that today's students visit regularly is YouTube. **YouTube** is an online video clearinghouse where students can watch, upload, and share online videos. Videos range from footage captured with a cell phone to high-end film productions. Users can establish profiles and share favorite videos with their friends. In addition to being a site for watching videos, YouTube is a form of online social networking because it can build a sense of community for users. Teachers are using YouTube in a variety of ways: to access international news coverage, political debates, and diverse opinions, and to enhance classroom lessons with stimulating content.

Blogs

A **blog** (short for *web log*) is an online journal constructed by an individual and reacted to by those who visit the blog. A blog usually consists of text, but it can include pictures, links to other websites, and media sources that support the author's views on various topics. Blogging can be interactive because the visitor can offer opinions about the author's statements. Figure 12.2 presents a blog created by a student for his high school English class.

Classroom Example *Mr. Sanchez uses a professional blog to recap the day's events in his seventh-grade classroom. He encourages students and their parents or guardians to join the conversation about activities in his classroom. He finds that blogging is a good way to connect with parents or guardians and to get them involved in their children's education.*

Wikis

A **wiki** is a website created, edited, and maintained by groups of people. A wiki website grows based on user creation and is validated by user reviews. Coming out of the

---

Jonah Trople's Overview of Senior English

Literature Discussion
Jonah's BLOG

Literary Essays

Comparative
Overviews

Character Analysis

Supporting Links

Home

I am a senior at River's Edge High School. This site provides an overview of my thoughts and learning on the works that I have read and discussed as part of Mr. Hegedus's Senior English class.

It is currently a work in progress. I will be updating links and adding information until June. Visit my BLOG to review my thoughts on the current novels.

Works Include:

Moby Dick, Jane Eyre, Tortilla Curtain, Grapes of Wrath, Hamlet, Paradise Lost

FIGURE 12.2 Sample individual student Web project

Source: Timothy D. Green, Abbie Brown, and LeAnne Robinson. Making the Most of the Web in Your Classroom: A Teacher's Guide to Blogs, Podcasts, Wikis, Pages, and Sites. Thousand Oaks, CA: Corwin Press, 2008, p. 12.

social networking movement, wikis follow the logic that many voices are better than one and allow collaborative work by various authors. A wiki website allows anyone or designated members of a group to create, delete, and/or edit the content on the website.

Classroom Example *Mrs. Rioas uses a wiki as a build-your-own-story writing assignment. She divides students into groups of five and then asks them to write a shared story on a classroom wiki space. The students have to come up with the topic, develop the story line, create and edit the work—all in their wiki space. As students work on the wiki, Mrs. Rioas examines different iterations of the story, checks progress, provides feedback, and shares the stories with parents and colleagues.*

3D Virtual Reality Worlds

Three-dimensional (3D) virtual reality worlds are a dynamic part of online social networking; **3D virtual reality worlds** can be a powerful learning tool for active, engaged learning with visually rich, hands-on experiences; trial-and-error activities; and virtual participation in events. For example, a teacher might assume the identity of a personal avatar (an online visual image) and take students on a virtual field trip to a museum, an active volcano, a chemistry lab, a spaceship, or other planets and galaxies. Participants are free to navigate, communicate, access resources, and in some cases manipulate the environment as they choose. Dozens of virtual reality worlds are available on the Internet. Among educators, one of the most popular virtual worlds is Second Life (http://www.secondlife.com).

Classroom Example *Ms. Wang, a history teacher, uses Second Life to help students understand past events and apply their understanding to life today. For example, when studying ancient Greece, she locates an "island" at the Second Life site that resembles ancient Athens. Then she develops roles that students can assume and a problem that confronts them—perhaps conflict with Sparta. Students then clothe their avatars according to their roles and then behave as people actually did in ancient Greek society. Ms. Wang, of course, assumes the role of Zeus and guides the action in the Second Life virtual world.*

Podcasts

A **podcast** is a digital media file delivered over the Internet. These files can be played on a computer or mobile device such as an MP3 player or cell phone. A podcast allows for a syndication feed, which delivers digital files to the user automatically once new content is loaded to the site. A podcast can be compared to online radio delivered on the Web, with the recipient able to decide what he or she will hear and when.

Classroom Example *Mr. Pendergrass uses podcasting in his AP chemistry class. He clips on a small wireless microphone at the beginning of the class period. The microphone is connected to his computer, which is set up to record audio. As he presents content and responds to students' questions, these interactions are recorded in an electronic file. When the session is finished, Mr. Pendergrass opens the audio file, looks for long periods of silence, and edits those out. He then publishes the file to his podcasting site. Students can then download and listen to material he has presented over a week, month, or year.*

E-Portfolios

An e-portfolio can serve many different functions; however, it is best known as an assessment tool. An **e-portfolio** allows students to place work they have completed, or resources they have gathered, in a Web-based portfolio. E-portfolios allow teachers and students to track growth and understanding.

Classroom Example *Susanna is a high school senior. She began using an e-portfolio during her freshman year. Originally, she saw the e-portfolio as a place where she could store her electronic artwork. As she began to publish her work in her portfolio space, however, she expanded the content to include all of her creative academic work. Susanna credits her e-portfolio for the scholarship she received to a prestigious university. In her e-portfolio, Susanna included her senior project, a photo-log of her service-learning activities for the victims of Hurricane Katrina. She included a story* *she had been working on since her freshman year. She included audio files of music she created and graphics of her artwork. Most impressive, though, are her personal reflections describing her philosophy of life and her professional goals for the future. As she says, "If you want to know who I am, what I can do, and where I can go, look at my e-portfolio."*

Digital Resources for Teaching and Learning

The digital resources available on the Web for teaching and learning are almost endless. Truly, the Web is like a giant candy store for teachers. So much is available, it can be hard to decide which resources to use. Knowing where to look for quality materials is as important as the materials themselves. Before entering this candy store, it is helpful to know about learning objects and open-source materials.

Learning Objects

Learning objects are digital resources that can be reused to support learning. Learning objects are small digital resources that:

- **Are self-contained**—Each learning object can be used independently.
- **Are reusable**—A single learning object may be used in multiple contexts for multiple purposes.
- **Can be aggregated**—Learning objects can be grouped into larger collections of content, including traditional course structures.
- **Are tagged with metadata**—Every learning object has descriptive information, allowing it to be found easily by a search (Beck, 2008).

The idea behind learning objects is simple. Large chunks of information are broken down into smaller bits of information. For example, a lesson on the Civil War might have smaller pieces consisting of a video on railroads in operation during the Civil War, an animated map of the Battle of Gettysburg, or ideas for activities related to Civil War era clothing. These objects are then made available to teachers. Teachers may use the objects sequenced in a manner that fits their instructional objectives.

Several online resources are devoted to creating and storing learning objects. Some are discipline-specific, such as the National Science Digital Library funded by the National Science Foundation. Others are very broad, such as PBS Teachers, which is described in the following excerpt from the PBS site:

> PBS Teachers is PBS' national web destination for high-quality preK–12 educational resources. Here you'll find classroom materials suitable for a wide range of subjects and grade levels. We provide thousands of lesson plans, teaching activities, on-demand video assets, and interactive games and simulations. These resources are correlated to state and national educational standards and are tied to PBS' award-winning on-air and online programming like *NOVA, Nature, Cyberchase, Between the Lions* and more. (PBS Teachers, 2008).

Classroom Example *Mr. Denta has been a substitute teacher at three local high schools during the past year. He is making quite a name for himself as a teacher prepared to teach any subject. Recently, the biology teacher at one of the high schools came down with the flu. The school district called Mr. Denta at 5:00 P.M. and asked him to sub for the teacher. Mr. Denta learned that the teacher was teaching about DNA.*

To prepare a lesson on DNA, Mr. Denta went to the site for MERLOT (Multimedia Educational Resource for Learning and Online Teaching), as he had done several times during the last few years. At merlot.org, he entered "DNA" in the search box. He located an excellent lesson on teaching DNA to high school students. The lesson included animations illustrating the formation of DNA and drag-and-drop animated DNA assessments.

Open Source

The open-source initiative grew out of the freeware or shareware approach to disseminating software and creating communities of users during the 1990s. **Open-source materials** are developed by a community of programmers and are distributed for free on the Internet. Users of the materials can, in turn, modify the materials and redistribute them. Although open source is usually associated with software development, the open-source movement is spreading to other areas of education as well, such as the open courseware initiative. The MIT OpenCourseWare project is one such example. MIT has made all of its 1,800 courses available for free online. Teachers can examine syllabi, lecture notes, resources, assessments, and teaching materials.

Classroom Example *Mrs. Banari is, by all accounts, obsessed with computers. She wants her high school students to become as passionate about computers as she is. She has offered elective computer science and advanced mathematics courses for several years. Usually, a small core of high-ability students take these courses. After visiting the MIT OpenCourseWare site, she decided to offer one of the MIT courses, Mathematics for Computer Science, as an elective. Students who signed up for the course knew about MIT's highly ranked programs and were eager to test their abilities at this advanced level.*

Digital Resources for Different Subject Areas

As the above classroom examples suggest, the Internet contains a vast amount of free, high-quality learning materials to use in your teaching. The following sections provide a brief sampling of the myriad ways these materials can be used in different subject areas.

The Fine Arts

The fine arts—art, music, theater, and dance—offer numerous opportunities to integrate technology into the fine arts classroom. Teachers have used technology in the fine arts classroom to provide students with opportunities to:

- View famous pieces of art in museums around the world.
- Create and share compilations of art, music, theater, and dance.
- View legendary performances by various fine artists.
- Experience diverse cultural styles of the fine arts.
- Express themselves artistically.
- Share ideas and thoughts about the fine arts with others.

Classroom Example *In smaller school districts, the opportunity to perform with other musicians can be limited. Technology, however, can be used to overcome the isolation of the artist. For example, Musigy makes it possible for people to perform live music together over the Internet. A performer at one location plugs a guitar, keyboard, microphone, or any other electronic instrument into a computer and connects with other musicians interested in jamming. Teachers have set up global jazz bands, string quartets, and rock-and-roll bands with partner schools around the world. In addition to the audio connection, Musigy includes a video connection that allows performers to view others who are performing at the same time.*

Language Arts

Language arts—reading, writing, oral communication—offer many opportunities for teachers to integrate technology. Language arts teachers have used technology in the classroom to:

- Access great works of literature from special or rare book collections.
- Show students videos of famous speeches.
- Improve student writing by using online writing labs.

These students are more engaged, motivated, and are acquiring twenty-first-century technology skills by using computers at school.

- Combat plagiarism by using online plagiarism detection programs.
- Access hard-to-find journals.
- Improve students' word recognition and pronunciation by using animation and audio.
- Increase students' reading comprehension by using audio textbooks or e-books.

To view a video of a teacher using gaming presentation software during a lesson on *Hamlet*, go to MyEducation Lab. The Teachers' Voices: Walk in My Shoes feature for this chapter describes how a ninth- and tenth-grade English teacher integrates technology into his teaching and promotes the development of his students' technology skills.

Classroom Example Good Readers, *a movie produced by April Payne's first-grade class at Highland Ranch Elementary School in San Diego, is a powerful example of technology integration in the language arts classroom. According to the website containing a link to the movie: "These amazing first graders created this movie to teach everyone what great readers do. Students were broken into teams that each had a cinematographer, a director, and a spokesperson. Each student had an opportunity to try each role. As the week progressed, they all wrote scripts highlighting six strategies of great readers. Next they memorized their lines, practiced speaking loudly and clearly, filmed scenes, and then edited the footage with Pinnacle Studio DV 8. The following week, they were ready to view the finished product! Not only are these students great readers, they are also great filmmakers. Since creating this movie, Mrs. Payne has noticed the students are far more aware of the strategies good readers use and apply them readily as they read new materials. Making this movie helped students "see" the strategies through a new visual filter. Evidently it was just what they needed to help the strategies stick. (Poway Unified School District, 2008)*

myeducationlab

Go to MyEducationLab, select Chapter 12 and then Activities and Applications to watch the video Presentation Software in Literature.

Mathematics

Technology has been a part of mathematics for centuries—from the abacus to the super computer. Mathematicians have long relied on technology to help solve complex problems. Similarly, mathematics teachers have integrated technology into their teaching to:

- Help students understand numerical relationships.
- Do math calculations such as addition, subtraction, multiplication, and division; find the square root; and solve trigonometry functions and linear equations.
- Help students estimate and measure.
- Help students deal with the symbolic manipulations needed in algebra and calculus.
- Reduce student anxiety about memorizing complex formulas in geometry and trigonometry.
- Help students understand more complex mathematical concepts and ideas.
- Allow for the application of mathematical solutions to real-world problems.

Classroom Example *Ms. Stone teaches third grade at the local elementary school. She uses mathematical computer games to reinforce basic mathematical concepts and*

TEACHERS' VOICES

Walk in My Shoes

Brad Kamradt adventured to Flagstaff, Arizona, for his first teaching position and a change from city life. Although studying and working in Chicago and Los Angeles had served him well, he was ready for a smaller place and the more manageable lifestyle of Flagstaff. Without knowing anyone in the area, Brad's first year of teaching was eased by the support of an assigned mentor, an informal mentor, and another first-year teacher who had also just moved to Flagstaff. All three helped Brad with resources, practical advice, and tips on navigating the school environment. The other new teacher and Brad peer-mentored each other at a more psychological and emotional level. "Without all of them it would have been an even greater struggle to get through last year," Brad reflected on the eve of his second year.

Brad's studies in Chicago at Northwestern University, DePaul University, and the University of Illinois prepared him well for the curricular and pedagogical aspects of teaching English, writing, and communication at the high school level. The University of Illinois, where he did his credential studies, emphasized multicultural and urban education. A series of practica in Chicago's inner-city schools and a semester of teaching in a suburban private Catholic school varied and enriched Brad's classroom experiences. All helped him when he was assigned to teach at Flagstaff's Coconino High School, a culturally diverse Title I school with a significant number of students on free or reduced lunch and many students who were not academically oriented toward college.

As a ninth- and tenth-grade English teacher, Brad was surprised by the relative lack of scope and sequence overview for the English curriculum. Each of the district's English teachers basically followed his or her own curriculum with little or no coordination with colleagues. Brad found that he needed to invent his courses as he went along. The disconnect from school to school concerned Brad enough to pull him into a leadership position. The district was beginning to do curriculum mapping, moving toward a standards-based and uniform curriculum across the schools, and Brad stepped in to help with it. He

"New teachers need to be advocates for themselves and their students."

facilitated a series of professional development days for all of the English teachers in the city's three high schools. "I won some converts from a group of resistant veteran teachers," he concludes, "and I would like to continue that work this year."

"New teachers need to be advocates for themselves and their students," Brad advises. Often they are given the "table scraps" in terms of furniture, books, and materials to support the curriculum. Unless they speak up as professionals and inform their department chairs and principals of their needs, nothing will happen. Brad is pleased with his own advocacy efforts and the resulting films, books, and other resources he now has to strengthen his teaching in his second year.

Brad values technology and is concerned about a deficiency he sees in his students' computer literacy skills: "If they want to compete in today's world, they need to be more advanced in their technology skills. To me, technology is vital; it has changed the way we communicate. English is about communication, and students need to understand how technology informs the way the world communicates." Brad's skills in this area are especially high because he worked in the multimedia world, creating corporate websites and CD-ROMS, before deciding to become a teacher. In his first year of teaching, he promoted technology by requiring his students to submit word-processed papers and getting them to the computer labs as often as possible. In his second year, he plans to incorporate students' development of web pages into the semester.

Brad's advice for first-year teachers is to be themselves and let their students be themselves as well. He has developed good relationships with really tough students and attributes his success to his being honest and real with them. "Students know when you are faking. If you want them to be real, then you need to be real. The more they see you as a real person, the more they are willing to work for and with you."

Brad Kamradt
Coconino High School

to introduce more advanced concepts. Games like "Timez Attack" allow students to navigate a subterranean dungeon, try to avoid scary beasts, and navigate out of tight spots, all by solving multiplication problems.

Science

Science teachers from the elementary through high school levels have made extensive use of technology in the classroom. Technology integration has enabled them to:

- Tour the solar system with students.
- Become miniaturized and travel throughout the human body.
- Visit the ocean floor.
- Experience an earthquake.

Classroom Example *Students at a rural high school use Second Life to study the human brain in biology class. Students and their teacher will have a virtual meeting with a neurosurgeon from a large urban hospital at a virtual model of the human brain located on a public island in Second Life. At a prearranged time, they meet at the brain stem. After a brief lecture by the doctor and a short question-and-answer session, the doctor leads them to the cerebrum, where she discusses the basic functions of the lobes. Students are able to manipulate the lobes and observe how the lobes react. From the cerebrum, they will visit the cerebellum for a similar experience.*

Social Studies

Social studies teachers have used technology to explore economics, geography, political science, psychology, and sociology. For example, social studies teachers have used technology to:

- Allow students to be floor traders on the Wall Street stock market.
- Enable students to become a leader of state and understand how their political decisions affect the countries they lead.
- Cope with the poverty, hunger, and political corruption that characterize the lives of people in many Third World countries.
- Help students experience how crime and violence affect the lives of victims.

To view a video that shows a world history teacher using a tablet PC and electronic pen to explain the migration of the Athenians, go to MyEducationLab.

Classroom Example *Mrs. Muralia's students have been studying the Israeli-Palestinian conflict for the past week. They have read the textbook, watched a video, listened to historical speeches online, researched articles and current events, and discussed the situation in class. However, it was not until students experienced a videogame that allowed them to role-play various characters in this historical conflict that they understood how complex and difficult the situation is. In the videogame, students assumed roles of the Israeli prime minister, local Palestinian political leaders, Israeli settlers, Palestinians working in Gaza, or Israeli soldiers. Each student's role called for an action followed by a reaction, followed by another action, and so on. Allowing students to navigate through this complex political landscape in various roles enabled them to begin to think critically and to understand the various points of view that make up the Israeli-Palestinian situation.*

PEARSON
myeducationlab

Go to MyEducationLab, select Chapter 12 and then Activities and Applications to watch the video Tablet Computers in World History.

TO WHAT DEGREE ARE TEACHERS INTEGRATING TECHNOLOGY INTO THEIR TEACHING?

As the preceding sections illustrate, a dazzling array of digital technologies is available for teachers to integrate into their teaching. However, to what degree are teachers actually using new technologies? As Figure 12.3 shows, the percentage of

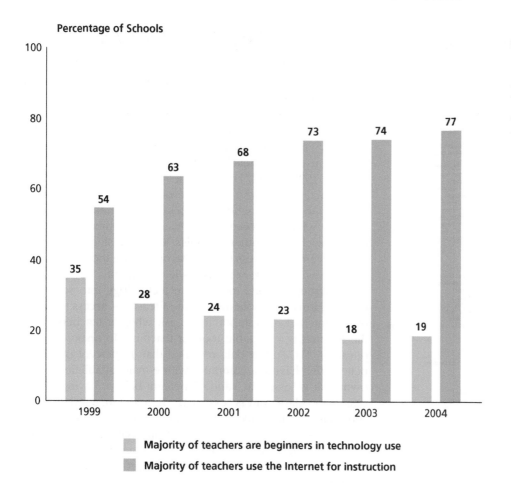

Percentage of Schools

FIGURE 12.3 Teacher technology use

Source: Data from Market Data Retrieval, Technology in Education 2001 *and* Technology in Education 2004. *As first appeared in* Education Week, Technology Counts 2005, *May 5, 2005. Used with permission.*

■ **Majority of teachers are beginners in technology use**

■ **Majority of teachers use the Internet for instruction**

schools reporting that a majority of their teachers use the Internet for instruction increased from 54 percent in 1999 to 77 percent in 2004. However, at schools that did not make AYP under the NCLB, the percentage of teachers who used the Internet during 2004 was only 69 percent (*Education Week*, 2005).

To determine how teachers use computers and how useful they find them, the U.S. Department of Education sponsored the Teaching, Learning, and Computing (TLC) survey, which gathered data from (1) 2,250 fourth- through twelfth-grade teachers at public and private schools, (2) 1,800 teachers at high-end technology schools and schools participating in educational reform programs, and (3) 1,700 principals and school-level technology coordinators (Anderson & Ronnkvist, 1999; Becker, 1999, 2001; Ravitz, Wong, & Becker, 1999).

Preparing Lessons

The Internet has been termed "the world's largest library" and, as such, it can be a remarkable resource for planning lessons. According to the TLC survey, 28 percent of teachers use the Internet weekly or more often to gather information and resources on the Internet for their teaching, and 40 percent do so occasionally. Among teachers who have access to the Internet at school as well as at home, 46 percent report weekly or more frequent use. In Washington state's Kent School District, for instance, teachers learn to use the district's Staff Toolbox website (see Figure 12.4), where they share lesson plans and gather information on students' progress in other classes. Kent teachers also use the Toolbox to complete previously onerous paperwork online and to sign up for in-service training.

Staff Toolbox

Communication Tools

- Outlook Web Access Check your e-mail and calendar online
  - Outlook Web Access Tutorial
- Groupwise is no longer available

Information Sources

- Staff Directory - phone, building, and e-mail search form
- Calendar - district and school activities
- EduPortal - district policies and procedures plus state and federal resources [password required - call Customer Support Center at x7030]
- Employee Newsletter - staff news and information
- Community Connections - newsletter, events, and cultural information
- Human Resources - applications, benefits, and human resources information
- Risk Management - workers' comp and safety program
- School Web Pages - view school maps, information and Web pages
- Staff Web Pages - directory of staff members' Web sites
- Technology - district technology resources and information
- Athletics and Activities - sports schedules and information
- Kent School District Library - search for school or district materials
- King County Library - catalog and other information online
- News Sources - ProQuest & other magazines, newspapers, radio & television
- Room to Learn - Moving Forward - Follow the progress on KSD's secondary school reconfiguration

Interactive Tools

- Staff Development - sign up online for classes, view transcripts and more
- Student Information - Star Gazer, online IEPs, attendance and grading
- Lunch Menu - order a sub sandwich or view the menu
- Mileage Manager - track your KSD mileage and print out a report
- InformAGENT - sign up for automatic e-mail from KSD sources
- Medicaid Administrative Match - Forms and assistance for Medicaid Match
- Warehouse Support Services Order Form - order tables, chairs, equipment, supplies, basically anything that needs to be moved from one location to another
- Debit Card - Review your Debit Card transactions

Classroom Tools

- Curriculum Resources - lesson plans and resources for teachers

District References

- Kent School District Policies - school board policies
- Kent School District Student Learning Objectives (SLOs)
- Copyright Information - copyright guidelines for educators

State and Community Resources

- Washington State Essential Learnings (EALRs)
- Office of the Superintendent of Public Instruction - OSPI in Olympia
- Emergency Information - school closure information
- Qwest Dex Directory

Site Search: [   ] [Go]

Advanced Search   Search Tips

FIGURE 12.4 Staff Toolbox, Kent School District

Source: Kent School District, Kent, Washington. Copyright © 1995–2005 by the Kent School District. Used with permission.

Communicating With Other Educators

Compared to their use of the Internet to prepare lessons and gather resources, teachers use the Internet less often to communicate with other educators, according to the TLC survey. Only 16 percent of teachers used e-mail to communicate with teachers in other schools, and 23 percent did so occasionally. However, "by far the most important variable in predicting teachers' Internet use is the teacher's level of classroom connectivity" (Becker, 1999, p. 29). For example, a comparison of e-mail use between teachers who had Internet access at home and at school with teachers who had access only at home revealed that teachers with classroom access were three times as likely to e-mail teachers at other schools. Not surprisingly, if teachers don't have ready access to the Internet during their daily professional lives, their use of e-mail is less frequent.

Although efforts to integrate technology into schools require information about the extent of teachers' access to and use of the Internet, it is important to ask whether teachers believe the Internet is a valuable tool for teaching. In response to this question, TLC survey data revealed that 49 percent of teachers believe that having a computer with e-mail capabilities on their own desk is "essential," and 47 percent believe having Web access in the classroom is "essential." In addition, another 38 percent believe e-mail access is "valuable," and 41 percent believe Web access is "valuable." These results echo comments made by a sixth-grade teacher who encourages teachers to make technology part of their daily lives: "As professionals, we (educators) . . . need to embrace the new technology. I am ready!" (Egbert, 2009, p. 17).

Posting Information and Student Work on the Web

In addition to using e-mail to communicate with other educators, 18 percent of teachers posted information, professional opinions, or student work at least once on the Web. For instance, as with the use of e-mail, the likelihood of teachers posting information, opinions, or student work was strongly related to connectivity in the classroom. As classroom access to the Internet continues to increase, teachers' use of the Internet to communicate with other educators and to post material will also increase.

Many school districts have taken steps to increase teacher professional communications via the Internet. As part of a "Reinventing Education" grant program, teachers in the San Jose Unified School District keep journals of their progress at integrating technology into instruction, and they share these with other teachers online. To ensure that teachers use their training in technology, the principal of Philadelphia's Hill-Freedman Middle School accepts lesson plans only by e-mail and posts daily announcements exclusively on the Internet.

Facilitating Students' Learning via Computers and Cyberspace

In previous sections of this chapter, we have seen several examples of how teachers are integrating technology into their teaching. Based on TLC survey data, Figure 12.5 documents the extent of this usage among teachers whose students typically use a computer more than 20 times during a school year. After word processing, the use of a Web

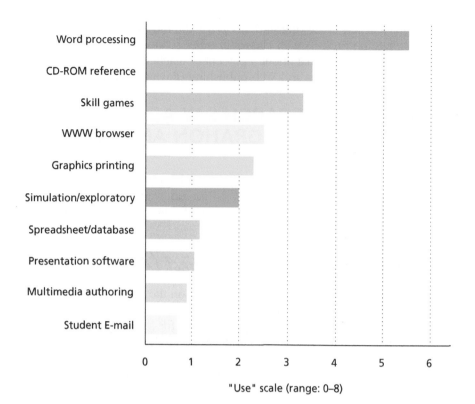

FIGURE 12.5 Software use by teachers who use computers frequently
Source: Adapted from Henry Jay Becker, How Are Teachers Using Computers in Education? Paper presented at the Annual Meeting of the American Educational Research Association, Seattle, April 2001, pp. 4, 12.

*Use is defined as teachers reporting that a typical student in one of their classes used computers more than 20 times during the school year. Percentage of teachers (by subject taught) who report "frequent computer use": computer, 80%; business, 70%; elementary self-contained, 43%; vocational, 42%; English, 24%; science, 17%; social studies, 12%; math, 11%; fine arts, 9%.

search engine is the most common teacher-directed use of computers by students. For example, many teachers have their students conduct **webquests**—online inquiry research projects that consist of five parts:

1. An introduction to spark students' interest in the quest
2. A task description explaining the purpose and outcomes of the quest
3. Steps to follow during the quest and resources to be used
4. Evaluation consisting of rubrics and assessment guidelines
5. Conclusion to provide closure

To view videos of two teachers giving students directions for using the Internet to gather information from various websites, go to MyEducationLab.

As with teachers' use of the Internet, student use is directly related to classroom connectivity; among teachers with Internet connectivity in the classroom, almost half had students use Web search engines on at least three occasions. Teachers whose classrooms had direct high-speed connections instead of much slower modem connections were 25 percent more likely to have students search the Web ten or more times. In the following, a science teacher comments on the benefits of having students search for information on the Internet:

> I think [the Internet] provides more opportunities for the kids than relying primarily on a textbook. I think that the Web allows them to go out and see things that the book just can't show them. If they want they can go out and see excellent schematics of the human cell. They can go out and see excellent photographs of cells. They can spend all day looking underneath a microscope and never see a cell as nice as they can find on line because they put the best ones out there. (Wallace, 2004, p. 462)

PEARSON myeducationlab

Go to MyEducationLab, select Chapter 12 and then Activities and Applications to watch the videos Model Inquiry Unit—Part 1 and Model Inquiry Unit—Part 2.

Increasingly, teachers are asking students to use the Internet to communicate with others, to collaborate on projects with classes at other schools, and to publish on the Web. The TLC survey revealed that about 5 percent of teachers have students involved in beyond-the-classroom projects and Web publishing (Ravitz et al., 1999).

WHAT DOES RESEARCH SAY ABOUT TECHNOLOGY INTEGRATION AND STUDENT LEARNING?

The integration of technology into teaching and learning has grown enormously since the early 1990s. Now, teachers and other educators want to know if technology integration enhances student learning. Regarding the effects of technology on learning, research results are just now beginning to appear.

Apple Classrooms of Tomorrow Project (ACOT)

One of the most informative research studies is based on the Apple Classrooms of Tomorrow (ACOT) project launched in seven K–12 classrooms in 1986. Participating students and teachers each received two computers—one for school and one for home. Eight years later, study results indicated that all ACOT students performed as well as they were expected to without computers, and some performed better. More important, perhaps, "the ACOT students routinely and without prompting employed inquiry, collaboration, and technological and problem-solving skills" (Mehlinger, 1996, p. 405). Also, 90 percent of ACOT students went on to college after graduating from high school, while only 15 percent of non-ACOT students did. Furthermore, the behavior of ACOT teachers also changed—they worked "more as mentors and less as presenters of information" (Mehlinger, 1996, p. 404).

An additional positive finding of the ACOT study was how teachers gradually began to use the computers in new ways in the classroom. "When [ACOT] teachers were able to move past that pervasive teacher-centered view of education, students and teachers, as communities of learners, were able to benefit from the range of individual areas of expertise represented by the entire group" (Bitter & Pierson, 2005, p. 95). Teachers rearranged their classrooms to enable students to work collaboratively on projects, and they frequently made arrangements for students who wished to stay after school to work on multimedia projects. Frequently, "students and teachers collaborated together, with the students often in the role of expert or resource person" (Schwartz & Beichner, 1999, pp. 33–34).

Integrating Technology

Teacher participants in the ACOT study were volunteers, many of whom had little experience with educational technology. As with teachers learning any new instructional strategy, the ACOT teachers frequently struggled to adjust to their new computer-filled rooms. Researchers found that the teachers progressed through five distinct stages as they integrated the technology into their teaching (Sandholtz, Ringstaff, & Dwyer, 1997):

1. **Entry stage**—For many teachers, this was a period of painful growth and discomfort; learning to use computers presented challenges similar to those faced by beginning teachers.
2. **Adoption stage**—Becoming more proactive toward the challenge of integrating computers, teachers began to teach students how to use the computers and software.
3. **Adaptation stage**—Teachers turned from teaching the technology to using the technology as a tool to teach content.
4. **Appropriation stage**—Teachers moved from merely accommodating computers in their daily routines to personally exploring new teaching possibilities afforded by the technology.

5. **Invention stage**—Eager to move beyond teacher-centered instruction, teachers began to collaborate with peers in developing authentic, inquiry-oriented learning activities.

As informative as the ACOT study has been, it is important to remember that it was funded by a computer manufacturer; thus, the outcomes might have been influenced by commercial bias and/or the expectation that computers could not have had anything other than a significant positive influence on teaching and learning. In fact, Schwartz and Beichner (1999, p. 34) suggest that the ACOT project "epitomizes what might be termed the 'Emperor's New Clothes' perspective on technology in education. [To] take the ACOT reports at face value would be to accept the notion that technology is the panacea that education has been searching for for ages."

Findings From Other Research Studies

A powerful way to determine whether certain educational practices actually influence students' learning is to conduct meta-analyses, that is, to "take the findings from single studies and calculate a way to compare them with each other. The goal is to synthesize the findings statistically and determine what the studies reveal when examined all together" (Kirkpatrick & Cuban, 1998). One such meta-analysis reviewed the results of 133 research studies on educational technology from 1990 through 1994. The results of that study follow:

- Educational technology has a significant positive impact on achievement in all subject areas, across all levels of school, and in regular classrooms as well as those for special-needs students.
- Educational technology has positive effects on student attitudes.
- The degree of effectiveness is influenced by the student population, the instructional design, the teacher's role, how students are grouped, and the levels of student access to technology.
- Technology makes instruction more student-centered, encourages cooperative learning, and stimulates increased teacher–student interaction.
- Positive changes in the learning environment evolve over time and do not occur quickly (Mehlinger, 1996, p. 405).

Another meta-analysis conducted by Heather Kirkpatrick and Larry Cuban (1998) at Stanford University also addressed the complications and difficulties involved in determining the effects of computers on learning, particularly when much of the research in that area is methodologically flawed. Research studies, they pointed out, "are of little use unless they elaborate the children's ages, the subject, the software used, the kinds of outcomes that were sought, and how the study was done." With these limitations in mind, the following is a brief summary of Kirkpatrick and Cuban's findings:

- Seven of the single studies of elementary and secondary students yielded positive findings related to achievement and attitude change, while seven studies yielded negative or mixed findings.
- Ten of the single studies on the effectiveness of computers to teach in core areas such as mathematics, reading, science, and social studies yielded results ranging from very positive to "cautiously negative."
- Ten meta-analyses found higher levels of student achievement in computer-using classrooms.
- Five meta-analyses found that student attitudes improved and students learned more in less time in computer-using classrooms.

On the basis of their meta-analysis of the research, much of it considered methodologically flawed due to a lack of scientific controls, Kirkpatrick and Cuban conclude that "we are unable to ascertain whether computers in classrooms have in fact been or will be the boon they have promised to be" (1998, p. 31).

The ambiguities of research on computer-based instruction aside, it is clear that educational technology can have positive effects on learning and teaching, and indications are that technology will influence all aspects of education even more as we enter the second decade of the twenty-first century. Thus, the question to be asked about the effectiveness of educational technology is not, Is it effective? Instead, the question should be, How and under what circumstances does educational technology enhance students' learning? As more funds are made available to purchase hardware and software, train teachers, and provide technical support, the benefits of educational technology will become even more widespread.

WHAT ARE THE CHALLENGES OF INTEGRATING TECHNOLOGY INTO TEACHING?

There continue to be challenges related to integrating technology into teaching. Failure to meet these challenges will shortchange students and prevent them from participating fully in the digital age. Four of the most significant challenges are Internet access for all schools, funding for technology and technical support, access to technology for all students, and training in technology for teachers.

Broadband Internet Access for All Schools

Internet access is a vital part of a school's capacity to benefit from the vast resources found in cyberspace. As we have seen throughout this chapter, the Internet enables teachers and students to draw from the world's best libraries, museums, universities, and cultural resources. In 1995, President Bill Clinton created the National Information Infrastructure (NII) to encourage all schools, libraries, hospitals, and law enforcement agencies to become connected to the "information superhighway." A year later, the Education rate (E-rate) program was established to help schools and libraries connect to the Internet. The E-rate program provides schools with Internet access at discounted rates based on the income levels of students' families and whether their location is urban or rural (rural communities receive up to a 10 percent discount). With increased purchasing power from the E-rate program, schools can purchase improved telephone service and greater bandwidth, thus allowing more data to travel across wires for Internet and e-mail use.

The percentage of the nation's public schools with Internet access has risen dramatically since the mid-1990s. Thirty-five percent of public schools had access to the Internet in 1994; by 2005, there was "virtually no difference in access between poor schools and their wealthier counterparts" (*Education Week,* 2005, p. 40).

Before the E-rate program, the richest schools had almost 50 percent more Internet-linked classrooms per teacher. This difference disappeared after the E-rate program began. By 2000, some poorer districts had more Internet connections than wealthier districts (Goolsbee & Guryan, 2002). However, a study of technology usage in all schools in California from 1996 to 2000 found that increased Internet access did not lead to better student scores on the math, reading, or science sections of the Stanford Achievement Test. Study results did point out that it may be too early to see the positive effects from increased Internet access because most teachers are "novice or completely inexperienced" with computers (Goolsbee & Guryan, 2002). Figure 12.6 shows that about 7 percent of public school classrooms did not have Internet access by 2003.

Funding for Technology and Technical Support

Funding provided by NCLB, Title II, Part D, is playing a key role in helping the states incorporate educational technology. Nearly a quarter of the states report that NCLB

Percentage

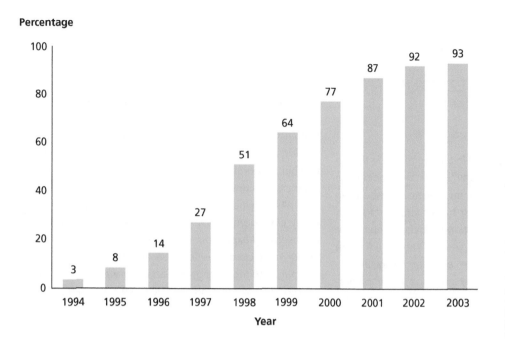

FIGURE 12.6 Percentage of public school instructional rooms with Internet access, 1994–2003

Note: Percentages are based on all public schools. Information on the number of instructional rooms with internet access was combined with information on the total number of instructional rooms in the school to calculate the percentage of instructional rooms with Internet access. All of the estimates in this report were recalculated from raw data files using the same computational algorithms. Consequently, some estimates presented here may differ trivially (i.e., 1 percent) from results published prior to 2001.

Source: Adapted from National Center for Education Statistics, Internet Access in U.S. Public Schools and Classrooms: 1994–2003. Washington, DC: Author, February 2005, p. 4.

funds are the only source of funds for technology, and half of the states report that these funds are their "primary" source for educational technology funding (State Educational Technology Directors Association, 2005). Only ten states have funding programs in place to regularly replace or update technology in all schools (*Education Week*, 2005, p. 50). As schools continue to incorporate technology, about 69 percent of their total technology spending is devoted to purchasing hardware, 15 percent to purchasing software, 9 percent to outside services, and 6 percent to providing staff development (*Education Week*, 2005, p. 8).

Although schools are getting more computer hardware, most cannot afford to hire sufficient support staff for technology. About 30 percent of schools employ a full-time coordinator of technology, about 40 percent employ a part-time coordinator, and about 30 percent have no on-site technical support personnel (Furger, 1999). As a result, most schools rely on central district personnel or computer-savvy teachers and/or students for support.

Access to Technology for All Students

Significant strides have been made toward reducing the digital divide between poor and more affluent schools in the United States. In 1999, only 25 percent of K–12 schools could be characterized as "high-end technology schools" with a student–computer ratio of 6:1 or less (Anderson & Ronnkvist, 1999). By 2004, however, the nationwide average was 3.8 students per instructional computer, with 3.9 students per computer at high-poverty schools (more than half of students are eligible for free or reduced-price lunches) and 4.1 students at high-minority schools (more than half of students belong to minority groups) (*Education Week*, 2005, p. 46).

While schools have reduced the number of students per computer, there is evidence of a digital divide if computer use at school and at home is compared to family income and minority-group status. In *A Nation Online: How Americans Are Expanding Their Use of the Internet*, the U.S. Department of Commerce (2002) reported that only 33.1 percent of children (ages 10 to 17) in the lowest income category use computers at home, compared with 91.7 percent of children in the highest income category. However, schools do help equalize the disparity in computer use among children from various income categories; according to *A Nation Online*, 80.7 percent of children in the lowest income category use computers at school, compared with 88.7 percent of children in the highest income category.

TEACHING ON YOUR FEET

RELEASING UNLIMITED STUDENT CREATIVITY WITH LIMITED TECHNOLOGY

"Mr. Lai, we're ready to film now" was a common phrase in my classroom when we first began integrating educational videos in curricular projects. That would seem like a great thing in this day and age of emphasizing project-based, student-centered learning. Unfortunately, that phrase was often followed up with *"Mr. Lai, there aren't any video cameras left"* or *"Mr. Lai, there's no microphone for this camera"* or *"Mr. Lai, I don't see any more tripods."* What does a teacher do when he or she wants to integrate 21st-century learning skills like collaboration, communication, and creativity, but most classrooms and schools have limited resources?

The truth is: Very few classes have unlimited access to equipment for multimedia projects. My main issues were with video equipment, but the same could be said for photo essays or projects with audio recordings. This reali-

zation truly hit home as I pondered how to continue developing multimedia projects when I had access to three or four video cameras but had six or seven collaborative learning groups. I knew that making the group sizes larger wouldn't be an effective solution because experience and teacher preparation training taught me that student learning increases when students participate more actively.

As with many of the brilliant solutions that originated in my classroom, the resolution came from the students themselves. I explained the situation to my fourth-graders at our next class meeting. We all agreed that we liked learning with technology projects, and we all realized that we didn't have the funds to buy more equipment. At the same time, we also knew that we couldn't take weeks on a project when there were so many curricular objectives to learn. After a bit of brainstorming and a lot of discussion, one student asked a simple question, *"Can my group do a different project instead of video? Maybe we can make a comic book instead with still photos."* Then another group added, *"We could record ourselves like a radio show!"*

As a few more ideas popped up, I realized that these were perfect solutions. Instead of being locked into a specific type of project, I could allow my students to choose their own way to complete the assignment. All that really changed were the parameters for how each group would creatively express what they know. Some could still create

High-quality, professional development opportunities are necessary if teachers are to integrate the latest technologies in their classrooms.

High-Quality, Continuous Training in Technology for Teachers

Using technology to enhance students' learning requires more than investing in the latest hardware, software, and connectivity to the Internet. E-mailing students, parents, and peers; conducting classroom demonstrations augmented with multimedia; using presentation graphics to address students' varied learning styles; and designing lessons that require students to use the Internet as a resource for inquiry should be second nature for teachers. Just as new technological skills are needed in the workplace, a high degree of technological literacy is needed in the classroom. Thus, acquiring proficiency in the ever-evolving array of technologies and developing the

TEACHING ON YOUR FEET

videos, while others could select a podcast or a photo essay or a multimedia presentation.

ANALYSIS

Teachers often get stuck in the mind-set of doing what's easiest for them. From high-stakes testing to the ever-present state standards, it often feels like there isn't enough time even to think and plan. It's understandable why many teachers make some choices based on what will help facilitate the *teaching*. Although there's nothing inherently wrong with that frame of mind, it's often beneficial to focus on what will enhance *student learning* instead of just the *teaching*.

In this situation, I believed that the entire class needed to create videos because this was a video project. But having each collaborative learning group create their own video in a timely manner was not feasible. The solution was only possible with a paradigm shift in what I believed my role should be as a teacher. By deciding that it's okay if I didn't have all the answers, the students were able to propose a better solution, and we created a partnership in learning. It was not only *okay*, it was *ideal* for me to allow students to select the type of project they would complete. We maximized the equipment while engaging students with a variety of options that would encompass a greater variety of multiple intelligences.

Creating a partnership in learning turned out to be a huge step in my classroom's integration of technology into the curriculum. Like a snowball, my students helped develop ideas for projects *and* become specialists in specific software, hardware, and troubleshooting. My paradigm shifted. I did what I do best: design curriculum. Students did what they do best: use technology to create and learn.

REFLECTION

- What other ways have you seen to resolve the problem of limited equipment?
- Describe a situation you experienced or observed when students suggested the solution to a classroom problem.
- What steps can teachers take to obtain more equipment for their classes?

Ted Lai
Former 3rd-grade teacher with Janson Elementary in Rosemead School District
Current Director of Technology & Media Services with Fullerton School District

myeducationlab *To answer these questions online, go to MyEducation Lab at www.myeducationlab.com, select the Activities and Application section, and click on this chapter's Teaching on Your Feet.*

ability to evaluate software and websites should be an important part of professional development for new and veteran teachers. However, teachers frequently complain of a lack of training in how to use technology to reach their curriculum goals. To help you evaluate computer-based instructional materials, Figure 12.7 presents criteria for evaluating software programs, and Figure 12.8 presents criteria for evaluating websites.

In the absence of high-quality, continuous training in how to integrate technology into teaching, some students will continue to make observations like the following two high school students quoted in a 2002 report entitled *The Digital Disconnect: The Widening Gap Between Internet-Savvy Students and Their Schools:*

Our teachers usually . . . don't really know what to do with [the Internet].

I never really got an assignment that specifically said you have to use the Internet. (Levin & Arafeh, 2002, p. 16)

Not surprisingly, 54 percent of school leaders who responded to a survey by the National School Boards Association (2002) reported that they rely on students to provide assistance with computers and advice about using the Internet. The Teaching on Your Feet feature in this chapter describes how one teacher's students came up with a solution to the shortage of equipment for the multimedia projects to be completed by small collaborative learning groups.

	Poor	Fair	Excellent
User Friendliness			
How easy is it to start the program?	❏	❏	❏
Is there an overview or site map for the program?	❏	❏	❏
Can students easily control the pace of the program?	❏	❏	❏
Can students exit the program easily?	❏	❏	❏
Can students create their own paths through the program and develop their own links among elements?	❏	❏	❏
After first-time use, can students bypass introductory or orientation material?	❏	❏	❏
Does the program include useful hotlinks to Internet sites?	❏	❏	❏
Inclusiveness			
Can students with hearing or visual impairments make full use of the program?	❏	❏	❏
Can students navigate the program by making simple keystrokes with one hand?	❏	❏	❏
Does the material avoid stereotypes and reflect sensitivity to racial, cultural, and gender differences?	❏	❏	❏
Textual Material			
How accurate and thorough is the content?	❏	❏	❏
Is the content well organized and clearly presented?	❏	❏	❏
Is the textual content searchable?	❏	❏	❏
Can the content be integrated into the curriculum?	❏	❏	❏
Images			
Is the image resolution high quality?	❏	❏	❏
Is the layout attractive, user friendly, and uncluttered?	❏	❏	❏
Do the graphics and colors enhance instruction?	❏	❏	❏
How true are the colors of the images?	❏	❏	❏
Are the images large enough?	❏	❏	❏
Does the program have a zoom feature that indicates the power of magnification?	❏	❏	❏
Does the program make effective use of video and animation?	❏	❏	❏
Audio			
Are the audio clips high quality?	❏	❏	❏
Does the audio enhance instruction?	❏	❏	❏
Technical			
Is installation of the program easy and trouble-free?	❏	❏	❏
Are instructions clear and easy to follow?	❏	❏	❏
Is user-friendly online help available?	❏	❏	❏
Are technical support people easy to reach, helpful, and courteous?	❏	❏	❏
Motivational			
Does the program capture and hold students' interest?	❏	❏	❏
Are students eager to use the program again?	❏	❏	❏
Does the program give appropriate, motivational feedback?	❏	❏	❏
Does the program provide prompts or cues to promote students' learning?	❏	❏	❏

FIGURE 12.7 Criteria for evaluating software programs

	Poor	Fair	Excellent
Authoritativeness			
The author(s) are respected authorities in the field.	❏	❏	❏
The author(s) are knowledgeable.	❏	❏	❏
The author(s) provide a list of credentials and/or educational background.	❏	❏	❏
The author(s) represent respected, credible institutions or organizations.	❏	❏	❏
Complete information on references (or sources) is provided.	❏	❏	❏
Information for contacting the author(s) and webmaster is provided.	❏	❏	❏
Comprehensiveness			
All facets of the subject are covered.	❏	❏	❏
Sufficient detail is provided at the site.	❏	❏	❏
Information provided is accurate.	❏	❏	❏
Political, ideological, and other biases are not evident.	❏	❏	❏
Presentation			
Graphics serve an educational, rather than decorative, purpose.	❏	❏	❏
Links are provided to related sites.	❏	❏	❏
What icons stand for is clear and unambiguous.	❏	❏	❏
The website loads quickly.	❏	❏	❏
The website is stable and seldom, if ever, nonfunctional.	❏	❏	❏
Timeliness			
The original website was produced recently.	❏	❏	❏
The website is updated and/or revised regularly.	❏	❏	❏
Links given at the website are up-to-date and reliable.	❏	❏	❏

FIGURE 12.8 Criteria for evaluating websites

In response to the uneven quality of professional development and technical support, several state departments of education, school districts, and individual schools are taking steps to ensure that teachers have the help they need to integrate technology fully into their teaching. Currently, 14 states require technology training and/or coursework for an initial teacher license, and 9 states require a technology test (*Education Week,* 2005, p. 50). In addition, the International Society for Technology in Education (ISTE) has developed professional standards for teachers related to integrating technology into teaching (2008). These standards are presented in Figure 12.9 . ISTE has also developed National Educational Technology and Performance Indicators for Students (ISTE, 2007).

Also, many teacher education programs have taken innovative steps such as the following to ensure that their graduates possess the ability to integrate technology into the classroom:

- At Washington State University, students develop an online portfolio of literacy strategies that are critiqued by teachers around the state.

- At the University of Virginia, students use the Internet to link with students at 11 other universities to analyze case studies based on commonly occurring problems in classrooms; students also write their own cases and post them on the Web.

- At San Diego State University, student teachers, along with classroom teachers and school administrators, participate in a weekly Multimedia Academy taught by university staff and former student teachers.

- At the University of Northern Iowa, students learn from television-mediated observations of "live" classrooms at a pre-K to 12 laboratory school and conduct question-and-answer sessions with the laboratory school teachers.

1. **Facilitate and Inspire Student Learning and Creativity**

   Teachers use their knowledge of subject matter, teaching and learning, and technology to facilitate experiences that advance student learning, creativity, and innovation in both face-to-face and virtual environments. Teachers:

   a. promote, support, and model creative and innovative thinking and inventiveness.
   b. engage students in exploring real-world issues and solving authentic problems using digital tools and resources.
   c. promote student reflection using collaborative tools to reveal and clarify students' conceptual understanding and thinking, planning, and creative processes.
   d. model collaborative knowledge construction by engaging in learning with students, colleagues, and others in face-to-face and virtual environments.

2. **Design and Develop Digital-Age Learning Experiences and Assessments**

   Teachers design, develop, and evaluate authentic learning experiences and assessment incorporating contemporary tools and resources to maximize content learning in context and to develop the knowledge, skills, and attitudes identified in the NETS•S. Teachers:

   a. design or adapt relevant learning experiences that incorporate digital tools and resources to promote student learning and creativity.

   b. develop technology-enriched learning environments that enable all students to pursue their individual curiosities and become active participants in setting their own educational goals, managing their own learning, and assessing their own progress.

   c. customize and personalize learning activities to address students' diverse learning styles, working strategies, and abilities using digital tools and resources.

   d. provide students with multiple and varied formative and summative assessment aligned with content and technology standards and use resulting data to inform learning and teaching.

FIGURE 12.9 National Education Technology Standards (NETS) for teachers, 2008
Source: © International Society for Technology in Education. Retrieved from http://www.iste.org/Content/ NavigationMenu/NETS/ForTeachers/2008Standards/NETS_for_Teachers_2008.htm. (accessed August 25, 2008).

3. **Model Digital-Age Work and Learning**

Teachers exhibit knowledge, skills, and work processes representative of an innovative professional in a global and digital society. Teachers:

a. demonstrate fluency in technology systems and the transfer of current knowledge to new technologies and situations.
b. collaborate with students, peers, parents, and community members using digital tools and resources to support student success and innovation.
c. communicate relevant information and ideas effectively to students, parents, and peers using a variety of digital-age media and formats.
d. model and facilitate effective use of current and emerging digital tools to locate, analyze, evaluate, and use information resources to support research and learning.

4. **Promote and Model Digital Citizenship and Responsibility**

Teachers understand local and global societal issues and responsibilities in an evolving digital culture and exhibit legal and ethical behavior in their professional practices. Teachers:

a. advocate, model, and teach safe, legal, and ethical use of digital information and technology, including respect for copyright, intellectual property, and the appropriate documentation of sources.

b. address the diverse needs of all learners by using learner-centered strategies providing equitable access to appropriate digital tools and resources.

c. promote and model digital etiquette and responsible social interactions related to the use of technology and information.

d. develop and model cultural understanding and global awareness by engaging with colleagues and students of other cultures using digital-age communication and collaboration tools.

5. **Engage in Professional Growth and Leadership**

Teachers continuously improve their professional practice, model lifelong learning, and exhibit leadership in their school and professional community by promoting and demonstrating the effective use of digital tools and resources. Teachers:

a. participate in local and global learning communities to explore creative applications of technology to improve student learning.

b. exhibit leadership by demonstrating a vision of technology infusion, participating in shared decision making and community building, and developing the leadership and technology skills of others.

c. evaluate and reflect on current research and professional practice on a regular basis to make effective use of existing and emerging digital tools and resources in support of student learning.

d. contribute to the effectiveness, vitality, and self-renewal of the teaching profession and of their school and community.

FIGURE 12.9 (Continued)

- At Indiana University, students, as well as visitors from around the world, learn about educational technology at the Center for Excellence in Education, a new state-of-the-art facility with 700 computers, an "enhanced technology suite," a building-wide video distribution system, and a two-way video distance-learning classroom.
- At Boise State University, students complete a 15-hour technology fieldwork internship in a public school classroom with a teacher who effectively integrates technology into the curriculum.

In spite of progress at integrating technology into schools, schools will need extensive support as they continue striving to meet the challenges outlined in this section. Teachers, professional associations, the private sector, state and federal governments, and local communities must continue to work together to enable digital technologies to enhance every student's learning.

Fortunately, teachers, along with others who have an interest in education, are becoming more sophisticated in understanding the strengths and limitations of technology as a tool to promote learning. They know full well that, like another educational tool—the book—computers and related technologies can be a powerful, almost unlimited medium for instruction and learning, if they carefully reflect on how it will further the attainment of the goals and aspirations they have for their students.

SUMMARY

How Is Technology Transforming Teaching and Learning?

- Today's students have grown up in a technology-rich environment and, with few exceptions, they are more comfortable with technology than their teachers.
- Anywhere, anytime learning is a reality for today's students.
- Many teachers are using blended learning—face-to-face instruction blended with online learning activities.
- E-learning and virtual schools are increasing in number, although a majority of the public does not think high school students should take at least one online course while in high school.

What Technologies Can Be Integrated Into Teaching?

- Increasingly, teachers are integrating online social networking methods such as FaceBook, MySpace, YouTube, blogs, wikis, 3D virtual reality worlds, podcasts, and e-portfolios into their teaching.
- Digital resources for teaching and learning in all academic areas include a vast array of learning objects on the Internet and open-source materials.

To What Degree Are Teachers Integrating Technology Into Their Teaching?

- Teachers use the Internet most frequently to gather information and resources for teaching. After word processing, CD-ROM references, and skill games, performing research on the Web is the most common teacher-directed use of computers by students.
- Teachers who have classroom access to the Internet are more likely than those without access to communicate via e-mail and to post information and student work on the World Wide Web.

What Does Research Say About Technology Integration and Student Learning?

- Although how and to what extent computers and other technologies are being used in schools differs greatly, research indicates that technology has a positive impact on students' achievement and attitudes, and the public believes that computers have increased students' learning.
- Teachers progress through five stages as they integrate technology into teaching: entry, adoption, adaptation, appropriation, and invention.

What Are the Challenges of Integrating Technology Into Teaching?

- Several challenges must be met so that all students can attend "high-end technology schools": (1) providing broadband Internet access for all schools; (2) funding for technology and technical support; (3) providing access to technology for all students; and (4) providing high-quality, continuous training in technology for teachers.
- Although school district spending on technology training for teachers is often inadequate and the quality of that training is uneven, state departments of education, school districts, and individual schools are developing new approaches to providing teachers with support for integrating technology.
- Many teacher education programs have developed innovative approaches to preparing technologically competent teachers. Many teachers, however, still believe they are ill-prepared to integrate technology into the curriculum.
- The International Society for Technology in Education (ISTE) has developed professional standards for teachers related to integrating technology into teaching.

PROFESSIONAL REFLECTIONS AND ACTIVITIES

Teacher's Journal

1. In addition to the content and processes students learn when technology is integrated into their learning activities, what "lessons" might they learn through the hidden curriculum created by educational technology?

2. With regard to the subject area and grade level for which you are preparing to teach, what are the advantages and disadvantages of integrating technology into teaching?

Teacher's Research

1. With regard to the subject area and grade level for which you are preparing to teach, identify several online learning objects that you might use in your teaching. Then, in a written narrative, explain how you would use them.

2. Construct a Web Quest on integrating technology into teaching with reference to the grade level and subject area for which you are preparing to teach.

Observations and Interviews

1. Interview two or more teachers at a local elementary, middle, or high school to find out how they integrate technology into their teaching. Ask them to describe their greatest successes at integrating technology. What do they see as the greatest challenges to using technology effectively in the classroom?

2. Visit a local elementary, middle, or high school and record the types of technologies used both inside and outside the classroom.

---

myeducationlab To complete additional observations and interviews, go to MyEducationLab at www.myeducationlab.com, select the Virtual Field Experience section, and click on this chapter's Observations and Interviews.

Professional Portfolio

Create an e-portfolio that includes at least three learning objects you developed using three different educational technologies. Include in your e-portfolio a statement that presents two or more principles for effectively integrating these learning objects into your teaching.

---

myeducationlab Now go to MyEducationLab at www.myeducationlab.com to test your understanding of chapter content by completing this chapter's Study Plan.

The Art of Teaching: Florida-Specific Resources
Florida iConnection

Objectives:
- Describe the curriculum that is taught in Florida schools.
- Identify how teachers evaluate student learning and assign grades in Florida.
- Identify which standardized tests are used in Florida, and how their results are used.
- Describe the technological tools that are available to enhance curriculum, instruction, and assessment in Florida schools.
- Explain how Florida teachers create a positive learning environment.
- Explain how Florida teachers develop a classroom management plan.

FEAP Competencies:

Assessment (FEAP #1): The preprofessional teacher collects and uses data gathered from a variety of sources. These sources include both traditional and alternate assessment strategies. Furthermore, the teacher can identify and match the students' instructional plans with their cognitive, social, linguistic, cultural, emotional, and physical needs.

Critical Thinking (FEAP #4): The preprofessional teacher is acquiring performance assessment techniques and strategies that measure higher order thinking skills in students and is building a repertoire of realistic projects and problem-solving activities designed to assist all students in demonstrating their ability to think creatively.

Knowledge of Subject Matter (FEAP #8): The preprofessional teacher has a basic understanding of the subject field and is beginning to understand that the subject is linked to other disciplines and can be applied to real-world integrated settings. The teacher's repertoire of teaching skills includes a variety of means to assist student acquisition of new knowledge and skills using that knowledge.

Learning Environments (FEAP #9): The preprofessional teacher understands the importance of setting up effective learning environments and has techniques and strategies to use to do so, including some that provide opportunities for student input into the processes. The teacher understands that she/he will need a variety of techniques and work to increase his/her knowledge and skills.

Planning (FEAP #10): Recognizing the importance of setting high expectations for all students, the preprofessional teacher works with other professionals to design learning experiences that meet students' needs and interests. The teacher candidate continually seeks advice/information from appropriate resources (including feedback), interprets the information, and modifies her/his plans appropriately. Planned instruction incorporates a creative environment and utilizes varied and motivational strategies and multiple resources for providing comprehensible instruction for all students. Upon reflection, the teacher continuously refines outcome assessment and learning experiences.

Technology (FEAP #12): The preprofessional teacher uses technology as available at the school site and as appropriate to the learner. She/he provides students with opportunities to actively use technology and facilitates access to the use of electronic resources. The teacher also uses technology to manage, evaluate, and improve instruction.

Important Concepts
- Curriculum
- Instruction
- Standards
- Pedagogy
- Classroom assessment
- Accountability
- Evaluation
- Educational technology
- Subject area organization technology standards
- Safety and privacy
- Classroom climate
- Classroom management

Activities

Objective 1: Describe the curriculum that is taught in Florida schools.

In Florida, like most states, one of the major aims of the school system is the ability for teachers to foster high levels of learning gains. For good or bad, this usually means performing well on a standardized achievement test.

Curriculum in Florida is geared to prepare students to meet the objectives and goals set out in the state-wide testing program.

The rigor of the Florida Comprehensive Assessment Testing (FCAT) and the challenge it represents to students whose graduation is at stake has led to a curriculum that is completely driven by that which is tested. FCAT preparation is a reality in every Florida classroom.

According to the Florida Department of Education, "A great tool for educators is the unveiling of the Sunshine Connections Website. This site affords a 'one-stop shopping' area for districts and teachers to access student data. Two types of information are accessible: performance data and instructional resources. The teacher can log in, review her students' scores, make decisions on instruction, access the resources and teach more effectively."

Teachers in a standards-based system of accountability rely on student data to make informed decisions, and the Sunshine Connections is a tool to support that perspective. Visit Sunshine Connections at http://www.sunshineconnections.org/.

Questions for Reflection

1. How might the Sunshine Connections Website be helpful in terms of curriculum development? How do you see yourself using these resources?
2. Click on Curricula at the top of the screen. Select a subject area and read through some of the curriculum resources. Is this a user-friendly resource? Imagine that you are teaching in a classroom. Describe how you would modify one of the lessons for your own classroom.
3. Click on Strategies at the top of the screen, and then Differentiated Instruction. Read through the articles and information. How will you incorporate differentiated instruction in your classroom?

Objective 2: Identify how teachers evaluate student learning and assign grades in Florida.

Evaluation makes judgments about and assigns value to the results of assessment. Every Florida teacher must prepare for evaluation of their student's learning by the FCAT. There are many other opportunities for formal and informal evaluation of learning. Effective instruction includes all types of evaluation. Examples include asking open-ended questions, monitoring student responses and attention, asking students to summarize content and learning, and providing practical application practice are all informal evaluation methods.

The Start With Success Website offers advice and information for new Florida teachers. Visit the assessment area of the site at http://www.startwithsuccess.com/Assessment/Planning.shtm

Questions for Reflection

1. After reading through the assessment tips, click on the link to the self-quiz at the bottom of the page. Reflect on each question.
2. Click on this link http://www.startwithsuccess.com/Assessment/AS_Competencies.shtm to read about building student competencies. Choose one of the tips. How will you incorporate this into your own assessment and evaluation plan?
3. Now read through the checklist for effective classroom assessment at http://www.startwithsuccess.com/Assessment/AS_ClassAssess.shtm . Choose one of the tips. Choose a grade level and subject, and pick a topic that interests you. Brainstorm and then list some very specific ways to implement this tip in your assessment planning.

Objective 3: Identify which standardized tests are used in Florida, and how their results are used.

The state of Florida utilizes the FCAT, or the Florida Comprehensive Assessment Test. The FCAT is administered in grades 3-10. Reading and math are assessed at each grade level. Writing is assessed in grades 4, 8, and 10. Science is assessed in grades 5, 8 and 10. The FCAT uses two types of testing: criterion-referenced and norm-referenced.

Visit http://www.startwithsuccess.com/Assessment/F_Additional.shtm to learn more about the scoring of the FCAT tests.

Questions for Reflection

1. What two types of questions are asked on the FCAT? How will you prepare your students for these kinds of questions?
2. Compare and contrast the criterion- and norm-referenced scoring. How are these scores used?
3. Look at the sample FCAT materials at http://fcat.fldoe.org/fcatsmpl.asp . Choose a grade level and subject, and look at the practice test. What is your initial reaction? Are you surprised by the types of questions? How will you use the sample tests to best prepare your students for the FCAT?

Objective 4: Describe the technological tools that are available to enhance curriculum, instruction, and assessment in Florida schools.

The turn-it-on, plug-it-in, or use-it-wireless revolution has evolved and Florida schools are equipped so that teachers and students have access to myriad technological applications. Possibilities for enhancing teaching and learning abound, limited only by teachers' imaginations. For instance, technological tools such as cameras, audio and video recorders, CD-ROMs, interactive white boards, laptops, e-books, and other computerized technologies are available in Florida's schools to support students as they create sophisticated representations of their knowledge.

Technology has changed the way teachers and parents communicate, as well. Classroom telephones, cell phones, email, PDAs, and Websites have become common vehicles for increased family involvement in the day-to-day life of Florida's classrooms.

Technology is a critical resource in terms of assisting Florida's students with special needs. Assistive technology exists to support students with dyslexia, hearing problems, cerebral palsy, Parkinson's disease, speech issues, or any other disability. Online classrooms, the use of voice recorders, adapted pencil grips, writing keyboards, and voice output devices are some of the technological tools that can be utilized.

Questions for Reflection

1. Each county in Florida has a network of local professionals called Local Assistive Technology Specials (LATS) to support students with special needs. Visit the LATS Network Website at http://www.aten.scps.k12.fl.us/LatsUsers.html . What are some ways that assistive technology is being used in Florida schools?
2. What resources are available to help teachers in their efforts to locate assistive technology that will help their students with special needs?
3. Locate the map of Florida and identify a regional site of the LATS Network. What kinds of services do the LATS Preview Centers offer to Florida teachers and families?

Objective 5: Explain how Florida teachers create a positive learning environment.

Because teaching is such a human endeavor, it is subject to unpredictability and requires a high degree of inter- and intrapersonal skills. Effective Florida teachers, no matter where they may work, are able to focus on learning and learners because they have certain attitudes toward their students, their subjects, and themselves. They are caring individuals, who set positive expectations for learning, believe that they are the decisive element in the classroom, and know how to be an enthusiastic model for learning.

According to sample key indicators for the Florida Educator Accomplished Practice # 9, a preprofessional "uses learning time effectively, maintains instructional momentum, and makes effective use of time for administrative and organization activities. He/she maintains academic focus of students by use of varied motivational devices."

Questions for Reflection

1. Imagine three very different students, perhaps modeled on family members or friends you may know. Assume these three students are in your Florida classroom. Name the students. For each student, describe the unique needs pertinent to each individual and how you might address each.
2. What are some methods you would use to communicate to these three students that you care about their learning, personally and socially, and not just about their preparation for FCAT?
3. Imagine you are in your own classroom. Describe how your classroom will look, sound, and smell.

Objective 6: Explain how Florida teachers develop a classroom management plan.

Because issues of classroom management are directly related to issues of instruction, the challenges of teaching in an urban setting are often solved best with effective teaching. However, it is estimated that one-half of all foreign-born Floridians live in the Miami and Ft. Lauderdale areas. Most Floridians born out of the United States come from Cuba, followed by Mexico, Haiti, Columbia, and Jamaica. Teaching diverse populations of students, found most often in Florida's larger cities, requires teacher sensitivity and respect for other cultures and traditions. What other issues are of special interest to Florida teachers?

Visit the page of Florida's Office of Safe and Healthy Schools at http://www.flboe.org/safeschools/. Read any two of the contemporary issues described on this website, such as hazing, school bullying, or the use of cell phones in the classroom.

Questions for Reflection

1. Which topics did you choose? Provide a brief summary of the information you read.
2. Imagine that you are a first-year teacher. How do you see these topics affecting your classroom and your students?
3. How will you include this information in your classroom management plan?

Important Sources

Just Read, Florida!
http://www.justreadflorida.com/
This is the Website for the literacy initiative called Just Read, Florida. This site offers literacy information for students, teachers, and parents.

Curriculum Support
http://www.fldoe.org/bii/curriculum/
The Florida Department of Education has a team of curriculum specialists available to help teachers, especially in the areas of music and fine arts, foreign languages, language arts, mathematics, science, social studies, physical education, health, and environmental education.

The Florida Instructional Technology Training Resource Unit
http://www.paec.org/fdlrstech/index.html
According to their Website, the FDLRS network "serves as the FDLRS network technology resource through coordination and delivery of information; support, coordination, and training services; identifying current technology; and through the support of technology labs at major conferences."

Start With Success

http://www.startwithsuccess.com/Classroom/Problems.shtm

This Website provides articles for new Florida teachers. Information about classroom management, organization, time management, and strategies is included.

Florida State Certification Exam Practice Questions

Directions: The following are 15 multiple-choice questions. Each question prompt is followed by 4 answer choices. Select the response that BEST answers the question.

Question #1

Mrs. Karp, the school's technology coordinator, is helping students conduct research for their upcoming multidisciplinary reports. Which task will facilitate students' work?

(A)   Demonstrating how to bookmark specific Web pages needed for their reports.
(B)   Designate a certain area in the school library for students to complete their work.
(C)   Create an online tutorial for students to work on and learn the programs.
(D)   Suggest students print resources found during their online searches.

****
The following scenario should be used in answering questions #2 and #3.

In a lesson on prime numbers, Ms. Waterman wrote 3 examples of prime numbers and 3 non-examples. She gave the students 2 minutes to write down numbers from 1 to 100 and circle the numbers that were prime. Then, she asked the students to share their examples and discuss non-examples while she wrote their response on the board.

Question #2

In reflecting on the responses that students gave at the end of the class period, which of these features should most concern Ms. Waterman?

(A)   Students asked questions to one another, rather than their teacher.
(B)   Students disregarded comments made by their peers.
(C)   Students often forgot to raise their hands before teaching.
(D)   Students spent the majority of their time debating examples and non-examples.

Question #3

Ms. Waterman plans to review the topic of prime numbers with her class before she begins the lesson. Tomorrow's class, will focus on division with remainders. What is the primary benefit of reinforcing students' understanding of prime numbers

(A)   It encourages students to evaluate their own learning and analyze potential misconceptions.
(B)   It allows teachers ample time to reiterate main concepts from a lesson across several days.
(C)   It helps students see how content discussed in math class is interconnected.
(D)   It provides teachers several opportunities to repeat the concept, using different words each time.

Question #4

Ms. Secrist plans to use the computer lab in an effort to integrate technology into a class project. She set up a template for students to use as they work on the computer. This template is similar to the one she already uses in class, but it is on the computer.

What is the best advantage of having students use a template in the computer lab?

(A)   The template reduces teacher preparation and grading.
(B)   The students are able to use the template for other lessons.
(C)   The template focuses student attention on completing the activity.
(D)   The students can incorporate technology into their work.

Question #5

Which of the following instructional strategies would best encourage high teacher expectations?

(A)   Emphasize academic strengths and reduce emphasis on challenging tasks.
(B)   Emphasize heterogeneous groupings with both group and individual evaluations.
(C)   Emphasize setting goals that will be challenging and provide necessary support to achieve goals.
(D)   Emphasize students' abilities by offering frequent praise, even when work is below acceptable standards.

Question #6

A math teacher plans to assign a problem-solving task to groups of mixed-ability students. She wants to implement the task in a way that will build students confidence in completing tasks using a variety of math skills, especially her low-ability math students. Which approach will most likely help her achieve this goal?

(A)   Provide options for students to self-select the task, the timeline, and procedures to complete the task.
(B)   Divide the tasks into smaller chunks and provide help to students as they have questions.
(C)   Pair high-ability students and low-ability math students in completing the tasks.
(D)   Design lessons and checklists that focus on the process skills underlying the task.

Question #7

A reading teacher plans to spend the first 10 minutes of her class reading aloud to her class of low-ability reading students. When she selects books for this purpose, Mr. Flagg is constantly reviewing reading material. What would be the primary goal of reading aloud?

(A)   Select books within the reading or vocabulary level of his students.
(B)   Select books with easy to understand plots and characters.
(C)   Select books that are enjoying and interesting for his students.
(D)   Select books with topics familiar to his students.

Question #8

When creating a problem-solving activity, which approach will help promote students understanding of an abstract concept?

(A)   Have students define unfamiliar concepts and terms based on personal experiences.
(B)   Give students a list of key terms and definitions they can use as a resource.
(C)   Provide enough time to introduce and reiterate concepts during an activity.
(D)   Use a variety of examples that students can relate to in their daily lives.

****

The following scenario should be used in answering questions #9 and #10.

Fiona is unsure of herself regarding anything in school. When assignments are given, she asks multiple questions and needs continuous support and prompting to complete them.

Question #9

In assessing Fiona's actions, what is the most important factor for her teachers to recognize?

(A)   Fiona may be the youngest student in her class.
(B)   Fiona may be seeking attention by acting more childlike.
(C)   Fiona's home environment and social history are irrelevant.
(D)   Fiona may be acting out when in stressful situations.

Question #10

Teachers are aware of the low expectations Fiona has for herself. What would be a likely way to improve her expectations and confidence?

(A)   Explain to her the notion of learned helplessness.
(B)   Help her see the cause as intrinsic.
(C)   Encourage her to use her locus-of-control.
(D)   Provide her with tasks that lead to success.

****

The following scenario should be used in answering questions #11 and #12.

In a science class, students begin talking about hazardous waste, more specifically PCBs in the ground near their local reservoir. Another student mentions that this type of waste was common biproduct among some commercial businesses or industries. As the class continues talking about the issue of contamination, students are curious to study the relationship. Ms. Bowling, asks the class "How can we organize this into a research project?" The class responds with a variety of perspectives.

One student, Khidhir, responds "If PCBs are made by businesses, how did they get in the ground?" Other students begin talking about how dumping PCBs is similar to littering trash and begin discussing what is currently being done for dumping that may have occurred many year ago.

Question #11

What opportunity is Ms. Bowling providing to her students when she allows them to select a topic and plan their own research?

(A) This type of project encourages organizational planning for students at a variety of academic levels.

(B) This type of project facilitates students by allowing them to take charge of their own learning.

(C) This type of project challenges teachers by reframing misconceptions about student learning.

(D) This type of project reorganizes the way students approach the learning task by making it more authentic.

Question #12

What is the best strategy for Ms. Bowling to keep students focused on a class research project?

(A) Encourage students to keep notes on the facts discussed in class.

(B) Provide structured questions to lead students to the correct answer.

(C) Ask students to recall the underlying issues inherent in Khidir's questions.

(D) Establish a general framework for continued student discussions.

Question #13

At the beginning of the year, Ms. LaForte wanted to encourage responsible homework habits. A teacher can best achieve this goal by using which of these approaches?

(A)   Creating a regular routine for study habits and turning in assignments.
(B)   Identifying students who regularly complete homework and use the students as examples.
(C)   Encourage students to be involved in the creation of homework assignments.
(D)   Foster students' understanding of their own personal strengths and weaknesses.

Question #14

The following statements give opinions on the topic of including students in the establishment of classroom rules. Which statement is supported by classroom-management research?

(A)   Primary students are cognitively unable.
(B)   Students may have more buy-in to follow rules if they have input.
(C)   Cost-benefit analysis suggests this process requires more effort than worth.
(D)   It works for constructivist teachers, but not for those who use direct instruction.

Question #15

Mrs. Mott wants her students to learn about the plants that surround their school by having them construct a school nature trail at the back of their school's grounds. Which of these best describes Mrs. Mott's instructional strategy?

(A)   Encourage students to ask questions about issues related to the task.
(B)   Scaffold students to determine their own understanding about the task.
(C)   Facilitate students in applying higher-order thinking skills to a real-world context.
(D)   Supply students with opportunities that will aid future learning.

ANSWER KEY

Question Number	Key
1	A
2	B
3	C
4	C
5	A
6	B
7	C
8	D
9	D
10	D
11	B
12	D
13	A
14	B
15	C

Becoming a Professional Teacher

17

Becoming a Professional Teacher

CLASSROOM CASE
The Realities of Teaching

THE CHALLENGE: Accepting the call to leadership that comes with being a professional teacher.

You are a lead teacher and a member of the site-based council (SBC) at your school. When you became a teacher three years ago, you never imagined that you would willingly take on a leadership role. At the beginning of last year, however, you decided to pursue a lead teacher position and a seat on the SBC. Now, after more than a year as a teacher-leader, you realize that being involved in leadership is exciting and satisfying. In fact, you plan to enroll in a principal certification program next year.

Two weeks before the school year ends, the SBC is meeting to discuss activities for next year. SBC members include the principal, two assistant principals, five teachers, and two parents. As you enter the conference room and take a seat, the chair of the SBC, a mathematics teacher, says, "Today, we've got to plan for next year. As we decided at our last meeting, today's meeting will be devoted to identifying priorities for next year."

One teacher—an active, vocal member of the teachers' union—nods her head in agreement and says, "Remember that other teachers, most of whom belong to the union, want the SBC to continue representing their interests next year. As professionals, all teachers play a key role in providing leadership for school improvement. That needs to be our guiding principle."

"I agree," adds another teacher. "We've worked hard for three years—developing a new curriculum, a mentoring program for new teachers, a peer coaching program . . . We've made a lot of progress."

The teacher next to you adds, "Teachers must be at the center of the change process. Teacher leadership is essential if we're going to continue improving as we have been during the last few years." Several members of the group, including the principal, who is very supportive of teacher leadership, nod in agreement.

Thinking about the leadership opportunities you've had since starting to teach three years ago, a feeling of satisfaction emerges within you. Granted, it will be a challenge to continue to improve the quality of education for all students at the school. However, the willingness of each SBC member to take on new leadership roles and responsibilities to attain that goal is impressive. You are proud to be a member of the teaching profession and anxious to share with the SBC your ideas for school improvement.

FOCUS QUESTIONS

1. Why is your induction into teaching important?
2. What can you learn from observing in classrooms?
3. How can you gain practical experience for becoming a teacher?
4. How can you develop your teaching portfolio?
5. What opportunities for continuing professional development will you have?
6. What new leadership roles for teachers are emerging?
7. How do teachers contribute to educational research?
8. How are teachers providing leadership for school restructuring and curriculum reform?
9. What can you expect as a beginning teacher?
10. How will your performance as a teacher be evaluated?

As the opening classroom case illustrates, school improvement efforts are continuing to change dramatically what it means to be a teacher. Steadily, the **professionalization of teaching** is taking place in the United States. National board certification, state-sponsored teacher networks, shared decision making, peer review, and teacher-mentor programs are among the changes that are providing unprecedented opportunities for teachers to assume leadership roles beyond the classroom. Along with these new opportunities for leadership, teaching as a profession is developing greater political influence and acquiring higher status in the public's eye.

In addition, school administration is becoming more collaborative and participatory, and teachers are playing a key role in school governance. For example, the National Policy Board for Educational Administration emphasized "the collaborative nature of school leadership" upon release of its Educational Leadership Policy Standards in 2008 (Council of Chief States School Officers, 2008, p. 8).

Near the end of your teacher education program, you will begin thinking about making the transition from being a student to being a teacher—and, eventually, a teacher-leader. It is natural that you feel both excited and a bit fearful when thinking about that transition. As a teacher, you will assume an entirely new role—one that requires some time before it becomes comfortable. In this chapter, you will learn how to make the first days and weeks of teaching productive and satisfying and how to become part of a professional, collaborative learning community. The following section focuses on one of the most critical phases of learning to become a professional teacher—your induction into the profession.

WHY IS YOUR INDUCTION INTO TEACHING IMPORTANT?

The retention of public school teachers has become a major problem in the United States. Each year, scores of beginning teachers enter classrooms with vigor and determination; regrettably, however, many soon leave the profession. Up to 50 percent of new teachers in the United States leave the profession within the first five years (National Commission on Teaching and America's Future, 2003). Clearly, beginning teachers need support, guidance, and encouragement to become confident, skilled professionals.

Some beginning teachers eventually give up their chosen profession because their problems and concerns go unattended. Veteran teachers, who recall their own early struggles as beginning teachers, often have a sink-or-swim attitude toward the difficulties encountered by those just entering the profession (Glickman, Gordon, & Ross-Gordon, 2007). "Since I learned to cope with the challenges of beginning teaching on my own, today's teachers either have to sink or swim," they reason. In addition, beginning teachers may think they should be as skilled as master teachers with many years of experience.

Feedback from new teachers suggests that they want to talk about the problems they encounter in their work. They want assistance to help them to be successful during the first few years of teaching. Instead, they may experience isolation and have few opportunities to share their experiences with colleagues.

Problems and Concerns of Beginning Teachers

The problems and concerns of beginning teachers can be extensive. The following problems cause some beginning teachers to think about leaving the profession: maintaining classroom discipline, motivating students, responding to individual differences, assessing students' work, maintaining positive relationships with parents, organizing classroom activities, securing adequate teaching materials and supplies, and dealing with the problems of individual students.

In some cases, teachers experience frustration related to lack of preparation time, conflicts with principals, difficulties with student misconduct, and undesirable teaching assignments (for example, larger class sizes than experienced teachers). Lack of dialogue with their peers about teaching, minimal involvement in schoolwide decisions about curriculum and instruction, and the absence of a shared technical culture are additional reasons why teachers leave the profession (Glickman, Gordon, & Ross-Gordon, 2007).

Induction Into the Profession

One solution to the problem of teacher attrition is to provide beginning teachers with induction programs that provide them with support during their first years in the profession. However, "in most school districts, there is no career path to identify, nurture, and reward the most effective teachers so that they remain in the classroom" (Olson, 2008, p. 12). In spite of the fact that high-quality teaching has the greatest influence on student achievement, some observers believe that "the current system for recruiting, developing, deploying, and keeping teacher talent in the nation's classrooms is broken" (Olson, 2008, p. 12).

Nevertheless, half of the states require and fund mentoring programs for new teachers (Olson, 2008), and many local school districts, often in collaboration with colleges and universities, have begun teacher induction programs. Among the programs that have received national attention are the Florida Beginning Teacher Program, the California Mentor Teacher Program, the Virginia Beginning Teacher Assistance Program, and the Kentucky Beginning Teacher Internship Program. Figure 13.1 indicates that among the 22 states that require and fund induction programs for beginning teachers, all have mentoring programs, most require a performance assessment, and only five require an individual growth plan.

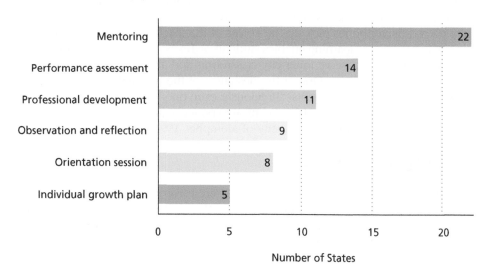

FIGURE 13.1 Elements of state-level teacher induction programs

Source: Lynn Olson. (2008). Human resources a weak spot. Quality counts: Tapping into teaching. Bethesda, MD: Education Week, p. 19.

Induction programs provide beginning teachers with continued assistance at least during the first year. Most induction programs serve the following purposes:

- Improving teaching performance
- Increasing the retention of promising beginning teachers during the induction years
- Promoting the personal and professional well-being of beginning teachers by improving teachers' attitudes toward themselves and the profession
- Satisfying mandated requirements related to induction and certification
- Transmitting the culture of the school system to beginning teachers

To accomplish these purposes, induction programs offer resources such as workshops based on teacher-identified needs, observations by and follow-up conferences with individuals not in a supervisory role, support from mentor (or buddy) teachers, and support group meetings for beginning teachers.

WHAT CAN YOU LEARN FROM OBSERVING IN CLASSROOMS?

Classroom observations are an excellent way to develop knowledge about teaching. Most teacher education programs require that students participate in **field experiences** that include classroom observations. Students report that these experiences help them make a final decision about becoming a teacher. Most become more enthusiastic about teaching and more motivated to acquire the essential knowledge and skills; however, a few decide that teaching is not for them.

Recognizing the value of observations, many teacher education programs are increasing the amount of field experiences and placing such fieldwork earlier in students' programs. For example, at Washington State University (WSU), students preparing to become elementary teachers complete one week of classroom observations as part of their first education course. Later in their program, WSU students complete two 45-hour blocks of observations in K–8 classrooms and a five-week advanced practicum (or field experience) that requires several hours of classroom observation each week.

Technology and Classroom Observations

Distance learning—the use of technology such as video transmissions that allows students to receive instruction at multiple, often remote sites—now enable preservice teachers on campus to observe in school classrooms off campus. For example, at the University of Nebraska, a two-way audio-video conferencing system called PictureTel allows remote viewing of any classroom with an Ethernet connection to the Internet (Austin & Adcock, 2002). The university instructor has a remote control so the camera at the school can follow the teacher around the room or zoom in on a small-group activity. The small camera makes almost no sound, so it does not disrupt the class. Strategically placed microphones pick up the voices of the teacher and the students.

Similarly, distance learning enables students at Texas A&M University and the University of Memphis to observe inner-city classrooms and afterward to discuss their observations with the teachers. One of the designers of the interactive video program at Memphis comments on its benefits: "Previously everyone visited different schools and saw very different things. [This] shared clinical experience [leads] to a more focused discussion of teaching methods" (University of Memphis, 1994/95, p. 2).

Focused Observations

Observations are more meaningful when they are focused and conducted with clear purposes. Observers may focus on the students, the teacher, the interactions between the two, the structure of the lesson, or the setting. More specifically, for example, observers may note differences between the ways boys and girls or members of different ethnic groups communicate and behave in the classroom. They may note student in-

Directions: *As you observe, note the ways that students are motivated intrinsically (from within) and extrinsically (from factors outside themselves).*

Intrinsic Motivation

What things seem to interest students at this age?

Which activities and assignments seem to give them a sense of pride?

When do they seem to be confused? Bored? Frustrated?

What topics do they talk about with enthusiasm?

In class discussions, when are they most alert and participating most actively?

What seems to please, amuse, entertain, or excite them?

What do they joke about? What do they find humorous?

What do they report as being their favorite subjects? Favorite assignments?

What do they report as being their least favorite subjects and assignments?

How do they respond to personalized lessons (e.g., using their names in exercises)?

How do they respond to activity-oriented lessons (e.g., fieldwork, project periods)?

How do they respond to assignments calling for presentations to groups outside the classroom (e.g., parents, another class, the chamber of commerce)?

How do they respond to being given a choice in assignments?

Extrinsic Motivation

How do teachers show their approval to students?

What phrases do teachers use in their praise?

What types of rewards do teachers give (e.g., grades, points, tangible rewards)?

What reward programs do you notice (e.g., points accumulated toward free time)?

What warnings do teachers give?

What punishments are given to students?

How do teachers arouse concern in their students?

How do students motivate other students?

What forms of peer pressure do you observe?

How do teachers promote enthusiasm for an assignment?

How do teachers promote class spirit?

How do teachers catch their students' interest in the first few minutes of a lesson?

Which type of question draws more answers—recall or open-ended?

How do teachers involve quiet students in class discussions?

How do teachers involve inactive students in their work?

In what ways do teachers give recognition to students' accomplishments?

FIGURE 13.2 Guiding questions for observing motivation

terests and ability levels, study student responses to a particular teaching strategy, or analyze the question-and-response patterns in a class discussion.

Observations may also be guided by sets of questions related to specific areas. For instance, because beginning teachers are frequently frustrated by their lack of success in motivating students to learn, asking questions specifically related to motivation can make an observation more meaningful and instructive. Figure 13.2 presents a helpful set of focused questions on motivation. Similar questions can be generated for other focus areas such as classroom management, student involvement, questioning skills, evaluation, and teacher–student rapport.

Observation Instruments

A wide range of methods can be used to conduct classroom observations, ranging from informal, qualitative descriptions to formal, quantitative checklists. With reform efforts to improve education in the United States has come the development of instruments to facilitate the evaluation of teacher performance, a task now widely required of school administrators. Students preparing to teach can benefit by using these evaluative instruments in their observations. An example is the Florida Performance Measurement System (FPMS) Screening/Summative Observation Instrument, which is presented in Figure 13.3.

The Florida instrument is based on educational research that has identified what effective teachers do. The Florida Performance Measurement System (FPMS) was the first research-based performance system to be implemented on a statewide basis. Beginning teachers in Florida must now demonstrate behaviors in six domains: planning, management of student conduct, instructional organization and development, presentation of subject matter, verbal and nonverbal communication, and testing (student preparation, administration, and feedback). Figure 13.3 presents the "effective" and "ineffective" behavioral indicators for four of those domains.

HOW CAN YOU GAIN PRACTICAL EXPERIENCE FOR BECOMING A TEACHER?

Your teacher education program is designed to give you opportunities to experience, to the extent possible, the real world of the teacher. Through field experiences and carefully structured experiential activities, you will be given limited exposure to various aspects of teaching, from curriculum development to classroom management. Observing, tutoring, instructing small groups, analyzing video cases, operating instructional media, performing student teaching, and completing various noninstructional tasks are among the most common activities.

Classroom Experiences

Opportunities to put theory into practice before student teaching are important. Thus, many teacher education programs enable students to participate in microteaching, teaching simulations, analyses of video cases, field-based practical and clinical experiences, and classroom aide programs.

Microteaching

Introduced in the 1960s, microteaching quickly became popular and is widely used today. When **microteaching,** students teach brief, single-concept lessons to a small group of students (five to ten). Microteaching gives students opportunities to practice specific teaching skills, such as positive reinforcement. Often the microteaching is videotaped for later study.

As originally developed, microteaching includes the following six steps:

1. Identify a specific teaching skill to learn about and practice.
2. Read about the skill in one of several pamphlets.
3. Observe a master teacher demonstrate the skill in a short movie or on videotape.
4. Prepare a three- to five-minute lesson to demonstrate the skill.
5. Teach the lesson, which is videotaped, to a small group of peers.
6. Critique, along with the instructor and student peers, the videotaped lesson.

Simulations

Simulations can provide opportunities for vicarious practice of a wide range of teaching skills. In **teaching simulations,** students analyze teaching situations that are written,

FRAME FACTOR INFORMATION (PLEASE PRINT)

Teacher's Name

_____ _____ _____
(Last)   (First)   (Middle)

SS# _ _ _ — _ _ — _ _ _ _

Institution of Graduation _____ Inst. # _____

Graduated from a College of Education ☐ 1. Yes   ☐ 2. No

Number of Complete Years of Teaching Experience _____

District Name _____ Number _____

School Name _____ Number _____

Observer's Name

_____ _____ ☐ _____
(Last)   (First)   (Middle)

SS# _ _ _ — _ _ — _ _ _ _

Position ☐1. Principal ☐2. Ass't Principal ☐3. Teacher ☐4. Other

Class _____ Grade Level (Specify one level only–For Adult Ed. mark level 13
For Kindergarten or Preschool mark Level 00.)

Subject Area Observed
☐ 1. Language Arts   ☐ 9. Home Economics
☐ 2. Foreign Language   ☐ 10. Other Vocational Ed.
☐ 3. Social Sciences   ☐ 11. Arts
☐ 4. Mathematics   ☐ 12. Music
☐ 5. Science   ☐ 13. Exceptional Stud. Ed.
☐ 6. Physical Education, ROTC ☐ 14. Other (Specify)
☐ 7. Business Education, DCT, CBE   _____
☐ 8. Industrial Arts/Education   _____

Type of Classroom/Facility in Which the Observation Occurred
☐ 1. Regular Classroom—Self-contained, Open, Pod
☐ 2. Laboratory or Shop
☐ 3. Field, Court, Gymnasium
☐ 4. Media Room or Library

Total Number of Students in Class _____

Observation Information   Date ___/___/___
Type of Observation ☐ 1. Prof. Orien. ☐ 2. Dis. Assess
                     ☐ 3. Other (Specify) _____
Screening Obs. ☐1. ☐2. ☐3. ☐4.
Summative Obs. ☐1. ☐2. ☐3. ☐4.

Time Observation Begins _ _:_ _   Observation Ends _ _:_ _
Test Begins _ _:_ _   Test Ends_ _:_ _

Methods Used in the Observed Lesson
☐ 1. Lecture
☐ 2. Interactive/Discussion
☐ 3. Independent Study/Lab or Shop Work

Teacher's Signature _____

Observer's Signature _____

Number of Students Not Engaged
1☐ 2☐ 3☐ 4☐

DOMAIN	EFFECTIVE INDICATORS		TOT. FREQ.	FREQUENCY	FREQUENCY	TOT. FREQ.	INEFFECTIVE INDICATORS
3.0 Instructional Organizatrion and Development	1. Begins instruction promptly						1. Delays
	2. Handles materials in an orderly manner						2. Does not organize materials systematically
	3. Orients students to classwork/maintains academic focus						3. Allows talk/activity unrelated to subject
	4. Conducts beginning/ending review						4.
	5. Questions: academic comprehension/ lesson development	a. single factual (Domain 5.0)					5a. Allows unison response
		b. requires analysis/reasons					5b. Poses multiple questions asked as one
							5c. Poses nonacademic questions/nonacademic procedural questions
	6. Recognizes response/amplifies/gives correct feedback						6. Ignores student or response/expresses sarcasm, disgust, harshness
	7. Gives specific academic praise						7. Uses general, nonspecific praise
	8. Provides practice						8. Extends discourse, changes topic with no practice
	9. Gives directions/assigns/checks comprehension of homework, seatwork assignments/gives feedback						9. Gives inadequate directions on homework/no feedback
	10. Circulates and assists students						10. Remains at desk/circulates inadequately
4.0 Presentation of Subject Matter	11. Treats concepts—definition/attributes/examples/ nonexamples						11. Gives definition or example only
	12. Discusses cause-effect/uses linking words/applies law or principle						12. Discusses either cause or effect only/uses no linking word(s)
	13. States and applies academic rule						13. Does not state or does not apply academic rule
	14. Develops criteria and evidence for value judgment						14. States value judgment with no criteria or evidence
5.0 Communication: Verbal and Nonverbal	15. Emphasises important points						15.
	16. Expresses enthusiasm verbally/challenges students						16.
	17.						17. Uses vague/scrambled discourse
	18.						18. Uses loud, grating, high pitched, monotone, or inaudible talk
	19. Uses body behavior that shows interest—smiles, gestures						19. Frowns, deadpan or lethargic
2.0 Management of Student Conduct	20. Stops misconduct						20. Delays desist/doesn't stop misconduct/desists punitively
	21. Maintains instructional momentum						21. Loses momentum—fragments nonacademic directions, over dwells

Observer's Notes: _____

Source: Florida Department of Education, Division of Human Resource Development, Tallahassee, FL. Copyright © 1989 State of Florida Department of State. Used with permission.

FIGURE 13.3 Florida Performance Measurement System Screening/Summative Observation Instrument

filmed, or videotaped. Typically, students are given background information about a hypothetical school or classroom and the pupils they must prepare to teach. After this orientation, students role-play the student teacher or the teacher who is confronted with the problem situation. Next, students discuss the appropriateness of solutions and work to increase their problem-solving skills and their understanding of the teacher's role as a decision maker in a complex setting.

Some teacher education programs are experimenting with computer-based simulations that enable students to hone their classroom planning and decision-making skills. Students at Nova Southwestern University in Florida, for example, learn to diagnose learning disabilities among children and youth by analyzing computer-simulated cases. In some cases, computer simulations are also being used for teacher professional development. For example, a three-dimensional virtual reality (VR) simulation model proved more effective than a workshop method for training kindergarten teachers to understand children's needs and perceptions (Katz, 1999), and a computer-based simulation has been used to train school personnel in crisis management (Degnan & Bozeman, 2001).

While progress is being made in the development of VR technology, "it is not possible to say how great the potential may actually be in the realm of teacher education" (Brown, 1999, p. 318). Current simulations are limited to specific skills such as classroom management or tutoring highly motivated individuals. As VR technology improves, however, one day we may see simulations of classrooms that show a variety of students with differing needs as learners.

Video Cases

Teacher education students who view, analyze, and then write about video cases have an additional opportunity to appreciate the ambiguities and complexities of real-life classrooms, to learn that "there are no clear-cut, simple answers to the complex issues teachers face" (Wasserman, 1994, p. 606). Viewing authentic video cases enables students to see how "teaching tradeoffs and dilemmas emerge in the video 'text' as do the strategies teachers use, the frustrations they experience, the brilliant and less-brilliant decisions they make" (Grant, Richard, & Parkay 1996, p. 5).

Practica

A **practicum** is a short-term field-based experience (usually about two weeks long) that allows teacher education students to spend time observing and assisting in classrooms. Though practica vary in length and purpose, students are often able to begin instructional work with individuals or small groups. For example, a cooperating teacher may allow a practicum student to tutor a small group of students, read a story to the whole class, conduct a spelling lesson, monitor recess, help students with their homework, or teach students a song or game.

Classroom Aides

Serving as a teacher aide is another popular means of providing field experience before student teaching. A teacher aide's role depends primarily on the unique needs of the school and its students. Generally, aides work under the supervision of a certified teacher and perform duties that support the teacher's instruction. Assisting teachers in classrooms familiarizes college students with class schedules, record-keeping procedures, and students' performance levels and provides ample opportunity for observations. In exchange, the classroom teacher receives much-needed assistance.

Student Teaching

The most extensive and memorable field experience in teacher preparation programs is student teaching. "Student teaching provide[s] student teachers with realistic evaluations of their strengths and weaknesses as prospective teachers and help[s] them to develop competencies in classroom management" (Wentz, 2001, p. 73). Student teaching will be a time of responsibility. As one student teacher put it,"I don't want to mess up [my students'] education!" It will also be an opportunity for growth, a chance to master critical skills.

States require students to have a five-week to semester-long student teaching experience in the schools before certifying them as teachers. The nature of student teaching varies considerably among teacher education programs. Some programs even pay student teachers during the student teaching experience. Most likely, you will be assigned to a cooperating (or master) teacher in the school, and a university supervisor will make periodic visits to observe you.

During your student teaching assignment, you will probably spend about half of your time teaching, with the remaining time devoted to observing and participating in classroom activities. The amount of time actually spent teaching, however, is not as important as your willingness to reflect carefully on your experiences. Two excellent ways to promote reflection during your student teaching experience are journal writing and maintaining a reflective teaching log.

Student Teaching Journal

Your supervisors may require you to keep a journal of your classroom experiences so that you can engage in reflective teaching. The following two entries—the first written by a student teacher in a fourth-grade classroom, the second by a student teacher in a high school English class—illustrate how journal writing can help student teachers develop strategies for dealing with the realities of teaching.

Entry 1: Today I taught a lesson on the geography of the Northeast, and the kids seemed so bored. I called on individuals to read the social studies text, and then I explained it. Some of them really struggled with the text. Mr. H. said I was spoon-feeding them too much. So tomorrow I am going to put them into groups and let them answer questions together rather than give them the answers. This ought to involve the students in the learning a bit more and enable some of the better readers to help out those who have difficulty, without the whole class watching. I feel bad when I see those glazed looks on their faces. I need to learn how to be more interesting. (Pitton, 1998, p. 120)

Entry 2: I had good feedback on small groups in their responses to questions on *Of Mice and Men*. They were to find a paragraph that might indicate theme and find two examples of foreshadowing. We found five!

The short story unit was awful during fourth hour. The kids just didn't respond. I quickly revamped my approach for the next hour. Fifth hour did seem to go better. (Mostly though, I think it was just that I was more prepared, having had one class to try things out.) I can see how experience really helps. Now that I've tried the story "The Tiger or the Lady," I would use the same material, but I would know HOW to use it more effectively! (Pitton, 1998, p. 143)

Unstructured, open-ended journals such as these enable student teachers to reflect on the student teaching experience.

Reflective Teaching Logs

To promote more analytical reflections, some supervisors ask student teachers to use a structured form of journal writing, the **reflective teaching log,** in which the student briefly describes the daily classroom activities, selects a single episode to analyze, explains the reason for selecting the episode, and discusses what was learned from the analysis and how that might be applied in the future. To illustrate a reflective teaching log, a partial entry for one episode follows. The entry shows how a college student can disagree with a supervising teacher's response to a classroom situation.

Log for December 1—Erin Tompkins

Sequence of Events

1. Arrival—end of eighth period

2. Ninth period—helped Sharad study science

487

3. After-school program—worked on science with Ricki, P.K., and Tom

4. Late bus duty with Ms. Soto

5. Departure

Episode

I was helping Ricki and P.K. fill out a table about the location and function of the different cell parts. P.K. asked me a question and two other students laughed at him. I began to answer his question when Ms. Soto came over to the table where we were working and yelled at P.K. She said, "P.K. I don't need you distracting other students who are trying to get their work done." He started to tell her what he asked me and she said, "I don't care. You can leave the room if you don't knock it off. Just do your work and be quiet or you're out!" She then apologized to me and went back to helping another student.

Analysis

I was very frustrated after this episode. This is the first time I've seen Ms. Soto raise her voice with a student and accuse him of causing problems when he was getting his work done and other students were being disruptive. P.K. had asked me a legitimate question; the other students who laughed at him were the problem. I was frustrated because Ricki and P.K. were working hard and asking me good questions. I was annoyed that P.K. was being reprimanded for asking a question that was relevant to the topic we were working on. I also felt helpless because I wanted to tell Ms. Soto that it wasn't P.K. who was the problem. I didn't feel it was my place to correct her in front of her students and kept quiet. I decided that my saying something would only make things worse because it would encourage P.K. to continue arguing with Ms. Soto and he would be in more trouble. (Posner, 2005, p. 122)

Although student teaching will be the capstone experience of your teacher education program, the experience should be regarded as an initial rather than a terminal learning opportunity—your first chance to engage in reflection and self-evaluation for a prolonged period. The benefits of reflection are illustrated in the following comment: "Being a good teacher means . . . thinking about teaching, in a long-term, systemic way. By asking the right questions, by continuously critiquing and improving your practice, and by continuing to examine the work you do in your classroom and how it connects with the larger world, you can achieve your vision and become the teacher you hope to be" (Salas, Tenorio, Walters, & Weiss, 2004, p. 8).

Substitute Teaching

Upon completion of your teacher education program and prior to securing a full-time teaching assignment, you may choose to gain additional practical experience by **substitute teaching.** If you are unable to locate a full-time position, you may decide to substitute, knowing that many districts prefer to hire from their pool of substitutes when full-time positions become available.

Substitute teachers replace regular teachers who are absent due to illness, family responsibilities, personal reasons, or professional workshops and conferences. Each day, approximately 270,000 substitutes are employed in schools across the United States, and one full year of a student's K–12 education is taught by substitute teachers (Substitute Teaching Institute, 2008).

Qualifications for substitutes vary from state to state and district to district. An area with a critical need for subs will often relax its requirements to provide classroom coverage. In many districts, it is possible to substitute-teach without regular certification. Some districts have less stringent qualifications for short-term, day-to-day substitutes and more stringent ones for long-term, full-time substitutes.

Advantages and Disadvantages of Substitute Teaching

Advantages

- Gain experience without all the nightly work and preparation
- Compare and contrast different schools and their environments
- Be better prepared for interviews by meeting administrators and teachers
- Teach and learn a variety of material
- Get to know people—network
- See job postings and hear about possible vacancies
- Gain confidence in your abilities to teach
- Practice classroom management techniques
- Learn about school and district politics—get the "inside scoop"
- Choose which days to work—flexible schedule

Disadvantages

- Pay is not as good as full-time teaching
- No benefits such as medical coverage, retirement plans, or sick days
- Lack of organized representation to improve wages or working conditions
- May receive a cool reception in some schools
- Must adapt quickly to different school philosophies
- Lack of continuity—may be teaching whole language one day, phonetics the next

FIGURE 13.4 Advantages and disadvantages of substitute teaching

Source: John F. Snyder, "The Alternative of Substitute Teaching," in 1999 Job Search Handbook for Educators. Evanston, IL: American Association for Employment in Education, p. 38.

In many districts, the application process for substitutes is the same as that for full-time applicants; in others, the process may be more brief. Often, substitutes are not limited to working in their area of certification; however, schools try to avoid making out-of-field assignments. If you decide to substitute-teach, contact the schools in your area to learn about the qualifications and procedures for hiring substitutes.

Despite the significant role substitutes play in the day-to-day operation of schools, "research tells us that they receive very little support, no specialized training, and are rarely evaluated. . . . In short, the substitute will be expected to show up to each class on time, maintain order, take roll, carry out the lesson, and leave a note for the regular teacher about the classes and events of the day without support, encouragement, or acknowledgment" (St. Michel, 1995, pp. 6–7). While working conditions such as these are certainly challenging, substitute teaching can be a rewarding, professionally fulfilling experience. Figure 13.4 presents several advantages and disadvantages of substitute teaching.

HOW CAN YOU DEVELOP YOUR TEACHING PORTFOLIO?

Now that you have begun your journey toward becoming a teacher, you should acquire the habit of assessing your growth in knowledge, skills, and attitudes. Toward this end, you may wish to collect the results of your reflections and self-assessment in a professional portfolio. A **professional portfolio** is a collection of work that documents an individual's accomplishments in an area of professional practice. An artist's portfolio, for example, might consist of a résumé, sketches, paintings, slides and photographs of exhibits, critiques of the artist's work, awards, and other documentation of achievement.

Recently, new approaches to teacher evaluation have included the professional portfolio. The National Board for Professional Teaching Standards, for example, uses portfolios and other evidence of performance prepared by applicants as one way of assessing whether teachers have met the high standards for board certification. Teacher education programs at several universities now use portfolios as one means of assessing the competencies of candidates for teacher certification. Also, many school districts are beginning to ask applicants to submit portfolios that document their effectiveness as teachers.

Portfolio Contents

What will your portfolio contain? In addition to the suggestions in the Professional Portfolio activities throughout this book, written materials might include the following: lesson plans and curriculum materials, reflections on your development as a teacher, journal entries, writing assignments given by your instructor, sample tests you have prepared, critiques of textbooks, evaluations of students' work at the level for which you are preparing to teach, sample letters to parents, and a résumé. Nonprint materials might include video- and audiotapes featuring you in simulated teaching and role-playing activities, audiovisual materials (PowerPoint presentations, charts, or other teaching aids), photographs of bulletin boards, charts depicting room arrangements for cooperative learning or other instructional strategies, a sample grade book, certificates of membership in professional organizations, and awards.

Your portfolio should represent your best work and give you an opportunity to become an advocate of who you are as a teacher. Because a primary purpose of the professional portfolio is to stimulate reflection and dialogue, you may wish to discuss what entries to place in your portfolio with your instructor or other teacher education students. In addition, the following questions from *How to Develop a Professional Portfolio: A Manual for Teachers,* 4th Edition (Campbell et al., 2007) can help you select appropriate portfolio contents:

> Would I be proud to have my future employer and peer group see this? Is this an example of what my future professional work might look like? Does this represent what I stand for as a professional educator? If not, what can I revise or rearrange so that it represents my best efforts? (p. 6)

Using a Portfolio

In addition to providing teacher education programs with a way to assess their effectiveness, portfolios can be used by students for a variety of purposes. A portfolio may be used as a(n):

- Way to establish a record of quantitative and qualitative performance and growth over time
- Tool for reflection and goal setting as well as a way to present evidence of your ability to solve problems and achieve goals
- Way to synthesize many separate experiences; in other words, a way to get the big picture
- Vehicle to help you collaborate with professors and advisers in individualizing instruction
- Vehicle for demonstrating knowledge and skills gained through outside-class experiences, such as volunteer experiences
- Way to share control and responsibility for your own learning
- Alternative assessment measure within the professional education program
- Potential preparation for national, regional, and state accreditation
- Interview tool in the professional hiring process
- Expanded résumé to be used as an introduction during the student-teaching experience

WHAT OPPORTUNITIES FOR CONTINUING PROFESSIONAL DEVELOPMENT WILL YOU HAVE?

Professional development is a lifelong process; any teacher, at any stage of development, has room for improvement. Indeed, "the continual deepening of knowledge and skills is an integral part of any profession [and] teaching is no exception" (Garet et al.,

2001, p. 916). To meet the need for professional development, many school systems and universities have programs in place for the continuing professional development of teachers.

Reflection and Self-Assessment for Professional Growth

Reflection and self-assessment are necessary first steps in pursuing opportunities for professional growth. Moreover, a continuation of these two processes is the hallmark of true professionalism in teaching. For example, three teachers comment on how reflection and self-assessment enabled them to earn certification by the National Board for Professional Teaching Standards:

> "The National Board Certification process was a powerful and worthwhile professional experience. It drastically refined my practice as an educator. It changed my thinking about curriculum." (Kim Oliver)

> "The National Board Certification process is a development program to investigate teaching and learning at the highest levels with the goal of providing students with the best education they can receive." (Meg Greiner)

> "I tell teachers that National Board Certification is the single most powerful process they'll ever go through, whether they achieve certification or not. The process makes teachers better. It's the ultimate measure of what great teaching means." (Pat Graff) (National Board for Professional Teaching Standards, 2007, pp. 3, 10–11)

Several questions can help you make appropriate decisions regarding your professional development as a teacher. In which areas am I already competent? In which areas do I need further development? How will I acquire the knowledge and skills I need? How will I apply new knowledge and practice new skills? Answers to such questions will lead you to a variety of sources for professional growth: teacher workshops, teacher centers, professional development schools, the opportunity to supervise and mentor student teachers, graduate programs, and Internet resources. Figure 13.5 illustrates the relationship of these professional development experiences to your teacher education program.

Finding a Mentor

When asked "[what] steps might be taken to attract good people into teaching and to encourage good teachers to remain in teaching," 82 percent of respondents to the MetLife Survey of the American Teacher said "providing mentoring and ongoing support for new teachers" would "help a lot" (Harris Interactive, 2001, p. 125). The following teacher-mentor explains how she provides help and support for beginning teachers:

> I go into their classrooms frequently to observe them and to give them feedback on what they ask for feedback on, or what they need feedback on. Mostly they will ask, "How am I doing with my questioning strategies?" or something like that.

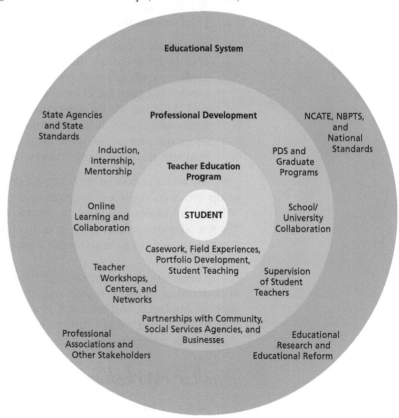

FIGURE 13.5 Professional development: From teacher education student to practitioner

A good mentor can make a significant difference in the professional life of a beginning teacher. What are the qualities of an effective mentor? The qualities a beginning teacher who takes full advantage of opportunities to develop a relationship with a mentor?

They will give me a focus that they want to look at. I let them know that I am on their side and want to help them. I will do whatever I can to facilitate their professional growth. (Peck, 2008, p. 123)

In reflecting on how a mentor contributed to his professional growth, Forrest W. Parkay defined **mentoring** as

an intensive, one-to-one form of teaching in which the wise and experienced mentor inducts the aspiring protégé [one who is mentored] into a particular, usually professional, way of life. . . . [T]he protégé learns from the mentor not only the objective, manifest content of professional knowledge and skills but also a subjective, nondiscursive appreciation for how and when to employ these learnings in the arena of professional practice. In short, the mentor helps the protégé to "learn the ropes," to become socialized into the profession. (Parkay, 1988, p. 196)

An urban middle school intern's description of how his mentor helped him develop effective classroom management techniques exemplifies "learning the ropes": "'You've got to develop your own sense of personal power,' [my mentor] kept saying. 'It's not something I can teach you. I can show you what to do. I can model it. But I don't know, it's just something that's got to come from within you'" (Henry et al., 1995, p. 114).

Those who have become highly accomplished teachers frequently point out the importance of mentors in their preparation for teaching. A mentor can provide moral support, guidance, and feedback to students at various stages of professional preparation. In addition, a mentor can model for the protégé an analytical approach to solving problems in the classroom.

Teacher Workshops

The quality of **in-service workshops** is uneven, varying with the size of school district budgets and the imagination and knowledge of the administrators and teachers who arrange them. It is significant that the most effective in-service programs tend to be the ones that teachers request—and often design and conduct. In addition, a national study of 1,027 mathematics and science teachers found that professional development activities such as workshops are most effective if they "(a) focus on content knowledge, (b) [provide] opportunities for active learning, and (c) [demonstrate] coherence with other learning activities" (Garet et al., 2001, p. 916).

Some workshops focus on topics that all teachers (regardless of subject or level) can benefit from: classroom management, writing across the curriculum, multicultural education, and strategies for teaching students with learning disabilities in the general education classroom, for example. Other workshops have a sharper focus and are intended for teachers of a subject at a certain level—for example, whole-language techniques for middle school students, discovery learning for high school science students, and student-centered approaches to teaching literature in the high school classroom. To view one teacher's description of the formal and informal professional development experiences that enabled her to integrate technology into her teaching, go to MyEducationLab.

myeducationlab

Go to MyEducationLab, select Chapter 13 and then Activities and Applications to watch the video Technology Improves Teaching.

Teacher Centers

Teacher centers "strengthen teamwork among teachers across disciplines" and "provide a location and atmosphere to foster sharing and increased understanding of resources, ideas, methods, approaches, information and materials among educators" (New York State Teacher Centers, 2008). In contrast to in-service programs, teacher centers are more clearly initiated and directed by teachers. Some centers cooperate with a local or neighboring college of education and include members of the faculty on their planning committees.

Many teachers find teacher centers stimulating because they offer opportunities for collegial interaction in a quiet, professionally oriented setting. Teachers often find that the busy, hectic pace of life in many schools provides little time for professional dialogue with peers. Furthermore, in the teacher center, teachers are often more willing to discuss openly areas of weakness in their performance. As one teacher told the first author of this book:

> At the teacher center I can ask for help. I won't be judged. The teachers who have helped me the most have had the same problems. I respect them, and I'm willing to learn from them. They have credibility with me.

Professional Development Schools

Professional development schools (PDSs) are a way to link school restructuring and the reform of teacher education in the United States. These school–university partnerships offer teachers the following opportunities:

- Fine learning programs for diverse students
- Practical, thought-provoking preparation for novice teachers
- New understanding and professional responsibilities for experienced educators
- Research projects that add to all educators' knowledge about how to make schools more productive (Holmes Group, n.d., p. 1)

For example, a teacher at a PDS might team with a teacher education professor and teach a university-level course, participate in a collaborative research project, offer a professional development seminar for other teachers, arrange for the teacher-educator to demonstrate instructional strategies in his or her classroom, or jointly develop relevant field experiences for prospective teachers.

Supervision and Mentoring of Student Teachers

After several years in the classroom, teachers may be ready to stretch themselves further by supervising student teachers. Some of the less obvious benefits of doing so are that teachers must rethink what they are doing so that they can explain and sometimes justify their behaviors to someone else, learning about themselves in the process.

TEACHERS' VOICES

Walk in My Shoes

Education offers teachers many opportunities to grow and ways to serve. Cheryl Bonner's professional journey illustrates that well. She has been a classroom teacher, summer school principal, teacher-mentor, action researcher, technology instructor, staff developer, adult education teacher, principal, and university adjunct professor. Her impressive career is due to Cheryl seeking to extend her knowledge and skills, and embracing opportunities that called for her to stretch herself and at times be uncomfortable.

She did her student teaching so well that she was called out of her assignment and given a long-term substitute teaching position in another school. She ended up teaching at that school for 15 years. While there, her school district was awarded a technology grant. Cheryl interviewed for a position to implement it and was one of the five teachers selected. The goals of the program were to help teachers, students, and parents develop computer literacy and learn to use computers as tools for learning.

Cheryl and the other four teachers taught in-service workshops in the district office, and then each went to an assigned school to assist teachers in carrying out what they had learned. They helped other teachers incorporate into their instruction several approaches to curriculum design: project-based learning, constructivism, and "backward planning."

One of the most satisfying opportunities Cheryl pursued was teaching English as a second language and citizenship in the adult education school. It was a second job for her and a good one. "Everyone there was working to better their lives, to communicate better, to get a better job. They'd come from working in a menial job every day to class four nights a week." At times Cheryl would be tired after teaching all day and not be enthusiastic about going to teach her class two nights a week. Her students had spent their day doing more physically demanding work; yet they were there, eager to learn. "I'd have students from ages 15 to 84. The 84-year-old couple worked in a Burger King as custodians and were learning English to communicate with their grandson." Cheryl appreciated the side benefits of teaching in the adult school: getting additional training in adult education, working with adults, and seeing a different part of the community she worked in.

She was a summer school principal for seven years. "I had taught summer school every summer, but it was getting harder and harder to get that job." She looked at what the summer school principal did and thought to herself, "I

Furthermore, because they become a model for their student teachers, they continually strive to offer the best example. In exchange, they gain an assistant in the classroom— another pair of eyes, an aid with record keeping—and more than occasionally, fresh ideas and a spirit of enthusiasm.

Graduate Study

One of the most challenging ways to become a more effective professional is to enroll in a graduate program at a nearby college or university. Most states now require teachers to take some graduate courses to keep their certifications and knowledge up-to-date.

Graduate-level class schedules are usually developed with teachers in mind, with most courses offered in the evenings, on Saturdays, and during the summer. If you pursue graduate study, not only will you find the professional dialogue with instructors and fellow students stimulating, but you will also acquire theories and practical approaches that you can implement in your classroom the next workday. Also, you might find some other area of education—administration and supervision, guidance and counseling, special education, or curriculum development—that you want to pursue in your long-term career development. The Teachers' Voices: Walk in My Shoes feature in this chapter profiles a teacher for whom graduate study eventually led to becoming a teacher-mentor, action researcher, staff developer, principal, and university adjunct professor.

can do that." So she decided to apply to be the summer school principal and was selected.

Cheryl also decided to be a teacher-mentor, which was a three-year commitment. Such teachers spend 75 percent of their time working with new teachers and doing staff development and 25 percent of the time on a new project. She helped new teachers prepare for their first week of school and guided them in classroom management. The project she worked on during her third year of the program was an action research study she conducted with a university professor. It focused on sustained silent reading and reader response journals. They presented their findings at a conference and a symposium. The experience made Cheryl realize that she wanted to do more work in higher education.

She applied for and was selected to teach adjunct courses in a master's degree program at a nearby university. Once again, Cheryl had pushed herself to grow, teaching adults working on graduate degrees. She has been an adjunct teacher for the last 10 years, combining the teaching with her full-time work in various administrative positions in the school system.

As the principal for Cullen Elementary School, Cheryl led her faculty in a collaborative process to apply for a special recognition. "Everyone who wanted to contribute could. We brainstormed, and then groups were chosen to write about the various themes within the 17-page application." The result was an excellent report of the outstanding work that had been going on in the school, and Cullen was selected as a 2006 Distinguished School.

Now in a position to hire teachers, Cheryl looks for a "person who seems to have a respect for kids and an enthusiasm for teaching kids and wanting to make a difference in the lives of children." She also wants to see them "take responsibility for being the person in charge of the classroom, getting the curriculum across, and helping students to believe in themselves." She also seeks people with a positive attitude. "Education is constantly being hammered, constantly being beat up about performance. We want education to not be the negative blurb in the news, but the positive light in people's lives." Being able to think for themselves is another criterion Cheryl factors into her selection process.

Cheryl's advice to new teachers is to take advantage of the training opportunities that come along and be aware of ways they can grow. "Some teachers may want to stay in the classroom their entire career. Some may want to add a role, being a trainer for the district or a special program." She notes that others may decide to leave the classroom to become principals, district administrators, or faculty at universities. Cheryl continues to be a school principal; however, she is also currently completing a doctoral degree.

The accomplishments of this gifted teacher, administrator, and adjunct professor are great. Her career path and her modest and down-to-earth account of it are an inspiration for others to follow.

Cheryl Bonner
Cullen Elementary School

WHAT NEW LEADERSHIP ROLES FOR TEACHERS ARE EMERGING?

The opening classroom case for this chapter provides an example of how today's professional teachers willingly respond to the call to leadership. As the opening quote for this chapter points out, teachers must become "vital contributors" to educational reform. Teachers' roles will continue to change in fundamental and positive ways during the 21st century.

Greater autonomy and an expanded role in educational policymaking will provide you with opportunities to extend your leadership roles beyond the classroom. To prepare for this future, you will need to develop leadership skills to a degree not needed in the past. In the Teachers' Voices: Research to Reality feature in this chapter, a school principal presents the case for teacher-led school improvement.

Teacher Involvement in Teacher Education, Certification, and Staff Development

Teacher input into key decisions about teacher preparation, certification, and staff development is on the rise. Through their involvement with professional development schools and the National Board for Professional Teaching Standards (NBPTS); state professional standards boards; and scores of local,

TEACHERS' VOICES RESEARCH TO REALITY

LaQuanda Brown
THE CASE FOR TEACHER-LED SCHOOL IMPROVEMENT

Retaining effective teachers and developing them into leaders is essential for school improvement. School principals must create a cadre of teacher-leaders for each grade level and for each content area. Teacher-leaders and members of the school's leadership teams should have an innate desire to serve, a high level of commitment to the total functioning of the school, and a spirit of dedicated volunteerism.

Teachers must have a voice in the types of training offered by teacher-leaders. Thus, teacher-leaders should provide and implement quality training systems that offer a balance for classroom teachers and that answer the data as well as the teachers' requests.

Teachers and school leaders can achieve amazing feats of school improvement when everyone works together. In some of the most challenging schools in the nation, teachers and students are thriving because teachers feel comfortable identifying problems, conversing together about solutions, and carrying out solutions that speak to those challenges.

Teachers and principals must be creative, systemic thinkers and learners, and collaborative leaders. They must be willing to implement solutions that are nontraditional, speak to the needs and interests of the students, and address the summative and formative data that answer the state and federal mandates and guidelines that outline the responsibilities of successful schools. Gabriel (2005) writes that teacher leadership "can transform schools from houses of detention to houses of attention—for both student and teacher." To allow this process to fully develop, administrators must maintain an open, responsive, and receptive attitude to new ideas, realizing that often the most effective strategies and suggestions come from sources within the school building.

QUESTIONS

1. How can teacher-leaders help to transform schools from "houses of detention to houses of attention—for both student and teacher"?
2. What educational, professional, or work experiences have you had that would help you to become a teacher-leader?

LaQuanda Brown is principal of King-Danforth Elementary School in Macon, GA. The preceding is excerpted and adapted from her article that appeared in *Principal*, March/April 2008, pp. 29–32.

state, and national education committees, teachers are changing the character of pre- and in-service education. For example, in the evaluation of the NBPTS authorized by the U.S. Congress, the prestigious National Research Council noted that "board-certified teachers are used as mentors, team leaders, and organizers of professional development activities; board certification is viewed as part of a broader commitment to improving professional development and meeting higher standards for teachers" (National Research Council, 2008, p. S-8).

In addition, the NBPTS established a network designed to allow nearly 7 percent of the nation's 2.5 million teachers to participate in field-testing various components of the NBPTS certification system. The NBPTS allocated $1 million to teachers, in the form of honoraria, for helping to field-test the NBPTS assessment materials. One of the first participants in the field test reflects on how teacher participation in the NBPTS can positively influence the profession of teaching:

> I am proud to say I was one of the first teachers in the country to participate in NBPTS. At its best, NBPTS can help us validate our skills as teachers; it can help us focus on areas of needed improvement; it can encourage a core of committed teacher-thinkers. . . . As more and more teachers participate and are certified, we will find our voices. We will be able to speak in an articulate fashion about what is important for us and our students. We will be heard. (Hletko, 1995, p. 36)

Since the NBPTS certification program began in 1993 through 2007, about 99,300 teachers applied for board certification, and 63,800 earned the credential (National Research Council, 2008, p. S-5). Teachers who have received National Board Certification are recognized as professionals not only in their schools, but also in their districts and beyond. For example, after receiving board certification, these teachers had the following professional opportunities:

- Helene Alolouf (Early Adolescence/English Language Arts certificate) of Yonkers, New York, was invited to teach at the Manhattanville Graduate School of Education as an adjunct professor.
- Sandra Blackman (Early Adolescence/English Language Arts certificate) of San Diego, California, was promoted to resource teacher for the humanities departments for 55 schools, where she provides staff development for a standards-based system.
- Edward William Clark Jr. (Early Childhood/Generalist certificate) of Valley, Alabama, helped the State Department of Education and the Alabama Education Association develop National Board Certification training modules to assist Alabama teachers with National Board Certification.
- Linda Lilja (Middle Childhood/Generalist certificate) of Scranton, Kansas, was invited to serve as a member of the task force for the National Teachers Hall of Fame.
- Donna W. Parrish (Early Adolescence/Generalist certificate) of Shelby, North Carolina, was appointed curriculum specialist at a middle school.

Teacher-Leaders

"One significant line of work to strengthen our nation's schools emphasizes teachers assuming greater leadership of the organizations in which they work, or what has come to be known as *teacher leadership*" (Murphy, 2005, p. 3). As the titles of a few of the many books on teacher leadership published since 2005 suggest, the term **teacher-leader** has become part of the vocabulary of educational reform:

- *Reframing Teacher Leadership to Improve Your School* (Reeves, 2008)
- *Developing Teacher Leaders: How Teacher Leadership Enhances School Success* (Crowther, Ferguson, & Hann, 2008)
- *Teacher Leadership in Context* (Gigante, 2008)
- *Leadership Strategies for Teachers* (Merideth, 2007)
- *Best Practices for Teacher Leadership: What Award-Winning Teachers Do for Their Professional Learning Communities* (Stone & Cuper, 2006)
- *Connecting Teacher Leadership and School Improvement* (Murphy, 2005)

A brief look at the professional activities of Sandra MacQuinn, a teacher-leader who worked with the author and a colleague on a major restructuring effort at Rogers High School in Spokane, Washington, illustrates the wide-ranging roles of a teacher-leader. In addition to teaching, here are just a few of MacQuinn's leadership activities while serving as liaison and on-site coordinator of a school-university partnership between Rogers High School and Washington State University's College of Education:

- Writing grant proposals for teacher-developed projects
- Helping other teachers write grant proposals
- Facilitating the development of an integrated school-to-work curriculum
- Preparing newsletters to keep faculty up-to-date on restructuring
- Organizing and facilitating staff development training
- Developing connections with area businesses and arranging job-shadowing sites for students
- Working with a community college to create an alternative school for Rogers High School students at the college

- Scheduling substitute teachers to provide Rogers High School teachers with release-time to work on restructuring
- Making presentations on the Rogers High School restructuring at state and regional conferences
- Arranging for Rogers High School students to visit Washington State University (WSU)
- Meeting with the principal, assistant principals, WSU professors, and others to develop short- and long-range plans for implementing site-based management
- Chairing meetings of the site-based council, the restructuring steering committee, and other restructuring-related committees

Three hundred and sixty teachers participated in the Teacher Leaders in Research-Based Science Education (TLRBSE) between 2002 and 2007. Funded by the National Science Foundation, TLRBSE enabled experienced teacher-leaders to mentor teachers new to the profession, participate in a year-round online course, and implement research-based science education in the classroom. The teacher-leaders also participated in a combination of in-residence workshops at Kitt Peak National Observatory and the National Solar Observatory. Participants also receive a stipend, airfare, room and board, and support to attend a meeting of the National Science Teachers Association (Rector, Jacoby, Lockwood, & McCarthy, 2002).

Dimensions of Teacher Leadership Beyond the Classroom

Currently, 17 states have incentives for teachers to assume leadership roles outside the classroom (Swanson, 2008, p. 38). Figure 13.6 illustrates 11 dimensions of teacher leadership beyond the classroom. The many teachers with whom we have worked on school restructuring projects during the last few years have used these skills to reach an array of educational goals. Teacher-leaders "view their responsibilities as extending beyond classroom teaching to include participation in the larger community of educators and administrators" (Becker, 2001). At schools around the country, teachers and principals are using a "collaborative, emergent" approach to leadership; that is,

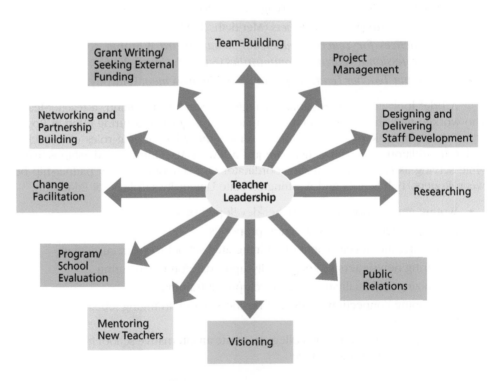

FIGURE 13.6 Eleven dimensions of teacher leadership beyond the classroom

the person who provides leadership for a particular schoolwide project or activity may or may not be the principal or a member of the administrative team (Parkay, Shindler, & Oaks, 1997).

HOW DO TEACHERS CONTRIBUTE TO EDUCATIONAL RESEARCH?

Today's teachers play an increasingly important role in educational research. By applying research to solve practical, classroom-based problems, teachers validate the accuracy and usefulness of educational research and help researchers identify additional areas to investigate. As consumers of educational research, teachers improve their teaching, contribute to educational reform, and enhance the professional status of teaching.

In addition, increasing numbers of teachers are becoming competent researchers in their own right and making important contributions to our understanding of teaching and learning. Until recently, teachers were the missing voice in educational research. For decades, we have had research *on* teachers; today, we have educational research *by* teachers. We have seen the emergence of the **teacher-researcher,** the professional teacher who conducts classroom research to improve his or her teaching.

Part of being a professional is the ability to decide how and when to use research to guide one's actions. For example, in her explanation to Courtney Rogers, a high school English teacher and coauthor of *Teacher Research for Better Schools*, one elementary teacher tells how she benefited from being a teacher-researcher:

> It opened my eyes to ways kids learn and think. . . . Conducting research makes you take the time to think about what you're doing and to kind of chart the course according to what happens and what you notice and the reactions or responses that your kids have. (Mohr et al., 2004, pp. 66, 69)

Conducting Classroom Action Research

More than four decades ago, Robert Schaefer (1967) posed the following questions in *The School as the Center of Inquiry*:

> Why should our schools not be staffed, gradually if you will, by scholar-teachers in command of the conceptual tools and methods of inquiry requisite to investigating the learning process as it operates in their own classroom? Why should our schools not nurture the continuing wisdom and power of such scholar-teachers? (p. 5)

Schaefer's vision for teaching has become a reality. Today, thousands of teachers are involved in action research to improve their teaching. Using their classrooms as laboratories, these teacher-researchers are systematically studying the outcomes of their teaching through the application of various research methods. In addition, they are disseminating the

This teacher is conducting classroom action research on the ways students come to understand a problem and to apply appropriate problem-solving skills. What are several ways the teacher might use this research as a professional?

results of their research at professional conferences and through publications, including *Networks: An On-line Journal for Teacher Research*.

Simply put, **action research** is the classroom-based study by teachers, individually or collaboratively, of how to improve instruction. As in the reflection-in-action approach described earlier in this chapter, action research begins with a teacher-identified question, issue, or problem. For example, Laura Jordan, a middle school teacher, explains how she designed an action research study (published in *Networks*) in response to her students' lack of involvement in class activities:

> The students enrolled in my sixth-grade advanced language arts class are particularly difficult to engage in discussions and frequently do not put forth their best efforts in completing assignments. [As] a result of my reflections, I discovered that I spend the majority of instructional time lecturing and directing students, as well as giving too few assignments that allow students to express their creativity and individual learning styles.
>
> In light of this realization, I came to the conclusion that I needed to seek a way to engage my students, making learning experiences meaningful and creating in students a spark of excitement for learning. [As] I began this project my goal was to determine whether students would take more ownership of their learning and produce higher quality work if they were allowed to choose responsive activities that reflected their individual learning styles. (Jordan & Hendricks, 2002)

Using an action research approach similar to Jordan's, the teacher profiled in the Technology in Action feature in this chapter figured out a way to improve his students' understanding of complex concepts. As a result of his classroom-based inquiry and reflection, he began to use Wondershare QuizCreator to create autograded self-assessments for his students.

Action research enables "teacher researchers [to] model for their students and colleagues a concept of learning that includes openly asking and systematically investigating questions that matter to them about teaching and learning" (Mohr et al., 2004, p. 81). Figure 13.7 presents five steps in the classroom-focused action research cycle.

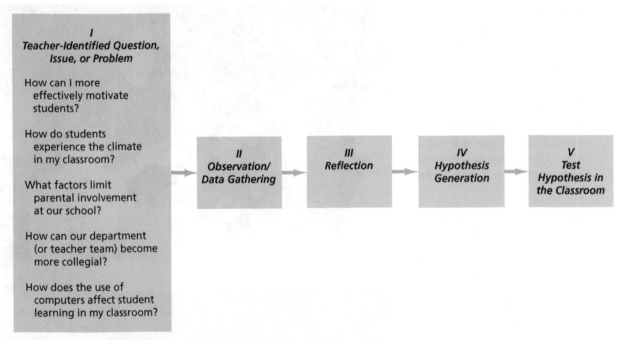

FIGURE 13.7 A classroom-focused action research cycle

TECHNOLOGY in *ACTION*

Autograded Quizzes and Exams in Eighth-Grade Social Studies

Mr. Winchell has been using Wondershare QuizCreator for the past year to create autograded self-assessments. (Autograded quiz-making tools allow teachers to construct their own assessments.) The QuizCreator allows Mr. Winchell to create Flash-driven quizzes that include audio, animation, and text. The quizzes can be true/false, short answer, clickable maps, multiple choice, and other autoreply formats. The tool allows him to create assessments that review classroom discussion, group projects, and current events, and it quickly and easily puts them in a format that allows students to access the assessments and receive immediate feedback on their responses—not just with right or wrong answers but with detailed explanations of the correct answer.

At the end of each lesson, Mr. Winchell has his students submit questions that cover the day's events. They provide the questions, the correct answers, and several not-so-correct answer choices. If Mr. Winchell uses a student's question in the daily quiz, then the student receives several extra credit points for that day. Mr. Winchell then loads the questions, the correct answers, and the incorrect choices into QuizCreator. The other students then access the questions, take the quiz, and see how they performed. They can take the quiz as many times as they want for as long as they want.

Mr. Winchell found that, as effective as the autograded quiz tool is, the exercise of having students write questions works equally well in helping students retain course-specific information. By the end of the year, Mr. Winchell has an extensive series of questions and answers that cover the entire term and that students can review anytime they need. And best of all, he never had to grade a single question!

AUTOGRADED TOOLS: Several quiz-making tools are available to teachers. Most of these tools allow teachers to import questions and answers from other sources like Excel or Word; insert screen shots, animation, music, and sound; randomize question-and-answer sets; provide automated feedback on performance and correct responses for each question; and provide detailed reporting to teachers.

VISIT: http://www.sameshow.com/quiz-creator.html. This site provides visitors with opportunities to try the quiz-creation tool, see examples of autograded assessment instruments, and obtain technical requirements for running the tool.

POSSIBLE USES: Teachers have used autograded assessments to improve student performance, save time, provide for diverse student self-assessment opportunities, and help students take control of their learning experience.

TRY IT OUT: Visit http://www.sameshow.com/quiz-creator.html and download the free trial version of the QuizCreator software. Once the software is installed on your computer, you will be able to create true/false, fill-in-the blank, multiple-choice, matching, and short essay self-assessment instruments.

■ ■ ■ ■ ■ ■ ■ ■ ■ ■

Not surprisingly, becoming a teacher-researcher is hard work, given the daily demands of teaching itself. However, more schools are redefining the teacher's role to include doing action research. These schools realize that action research can provide data on the effectiveness of educational programs, enhance student learning, and energize teachers for professional growth. Four teachers who are members of the Action Research Laboratory at Highland Park High School near Chicago comment on the benefits of action research:

> By far the most rewarding part of working on an action research team was the opportunity to learn and grow with a small group of teacher colleagues. This experience of mutual commitment provided a wonderful staff development experience; by working with these colleagues consistently throughout the year, we were able to explore new ideas and take risks in the classroom with a type of "safety net" in place. For that reason alone, as well as our desire to explore the new questions and challenges raised by our research, we will continue to conduct action research into the effectiveness of our teaching and grading practices. (Mills, 2000, p. 97)

HOW ARE TEACHERS PROVIDING LEADERSHIP FOR SCHOOL RESTRUCTURING AND CURRICULUM REFORM?

Today's teachers welcome opportunities to provide leadership for school restructuring and curriculum reform. Although teachers may have played a limited role in school governance in the past, teachers have many opportunities now to become educational leaders beyond the classroom. Figure 13.8 presents five clusters of educational reform, each of which offers teachers opportunities to shape policies during the future.

Leadership and Collaboration for School Reform

The key to successful school restructuring and curriculum reform is teacher leadership and collaboration. At the National Teacher Forum on Leadership, sponsored by the U.S. Department of Education, participating teachers identified the following ways in which teachers can lead and collaborate for school reform. To illustrate each form of leadership, one example from among the thousands of teachers exercising similar leadership is provided.

- *Participating in professional teacher organizations*—As president of the Wisconsin Science Teachers' Association, Sharon Nelson worked with the National

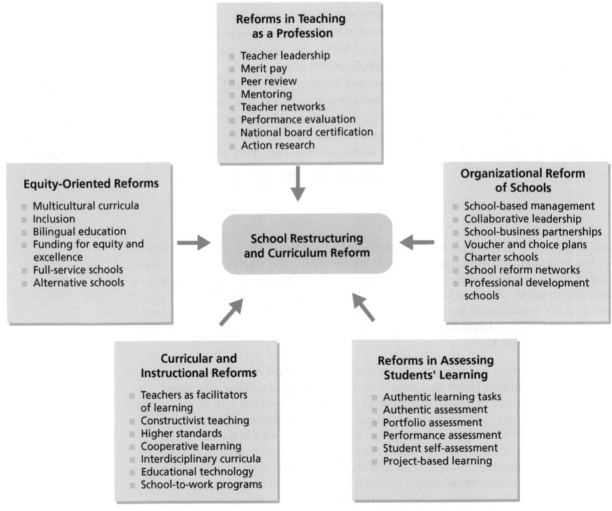

FIGURE 13.8 Opportunities for teacher leadership in school restructuring and curriculum reform

Science Teachers Association, Goals 2000, to disseminate national science education standards in her state.

- *Taking part in school decisions*—Melisa Hancock, an elementary school teacher in Kansas, became a clinical instructor at Kansas State University and played a key role in engineering a partnership with the university that led to her school becoming a professional development school.

- *Defining what students need to know and be able to do*—Delaware teacher Jan Parsons was one of several teachers who took leadership roles on Delaware commissions that wrote standards for mathematics, science, social studies, and language arts; teachers also wrote and piloted new statewide assessments in line with the new standards.

- *Sharing ideas with colleagues*—Tom Howe and other Wisconsin teachers developed a Share Net Program that allows teachers to make formal presentations to their peers on effective instructional practices.

- *Being a mentor to new teachers*—Science teacher Fie Budzinsky serves as a teacher mentor for the state of Connecticut; Budzinsky had, in turn, been mentored earlier in her career by Dick Reagan, another science teacher.

- *Helping to make personnel decisions*—North Carolina teacher Mary Ostwalt served on a selection committee formed to replace a teacher who resigned; other teachers in her district serve on selection committees for the hiring of new principals.

- *Improving facilities and technology*—Ray Hasart and other teachers were the driving force behind the creation of a new $3.5 million technology facility at a Redmond, Oregon, high school; the facility is visited regularly by people throughout the West Coast.

- *Working with parents*—Martina Marquez and a team of colleagues in New Mexico visit Native American villages and surrounding communities to disseminate math and reading activities that parents can do with their children.

- *Creating partnerships with the community*—North Carolina teacher Scott Griffin became a member of his community's volunteer fire department and spearheaded the redesign of the fire safety curriculum presented at schools in the community.

- *Creating partnerships with businesses and organizations*—Georgia teacher Stephanie Blakney took the lead in developing a systemwide Partnership with Education program that led to the creation of a food bank and the Atlanta Coca-Cola Bottling Company adopting her school.

- *Creating partnerships with colleges and universities to prepare future teachers*—Former Kansas Teacher of the Year Christy McNally and other award-winning teachers organized a partnership with teacher education programs throughout Kansas.

- *Becoming leaders in the community*—Teacher Jacqueline Omland is president of the Legion auxiliary in Aberdeen, South Dakota, and a colleague is chair of the Legion.

- *Becoming politically involved*—Washington state teacher Ivy Chan served as treasurer for a person who ran for state superintendent of public instruction.

- *Leading efforts to make teachers more visible and communicate positive information*—High school teacher Larry Torres started a weekly news column in his New Mexico community paper that focuses on positive articles about education; the column has now expanded to a full page.

Collaborative School Reform Networks

Many teachers are involved in restructuring and curriculum change through their schools' participation in collaborative networks for reform. Networks provide teachers with training and resources for restructuring, and they create opportunities for teachers at network schools to help teachers at non–network schools with their restructuring

These teachers have been selected by their peers to provide leadership for the collaborative school reform network their school has joined. What are some forms of professional collaboration in which you will participate as a teacher?

efforts. Among the many collaborative reform networks are the Coalition of Essential Schools, the National Network for Educational Renewal, Accelerated Schools, and state-based networks such as the League of Professional Schools.

Coalition of Essential Schools

The **Coalition of Essential Schools (CES),** started by Theodore R. Sizer at Brown University, consists of 19 regional centers that offer direct support to hundreds of schools in the areas of school organization, classroom practice, leadership, and community connections. The regional centers, with the support of CES National, coach schools through a systematic process of change at the school site. No two coalition schools are alike; each develops an approach to restructuring suited to its students, faculty, and community. However, the efforts of coalition schools to restructure are guided by ten common principles extrapolated from Sizer's (1997a, 1997b, 1997c; Sizer & Sizer, 1999) books on redesigning U.S. schools and the beliefs that top-down, standardized solutions to school problems don't work and that teachers must play a key role in the operation of their schools. Recently, the coalition organized resource centers so teachers at coalition schools can provide non–coalition schools with restructuring assistance.

National Network for Educational Renewal

The Center for Educational Renewal at the University of Washington created the **National Network for Educational Renewal (NNER)** to encourage new opportunities for teachers to become involved in school restructuring, curriculum reform, and the preparation of teachers. The NNER consists of 19 settings in 18 states, and its members include 41 colleges and universities, more than 100 school districts, and over 750 partner schools. The NNER is based on 20 postulates for reforming teacher education that John Goodlad originally presented in *Educational Renewal: Better Teachers, Better Schools* (1994). "The members of [the National Network for Educational Renewal], called settings, include partnerships of university faculty in the arts, sciences, and education, and public school educators. All are engaged as equal partners as [the Network] strives to pursue the Agenda for Education in a Democracy (National Network for Educational Renewal, 2008).

Accelerated Schools

Stanford economist Henry M. Levin developed a nationwide network of **accelerated schools** that provide enriched, rigorous curricula to speed up the learning of students at risk. Instead of placing at-risk students into remedial classes, accelerated schools provide students with challenging learning activities traditionally reserved for gifted and talented students. Accelerated schools are based on the belief that teachers—in collaboration with administrators, parents, and community members—must be able to make important educational decisions, take responsibility for implementing those decisions, and take responsibility for the outcomes of those decisions. The National Center for Accelerated Schools PLUS (Powerful Learning Unlimited Success), now located at the University of Connecticut, operates 13 regional centers across the country. The regional centers provide assistance to teachers and administrators who wish to restructure their schools according to the accelerated schools model.

State-Based Educational Partnerships

Many states have established state-based partnerships between a state university or college and a coalition of public schools. Several of these partnerships are patterned after the League of Professional Schools started by Carl Glickman at the University of Georgia. The overall goal of the league is to improve student learning by using shared governance and action research to focus on instructional and curricular issues. Following guidelines Glickman has outlined in *Leadership for Learning* (2002) and *Holding Sacred Ground: Leadership, Courage, and Endurance in Our Schools* (2003), league schools usually begin the restructuring process by developing a *covenant,* a set of mutually agreed-on beliefs about how students learn best, and a *charter,* a set of democratically developed guidelines for how shared governance will operate at the school. Presently, nearly 100 league schools exchange resources and ideas and support one another in their restructuring efforts.

WHAT CAN YOU EXPECT AS A BEGINNING TEACHER?

Once you accept the professional challenge of teaching, it is important to prepare well in advance of the first day of school. In addition to reviewing the material you will teach, you should use this time to find out all you can about the school's students, the surrounding community, and the way the school operates. Also reflect on your expectations. To view a video that demonstrates how one teacher organizes his fourth-grade classroom to convey his expectations regarding student accountability, go to MyEducationLab. The video shows how students are made aware of their responsibilities related to tasks such as homework assignments and arranging themselves for the next lesson.

PEARSON
myeducationlab
Go to MyEducationLab, select Chapter 13 and then Activities and Applications to watch the video Modeling Mutual Respect, Routines, and Transitions.

The First Day

The first day of school can be frightening, as the following beginning teacher admits:

> My first day of teaching in the classroom—alone! All of the other teachers look calm and are even smiling. I'm so nervous about fitting in at this school, making friends with my colleagues, and being respected by my students. What if the students misbehave and I don't handle it properly? Or what if the principal walks in unannounced? (Hauser & Rauch, 2002, p. 35)

Veteran teachers can also feel anxious on the first day of school; however, anxiety can be used to set a positive tone for the rest of the school year, as the following experienced teacher points out:

> The anxiety level for both teachers and students about [the] first day is high. Taking advantage of these feelings can make for a good beginning.

> Students like to have guidelines on how the class will be run as well as what is expected of them academically. I always begin by welcoming the students into my class and immediately giving them something to do. I hand them their textbook and an index card. On the card, they write their name, address, telephone number, and book number.

> While the students are filling out their cards and looking at the textbook, I set up my seating chart and verify attendance. Within ten minutes of meeting the students, I begin my first lesson. By keeping clerical chores to a minimum, I try to have more time on task. After a closure activity, somewhere in the middle of the class period I take a few minutes to explain how their grade will be determined, the rules of the class, and when extra help sessions are available.

> Next, we deal with some curriculum content, and then I make a homework assignment. I tell the students that any homework assignment will be written on the chalkboard every day in the same location.

This teacher has planned well for the first day of school. What kinds of planning and classroom management practices have enabled this teacher to be successful at the beginning of the school year?

Setting high standards on the first day makes the following days easier. We will always need to monitor and adjust, but this will be within the framework set on the first day. (Burden & Byrd, 2007, p. 177)

Creating a pleasant, learning-oriented climate on the first day, as this teacher has done, will contribute greatly to your success during the first year. On the first day, students are eager to learn and are hopeful that the year will be a productive one. In addition, nearly all students will be naturally receptive to what you have to say. To them, you are a new, unknown quantity, and one of their initial concerns is to find out what kind of teacher you will be. Therefore, it is critical that you be well organized and ready to take charge. The Teaching on Your Feet feature in this chapter illustrates how an Algebra 1 teacher used the first day of class to communicate positive expectations and support to a student who, at first, doubted his ability to be successful.

Advice From Experienced Teachers

In our work with schools and teachers, we have gathered recommendations on preparing for the first day from experienced K–12 teachers in urban, suburban, and rural schools. Teachers' recommendations focus on planning, establishing effective management practices, and following through on decisions.

There are little things you can do, such as having a personal note attached to a pencil welcoming each child. You may want to do a few little tricks in science class or read them your favorite children's story. But don't put all your energy into the first day and have that day be the highlight of the year. Be well prepared and have plenty of things to do. Don't worry if you don't get everything done. Remember, you have all year.

—Middle school science teacher

It really helps on the first day to have plenty of material to cover and things to do. I'd recommend taking the material you plan to cover that day and doubling it. It's better to have too much than to run out. What you don't use the first day, you use the next. It takes awhile to get a feeling for how fast the kids are going to go.

—Third-grade teacher

The first day is a good time to go over rules and procedures for the year. But don't overdo it. Be very clear and specific about your expectations for classroom behavior.

—Sixth-grade teacher

From the beginning, it's important to do what you're there to do—teach. Teach the class something, maybe review material they learned last year. That lets them know that you're in charge, you expect them to learn. They'll look to you for direction—as long as you give it to them, you're fine.

—Junior high language arts teacher

"I NOW BELIEVE I CAN FLY!"

It was a hot day in the middle of August and another school year was beginning. Each period, as I greeted the new ninth-grade students coming into my Algebra 1 classes, I couldn't help but wonder what kind of hand I had been dealt for the year. It was a surprise to see a student from the previous year come into one of my classes, and all I could think was, "Is he going to fail—again?"

I liked this young man and I wanted to see him succeed. I knew he was intelligent, but the year before, his immaturity and lack of confidence kept him from passing my class. I told him that, because he failed my class the past year, he should give serious thought to having a different teacher this year. A different teacher with a different approach might be his key to success.

I also made it clear that he was welcome to stay in my class. I told him that my perception of him was that he was an intelligent young man and that I believed he could pass Algebra 1. With his head down, he said, "I just can't understand it."

I said, "I think you can, and I am willing to do whatever it takes to help you pass."

He chose to stay in my class, so I talked with him about some things he needed to do differently this year, but I did not make demands. I wanted him to have the autonomy to choose. My main goal was to help him become successful with a few simple tasks at the beginning. I hoped this would grow into a confidence that he could understand Algebra 1 concepts.

So as we started the year, I made certain that he understood procedures and meaning. From the very beginning, he started exclaiming, "This stuff is easy, Mr. Quine." He began completing his classwork before anyone else, and his work was exemplary. I encouraged him appropriately every day, hoping to build his confidence and to build a relationship with him. To let him know how interested I was in him, I greeted him every day when he came to class and always made conversation with him about something other than Algebra 1.

Now he was experiencing success, and so he chose to do the things I had suggested. For example, he began sitting at a place in the room where he would not be distracted by others. Whenever I gave an assignment, he worked at it diligently and always asked me questions if he didn't understand something. If he did poorly on an assessment, he would always review the material and take it again. This was my policy for everyone, but not everyone took advantage of the opportunity. It wasn't long before he was the first to class every day. His grades went from C's and D's at the beginning of the year to A's and B's by the second quarter. He was doing so well that he rarely took an assessment over.

By the middle of the third quarter, I started differentiating with him by giving him more challenging problems. I knew he would rise to the occasion, and I wanted to sustain his success. I also encouraged him because of the quality of his new attitude. Near the middle of the fourth quarter, I started having him work in the geometry text to give him a head start for the next year. One day he asked me, "Mr. Quine, can I have you for Geometry next year? I now believe I can fly!"

ANALYSIS

Effective teachers like Doug Quine understand how teacher expectations can have a powerful, positive influence on student learning. At the beginning of the Algebra 1 class, Quine's student believes that he "just can't understand" algebra; however, his teacher believes otherwise. Buoyed by Quine's belief in his ability to learn, the student gradually experiences success and comes to see himself as a capable learner. In addition, Quine takes responsibility for student learning. In other words, he focuses on what *he* can do as a teacher to increase his student's learning. Furthermore, the student knows that his teacher really cares—that he will do whatever it takes for him to be successful.

REFLECTION

- What can a teacher do to motivate a student who has had a pattern of failing and thinks he or she cannot understand a subject?
- How can a teacher help a student understand abstract concepts?
- What strategies and approaches can a teacher use to sustain students' growth in achievement so they can progress?

Doug Quine
Ninth-Grade Algebra Teacher
Silverado High School

To answer these questions online, go to MyEducationLab **myeducationlab** *at www.myeducationlab.com, select the Activities and Application section, and click on this chapter's Teaching on Your Feet.*

myeducationlab

Go to MyEducationLab, select Chapter 13 and then Activities and Applications to watch the video Classroom Rules.

To view a teacher conducting a discussion with her students regarding why they need a set of rules for the classroom, go to MyEducationLab. After listening to their suggestions, the teacher displays a list of rules and discusses them with students. A week later, she reviews the rules with her students.

HOW WILL YOUR PERFORMANCE AS A TEACHER BE EVALUATED?

Most teachers are evaluated on a regular basis to determine whether their performance measures up to acceptable standards, whether they can create and sustain effective learning environments for students. Performance criteria used to evaluate teachers vary and are usually determined by the school principal, district office, the school board, or a state education agency. In most schools, the principal or a member of the leadership team evaluates teachers.

Teacher evaluations serve many purposes: to determine whether teachers should be retained, receive tenure, or be given merit pay. Evaluations also help teachers assess their effectiveness and develop strategies for self-improvement. In fact, "teachers who receive the most classroom feedback are also most satisfied with teaching" (Glickman, Gordon, & Ross-Gordon, 2007, p. 301).

Quantitative and Qualitative Evaluation

Typically, supervisors use quantitative or qualitative approaches (or a combination) to evaluate teachers' classroom performance. **Quantitative evaluation** includes pencil-and-paper rating forms that the supervisor uses to record classroom events and behaviors objectively in terms of their number or frequency. For example, a supervisor might focus on the teacher's verbal behaviors—questioning, answering, praising, giving directions, and critiquing.

Figure 13.9 presents an observation instrument a supervisor can use to focus on on-task and off-task student behaviors. The supervisor conducts a sweep of the classroom every five minutes, focusing on each student for approximately 20 seconds and then recording the student's behavior according to the key at the bottom of the chart. The results of sweeps conducted between 9:00 and 9:35 indicate that John was frequently off-task, playing; Mark was usually disturbing others; and Shawn G. was always on-task.

Since the late 1980s, several states and a few large cities have developed their own lists of research-based competencies that beginning teachers must demonstrate. These competencies are derived from educational research that has identified what effective teachers do. Typically, the states have developed behavioral indicators for each competency. Trained observers from universities and school districts then use these to determine to what extent teachers actually exhibit the target behaviors in the classroom. The Florida Performance Measurement System (FPMS) was presented in Figure 13.3 and is one example of a research-based observation instrument.

Qualitative evaluation, in contrast, includes written, open-ended narrative descriptions of classroom events in terms of their qualities. These more subjective measures are equally valuable in identifying teachers' weaknesses and strengths. In addition, qualitative evaluation can capture the complexities and subtleties of classroom life that might not be reflected in a quantitative approach to evaluation. For example, read the following excerpt from a supervisor's open-ended narrative; how might the teacher, Mr. X, improve his teaching?

> Students begin arriving at 10:13; the teacher is at his desk correcting papers. The bell rings at 10:15 to begin third period. Students keep arriving. Mr. X gets up from his desk to begin class at 10:25. In the meantime, students have put away their school bags and are awaiting instruction, except three girls in the back corner who are talking, combing their hair, and spreading the contents of their pocketbooks on their desks. Five minutes after Mr. X begins, he talks to them and they put away their combs and pocketbooks. Mr.

	Time When Sweep Began							
Student	**9:00**	**9:05**	**9:10**	**9:15**	**9:20**	**9:25**	**9:30**	**9:35**
Andrew	A	C	D	E	E	A	B	B
Shawn G.	A	A	D	E	E	A	C	B
Maria	A	A	D	E	E	C	B	B
Sam	I	F	F	E	F	A	B	C
Barbara	H	F	D	E	E	F	F	B
Angie	C	G	G	C	E	G	G	G
Jeff	A	A	C	E	E	A	B	B
Jessica	F	F	D	E	E	A	B	E
Shawn L.	A	A	D	E	H	H	B	B
Chris	F	F	D	E	E	A	B	C
Michele	A	A	D	E	H	H	B	B
Mark	A	I	I	F	I	I	I	F
Melissa	C	A	D	E	E	C	H	B
John	J	A	J	I	J	J	J	J
Rolanda	A	C	D	E	E	A	B	F

key

A = on task, listening/watching   F = off task, passive

B = on task, writing   G = off task, doing work for another class

C = on task, speaking   H = off task, listening to others

D = on task, reading   I = off task, disturbing others

E = on task, hands-on activity   J = off task, playing

FIGURE 13.9 Student on-task and off-task behavior
Source: From Glickman, Carl D., Stephen P. Gordon & Jovita M. Ross-Gordon. Supervision and Instructional Leadership: A Developmental Approach, 7e. Published by Allyn & Bacon, Boston, MA. Copyright © 2007 by Pearson Education. Reprinted by permission of the publisher.

X describes the activities for the day but then cannot find his prepared hand-outs. After two minutes of looking, he finds the papers in his desk drawer.

The intercom comes on at 10:30 with two announcements by the principal. Mr. X gives the assignments, and the class begins to read at 10:33. Two students are reprimanded for talking, and occasional student talk can be heard as Mr. X moves around and reviews yesterday's homework with students. He talks with 12 students before asking for class attention at 10:45. He then lectures on the classification of insects. The overhead projection on the board is difficult for students in the back to read. One student asks if he can darken the lights. (Glickman et al., 2007, pp. 256–257)

Clinical Supervision

Many supervisors follow the four-step **clinical supervision** model in which the supervisor first holds a preconference with the teacher, then observes in the classroom, analyzes and interprets observation data, and finally holds a postconference with the teacher (Acheson & Gall, 1997; Glickman et al., 2007; Goldhammer, Anderson, & Krajewski, 1993; Pajak, 1999; Smyth, 1995; Snyder & Anderson, 1996). During the preconference, the teacher and supervisor schedule a classroom observation and determine its purpose and focus and the method of observation to be used. At the postconference, the teacher and supervisor discuss the analysis of observation data and jointly develop a plan for instructional improvement. For example, Pam Johnson, a math-science coordinator, describes the preconference and postconference she had with a fourth-grade teacher:

> During the preconference, to clarify expectations, we discussed what constituted a closed question as opposed to an open-ended question. Together

we designed a chart to denote whether the questions were directed to the whole class, groups, or individuals. The simple, handwritten chart would allow for me to tally the types of questions, and it provided a space for me to script examples of open-ended and closed questions I observed . . . .

During our postobservation discussion, Miss Rogers noticed that some of the closed questions that I recorded could have been asked differently to create open-ended questions by simply adding a phrase of "why" or "explain your thinking." As we discussed the data, we debated different questions and further discussed what constituted closed versus open-ended questions. As the observer and supervisor, I was learning too. We were on common ground and having a rich conversation about student participation. (Glickman et al., 2007, p. 315)

Fulfilling the clinical supervision model is time-consuming, and time-pressed administrators must often modify the approach. For example, when Kim Marshall was a principal at a Boston elementary school with 39 teachers, he made four random, unannounced five-minute visits to classrooms each day. This schedule allowed him to observe every teacher during a two-week period, and each teacher about 19 times during a year. According to Marshall:

[A] regular cycle of five-minute classroom visits with a follow-up conversation after each one is the most efficient way for a principal to monitor classrooms and find the answers to [the following] key questions:

- Are teachers on track with the curriculum?
- Are the students learning?
- Are teachers "happy campers" in terms of their jobs and their lives?
- Do some teachers deserve special praise?
- Do some teachers need redirection, emergency support, or a negative evaluation? (Marshall, 2003, p. 703)

Regardless of the approach a school district uses to evaluate your performance as a beginning teacher, remember that evaluation will assist your professional growth and development. Experienced teachers report that periodic feedback and assistance from knowledgeable, sensitive supervisors is very beneficial; such evaluation results in "improved teacher reflection and higher-order thought, more collegiality, openness, and communication, greater teacher retention, less anxiety and burnout, greater teacher autonomy and efficacy, improved attitudes, improved teaching behaviors, and better student achievement and attitudes" (Glickman et al., 2001, p. 329).

SUMMARY

Why Is Your Induction Into Teaching Important?

- In response to the problem of teacher attrition, many states and school districts provide beginning teachers with induction programs that offer support during their first years in the profession.
- Induction programs offer beginning teachers various types of support, including workshops based on teacher-identified needs, observations and feedback from experienced teachers, mentoring, and support group meetings.

What Can You Learn From Observing in Classrooms?

- You can gain practical experience through field experiences, focused classroom observations, and the use of various observation instruments.
- Observation instruments range from informal, qualitative descriptions to formal, quantitative checklists.

How Can You Gain Practical Experience for Becoming a Teacher?

- Microteaching, teaching simulations, analyses of video cases, field-based practica and clinical experiences, classroom aide programs, student teaching, and substitute teaching are among the ways teacher education students can gain practical experience.

How Can You Develop Your Teaching Portfolio?

- A teaching portfolio documents professional growth and development over time and can be used in teacher evaluation, self-evaluation, and hiring.

What Opportunities for Continuing Professional Development Will You Have?

- Reflection and self-assessment are necessary first steps in pursuing opportunities for professional growth.
- Mentoring can be a source of professional growth for experienced teachers and enables the protégé to learn about the profession.
- Opportunities for professional development include teacher workshops, teacher centers, professional development schools, supervision and mentoring of student teachers, and graduate study.

What New Leadership Roles for Teachers Are Emerging?

- Teachers are assuming new leadership roles beyond the classroom as educational systems become more decentralized and approaches to school leadership become more collaborative and participatory.
- Through their involvement with professional development schools; the National Board for Professional Teaching Standards; and local, state, and national education committees, teachers participate in making key decisions about teacher preparation, certification, and staff development.
- Teachers who work collaboratively with principals on school improvement are involved in 11 dimensions of teacher leadership beyond the classroom: team-building, project management, designing and delivering staff development, researching, public relations, visioning, mentoring new teachers, program/school evaluation, change facilitation,

networking and partnership building, and grant writing/seeking external funding.

How Do Teachers Contribute to Educational Research?

- Teachers validate the accuracy and usefulness of educational research and identify additional areas to research when they put "research into practice."
- Many teachers have become teacher-researchers who conduct action research to improve their teaching.
- The five steps in the classroom-focused action research cycle are (1) teacher-identified question, issue, or problem; (2) observation/data gathering; (3) reflection; (4) hypothesis generation; and (5) testing the hypothesis in the classroom.

How Are Teachers Providing Leadership for School Restructuring and Curriculum Reform?

- Teachers have many opportunities to provide leadership for school reform, including in areas such as teaching as a profession, equity, school organization, assessment of student learning, and curriculum and instruction.

What Can You Expect as a Beginning Teacher?

- Beginning teachers should prepare instructional strategies and materials and learn about their students and the community well in advance of the first day of school.
- Experienced teachers' recommendations for beginning teachers focus on planning, organizing, and following through.

How Will Your Performance as a Teacher Be Evaluated?

- Criteria for evaluating teachers are developed by school principals, districts, school boards, or states and encompass both quantitative and qualitative approaches.
- One approach to teacher performance evaluation is the four-step clinical supervision model in which the supervisor first holds a preconference with the teacher, then observes in the classroom, analyzes and interprets observation data, and finally holds a postconference with the teacher.

PROFESSIONAL REFLECTIONS AND ACTIVITIES

Teacher's Journal

1. Imagine your first day as a teacher. Describe what you see.
2. Do you think there are any limitations regarding the extent to which a teacher should become involved in the 11 dimensions of leadership beyond the classroom that was presented in Figure 13.6? Explain your answer. As a teacher, which leadership activities might you become involved in?

Teacher's Research

1. Use your favorite search engine to gather online information and resources about teacher networking and mentoring. How might online networking provide you with mentoring support and resources during your induction into teaching?
2. Use your favorite search engine to find examples of teachers who are exhibiting one or more of the 11 dimensions of leadership beyond the classroom that was presented in Figure 13.6. To what extent can these teachers serve as role models for developing your own leadership abilities as a teacher?

Observations and Interviews

1. Refer again to the student on-task and off-task observation checklist that was presented in Figure 13.9. Observe two students in a classroom at the level for which you are preparing to teach. What differences do you note between the behaviors of the two students? Are both students about equally engaged in the learning activities?

2. Interview two or more teachers about their involvement in leadership activities outside the classroom. With which of the 11 dimensions of teacher leadership presented in Figure 13.6 are they involved? What benefits do they obtain from their leadership activities?

PEARSON myeducationlab To complete additional observations and interviews, go to MyEducationLab at www.myeducationlab.com, select the Virtual Field Experience section, and click on this chapter's Observations and Interviews.

Professional Portfolio

With reference to the grade level for which you are preparing to teach, compile a set of rules related to classroom conduct and academic work that you would want to present to students on the first day of class. Classroom conduct rules might address areas such as seat assignments; food, drinks, and gum in class; passes to use the washroom; and talking during class. Rules related to academic work might address areas such as materials required for each class, homework, incomplete work, missed quizzes or examinations, assignments turned in late, and makeup work.

PEARSON myeducationlab Now go to MyEducationLab at www.myeducationlab.com to test your understanding of chapter content by completing this chapter's Study Plan.

Growing Toward the Teaching Profession: Florida-Specific Resources

Objectives:
- Describe a Florida teacher's responsibilities and opportunities regarding family involvement.
- Describe a Florida teacher's responsibilities and opportunities regarding self-growth.
- Identify ways to make the most of teacher preparation in Florida.
- Describe how to make the most of searching for a teaching position in Florida.
- Evaluate ways to thrive, not merely survive, during the first year in a Florida classroom.

FEAP Competencies:

Communication (FEAP #2): The preprofessional teacher recognizes the need for effective communication in the classroom and is in the process of acquiring techniques which she/he will use in the classroom.

Continuous Improvement (FEAP #3): The preprofessional teacher realizes that she/he is in the initial stages of a lifelong learning process and that self reflection is one of the key components of that process. While her/his concentration is, of necessity, inward and personal, the role of colleagues and school-based improvement activities increases as time passes. The teacher's continued professional improvement is characterized by self-reflection, working with immediate colleagues and teammates, and meeting the goals of a personal professional development plan.

Role of the Teacher (FEAP #11): The preprofessional teacher communicates and works cooperatively with families and colleagues to improve the educational experiences at the school.

Important Concepts
- Parental involvement
- Community involvement
- Systemic involvement
- Collegial involvement
- Professional development
- Teacher preparation
- Field experience
- Finding a teaching position
- Thriving during the first year of teaching

Activities

Objective 1: Describe a Florida teacher's responsibilities and opportunities regarding family involvement.

Parental and/or family involvement in a child's education has been linked to increased academic achievement and achievement rates, positive attitudes towards school, and improved behavior of students in the classroom. Parental involvement can take many forms, such as attendance at parent-teacher conferences, chaperoning events or field trips, helping students with homework and/or reading aloud, and serving in a leadership capacity.

Roadblocks to parental involvement include work conflicts, socioeconomic differences, and language and/or cultural barriers.

In 2005, there were over 225,000 students enrolled in Florida public school who were classified as Limited English Proficient (LEP). This is approximately 8.4% of the student population. According to the 2000 census, 23% of Floridians speak a language other than English at home. 16.5% of these people speak Spanish.

Questions for Reflection

1. Browse through the Office of Economic and Demographic Research's report about student characteristics at
   http://edr.state.fl.us/reports/education/Characteristics%20of%20students%202003-04%20-%20Final%20-%20Aug%2029%202005.pdf . Look at page 30 of the report and select a district. Using the report, find the percentage of students who speak a language other than English. Brainstorm some ways that language barriers will affect your future classroom. What are some ways that you will help meet the needs of your students who speak other languages?
2. Using the same district, research the number of students who were born in a country other than the U.S. How will cultural barriers affect your classroom? What are some ways you will try to overcome these barriers?
3. How will you seek to get parents involved in your classroom that might have cultural and language barriers?

Objective 2: Describe a Florida teacher's responsibilities and opportunities regarding self-growth.

Membership in an organization such as Florida Education Association can provide invaluable professional development opportunities. There are a number of subject area organizations in Florida that are also excellent resources for self-growth.

For example, Florida Council of Teachers of Mathematics provides support, advocacy, and communication for math teachers in Florida.

Similarly, Florida Council of Teachers of English provides "knowledge, communication, and cooperation among those responsible for teaching English and Language Arts in Florida", according to their Website.

Here are the Websites for the Florida chapters of the professional organizations for each of the four core subject areas:

Florida Council of Teachers of Mathematics
http://www.fctm.net/index.htm

Florida Council for the Social Studies
http://www.fcss.org/index.cfm/fuseaction/Awards.Warren_Tracy

Florida Association of Science Teachers
http://www.fastscience.org/

Florida Council of Teachers of English
http://www.fcte.org/

Questions for Reflection

1. Choose a subject from the list above and visit the Website for the Florida professional organization of your choice. Which did you choose and why?
2. What kinds of information and resources did you find at the Website? How do you see yourself using this information in your future classroom?
3. Does your chosen organization sponsor a regular event for members? Describe the event. How could this kind of event be useful in the area of self-growth?

Objective 3: Identify ways to make the most of teacher preparation in Florida.

Teacher preparation programs in Florida are numerous and diverse. How can you make sure that you are selecting an appropriate program that will best prepare you for the classroom?

Education Preparation Institutes are a fairly new opportunity for people interested in gaining teacher certification. According to the Florida Department of Education Website, EPIs offer any or all of the following:

1) professional development for teachers for classroom improvement and for recertification
2) training for substitute teachers
3) paraprofessional instruction
4) competency-based instruction for Bachelor Degree holders leading to temporary and full teacher certification

The goal of an EPI is to provide "programs with the highest professional and academic standards, with the goal of helping to increase the number of highly qualified teachers in the state."

Questions for Reflection

1. Visit the Florida Academic Counseling and Tracking for Students (FACTS) Website at http://facts23.facts.org/epi_portfolio/index.jsp . This site offers a place for EPI students to create and display portfolios. View some of the sample portfolios. Use both the student and employer views to get a sense of what is available. What are some ways that this tool could be beneficial for teacher preparation students?

2. Visit the Florida Department of Education's EPI site at http://www.fldoe.org/cc/OSAS/APTP/epi.asp and read through the resources. What are your feelings about EPI as an alternative to traditional teacher preparation programs? What are some benefits and drawbacks of this kind of program?

3. Look through the approved EPI program list at http://www.teachinflorida.com/Preparation/EducatorPreparationInstitutes/tabid/187/Default.aspx . Choose one of the institutions and visit their Website. Research their EPI program. What is the general structure of the program? What types of classes are required for successful completion? How would an EPI program at this institution benefit an aspiring teacher?

Objective 4: Describe how to make the most of searching for a teaching position in Florida.

Looking for your first teaching position can be a scary and overwhelming process. Where do you begin? Who do you contact?

The Florida Department of Education offers several resources for teachers looking for teaching opportunities. One of the most helpful is the Teach in Florida Website. This site offers job search engines, job fair listings, recruitment contacts, and a "tool kit" for new teachers.

Questions for Reflection

1. Visit the Teach in Florida Website. Which resource do you think will be the most helpful in your job search?

2. Click on 'Job Search' on the left side of the screen. Fill in the search criteria for your ideal position. If you have an idea about the district you would like to teach in, select it. If not, select 'All Counties'. How many positions did you find? What is your reaction to your search results?

3. Using the results from reflection 2, select one of the positions that came up through your search. What kind of information is provided about the position? How would you follow up on this position?

Objective 5: Evaluate ways to thrive, not merely survive, during the first year in a Florida classroom.

An alarming trend in all states, including Florida, is the increasing rate of teacher turnover. The Florida Department of Education reports that 11% of new teachers leave the classroom after one year of teaching. The attrition rate is high for all categories of teachers, but is highest for recent college graduates and young teachers. A large number of first-year teachers who decide to remain in the field of education will relocate to another school or district after only one year of teaching.

Because of this trend, the Florida Department of Education has developed strategies and resources to support new teachers throughout the state. Their goal is to help new teachers to find success and satisfaction in their teaching careers. They recommend that individual school districts take an active role in mentoring new teachers. Many districts assign veteran teachers to notice teachers for the duration of one or two years.

The Department of Education has also developed a Website with resources for teachers.

Questions for Reflection

1. Visit the Florida DOE Professional Development site at http://www.fldoe.org/profdev/inserv.asp . What kinds of resources are available? Why do you suppose the DOE selected this set of resources?

2. Imagine that you are beginning your first teaching position in a Florida school. Which resources from the DOE site are you most likely to utilize? List the specific resources you find useful and describe your reasoning.

3. As a new teacher, what are some additional resources you would like to see made available?

Important Sources

Florida Comprehensive Assessment Test:
http://fcat.fldoe.org/
"The FCAT, administered to students in Grades 3–11, contains two basic components: criterion-referenced tests (CRT) measuring selected benchmarks in Mathematics, Reading,

Science, and Writing from the Sunshine State Standards (SSS); and norm-referenced tests (NRT) in Reading and Mathematics, measuring individual student performance against national norms."

Keys to FCAT
http://fcat.fldoe.org/fcatkeys.asp
These booklets are distributed by the DOE to teachers each January and contain information for parents and students preparing for FCAT testing.

Teach In Florida
http://www.teachinflorida.com/
This is a rich resource for new and aspiring teachers. Information is available for job seekers and those looking for professional development resources.

Start With Success
http://www.startwithsuccess.com/
This Website was created as a resource for new Florida teachers. The site includes tips, suggestions, and strategies for first-year teachers. It also includes a number of links and resources that are of interest to novice teachers.

Florida State Certification Exam Practice Questions

Directions: The following are 13 multiple-choice questions. Each question prompt is followed by 4 answer choices. Select the response that BEST answers the question.

Question #1

LaQuaker, a ninth-grade student, is having difficulty paying attention and learning new information. What is the best adaptation a teacher could make to help this student?

(A)   Provide her with a Teacher's Aid and materials that are at her reading level.
(B)   Supply her with manipulatives that will make the learning task more concrete.
(C)   Let her practice as a peer tutor with less-skilled students.
(D)   Have her work with peers who understand and can explain the new information.

****

The following scenario should be used in answering questions #2 and #3.

Mr. Kmetz's students keep weekly logs that record information about their learning progress. He requires the following:

- Identify what they learned;
- Describe the strategies used to learn the information or task; and
- List any new ideas or questions that came about as a result of learning the information.

Question #2

What is the most important advantage of having students reflect on the completed task?

(A)   Allow students to share their thoughts openly with the group.
(B)   Identify students who lack leadership abilities and give them responsibilities.
(C)   Help students how their group worked and talk about why things worked.
(D)   Evaluate student work based on the effectiveness of the group's effort

Question #3

What principle supports Mr. Kmetz reasoning for using a learning log?

(A)   Learning logs ask students to generate rules or principles based on their understanding.
(B)   Learning logs have students identify how the lesson was meaningful and relevant.
(C)   Learning logs prompt students to be conscious of the skills and processes they used in a new task.
(D)   Learning logs grade students on the types of examples they give in class.

****

Question # 4

Mr. Outten set up a classroom bulletin board where the students could become part of a three-tiered book club. Students received a certificate for each level they completed. Students earned this honor after submitting a certain number of book reports based on the level of the club. Mr. Outten met monthly with students to review and revise goals.

Lucia, a student in Mr. Outten's class, needs to improve her goal-setting abilities. How will this plan most likely help her achieve this task?

(A)   The plan will encourage a better outlook on school and learning.
(B)   The plan will encourage self-monitoring of both progress and performance.
(C)   The plan will build on personal strengths and focus on skills that best suit her needs.
(D)   The plan will build on the knowledge she already has and reinforce her subset of skills.

Question #5

How will the results from the Weschler Intelligence Scale be best used by a classroom teacher?

    (A)   The results will guide the broad development of lessons.
    (B)   The results will state students' fixed intellectual abilities.
    (C)   The results will identify strengths and weaknesses by content area.
    (D)   The results cannot be used by a classroom teacher.

Question #6

Which of the following best reflects a behavior commonly used for identifying gifted and talented students?

    (A)   limited social skills
    (B)   advanced reading level
    (C)   complex understanding of a content area
    (D)   overachievement in academic tasks

Question #7

Which of the following best represents current research about praise in the classroom?

    (A)   It enhances extrinsic motivation.
    (B)   It provides effective feedback.
    (C)   It builds trust and relationships.
    (D)   It should be continuous and genuine.

Question #8

An eighth-grade teacher plans to share the following concept with her Spanish-language class.

In romance languages, such as Spanish, French, Italian, have a special order of placement for words in a sentence. For example, in English, the article always comes before the noun.

Which of the following strategies is most likely to help the Spanish teacher explain this concept and its implications to her class?

    (A)   Reiterate the concept regularly throughout the semester, using different parts of speech.
    (B)   Require that students diagram Spanish and English sentences.
    (C)   Use a phrase to illustrate the concept and parallels across languages.
    (D)   Hang a poster with a diagrammed sentence showing the placements.

Question #9

While working on 3rd grade math problems, Suzanne stated that she did not like doing all this stuff. She said, "I just can't do it, and it makes me feel stupid." According to theories on motivation, her teacher would first need to work on Suzanne's:

(A) math ability
(B) self-concept
(C) language ability
(D) deductive thinking

Question #10

The effectiveness of a performance assessment would be improved by a teacher doing which of the following?

(A) Evaluating learning by having students complete a predetermined task
(B) Observing students behavior while taking a test
(C) Recording the number of times students' respond to a teacher's questions
(D) Gathering information about student behavior from a variety of sources

Question #11

Mrs. Ryser is preparing an open house for parents and guardians at the beginning of the school year. This will be her first opportunity to establish a partnership and a good rapport with many of the attendees. Which of these would achieve this goal?

(A) Stating the goals for all students and the roles needed by teachers, students, and families to attain the goals.
(B) Discuss ways to establish positive connections between home and school.
(C) Identifying age-appropriate developmental issues that students may face.
(D) Review her teaching background, credentials, and approach to teaching.

Question #12

Mr. Harrell, a new teacher, decides to subscribe to a new professional teaching journal in his field. What is the primary benefit of this decision?

(A) He will read effective strategies for working with challenging students.
(B) It will teach him information he may not know in his content area.
(C) He will become aware of a network of available teachers.
(D) It will keep him aware of current research and trends in education.

Question #13

Mrs. Kang will have a teacher's aide assisting her during mornings. Which steps will help ensure effective communication and planning?

(A)   Divide the curriculum, giving each equal responsibility for specific content areas.
(B)   Use a similar teaching style to meet the needs of the students.
(C)   Set aside time each day to coordinate and discuss issues impacting student learning.
(D)   Identify specific tasks and responsibilities for the aid to accomplish each day.

ANSWER KEY

Question Number	Key
1	D
2	C
3	B
4	B
5	A
6	C
7	D
8	C
9	B
10	D
11	A
12	D
13	C

APPENDIX

PREPARING FOR CERTIFICATION: *Your Guide to Licensure*

LEARNING ABOUT THE *PRAXIS SERIES*™ STATEWIDE TESTING LICENSURE

Many states require prospective teachers to take standardized tests for licensure. The questions and answers in this appendix will help you learn more about this important step to becoming a teacher.

What kinds of tests do states require for certification?

Some tests assess students' competency in the basic skills of reading, writing, and mathematics, often prior to admission to a professional teacher education program. Many states also require standardized tests at the end of a teacher education program; these tests assess prospective teachers' competency and knowledge in their subject area and about teaching and learning.

Do all states use the same test for certification?

No. Some states have developed their own tests. The most commonly used test is the *Praxis Series*™, published by the Educational Testing Service (ETS); as of August 2008, 35 states required some form of the *Praxis Series*™ for certification. You can learn about each state's testing requirements by checking its department of education website or contacting the state department of education by mail or telephone. The University of Kentucky has developed a website with the web addresses for all 50 states' and the District of Columbia's certification requirements (www.uky.edu/Education/TEP/usacert.html).

What is the Praxis Series™, and what is the difference between Praxis I, Praxis II, and Praxis III?

The *Praxis Series*™ is a set of three levels of standardized tests developed by the Educational Testing Service.

Praxis I assesses reading, writing, and mathematics skills. Many states require minimum passing scores on the three Praxis I subtests (also sometimes called the **Preprofessional Skills Test**, or **PPST**) prior to admission to a teacher education program.

Praxis II measures prospective teachers' knowledge of the teaching and learning process and the subjects they will teach. Praxis II includes tests on Principles of Learning and Teaching, specific subject assessments, and multiple subject assessments. Many states require that prospective teachers pass both a subtest on principles of teaching and learning appropriate to the grade level to be taught and either a single-subject or multiple-subject test appropriate to the area of certification. It is important to check with an adviser, testing center, or state certification office about the appropriate Praxis II tests to take for certification.

Praxis III focuses on classroom performance assessment and is usually taken by teachers in their first year of teaching. Prospective teachers who are applying for initial certification are not required to take Praxis III.

If my state uses the Praxis Series™, how do I know which tests to take?

Contact your adviser or student services center if you are currently a student in a teacher education program. If you are applying for certification through an alternative certification program, contact the state department of education's certification office.

What is the format of the Principles of Learning and Teaching (PLT) test?

The Principles of Learning and Teaching tests are two hours in length, and consist of 45 multiple-choice questions and six constructed-response (short-answer) questions. Each test includes three case histories followed by seven multiple-choice and two short-answer questions and 24 additional multiple-choice questions.

What does the PLT test cover?

The PLT covers four broad content categories:

- Organizing Content Knowledge for Student Learning
- Creating an Environment for Student Learning
- Teaching for Student Learning
- Teacher Professionalism

ETS provides descriptions of topics covered in each category on its website (www.ets.org/praxis) and in its free *Test at a Glance* booklet.

What courses in my teacher preparation program might apply to the PLT?

Almost all of your teacher preparation courses relate to the PLT in some way. This text addresses many concepts that are assessed in the PLT tests, particularly in the areas of Creating an Environment for Student Learning and Teacher Professionalism. You have probably studied or will study concepts and knowledge related to the four content categories in courses such as educational foundations, educational psychology or human growth and development, classroom management, curriculum and methods, and evaluation and assessment. You may have had or will have field experiences and seminars that provide knowledge about these concepts.

How should I prepare for the PLT?

Test-taking tips are provided in the next section.

TEST-TAKING TIPS FOR THE *PRAXIS SERIES*™ AND STATE CERTIFICATION TESTS

Test-taking tip 1: Know the test

- **Review the topics covered in the exam.** For the Praxis Series™, the ETS booklet *Test at a Glance* (available online at www.ets.org/praxis or free by mail) includes detailed descriptions of topics covered in each of the four content categories.
- **Take the sample tests.** The ETS provides sample tests for the Praxis Series™ on its website and in its print materials. Analyze the kinds of questions asked, the correct answers, and the knowledge necessary to answer the questions correctly.

- **Analyze the sample questions and the standards used for scoring the responses to open-ended (constructed response) questions.** Read the scoring guides carefully; the test readers will use these criteria to score your written responses. Write your own responses to the sample questions and analyze them using the test-scoring guide. If your responses do not meet all the criteria for a score of 3 on Praxis (or the highest score for your test), revise them.

Test-taking tip 2: Know the content

- **Plan ahead.** You can begin preparing for Praxis and other standardized teacher certification tests early in your program. Think about how each of your courses relates to the concepts and content of the exam.
- **Review what you learned in each course in relation to the topics covered in the test.** Review course textbooks and class notes for relevant concepts and information. At the end of each course, record reminders of how the course's content and knowledge relate to concepts on the test.
- **Think across courses.** The Praxis case studies draw on knowledge from several courses. As you prepare for the exam, think about how knowledge, skills, and concepts from the courses that you took relate to each other. For example, you might have learned about aspects of working with parents in a foundations course, an educational psychology course, or a methods course. Be prepared to integrate that knowledge.
- **Review the content with others.** Meet with a study group and review the test and your course work together. Brainstorm about relevant content using the ETS descriptions or other descriptions of each test's categories and representative topics as a guideline.

Test-taking tip 3: Apply good test-taking strategies

- **Read the test directions carefully.** Even though you have previewed the test format and directions as part of learning about the test, make sure you understand the directions for this test.

For multiple-choice questions:

- **Read each question carefully.** Pay attention to key words such as *not, all, except, always,* or *never*.

- **Try to anticipate the answer to the question before looking at the possible responses.** If your answer is among the choices, it is likely to be correct. Before automatically choosing it, however, carefully read the alternative answers.
- **Answer questions you are certain of first.** Return to questions you are uncertain about later.
- **If you are unsure of the answer, eliminate obviously incorrect responses first.**

For short open-ended response questions:

- **Read the directions carefully.** Look for key words and respond directly to exactly what is asked.
- **Repeat key words from the question to focus your response.** For example, if you are asked to list two advantages of a method, state "Two advantages are (1) . . . and (2) . . ."
- **Be explicit and concrete.** Short-answer responses should be direct and to the point.

For essay questions:

- **Read the question carefully and pay close attention to key words, especially verbs.** Make sure you understand all parts of the question. For example, if the question asks you to list advantages and disadvantages, be sure to answer both parts.
- **Before you write your response, list key points or make an outline.** The few minutes you take to organize your thoughts will pay off in a better-organized essay.
- **Use the question's words in your response.** For example, if the question asks for three advantages, list each in a sentence, "The first advantage is . . . ," "The second advantage is . . . ," and "The third advantage is. . . ." Make it easy for the reader to score your response.
- **Stay on topic.** Answer the question fully and in detail, but do not go beyond what the question asks or add irrelevant material.

SAMPLE STATE LICENSURE TEST QUESTIONS

The following sample questions illustrate the kinds of questions in the Praxis Series™ Principles of Learning and Teaching tests and other state licensure tests. The case study focuses on elementary education, which is the focus of Principles of Learning and Teaching: Grades K–6 (0522). Praxis tests for Principles of Learning and Teaching: Grades 5–9 (0523) and Principles of Learning and Teaching: Grades 7–12 (0524) would include case histories appropriate to those grade levels.

The Principles of Learning and Teaching tests focus on four broad content categories:

- Organizing Content Knowledge for Student Learning
- Creating an Environment for Student Learning
- Teaching for Student Learning
- Teacher Professionalism

The sample questions that follow include one case study followed by three related multiple-choice questions, two short-answer constructed-response questions, and three additional discrete multiple-choice questions. An actual Praxis Principles of Learning and Teaching test would include three case histories, each with seven related multiple-choice questions, two constructed-response questions, and 24 additional discrete multiple-choice questions. It would draw from many courses and field experiences in your teacher education program.

These sample questions focus only on content and issues presented in this text; they are not representative of the actual test in scope, content, or difficulty. Learn more about Praxis and try more sample questions on the Educational Testing Service website at www.ets.org/praxis.

Following the sample questions are answers with explanations and references to Praxis topics and appropriate parts of this book.

SAMPLE CASE STUDY AND RELATED QUESTIONS

Case History: K–6

Columbus, New Mexico, is an agricultural community near the international boundaries separating Mexico and the United States. It's a quiet town where traditional views of community and territory are being challenged. Just three miles from the border is Columbus Elementary School, a bilingual school for kindergarten through fifth-grade students. Of the some 340 students enrolled at Columbus Elementary, approximately 97 percent are on free or reduced price lunches. The school is unique because about 49 percent of the students live in Mexico and attend Columbus Elementary at U.S. taxpayer expense. Columbus Elementary is a fully bilingual school. In the early grades, basic skills are taught in Spanish, but by the third-grade level, students have begun to make the transition to English. Most of the teachers at Columbus Elementary School are English speakers; some have limited Spanish skills. The school also employs teaching assistants who are fluent in Spanish and can assist the teachers in these bilingual classrooms.

Dennis Armijo, the principal of Columbus Elementary School, describes the unique relationship between Columbus and its neighboring community, Palomas, Mexico. "Most of the people who live in Columbus, New Mexico, have relatives in Palomas, Mexico. At one point or another, many Columbus residents were Mexican residents and they came over and established a life here. And so they still have ties to Mexico and a lot of uncles and aunts and grandparents still live in Palomas. They have a kind of family togetherness, where they just go back and forth all the time. The kids that are coming over from Mexico, most of those are U.S. citizens who have been born in the United States. Now the parents may not be able to cross because of illegal status, but the kids are U.S. citizens; they have been born in U.S. hospitals."

Columbus Elementary School's international enrollment poses special challenges for family and parental involvement. Mr. Armijo notes that parental contact is often not as frequent as he would like it to be. The school occasionally runs into problems reaching parents because many don't have telephones and must be reached through an emergency number in Mexico that might be as far as three blocks away or through a relative on the United States side of the border. In many cases, school personnel go into Mexico and talk to the parents or write them a letter so they can cross the border legally to come to the school. Despite these barriers, however, Mr. Armijo says that cooperation from the parents is great. "They'll do anything to help out this school."

The parents who send their children across the border to Columbus Elementary are willing to face the logistical difficulties of getting their children to Columbus each day because they want their children to have the benefits of a bilingual education. Mr. Armijo notes that the only reason that many parents from across the border send their kids to Columbus is to learn English. He describes a potential conflict that sometimes arises from this expectation:

There's—I wouldn't call it a controversy, but there's some misunderstanding, mainly because parents don't understand what a bilingual program is. Some of them don't want their children to speak Spanish at all; they say they are sending the children to our school just to learn English. A true bilingual program will take kids that are monolingual speakers of any language and combine them together. At Columbus Elementary, for example, if you have a monolingual English speaker and a monolingual Spanish speaker, if they are in a true bilingual program you hope that the Spanish speaker will learn English and the English speaker will learn Spanish. And if they live here for the rest of their lives, they will be able to communicate with anybody. So when the students from Mexico come over, they need, as far as I know, they need to learn the skills or the way of life, the American way of life, the American dream, if you will, of an education. Because at some point or another, they might want to come over. Remember, these students are United States citizens, even though they live with their parents in Mexico. I'm almost sure that most of those kids are going to come over across to the United States and live here and so they need to have this education.

Perspective of Linda Lebya, Third-Grade Teacher

Linda Lebya is [in] her third year of teaching third grade at Columbus Elementary School. She lives nearby on a ranch with her husband, who is a deputy sheriff. She speaks conversational Spanish, although she is not a native Spanish speaker. About 95 percent of her third-grade students are Spanish-speaking.

Linda's classroom is small but inviting. Colorful posters and pictures on the wall reflect the students' culture, and many words and phrases are posted in Spanish and English. Desks are grouped in clusters of four so students can sit together facing one another. A list of vocabulary words, written in English and Spanish, is on the blackboard.

Linda describes her teaching approaches and some of the challenges she faces. First, she describes a typical spelling lesson:

On Monday as an introduction for spelling vocabulary we have 10 vocabulary words written in English and Spanish. The intent is for [students] to learn it in English; I also put up the Spanish words with the intent of helping them to learn what the English word means. We discuss the words in English and Spanish, then use them in sentences in each language.

Columbus Elementary is a poor school, and Linda reports that resources are limited:

Lack of books is a problem because we're supposed to be teaching in Spanish for part of the day but the only thing we have in Spanish are the readers. All the other materials are in English so that is a problem.

One resource that Ms. Lebya does have is a Spanish-speaking instructional assistant. She describes the assistant's role in her classroom:

All of the teachers here at Columbus K–3 have an instructional assistant to help out with different things. My assistant this year is really wonderful; she helps out a great deal. She teaches the Spanish reading to the students because I'm not as fluent to teach it. I can speak it and I can understand, but to actually teach it, I wouldn't know how; my Spanish is not strong enough.

Linda describes her understanding of multicultural education:

Multicultural education here means that most of the students are from a different culture. We have a few Anglos but most of the students are Mexicans or Hispanics, and when you are teaching multicultural education, you want to make sure that the students understand that their culture is just as important as the dominant culture. For example, one of our vocabulary words was "fiesta" or "party." Some of our students were not in school that day because they were making their First Holy Communion and their families were having a big celebration. We talked about official fiestas like Cinco de Mayo and family or traditional fiestas like today and the students made English and Spanish sentences about fiestas and parties. It all helps them to value their culture while they learn about the culture of the United States.

And as far as the Spanish sentences, that's just giving them an opportunity to do something well because they already know it in Spanish. They have the vocabulary in Spanish, so they're able to do a good job in making the sentences, and that's something they can feel good about and help their self-esteem. (Kent, Larsen, & Becker, 1998)

SAMPLE TEST QUESTIONS

Sample multiple-choice questions

DIRECTIONS: Each of the multiple-choice questions below is followed by four choices. Select the one that is best in each case.

1. Which approach best describes the philosophy of the bilingual program at Columbus Elementary School?
   A. Children should receive instruction in both English and their native language and culture throughout their school years, making a gradual transition to English.
   B. Students should make the transition to English through ongoing, intensive instruction in English as a second language.
   C. Students should be removed from their regular classes to receive special help in English or in reading in their native language.
   D. Students should be immersed in English, then placed in English-speaking classes.

2. Sleeter and Grant describe five approaches to multicultural education. Which approach best characterizes the Columbus Elementary School program, based on the comments of Ms. Lebya?
   A. Human relations approaches
   B. Single-group studies
   C. Teaching the exceptionally and culturally different
   D. Education that is multicultural and social reconstructionist

3. Ms. Lebya's instructional approach to teaching vocabulary could best be described as
   A. Individualized instruction
   B. Cooperative learning
   C. Inquiry learning
   D. Direct instruction

Sample short-answer questions

The Principles of Learning and Teaching tests include two open-ended short-answer questions related to the case study. A well-constructed short-answer response demonstrates an understanding of the aspects of the case that are relevant to the question; responds to all parts of the question; supports explanations with relevant evidence; and demonstrates a strong knowledge of appropriate concepts, theories, or methodologies relevant to the question. Two readers who are practicing teachers will score the responses according to an ETS scoring guide. (To view the scoring guide, go to the ETS web page: www.ets.org/praxis)

The following sample open-ended questions draw from knowledge and concepts covered in this text only. In an actual Praxis Principles of Learning and Teaching test, respondents should use knowledge and concepts derived from all parts of their teacher education program.

4. Ms. Lebya says that she relies on her instructional assistant to teach reading in Spanish because "I'm not as fluent to teach it. I can speak it and I can understand, but to actually teach it, I wouldn't know how." List at least one positive and one negative possible consequence of this teaching arrangement.

5. Is it possible to teach well without textbooks? If so, in what situations? If not, why not?

Sample discrete multiple-choice questions

The Principles of Learning and Teaching tests include 24 discrete multiple-choice questions that cover an array of teaching and learning topics. In an actual Praxis Principles of Learning and Teaching test, respondents would draw from knowledge and concepts learned in all aspects of an undergraduate teacher preparation program. In this sample test, items are drawn from concepts discussed in *Becoming a Teacher*.

6. On the first day of school, Mr. Jones told his eighth-grade class that all students must arrive at class on time and with all their materials. He posted the same rule on the bulletin board by the door.

   On Tuesday of the second week of school, a classroom visitor observed the following: two students arrived about five minutes late for class and took their seats without any comment from Mr. Jones; one student received permission to go to his locker to get an assignment the class was reviewing; another student borrowed a pen from Mr. Jones so she could complete an in-class activity.

The student actions and teacher response suggest which of the following:

A. Mr. Jones did not establish a set of expectations at the beginning of the year.

B. Mr. Jones did not make consequences clear and apply them consistently.

C. Mr. Jones taught and retaught desired behaviors.

D. Mr. Jones demonstrated "with-it-ness" when working with the students.

7. Mr. Williams placed a pitcher of water and several containers of different sizes and shapes on a table. He asked a small group of students, "Which container holds the most water? Which holds the least? How can you figure it out?"

Mr. Williams's philosophical orientation probably is:

A. behaviorism

B. perennialism

C. constructivism

D. essentialism

8. Ms. Jackson was planning a unit of study for her eleventh-grade American history class. She wanted to determine what students already know and want to know about the topic prior to beginning the unit. Which forms of pre-assessment would be most useful?

A. a norm-referenced test

B. a teacher-made assessment

C. a criterion-referenced test

D. a summative assessment

Answers

1. The best answer is A. In the Columbus School's bilingual program, children learn primarily in Spanish during their first few grades and then begin the transition to English in the third grade. They are not experiencing an intensive English instruction or pullout program, nor are they immersed in English.

    Related Praxis Topics: I. Organizing Content Knowledge for Student Learning/Needs and characteristics of students from diverse populations; II. Creating an Environment for Student Learning/ Appropriate teacher responses to individual and cultural diversity; III. Teaching for Student Learning/Needs and characteristics of students from diverse populations

2. The best answer is C. Both Mr. Armijo and Ms. Lebya emphasize that the purpose of their bilingual program is to help the students assimilate into American culture and acquire language and skills that will help them be successful if they choose to live in the United States.

Related Praxis Topics: I. Organizing Content Knowledge for Student Learning/Needs and characteristics of students from diverse populations; II. Creating an Environment for Student Learning/Appropriate teacher responses to individual and cultural diversity

3. The best answer is D. Ms. Lebya uses a teacher-directed approach, in which she asks specific questions of the students and provides praise or corrective feedback.

    Related Praxis Topics: I. Organizing Content Knowledge for Student Learning/Creating or selecting teaching methods, learning activities, and instructional materials or other resources that are appropriate for the students and are aligned with the goals of the lesson; III. Teaching for Student Learning/Repertoire of flexible teaching and learning strategies

4. A strong response to this open-ended question will explicitly state at least one potential positive consequence and one potential negative consequence to the teaching arrangement. The respondent will use or paraphrase the question and answer explicitly in complete sentences.

    Sample Response: One potential positive consequence of having the Spanish-speaking teaching assistant teach reading in Spanish is that the students will acquire better reading skills in Spanish. If they become good readers in Spanish, they may find it easier to become good readers in English later. One potential negative consequence of having the Spanish-speaking teaching assistant teach reading in Spanish is that she may not have the knowledge or skills to teach reading. (Many teaching assistants have not had the educational preparation that licensed teachers have.) Ms. Lebya's Spanish may not be strong enough to pick up on those problems or correct them. Thus, the children may not become strong readers in Spanish.

    Related Praxis Topic: III. Teaching for Student Learning/Making content comprehensible to students; IV. Teacher Professionalism/Reflecting on the extent to which learning goals were met

5. A strong response to this open-ended question will explicitly take a position on the necessity of textbooks and will defend that position. The respon-

dent will use or paraphrase the question and answer explicitly in complete sentences.

Sample Response: It is entirely possible to teach well without textbooks. Although textbooks can be an invaluable resource for teachers, they are only one kind of resource that can be used for instruction. Instead of textbooks, teachers could use a collection of printed materials, such as articles or primary resources, or websites from the Internet. The teacher could also use multimedia resources, such as films, videotapes, or audiotapes. To teach well without textbooks, however, the teacher must have clear goals and spend time looking for good alternative materials.

Related Praxis Topic: I. Organizing Content Knowledge for Student Learning/Creating or selecting teaching methods, learning activities, and instructional materials or other resources that are appropriate for the students and are aligned with the goals of the lesson

6. The best answer is B. Although Mr. Jones established and posted classroom procedures at the beginning of the school year, he did not make consequences clear. When students did not follow the procedures, he did not correct the students or remind them of the established classroom expectations.

Related Praxis Topic: II. Creating an Environment for Student Learning/Establishing and maintaining consistent standards of classroom behavior

7. The best answer is C. Mr. Williams encouraged the students to construct meaning or make sense of information for themselves, one of the characteristics of constructivism.

Related Praxis Topic: I. Organizing Content Knowledge for Student Learning/Major theories of human development and learning; III. Teaching for Student Learning/Stages and patterns of cognitive and cultural development

8. The best answer is B. Ms. Jackson can best find out what students know and want to know by designing her own instrument.

Related Praxis Topic: I. Organizing Content Knowledge for Student Learning/Structuring lessons based on the knowledge, experiences, skills, strategies, and interests of the students in relation to the curriculum.

REFERENCES

Educational Testing Service (ETS). (2002). *Tests at a glance: Praxis II Subject Assessments/Principles of Learning and Teaching.* Available online: www.ets.org/praxis/prxtest.html

Kent, T. W., Larsen, V. A., & Becker, F. J. (1998). *Educational border culture in New Mexico.* Boston: Allyn & Bacon.

GLOSSARY

A

academic freedom: the right of teachers to teach, free from external constraint, censorship, or interference.

academic learning time: the amount of time students spend working on academic tasks with a high level of success (80 percent or higher).

academies: early secondary schools with broader and more practical curricula than those found in grammar schools of the previous era.

accelerated schools: a national network of schools that provide enriched, rigorous curricula to speed up the learning of students at risk.

acceleration: the process of providing academically enriched programs to meet the needs of intellectually advanced students—for example, early entrance, grade skipping, rigorous curricula, credit by examination, and early entrance to college.

accountability: the practice of holding teachers responsible for adhering to high professional and moral standards and creating effective learning environments for all students.

achievement gap: the continuing gap in academic achievement between White students and Hispanic, African American, and American Indian/Alaska Native students.

action research: classroom-based study, by teachers, of how to improve their instruction.

adequate yearly progress (AYP): a provision of the No Child Left Behind Act of 2001 requiring that schools provide evidence each year that students are making "adequate yearly progress."

aesthetics: the branch of axiology concerned with values related to beauty and art.

Afrocentric schools: schools that focus on African American history and cultures for African American pupils.

allocated time: the amount of time teachers allocate for instruction in various areas of the curriculum.

alternate assessment: an alternative way of measuring the performance of students who are unable to participate in traditional approaches to assessment.

alternative assessments: approaches that assess students' ability to complete real-life tasks rather than merely regurgitate facts.

alternative school: a small, highly individualized school separate from a regular school; designed to meet the needs of students at risk.

alternative teacher certification: a provision allowing people who have completed college but not a teacher education program to become certified teachers.

Amendments to the Individuals with Disabilities Education Act (IDEA 97): amendments to IDEA that emphasize educational outcomes for students with disabilities and provide greater access through changes in eligibility requirements, IEP guidelines, public and private placements, student discipline guidelines, and procedural safeguards.

American Federation of Teachers (AFT): a national professional association for teachers, affiliated with the AFL-CIO.

analytic rubric: a rating scale, or scoring guide, for evaluating part of a student's product or performance.

assertive discipline: an approach to classroom discipline requiring that teachers establish firm, clear guidelines for student behavior and follow through with consequences for misbehavior.

assessment: the process of gathering information related to how much students have learned.

assistive technology: technological advances (usually computer-based) that help exceptional students learn and communicate.

Association for Supervision and Curriculum Development (ASCD): a professional organization for educators interested in school improvement at all levels.

attention deficit disorder (ADD): a learning disability characterized by difficulty in concentrating on learning.

attention deficit hyperactivity disorder (ADHD): a learning disability characterized by difficulty in remaining still so that one can concentrate on learning.

authentic assessment: an approach to assessing students' learning that requires them to solve problems or work on tasks that approximate as much as possible those they will encounter beyond the classroom.

authentic learning tasks: learning activities that enable students to see the connections between classroom learning and the world beyond the classroom.

axiology: the study of values, including the identification of criteria for determining what is valuable.

B

back-to-basics: a movement begun in the mid-1970s to establish the basic skills of reading, writing, speaking, and computation as the core of the school curriculum.

behaviorism: based on behavioristic psychology, this philosophical orientation maintains that environmental factors shape people's behavior.

benchmarks: statements of what students should understand and be able to do at specific grade levels or developmental stages.

between-class ability grouping: the practice of grouping students at the middle and high school levels for instruction on the basis of ability or achievement, often called tracking.

bicultural: the ability to function effectively in two or more linguistic and cultural groups.

bilingual education: a curriculum for non-English-speaking and English-speaking students in which two languages are used for instruction and biculturalism is emphasized.

blended learning: a blending of online and face-to-face instruction.

block grants: a form of federal aid given directly to the states, which a state or local education agency may spend as it wishes with few limitations.

block scheduling: a high school scheduling arrangement that provides longer blocks of time each class period, with fewer periods each day.

blog: an online journal constructed by an individual and reacted to by those who visit the blog (short for *web log*).

***Brown v. Board of Education of Topeka*:** a 1954 landmark U.S. Supreme Court case rejecting the separate but equal doctrine used to prevent African Americans from attending schools with whites.

Buckley Amendment: a 1974 law, the Family Educational Rights and Privacy Act, granting parents of students under 18 and students over 18 the right to examine their school records.

C

caring classroom: a classroom in which the teacher communicates clearly an attitude of caring about students' learning and their overall well-being.

categorical aid: state-appropriated funds to cover the costs of educating students with special needs.

censorship: the act of removing from circulation printed material judged to be libelous, vulgar, or obscene.

character education: an approach to education that emphasizes the teaching of values, moral reasoning, and the development of "good" character.

charter: an agreement between a charter school's founders and its sponsors specifying how the school will operate and what learning outcomes students will master.

charter schools: independent schools, often founded by teachers, that are given a charter to operate by a school district, state, or national government, with the provision that students must demonstrate mastery of predetermined outcomes.

chief state school officer: the chief administrator of a state department of education and head of the state board of education, often called the commissioner of education or superintendent of public instruction.

choice theory: an approach to classroom management, developed by psychiatrist William Glasser, based on a belief that students will usually make good choices (i.e., behave in an acceptable manner) if they experience success in the classroom and know that teachers care about them.

classroom climate: the atmosphere or quality of life in a classroom, determined by how individuals interact with one another.

classroom culture: the way of life characteristic of a classroom group; determined by the social dimensions of the group and the physical characteristics of the setting.

classroom management: day-to-day teacher control of student behavior and learning, including discipline.

classroom organization: how teachers and students in a school are grouped for instruction and how time is allocated in classrooms.

clinical supervision: a four-step model supervisors follow in making teacher performance evaluations.

Coalition of Essential Schools: a national network of public and private high schools that have restructured according to nine Common Principles.

code of ethics: a set of guidelines that defines appropriate behavior for professionals.

cognitive development: the process of acquiring the intellectual ability to learn from interaction with one's environment.

cognitive science: the study of the learning process that focuses on how individuals manipulate symbols and process information.

collaboration: the practice of working together, sharing decision making, and solving problems among professionals.

collaborative consultation: an approach in which a classroom teacher meets with one or more other professionals (such as a special educator, school psychologist, or resource teacher) to focus on the learning needs of one or more students.

collective bargaining: a process followed by employers and employees in negotiating salaries, hours, and working conditions; in most states, school boards must negotiate contracts with teacher organizations.

collectivistic cultures: cultures that tend to emphasize group membership and a sense of "we" rather than "I"—in contrast to individualistic cultures that emphasize the individual and his or her success and achievement.

collegiality: a spirit of cooperation and mutual helpfulness among professionals.

collegial support team (CST): a team of teachers—created according to subject area, grade level, or teacher interests and expertise—who support one another's professional growth.

Commission on the Reorganization of Secondary Education: an NEA committee that called for a high school curriculum designed to accommodate individual differences in scholastic ability and based on seven educational goals, or "cardinal principles" (1913).

Committee of Fifteen: an NEA committee that recommended an academically rigorous curriculum for elementary students (1895).

Committee of Ten: an NEA committee that recommended an academically rigorous curriculum for high school students (1893).

common schools: free state-supported schools that provide education for all students.

compensatory education programs: federally funded educational programs designed to meet the needs of low-ability students from low-income families.

concrete operations stage: the stage of cognitive development (7 to 11 years of age) proposed by Jean Piaget in which the individual develops the ability to use logical thought to solve concrete problems.

constructive assertiveness: an approach to classroom management that calls for the teacher to communicate to misbehaving student(s) a direct, clear statement of the problem; maintain direct eye contact with the student(s); and insist upon correct behavior.

constructivism: a psychological orientation that views learning as an active process in which learners construct understanding of the material they learn—in contrast to the view that teachers transmit academic content to students in small segments.

constructivist teaching: a method of teaching based on students' prior knowledge of the topic and the processes they use to construct meaning.

content standards: the content—or knowledge and skills—students should acquire in various academic disciplines.

cooperative learning: an approach to education in which students work in small groups, or teams, sharing the work and helping one another complete assignments.

copyright laws: laws limiting the use of photocopies, videotapes, and computer software programs.

corporal punishment: physical punishment applied to a student by a school employee as a disciplinary measure.

cost of living: the amount of money needed, on average, for housing, food, transportation, utilities, and other living expenses in a given locale.

co-teaching: an arrangement whereby two or more teachers teach together in the same classroom.

criterion-referenced assessments: assessments of achievement that compare students' performance with clearly defined criteria or standards.

critical pedagogy: an educational orientation that emphasizes education as a way to promote social justice and equity for those who do not enjoy positions of power and influence in society.

cross-age tutoring: a tutoring arrangement in which older students tutor younger students; evidence indicates that cross-age tutoring has positive effects on the attitudes and achievement of tutee and tutor.

cultural identity: an overall sense of oneself, derived from the extent of one's participation in various subcultures within the national macroculture.

cultural pluralism: the preservation of cultural differences among groups of people within one society. This view is in contrast to the melting-pot theory that says that ethnic cultures should melt into one.

culture: the way of life common to a group of people; includes knowledge deemed important, shared meanings, norms, values, attitudes, ideals, and view of the world.

curriculum: the school experiences, both planned and unplanned, that enhance (and sometimes impede) the education and growth of students.

curriculum alignment: the process of ensuring that the content of curricula and textbooks reflects desired learning outcomes, or academic standards, for students.

curriculum framework: a document that provides guidelines, instructional and assessment strategies, resources, and models for teachers to use as they develop curricula aligned with academic standards.

cyberbullying: using information and/or communication technologies to harass or threaten an individual or group.

D

dame schools: colonial schools, usually held in the homes of widows or housewives, for teaching children basic reading, writing, and mathematical skills.

democratic classroom: a classroom in which the teacher's leadership style encourages students to take more power and responsibility for their learning.

departmentalization: an organizational arrangement for schools in which students move from classroom to classroom for instruction in different subject areas.

desegregation: the process of eliminating schooling practices based on the separation of racial groups.

Digital Millennium Copyright Act (DMCA): an amendment to the Copyright Act of 1998, making it illegal to reproduce copyrighted material in digital format.

direct instruction: a systematic instructional method focusing on the transmission of knowledge and skills from the teacher to the students.

discovery learning: an approach to teaching that gives students opportunities to inquire into subjects so that they "discover" knowledge for themselves.

dismissal: the involuntary termination of a teacher's employment; termination must be made for a legally defensible reason with the protection of due process.

distance learning: the use of technology such as video transmissions that enables students to receive instruction at multiple, often remote, sites.

diversity: differences among people in regard to gender, race, ethnicity, culture, and socioeconomic status.

due process: a set of specific guidelines that must be followed to protect individuals from arbitrary, capricious treatment by those in authority.

E

early childhood education: educational programs for children from birth to age 8, also termed *pre-K education*.

educational malpractice: liability for injury that results from the failure of a teacher, school, or school district to provide a student with adequate instruction, guidance, counseling, and/or supervision.

educational philosophy: a set of ideas and beliefs about education that guide the professional behavior of educators.

educational politics: how people use power, influence, and authority to affect instructional and curricular practices within a school or school system.

educational reform movement: a comprehensive effort made during the 1980s and into the 1990s to improve schools and the preparation of teachers.

Education Consolidation and Improvement Act (ECIA): a 1981 federal law giving the states a broad range of choices for spending federal aid on education.

Education for All Handicapped Children Act (Public Law 94-142): a 1975 federal act that guarantees a free and appropriate education to all children with handicaps (often referred to as the mainstreaming law or Public Law 94-142).

e-learning: education that is delivered via the Internet, satellite broadcast, interactive TV, or CD-ROM.

Elementary and Secondary Education Act: part of President Lyndon B. Johnson's Great Society Program, this act allocated federal funds on the basis of the number of poor children in school districts.

emergency certification: temporary, substandard certification requirements set by a state in response to a shortage of teachers.

emotional intelligence: the capacity to be aware of and to manage one's feelings.

English-language learners (ELLs): students whose first language is not English.

entitlements: federal programs to meet the educational needs of special populations.

epistemology: a branch of philosophy concerned with the nature of knowledge and what it means to know something.

e-portfolio: an online site where an individual can place products that represent accomplishments in an area of interest.

e-rate: a controversial program that uses fees from telecommunications companies to provide discounts on telecommunications services and wiring to schools and libraries.

essentialism: formulated in part as a response to progressivism, this philosophical orientation holds that a core of common knowledge about the real world should be transmitted to students in a systematic, disciplined way.

ethical dilemmas: problem situations in which an ethical response is difficult to determine; that is, no single response can be called "right" or "wrong."

ethics: a branch of philosophy concerned with principles of conduct and determining what is good and evil, right and wrong, in human behavior.

ethnic group: individuals within a larger culture who share a racial or cultural identity and a set of beliefs, values, and attitudes and who consider themselves members of a distinct group or subculture.

ethnicity: a shared feeling of common identity that derives, in part, from a common ancestry, common values, and common experiences.

evaluation: making judgments about, or assigning a value to, measurements of students' learning.

exceptional learners: students whose growth and development deviate from the norm to the extent that their educational needs can be met more effectively through a modification of regular school programs.

existentialism: a philosophical orientation that emphasizes the individual's experiences and maintains that each individual must determine his or her own meaning of existence.

expenditure per pupil: the amount of money spent on each pupil in a school, school district, state, or nation; usually computed according to average daily attendance.

explicit curriculum: the behavior, attitudes, and knowledge that a school intends to teach students.

extracurricular/cocurricular programs: activities perceived as additions to the academic curriculum.

F

FaceBook: a popular form of online social networking that people use to communicate with a network of friends who have common interests.

fair use: the right of an individual to use copyrighted material in a reasonable manner without the copyright holder's consent, provided that use meets certain criteria.

female seminaries: schools established in the early nineteenth century to train women for higher education and public service outside the home.

feminist pedagogy: a philosophical orientation that emphasizes caring, respect for individual differences, and collaboration to achieve the aims of a democratic and just society.

field experiences: opportunities for teachers-in-training to experience firsthand the world of the teacher by observing, tutoring, and instructing small groups.

formal operations stage: the stage of cognitive development (11 to 15 years of age) proposed by Jean Piaget in which cognitive abilities reach their highest level of development.

formative evaluation: an assessment, or diagnosis, of students' learning for the purpose of planning instruction.

for-profit schools: schools that are operated, for profit, by private educational corporations.

Freedmen's Bureau: a U.S. government agency to provide assistance to former slaves after the Civil War.

freedom of expression: freedom, granted by the First Amendment to the Constitution, to express one's beliefs.

fringe benefits: benefits (i.e., medical insurance, retirement, and tax-deferred investment opportunities) that are given to teachers in addition to base salary.

full-funding programs: state programs to ensure statewide financial equity by setting the same per-pupil expenditure level for all schools and districts.

full inclusion: the policy and process of including exceptional learners in general education classrooms.

full-service community schools: schools that provide students and their families with medical, social, and human services, in addition to their regular educational programs.

G

gender bias: subtle bias or discrimination on the basis of gender; reduces the likelihood that the target of the bias will develop to the full extent of his or her capabilities.

gender-fair classroom: education that is free of bias or discrimination on the basis of gender.

G.I. Bill of Rights: a 1944 federal law that provides veterans with payments for tuition and room and board at colleges and universities and special schools; formally known as the Servicemen's Readjustment Act.

gifted and talented: exceptional learners who demonstrate high intelligence, high creativity, high achievement, or special talents.

grievance: a formal complaint filed by an employee against his or her employer or supervisor.

group investigation: an approach to teaching in which the teacher facilitates learning by creating an environment that allows students to determine what they will study and how.

H

hidden curriculum: the behaviors, attitudes, and knowledge that the school culture unintentionally teaches students.

hierarchy of needs: a set of seven needs, from the basic needs for survival and safety to the need for self-actualization, that motivate human behavior as identified by Abraham Maslow.

highly qualified teachers (HQTs): teachers who have the following qualifications as contained in No Child Left Behind legislation: bachelor's degree, full state certification, and knowledge of the subject(s) they teach.

High School: A Report on Secondary Education in America: a book by Ernest Boyer calling for a strengthened academic core curriculum in high schools (1983).

high-stakes tests: achievement tests that have high-stakes consequences for students, teachers, and administrators—for example, a test that determines if a student is eligible to graduate or whether educators receive merit pay increases.

holistic rubric: a rating scale, or scoring guide, for evaluating a student's overall product or performance.

horn book: a copy of the alphabet covered by a thin transparent sheet made from a cow's horn.

humanism: a philosophy based on the belief that individuals control their own destinies through the application of their intelligence and learning.

humanistic psychology: an orientation to human behavior that emphasizes personal freedom, choice, awareness, and personal responsibility.

I

inclusion: the practice of integrating all students with disabilities into general education classes.

Indian Education Act of 1972 and 1974 Amendments: a federal law and subsequent amendment designed to provide direct educational assistance to Native American tribes and nations.

individualistic cultures: cultures that tend to emphasize the individual, his or her success and achievement, and a sense of "I"—in contrast to collectivistic cultures that emphasize group membership and a sense of "we."

individualized education plan (IEP): a plan for meeting an exceptional learner's educational needs, specifying goals, objectives, services, and procedures for evaluating progress.

individual racism: the prejudicial belief that one's ethnic or racial group is superior to others.

Individuals with Disabilities Education Act (IDEA): a 1990 federal act providing a free, appropriate education to disabled youth between 3 and 21 years of age. IDEA

superseded the earlier Education for All Handicapped Children Act (Public Law 94-142).

induction programs: programs of support for beginning teachers, usually during their first year of teaching.

information processing: a branch of cognitive science concerned with how individuals use long- and short-term memory to acquire information and solve problems.

inquiry learning: an approach to teaching that gives students opportunities to explore or inquire into subjects so that they develop their own answers to problem situations.

in-service workshops: on-site professional development programs in which teachers meet to learn new techniques, develop curricular materials, share ideas, or solve problems.

institution: any organization a society establishes to maintain and improve its way of life.

institutional racism: institutional policies and practices, intentional or not, that result in racial inequities.

integrated curriculum: a school curriculum that draws from two or more subject areas and focuses on a theme or concept rather than on a single subject.

intelligence: the ability to learn; the cognitive capacity for thinking.

International Assessment of Educational Progress (IAEP): a program established in 1991 for comparing the achievement of students in the United States with that of students from other countries.

internship programs: programs of assistance and training for beginning teachers, usually for those who have not gone through a teacher education program.

Interstate New Teacher Assessment and Support Consortium (INTASC): an organization of states established in 1987 to develop performance-based standards for what beginning teachers should know and be able to do.

K

Kentucky Education Reform Act (KERA): comprehensive school-reform legislation requiring all Kentucky schools to form school-based management councils with authority to set policies in eight areas.

kindergarten: a school for children before they begin formal schooling at the elementary level; based on the ideas of German educator Friedrick Fröebel, *kindergarten* means "garden where children grow."

L

Lanham Act: a U.S. government program during World War II that provided funding for training workers in war plants, construction of schools, and child care for working parents.

latchkey children: children who, because of family circumstances, must spend part of each day unsupervised by a parent or guardian.

Latin grammar school: colonial schools established to provide male students with a precollege education; comparable to today's high schools.

learning disability (LD): a limitation in one's ability to take in, organize, remember, and express information.

learning management system: software tools that enable teachers to organize and manage various types of information and data related to their teaching—for example, students' test scores, individual learning needs.

learning objects: digital resources containing a small amount of information that can be reused to support learning—for example, learning objects stored at the National Science Digital Library or at PBS Teachers.

learning styles: cognitive, affective, and physiological behaviors through which an individual learns most effectively; determined by a combination of hereditary and environmental influences.

least restrictive environment: an educational program that meets a disabled student's special needs in a manner that is identical, insofar as possible, to that provided to students in general education classrooms.

Lemon test: a three-part test, based on *Lemon v. Kurtzman*, to determine whether a state has violated the separation of church and state principle.

lesbian, gay, bisexual, and transgender (LGBT) students: students whose sexual orientation may subject them to discrimination and/or harassment in school settings.

limited English proficiency (LEP): a designation for students with limited ability to understand, read, or speak English and who have a first language other than English.

local school council (LSC): a group of community members that is empowered to develop policies for the operation of local schools.

local school district: an agency at the local level that has the authority to operate schools in the district.

logic: a branch of philosophy concerned with the processes of reasoning and the identification of rules that will enable thinkers to reach valid conclusions.

M

magnet school: a school offering a curriculum that focuses on a specific area such as the performing arts, mathematics, science, international studies, or technology. Magnet schools, which often draw students from a larger attendance area than regular schools, are frequently developed to promote voluntary desegregation.

mainstreaming: the policy and process of integrating disabled or otherwise exceptional learners into regular classrooms with nonexceptional students.

Massachusetts Act of 1642: a law requiring each town to determine whether its young people could read and write.

Massachusetts Act of 1647: a law mandating the establishment and support of schools; often referred to as the Old Deluder Satan Act because education was seen as the best protection against the wiles of the devil.

mastery learning: an approach to instruction based on the assumptions that (1) nearly all students can learn material if given enough time and taught appropriately and (2) learning is enhanced if students can progress in small, sequenced steps.

McGuffey readers: an immensely popular series of reading books for students in grades 1 through 6, written in the 1830s by Reverend William Holmes McGuffey.

McKinney-Vento Act: the nation's first law to provide assistance to homeless persons, including free public education for children.

measurement: the gathering of data that indicate how much students have learned.

mentor: a wise, knowledgeable individual who provides guidance and encouragement to someone.

mentoring: an intensive form of teaching in which a wise and experienced teacher (the mentor) inducts a student (the protégé) into a professional way of life.

metaphysics: a branch of philosophy concerned with the nature of reality.

microcomputer-based laboratories (MBLs): the use of computers to gather and then analyze data that students have collected in a school laboratory or in the field.

microteaching: a brief, single-concept lesson taught by a teacher education student to a small group of students; usually designed to give the education student an opportunity to practice a specific teaching skill.

minorities: groups of people who share certain characteristics and are smaller in number than the majority of a population.

modeling: the process of thinking out loud that teachers use to make students aware of the reasoning involved in learning new material.

Montesorri method: a method of teaching, developed by Maria Montessori, based on a prescribed set of materials and physical exercises to develop children's knowledge and skills.

moral reasoning: the reasoning process people follow to decide what is right or wrong.

Morrill Land-Grant Act: an 1862 act that provided federal land that states could sell or rent to raise funds to establish colleges of agriculture and mechanical arts.

multiage classrooms: elementary classrooms with students from different grade levels.

multicultural curriculum: a school curriculum that addresses the needs and backgrounds of all students regardless of their cultural identity and includes the cultural perspectives, or voices, of people who have previously been silent or marginalized.

multicultural education: education that provides equal educational opportunities to all students—regardless of socioeconomic status; gender; or ethnic, racial, or cultural backgrounds—and is dedicated to reducing prejudice and celebrating the rich diversity of U.S. life.

multiculturalism: a set of beliefs based on the importance of seeing the world from different cultural frames of reference and valuing the diversity of cultures in the global community.

multiple intelligences: a perspective on intellectual ability, proposed by Howard Gardner, suggesting that there are at least eight, and maybe as many as ten, types of human intelligence.

MySpace: a popular form of online social networking that people use to communicate with a network of friends who have common interests.

N

NASDTEC Interstate Agreement: a reciprocity agreement among approximately 47 states and the District of Columbia whereby a teaching certificate obtained in one state will be honored in another; developed by the National Association of State Directors of Teacher Education and Certification (NASDTEC).

National Board for Professional Teaching Standards (NBPTS): a board established in 1987 that began issuing professional certificates in 1994–95 to teachers who possess extensive professional knowledge and the ability to perform at a high level.

National Council for Accreditation of Teacher Education (NCATE): an agency that accredits, on a voluntary basis, almost half of the nation's teacher education programs.

National Defense Education Act: a 1958 federally sponsored program to promote research and innovation in science, mathematics, modern foreign languages, and guidance.

National Education Association (NEA): the oldest and largest professional association for teachers and administrators.

National Governor's Association (NGA): an association of state governors that influences policies in several areas, including teacher education and school reform.

National Information Infrastructure (NII): a federal plan to create a telecommunications infrastructure linking all schools, libraries, hospitals, and law enforcement agencies to the Internet and the World Wide Web.

National Network for Educational Renewal (NNER): a national network of colleges and universities that collaborate with school districts and partner schools to reform education according to 19 postulates in John Goodlad's *Teachers for Our Nation's Schools* (1990).

A Nation at Risk: a 1983 national report critical of U.S. education.

NEAFT Partnership: an agreement between the National Education Association and the American Federation of Teachers to work collaboratively to attain mutually desired goals for the teaching profession.

negligence: failure to exercise reasonable, prudent care in providing for the safety of others.

No Child Left Behind (NCLB) Act of 2001: a federal law that mandates statewide testing in reading and mathematics each year in grades 3–8 and holds schools accountable for students' performance on state proficiency tests.

nondiscrimination: conditions characterized by the absence of discrimination; for example, employees receive compensation, privileges, and opportunities for advancement without regard for race, color, religion, sex, or national origin.

normal schools: schools that focus on the preparation of teachers.

norm-referenced assessments: achievement tests that compare students' scores with scores of other students who are similar.

null curriculum: the intellectual processes and subject content that schools do not teach.

O

observations: field experiences wherein a teacher education student observes a specific aspect of classroom life such as the students, the teacher, the interactions between the two, the structure of the lesson, or the setting.

Office of Educational Research and Improvement (OERI): a federal agency that promotes educational research and improving schools through the application of research results.

online social networking: an online community of people who share common interests and use methods such as e-mail, chat rooms, blogging, voice chat, and discussion groups to communicate.

open source materials: software, learning materials, and other digital resources that are available for free on the Internet.

open-space schools: schools that have large instructional areas with movable walls and furniture that can be rearranged easily.

opportunity to learn (OTL): the time during which a teacher provides students with challenging content and appropriate instructional strategies to learn that content.

outcome-based teacher education: an approach to teacher education emphasizing outcomes (what teachers should be able to do, think, and feel) rather than the courses they should take.

out-of-school time (OST) activities: growth-oriented activities for students that take place beyond the school day; often called extracurricular activities.

P

Paideia Proposal: a book by philosopher Mortimer Adler calling for a perennialist core curriculum based on the Great Books (1982).

parochial schools: schools founded on religious beliefs.

pedagogical content knowledge: the knowledge accomplished teachers possess regarding how to present subject matter to students through the use of analogies, metaphors, experiments, demonstrations, illustrations, and other instructional strategies.

peer assessment: the practice of having students assess one another's work; usually done informally and during a class session.

peer coaching: an arrangement whereby teachers grow professionally by observing one another's teaching and providing constructive feedback.

peer counseling: an arrangement whereby students, monitored by a school counselor or teacher, counsel one another in areas such as low achievement, interpersonal problems, substance abuse, and career planning.

peer-mediated instruction: approaches to teaching, such as cooperative learning and group investigation, that use the social relationships among students to promote their learning.

peer mediation: experiential activities, such as role-playing and simulations, that encourage students to be more accepting of differences and to develop empathy, social skills, and awareness of prejudice.

peer tutoring: an arrangement whereby students tutor other students in the same classroom or at the same grade level.

perennialism: a philosophical orientation that emphasizes the ideas contained in the Great Books and maintains that the true purpose of education is the discovery of the universal, or perennial, truths of life.

performance-based assessment: the process of determining students' ability to apply knowledge, skills, and work habits to the performance of specific learning tasks; determining what students can do as well as what they know.

performance-based teacher education: an approach to teacher education emphasizing performances (what teachers should be able to do, think, and feel) rather than the courses they should take.

performance expectations: established levels of achievement, quality of performance, or level of proficiency.

performance standard: academic standards that reflect levels of proficiency—for example, "1 = outstanding, 2 = exemplary, 3 = proficient, 4 = progressing, and 5 = standard not met."

Phi Delta Kappa (PDK): a professional and honorary fraternity of educators with 650 chapters and 130,000 members.

philosophy: the use of logical reasoning to inquire into the basic truths about being, knowledge, and conduct.

podcast: delivery of digital-media files over the Internet and played back on portable media players such as iPods.

portfolio assessment: the process of determining how much students have learned by examining collections of work that document their learning over time.

postmodernism: a philosophical orientation that maintains there are no absolute truths; instead, there are many truths and many voices that need to be heard.

practicum: a short field-based experience during which teacher education students spend time observing and assisting in classrooms.

Praxis Series: Professional Assessments for Beginning Teachers: a battery of tests available to states for the initial certification of teachers. Consists of assessments in three areas: academic skills, knowledge of subject, and classroom performance.

pre-K education: educational programs for children from birth to age 8, also termed early childhood education.

preoperational stage: the stage of cognitive development (2 to 7 years of age) proposed by Jean Piaget in which the individual begins to use language and symbols to think of objects and people outside the immediate environment.

privatization movement: umbrella term for reform initiatives that seek to run public schools as private enterprises.

problem-solving orientation: an approach to teaching that places primary emphasis on the teacher's role as a decision maker and problem solver.

profession: an occupation that requires a high level of expertise, including advanced study in a specialized field, adherence to a code of ethics, and the ability to work without close supervision.

professional development schools (PDSs): schools that have formed partnerships with a college or university for the purpose of improving the schools and contributing to the improvement of teacher preparation programs. Activities at a PDS may include collaborative research, team teaching, demonstration lessons by teacher education faculty, and

various professional growth opportunities for teachers and teacher educators.

professionalization of teaching: the steadily increasing political influence and status of teaching as a profession; increased political influence and status reflect changes such as expanding leadership opportunities for teachers, national board certification, peer review, shared decision making, and teacher-mentor programs.

professional portfolio: a collection of various kinds of evidence (for example, projects, written work, and video demonstrations of skills) documenting the achievement and performance of individuals in an area of professional practice.

professional standards boards: state agencies to regulate and improve the professional practice of teachers, administrators, and other education personnel.

Progress in International Reading Literacy Study (PIRLS): an international assessment of students' reading and literacy skills in 44 nations.

progressive movement: a movement during the 1920s and 1930s to create schools that emphasized democracy, children's interests and needs, and closer connections between school and community.

progressivism: a philosophical orientation based on the belief that life is evolving in a positive direction, that people may be trusted to act in their own best interests, and that education should focus on the needs and interests of students.

project-based learning (PBL): an approach to learning in which students work in teams on complex, real-world projects that allow them to develop and apply skills and knowledge.

property taxes: local taxes assessed against real estate and, in some areas, against personal property in the form of cars, household furniture and appliances, and stocks and bonds.

prosocial values: values such as honesty, patriotism, fairness, and civility that promote the well-being of a society.

psychosocial crisis: a life crisis at one of eight different stages of growth and development. According to psychologist Erik Erikson, individuals must resolve each crisis to reach the next stage.

psychosocial developmen: the progression of an individual through various stages of psychological and social development.

Q

qualitative assessments: subjective assessments of student learning—for example, formal and informal observations of students' performance on learning tasks and/or the manner in which they approach those tasks.

qualitative evaluation: the appraisal of teacher performance through the use of written, open-ended descriptions of classroom events in terms of their qualities.

quantitative assessments: assessments of student learning that yield numerical scores that teachers use to evaluate student learning as well as the effectiveness of their teaching.

quantitative evaluation: the appraisal of teacher performance by recording classroom events in terms of their number or frequency—for example, teacher verbal behaviors such as questioning, praising, or critiquing.

R

race: a concept of human variation used to distinguish people on the basis of biological traits and characteristics.

reading and writing schools: colonial schools, supported by public funds and fees paid by parents, that used a religiously oriented curriculum to teach boys reading and writing skills and, to a lesser degree, mathematics.

recertification: the practice in some states of requiring experienced teachers to undergo periodic testing to maintain their teaching certificates.

redistricting: the practice of redrawing district boundaries to equalize educational funding by reducing the range of variation in the ability of school districts to finance education.

reflection: the process of thinking carefully and deliberately about the outcomes of one's teaching.

reflection-in-action: the process of engaging in serious, reflective thought about improving one's professional practice while one is engaged in that practice.

reflective teaching log: a journal of classroom observations in which the teacher education student systematically analyzes specific episodes of teaching.

Regional Educational Laboratories : nine federally supported, nonprofit agencies that serve a region of the country and work directly with educators to improve schools.

Regional Educational Service Agency (RESA): a state educational agency that provides supportive services to two or more school districts; known in some states as education service centers, intermediate school districts, multicounty education service units, boards of cooperative educational services, or educational service regions.

reliability: the degree to which an assessment provides results that are consistent over time.

Research and Development Centers: 14 federally supported, university-based centers, each conducting research and development activities in a different area of education.

research-based competencies: specific behaviors that educational research has identified as characteristic of effective teachers.

restructuring: reorganizing how schools are controlled at the local level so that teachers, principals, parents, and community members have greater authority.

S

scaffolding: an approach to teaching based on the student's current level of understanding and ability; the teacher varies the amount of help given (for example, clues, encouragement, or suggestions) to students based on their moment-to-moment understanding of the material being learned.

school-based interprofessional case management: an approach to education in which professionally trained case managers work directly with teachers, the community, and families to coordinate and deliver appropriate services to at-risk students and their families.

school-based management (SBM): various approaches to school improvement in which teachers, principals, students, parents, and community members manage individual schools and share in the decision-making processes.

school-based teacher education: a model of teacher preparation through which professional coursework is presented on site at a school, usually to students who have a bachelor's degree.

school board: the primary governing body of a local school district.

school choice: various proposals that would allow parents to choose the schools their children attend.

school culture: the collective way of life characteristic of a school; a set of beliefs, values, traditions, and ways of thinking and behaving that distinguish it from other schools.

school traditions: those elements of a school's culture that are handed down from year to year.

school-within-a-school: an alternative school (within a regular school) designed to meet the needs of students at risk.

scientifically based research (SBR): research that meets the following scientific standards: use of scientific method, replication of results, ability to generalize, rigorous standards and peer review, and consistency of results.

scientific management: the application of management principles and techniques to the operation of big business and large school districts.

scoring rubrics: rating scales that consist of preestablished criteria for evaluating student performance on learning tasks.

screen capture: software that allows the user to capture an image from a computer monitor and save it to a file that can later be e-mailed or used in a presentation or printed document.

search and seizure: the process of searching an individual and/or his or her property if that person is suspected of an illegal act; reasonable or probable cause to suspect the individual must be present.

self-assessment: the process of measuring one's growth in regard to the knowledge, skills, and attitudes possessed by professional teachers.

self-contained classroom: an organizational structure for schools in which one teacher instructs a group of students (typically, 20 to 30) in a single classroom.

service learning: an approach to teaching in which students participate in community-based service activities and then reflect on the meaning of those experiences.

sex role socialization: socially expected behavior patterns conveyed to individuals on the basis of gender.

sex role stereotyping: beliefs that subtly encourage males and females to conform to certain behavioral norms regardless of abilities and interests.

sexual harassment: unwanted and unwelcome sexual behavior directed toward another person, whether of the same or opposite sex.

social justice: a philosophical orientation that emphasizes equity and equal social benefits for all individuals and groups.

social reconstructionism: a philosophical orientation based on the belief that social problems can be solved by changing, or reconstructing, society.

Socratic questioning: a method of questioning designed to lead students to see errors and inconsistencies in their thinking, based on questioning strategies used by Socrates.

special education: a teaching specialty for meeting the special educational needs of exceptional learners.

stages of development: predictable stages through which individuals pass as they progress through life.

standardized assessments: pencil-and-paper achievement tests taken by large groups of students and scored in a uniform manner—some examples are the Iowa Test of Basic Skills, California Achievement Test, and the Scholastic Aptitude Test.

standards: statements that reflect what students should know and be able to do within a particular discipline or at a particular grade level.

standards-based education (SBE): basing curricula, teaching, and assessment of student learning on rigorous academic standards.

state aid: money given by a state to its cities and towns to provide essential services, including the operation of public schools.

state board of education: the highest educational agency in a state, charged with regulating the state's system of education.

state department of education: the branch of state government, headed by the chief state school officer, charged with implementing the state's educational policies.

state takeover: takeover of a chronically low-achieving school or district by the state.

stereotyping: the process of attributing behavioral characteristics to all members of a group; formulated on the basis of limited experiences with and information about the group, coupled with an unwillingness to examine prejudices.

student-centered curriculum: curriculum that is organized around students' needs and interests.

student diversity: differences among students in regard to gender, race, ethnicity, culture, and socioeconomic status.

student mobility rates: the proportion of students within a school or district who move during an academic year.

students at risk: students whose living conditions and backgrounds place them at risk for dropping out of school.

students with disabilities: students who need special education services because they possess one or more of the following disabilities: learning disabilities, speech or language impairments, mental retardation, serious emotional disturbance, hearing impairments, orthopedic impairments, visual impairments, or other health impairments.

student variability: differences among students in regard to their developmental needs, interests, abilities, and disabilities.

subject-centered curriculum: a curriculum that emphasizes learning an academic discipline.

substitute teaching: instruction provided by temporary teachers who replace regular teachers absent due to illness, family responsibilities, personal reasons, or attendance at professional workshops and conferences.

summative evaluation: an assessment of student learning made for the purpose of assigning grades at the end of a unit, semester, or year and deciding whether students are ready to proceed to the next phase of their education.

superintendent: the chief administrator of a school district.

T

teacher accountability: society's expectations that teachers will adhere to high professional and moral standards and create effective learning environments for all students.

teacher centers: centers where teachers provide other teachers with instructional materials and new methods and where teachers can exchange ideas.

teacher-leader: a teacher who assumes a key leadership role in the improvement and/or day-to-day operation of a school.

teacher-researcher: a teacher who regularly conducts classroom research to improve his or her teaching.

teachers' craft knowledge: the knowledge teachers develop about teaching that derives from their experiences in the classroom, particularly the actions they have taken to solve specific problems of practice.

teachers' thought processes: the thoughts that guide teachers' actions in classrooms. These thoughts typically consist of thoughts related to planning, theories and beliefs, and interactive thoughts and decisions.

teacher–student ratios: a ratio that expresses the number of students taught by a teacher.

teacher supply and demand: the number of school-age students compared to the number of available teachers; may also be projected on the basis of estimated numbers of students and teachers.

Teach for America: a program that enables recent college graduates without a teaching certificate to teach in districts with critical shortages of teachers and, after taking professional development courses and after supervision by state and school authorities, earn a teaching certificate.

teaching certificate: a license to teach issued by a state or, in a few cases, a large city.

teaching contract: an agreement between a teacher and a board of education that the teacher will provide specific services in return for a certain salary, benefits, and privileges.

teaching simulations: an activity in which teacher education students participate in role-plays designed to create situations comparable to those actually encountered by teachers.

team teaching: an arrangement whereby a team of teachers teaches a group of students equal in number to what the teachers would have in their self-contained classrooms.

tenure: an employment policy in which teachers, after serving a probationary period, retain their positions indefinitely and can be dismissed only on legally defensible grounds.

text-to-speech (TTS) program: a computer software program that converts speech into text.

3D virtual reality worlds: computer-based simulated environments that a user inhabits through use of an avatar, a user's representation of himself or herself; a popular 3D virtual reality program is Second Life.

time on task: the amount of time students are actively and directly engaged in learning tasks.

Title IX: a provision of the 1972 Education Amendments Act prohibiting sex discrimination in educational programs.

tort liability: conditions that would permit the filing of legal charges against a professional for breach of duty and/or behaving in a negligent manner.

Trends in International Mathematics and Science Study (TIMSS): an international assessment of mathematics and science achievement among fourth-, eighth-, and twelfth-grade students in 41 nations.

Tyler rationale: a four-step model for curriculum development in which teachers identify purposes, select learning experiences, organize experiences, and evaluate.

V

validity: the degree to which assessments measure what they are supposed to measure.

vertical equity: an effort to provide equal educational opportunity within a state by providing different levels of funding based on economic needs within school districts.

virtual labs: computerized, online simulations of scientific laboratories that enable students to conduct scientific inquiry in a virtual environment.

virtual schools: educational institutions that offer K–12 courses through the Internet or by means of Web-based methods; an online learning space where teachers and students interact.

voucher system: funds allocated to parents that they may use to purchase education for their children from public or private schools in the area.

W

webconferencing: a meeting, presentation, or conference held over the Internet, with participants connected to other participants via the Internet.

WebQuests: online inquiry research projects for students that require them to gather material from the Web.

wiki: a website created, edited, and maintained by a group of people with a common interest.

within-class ability grouping: the practice of creating small, homogeneous groups of students within a single classroom for the purpose of instruction, usually in reading or mathematics, at the elementary level.

Women's Educational Equity Act (WEEA): a 1974 federal law that guarantees equal educational opportunity for females.

work habits: dispositions important for effective thinking and learning—for example, reading with curiosity and willingness to work hard.

Y

YouTube: an online video clearinghouse where people watch, upload, and share videos.

Z

zero tolerance: school policies related to discipline and safety that provide for automatic, severe consequences for certain types of misbehavior—misbehavior that involves drugs, violence, sexual harassment, or bullying, for example.

REFERENCES

Abernathy, S. F. (2007). *No Child Left Behind and the public schools*. Ann Arbor: University of Michigan Press.

Abrahamsson, B. (1971). *Military professionalization and political power*. Stockholm: Allmanna Forlagret.

Acheson, A. A., & Gall, M. D. (1997). *Techniques in the clinical supervision of teachers: Preservice and inservice applications* (4th ed.). New York: Longman.

Achieve, Inc. (2005). *America's high schools: The front line in the battle for our economic future*. Retrieved April 30, 2008, from http://www.achieve.org

Acton v. Vernonia School District, 66 F.3d 217 (9th Cir.), *rev'd*, 515 U.S. 646, 115 S. Ct. 2386 (1995).

Adler, M. (1982). *The paideia proposal: An educational manifesto*. New York: Macmillan.

African American Academy. (2008, June 9). Retrieved from http://www.seattleschools.org/schools/aaa/mission.htm

Agostini v. Felton, 521 U.S. 203 (1997).

Aguilar v. Felton, 473 U.S. 402 (1985).

Alan Guttmacher Institute. (2006). *Facts on American teens' sexual and reproductive health*. New York: Author.

Alexander, K., & Alexander, M. D. (2009). *American public school law* (7th ed.). Belmont, CA: Wadsworth, Cengage Learning.

Alfonso v. Fernandez, 606 N.Y.S.2d 259 (N.Y. App. Div. 1993).

Alvin Independent School District v. Cooper, 404 S.W.2d 76 (Tex. Civ. App. 1966).

American Academy of Child and Adolescent Psychiatry. (2004, July). *When children have children, No. 31*. Retrieved May 1, 2008 from http://www.aacap.org/cs/root/facts_for_families/when_children_have_children

American Association of University Women (AAUW). (1991). *Shortchanging girls, shortchanging America*. Washington, DC: Author.

American Association of University Women (AAUW). (1992). *How schools shortchange girls: The AAUW report*. Researched by Wellesley College Center for Research on Women. Washington, DC: The AAUW Educational Foundation.

American Association of University Women. (2002). *Harassment-free hallways: How to stop sexual harassment in schools: A guide for students, parents, and teachers, Section III for schools*. Washington, DC: Author.

American Association of University Women. (May 2008). *Where the girls are: The facts about gender equity in education*. Washington, DC: Author.

American Federation of Teachers. (1998). *Student achievement in Edison schools: Mixed results in an ongoing experiment*. Washington, DC: Author.

American Federation of Teachers. (2002, July). *Do charter schools measure up? The charter school experiment after 10 years*. Washington, DC: Author.

American Institutes of Research. (2003). *Effects of the implementation of Proposition 227 on the education of English learners, K-12, year 3 report*. Submitted to the California Department of Education, October 29, 2003.

Anderson, R. E., & Ronnkvist, A. (1999). *The presence of computers in American schools*. University of California, Irvine, and University of Minnesota: Center for Research on Information Technology and Organizations.

Annie E. Casey Foundation. (2007). *Lifelong family connections: Supporting permanence for children in foster care*. Baltimore, MD: Author. Retrieved May 1, 2008, from http://www.kidscount.org/datacenter/db_07pdf/essay.pdf

Ansary, T. (2004, November). The muddle machine: Confessions of a textbook editor *Edutopia*, 30–35.

Anyon, J. (1996). Social class and the hidden curriculum of work. In E. Hollins (Ed.), *Transforming curriculum for a culturally diverse society* (pp. 179–203). Mahwah, NJ: Lawrence Erlbaum.

Appalachia Educational Laboratory. (1993). *Alternative assessment in math and science: Moving toward a moving target*. Charleston, WV: Author.

Ariza, E. N. W. (2006). *Not for ESOL teachers: What every classroom teacher needs to know about the linguistically, culturally, and ethnically diverse student*. Boston: Pearson.

Armour, R. (2006). *We can finally close the achievement gap*. Retrieved August 9, 2008, from http://armourachievement.blogspot.com/

Armstrong, P. A. (2008). *What teachers expect in reform: Making their voices heard*. Lanham, MD: Rowman & Littlefield Education.

Aronson, E., & Gonzalez, A. (1988). Desegregation, jigsaw, and the Mexican-American experience. In P. A. Katz & D. A. Taylor (Eds.), *Eliminating racism: Profiles in controversy*. New York: Plenum Press.

Artz, S. (1999). *Sex, power, and the violent school girl*. New York: Teachers College Press.

Ashton-Warner, S. (1963). *Teacher*. New York: Simon & Schuster.

Asian Americans/Pacific Islanders in Philanthropy. (1997). *An invisible crisis: The educational needs of Asian Pacific American youth*. New York: Author.

Associated Press. (2004, June 10). *Study: High school exit tests flimsy*. Retrieved from www.cnn.com/2004/EDUCATION/06/10/graduation.tests.ap/

Avramidis, E., Bayliss, P., & Burden, R. (2000). A survey into mainstream teachers' attitudes towards the inclusion of children with special educational needs in the ordinary school in one local education authority. *Educational Psychology, 20*(2), 191–211.

Ayers, W. C., & Miller, J. L. (Eds.). (1998). *A light in dark times: Maxine Greene and the unfinished conversation*. New York: Teachers College Press.

Babbage, K. (2008). *What only teachers know about education*. Lanham, MD: Rowman & Littlefield Education.

Baker, B. D., Green, P., & Richards, C. E. (2008). *Financing education systems*. Upper Saddle River, NJ: Pearson.

Ballantine, J. H. (1997). *The sociology of education: A systematic analysis* (4th ed.). Upper Saddle River, NJ: Prentice Hall.

Banks, J. A. (2008). *An introduction to multicultural education* (4th ed.). Boston: Allyn & Bacon.

Banks, J. S. (2006). *Cultural diversity and education: Foundations, curriculum and teaching* (5th ed.). Boston: Allyn & Bacon.

Banks, J. S. (2009). *Teaching strategies for ethnic studies* (8th ed.). Boston: Allyn & Bacon.

REFERENCES

Battles v. Anne Arundel County Board of Education, 904 F. Supp. 471 (D. Md. 1995), *aff'd*, 95 F.3d 41 (4th Cir. 1996).

Beck, R. J. (2008). *What are learning objects?* Retrieved from http://www.uwm.edu/Dept/CIE/AOP/LO_what.html

Becker, H. J. (1999). *Internet use by teachers: Conditions of professional use and teacher-directed student use.* University of California, Irvine, and University of Minnesota: Center for Research on Information Technology and Organizations.

Becker, H. J. (2001, April). *How are teachers using computers in instruction?* Paper presented at the annual meeting of the American Educational Research Association, Seattle, WA.

Bennett, C. I. (1990). *Comprehensive multicultural education: Theory and practice* (2nd ed.). Boston: Allyn & Bacon.

Bennett, C. I. (2003). *Comprehensive multicultural education: Theory and practice* (5th ed.). Boston: Allyn & Bacon.

Bennett, C. I. (2006). *Comprehensive multicultural education: Theory and practice* (6th ed.). Boston: Allyn & Bacon.

Bennett, L. (1997). Break the silence: Gay and straight students in Massachusetts team up to make a difference. *Teaching Tolerance, 6*, 24–31.

Bennett, W. (1987). *James Madison High School: A curriculum for American students.* Washington, DC: U.S. Department of Education.

Bernstein, B. B. (1996). *Pedagogy, symbolic control and identity: Theory, research, critique (critical perspectives on literacy and education).* New York: Taylor and Francis.

Bertocci, P. A. (1960). *Education and the vision of excellence.* Boston: Boston University Press.

Besner, H. F., & Spungin, C. I. (1995). *Gay and lesbian students: Understanding their needs.* Washington, DC: Taylor and Francis.

Bitter, G. G., & Pierson, M. E. (2005). *Using technology in the classroom* (6th ed.). Boston: Allyn & Bacon.

Black, P., Harrison, C., Lee, C., Marshall, B., & Wiliam, D. (2004, September). Working inside the black box: Assessment for learning in the classroom. *Phi Delta Kappan,* 9–21.

Blair, K. (2005, November/December). Teacher diary #2: A chronicle of a first-time ELL teacher. *The ELL Outlook.* Retrieved April 17, 2008, from http://www.coursecrafters.com/ELL-Outlook/2005/nov_dec/ELLOutlookITIArticle4.htm

Blau v. Fort Thomas Pub. Sch. Dist., 401, F.3d 381, 395–96 (6th Cir. 2005).

Bloom, B. S. (1981). *All our children learning: A primer for parents, teachers, and other educators.* New York: McGraw-Hill.

Board of Education of Oklahoma City Public Schools v. Dowell, 498 U.S. 237, 249–250 (1991).

Board of Education of Westside Community Schools v. Mergens, 496 U.S. 226 (1990).

Board of Education, Sacramento City Unified School District v. Holland, 786 F. Supp. 874 (E.D. Cal. 1992).

Borich, G. D. (2007). *Effective teaching methods: Research-based practice.* Upper Saddle River, NJ: Pearson Education.

Boser, U. (2000, May 3). States stiffening recertification for teachers. *Education Week on the Web.*

Boyer, E. (1983). *High school: A report on secondary education in America.* New York: Harper & Row.

Boyer, E. (1995). *The basic school: A community for learning.* Princeton, NJ: Carnegie Foundation for the Advancement of Teaching.

Bradley, A. (1998, February 4). Unions agree on blueprint for merging. *Education Week on the Web.*

Brameld, T. (1956). *Toward a reconstructed philosophy of education.* New York: Holt, Rinehart and Winston.

Bran, A., Gray, T., & Silver-Pacuila, H. (2008, June 10). Berberi's tools: Technology can level the learning field. George Lucas Educational Foundation. Retrieved from http://www.edutopica.org/assistive-technology-devices-visually-impaired

Brock, B. L., & Grady, M. L. (2001). *From first-year to first-rate: Principals guiding beginning teachers.* Thousand Oaks, CA: Corwin Press.

Broudy, H. S. (1979). Arts education: Necessary or just nice? *Phi Delta Kappan, 60*, 347–350.

Brown, A. H. (1999). Simulated classrooms and artificial students: The potential effects of new technologies on teacher education. *Journal of Research on Computing in Education, 32*(2), 307–318.

Brown, F. B., Kohrs, D., & Lanzarro, C. (1991). *The academic costs and consequences of extracurricular participation in high school.* Paper presented at the Annual Meeting of Educational Research Association.

Brown v. Board of Education of Topeka, Kansas, 347 U.S. 483 (1954).

Brown v. Hot, Sexy and Safer Productions, Inc., 68 F.3d 525 (1st Cir. 1995), *cert. denied*, 516 U.S. 1159 (1996).

Brown v. Unified School District No. 501, 56 F. Supp. 2d 1212 (D. Kan. 1999).

Brunelle v. Lynn Public Schools, 702 N.E.2d 1182 (Mass. 1998).

Buckney, C. (2004). A final word: Ten questions for Paul Vallas' right-hand woman. In A. Russo (Ed.), *School reform in Chicago: Lessons in policy and practice* (pp. 151–162). Cambridge, MA: Harvard Education Press.

Bucky, P. A. (1992). *The private Albert Einstein.* Kansas City: Andrews and McMeel.

Burch v. Barker, 651 F. Supp. 1149 (W.D. Wash. 1987).

Burch v. Barker, 861 F.2d 1149 (9th Cir. 1988).

Bureau of Justice Statistics and National Center for Education Statistics. (2007). *Indicators of schools, crime and safety, 2007.* Washington, DC: Author.

Burns, J. (2003, September 20). Immersion aims to undo damage of assimilation policies. Associated Press.

Burton v. Cascade School District Union High School No. 5, 512 F.2d 850 (9th Cir. 1975).

Bush v. Holmes, 767 So. 2d 668, 675 (2006).

Button, H. W., & Provenzo, E. F. (1983). *History of education and culture in America.* Englewood Cliffs, NJ: Prentice Hall.

Button, H. W., & Provenzo, E. F. (1989). *History of education and culture in America* (2nd ed.). Englewood Cliffs, NJ: Prentice Hall.

Cantor, L. (1989). Assertive discipline—more than names on the board and marbles in a jar. *Phi Delta Kappan, 71*(1), 57–61.

Carnegie Corporation of New York. (2008). *Teachers for a new era.* Retrieved February 28, 2008, from http://www.teachersforanewera.org/index.cfm?fuseaction=home.home

Carnegie Council on Adolescent Development. (1989). *Turning points: Preparing American youth for the 21st century.* New York: Author.

Carroll, J. (1963). A model of school learning. *Teachers College Record, 64.*

Cauthen, N. K., & Fass, S. (2007). *Measuring income and poverty in the United States.* New York: National Center for Children in Poverty. Retrieved from http://www.nccp.org/publications/pdf/text_707.pdf

Center for Educational Reform. (2007, April). *Annual Survey of America's Charter Schools 2007.* Washington, DC: Author.

Center for Immigration Studies. (2007). *Immigrants in the United States, 2007: A profile of America's foreign-born population.* Washington, DC: Author.

Center for Research on Effective Schooling for Disadvantaged Students. (1992). *Helping students who fall behind,* Report no. 22. Baltimore: Johns Hopkins University.

Centers for Disease Control and Prevention. (2008, Summer). *Suicide: Facts at a glance.* Atlanta: Author.

Chicago Public Schools. (2008, April 30). *Guidelines: Service learning.* Retrieved from http://servicelearning.cps.kl2.il.us/Guidelines.html

Cohen, S. (Ed.). (1974). *Massachusetts school law of 1648. Education in the United States.* New York: Random House.

Coladarci, T., & Cobb, C. D. (1996). Extracurricular participation, school size, and achievement and self-esteem among high school students: A national look. *Journal of Research in Rural Education, 12*(2), 92–103.

Coleman, J. S., Campbell, E. Q., Hobson, C. J., McPartland, J., Mood, A. L., Weinfeld, F. D., et al. (1966). *Equality of educational opportunity.* Washington, DC: U.S. Government Printing Office.

Collier-Thomas, B. (1982, Summer). Guest editorial: The impact of black women in education: An historical overview. *The Journal of Negro Education 51*(3), 173–180.

Colucci, K. (2000). Negative pedagogy. In J. L. Paul & K. Colucci (Eds.), *Stories out of school: Memories and reflections on care and cruelty in the classroom* (pp. 27–44). Stamford, CT: Ablex.

Comer, J. P. (1997). *Waiting for a miracle: Why schools can't solve our problems—and how we can.* New York: Dutton.

Commager, H. S. (1958, October). Noah Webster, 1758–1958. *Saturday Review 41,* 18.

Commager, H. S. (1962). *Noah Webster's American spelling book.* New York: Teachers College Press.

Consortium for School Networking. (2008). *Executive summary: Collaboration in K-12 schools: Anywhere, anytime, any way.* Washington, DC: Author. Retrieved from http://www.cosn.org/resources/emerging_technologies/collaboration.cfm

Cosby, B. (2004). Where do we start to sweep? In C. Glickman (Ed.), *Letters to the next president: What we can do about the real crisis in public education* (pp. xi–xiv). New York: Teachers College Press.

Cossentino, J., & Whitcomb, J. A. (2007). In D. T. Hansen (Ed.), *Ethical visions of education: Philosophies in practice.* New York: Teachers College Press.

Costa, A. L. (1984). A reaction to Hunter's knowing, teaching, and supervising. In P. L. Hosford (Ed.), *Using what we know about teaching.* Alexandria, VA: Association for Supervision and Curriculum Development.

Coughlin, E. K. (1993, March 24). Sociologists examine the complexities of racial and ethnic identity in America. *Chronicle of Higher Education.*

Council of Chief State School Officers. (2008, May 26). *Chief state school officers: Method of selection.* Retrieved from http://www.ccsso.org/chief_state_school_officers/method_of_selection/index.cfm

Council of the Great City Schools. (2005, October). *Urban school board survey.* Washington, DC: Author.

Counts, G. (1932). *Dare the school build a new social order?* New York: John Day.

Crawford, J. (2004). *Education of English learners: Language diversity in the classroom* (5th ed.). Los Angeles: Bilingual Education Services.

Crawford, J. (2007). The decline of bilingual education: How to reverse a troubling trend. *International Multilingual Research Journal, 1*(1), 33–37.

Cremin, L. A. (1961). *The transformation of the school: Progressivism in American education, 1876–1957.* New York: Alfred A. Knopf.

Crowther, F., Ferguson, M., & Harm, L. (2008). *Developing teacher leaders: How teacher leadership enhances school success* (2nd ed.). Thousand Oaks, CA: Corwin Press.

Cuban, L. (2003). *Why is it so hard to get good schools?* New York: Teachers College Press.

Cunningham, C. (2003). *Trends and issues: Social and economic context.* Eugene: University of Oregon, Clearinghouse on Educational Management.

Curtis, D. (2000, October 1). Treating teachers as professionals. *Edutopia.* San Rafael, CA: George Lucas Educational Foundation. Retrieved from http://glef.org/orlandpk.html

Curtis v. School Committee of Falmouth, 652 N.E.2d 580 (Mass. 1995), *cert. denied,* 516 U.S. 1067 (1996).

Curwin, R., & Mendler, A. (1988). Packaged discipline programs: Let the buyer beware. *Educational Leadership, 46*(2), 68–71.

Curwin, R., & Mendler, A. (1989, March). We repeat, let the buyer beware: A response to Canter. *Educational Leadership, 46*(6), 83.

Davis v. Meek, 344 F. Supp. 298 (N.D. Ohio 1972).

Deal, T. E., & Peterson, K. D. (1999). *Shaping school culture: The heart of leadership.* San Francisco: Jossey-Bass.

Degnan, E., & Bozeman, W. (2001). An investigation of computer-based simulations for school crisis management. *Journal of School Leadership, 11*(4), 296–312.

Dell'Olio, J. M., & Donk, T. (2007). *Models of teaching: Connecting student learning with standards.* Thousand Oaks, CA: Sage.

DeRoche, E. F., & Williams, M. M. (2001). *Character education: A guide for school administrators.* Lanham, MD: Scarecrow Press.

Dewey, J. (1900). *The school and society.* Chicago: University of Chicago Press.

Dewey, J. (1902). *The child and the curriculum.* Chicago: University of Chicago Press.

Dewey, J. (1916). *Democracy and education: An introduction to the philosophy of education.* New York: Macmillan.

Dewey, J. (1955). Quoted in *Organizing the teaching profession: The story of the American Federation of Teachers.* Glencoe, IL: Commission on Educational Reconstruction.

Doe v. Renfrow, 631 F.2d 91, *reh'g denied,* 635 F.2d 582 (7th Cir. 1980), *cert. denied,* 451 U.S. 1022 (1981).

Dryfoos, J. G. (1998). *Safe passage: Making it through adolescence in a risky society.* New York: Oxford University Press.

Dryfoos, J. G., & Maguire, S. (2002). *Inside full-service community schools.* Thousand Oaks, CA: Corwin Press.

Dubuclet v. Home Insurance Co., 660 So. 2d 67 (La. Ct. App. 1995).

Dunklee, D. R., & Shoop, R. J. (2002). *The principal's quick-reference guide to school law: Reducing liability, litigation, and other potential legal tangles.* Thousand Oaks, CA: Corwin Press.

Durkheim, E. (1956). *Education and sociology* (S. D. Fox, Trans.). Glencoe, IL: The Free Press.

Eamon, M. K. (2001, July). The effects of poverty on children's socio/emotional development: An ecological systems analysis. *Social Work, 46*(3), 256–266.

Edelman, M. W. (April 11, 2008). *Child watch column: Celebrating young people who beat the odds.* Retrieved May 1, 2008, from http://www.childrensdefense.org/site/MessageViewer?em_id=7901.0

Edison Schools, Inc. (2004). *Annual report.* New York: Author.

Education Commission of the States. (April 20, 2007). *High school-level assessments: Purpose(s) of exams.* Retrieved from http://mb2.ecs.org/reports/Report.aspx?id=1163

Educational Testing Service. (1995). Bringing volunteers into teacher education programs. *ETS Policy Notes,* pp. 8–9.

Educational Testing Service. (2007, December 17). *Teacher quality in a changing policy landscape: Improvements in the teacher pool.* Princeton, NJ: Author.

Education Trust. (2002). *All talk, putting an end to out-of-field teaching.* Washington, DC: Author.

Education Week. (2005, May 5). *Technology counts 2005: Electronic transfer: Moving technology dollars in new directions.*

Educators with Disabilities Caucus, Council for Exceptional Children. (2008). CEC's Educators with Disabilities Caucus (EDC). Retrieved April 27, 2008, from http://www.cec.sped.org/Content/NavigationMenu/AboutCEC/Communities/Caucuses/EducatorswithDisabilities/default.htm

Eduventures. (2003, August). *Learning markets and opportunities 2003: New models for delivering education and services drive pre–K and postsecondary sector growth*. Boston: Author.

Edwards v. Aguillard, 482 U.S. 578 (1987).

Egbert, J. (2009). *Supporting learning with technology: Essentials of classroom practice*. Upper Saddle River, NJ: Pearson Education.

Eggen, P., & Kauchak, D. (2007). *Educational psychology: Windows on classrooms* (7th ed.). Upper Saddle River, NJ: Pearson Education.

Eisner, E. (2002). *The educational imagination: On the design and evaluation of school programs* (3rd ed.). New York: Macmillan College.

Eisner, E. (March 2006). The satisfactions of teaching: How we teach is ultimately a reflection of why we teach. *Educational Leadership*, 44–46.

Eisner, E. W. (1998). *The kind of schools we need: Personal essays*. Portsmouth, NH: Heinemann.

Emmer, E. T., & Evertson, C. M. (2009). *Classroom management for middle and high school teachers* (8th ed.). Boston: Pearson Education.

Engel v. Vitale, 370 U.S. 421 (1962).

Enlow, R. (2004). *Grading vouchers: Ranking America's school choice programs*. Indianapolis: Milton and Rose D. Friedman Foundation.

Epperson v. Arkansas, 393, U.S. 97 (1968).

Erickson, H. L. (2008). *Stirring the head, heart, and soul: Redefining curriculum, instruction, and concept-based learning*. Thousand Oaks, CA: Corwin Press.

Erikson, E. H. (1963). *Childhood and society* (2nd ed.). New York: Norton.

Erikson, E. H. (1997). *The life cycle completed: Extended version with new chapters on the ninth stage of development by Joan M. Erikson*. New York: W. W. Norton.

Essex, N. L. (1999). *School law and the public schools: A practical guide for educational leaders*. Boston: Allyn & Bacon.

Essex, N. L. (2008). *School law and the public schools: A practical guide for educational leaders* (4th ed). Boston: Pearson.

Etzioni, A. (1969). *The semi-professions and their organization: Teachers, nurses, social workers*. New York: The Free Press.

Etzioni, A. (1999, June 9). The truths we must face to curb youth violence. *Education Week on the Web*.

Evans, L. (2002). Teacher attraction: Are magnet school teachers more professionalized than traditional schoolteachers in urban secondary schools? *Education and Urban Society, 34* (3), 312–333.

Evertson, C. M., & Emmer, E. T. (2009). *Classroom management for elementary teachers* (8th ed.). Boston: Pearson Education.

Fagen v. Summers, 498 P.2d 1227 (Wyo. 1972).

FairTest. (June 2, 2008). *What the presidential candidates are saying about NCLB*. Retrieved from http://www.fairtest.org/what-presidential-candidates-are-saying-about-nclb

Falk, B. (2002, April). Standards-based reforms: Problems and possibilities. *Phi Delta Kappan*, 612–620.

Falvo v. Owasso Independent School District, 233 F.3d 1203 (10th Cir. 2000).

Fashola, O. (1999). *Review of extended-day and after-school programs and their effectiveness*. Baltimore: Johns Hopkins University, Center for Research on the Education of Students Placed at Risk.

Fass, S., & Canthen, N. K. (2007, November). *Who are America's poor children? The official story*. New York: Columbia University, Mailman School of Public Health, National Center for Children in Poverty.

Feistritzer, C. E., & Haar, C. K. (2008). *Alternate routes to teaching*. Upper Saddle River, NJ: Pearson Education.

Feistritzer, E. (1999). *A report on teacher preparation in the United States*. Washington, DC: National Center for Education Information.

Feistritzer, E. (2002). *Alternative teacher certification: A state-by-state analysis*. Washington, DC: National Center for Education Information.

Feller, B. (2003, August 14). High school exit exams are here to stay. *The Detroit News*. Retrieved from www.detnews.com/2003/schools/0308/14/a02-244824.htm

Ferguson, C. (2003, August 30). Gay high school draws criticism from conservatives and civil libertarians. Associated Press.

Ferris, S. (2008). A teacher's voice: Lost and found in paradox. *Curriculum in Context, 35*(1), 16–17.

Fetler, M. (2001). Student mathematics achievement test scores, dropout rates, and teacher characteristics. *Teacher Education Quarterly, 28*(1), 151–168.

Firestone, D. (2008). Alternative schools: When teachers unite to run school. *New York Times*. Retrieved April 12, 2008, from http://query.nytimes.com/gst/fullpage.html?res=990CE1DF1039F937A15756C0A963958260

Flores vs. Morgan Hill Unified School District, 324 F.3d 1130 (9th Cir. 2003).

Fong, T. P. (2007). *The contemporary Asian American experience: Beyond the model minority* (3rd ed.). Upper Saddle River, NJ: Prentice Hall.

Franklin, B. (1931). Proposals relating to the education of youth in Pennsylvania. In T. Woody (Ed.), *Educational views of Benjamin Franklin*. New York: McGraw-Hill.

Franklin v. Gwinnett County Public Schools, 503 U.S. 60 (1992).

Freeman v. Pitts, 503 U.S. 467 (1992).

Freire, P. (1970). *Pedagogy of the oppressed*. New York: Continuum.

Freire, P., & Macedo, D. (1987). *Literacy: Reading the word and the world*. South Hadley, MA: Bergin & Garvey.

Friedman, M. (2003, March 24). Milton Friedman interview on CNBC: Friedman on school vouchers.

Friend, M., & Bursuck, W. D. (2002). *Including students with special needs: A practical guide for classroom teachers*. Boston: Allyn & Bacon.

Fulton, K. P., & Riel, M. (1999, May 1). Professional development through learning communities. *Edutopia, 6*(2), 8–9. San Rafael, CA: George Lucas Educational Foundation.

Furger, R. (1999, September). Are wired schools failing our kids? *PC World*.

Gagné, R. M. (1974). *Essentials of learning for instruction*. Hinsdale, IL: Dryden.

Gagné, R. M. (1977). *The conditions of learning* (3rd ed.). New York: Holt, Rinehart and Winston.

Gaines, G. F. (2007). *Focus on teacher pay and incentives: Recent legislative action and update on salary averages*. Atlanta: Southern Regional Education Board.

Gandara, P., & Fish, J. (1994, Spring). Year-round schooling as an avenue to major structural reform. *Educational Evaluation and Policy Analysis*, p. 16.

Garbarino, J. (1999). *Lost boys: Why our sons turn violent and how we can save them*. New York: The Free Press.

Gardner, H. (1983). *Frames of mind*. New York: Basic Books.

Gardner, H. (1997, September). Multiple intelligences as a partner in school improvement. *Educational Leadership*, pp. 20–21.

Gardner, H. (1999). *The disciplined mind: What all students should understand*. New York: Simon & Schuster.

Garet, M. S., Porter, A. C., Desimone, L., Birman, B. F., & Yoon, K. S. (2001). What makes professional development effective? Results from a national sample of teachers. *American Educational Research Journal, 38*(4), 915–945.

Gates, B., & Gates, M. (May 28, 2008). Letter from Bill and Melinda Gates. Retrieved from http://www.gatesfoundation.org/AboutUs/OurValues/GatesLetter/

Gaylord v. Tacoma School District No. 10, 599 P.2d 1340 (Wash. 1977).

Gebser v. Lago Vista Independent School District, 524 U.S. 274 (1998).

George Lucas Educational Foundation. (2004a, February 9). *From hula to high tech*. Retrieved from www.glef.org/php/article.php?id=Art_1126&key=137

George Lucas Educational Foundation. (2004b, January 19). *Laptops on expedition*. Retrieved from www.glef.

org/php/article.php?id=Art_1127&key=137

George Lucas Educational Foundation. (2005, September 26). *Synching up with the iKid: Connecting to the twenty-first century student*. Retrieved February 6, 2008, from www.edutopia.org/node/1335/print

George Lucas Educational Foundation. (2008, February 9). *Visual acuity: From consumers to critics and creators*. Retrieved from http://www.edutopia.org/media-literacy-skills

George Lucas Educational Foundation. (2008, June). *A word from George Lucas: Edutopia's role in education*. Retrieved from http://www.edutopia.org/lucas

Gerber, S. B. (1996). Extracurricular activities and academic achievement. *Journal of Research and Development in Education, 30*(1), 42–50.

Gigante, N. (2008). *Teacher leadership in context*. Saarbrücken, Germany: Vdm Verlog.

Gill, B., Zimmer, R., Christman, J., & Blanc, S. (2007). *State takeover, school restructuring, private management, and student achievement in Philadelphia*. Santa Monica, CA: Rand Corporation.

Gilligan, C. (1993). *In a different voice: Psychological theory and women's development*. Cambridge, MA: Harvard University Press.

Gipp, G. (1979, August–September). Help for Dana Fast Horse and friends. *American Education*, p. 15.

Glasser, W. R. (1997, April). A new look at school failure and school success. *Phi Delta Kappan*, 596–602.

Glasser, W. R. (1998a). *Quality school* (3rd ed.). New York: Harper Perennial.

Glasser, W. R. (1998b). *The quality school teacher: Specific suggestions for teachers who are trying to implement the lead-management ideas of the quality school*. New York: Harper Perennial.

Glasser, W. R. (1998c). *Choice theory: A new psychology of personal freedom*. New York: HarperCollins.

Glasser, W. R., & Dotson, K. L. (1998). *Choice theory in the classroom*. New York: Harper Perennial.

Glickman, C. (2002). *Leadership for learning: How to help teachers succeed*. Alexandria, VA: Association of Supervision and Curriculum Development.

Glickman, C. (2003). *Holding sacred ground: Essays on leadership, courage, and sustaining great schools*. San Francisco: Jossey-Bass.

Glickman, C. (Ed.). (2004). *Letters to the next president: What we can do about the real crisis in public education*. New York: Teachers College Press.

Glickman, C., Gordon, S. P., & Ross-Gordon, J. M. (2001). *SuperVision and instructional leadership* (5th ed.). Boston: Allyn & Bacon.

Glickman, C., Gordon, S. P., & Ross-Gordon, J. M. (2004). *Supervision and instructional leadership* (6th ed.). Boston: Allyn & Bacon.

Glickman, C., Gordon, S. P., & Ross-Gordon, J. (2007). *Supervision and instructional leadership: A developmental approach* (7th ed.). Boston: Allyn & Bacon.

Gmelch, W. H., & Parkay, F. W. (1995). Changing roles and occupational stress in the teaching profession. In M. J. O'Hair & S. J. Odell, *Educating teachers for leadership and change: Teacher education yearbook III*. Thousand Oaks, CA: Corwin Press.

Goldhammer, R., Anderson, R. H., & Krajewski, R. J. (1993). *Clinical supervision: Special methods for the supervision of teachers* (3rd ed.). Fort Worth: Harcourt Brace Jovanovich.

Gollnick, D. M., & Chinn, P. C. (2009). *Multicultural education in a pluralistic society* (8th ed.). Upper Saddle River, NJ: Merrill.

Good, T. E., & Brophy, J. E. (2003). *Looking in classrooms* (9th ed.). Boston: Allyn & Bacon.

Good, T. L., & Brophy, J. E. (2008). *Looking in classrooms* (10th ed.). Boston: Pearson Education.

Good, T. E., & Grouws, D. (1979). The Missouri mathematics effectiveness project: An experimental study in fourth-grade classrooms. *Journal of Educational Psychology, 71*, 355–362.

Goodlad, J. (1994). *Educational renewal: Better teachers, better schools*. San Francisco: Jossey-Bass.

Good News Club v. Milford Central School, 533 U.S. 98 (2001).

Goolsbee, A., & Guryan, J. (2002). *The impact of Internet subsidies in public schools*. Working Paper 9090. Cambridge, MA: National Bureau of Economic Research.

Goss v. Lopez, 419 U.S. 565 (1975).

Graham, P. A. (1967). *Progressive education: From Arcady to academe: A history of the Progressive Education Association, 1919–1955*. New York: Teachers College Press.

Grant, G., & Murray, C. E. (1999). *Teaching in America: The slow revolution*. Cambridge, MA: Harvard University Press.

Grant, P. G., Richard, K. J., & Parkay, F. W. (1996, April). *Using video cases to promote reflection among preservice teachers: A qualitative inquiry*. Paper presented at the annual meeting of the American Educational Research Association, New York.

Green, T. D., Brown, A., & Robinson, L. (2008). *Making the most of the Web in your classroom: A teacher's guide to blogs, podcasts, wikis, pages, and sites*. Thousand Oaks, CA: Corwin Press.

Greene, M. (1995a). *Releasing the imagination*. San Francisco: Jossey-Bass.

Greene, M. (1995b). What counts as philosophy of education? In W. Kohli (Ed.), *Critical conversations in philosophy of education*. New York: Routledge.

Greenfield, P. M. (1994). Independence and interdependence as developmental scripts: implications for theory, research, and practice. In P. M. Greenfield & R. R. Cocking (Eds.), *Cross-cultural roots of minority child development* (pp. 1–37). Mahwah, NJ: Lawrence Erlabaum.

Gross, M. U. M. (2008). Highly gifted children and adolescents. In J. A. Plucker & C. M. Callahan (Eds.), *Critical issues and practices in gifted education: What the research says* (pp. 241–251). Waco, TX: Prufrock Press.

Guenemoen, R. F., Thompson, S. J., Thurlow, M. L., & Lehr, C. A. (2001). *A self-study guide to implementation of inclusive assessment and accountability systems: A best practice approach*. Minneapolis: University of Minnesota, National Center on Educational Outcomes.

Gurian, M., & Stevens, K. (2007). *The minds of boys: Saving our sons from falling behind in school and life*. San Francisco: Jossey-Bass.

Hakuta, K. (2001a). Follow-up on Oceanside: Communications with Ron Unz. Retrieved June 10, 2008, from http://www.stanford/edu/~hakuta/SAT9/Silence%20from%20Oceanside%202.htm

Hakuta, K. (2001b). Silence from Oceanside and the future of bilingual education. Retrieved June 10, 2008, from http://faculty.ucmerced.edu/khakuta/research/SAT9/silence1.html

Hale-Benson, J. E. (1986). *Black children: Their roots, culture, and learning styles*. Baltimore: Johns Hopkins University Press.

Hallahan, D. P., & Kauffman, J. M. (2000). *Exceptional children: Introduction to special education* (8th ed.). Boston: Allyn & Bacon.

Hallahan, D. P., &, Kauffman, J. M. (2006). *Exceptional learners: Introduction to special education*. Boston: Pearson Education.

Hansen, D. T. (1995). *The call to teach*. New York: Teachers College Press.

Hanson, J. R., & Silver, H. F. (2000). *Learning preference inventory*. Woodbridge, NJ: Thoughtful Education Press.

Hardman, M. L., Drew, C. J., & Egan, M. W. (2002). *Human exceptionality: Society, school, and family* (7th ed.). Boston: Allyn & Bacon.

Hardman, M. L., Drew, C. J., & Egan, M. W. (2005). *Human exceptionality: School, community, and family* (8th ed.). Boston: Allyn & Bacon.

Hardman, M. L., Drew, C. J., & Egan, M. W. (2007). *Human exceptionality:*

Society, school, and family (9th ed.). Boston: Houghton Mifflin.

Harrington, M. (1962). *The other America: Poverty in the United States*. New York: MacMillan.

Harris Interactive, Inc. (2001). *The MetLife survey of the American teacher: Key elements of quality schools*. New York: Author.

Harris Interactive, Inc. (2006). *The MetLife survey of the American teacher: Expectations and experiences*. New York: Author.

Harry A. v. Duncan, 351 F.Supp 2d 1060 (Mont. 2005).

Hart, P., & Teeter, R. (2002). *A national priority: Americans speak on teacher quality*. Princeton, NJ: Educational Testing Service.

Hartman, A. (2008). *Education and the cold war: The battle for the American school*. New York: Palgrave Macmillan.

Hauser, M., & Rauch, S. (2002). *New teacher! An exciting and scary time. 2002 job search handbook for educators*. Columbus, OH: American Association for Employment in Education.

Hawking, S. W. (1988). *A brief history of time: From the big bang to black holes*. New York: Bantam Books.

Hawkins-Simons, D. (2008, May 8). Where Clinton, Obama, and McCain stand on education. *U.S. News and World Report*. Retrieved from http://www.usnews.com/articles/news/campaign-2008/2008/05/08/where-clinton-obama-and-mccain-stand-on-education.html

Hazelwood School District v. Kuhlmeier, 484 U.S. 260 (1988).

Heath, S. B. (1983). *Ways with words*. Cambridge, UK: Cambridge University Press.

Hedges, L. V. (1996). Quoted in Hedges finds boys and girls both disadvantaged in school. *Education News*. University of Chicago, Department of Education.

Heffter, E. (2007, August 27). Seattle's African American Academy gets one more try. *Seattle Times*. Retrieved from http://seattletimes.nwsource.com/html/localnews/2003855108_aaa22m.html

Heilman, E. (2008). Hegemonies and "transgressions" of family: Tales of pride and prejudice. In T. Turner-Vorbeck & M. M. Marsh (Eds.), *Other kinds of families: Embracing diversity in schools*. New York: Teachers College Press.

Hendrie, C. (1999, May 5). Battle over principals in Chicago: Administration vs. local councils. *Education Week on the Web*.

Henriques, M. E. (1997, May). Increasing literacy among kindergartners through cross-age training. *Young Children*, pp. 42–47.

Henry, E., Huntley, J., McKamey, C., & Harper, L. (1995). *To be a teacher: Voices from the classroom*. Thousand Oaks, CA: Corwin Press.

Herndon, J. (1969). *The way it spozed to be*. New York: Bantam Books.

Hess, F. M. (2002). *Revolution at the margins: The impact of competition on urban school systems*. Washington, DC: Brookings Institution Press.

Hess, F. M. (2004, March). The political challenge of charter school regulation. *Phi Delta Kappan*, 508–512.

Hess, G. A. (2000). *Changes in student achievement in Illinois and Chicago, 1990–2000*. Chicago: Northwestern University, Center for Urban School Policy.

Hiebert, J., Gallimore, R., & Stigler, J. W. (2002). A knowledge base for the teaching profession: What would it look like and how can we get one? *Educational Researcher, 31*(5), 3–15.

Hills, G., & Hirschhorn, J. (2007, May). *Best in class: How top corporations can help transform public education*. New York: Ernst & Young.

Hirschfelder, A. B. (1986). *Happily may I walk: American Indians and Alaska Natives today*. New York: Scribner.

Hletko, J. D. (1995). Reflections on NBPTS. *Voices from the Middle, 2*(4), 33–36.

Hoekstra, M. (Ed.). (2002) *Am I teaching yet? Stories from the teacher-training trenches*. Portsmouth, NH: Heinemann.

Hofstede, G. (2001). *Culture's consequences: Comparing values, behaviors, institutions and organizations across nations* (2nd ed.). Thousand Oaks, CA: Sage.

Hoh, P. S. (2008). Cognitive characteristics of the gifted. In J. A. Plucker & C. M. Callahan (Eds.), *Critical issues and practices in gifted education: What the research says* (pp. 57–83). Waco, TX: Prufrock Press.

Holland, A., & Andre, T. (1987, Winter). Participation in extracurricular activities in secondary schools. *Review of Educational Research*, pp. 437–466.

Holmes, M., & Weiss, B. J. (1995). *Lives of women public schoolteachers: Scenes from American educational history*. New York: Garland.

The Holmes Group. (n.d.). *Tomorrow's schools: Principles for the design of professional development schools*. East Lansing, MI: Author.

Holt, J. (1964). *How children fail*. New York: Delta.

Holt v. Shelton, 341 F. Supp. 821 (M.D. Tenn. 1972).

Holt-Reynolds, D. (1999). Good readers, good teachers? Subject matter expertise as a challenge in learning to teach. *Harvard Educational Review, 69*(1), 29–50.

hooks, b. (1989). *Talking back: Thinking feminist, thinking black*. Toronto: Between the Lines.

hooks, b. (1994). *Teaching to transgress: Education as the practice of freedom*. New York: Routledge.

hooks, b. (2003) *Teaching community. A pedagogy of hope*. New York: Routledge.

Hopson, J. L., Hopson, E., & Hagen, T. (2002, May 8). Take steps to protect latchkey children. Knight Ridder/Tribune News Service.

Hortonville Joint School District No. 1 v. Hortonville Education Association, 426 U.S. 482 (1976).

Howard, V. F., Williams, B. F., Port, P. D., & Lepper, C. (2001). *Very young children with special needs*. Upper Saddle River, NJ: Merrill Prentice Hall.

Hoxby, C. M. (2004). *Achievement in charter schools and regular public schools in the United States: Understanding the differences*. Cambridge, MA: Harvard University and National Bureau of Economic Research.

Hoy, A. W., & Hoy, W. K. (2009). *Instructional leadership: A research-based guide to learning in schools*. Boston: Pearson.

Hoy, W. K., & Miskel, C. G. (2001). *Educational administration: Theory, research and practice* (6th ed.). Boston: McGraw-Hill.

Hoyt, W. H. (1999). An evaluation of the Kentucky Education Reform Act. In *Kentucky Annual Economic Report 1999* (pp. 21–36). Lexington: University of Kentucky, Center for Business and Economic Research.

Hurwitz, S. (1999, April). New York, New York: Can Rudy Crew hang tough on vouchers and pull off a turnaround in the nation's biggest school system? *The American School Board Journal*, pp. 36–40.

Idol, L. (1998). Optional extended year program, Feedback, Publication No. 97.20. Austin, TX: Austin Independent School District, Office of Program Evaluation.

Igoa, C. (1995). *The inner world of the immigrant child*. New York: Lawrence Erlbaum.

Imber, M., & van Geel, T. (2005). *A teacher's guide to education law* (3rd ed.). Mahwah, NJ: Lawrence Erlbaum.

Indiana University. (2008, March 14). *Teaching without distractions*, news release. Bloomington, IN: Author. Retrieved from http://info.iu.edu/news/page/print/7733.html

Ingraham v. Wright, 430 U.S. 651 (1977).

Inlay, L. (2003, March). Values: The implicit curriculum. *Educational Leadership 60*(6), 69–71.

Institute for Educational Leadership. (2002). *Community schools: Improving student learning/strengthening schools, families, and communities*. Washington, DC: Author.

REFERENCES

Institute for Government Research: Studies in Administration. (1928). *The problem of Indian administration: Report of a survey made at the request of Honorable Hubert Work, Secretary of the Interior, and submitted to him, February 21, 1928*. Baltimore, MD: Johns Hopkins Press.

Institute for Social Research. (2006). *Monitoring the future: National results on adolescent drug abuse*. Ann Arbor: University of Michigan, Institute for Social Research.

International Society for Technology in Education. (2007). *National educational technology and performance indicators for students*. Eugene, OR: Author.

International Society for Technology in Education. (2008). *National educational technology standards (NETS) for teachers 2008*. Retrieved from http://www.iste.org/Content/NavigationMenu/NETS/ForTeachers/2008Standards/NETS_for_Teachers_2008.htm

Jackson, P. (1965). The way teaching is. *NEA Journal*.

Jackson, P. (1990). *Life in classrooms*. New York: Teachers College Press.

Jeglin v. San Jacinto Unified School District, 827 F. Supp. 1459 (C.D. Cal. 1993).

Jencks, C., et al. (1972). *Inequality: A reassessment of the effect of family and schooling in America*. New York: Basic Books.

Jencks, C., & Phillips, M. (Eds.). (1998). *The black-white test score gap*. Washington, DC: Brookings Institution Press.

Johanningmeier, E. V. (1980). *Americans and their schools*. Chicago: Rand McNally.

Johnson, D. W., & Johnson, R. T. (1999). *Learning together and alone: Cooperative, competitive, and individualistic learning* (5th ed.). Boston: Allyn & Bacon.

Johnson, J., & Immerwahr, J. (1994). *First things first: What Americans expect from the public schools, a report from Public Agenda*. New York: Public Agenda.

Johnson, M. J., & Brown, L. (1998). Collegial support teams. In D. J. McIntyre & D. M. Byrd (Eds.), *Strategies for career-long teacher education: Teacher education yearbook VI*. Thousand Oaks, CA: Corwin Press.

Jonassen, D. H., Howland, J., Moore, J., & Marra, R. (2003). *Learning to solve problems with technology: A constructivist perspective*. Upper Saddle River, NJ: Merrill Prentice Hall.

Jones, K., & Whitford, K. (1997, December). Kentucky's conflicting reform principles: High-stakes accountability and student performance assessment. *Phi Delta Kappan*, 276–281.

Jordan, L., & Hendricks, C. (2002, March). Increasing sixth-grade students' engagement in literacy learning. *Networks: An on-line journal for teacher research*.

Jordan, W. J., & Nettles, S. M. (1999). *How students invest their time out of school: Effects on school engagement, perceptions of life chances, and achievement*. Baltimore: Center for Research on the Education of Students Placed at Risk.

Jorgensen, O. (2001). Supporting a diverse teacher corps. *Educational Leadership 58*(8), 64–67.

Joyce, B., Weil, M., & Calhoun, E. (2000). *Models of teaching* (6th ed.). Boston: Allyn & Bacon.

Joyce, B., Weil, M., & Calhoun, E. (2004). *Models of teaching* (7th ed.). Boston: Allyn & Bacon.

Joyce, B., Weil, M., & Calhoun, E. (2009). *Models of teaching,* (8th ed.). Boston: Allyn & Bacon.

Karr v. Schmidt, 401 U.S. 1201 (1972).

Katz, Y. J. (1999). Kindergarten teacher training through virtual reality: Three-dimensional simulation methodology. *Educational Media International, 36*(2), 151–156.

Kaye, E. A. (Ed.). (2001). *Requirements for certification of teachers, counselors, librarians, administrators for elementary and secondary schools—66th edition, 2001–2002*. Chicago: University of Chicago Press.

Kelly, M. (2000, September 8). Indian Affairs head makes apology. Associated Press.

Kellner, D. (2000). Multiple literacies and critical pedagogies. In P. P. Trifonas (Ed.), *Revolutionary pedagogies—cultural politics, instituting education, and the discourse of theory*. New York: Routledge.

Kennedy, M. (1999). Ed schools and the problem of knowledge. In J. D. Raths & A. C. McAninch (Eds.), *Advances in teacher education: Vol. 5. What counts as knowledge in teacher education?* (pp. 29–45). Stamford, CT: Ablex.

Kentucky Institute for Education Research. (2001). *KIER 2000 review of research*. Georgetown, KY: Georgetown College Conference and Training Center.

King, M. (2008, February 3). Tribes confront painful legacy of Indian boarding schools. *Seattle Times*. Retrieved from http://seattletimes.nwsource.com/html/localnews/2004161238_boardingschool03m.html

Kirkpatrick, H., & Cuban, L. (1998). Computers make kids smarter—right? *TECHNOS Quarterly, 7*(2), 26–31.

Kitzmiller v. Dover Area School District, 400 F. Supp. 2d 707 (2005).

Kleiner, B., Porch, R., & Farris, E. (2002). *Public alternative schools and programs for students at risk of education failure: 2000–01* (NCES 2002–04). Washington, DC: U.S. Department of Education, National Center for Education Statistics.

Kleinfeld, J. (1998). *The myth that schools shortchange girls: Social science in the service of deception*. Washington, DC: Women's Freedom Network.

Kohl, H. R. (1968). *36 children*. New York: Signet.

Kohlberg, H. (2006). The cognitive-developmental approach to moral education. In F. W. Parkay, E. J. Anctil, & G. Hass, *Curriculum planning: A contemporary approach* (8th ed., pp. 136–148). Boston: Pearson.

Kosciw, J. G. & Diaz., E. M. (2006). *The 2005 national school climate survey: The experiences of lesbian, gay, bisexual, and transgender youth in our nation's schools*. New York: Gay, Lesbian and Straight Education Network.

Kostelnik, M. J., Onaga, E., Rohde, B., & Whiren, A. (2002). *Children with special needs: Lessons for early childhood professionals*. New York: Teachers College Press.

Kounin, J. (1970). *Discipline and group management in classrooms*. New York: Holt, Rinehart and Winston.

Kozol, J. (1967). *Death at an early age*. Boston: Houghton Mifflin.

Kozol, J. (1991). *Savage inequalities: Children in America's schools*. New York: Crown.

Kozol, J. (2005). *The shame of the nation: The restoration of apartheid schooling in America*. New York: Three Rivers Press.

Krashen, S., & McField, G. (2005). What works? Reviewing the latest evidence on bilingual education. *Language Learner, 1*(2), 7–10.

Krizek v. Cicero-Stickney Township High School District No. 201, 713 F. Supp. 1131 (N.D. Ill. 1989).

Krogh, S. L. (2000). Weaving the web. In F. W. Parkay & G. Hass (Eds.), *Curriculum planning: A contemporary approach* (7th ed., pp. 338–341). Boston: Allyn & Bacon.

Kulik, J. A. (2004). Meta-analytic studies of acceleration. In N. Colangelo, S. G. Assouline, & M. U. M. Gross (Eds.), *A nation deceived: How schools hold back America's brightest students* (Vol. 2, pp. 13–22). Iowa City, IA: The Connie Belin and Jacqueline N. Blank International Center for Gifted Education and Talent Development.

Ladson-Billings, G. (2005). Is the team all right? Diversity and teacher education. *Journal of Teacher Education, 56*(3), 229–234.

LaMorte, M. W. (2008). *School law: Cases and concepts* (9th ed.). Boston: Pearson.

Lange, C. M., & Sletten, S. J. (2002). *Alternative education: A brief history and research synthesis*. Alexandria, VA: Project Forum at National Association of

State Directors of Special Education. Retrieved April 12, 2008, from http://www.nasdse.org/forum.htm

Larry P. v. Riles, 793 F.2d 969 (9th Cir. 1984).

Lau v. Nichols, 414 U.S. 563 (1974).

Laurence, D. (2000). *NEA: The grab for power: A chronology of the National Education Association*. Hearthstone.

Le, C. N. (2008). *Population statistics & demographics, Asian-nation: The landscape of Asian America*. Retrieved from http://www.asian-nation.org/population.shtm

Leahy, T., & Harris, R. (2001). *Learning and cognition* (5th ed.). Upper Saddle River, NJ: Merrill/Prentice Hall.

Learning in Deed. (2004). *Learning in deed: Service learning in action*. New York: National Service-Learning Partnership, Academy for Educational Development. Retrieved from http://www.learningindeed.org/tools/examples.html

Lee, V. E., Chen, X., & Smerdon, B. A. (1996). *The influence of school climate on gender differences in the achievement and engagement of young adolescents*. Washington, DC: American Association of University Women.

Leinhardt, G. (1990). Capturing craft knowledge in teaching. *Educational Researcher, 19*(2), 18–25.

Lemon v. Kurtzman, 403 U.S. 602 (1971).

Levin, D., & Arafeh, S. (2002). *The digital disconnect: The widening gap between Internet-savvy students and their schools*. Washington, DC: The Pew Internet and American Life Project.

Lewis, C. (2003, August 13). Is it time for cameras in classrooms? *Philadelphia Inquirer*. Retrieved from www.philly.com

Lewis, R. B., & Doorlag, D. H. (2006). *Teaching special students in general education classrooms* (7th ed.). Upper Saddle River, NJ: Pearson Education.

Lickona, T. (2008). *A 12-point comprehensive approach to character education*. Cortland, NY: SUNY Cortland School of Education, Center for the 4th and 5th Rs. Retrieved August 10, 2008, from http://www.cortland.edu/character/12pts.asp

Lightfoot, S. L. (1978). *Worlds apart: Relationships between families and schools*. New York: Basic Books.

Lindjord, D. (2000). Families at the century's turn: The troubling economic trends. *Family Review, 7*(3), 5–6.

Lindsay, D. (1996, March 13). N.Y. bills give teachers power to oust pupils. *Education Week*.

Lipsman v. New York City Board of Education, 1999 WL 498230 (N.Y.).

Littky, D. (2004). *The big picture: Education is everyone's business*. Alexandria, VA: Association for Supervision and Curriculum Development.

Little, P. M. D., & Harris, E. (2003, July). A review of out-of-school time program quasi-experimental and experimental evaluation results. Cambridge, MA: Harvard University, Harvard Family Research Project.

Lloyd, S. C. (June 22, 2006). A road map to state graduation policies. *Education Week, 25*(41S), 25, 29.

Lortie, D. (1975). *School teacher: A sociological study*. Chicago: University of Chicago Press.

Louis Harris and Associates, Inc. (1995). *The Metropolitan Life survey of the American teacher, 1984–1995: Old problems, new challenges*. New York: Author.

MacKinnon, C. (1994). Quoted in bell hooks, *Teaching to transgress: Education as the practice of freedom*. New York: Routledge.

Mack-Krisher, A. (2004). *Powerful classroom stories from accomplished teachers*. Thousand Oaks, CA: Corwin Press.

MacLeod, J. (1995). *Ain't no makin' it: Aspirations & attainment in a low-income neighborhood*. Boulder, CO: Westview Press.

MacNaughton, R. H., & Johns, F. A. (1991, September). Developing a successful schoolwide discipline program. *NASSP Bulletin*, pp. 47–57.

Mahoney, J., & Cairns, R. B. (1997). Do extracurricular activities protect against early school dropout? *Developmental Psychology, 33*(2), 241–253.

Mailloux v. Kiley, 323 F. Supp. 1387, 1393 (D. Mass.), *aff'd*, 448 F.2d 1242 (1st Cir. 1971).

Mann, H. (1848). Twelfth annual report. In L. A. Cremin (Ed.), *The republic and the school: Horace Mann on the education of free men*. New York: Teachers College Press, 1957.

Mann, H. (1868). Annual reports on education. In M. Mann (Ed.), *The life and works of Horace Mann* (Vol. 3). Boston: Horace B. Fuller.

Mann, H. (1957). Twelfth annual report. In L. A. Cremin (Ed.), *The republic and the school: Horace Mann on the education of free men*. New York: Teachers College Press.

Marcus v. Rowley, 695 F.2d 1171 (9th Cir. 1983).

Markus, H., & Kitayama, S. (1991). Conflictways: Culture and the self: Implications for cognition, emotion, and motivation. *Psychological Review, 98*, 224–253.

Marshall, K. (2003, May). Recovering from HSPS (hyperactive superficial principal syndrome): A progress report. *Phi Delta Kappan*, 701–709.

Martinez, M. E. (2006). What is metacognition? *Phi Delta Kappan, 87*(9), 696–699.

Marzano, R. J. (1997). *Eight questions you should ask before implementing standards-based education at the local level*. Aurora, CO: Mid-Continent Research for Education and Learning.

Maslow, A. (1954). *Motivation and personality*. New York: Basic Books.

Maslow, A. (1962). *Toward a psychology of being*. New York: Basic Books.

Maslow, A. H. (1959). *Toward a psychology of being* (3rd ed.). New York: John Wiley & Sons.

Maslow, A. H. (1987). *Motivation and personality* (3rd ed.). Boston: Addison-Wesley.

Mayhew, K. C., & Edwards, A. C. (1936). *The Dewey School: The University Laboratory School of the University of Chicago, 1896–1903*. New York: D. Appleton-Century.

McCain, T., & Jukes, I. (2001). *Windows on the future: Education in the age of technology*. Thousand Oaks, CA: Corwin Press.

McCourt, F. (2005). *Teacher man: A memoir*. New York: Simon & Schuster.

McHugh, J. (2005, October). Synching up with the iKid: Connecting to the twenty-first-century student. *Edutopia Magazine*.

McMillan, J. H. (2001). *Classroom assessment: Principles and practice for effective instruction* (2nd ed.). Boston: Allyn & Bacon.

Meek, C. (2003, April). Classroom crisis: It's about time. *Phi Delta Kappan*, 592–595.

Mehlinger, H. D. (1996, February). School reform in the information age. *Phi Delta Kappan*, 400–407.

Metcalf, K. K. (2003, March). *Evaluation of the Cleveland scholarship and tutoring program*. Bloomington: Indiana Center for Evaluation.

Michie, G. (1999). *Holler if you hear me: The education of a teacher and his students*. New York: Teachers College Press.

Miller, S. R., Allensworth, E. M., & Kochanek, J. R. (2002). *Student performance: Course taking, test scores, and outcomes*. Chicago: Consortium on Chicago School Research.

Mills, G. E. (2000). *Action research: A guide for the teacher researcher*. Upper Saddle River, NJ: Merrill.

Missouri v. Jenkins, 515 U.S. 70 (1995).

Mitchell v. Helms, 530 U.S. 793 (2000).

Modi, M., Konstantopoulos, S., & Hedges, L. V. (1998). *Predictors of academic giftedness among U.S. high school students: Evidence from a nationally representative multivariate analysis*. Paper presented at the annual meeting of the American Educational Research Association, San Diego. (Eric Document No. ED422 356).

Mohammed ex rel. Mohammed, v. School District of Philadelphia, 355 F. Supp. 2d 779 (Pa. 2005).

Mohr, M., Rogers, C., Sanford, B., Nocerino, M. A., MacLean, M. S., & Clawson, S.

(2004). *Teacher research for better schools*. New York: Teachers College Press.

Molino, F. (1999). My students, my children. In M. K. Rand & S. Shelton-Colangelo, *Voices of student teachers: Cases from the field* (pp. 55–56). Upper Saddle River, NJ: Merrill.

Molnar, A., Wilson, G., & Allen, D. (2004). *Profiles of for-profit education management companies: Sixth annual report*. Arizona State University: Education Policy Studies Laboratory, Commercialism in Education Research Unit.

Montagu, A. (1974). *Man's most dangerous myth: The fallacy of race* (5th ed.). New York: Oxford University Press.

Moran v. School District No. 7, 350 F. Supp. 1180 (D. Mont. 1972).

Morris, J. E., & Curtis, K. E. (1983, March/April). Legal issues relating to field-based experiences in teacher education. *Journal of Teacher Education*, 2–6.

Morris, V. C., & Pai, Y. (1994). *Philosophy and the American school: An introduction to the philosophy of education*. Lanham, MD: University Press of America.

Morrison v. State Board of Education, 461 P.2d 375 (Cal. 1969).

Moskal, B. M. (2000). Scoring rubrics: What, when, and how? *Practical Assessment, Research, & Evaluation*, 7(3).

Mozert v. Hawkins County Board of Education, 827 F.2d 1058 (6th Cir. 1987), *cert. denied*, 484 U.S. 1066 (1988).

MTV and American Psychological Association. (n.d.) *Warning signs: A violence prevention guide for youth from MTV and APA*. New York: MTV; Washington, DC: American Psychological Association.

Mueller v. Allen, 463 U.S. 388 (1983).

Mukhopadhyay, C., & Henze, R. C. (2003, May). How real is race? Using anthropology to make sense of human diversity. *Phi Delta Kappan*, 84(9), 669–678.

Murphy, J. (2005). *Connecting teacher leadership and school improvement*. Thousand Oaks, CA: Corwin Press.

Murray v. Pittsburgh Board of Public Education, 919 F. Supp. 838 (W.D. Pa. 1996).

National Association of School Psychologists. (2008). *Zero tolerance and alternative strategies: A fact sheet for educators and policymakers*. Bethesda, MD: Author. Retrieved from http://www.nasponline.org/educators/zero_alternative.pdf

National Association for Year-Round Education. (2008). *Statistical summaries of year-round education programs*. Retrieved February 28, 2008 from http://www.nayre.org/

National Board for Professional Teaching Standards (NBPTS). (2002). *What teachers should know and be able to do*. Arlington, VA: Author.

National Board for Professional Teaching Standards. (2007). *Making the commitment to accomplished teaching: Q & A for 2007 National Board Certification*. Arlington, VA: Author.

National Board for Professional Teaching Standards. (2007, December 3). *Largest one-year gain of National Board certified teachers advances teaching quality movement in the U.S.*, [press release]. Arlington, VA: Author.

National Catholic Education Association. (2008, April 11). *Catholic education questions*. Retrieved from http://www.ncea.org/FAQ/CatholicEducationFAQ.asp

National Center for Children in Poverty. (2008). *Who are America's poor children: The official story*. Retrieved from http://www.nccp.org/

National Center for Education Statistics. (1980). *High school and beyond study*. Washington, DC: U.S. Department of Education.

National Center for Education Statistics. (2002, July 2). *The condition of education 2002*. Washington, DC: Author.

National Center for Education Statistics. (2002, August). *Public alternative schools and programs for students at risk of education failure: 2000–01*. Washington, DC: Author.

National Center for Education Statistics. (2006, February). *Public elementary and secondary students, staff, schools, and school districts: School year 2003–04*. Washington, DC: Author.

National Center for Education Statistics. (2006, September). *Projections of education statistics to 2015*. Washington, DC: U.S. Department of Education.

National Center for Education Statistics. (2006, October). *State profiles: The nation's report card*. Washington, DC: Author.

National Center for Education Statistics. (2007, January). *Projections of education statistics to 2016*. Washington, DC: U.S. Department of Education.

National Center for Education Statistics. (2007, May). *Digest of education statistics 2007*. Washington, DC: Author.

National Center for Education Statistics. (2007, September). *Private school universe survey*. Washington, DC: U.S. Department of Education.

National Center for Education Statistics. (2007, September). *Status and trends in the education of racial and ethnic minorities*. Washington, DC: Author.

National Center for Education Statistics. (2007, December). *Indicators of school crime and safety*. Washington, DC: Author.

National Center for Education Statistics. (2007, December). *Projections of education statistics to 2016*. Washington, DC: U.S. Department of Education.

National Center for Education Statistics. (2008). *The condition of education 2008*. Washington, DC: U.S. Department of Education.

National Center for Education Statistics. (2008, February 28). *Fast facts*. Retrieved from http://nces.ed.gov/fastfacts/display.asp?id=372

National Center for Education Statistics. (2008, March 25). *Digest of Education Statistics, 2007*. Washington, DC: Author.

National Center for Education Statistics. (2008, April). *Revenues and expenditures for public elementary and secondary education, school year 2005–06*. Washington, DC: Author.

National Center for Education Statistics. (2008, May 29). *The condition of education 2008*. Washington, DC: Author.

National Clearinghouse for English Language Acquisition. (2008). *The growing numbers of limited English proficient students: 1995/96–2005/06*. Washington, DC: Author.

National Clearinghouse on Child Abuse and Neglect. (2002). *National child abuse and neglect data system (NCANDS): Summary of key findings from calendar year 2000*. Washington, DC: Author.

National Coalition for the Homeless. (2008). *Who is homeless?* Retrieved August 9, 2008, from http://www.nationalhomeless.org/publications/facts/Whois.pdf

National Commission on Excellence and Education. (1983). *A nation at risk: The imperative for educational reform*. Washington, DC: U.S. Government Printing Office.

National Commission on Teaching and America's Future. (2003). *What matters most: Teaching for America's future*. New York: Author.

National Council for Accreditation of Teacher Education (NCATE). (2002). *Professional standards for the accreditation of schools, colleges, and departments of education—2002 edition*. Washington, DC: Author.

National Council for Accreditation of Teacher Education (NCATE). (2008, February 28). *About NCATE*. Retrieved from http://www.ncate.org/public/aboutNCATE.asp

National Education Association. (2002). *Status of the American public school teacher*. Washington, DC: Author.

National Education Association. (2003). *Status of the American public school teacher*. Washington, DC: Author.

National Education Association. (2007, December). *Rankings and estimates: Rankings of the states 2006 and estimates of school statistics 2007.* Washington, DC: Author.

National Education Association. (2008). *Attracting and keeping quality teachers.* Retrieved February 28, 2008, from http://www.nea.org/teachershortage/index.html

National Education Association. (2008, April 29). *About NEA.* Retrieved from http://www.nea.org/index.html

National Governors' Association and NGA Center for Best Practices. (2002). *After-school plus (+) program: Hawaii.* Washington, DC: Author.

National Joint Committee on Learning Disabilities. (2008). *LD basics: What is a learning disability?* Retrieved from http://www.ldonline.org/ldbasics/whatisld

National School Boards Association. (2002). *Are we there yet? Research and guidelines on school's use of the Internet.* Alexandria, VA: Author.

National trade and professional associations of the United States 2008. New York: Columbia Books.

Navarro, M. (2008, March 31). New dialogue on mixed race: Many of mixed parentage feel Obama's path similar to theirs. *New York Times.* Retrieved from http://www.msnbc.msn.com/id/23875822/

NEA Today. (2003, May). New federal rule supports school prayer, p. 13.

NEAFT Partnership. (2002, April 23–24). *NEAFT Partnership Joint Council communique.* Washington, DC: Author.

Neill, A. S. (1960). *Summerhill: A radical approach to child rearing.* New York: Hart.

Nelson, J. L., Carlson, K., & Palonsky, S. B. (2000). *Critical issues in education: A dialectic approach* (4th ed.). New York: McGraw-Hill.

New Jersey v. Massa, 231 A.2d 252 (N.J. Sup. Ct. 1967).

New Jersey v. T.L.O., 469 U.S. 325 (1985).

Newmann, F. M., et al. (Eds.). (1996). *Authentic achievement: Restructuring schools for intellectual quality.* San Francisco: Jossey-Bass.

Newmann, F. M., & Wehlage, G. G. (1995). *Successful school restructuring: A report to the public and educators by the Center on Organization and Restructuring of Schools.* Madison: University of Wisconsin, Center on Organization and Restructuring of Schools.

Nieto, S. (2002). *Language, culture, and teaching: Critical perspectives for a new century.* Mahwah, NJ: Lawrence Erlbaum.

Nieto, S. (2003). *What keeps teachers going?* New York: Teachers College Press.

Nitko, A. J. (2001). *Educational assessment of students* (3rd ed.). Upper Saddle River, NJ: Merrill.

Noddings, N. (2002). *Educating moral people: A caring alternative to character education.* New York: Teachers College Press.

Noddings, N. (2007). *When school reform goes wrong.* New York: Teachers College Press.

Nord, C. W., & West, J. (2001). *National household education survey: Fathers' and mothers' involvement in their children's schools by family type and resident status.* Washington, DC: U.S. Department of Education, National Center for Education Statistics.

Null v. Board of Education, 815 F. Supp. 937 (D. W. Va. 1993).

Oakes, J., & Lipton, M. (2007). *Teaching to change the world* (3rd ed.). Boston: McGraw-Hill.

Oberti v. Board of Education of the Borough of Clementon School District, 789 F. Supp. 1322 (D.N.J. 1992).

Obiakor, F. E. (2007). *Multicultural special education: Culturally responsive teaching.* Upper Saddle River, NJ: Pearson Education.

Oh Day Aki. (2008). *Oh Day Aki Charter School, school information.* Retrieved from http://www.americanindianeducation.org/school_information.htm

Ohman v. Board of Education, 93 N.E.2d 927 (N.Y. 1950).

Orfield, G., & Yun, J. T. (1999). *Re-segregation in American schools.* Cambridge, MA: Harvard University, Civil Rights Project.

Ormrod, J. E. (2003). *Educational psychology: Developing learners* (4th ed.). Upper Saddle River, NJ: Merrill Prentice Hall.

Ormrod, J. E. (2006). *Essentials of educational psychology.* Upper Saddle River, NJ: Pearson Education.

Ormrod, J. E., & McGuire, D. J. (2007). *Case studies: Applying educational psychology.* Upper Saddle River, NJ: Pearson Education.

Ortiz, M. G. (1999, April 19). Urban schools lag in technology. *Detroit Free Press.*

Ovando, C. J., Combs, M. C., & Collier, V. P. (2006). *Bilingual and ESL classrooms: Teaching in multicultural contexts.* Boston: McGraw-Hill.

Owasso Independent School District v. Falvo, 233 F.3d 1203 (10th Cir. 2002).

Ozmon, H. W., & Craver, S. M. (2007). *Philosophical foundations of education* (8th ed.). Upper Saddle River, NJ: Prentice Hall.

Paglin, C., & Fager, J. (1997). *Grade configuration: Who goes where? By request series.* Portland, OR: Northwest Regional Educational Laboratory. (ERIC Document Reproduction Service No. ED 432 033).

Pajak, E. (1999). *Approaches to clinical supervision: Alternatives for improving instruction.* Norwood, MA: Christopher-Gordon.

Parkay, F. W. (1983). *White teacher, black school: The professional growth of a ghetto teacher.* New York: Praeger.

Parkay, F. W. (1988, Summer). Reflections of a protégé. *Theory into Practice,* pp. 195–200.

Parkay, F. W., Anctil, E., & Hass, G. (2006). *Curriculum planning: A contemporary approach* (8th ed.). Boston: Allyn & Bacon.

Parkay, F. W., Potisook, P., Chantharasa-kul, A., & Chunsakorn, P. (1999). *New roles and responsibilities in educational reform: A study of Thai and U.S. principals' attitudes toward teacher leadership.* Bangkok: Kasetsart University, Center for Research on Teaching and Teacher Education.

Parkay, F. W., Shindler, J., & Oaks, M. M. (1997, January). Creating a climate for collaborative, emergent leadership at an urban high school: Exploring the stressors, role changes, and paradoxes of restructuring. *International Journal of Educational Reform,* 64–74.

Parker, L., & Shapiro, J. P. (1993). The context of educational administration and social class. In C. A. Capper (Ed.), *Educational administration in a pluralistic society* (pp. 36–65). Albany: State University of New York Press.

PASE (Parents in Action on Special Education) v. Hannon, 506 F. Supp. 831 (E.D. Ill. 1980).

Pashler, H., & Carrier, M. (1996). Structures, processes, and the flow of information. In E. Bjork & R. Bjork (Eds.), *Memory* (pp. 3–29). San Diego, CA: Academic Press.

Patchin, J. W., & Hinduja, S. (2006). Bullies move beyond the schoolyard: A preliminary look at cyberbullying. *Youth Violence and Juvenile Justice, 4*(2), 148–169.

Patchogue-Medford Congress of Teachers v. Board of Education of Patchogue-Medford Union Free School District, 510 N.E.2d 325 (N.Y. 1987).

Paul, J. L., Christensen, L., & Falk, G. (2000). Accessing the intimate spaces of life in the classroom through letters to former teachers: A protocol for uncovering hidden stories. In J. L. Paul & T. J. Smith (Eds.), *Stories out of school: Memories and reflections on care and cruelty in the classroom* (pp. 15–26). Stamford, CT: Ablex.

Paul, J. L., & Colucci, K. (2000). Caring pedagogy. In J. L. Paul & T. J. Smith (Eds.), *Stories out of school: Memories and reflections on care and cruelty in the classroom* (pp. 45–63). Stamford, CT: Ablex.

Paul, R., & Elder, L. (2006). *The thinker's guide to the art of Socratic questioning.* Dillon Beach: Foundation for Critical Thinking.

PBS Teachers. (2008). *About*. Retrieved from http://www.pbs.org/teachers/about/

People for the American Way. (2008, May 25). *Schools and censorship*. Retrieved from http://www.pfaw.org/pfaw/general/default.aspx?oid=10038#

Peter Doe v. San Francisco Unified School District, 131 Cal. Rptr. 854 (Ct. App. 1976).

Pew Forum on Religion & Public Life. (2008, February 25). *The U.S. religious landscape survey*. Washington, DC: Author.

Picarella v. Terrizzi, 893 F. Supp. 1292 (M.D. Pa. 1995).

Pitton, D. E. (1998). *Stories of student teaching: A case approach to the student teaching experience*. Upper Saddle River, NJ: Merrill.

Portner, J. (1999, May 12). Schools ratchet up the rules on student clothing, threats. *Education Week on the Web*.

Posner, G. J. (2005). *Field experience: A guide to reflective teaching* (6th ed.). Boston: Pearson Education.

Poway Unified School District. (2008). *Ed tech central*. Retrieved from http://powayusd.sdcoe.k12.ca.us/projects/edtechcentral/DigitalStorytelling/default.htm

Power, E. J. (1982). *Philosophy of education: Studies in philosophies, schooling, and educational policies*. Englewood Cliffs, NJ: Prentice Hall.

Power, F. C., et al. (Eds.). (2008). *Moral education: A handbook* (Vol. 1). Westport, CT: Praeger.

Prensky, M. (2008). Young minds, fast times: How tech-obsessed iKids would improve our schools. *Edutopia: What Works in Public Education, 33–36.*

President's Commission on Excellence in Special Education. (2002). *A new era: Revitalizing special education for children and their families*. Washington, DC: Author.

Protheroe, N., Lewis, A., & Paik, S. (2002, Winter). Promoting quality teaching. *ERS Spectrum*. Retrieved from www.ers.org/spectrum/wino2a.htm

Rand, M. K., & Shelton-Colangelo, S. (1999). *Voices of student teachers: Cases from the field*. Upper Saddle River, NJ: Merrill.

Randall, V. R. (2001). *Institutional racism*. Dayton, OH: University of Dayton School of Law.

Ravitch, D. (1983). *The troubled crusade: American education, 1945–1980*. New York: Basic Books.

Ravitch, D. (1985). *The schools we deserve: Reflections on the education crises of our times*. New York: Basic Books.

Ravitch, D. (1996). *National standards in American education: A citizen's guide*. Washington, DC: Brookings Institution.

Ravitch, D. (1997, December 15). The fight for standards. *Forbes, 160* (13), 106.

Ravitz, J. L., Wong, Y. T., & Becker, H. J. (1999). *Report to participants*. University of California, Irvine, and University of Minnesota: Center for Research on Information Technology and Organizations.

Ray v. School District of DeSoto County, 666 F. Supp. 1524 (M.D. Fla. 1987).

RCM Research Corporation. (1998). *Time: Critical issues in educational change*. Portsmouth, NH: Author.

Rector, T. A., Jacoby, S. H., Lockwood, J. F., & McCarthy, D. W. (2002, January 7). *Teacher leaders in research based science education*. Paper presented at the 199th meeting of the American Astronomical Society, Washington, DC.

Reeves, D. B. (2008). *Reframing teacher leadership to improve your school*. Alexandria, VA: Association for Supervision and Curriculum Development.

Renzulli, J. S. (1998). The three-ring conception of giftedness. In S. M. Baum, S. M. Reis, & L. R. Maxfield (Eds.), *Nurturing the gifts and talents of primary grade students*. Mansfield Center, CT: Creative Learning Press.

Richard, A. (2002a, January 9). Report card days. *Education Week on the Web*.

Richard, A. (2002b, May 15). Memphis school board wants uniforms for all. *Education Week on the Web*.

Rickover, H. G. (1959). *Education and freedom*. New York: E. P. Dutton.

Rideout, V., Roberts, D. F., & Foehr, U. G. (2005). *Generation M: Media in the lives of 8–18-year olds*. Menlo Park, CA: Kaiser Family Foundation.

Rieger, L. (2008). A welcoming tone in the classroom: Developing the potential of diverse students and their families. In T. Turner-Vorbeck. & M. M. Marsh (Eds.), *Other kinds of families: Embracing diversity in schools* (pp. 64–80). New York: Teachers College Press.

Rippa, S. A. (1984). *Education in a free society*. New York: Longman.

Rippa, S. A. (1997). *Education in a free society: An American history* (8th ed.). New York: Longman.

Ripple, R. E., & Rockcastle, V. E. (Eds.). (1964). *Piaget rediscovered: A report of the conference on cognitive studies and curriculum development*. Ithaca, NY: Cornell University, School of Education.

Roach, V., & Cohen, B. A. (2002). *Moving past the politics: How alternative certification can promote comprehensive teacher development reforms*. Alexandria, VA: National Association of State Boards of Education.

Robinson, A. (2008). Teacher characteristics. In J. A. Plucker & C. M. Callahan (Eds.), *Critical issues and practices in gifted education: What the research says* (pp. 669–680). Waco, TX: Prufrock Press.

Robinson, M. W. (2008, February/March). Scared not to be straight. *Edutopia: The New World of Learning, 4*(1), 56–58.

Rogers, C. (1961). *On becoming a person*. Boston: Houghton Mifflin.

Rogers, C. (1982). *Freedom to learn in the eighties*. Columbus, OH: Merrill.

Romans v. Crenshaw, 354 F. Supp. 868 (S.D. Tex. 1972).

Rose, L. C., & Gallup, A. M. (2005, September). The 37th annual Phi Delta Kappa/Gallup poll of the public's attitudes toward the public schools. *Phi Delta Kappan*, 41–57.

Rose, L. C., & Gallup, A. M. (2006, September). The 38th annual Phi Delta Kappa/Gallup Poll of the public's attitudes toward the public schools. *Phi Delta Kappan,* 41–56.

Rose, L. C., & Gallup, A. M. (2007, September). The 39th annual Phi Delta Kappa/Gallup Poll of the public's attitudes toward the public schools. *Phi Delta Kappan,* 33–43.

Rosenkranz, T. (2002). *2001 CPS test trend review: Iowa Tests of Basic Skills*. Chicago: Consortium on Chicago School Research.

Rosenshine, B. (1988). Explicit teaching. In D. Berliner & B. Rosenshine (Eds.), *Talks to teachers*. New York: Random House.

Rosenshine, B., & Stevens, R. (1986). Teaching functions. In M. C. Wittrock (Ed.), *Handbook of research on teaching* (3rd ed.). New York: Macmillan.

Rothstein-Fisch, C., & Trumbull, E. (2008). *Managing diverse classrooms: How to build on students' cultural strengths*. Alexandria, VA: Association for Supervision and Curriculum Development.

Rury, J. L. (2002). *Education and social change: Themes in the history of American schooling*. Mahwah, NJ: Lawrence Erlbaum.

Russo, A. (Ed.). (2004). *School reform in Chicago: Lessons in policy and practice*. Cambridge, MA: Harvard Education Press.

Salovey, P., & Feldman-Barrett, L. (Eds.). (2002). *The wisdom of feelings: Psychological processes in emotional intelligence*. New York: Guilford Press.

Salovey, P., Mayer, J. D., & Caruso, D. (2002). The positive psychology of emotional intelligence. In C. R. Snyder & S. J. Lopez (Eds.), *The handbook of positive psychology* (pp. 159–171). New York: Oxford University Press.

Salovey, P., & Sluyter, D. J. (Eds.). (1997). *Emotional development and emotional intelligence: Educational implications*. New York: Basic Books.

Sandham, J. L. (2002, February 6). Board to close Fla. "voucher" school. *Education Week on the Web*.

Sandholtz, J. J., Ringstaff, C., & Dwyer, D. C. (1997). *Teaching with technology:*

Creating student-centered classrooms. New York: Teachers College Press.

Santa Fe Independent School District v. Jane Doe, 530 U.S. 290 (2000).

Santayana, G. (1954). *The life of reason; or, The phases of human progress.* New York: Scribner.

Sartre, J. P. (1972). Existentialism. In J. M. Rich (Ed.), *Readings in the philosophy of education.* Belmont, CA: Wadsworth.

Scales, P. C. (2001). The public image of adolescents. *Society 38*(4), 64–70.

Scering, G. E. S. (1997, January–February). Theme of a critical/feminist pedagogy: Teacher education for democracy. *Journal of Teacher Education, 48*(1), 62–68.

Schaefer, R. (1967). *The school as the center of inquiry.* New York: Harper & Row.

Schaill v. Tippecanoe School Corp., 864 F.2d 1309 (7th Cir. 1988).

Schmuck, R. A., & Schmuck, P. A. (2001). *Group processes in the classroom* (8th ed.). Boston: McGraw-Hill.

Schneider, R. B., & Barone, D. (1997, Spring). Cross-age tutoring. *Childhood Education,* 136–143.

School District of Abington Township v. Schempp, 374 U.S. 203 (1963).

Schunk, D. (2004). *Learning theories: An educational perspective* (4th ed.). Upper Saddle River, NJ: Merrill/Prentice Hall.

Schwartz, J. E., & Beichner, R. J. (1999). *Essentials of educational technology.* Boston: Allyn & Bacon.

Scopes, J. (1966). *Center of the storm.* New York: Holt, Rinehart and Winston.

Scoville v. Board of Education of Joliet Township High School District 204, 425 F.2d 10 (7th Cir.), *cert. denied,* 400 U.S. 826, (1970).

Search Institute. (2002). *Help your youth grow up healthy.* Minneapolis: Author.

Sears, J. T. (1991). Educators, homosexuality and homosexual students: Are personal feelings related to professional beliefs? *Journal of Homosexuality, 22.*

Shade, B. J. (1982). Afro-American cognitive style: A variable in school success? *Review of Educational Research, 52*(2), 219–238.

Shanley v. Northeast Independent School District, 462 F.2d 960 (5th Cir. 1972).

Sharan, Y., & Sharan, S. (1989/90, December/January). Group investigation expands cooperative learning. *Educational Leadership,* 17–21.

Sheuerer, D., & Parkay, F. W. (1992). The new Christian right and the public school curriculum: A Florida report. In J. B. Smith & J. G. Coleman, Jr. (Eds.), *School library media annual: 1992* (Vol. 10). Englewood, CO: Libraries Unlimited.

Shulman, L. (1987, August). *Teaching alone, learning together: Needed agendas for the new reform.* Paper presented at the Conference on Restructuring Schooling for Quality Education, San Antonio.

Simonetti v. School District of Philadelphia, 454 A.2d 1038 (Pa. Super. 1982).

Simpkins, S. (2003, Spring). Does youth participation in out-of-school time activities make a difference? *The evaluation exchange,* Vol. IX, No. 1. Harvard Graduate School of Education, Harvard Family Research Project (HFRP).

Sizer, T. (1997a). *Horace's compromise: The dilemma of the American high school* (3rd ed.). Boston: Houghton Mifflin.

Sizer, T. (1997b). *Horace's hope: What works for the American high school.* Boston: Houghton Mifflin.

Sizer, T. (1997c). *Horace's school: Redesigning the American high school.* Boston: Houghton Mifflin.

Sizer, T., & Sizer, N. F. (1999). *The students are watching: Schools and the moral contract.* Boston: Beacon Press.

Skinner, B. F. (1972). Utopia through the control of human behavior. In J. M. Rich (Ed.), *Readings in the philosophy of education.* Belmont, CA: Wadsworth.

Slavin, R. E. (2000). *Educational psychology: Theory and practice* (6th ed.). Boston: Allyn & Bacon.

Slavin, R. E. (2003). *Educational psychology: Theory and practice* (7th ed.). Boston: Allyn & Bacon.

Smith, D. D. (2007). *Introduction to special education: Making a difference* (6th ed.). Boston: Pearson.

Smith, L. G., & Smith, J. K. (1994). *Lives in education: A narrative of people and ideas* (2nd ed.). New York: St. Martin's Press.

Smith v. Board of School Commissioners of Mobile County, 655 F. Supp. 939 (S.D. Ala.), *rev'd,* 827 F.2d 684 (11th Cir. 1987).

Smyth, J. W. (1995). *Clinical supervision: Collaborative learning about teaching.* New York: State Mutual Book and Periodical Service.

Snipes, J., Soga, K., & Uro, G. (2007). *Improving teaching and learning for English language learners in urban schools.* Council of the Great City Schools, Research Brief. Washington, DC: Author.

Snyder, J. F. (1999). The alternative of substitute teaching. *1999 job search handbook for educators* (p. 38). Evanston, IL: American Association for Employment in Education.

Snyder, K. J., & Anderson, R. H. (Eds.). (1996). *Clinical supervision: Coaching for higher performance.* Lanham, MD: Scarecrow Press.

Sommers, C. H. (1994). *Who stole feminism? How women have betrayed women.* New York: Simon & Schuster.

Sommers, C. H. (1996, June 12). Where the boys are. *Education Week on the Web.*

Sommers, C. H. (2000). *The war against boys: How misguided feminism is harming our young men.* New York: Simon & Schuster.

Spokesman Review. (1993, June 4). Harassment claims vex teachers.

Spring, J. (1997). *The American school 1642–1996* (4th ed.). New York: McGraw-Hill.

Spring, J. (2005). *The American school: 1642–2004.* Boston: McGraw-Hill.

Spring, J. (2008a). *American education* (13th ed.). Boston: McGraw-Hill.

Spring, J. (2008b). *The American school: From the Puritans to No Child Left Behind.* Boston: McGraw-Hill.

St. Michel, T. (1995). *Effective substitute teachers: Myth, mayhem, or magic?* Thousand Oaks, CA: Corwin Press.

Stanford, B. H. (1992). Gender equity in the classroom. In D. A. Byrnes & G. Kiger (Eds.), *Common bonds: Anti-bias teaching in a diverse society.* Wheaton, MD: Association for Childhood Education International.

State v. Rivera, 497 N.W.2d 878 (Iowa 1993).

State Educational Technology Directors Association. (2005). *National trends: Enhancing education through technology: No Child Left Behind, Title IID-year two in review.* Los Angeles: Metri Group.

Station v. Travelers Insurance Co., 292 So. 2d 289 (La. Ct. App. 1974).

Stecher, B., & Hamilton, L. (2002, February 20). Test-based accountability: Making it work better. *Education Week on the Web.* Retrieved from www.edweek.org/ew/newstory.cfm?slug=23Stecher.h21

Stengel, B. S., & Tom, A. R. (2006). *Moral matters: Five ways to develop the moral life of schools.* New York: Teachers College Press.

Sternberg, L., Dornbusch, S., & Brown, B. (1996). *Beyond the classroom: Why school reform has failed and what parents need to do.* New York: Simon & Schuster.

Sternberg, R. J. (2002). Beyond g: The theory of successful intelligence. In R. J. Sternberg & E. L. Grigorenko (Eds.), *The general factor of intelligence: How general is it?* (pp. 447–479). Mahwah, NJ: Lawrence Erlbaum.

Stiggins, R. J. (2004, September). New assessment beliefs for a new school mission. *Phi Delta Kappan,* 22–27.

Stiggins, R. J. (2005). *Student-involved assessment for learning* (4th ed.). Upper Saddle River, NJ: Pearson/Merrill Prentice Hall.

Stone, R., & Cuper, P. H. (2006). *Best practices for teacher leadership: What award-winning teachers do for their professional learning communities.* Thousand Oaks, CA: Corwin Press.

Stone v. Graham, 599 S.W.2d 157 (Ky. 1980).

Stover, D. (1992, March). The at-risk kids schools ignore. *The Executive Educator,* pp. 28–31.

Strike, K. A. (2007). *Ethical leadership in schools: Creating community in an environment of accountability.* Thousand Oaks, CA: Corwin Press.

Strike, K. A., & Soltis, J. F. (1985). *The ethics of teaching.* New York: Teachers College Press.

Strong, R., Silver, H., & Perini, M. (2001). *Teaching what matters most: Standards and strategies for raising student achievement.* Alexandria, VA: Association for Supervision and Curriculum Development.

Stuckey, M. (2008, May 28). Multiracial Americans surge in numbers. Voice: Obama candidacy focuses new attention on their quest for understanding. MSNBC Interactive. Retrieved from http://www.msnbc.msn.com/id/24542138/

Sullivan v. Houston Independent School District, 475 F.2d 1071 (5th Cir.), cert. denied, 414 U.S. 1032 (1969).

Swanson v. Guthrie Independent School District No. 1, 135 F.3d 694 (10th Cir. 1998).

Swisher, K., & Deyhle, D. (1987). Styles of learning and learning styles: Educational conflicts for American Indian/Alaskan Native youth. *Journal of Multilingual and Multicultural Development, 8*(4), 345–360.

Teach for America. (2008). *About us.* Retrieved February 28, 2008, from www.teachforamerica.org

Tellijohann, S. K., & Price, J. H. (1993). A qualitative examination of adolescent homosexuals' life experiences: Ramifications for secondary school personnel. *Journal of Homosexuality, 26.*

Terman, L. M., Baldwin, B. T., & Bronson, E. (1925). Mental and physical traits of a thousand gifted children. In L. M. Terman (Ed.), *Genetic studies of genius* (Vol. 1). Stanford, CA: Stanford University Press.

Terman, L. M., & Oden, M. H. (1947). The gifted child grows up. In L. M. Terman (Ed.), *Genetic studies of genius* (Vol. 4). Stanford, CA: Stanford University Press.

Terman, L. M., & Oden, M. H. (1959). The gifted group in mid-life. In L. M. Terman (Ed.), *Genetic studies of genius* (Vol. 5). Stanford, CA: Stanford University Press.

Thelen, H. A. (1960). *Education and the human quest.* New York: Harper & Row.

Tileston, D. W. (2004). *What every teacher should know about student assessment.* Thousand Oaks, CA: Corwin Press.

Tinker v. Des Moines Independent Community School District, 393 U.S. 503 (1969).

Torres, C. A. (1994). Paulo Freire as Secretary of Education in the municipality of Sao Paula. *Comparative Education Review, 38*(2), 181–214.

Triandis, H. (1989). Cross-cultural studies of individualism and collectivism. *Nebraska Symposium of Motivation, 37,* 43–133.

Trotter, A. (2002, May 9). E-learning goes to school. *Education Week on the Web.*

Tyler, R. (1949). *Basic principles of curriculum and instruction.* Chicago: University of Chicago.

Unified School District No. 241 v. Swanson, 717 P.2d 526 (Kan. Ct. App. 1986).

University of Memphis. (1994/95, Winter). Technology provides field experiences. *Perspectives.* Memphis: University of Memphis, College of Education.

Urban, W. J., & Wagoner, J. L. (2004). *American education: A history* (3rd ed.). Boston: McGraw-Hill.

Uribe, V., & Harbeck, K. M. (1991). Addressing the needs of lesbian, gay and bisexual youth. *Journal of Homosexuality, 22.*

U.S. Bureau of Census. (2008). *Statistical abstract of the United States* (128th ed.). Washington, DC: U.S. Government Printing Office.

U.S. Census Bureau. (2004, June). *Educational attainment in the United States: 2003.* Washington, DC: Author.

U.S. Census Bureau. (2008). *2007 population estimates.* Washington, DC: Author.

U.S. Charter Schools. (2008, May 28). *Charter schools: Frequently asked questions.* Retrieved from http://www.uscharterschools.org/pub/uscs_docs/o/faq.htm1#8

U.S. Department of Commerce. (2002). *A nation online: How Americans are expanding their use of the Internet.* Washington, DC: Author.

U.S. Department of Education. (2001, July 27). *Ready to read, ready to learn* [news release]. Washington, DC: Author.

U.S. Department of Education. (2002a, July 28). Paige announces new "No Child Left Behind-Blue Ribbon Schools" program [news release]. Washington, DC: Author.

U.S. Department of Education. (2002b, October). *Student achievement and school accountability conference.* Washington, DC: Author.

U.S. Department of Education. (2006). *Answering the challenge of a changing world: Strengthening education for the 21st century.* Washington, DC: Author.

U.S. Department of Education. (2008, March/April). President urges Congress to reauthorize law. *The Achiever, 7*(2).

U.S. Department of Education. (2008, April 22). U.S. Secretary of Education Margaret Spellings' prepared remarks at the Detroit Economic Club, where she announced proposed regulations to strengthen No Child Left Behind [news release]. Washington, DC: Author.

U.S. Department of Education, Institute for Education Sciences, National Center for Education Statistics. (2004). *The nation's report card: America's charter school report,* NCES 2005–456, by National Center for Education Statistics. Washington, DC: Author.

U.S. Department of Education, Office of Postsecondary Education. (2005, August).

The Secretary's fourth annual report on teacher quality: A highly qualified teacher in every classroom. Washington, DC: Author.

U.S. Department of Justice. (2002). *Highlights of the 2000 national youth gang survey.* Washington, DC: Author.

U.S. Department of Labor. (2008). *Occupational outlook handbook 2008–09 edition. Teachers—preschool, kindergarten, elementary, middle, and secondary.* Washington, DC: Author.

U.S. English. (2008). *About U.S. English: History.* Retrieved August 10, 2008, from http://www.us-english.org/view/3

U.S. Secret Service. (2000, October). *Safe school initiative: An interim report on the prevention of targeted violence in schools.* Washington, DC: Author.

USA Today. (2003, June 17). Teens flunk Mass. exam, won't graduate.

Utay, C., & Utay, J. (1997). Peer-assisted learning: The effects of cooperative learning and cross-age peer tutoring with word processing on writing skills of students with learning disabilities. *Journal of Computing in Childhood Education, 8.*

Valli, L., & Buese, D. (2007, September). The changing roles of teachers in an era of high-stakes accountability. *American Educational Research Journal, 44*(3), 519–558.

Van Reusen, A. K., Shoho, A. R., & Barker, K. S. (2000). High school teacher attitudes toward inclusion. *High School Journal, 84*(2), 7–20.

Vaughn, S., Bos, C. S., & Schumm, J. S. (1997). *Teaching mainstreamed, diverse, and at-risk students in the general education classroom.* Boston: Allyn & Bacon.

Vedder, R. K. (2003). *Can teachers own their own schools? New strategies for educational excellence.* Chicago: Paul & Co.

Vygotsky, L. S. (1978). *Mind in society: The development of higher mental process.* Cambridge, MA: Harvard University Press.

Vygotsky, L. S. (1986). *Thought and language.* Cambridge, MA: MIT Press.

Walberg, H. J. (Ed.). (2007). *Handbook on restructuring and substantial school improvement.* Lincoln, IL: Center on Innovation & Improvement.

Walberg, H. J., & Greenberg, R. C. (1997, May). Using the learning environment inventory. *Educational Leadership,* pp. 45–47.

Wallace, R. M. (2004, Summer). A framework for understanding teaching with the Internet. *American Educational Research Journal, 41*(2), 447–488.

Wallace v. Jaffree, 472 U. S. 38 (1985).

Waller, W. (1932). *The sociology of teaching.* New York: John Wiley.

Walsh, M. (1999, April 14). Most Edison schools report rise in test scores. *Education Week on the Web.*

REFERENCES

Waltman. J. L., & Bush-Bacelis, J. L. (1995), Contrasting expectations of individualists and collectivists: Achieving effective group interaction. *Journal of Teaching in International Business,* 7(1), 61–76.

Ward, C., & Griffin, A. (2006, March 21). *Five characteristics of an effective school board: A multifaceted role, defined.* San Rafael, CA: George Lucas Educational Foundation.

Washington, W. (1998). *Optional extended year program feedback.* Austin, TX: Austin Independent School District, Department of Accountability, Student Services, and Research.

Wasserman, S. (1994, April). Using cases to study teaching. *Phi Delta Kappan,* 602–611.

Watson, J. B. (1925). *Behaviorism* (2nd ed.). New York: People's Institute.

Webb, L. D., Metha, A., & Jordan, K. F. (1999). *Foundations of American education* (3rd ed.). Englewood Cliffs, NJ: Prentice Hall.

Wechsler, D. (1958). *The measurement and appraisal of adult intelligence* (4th ed.). Baltimore: Williams and Wilkins.

Wentz, P. J. (2001). *The student teaching experience: Cases from the classroom.* Upper Saddle River, NJ: Merrill Prentice Hall.

West v. Board of Education of City of New York, 8 A.D.2d 291 (N.Y. App. 1959).

Wills, K. (2007, September). The advantage of disadvantage: Teachers with disabilities not a handicap. *Edutopia.* Retrieved April 27, 2008, from http://www.edutopia.org/disabled-teachers

Wilson, B. L., & Corbett, H. D. (2001). *Listening to urban kids: School reform and the teachers they want.* Albany: State University of New York Press.

Wirt, F. M., & Kirst, M. W. (1997). *The political dynamics of American education.* Berkeley: McCutchan.

Wisconsin v. Yoder, 406 U.S. 205 (1972).

Wiske, M. S., Rennebohm Franz, K., & Breit, L. (2005). *Teaching for understanding with technology.* San Francisco: Jossey-Bass.

Wolfgang, C. H. (2001). *Solving discipline problems: Methods and models for today's teachers* (5th ed.). Boston: Allyn & Bacon.

Woodman, B. (2007, October 18). Magnet school teacher receives national recognition. *Bloomfield Journal.com.* Retrieved April 9, 2008, from http://www.zwire.com/site/news.cfm?newsid=18931594&BRD=1650&PAG=461&deptid=12156&rfi=6

Woolfolk, A. E. (2007). *Educational psychology* (10th ed.). Boston: Allyn & Bacon.

Wright, R. J. (2008). *Educational assessment: Tests and measurements in the age of accountability.* Los Angeles: Sage.

Yamamoto, K., Davis, Jr., O. L., Dylak, S., Whittaker, J., Marsh, C., & van der Westhuizen, P. C. (1996, Spring). Across six nations: Stressful events in the lives of children. *Child Psychiatry and Human Development,* 139–150.

Yap v. Oceanside Union Free School District, 303 F.Supp 2d 284 (N.Y. 2004).

Young, C. (1999). *Ceasefire! Why women and men must join forces to achieve true equality.* New York: The Free Press.

Zehm, S. J., & Kottler, J. A. (1993). *On being a teacher: The human dimension.* Newbury Park, CA: Corwin Press.

Zelman v. Simmons-Harris, 536 U.S. 639 (2002).

Zhang, L., & Sternberg, R. J. (2001). Thinking styles across cultures: Their relationships with student learning. In R. J. Sternberg & L. Zhang (Eds.), *Perspectives on thinking, learning, and cognitive styles* (pp. 197–226). Mahwah, NJ: Lawrence Erlbaum.

Zobrest v. Catalina Foothills School District, 509 U.S. 1 (1993).

Zucker v. Panitz, 299 F. Supp. 102 (S.D.N.Y. 1969).

Zukowski, V. (1997, Fall). Teeter-totters and tandem bikes: A glimpse into the world of cross-age tutors. *Teaching and Change,* 71–91.

Index